JOHN MILTON

The Complete Poems

TEXT EDITED BY B. A. WRIGHT

INTRODUCTION AND NOTES BY GORDON CAMPBELL
Department of English, University of Leicester

J M DENT & SONS LTD
London Melbourne Toronto
E P DUTTON & CO INC
New York

© Introduction and notes, J. M. Dent & Sons Ltd, 1980
All rights reserved
Printed in Great Britain by Billing & Sons Ltd
London, Guildford, Oxford, Worcester for
J. M. DENT & SONS LTD
Aldine House, 33 Welbeck St, London
First published in Everyman's Library 1909
B. A. Wright's edition first published 1956
New edition 1980

Published in the USA by arrangement with
J. M. Dent & Sons Ltd

British Library Cataloguing in Publication Data
Milton, John
The complete poems – (Everyman's Library)
I Campbell, Gordon II Series
821′4   PR3550
ISBN 0–460–10384–9
ISBN 0–460–11384–4 Pbk

CONTENTS

Psalms

Latin Poems

PARADISE LOST

PARADISE REGAIN'D

SAMSON AGONISTES 437

ACKNOWLEDGMENTS

Any editor of Milton who is not a monster of erudition must inevitably be indebted to the learned labours of his predecessors. In preparing my annotations I have drawn on the humane scholarship of Milton's editors from Patrick Hume, whose annotations on *Paradise Lost* were published in 1695, to such recent editors as M. Y. Hughes, D. Bush, J. Carey, and A. D. S. Fowler. I owe a debt of equal magnitude to the original editors of the *Oxford English Dictionary*, who chose to include thousands of illustrations from Milton's verse in their dictionary, and so have very much eased the task of annotation; even in those instances where I have chosen to dissent from the meaning suggested in the *OED*, I have done so on the basis of the close and clear discriminations which characterize its definitions.

Many of Milton's early poems were written in Latin. The translations of Milton's Latin verse included in the notes were prepared by my wife, Mary Campbell, and I am pleased to record my thanks for her labours. The translations of the Greek and Italian verse and of the Hebrew annotations of the Psalms are my own.

I assumed responsibility for this edition at the suggestion of Professor C. A. Patrides, and I should like to thank him for this characteristic act of kindness. I prepared the edition while on the staff of the University of Liverpool, and have often had occasion to be grateful for the readiness with which my colleagues have placed their specialized knowledge at my disposal. In particular Mr A. M. Bowie and Mr A. R. Millard have saved me from many foolish errors in Hellenic and Semitic matters. Mrs Annette Butler, Mrs Joan Welford and Miss Catherine Rees typed my palimpsestic manuscript quickly and carefully.

I should like to dedicate this edition to three men who many years ago stimulated and disciplined my enthusiasm for Milton: W. J. Barnes, R. R. Dubinski, and J. C. Gray.

1979   G.C.

TEXT AND TEXTUAL NOTES

The text of this edition was prepared by the late Professor B. A. Wright for the 1956 'Everyman' edition, and is here reprinted with a few minor corrections. Professor Wright's twenty-eight page textual introduction is not reprinted here, for although it constitutes an important contribution to the debate about Milton's spelling and punctuation, that debate had run its course by the early 1960s, and is now part of the history of Milton criticism. The interested reader may follow the debate through the four most important essays on the subject: Helen Darbishire's introduction to her edition of Milton's *Poetical Works* (2 vols., Oxford, 1952, 1955), R. M. Adams, 'The Text of *Paradise Lost*: Emphatic and Unemphatic Spellings', *Modern Philology* 52 (1954), 84–91, Professor Wright's essay, and J. T. Shawcross, 'One Aspect of Milton's Spelling: Idle Final "E" ', *PMLA* 78 (1963) 501–10.

Professor Wright believed that Milton took advantage of the lack of uniformity in seventeenth-century spelling by using variant spellings to mark differences in pronunciation and meaning, and to point his prosody. Thus such spellings as *towr*, *flowr*, *bowr* show that these words are metrical monosyllables, and *corporal* (bodily) is distinguished from *corporeal* (opposite of spiritual). Similarly, an initial capital distinguishes *Spirits* (supernatural beings) from *spirits* (in physiological sense), *Vertues* (angels) from *vertues* (moral qualities), and so on. Milton was also believed to have distinguished emphatic forms of personal pronouns (*hee*, *mee*, *wee*, *yee*, *you*, *their*) from unemphatic forms (*he*, *me*, *we*, *ye*, *thir*).

The punctuation in the text attempts to rescue Milton's pointing from the stately correctness of Victorian editions by restoring in large part Milton's own punctuation. Milton's punctuation served a grammatical function, but it was also used as a prosodic device, and so was the servant of rhetoric as well as grammar.

The text is based on the last edition of Milton's poems published during his lifetime, and the textual notes record variants from earlier editions. Thus the second edition of Milton's *Poems* (1673) forms the basic text, and the notes record variants from the first edition (1645), the Trinity MS, the 1637 edition of *Comus* published by Henry Lawes, the 1638 edition of *Lycidas* (in *Justa Eduardo King*), and other MSS and earlier publications. In the case of *Paradise Lost* the revised edition of 1674 forms the basic text, and variants from the first edition (1667) and the MS of Book I are recorded in the notes. The texts of *Paradise Regain'd* and *Samson Agonistes* are based on the 1671 edition.

CHRONOLOGY OF MILTON'S LIFE

1608, December 9. Born in Bread Street, Cheapside, London.

1620(?) Entered St Paul's School.

1625, February 12. Matriculated at Christs College, Cambridge.

1629, March. Took BA degree.

1629, December. *On the Morning of Christs Nativity*.

1632, July. Took MA degree.

1632, July–1638, April. Lived at Hammersmith and Horton.

1634, September 29. *Comus* performed at Ludlow.

1637, November. *Lycidas*.

1638, April–1639, August. Continental tour.

1639–1640. Settled in London.

1641–1642. Begins pamphleteering. Five anti-prelatical tracts: *Of Reformation in England; Of Prelatical Episcopacy; Animadversions upon the Remonstrant's Defence; The Reason of Church Government; Apology for Smectymnuus*.

1642, May–June. Married Mary Powell, who left him about a month later.

1643–1645 *The Doctrine and Discipline of Divorce; Of Education; The Judgement of Martin Bucer Concerning Divorce; Areopagitica; Tetrachordon; Colasterion*.

1645. Milton's wife returns. *Miscellaneous Poems* published.

1649. *The Tenure of Kings and Magistrates* (February). Appointed Secretary for Foreign Tongues to the Council of State (March). *Eikonoklastes* (October).

1651. *Defensio pro Populo Anglicano*.

1652. Milton totally blind. Death of his first wife.

1654. *Defensio Secunda*.

1655. *Defensio Pro Se*.

1656, November. Married Katherine Woodcock.

1658, February. Death of Katherine Woodcock.

1660, March. *The Ready and Easy Way to Establish a Free Commonwealth*.

1663, February. Married Elizabeth Minshull.

1667. *Paradise Lost* published.

1671. *Paradise Regained* and *Samson Agonistes* published.

1673. Second edition of *Miscellaneous Poems*.

1674. Second edition of *Paradise Lost*.

1674, November 8. Died; buried in St Giles' Church, Cripplegate.

BIOGRAPHICAL NOTE

The flyleaf of Milton's family Bible, which is now preserved in the British Library, records in the poet's own hand that 'John Milton was born the 9th of December 1608 die Veneris [i.e. Friday] half an howr after 6 in the morning'. His birthplace and childhood home was the Spread Eagle, on the east side of Bread Street, in Cheapside. The family home contained a small shop in which Milton's father, who was also called John, conducted his business as a scrivener, a profession which by the seventeenth century had extended beyond the work of a scribe to include the functions of notary, money-lender, and investment broker.

Milton's early education was entrusted to private tutors, and some-time between 1615 and 1620 he began to attend a nearby school, St Paul's, which adjoined the cathedral. In 1621 John Donne was appointed Dean of St Paul's Cathedral, and Milton probably heard Donne preach on several occasions between 1621 and 1624. Milton's parents encouraged studious habits in their young son. In *Ad Patrem* Milton thanks his father for the gift of five languages – Latin, Greek, Hebrew, French and Italian – and in his *Defensio Secunda* Milton asserts that from the age of twelve he habitually studied until midnight; his school day began at seven o'clock.

Milton was formally admitted to Christ's College, Cambridge on Saturday 12 February 1625, though he may have begun attending on Thursday 13 January, the first day of the Lent Term. Each morning the members of Christ's assembled at five o'clock for chapel, and later in the morning undergraduates met their tutors for instruction, which was given through the medium of Latin. Milton's first tutor was William Chappell, Fellow of Christ's and Lecturer in Hebrew. For unknown reasons Milton soon fell out with Chappell, who, according to John Aubrey, whipped Milton. Milton was sent down from the university. After a brief period of rustication he was re-admitted to the college and assigned to a new tutor, Nathaniel Tovey, with whom Milton was evidently able to forge a satisfactory relationship. A few years later Milton's brother Christopher was admitted to Christ's and Tovey became his tutor.

At Christ's Milton was an assiduous student. When he graduated in 1629 he was placed fourth in the honours list of twenty-four under-graduates who were deemed to have been the most distinguished of the 259 students who graduated that year. The three young scholars whose learning was judged to be superior to Milton's have left nothing which enables posterity to comment on the judgement of the examiners. Three years later, on 3 July 1632, Milton was awarded the MA degree. The award of the BA and MA degrees was contingent on a written declara-tion to the effect that the candidate subscribed to the doctrines of the

Church of England and acknowledged the supremacy of the king. Milton's willingness to sign the graduation-book suggests that he did not yet espouse the heterodox theological principles and the republican views of his maturity. For the MA degree Milton also swore to continue his university studies for an additional five years; two years after this 'regency' he would have been eligible to apply for the degree of BD. In the seventeenth century this second oath was merely a vestige of an earlier custom, and it is characteristic of Milton that he alone seems to have taken it seriously, for he chose to spend the next five years in private study. Milton's father retired from business at about the same time that Milton left Cambridge, and Milton joined his family in Hammersmith, devoting his time to reading Greek and Latin authors. In 1635 he moved with his family further into the countryside, to Horton, and there continued his programme of study until 1638.

Milton's education was completed with a continental tour which was to be a decisive influence on his vocation as a poet. When Milton left England in the spring of 1638 he had already written some of the greatest poems in the English language. He had composed many of his early poems for specific occasions, but when he read them to his new friends in Italy, the warmth with which they were received encouraged him to recognize that his poems had a life beyond the occasions which had prompted them. In Italy Milton resolved to become a great national poet. It is perhaps fortunate that he did not know that many years would pass before that ideal could be realized.

In the summer of 1639 Milton returned to England, and took lodgings in London, near Fleet Street. He once again took up his serious reading, and in his leisure hours began to teach his two nephews, John and Edward Phillips, who were then eight and nine years old respectively. Within a year the boys could read Latin authors with reasonable ease. Out of this practical experience of teaching emerged one of Milton's finest pamphlets, *Of Education*, which he published in 1644. Reading this pamphlet in conjunction with Edward Phillips' account of the books which he and his brother studied under their uncle's supervision is a humbling experience, for one realizes how far our expectations of the amount young children can learn have fallen since Milton's time. And in this matter Milton was not out of step with his age. The tone of *Of Education* is not one of strident advocacy, but rather assumes the reasonableness of his standards.

The tone of Milton's other great tract, *Areopagitica* (1644) provides a good contrast to the calm assurance which pervades *Of Education*, for in *Areopagitica* Milton was addressing a hostile audience. Parliament had decided that books should be censored prior to publication, and whilst Milton advocated the suppression of libellous books after publication, he could not abide the prospect of licensing before publication. He cast his pamphlet in the form of a classical oration addressed to Parliament, and it is by common consent one of the most eloquent books in the English language.

The other pamphlets of the 1640s and 1650s are important for the student of Milton, but their subject matter is so rooted in the concerns of the seventeenth century that it is difficult for a modern student to be enthusiastic about them. In the early 1640s Milton wrote several pamphlets on episcopacy and divorce. On 15 March 1649 Milton was appointed Secretary for Foreign Tongues to the Council of State, and turned his polemical energies to the defence of the execution of Charles I.

Milton's tumultuous life as a public figure during the 1640s and 1650s distracted him from his activities as a poet, and a series of personal crises disturbed his domestic peace. Early in the summer of 1642 Milton had married Mary Powell, who a few weeks later left her husband to return to her parents' home, and was not re-united with her husband until 1645. Before his wife returned Milton realized that he was losing the sight in his left eye, and by 1648 his left eye had ceased to function. Early in 1652 his right eye collapsed, and he became permanently blind. In May of the same year his wife died giving birth to their fourth child, and Milton was left, alone and blind, to care for four young children. Six weeks later his only son, John, died. In 1656 Milton married Katherine Woodcock, and in October of the following year Katherine gave birth to a daughter. Four months later Katherine died, and a month after that their daughter was buried beside her.

These personal calamities were shortly followed by public events which affected Milton deeply. On 3 September 1658 Cromwell died, and the foundations of the government to which Milton had dedicated many years were shaken. When Charles II entered London on 19 May 1660 Milton feared punishment, and was in hiding. He narrowly missed being condemned to death, but the mediation of friends such as Andrew Marvell, and the common opinion that God had already punished Milton by striking him blind, led eventually to his exemption from the death-list, and to a pardon in December 1660. Milton retired to private life, and concentrated on the composition of his epic, *Paradise Lost*. In 1663 he married Elizabeth Minshull, who was to outlive her husband by over 50 years. In 1667 Milton published *Paradise Lost*, and in 1671 *Paradise Regain'd* and *Samson Agonistes*. He died early in November 1674 and on 12 November was buried in St Giles' Cripplegate.

INTRODUCTION

Milton is the most learned poet in the English literary tradition, and it is remarkable that the weight of his erudition did not crush his genius for writing poetry. In some of Milton's early Latin poems, such as the poem addressed to Thomas Young (*Elegia quarta*) and the poem written to commemorate the death of the Vice-Chancellor of Cambridge University (*In obitum Procancellarii medici*), an excess of allusion leads one to suspect a rather self-conscious attitude to learning on the part of the poet. But by the time Milton had emerged from his years as a primarily Latin poet at the age of twenty-one he was capable of writing poems in which his gifts as a poet are untrammelled by his learning. Milton was a learned poet, but he did not write learned poems. His poems contain very few allusions that would not be instantly understood by any seventeenth-century reader. Some of the minor poems of his youth are addressed to a university audience, but the poems of his maturity are not addressed to a highly educated audience. Anyone who had enjoyed a grammar school education would be able to read his Latin poems with ease and pleasure, and would be able to respond directly to the classical and Biblical allusions embodied in his English poems without recourse to learned footnotes.

Milton's earliest dated poems are his paraphrases of Psalms cxiv and cxxxvi. In a headnote to the poems in the 1645 collection Milton explains that they 'were done by the Author at fifteen years old'. Milton was fifteen in 1624, and was completing his final year as a pupil at St Paul's School in London. In that year he had begun his formal study of the Hebrew language and the Psalter, and he doubtless consulted the Hebrew text as well as the Greek and Latin versions of the psalms. The singing of psalms was an important part of Protestant congregational and domestic worship, and many Protestants published translations and paraphrases of the psalms in metres suitable for singing. Indeed, Milton's own father, who was a gifted amateur composer, had set some psalms to music for Ravenscroft's Psalter of 1621. The quality of Milton's paraphrases is not exceptional, but they are valuable in that they embody in a simple form some of the features that were later to characterize some of Milton's greatest poems. Although he regarded every word of the original Hebrew texts as literally inspired by God, Milton felt free to elaborate many of the phrases of the Hebrew originals. The hand of Joshua Sylvester lies heavily on some of these embellishments, but one can none the less see in them something of Milton's own tastes. His use of the phrases '*Pharian* Fields' and '*Erythræan* main' to refer to Egypt and the Red Sea, for example, indicates a nascent sense of the rhetorical advantages to be reaped from the use of classical place-names.

Most of the poems which Milton wrote while an undergraduate at Cambridge were composed in Latin. The choice of Latin as a literary medium was not at all unusual, for Latin composition formed part of the education of every school-boy and undergraduate. The fact that many of Milton's poems are written in Latin is not a mark of any exceptional learning on his part, but is symptomatic of the literary conventions of an age more learned than our own. What should attract our attention, however, is the quality of Milton's Latin poems, for although some of his tributes to deceased dignitaries fail to distinguish themselves from the indifferent poems of many of his contemporaries, some of Milton's Latin poems clearly display the vigorous powers of his developing poetic imagination. Of his early Latin poems *Elegia quinta* is probably the finest, for in that poem Milton takes a traditional subject, the advent of spring, and creates a poem of such voluptuous exuberance that one can scarcely believe it was written by a young student of theology. Milton's two greatest Latin poems, *Mansus* and *Epitaphium Damonis*, were written after he left university.

Mansus, like the *Elegia quinta*, is a poem on a conventional theme, in this case expressing gratitude to a kind host. But once again Milton's poetic energy bursts the constraints of his ostensible subject, and he writes an impassioned poem which begins with the praise of Manso and culminates in a magnificent passage in which Milton pours out his ambition to become a great English poet. Civil war and the obligation of public service were to postpone the realization of this ambition to write immortal poetry, but the intensity of this vision was sufficient to sustain Milton throughout these years until he at last had the leisure and maturity of mind requisite for the composition of *Paradise Lost*.

Epitaphium Damonis is also an intensely personal poem, for in it Milton articulates his grief at the death of the dearest friend of his youth, Charles Diodati. The poem is a pastoral elegy, a form which will be discussed below in connection with *Lycidas*. The control of emotion which this artificial form affords enabled Milton to articulate poignant recollections of his friendship with Diodati. In the course of the poem Milton's grief gradually yields to a vision of immortality that culminates in an ecstatic depiction of Diodati's heavenly reward.

Throughout Milton's years as a Latin poet he nourished ambitions to write in his native tongue. One of the earliest and most remarkable outpourings of this ambition occurs in *At a Vacation Exercise*, which Milton recited to the undergraduates of Christ's College in July 1628. The poem begins as a light-hearted address to Milton's native language, which was to be the medium of the satirical play which follows Milton's poem. In the course of this poem Milton digresses to announce that he aspires to use his native language for more exalted purposes:

> Yet I had rather if I were to chuse,
> Thy service in som graver subject use
> Such as may make thee search thy coffers round
> Before thou clothe my fancy in fit sound.

The tone of the ensuing description of Milton's poetical ambition is delicately poised, for it is at once a serious catalogue of ambitions and a nimble display of poetic virtuosity.

The first poem in which Milton achieved the greatness to which he aspired was his ode *On the Morning of Christ's Nativity*. At the end of *Elegia sexta* Milton explained to Diodati that he had written a poem as a birthday gift for Christ. The context of this remark suggests that Milton may have seen the *Nativity Ode* as the first serious poem of a man who has dedicated his life to the composition of heroic poetry. The *Nativity Ode* was Milton's first English poem on a religious theme, and in order to indicate its importance in his spiritual and poetic development he placed it first in his 1645 and 1673 *Poems*.

The *Nativity Ode* partakes of a tradition that originates with Virgil's *Eclogue* IV, the 'Messianic' Eclogue, which associates the birth of a child with the return of the Golden Age in the reign of Augustus. The use of pastoral imagery in a poem which celebrates the birth of a child was congenial to Christian thought, in which Christ was the Good Shepherd. In Christian poetry Christ was commonly compared to Pan the guardian of sheep.

Milton refers to his poem as an ode (line 24), and it has long been known as the *Nativity Ode*, though this was not Milton's title. The term 'ode' would suggest to Milton the poems of Pindar, Anacreon and Horace. The canon of Pindar and Anacreon in Milton's time was very different from the modern canon, for new poems have been re-discovered and many others re-attributed, and the differences in structure, tone, and style that distinguish the works of these three poets would have seemed even sharper to Milton than they do to a modern reader. The form of Milton's poem does not descend from the odes of any of these three poets. On the contrary, Milton takes advantage of the diversity of the ancient tradition and creates a new form that suits his own poetic temperament.

The *Nativity Ode* has a five-part structure. It begins with a four-stanza prelude in rhyme royal, the metre which Milton had used earlier for *On the Death of a Fair Infant*. In both poems he expands the final line of each stanza into an alexandrine, presumably in imitation of Spenser. In the prelude Milton establishes the subject, occasion, and time of the poem, and also creates the sense of a journey within the poem. This last feature is one of several masque-like aspects of the poem; the descent of Peace in stanza III of the Hymn is another masque-like moment, for allegorical and mythological characters often descend onto the stage in masques, as for example, does Juno in the masque in Act IV of Shakespeare's *Tempest*.

The other four sections of the *Nativity Ode* are grouped in a Hymn written in a stanza form which Milton devised for the occasion, a form which recalls the grouping of trimeter and pentameter lines in the *canzone* tradition, and in its final alexandrine again recalls Spenser. The first eight stanzas of the Hymn constitute the second section of the poem, and in these stanzas Milton sketches the setting of the nativity, using images of subdued colour, light, and sound to emphasize the peacefulness of the scene. In the third section, stanzas IX-XVII, Milton describes the song of the angelic choir, deploying images of intense colour, bright light, and harmonious sound. In the fourth section, stanzas XVIII-XXVI, Milton depicts the flight of the pagan gods, using images of cacophony and shadow, in sharp contrast to the previous section. The final section is the concluding stanza of the poem, in which the tranquil scene of the nativity is illuminated by the clear light of the star of Bethlehem and the radiance of the 'Bright-harnest Angels'.

Much of the power of the poem derives from Milton's concern to transcend the details of the nativity in order to assert the significance of the event. The image of the smiling baby in stanza XVI, for example, dissolves into a reminder of his destiny, for the baby is the Christ

> That on the bitter cross
> Must redeem our loss.

For Milton the importance of the nativity was that it constituted the essential prerequisite to the redemption of our loss. Milton's imagination seemed to respond more easily to an event highly charged with future significance than to the future event itself. When in *The Passion* he tried to contemplate the redemptive act directly, he was unable to complete the poem. In the *Nativity Ode* Milton succeeds because he concentrates on an event distanced from the redemption. He was to repeat this success in a modest way in *Upon the Circumcision*, for he was able to seize on the theological significance of the circumcision: the shedding of the blood of the infant Christ was the first act in the passion, and prefigured the day when

> Huge pangs and strong
> Will pierce more near his heart.

The companion poems *L'Allegro* and *Il Penseroso* must be counted among the finest poems of Milton's youth. Companion poems were popular in the late sixteenth and early seventeenth centuries. It should be remembered that the second poem in the pair was not always written at the same time, or even by the same person, as the first poem. Marlowe's *Passionate Shepherd to his Love*, for example, was written as an autonomous poem, and later Raleigh wrote a companion poem, *The Nymph's Reply to the Shepherd*. Marlowe's poem concludes with the couplet

> If these delights thy mind may move,
> Then live with me and be my love

and Raleigh's with a similar couplet. These invitations are clearly the originals of the couplets which conclude Milton's poems.

L'Allegro, or a portion of it, may have been written as an independent poem, though attempts to argue this hypothesis on prosodic grounds have proved inconclusive. If, however, *Il Penseroso* does represent a later stage in Milton's poetic development, then it would seem fitting to view the thought in the poems as progressing from *L'Allegro* to *Il Penseroso* rather than to see the points of view as two carefully-balanced alternatives. There are many exact parallels between the poems: the metre of *Il Penseroso* imitates that of *L'Allegro*, the preludes are similar, and the catalogues of pleasures contain many exact oppositions. On the other hand there are some indications that *Il Penseroso* has the upper hand. In the ten-line preludes to the poems, for example, one notes that whilst the deluding joys banished by *Il Penseroso* bear some resemblance to the joys celebrated in *L'Allegro*, the melancholy banished by *L'Allegro* is of a different kind from that celebrated by *Il Penseroso*. *Il Penseroso* welcomes the melancholy of Aristotle and Ficino, who associated it with an artistic or philosophical temperament, but *L'Allegro* condemns the melancholy of Galen and Burton, who associated it with a medical imbalance causing torpor, madness, and fear. A similar weighting of the scales in favour of *Il Penseroso* is evident in the final movements of the poems, for not only is *Il Penseroso* longer, but it also concludes with a religious experience that has no parallel in the earlier poem.

 A Maske Presented at Ludlow Castle, which since the late seventeenth century has been known as *Comus*, was performed before the Earl of Bridgewater and his guests on 29 September 1634. Although both Milton and Lawes termed *Comus* a masque, it is not a representative Stuart masque, as a comparison with Jonson's masques or the masques incorporated in Shakespeare's plays makes readily apparent. *Comus* is not alone among masques in absorbing into its fabric elements from related forms such as the moral interlude and the pastoral play, but the dominance of dramatic dialogue over the music and spectacle is unusual in a play that retains so many of the traditional features of the masque. The journey to Ludlow in *Comus* reflects the processional element in traditional masques. The element of compliment in court masques is presented indirectly in *Comus* through a portrayal of the virtue of Lord Bridgewater's children, who at the dramatic climax of the masque are presented to the Earl and Countess as 'three fair branches of your own'; the virtue of the children is a compliment to their parents.

 The subject of *Comus* is virtue. As virtue in women was thought to manifest itself in chastity, which for an unmarried woman meant virginity, and as the central character in the play is the Lady, Milton's exposition of virtue is couched in terms of chastity and virginity. While Comus is on the stage virtue is tested; this portion of the play constitutes Milton's first dramatic exposition of the theme of temptation, a theme to which he was to return in *Paradise Lost*, *Paradise Regain'd*, and *Samson Agonistes*. When Comus is replaced by Sabrina – the parts may have been played by the same actor – chastity is celebrated rather than tested, and becomes a positive virtue rather than an inhibiting one. The dramatic realization of this aspect of virtue is reserved until the end of the masque, but Milton had allowed the Lady to articulate the positive aspect of chastity in her first speech:

> O welcom pure-ey'd Faith, white-handed Hope,
> Thou hovering Angel girt with golden wings,
> And thou unblemisht form of Chastity.

The mention of faith and hope in line 212 naturally leads Milton's readers or listeners to expect a description of charity. Milton skilfully prolongs the expectation by spending his next line on a visual image of hope, and at the end of line 214 suddenly fulfils the anticipation of charity with a presentation of chastity. The effect of this paranomasia is an alteration in the meaning of chastity. The word normally carries the suggestion of a withholding or suppressing of natural desires in the interests of a lofty ideal, and later in the poem Comus exploits this negative idea of chastity. The Lady's speech anticipates these arguments by forcefully conjoining charity and chastity, and so removes the stigma of withholding from chastity, which becomes an image of love. The Lady has transformed chastity into a positive virtue which represents the giving of love rather than its denial.

The greatest of Milton's minor poems is *Lycidas*, which is justly regarded as one of the finest poems in the English language. *Lycidas* was first published in a collection of poems commemorating the death of Edward King, a Fellow of Christ's College. Milton had probably not known King well, but was none the less deeply moved by his premature death. Milton's poem originated in a desire to lament this specific death, but in the act of composition Milton transcended his ostensible subject to produce a meditation on personal mortality that retains the power to move readers centuries after King and his mourners have turned to dust.

Lycidas is a pastoral elegy, a form that was absorbed into the literary tradition in the third century BC when Theocritus composed his lament for Daphnis (*Idyll* I). The authors of *Lament for Adonis* and *Lament for Bion* (traditionally attributed to Bion and Moschus respectively) sustained the tradition in Greek poetry, and Virgil imitated Theocritus' *Idyll* I in his *Eclogue* X. The pastoral elegy was a popular form in the late Middle Ages and the Renaissance, and even in the nineteenth century the pastoral elegy was chosen by Shelley for *Adonais* and by Arnold for *Thyrsis*, their laments for Keats and Clough.

In pastoral elegy the poet and his subject are described as shepherds or goatherds. As the form evolved it became increasingly distanced from shepherd life in ancient Sicily. Virgil elevated the style of pastoral elegy and included in it personal and public comments unrelated to the death of the person represented as a shepherd. Christian writers of the late Middle Ages and the Renaissance seized on the joyous conclusion of Virgil's *Eclogue* V as a model for the Christian consolation at the end of their elegies. In the Renaissance pastoral these innovations were combined with traditional features such as the procession of mourners and the lament of nature, and with features that had appeared in other pastoral poems, such as the ecclesiastical satire in the eclogues of Petrarch (VI and VII) and Mantuan (IX). The pastoral elegy was established in England by Spenser in the November eclogue of the *Shepheardes Calender* and in *Astrophel*, his lament for Sidney. Both *Lycidas* and *Epitaphium Damonis* are firmly rooted in the tradition of pastoral elegy and display many of its characteristic features. Milton was not bound by the tradition – in *Lycidas*, for example, he omitted the refrain which was a prominent feature of ancient pastoral elegies – but drew on it to shape and temper his emotions and poetical impulses.

The composition of a lament for Edward King prompted Milton to reflect on the meaning and purpose of human life. King was a young man who had shared with Milton the experience of the same tutor in the same college, who had shared Milton's commitment to the Protestant faith, and who, like Milton, had published a few poems. King's premature death called into question Milton's ambition to become a great Christian poet:

> Alas! What boots it with uncessant care
> To tend the homely slighted Shepherds trade,
> And strictly meditate the thankless Muse?

Lycidas is a quest for an answer to that question. At the beginning of the poem Milton's imagination is constrained by the thought of his own death:

> So may som gentle Muse
> With lucky words favour my destind Urn,
> And as he passes, turn
> And bid fair peace be to my sable shroud.

At this moment the poem is saved from what seems an inevitable plunge into self-pity by the impersonality of the pastoral mode. Milton gradually transcends not only the death of King but also the brutal reminder of his own mortality that King's death afforded. At its most profound level the poem considers the purpose of human existence and effort in a world in which evil is allowed to flourish and virtuous men like King are allowed to die. Milton's characteristic integrity of mind prevents him from accepting the platitudinous assurances of Phoebus, and from acquiescing in the consolation offered by the ceremony of throwing poetical flowers on the hearse of Lycidas. Consolation finally comes with the realization that Lycidas 'is not dead', for he is experiencing the inexpressible joy of heaven and as the 'Genius of the shore' is continuing to minister to mankind as he did on earth. Milton's calm of mind is restored, and his detachment from his grief is marked by a change of poetic voice in the last stanza of the poem. Milton is reconciled to mortality, and has summoned up the strength to enter 'fresh Woods and Pastures new'.

In 1641 and 1642 Milton published his five anti-episcopal pamphlets, and so began his career as a writer of prose. *Of Education*, *Areopagitica* and the four tracts in defence of divorce followed in the next three years. In 1649 he was appointed Secretary of Foreign Tongues to the Council of State, and his formidable abilities as a pamphleteer were turned to the defence of the Commonwealth, and in particular to the defence of the execution of Charles I. Milton continued to defend his republican principles until the eve of the Restoration in 1660. During these two decades of pamphleteering Milton continually reminded his readers of his plans to write a national epic. But his only finished English poems composed during this period are his sonnets.

Milton's sonnets constitute an important contribution to the English sonnet tradition. Sometimes his subject so inflamed his imagination that his sonnets achieved greatness. In Sonnet XIX his horror at the barbarity of the recent massacre in Piedmont is condensed into an explosive sonnet; in Sonnet XX, on the other hand, quiet reflection on his blindness has impelled him to write a sonnet that begins in despair and frustration and rises to a sense of spiritual calmness that recalls the ending of *Lycidas*.

Milton's English predecessors in the art of the sonnet had developed conventions that had originated in Petrarch's sonnets and then been modified by poets adapting the form to their own purposes. Shakespeare, for example, turned the Petrarchan sestet into a third quatrain and an independently rhymed couplet. Milton continued this tradition of innovation, but experimented with one eye on Italian poets (particularly Giovanni Della Casa) who had attempted similar variations. Like these Italian poets, Milton often chose to blur the distinction between octave and sestet by making both sense and syntax continuous between the eighth and ninth lines. The fluidity and continuity of thought which Milton is able to achieve by allowing his sentences to come to a natural conclusion remind one of the style of Shakespeare's last plays, in which the sense flows from line to line with scarcely any end-stopping. Milton's poetry similarly flourished when he over-rode the constraints of form. The exploration of this freedom is an important element in the poetic accomplishment of *Paradise Lost*, in which, as Milton explains in his prefatory note on the verse (p. 156), 'the sense [is] variously drawn out from one Verse into another'.

Paradise Lost represented for Milton the fulfilment of two aspirations. He had for several decades wanted to write an epic, and for a similar length of time had wanted to re-create the story of the fall of man. Originally these were separate projects; the epic was to be an Arthuriad, and the exposition of the fall of man was to be a tragedy. Disenchantment about the historicity of Arthur gradually led to the abandonment of the plan to write an Arthurian epic, and the two projects merged into the composition of an epic which dealt with the tragedy of the fall of man. The decision to explore his chosen theme in an epic rather than a tragedy gave Milton licence to range over vast tracts of human experience. Thus the poem extends chronologically from the exaltation of Christ (V 575 ff.) before the creation of the universe through human history to the second coming of Christ (XII 458–465). Geographically the poem ranges over the entire world, and Milton delights in cataloguing place-names culled from contemporary atlases, the Bible and Biblical commentaries, and the works of classical antiquity. Two of the competing cosmologies of the seventeenth century are incorporated into the poem, and Milton has also invented splendid prelapsarian versions of both the Ptolemaic and Copernican cosmologies.

The presence of these two competing theories of the universe is suggestive of the public nature of the poem. Milton did not use the poem as a vehicle for his own opinions, but allowed it to voice the range of opinions represented in Protestant England. Thus when the poem approaches controversial issues of theology, Milton sets aside his own theological opinions (which he expresses elsewhere in his systematic theology, *De Doctrina Christiana*) in favour of a public statement phrased in the language of the Bible. In Book III, for example, God the Father explains his position regarding election to salvation and damnation (ll. 173–90). Some critics have claimed that the passage is wholly Calvinistic, others have found it to be uncompromisingly Arminian, and still others have seen it as an attempt to tread a middle way between these extremes. This ambiguity suggests that God's words were not meant to endorse any particular doctrine. On the contrary, the fact that Milton has grounded virtually every phrase on the Scriptures would enable every seventeenth-century reader to respond to the passage in accordance with the doctrinal interpretation he gave to the Biblical passages which underlie it. The freedom of interpretation which the Biblical texture of the language allows the reader recalls the insistence of Milton and his contemporaries on the freedom of the individual to interpret the Bible under the guidance of the Spirit. In the invocations to *Paradise Lost* Milton makes it clear that he thinks of his poem as divinely inspired, and it is therefore fitting that he encourage in his readers the Protestant virtue of individual interpretation.

The Bible and Biblical commentaries account for much of the substance of the poem; the form of the poem, however, is that of classical epic. The ten books of the first edition of *Paradise Lost* recall Milton's original intention to present the story as a tragedy, for the ten books comprise five acts of two books each. In the second edition Milton divided the poem into twelve books in imitation of classical epic, particularly Virgil's *Æneid*. The debt to classical epic extends far beyond this structural imitation, for *Paradise Lost* almost continuously alludes to incidents in the epics of Homer and Virgil. Milton attempts to renovate the epic tradition, and he does so by setting his own poem firmly within that tradition, and then distinguishing it from its predecessors. At the beginning of Book IX Milton announces that his subject will be the tragedy of the fall, and asserts that this theme is 'Not less but more Heroic' than the subjects of the epics of Homer and Virgil.

In *Paradise Lost* Milton attempts to

> assert Eternal Providence,
> And justifie the wayes of God to men.   (I 25–6)

A reading of the narrative of the fall in Books IX and X might lead one to conclude that Milton's actual purpose was the opposite of his stated purpose, for in those Books Milton's exquisite portrayal of the motives and reactions of Adam and Eve seems to constitute an attempt to justify the ways of men to God. In the first eight books, however, Milton educates the reader in the values which must be brought to bear on the tragedy of Adam and Eve. The clearest statement of these values occurs in Book III, in which Milton boldly presents God the Father and God the Son as dramatic characters. The Son volunteers to redeem mankind, and at the conclusion of his speech the narrator says

> His words here ended, but his meek aspect
> Silent yet spake, and breath'd immortal love
> To mortal men, above which only shon
> Filial obedience: as a sacrifice
> Glad to be offerd, he attends the will
> Of his great Father.   (III 266–71)

In this passage Milton asserts the pre-eminence of obedience over love, and so establishes a priority of values which informs the action of Book IX, where the fallen Eve presents Adam's temptation as a 'glorious trial of exceeding Love' (961). There is an apparent similarity between Christ's willingness to die for mankind, and Adam's willingness to die for Eve, but the values of Book III make it clear that the similarity is an illusion. Christ's act entailed obedience; Adam's, disobedience. Christ's act was heroic; Adam's had only the illusion of heroism. Christ's sacrifice has shown the reader a truly heroic act.

The reader has also been prepared for Adam's falsely heroic pose, for in the first two books of the poem Milton presents Satan, the master of illusory heroism. The seventeenth-century reader shared with Milton an unshakeable conviction of the total and irredeemable depravity of Satan. This conviction underlies Milton's description of Satan in heroic terms in the opening books of the poem. The falseness of his heroism becomes more apparent as the poem progresses, and the last illusions are shattered in Book IV, where the imagery deployed to describe Satan is bestial, and he is variously compared to such animals as a wolf (183), a cormorant (196), a lion (402), a tiger (403), and a toad (800). Although the first four animals are capable of heroic representation, in the pastoral world of Eden they are animals of rapine; and it is difficult to imagine an heroic toad.

The justification of God's ways must of course extend beyond an account of the fall of man to an affirmation of his redemption. In the first sentence of the poem Milton had linked the fall with man's eventual restoration by 'one greater Man', and as the narrative progresses Christ's presence is increasingly felt in the poem. At the earliest point in the poem Christ is exalted, and this exaltation initiates the action of the poem, for Satan reacts with envy and malice (V 662–6). In Book VI Milton organizes his account of the war in heaven so that its climax is the heroic intervention of the Son. Similarly, the account of creation in Book VII culminates in a celebration of Christ as creator. The centrality of Christ in the poem is the reason that it does not end with the description of the immediate consequences of the fall in Book X. Books XI and XII show how the fall leads to the redemptive act of Christ by presenting a series of visions which demonstrate to Adam and the reader the historical effects of the fall and prefigure man's eventual restoration. In Book XII Adam learns that the ultimate effect of the fall will be the triumph of Christ, and suddenly realizes that God will turn the evil of the fall into an instrument of his greater glory. Adam's impulse to repent of his sin is now mingled with an urge to

> rejoice
> Much more, that much more good thereof shall spring,
> To God more glory, more good will to Men
> From God, and over wrauth grace shall abound.   (XII 475–8)

The loss of Paradise is the cause of 'all our woe', but it also prompts God's exercise of grace and leads to his greater glorification, which is the ultimate justification of his mysterious ways.

The texture of *Paradise Lost* is remarkable for its suppleness, which derives from its syntactical range and the nature of its vocabulary. One of the most remarkable aspects of its syntactical flexibility is the recurrent use of double syntax. Thus in the first line of the poem – 'Of Mans First Disobedience, and the Fruit' – the word 'Fruit' seems at first to be connected with 'Disobedience', and to mean 'result', but as one reads on it becomes apparent that 'Fruit' is grammatically connected to 'Of that Forbidden Tree'. The last word in a line often acts as a syntactical pivot, completing one grammatical sequence and initiating another. The vocabulary of the poem is similarly fluid, for although the contemporary English meaning of a word is almost inevitably the primary meaning, the etymological sense of a word – usually Latin but sometimes Greek or Hebrew – often contributes a secondary meaning. Thus in Book IX 'sapient' means 'wisdom', but retains an etymological connection with 'taste' (IX 442, 797, 1018).

Paradise Lost portrays the disobedience of Adam in yielding to temptation; *Paradise Regain'd* portrays the obedience of Christ, the second Adam, in resisting temptation. This exact correspondence in subject is not matched by a similarity in style or scope. Some indication of the nature of the differences between the poems may be gleaned from the preface to the second book of *Reason of Church-government* (1641), in which Milton mentions his ambition to write an epic, and distinguishes 'diffuse' epics such as Homer's *Iliad* and *Odyssey*, Virgil's *Æneid*, and Tasso's *Gerusalemme Liberata*, from 'brief' epics such as 'the book of *Job*'. Milton was not predicting the composition of *Paradise Lost* and

Paradise Regain'd, but was simply elaborating Aristotle's distinction between a brief epic with an abrupt ending and a lengthier epic in which the subject is diffuse, or 'watery' (*Poetics* xxvi). In the event Milton's epic did conform to this distinction, and *Paradise Regain'd* became Milton's brief epic. As a young man Milton had written another brief epic, *In Quintum Novembris*. The two works have in common a scheming Satan whose plans are eventually frustrated. The great weakness of the earlier piece is its ending, the abruptness of which seems to follow Aristotle's description of the brief epic rather too enthusiastically. The ending of *Paradise Regain'd*, on the other hand, is carefully shaped to provide a dramatic climax to the poem. Medieval and Renaissance artistic and theological presentations of the temptation had traditionally followed the order of temptation as presented in Matthew iv, in which Christ's first temptation is to turn stones into bread, his second to cast himself down from the pinnacle of the temple, and his third to worship Satan in exchange for the kingdoms of the world. Milton chose to follow instead the order outlined in Luke iv, in which the second and third temptations are reversed, thus enabling him to finish his poem with the climactic episode of the pinnacle. Milton chose to follow Matthew, however, in placing all the temptations after the forty days of fasting, and thus transformed brevity into intensity. He also interpolated two temptations of his own devising into the series – the banquet and the storm – and greatly elaborated the temptation of the kingdoms.

Milton divides the temptation of the kingdoms into a series of related temptations, and Christ's responses to two of these may seem puzzling to the modern reader. At the beginning of Book III Satan tempts Christ with glory. Jesus replies that glory is merely the people's praise, and then remarks

> And what the people but a herd confus'd,
> A miscellaneous rabble, who extoll
> Things vulgar, and well weighd, scarce worth the praise?

Milton's Christ has little in common with the sentimentalized figure of more recent centuries, and he here reflects an attitude that has since gone out of fashion. Milton's political radicalism did not extend to an enthusiasm for popular democracy, and he shared with many of his contemporaries a disdain for the multitude. The undemocratic remarks of Milton's Christ would have seemed quite unexceptionable to Milton's seventeenth-century readers.

The second puzzling response is Christ's reply to the temptation of wisdom, which Satan illustrates by reference to Athens (IV 221–284). Christ replies with a breath-taking denunciation of the accomplishments of ancient Greece (ll. 285–364). One of the central civilizing forces in Milton's life had been his close study of the literature and philosophy of classical antiquity, and it does seem odd that his Christ should articulate barbarian sentiments with such ferocity. Milton was aware, however, that the historical Christ had good reason to be anti-Hellenic, and his fictional Christ compares Roman violations of the Temple and the Law to the earlier abominations of Antiochus IV (III 160–3). The forced Hellenization of Judaea which Antiochus had inaugurated was still government policy at the time of Christ, and he therefore had good reason to be anti-Hellenic. The fact that the historical element in Milton's portrayal of Christ probably lies behind Christ's remarks does not, however, entitle one to drive a wedge between Milton's own attitudes and those of his fictional Christ, for Milton would not allow his Christ to articulate ideas which Milton thought perverse. The judgement that the literature of Greece is 'unworthy to compare/With *Sions* songs, to all true tastes excelling' (IV 346–7) does seem perverse to a modern reader, but it should be remembered that for Milton and his contemporaries 'true tastes' were those tempered by the conviction that Hebrew literature was 'from God inspir'd'. One must also respect the fact that the judgement of Milton's generation was based on a reading of both literatures in the original languages.

Samson Agonistes was Milton's third dramatic poem. In his youth he had written *Arcades* and *Comus*, both of which are indebted to the masque tradition and accordingly partake of the masque convention of the delayed journey. When Milton returned to poetic drama to write *Samson* (at an unknown date) he again incorporated an interrupted journey into the fabric of his poem, but transformed the outward journey of the masque into an interior journey, Samson's progress towards spiritual regeneration.

Samson Agonistes is a play about an episode in Hebrew history written by a Christian in the style of Greek drama. The extraordinary result of this blend of Hellenism, Hebraism, and Christianity is a play in which these elements coalesce with a minimum of compromise. Of the three elements Christianity is probably the most difficult for the modern reader to recognize, but an encounter with the tough-minded Christ of *Paradise Regain'd* (which appeared in the same volume as *Samson Agonistes*) helps one to appreciate the nature of the Christian elements in Milton's play. Milton's Christ was not a pacifist: he 'came not to send peace, but a sword'. The Christ of *Paradise Regain'd* would have viewed the death of the Philistines at the end of *Samson Agonistes* with satisfaction. The fact that some Philistine Lords could be described by Manoah as generous, civil, and magnanimous (ll. 1467–70) would not have muddied the moral water for a seventeenth-century Christian reader: worshippers of Dagon must die. If the ending of the play now seems to be a celebration of primitive savagery, that is because our sensibility has changed in the three centuries since Milton wrote the play.

In the seventeenth century the Old Testament was thought to be not only a record of historical events, but also a foreshadowing of New Testament events. The tradition which represented Samson as a type of Christ originated with Ambrose in the fourth century, and by Milton's time was highly diffuse. Milton draws no specific parallels between

Samson and Christ, so it would be incautious to argue that Milton has shaped details of specific episodes, such as the death of Samson, to remind us of parallels in the life of Christ. On the other hand one must remember that Milton shared with his contemporaries the belief that in some sense the life of Samson prefigured that of Christ, and that Milton's contemporaries would read the poem with this parallel in mind. To the modern reader the Hebraic element seems irreconcilable with Christianity; Milton's seventeenth-century readers would not have sensed a gulf between the Hebraic and Christian elements.

Milton's play is modelled on the tragedies of ancient Greece. But like Racine, who was at the height of his powers when Milton published *Samson Agonistes*, Milton used the traditional form of Greek drama to create highly original art. Racine and Milton both made their characters more self-conscious than the characters of antiquity, though Milton checked this modernizing tendency to some extent by limiting Samson's intelligence (ll. 52, 207), and both authors concentrate their attention on the debilitating effects of passion in a way that recalls the intellectual temper of the authors' backgrounds more readily than the attitudes implied in ancient Greek drama.

For a reader accustomed to Shakespearian tragedy, Samson's absence in the last scene of the play may seem strange. In English Renaissance tragedy the hero dies on stage, often amidst a litter of bodies. In Greek tragedy the hero leaves the stage before the final scene and is replaced by a messenger (often played by the same actor) who reports the fate of the hero. The description of Samson's death in the Book of Judges does not readily lend itself to presentation on the stage, but it is easily accommodated to the convention of Greek tragedy.

The conventions of Greek drama were admirably suited to Milton's purposes. The fate that dominates Greek tragedy becomes for Samson the promise that he will deliver '*Israel* from *Philistian* yoke' (39). Greek fate would have been readily translated into Christian providence by Milton's contemporary readers, and his Puritan readers would have believed, with Milton, that they had a sacred obligation to search themselves for indications of God's plan for their lives. Samson's cast of mind would not have seemed remote. Because the audience of a Greek play knew at the outset how fate was going to direct the course of a play, the playwrights of antiquity could make full use of dramatic irony. Milton's readers were similarly familiar with God's plan for the life of Samson, and Milton follows the ancients by imbuing his play with dramatic irony. In Milton's case this irony does not entirely replace narrative suspense, for his interpolation of imagined incidents into the story creates local uncertainties about the resolution of individual scenes. We do not know if Samson will forgive Dalila, and the knowledge that violence was not permitted on the Greek stage does not abate the feeling that the scene with Harapha could erupt into a brawl at any moment.

In the preface to *Samson Agonistes* Milton discusses the idea of catharsis, and the details of his account show that he has drawn not only on Aristotle but also on recent Italian criticism. His view that tragedy has the power 'to purge the mind' is illustrated by analogy to 'Physic', and so reflects the Italian idea that catharsis is a medical metaphor (though his use on the title-page of *lustratio* rather than *purgatio* to translate *catharsis* suggests resistance to the Italian theory in favour of a more ancient interpretation). Aristotle had outlined a theory of catharsis in the *Poetics*, and had discussed the notion of an ideal state of mind – the 'Aristotelian mean' – in the *Politics*. Italian theorists had linked these two ideas, and Milton's assertion that tragedy has the power to temper and reduce the passions 'to just measure' reflects the Italian idea that catharsis should lead to the ideal of emotional harmony. Milton concludes the play with an expression of the connection between catharsis and inner harmony that articulates his hope for the effect of the play on the sympathetic reader: 'And calm of mind all passion spent'.

The theme which unites Milton's greatest poems is temptation. In *Comus* and the epics temptation is central to the plot, and in those poems Milton exalts the virtue of resisting temptation. His fondness for this theme is related to the moral and intellectual integrity that is such a prominent feature of Milton's own character, and that shapes the character of his poems. This integrity was tested in Milton's youth by the death of Edward King, and he responded to the questions raised by his death with a poem that steadfastly resists easy consolations. The question of how a just God could permit an unjust event to occur was raised again when God permitted the restoration of the monarchy in 1660. There is a sense in which *Paradise Lost*, *Paradise Regain'd*, and *Samson Agonistes* represent Milton's attempt to understand the moral issues raised by the Restoration, and the integrity with which Milton responded to these complex questions contributes substantially to the greatness of these poems.

SELECT BIBLIOGRAPHY

MANUSCRIPTS

MS preserved in Trinity College, Cambridge: holographs of many of the poems published in 1645, including *Comus* and *Lycidas*; also of many of the sonnets first published in 1673, but those from about 1652 are in the hands of amanuenses. Facsimile edition by Scolar Press, 1970.

A Maske: fair copy by an amanuensis of the acting version of *Comus* preserved in the Bridgewater Library.

The five songs of *Comus*, with musical score: British Museum, Additional MS II 518.

Ode to John Rouse (not holograph) in Bodleian Library, MS Lat. Misc. f. 15.

Paradise Lost, Book I, now in Pierpont Morgan Library, New York; facsimile edition by H. Darbishire, Oxford, 1913.

There are facsimiles of all these MSS in H. F. Fletcher's *Facsimile Edition of the Poetical Works of Milton*, Illinois, 4 vols., 1943–8.

FIRST EDITIONS

On Shakespear: second folio of Shakespeare, 1632.

A Maske (*Comus*), 1637; published by Henry Lawes.

Lycidas, in volume of elegies *Justa Eduardo King*, Cambridge, 1638; a copy in the Cambridge University Library and another in the British Museum contain corrections in Milton's hand.

Epitaphium Damonis, c. 1639–40; British Museum, C. 57 d. 48.

Upon Old Hobson the Carrier of Cambridge (second of the poems on *The University Carrier*) in a miscellany, *Banquet of Jests*, London, 1640.

Poems of Mr. John Milton, Both English and Latin, 1645. Second edition, *Poems, etc. Upon Several Occasions*, 1673.

Sonnets: *To Mr. H. Lawes* in *Choice Psalms*, 1648; *To Sr. Henry Vane* in *The Life and Death of Sir Henry Vane*, 1662; *On Lord Gen. Fairfax*, *To the Lord General Cromwell*, *To Mr. Cyriack Skinner*, *To Sr. Henry Vane* in *Letters of State*, 1694.

Paradise Lost, 1667; second edition, 1674.

Paradise Regain'd and *Samson Agonistes*, 1671.

LATER EDITIONS

Poetical Works, with Patrick Hume's commentary on *Paradise Lost*, published by Jacob Tonson, 1695.

Paradise Lost, ed. Richard Bentley, 1732.

    Zachary Pearce: *Review of the text of . . . 'Paradise Lost'* (viz. Bentley's), 1733.

Jonathan Richardson: *Explanatory Notes and Remarks on 'Paradise Lost'*, 1734.

Poetical Works, ed. Thomas Newton, 1749–52.

Poems upon Several Occasions, ed. Thomas Wharton, 2nd edition, 1791.

Poems, ed. William Cowper, 4 vols. 1810.

Poetical Works, variorum edition, ed. H. J. Todd, 1826.

Poems, ed. T. Keightley, 1859.

Poetical Works, ed. D. Masson, 1874.

The Cambridge Milton for Schools, ed. A. W. Verity, 1891–6.

IMPORTANT MODERN EDITIONS

The Works of John Milton, gen. ed. F. A. Patterson, 18 vols., 1931–38.

Complete Prose Works, gen. ed. D. M. Wolfe, 8 vols., 1953 ff.

Sonnets, ed. J. S. Smart, 1921, ed. E. A. J. Honigmann, 1966.

Latin Poems, ed. W. MacKellar, 1930.

Shorter Poems, ed. B. A. Wright, 1938.

Complete Poems and Major Prose, ed. M. Y. Hughes, 1957.

Poetical Works, ed. H. Darbishire, 2 vols., 1952–5.

Poetical Works, ed. D. Bush, 1966.

Poems, ed. J. Carey and A. D. S. Fowler, 1968.

Poems of 1645 and Comus, ed. B. Nellist, 1974.

BIOGRAPHY

Milton's autobiographical remarks have been assembled by J. S. Diekhoff, *Milton on Himself*, 1939. The six early accounts have been collected by H. Darbishire in *Early Lives of Milton*, 1932; her attribution of the anonymous *Life* to John Phillips has not been received uncritically. Of later biographies Dr Johnson's version in *Lives of the Poets* is remarkable for its insights and prejudices. The great Victorian biography, D. Masson's *Life of John Milton* (7 vols., 1859–94) remains indispensable. *The Life Records of John Milton* have been collected by J. M. French (5 vols., 1949–58). The authoritative modern biography is W. R. Parker's *Milton: A Biography* (2 vols., 1968).

BIBLIOGRAPHICAL GUIDES

D. H. Stevens, *A Reference Guide to Milton from 1800 to the Present Day*, 1930.

H. F. Fletcher, *Contributions to a Milton Bibliography 1800—1930*, 1931.

C. Huckaby, *John Milton, An Annotated Bibliography 1929—1968*, 1969.

J. H. Hanford, *Milton* (Goldentree Bibliographies) 1966, 1979.

Bibliographies are published annually in the English Association's *Year's Work in English Studies*, the Modern Humanities Research Association's *Annual Bibliography of English Language and Literature*,

PMLA, Studies in Philology, and *Studies in English Literature 1500–1900*.

The best source of information about current publications is the invaluable *Milton Quarterly*, which contains reviews of all new books on Milton, and abstracts of all articles on Milton.

REFERENCE BOOKS

J. Bradshaw, *A Concordance to the Poetical Works of John Milton*, 1894.
C. G. Osgood, *The Classical Mythology of Milton's English Poems*, 1900.
L. E. Lockwood, *Lexicon to the English Poetical Works of John Milton*, 1907.
A. H. Gilbert, *A Geographical Dictionary of Milton*, 1919.
E. S. LeComte, *A Milton Dictionary*, 1961.
J. C. Boswell, *Milton's Library*, 1975.
Milton Encyclopedia, gen. ed. W. B. Hunter, 8 vols., 1978 ff.

CRITICISM

The Variorum Commentary on the Poems of John Milton gen. ed. M. Y. Hughes (8 vols., 1970 ff.) contains summaries of criticism and line-by-line commentaries. Early criticism has been collected by J. T. Shawcross, *Milton: The Critical Heritage* (2 vols., 1970, 1972) and J. A. Wittreich Jr, *The Romantics on Milton* (1970). Many journals publish articles on Milton, and two – *Milton Quarterly* and *Milton Studies* – are wholly devoted to Milton. There are many excellent books on Milton, a few of which are listed below.

E. M. W. Tillyard, *Milton*, 1930.
W. R. Parker, *Milton's Debt to Greek Tragedy in 'Samson Agonistes'*, 1937.
M. Kelley, *This Great Argument*, 1941.
A. Barker, *Milton and the Puritan Dilemma*, 1942.
B. Rajan, *'Paradise Lost' and the Seventeenth-Century Reader*, 1947.
A. J. A. Waldock, *'Paradise Lost' and Its Critics*, 1947.
E. M. Pope, *'Paradise Regain'd': The Tradition and the Poem*, 1947.
F. M. Krowse, *Milton's Samson and the Christian Tradition*, 1949.
F. T. Prince, *The Italian Element in Milton's Verse*, 1954.
C. Brooks and J. E. Hardy, *Poems of Mr. John Milton*, 1957.
R. Tuve, *Images and Themes in Five Poems by Milton*, 1957.
W. Empson, *Milton's God*, 1961.
C. Ricks, *Milton's Grand Style*, 1963.
H. Gardner, *A Reading of Paradise Lost*, 1965.
C. A. Patrides, *Milton and the Christian Tradition*, 1966.
B. K. Lewalski, *Milton's Brief Epic*, 1966.
D. Burden, *The Logical Epic*, 1967.
J. M. Evans, *'Paradise Lost' and the Genesis Tradition*, 1968.
J. B. Leishman, *Milton's Minor Poems*, 1969.

B. Rajan, *The Lofty Rhyme*, 1970.
M. Treip, *Milton's Punctuation*, 1970.
A. Low, *The Blaze of Noon: A Reading of Samson Agonistes*, 1974.
J. M. Steadman, *Epic and Tragic Structure in Paradise Lost*, 1976.
C. Hill, *Milton and the English Revolution*, 1977.
R. M. Frye, *Milton's Imagery and the Visual Arts*, 1978.
M. A. Radzinowicz, *Toward Samson Agonistes*, 1978.

MISCELLANEOUS POEMS

POEMS

OF

Mr. *John Milton*,

BOTH

ENGLISH and LATIN,

Compos'd at several times.

Printed by his true Copies.

The S o n g s were set in Musick by
Mr. HENRY LAWES Gentleman of
the KINGS Chappel, and one
of His MAIESTIES
Private Musick.

———*Baccare frontem*
Cingite, ne vati noceat mala lingua futuro,
Virgil, Eclog. 7.

Printed and publish'd according to
ORDER.

LONDON,
Printed by *Ruth Raworth* for *Humphrey Moseley*,
and are to be sold at the signe of the Princes
Arms in S. *Pauls* Church-yard. 1645.

POEMS, &c.

UPON

Several Occasions.

BY

Mr. *JOHN MILTON:*

Both E N G L I S H and L A T I N, &c.
Composed at several times.

With a small Tractate of
EDUCATION
To Mr. HARTLIB

LONDON,
Printed for *Tho. Dring* at the *Blew Anchor*
next *Mitre Court* over against *Fetter*
Lane in *Fleet-street.* 1673.

THE STATIONER
TO THE READER

It is not any private respect of gain, Gentle Reader, *for the slightest Pamphlet is now adayes more vendible then the Works of learnedest men; but it is the love I have to our own Language that hath made me diligent to collect, and set forth such* Peeces *both in Prose and Vers as may renew the wonted honour and esteem of our English tongue: and it's the worth of these both English and Latin* Poems, *not the flourish of any prefixed* encomions *that can invite thee to buy them, though these are not without the highest Commendations and Applause of the learnedst* Academicks, *both domestick and forrein: And amongst those of our own Countrey, the unparallel'd attestation of that renowned Provost of* Eaton, *Sir Henry Wootton: I know not thy palat how it relishes such dainties, nor how harmonious thy soul is; perhaps more trivial Airs may please thee better. But howsoever thy opinion is spent upon these, that incouragement I have already received from the most ingenious men in their clear and courteous entertainment of Mr* Wallers *late choice Peeces, hath once more made me adventure into the World, presenting it with these ever-green, and not to be blasted Laurels. The Authors more peculiar excellency in these studies, was too well known to conceal his Papers, or to keep me from attempting to sollicit them from him. Let the event guide it self which way it will, I shall deserve of the age, by bringing into the Light as true a Birth, as the Muses have brought forth since our famous* Spencer *wrote; whose Poems in these English ones are as rarely imitated, as sweetly excell'd. Reader, if thou art Eagle-eied to censure their worth, I am not fearful to expose them to thy exactest perusal.*

Thine to command

HUMPH. MOSELEY.

[This preface to the 1645 edition was omitted in 1673.]

ON THE MORNING OF
CHRISTS NATIVITY

Compos'd 1629

I

THIS is the Month and this the happy morn
Wherein the Son of Heav'ns eternal King,
Of wedded Maid and Virgin Mother born,
Our great Redemption from above did bring;
For so the holy Sages once did sing, 5
    That he our deadly forfeit should release,
And with his Father work us a perpetual peace.

II

That glorious Form, that Light unsufferable,
And that far-beaming blaze of Majesty,
Wherewith he wont at Heav'ns high Councel-Table 10
To sit the midst of Trinal Unity,
He laid aside; and here with us to be,
    Forsook the Courts of everlasting Day,
And chose with us a darksom House of mortal Clay.

III

Say Heav'nly Muse, shall not thy sacred vein 15
Afford a Present to the Infant God?
Hast thou no verse, no hymn or solemn strein
To welcome him to this his new abode,
Now while the Heav'n by the Suns team untrod
    Hath took no print of the approaching light, 20
And all the spangled host keep watch in squadrons bright?

IV

See how from far upon the Eastern rode
The Star-led Wizards haste with odours sweet,
O run, prevent them with thy humble ode,
And lay it lowly at his blessed feet; 25
Have thou the honour first, thy Lord to greet,
    And join thy voice unto the Angel Quire,
From out his secret Altar toucht with hallowd fire.

THE HYMN

I

It was the Winter wilde,
While the Heav'n-born-childe
 All meanly wrapt in the rude manger lies;   30
Nature in awe to him
Had doft her gaudy trim,
 With her great Master so to sympathize:
It was no season then for her   35
To wanton with the Sun her lusty Paramour.

II

Onely with speeches fair
She woo's the gentle Air
 To hide her guilty front with innocent Snow,
And on her naked shame,   40
Pollute with sinful blame,
 The Saintly Veil of Maiden white to throw,
Confounded that her Makers eyes
Should look so near upon her foul deformities.

III

But he her fears to cease   45
Sent down the meek-ey'd Peace,
 She crownd with Olive green, came softly sliding
Down through the turning sphear
His ready Harbinger,
 With Turtle wing the amorous clouds dividing, 50
And waving wide her mirtle wand
She strikes a universal Peace through Sea and Land.

IV

No War, or Battels sound
Was heard the World around,
 The idle Spear and Shield were high up hung, 55
The hooked Chariot stood
Unstaind with hostile blood,
 The Trumpet spake not to the armed throng,
And Kings sate still with awful eye,
As if they surely knew their sovran Lord was by. 60

V

But peaceful was the night
Wherein the Prince of light

His reign of peace upon the earth began:
The Windes with wonder whist
Smoothly the waters kist,   65
   Whispering new joyes to the milde Ocean,
Who now hath quite forgot to rave,
While Birds of Calm sit brooding on the charmed wave.

VI

The Stars with deep amaze
Stand fixt in stedfast gaze,   70
   Bending one way their precious influence,
And will not take their flight,
For all the morning light,
   Or *Lucifer* that often warnd them thence;
But in their glimmering Orbs did glow,   75
Untill their Lord himself bespake, and bid them go.

VII

And though the shady gloom
Had given day her room,
   The Sun himself withheld his wonted speed,
And hid his head for shame,   80
As his inferior flame
   The new enlightend world no more should need;
He saw a greater Sun appear
Than his bright Throne or burning Axletree could bear.

VIII

The Shepherds on the Lawn,   85
Or ere the point of dawn,
   Sate simply chatting in a rustic row;
Full little thought they than,
That the mighty *Pan*
   Was kindly come to live with them below;   90
Perhaps their loves, or else their sheep,
Was all that did their silly thoughts so busie keep.

IX

When such music sweet
Their hearts and ears did greet
   As never was by mortal finger strook,   95
Divinely-warbl'd voice
Answering the stringed noise,
   As all their souls in blissful rapture took:
The Air such pleasure loth to lose
With thousand echoes still prolongs each heav'nly close.   100

X

Nature that heard such sound
Beneath the hollow round
  Of *Cynthia's* seat, the Airy region thrilling,
Now was almost won
To think her part was don,   105
  And that her reign had here its last fulfilling;
She knew such harmony alone
Could hold all Heav'n and Earth in happier union.

XI

At last surrounds their sight
A Globe of circular light,   110
  That with long beams the shame-fac't night arrayd,
The helmed Cherubim
And sworded Seraphim
  Are seen in glittering ranks with wings displayd,
Harping in loud and solemn quire,   115
With unexpressive notes to Heav'ns new-born Heir.

XII

Such Music (as 'tis said)
Before was never made,
  But when of old the sons of morning sung,
While the Creator great   120
His Constellations set,
  And the well-ballanc't world on hinges hung,
And cast the dark foundations deep,
And bid the weltring waves their oozy channel keep.

XIII

Ring out ye Crystal sphears,   125
Once bless our human ears,
  (If ye have power to touch our senses so)
And let your silver chime
Move in melodious time;
  And let the Base of Heav'ns deep Organ blow,   130
And with your ninefold harmony
Make up full consort to th'Angelic symphony.

XIV

For if such holy Song
Enwrap our fancy long,
  Time will run back, and fetch the age of gold,   135
And speckl'd vanity
Will sicken soon and die,
  And leprous sin will melt from earthly mould,

126 human *Ed. 1*] humane *Ed. 2*

And Hell it self will pass away,
And leave her dolorous mansions to the peering day. 140

XV

Yea Truth and Justice then
Will down return to men,
  Orbd in a Rain-bow; and like glories wearing
Mercy will sit between,
Thron'd in Celestial sheen, 145
  With radiant feet the tissued clouds down stearing,
And Heav'n as at some Festivall
Will open wide the Gates of her high Palace Hall.

XVI

But wisest Fate sayes no,
This must not yet be so, 150
  The Babe lies yet in smiling Infancy,
That on the bitter cross
Must redeem our loss;
  So both himself and us to glorifie:
Yet first to those ychain'd in sleep, 155
The wakeful trump of doom must thunder through the deep,

XVII

With such a horrid clang
As on mount *Sinai* rang
  While the red fire and smouldring clouds out brake:
The aged Earth agast 160
With terror of that blast
  Shall from the surface to the center shake,
When at the worlds last session
The dreadful Judge in middle Air shall spread his throne.

XVIII

And then at last our bliss 165
Full and perfet is,
  But now begins; for from this happy day
Th'old Dragon under ground
In straiter limits bound
  Not half so far casts his usurped sway, 170
And wroth to see his Kingdom fail,
Swindges the scaly Horror of his folded tail.

143–4 Th'enameld *Arras* of the Rainbow wearing
          And Mercy set between, *Ed. 1*
156 deep, *Ed. 1*] deep. *Ed. 2*

XIX

The Oracles are dumm,
No voice or hideous humm
   Runs through the arched roof in words deceiving.   175
Apollo from his shrine
Can no more divine,
   With hollow shriek the steep of *Delphos* leaving.
No nightly trance, or breathed spell,
Inspires the pale-ey'd Priest from the prophetic cell.   180

XX

The lonely mountains ore,
And the resounding shore,
   A voice of weeping heard, and loud lament;
From haunted spring, and dale
Edg'd with poplar pale,   185
   The parting Genius is with sighing sent,
With flowr-inwoven tresses torn
The Nymphs in twilight shade of tangl'd thickets mourn.

XXI

In consecrated Earth,
And on the holy Hearth   190
   The *Lars* and *Lemures* moan with midnight plaint,
In Urns, and Altars round,
A drear and dying sound
   Affrights the *Flamins* at their service quaint;
And the chill Marble seems to sweat,   195
While each peculiar power forgoes his wonted seat.

XXII

Peor and *Baälim*
Forsake their Temples dim,
   With that twice-batterd god of *Palestine*,
And mooned *Ashtaroth*,   200
Heav'ns Queen and Mother both,
   Now sits not girt with Tapers holy shrine,
The Libyc *Hammon* shrinks his horn,
In vain the *Tyrian* Maids their wounded *Thamuz* mourn.

XXIII

And sullen *Moloch* fled   205
Hath left in shaddows dred
   His burning Idol all of blackest hue;
In vain with Cymbals ring
They call the grisly King,
   In dismal dance about the furnace blue;   210

The brutish gods of *Nile* as fast,
Isis and *Orus*, and the Dog *Anubis* hast.

XXIV

Nor is *Osiris* seen
In *Memphian* Grove or Green,
  Trampling the unshowr'd Grass with lowings loud: 215
Nor can he be at rest
Within his sacred chest,
  Naught but profoundest Hell can be his shroud;
In vain with Timbrel'd Anthems dark
The sable-stoled Sorcerers bear his worshipt Ark.   220

XXV

He feels from *Juda's* Land
The dreaded Infants hand,
  The rays of *Bethlehem* blind his dusky eyn;
Nor all the Gods beside
Longer dare abide,   225
  Not *Typhon* huge ending in snaky twine:
Our Babe to shew his Godhead true
Can in his swadling bands controul the damned crew.

XXVI

So when the Sun in bed,
Curtaind with cloudy red,   230
  Pillows his chin upon an Orient wave,
The flocking shaddows pale
Troop to th'infernal Jail,
  Each fetterd Ghost slips to his several grave,
And the yellow-skirted *Fays*   235
Fly after the Night-steeds, leaving their Moon-lov'd maze.

XXVII

But see the Virgin blest
Hath laid her Babe to rest.
  Time is our tedious Song should here have ending:
Heav'ns youngest teemed Star   240
Hath fixt her polisht Car,
  Her sleeping Lord with Handmaid Lamp attending:
And all about the Courtly Stable,
Bright-harnest Angels sit in order serviceable.

A PARAPHRASE ON *PSALM 114*

This and the following *Psalm* were done
by the Author at fifteen years old.

When the blest seed of *Terah*'s faithful Son
After long toil their liberty had won,
And passd from *Pharian* Fields to *Canaan* Land,
Led by the strength of the Almightys hand,
Jehovah's wonders were in *Israel* shown,   5
His praise and glory was in *Israel* known.
That saw the troubl'd Sea, and shivering fled,
And sought to hide his froth-becurled head
Low in the earth, *Jordans* clear streams recoil,
As a faint Host that hath receiv'd the foil.   10
The high, huge-bellied Mountains skip like Rams
Amongst their Ewes, the little Hills like Lambs.
Why fled the Ocean?   And why skipd the Mountains?
Why turned *Jordan* toward his Crystal Fountains?
Shake earth, and at the presence be agast   15
Of him that ever was, and ay shall last,
That glassy floods from rugged rocks can crush,
And make soft rills from fiery flint-stones gush.

PSALM 136

Let us with a gladsom mind
Praise the Lord, for he is kind,
    For his mercies ay endure,
    Ever faithful, ever sure.

Let us blaze his Name abroad,   5
For of gods he is the God;
    For his, etc.

O let us his praises tell,
Who doth the wrathful tyrants quell.   10
    For his, etc.

Who with his miracles doth make
Amazed Heav'n and Earth to shake.
    For his, etc.   15

Psalm 136. 10, 13 Who] That *Ed. 1*

Who by his wisdom did create
The painted Heav'ns so full of state.
  For his, etc.   20

Who did the solid Earth ordain
To rise above the watry plain.
  For his, etc.

Who by his all-commanding might   25
Did fill the new-made world with light.
  For his, etc.

And caus'd the Golden-tressed Sun
All the day long his course to run.   30
  For his, etc.

The horned Moon to shine by night,
Amongst her spangl'd sisters bright.
  For his, etc.   36

He with his thunder-clasping hand
Smote the first-born of *Egypt* Land.
  For his, etc.
                                                  40
And in despite of *Pharaoh* fell,
He brought from thence his *Israël*.
  For his, etc.

The ruddy waves he cleft in twain   45
Of the *Erythræan* main.
  For his, etc.

The floods stood still like Walls of Glass,
While the Hebrew Bands did pass.   50
  For his, etc.

But full soon they did devour
The Tawny King with all his power.
  For his, etc.   56

His chosen people he did bless
In the wasteful Wilderness.
  For his, etc.   60

In bloody battel he brought down
Kings of prowess and renown.
  For his, etc.

17, 21, 25 Who] That *Ed. 1*

He foild bold *Seon* and his host,   65
That rul'd the *Amorrean* coast.
    For his, etc.

And large-limbd *Og* he did subdue,
With all his over-hardy crew.   70
    For his, etc.

And to his Servant *Israël*
He gave their Land therein to dwell.
    For his, etc.   76

He hath with a piteous eye
Beheld us in our misery.
    For his, etc.   80

And freed us from the slavery
Of the invading enemy.
    For his, etc.

All living creatures he doth feed,   85
And with full hand supplies their need.
    For his, etc.

Let us therefore warble forth
His mighty Majesty and worth.   90
    For his, etc.

That his mansion hath on high
Above the reach of mortal eye.
    For his mercies ay endure,   95
    Ever faithful, ever sure.

Anno ætatis 17

ON THE DEATH OF A FAIR INFANT
DYING OF A COUGH

I

O fairest flowr no sooner blown but blasted,
Soft silken Primrose fading timelesslie,
Summers chief honour if thou hadst out-lasted
Bleak winters force that made thy blossom drie;
    For he being amorous on that lovely die   5
That did thy cheek envermeil, thought to kiss
But killd alas, and then bewaild his fatal bliss.

II

For since grim Aquilo his charioter
By boistrous rape th' Athenian damsel got,
He thought it touchd his Deitie full neer   10
If likewise he some fair one wedded not,
Thereby to wipe away th' infamous blot
    Of long-uncoupl'd bed and childless eld,
Which 'mongst the wanton gods a foul reproach was held.

III

So mounting up in icie-pearled carr,   15
Through middle empire of the freezing aire
He wanderd long, till thee he spi'd from farr,
There ended was his quest, there ceas'd his care.
Down he descended from his Snow-soft chaire,
    But all unwares with his cold-kind embrace   20
Unhous'd thy Virgin Soul from her fair biding place.

IV

Yet art thou not inglorious in thy fate;
For so *Apollo*, with unweeting hand
Whilome did slay his dearly-loved mate
Young *Hyacinth* born on *Eurotas* strand,   25
Young *Hyacinth* the pride of *Spartan* land;
    But then transformd him to a purple flower:
Alack that so to change thee winter had no power.

[*On the death of a fair Infant* first printed 1673]

V

Yet can I not persuade me thou art dead
Or that thy corse corrupts in earths dark wombe, 30
Or that thy beauties lie in wormie bed,
Hid from the world in a low delved tombe;
Could Heav'n for pittie thee so strictly doom?
  Oh no! for something in thy face did shine
Above mortalitie that shewd thou wast divine. 35

VI

Resolve me then oh Soul most surely blest
(If so it be that thou these plaints dost hear),
Tell me bright Spirit where e're thou hoverest,
Whether above that high first-moving Sphear
Or in th' Elisian fields (if such there were), 40
  Oh say me true if thou wert mortal wight
And why from us so quickly thou didst take thy flight.

VII

Wert thou som Starr which from the ruind roofe
Of shak't Olympus by mischance didst fall;
Which careful *Jove* in natures true behoofe 45
Took up, and in fit place did reinstall?
Or did of late earths Sons besiege the wall
  Of sheenie Heav'n, and thou som goddess fled
Amongst us here to hide thy nectard head?

VIII

Or wert thou that just Maid who once before 50
Forsook the hated earth, O tell me sooth,
And cam'st again to visit us once more?
Or wert thou Mercy that sweet smiling Youth?
Or that crownd Matron sage white-robed Truth?
  Or any other of that heav'nly brood 55
Let down in cloudie throne to do the world som good?

IX

Or wert thou of the golden-winged host,
Who having clad thy self in human weed,
To earth from thy prefixed seat didst post,
And after short abode flie back with speed, 60
As if to shew what creatures Heav'n doth breed,
  Thereby to set the hearts of men on fire
To scorn the sordid world, and unto Heav'n aspire.

40 were *Ed. 1*] were. *Ed. 2*
53 Or wert thou that sweet smiling Youth! *Ed. 2*

X

But oh why didst thou not stay here below
To bless us with thy heav'n-lov'd innocence,   65
To slake his wrath whom sin hath made our foe,
To turn Swift-rushing black perdition hence,
Or drive away the slaughtering pestilence,
 To stand 'twixt us and our deserved smart?
But thou canst best perform that office where thou art. 70

XI

Then thou the mother of so sweet a child
Her false imagind loss cease to lament,
And wisely learn to curb thy sorrows wild;
Think what a present thou to God hast sent,
And render him with patience what he lent;   75
 This if thou do he will an offspring give,
That till the worlds last-end shall make thy name to live.

Anno Ætatis 19

AT A VACATION EXERCISE
IN THE COLLEDGE,
PART LATIN PART ENGLISH.
THE LATIN SPEECHES ENDED,
THE ENGLISH THUS BEGAN

Hail native Language, that by sinews weak
Didst move my first endevoring tongue to speak,
And mad'st imperfet words with childish trips,
Half unpronounc't, slide through my infant lips,
Driving dumb silence from the portal dore,   5
Where he had mutely sate two years before:
Here I salute thee and thy pardon ask,
That now I use thee in my latter task:
Small loss it is that thence can come unto thee,
I know my tongue but little Grace can do thee: 10
Thou needst not be ambitious to be first,
Believe me I have thither packt the worst:
And, if it happen as I did forecast,
The daintest dishes shall be serv'd up last.
I pray thee then deny me not thy aide   15
For this same small neglect that I have made:
But haste thee straight to do me once a Pleasure,
And from thy wardrope bring thy chiefest treasure;
Not those new fangled toys, and trimming slight
Which takes our late fantastics with delight,   20
But cull those richest Robes and gay'st attire
Which deepest Spirits and choicest Wits desire:
I have some naked thoughts that rove about
And loudly knock to have their passage out;
And wearie of their place do only stay   25
Till thou hast deckt them in thy best array;
That so they may without suspect or fears
Fly swiftly to this fair Assemblys ears;
Yet I had rather if I were to chuse,
Thy service in som graver subject use,   30
Such as may make thee search thy coffers round
Before thou clothe my fancy in fit sound:
Such where the deep transported mind may soare
Above the wheeling poles, and at Heav'ns dore

[*At a Vacation Exercise* first printed 1673.   *Errata* directs that it should be placed here]

Look in, and see each blissful Deitie   35
How he before the thunderous throne doth lie,
List'ning to what unshorn *Apollo* sings
To th'touch of golden wires, while *Hebe* brings
Immortal Nectar to her Kingly Sire:
Then passing through the Sphears of watchful fire,   40
And mistie Regions of wide air next under,
And hills of Snow and lofts of piled Thunder,
May tell at length how green-ey'd *Neptune* raves,
In Heav'ns defiance must'ring all his waves;
Then sing of secret things that came to pass   45
When Beldam Nature in her cradle was;
And last of Kings and Queens and Heroes old,
Such as the wise *Demodocus* once told
In solemn Songs at King *Alcinous* feast,
While sad *Ulysses* soul and all the rest   50
Are held with his melodious harmonie
In willing chains and sweet captivitie.
But fie my wandring Muse how thou dost stray!
Expectance calls thee now another way,
Thou knowst it must be now thy only bent   55
To keep in compass of thy Predicament:
Then quick about thy purpos'd buisness come,
That to the next I may resign my Roome.

Then Ens *is represented as Father of the Praedicaments his ten Sons, whereof the Eldest stood for* Substance *with his Canons, which* Ens *thus speaking, explains.*

Good luck befriend thee Son; for at thy birth
The Fairy Ladies danc'd upon the hearth;   60
Thy drowsie Nurse hath sworn she did them spie
Come tripping to the Room where thou didst lie;
And sweetly singing round about thy Bed
Strew all their blessings on thy sleeping Head.
She heard them give thee this, that thou shouldst still   65
From eyes of mortals walk invisible,
Yet there is something that doth force my fear,
For once it was my dismal hap to hear
A *Sybil* old, bow-bent with crooked age,
That far events full wisely could presage,   70
And in Times long and dark Prospective Glass
Foresaw what future dayes should bring to pass,
Your Son, said she, (nor can you it prevent)
Shall subject be to many an Accident.
Ore all his Brethren he shall Reign as King,   75
Yet every one shall make him underling,
And those that cannot live from him asunder
Ungratefully shall strive to keep him under,

In worth and excellence he shall outgo them,
Yet being above them, he shall be below them;   80
From others he shall stand in need of nothing,
Yet on his Brothers shall depend for Clothing.
To find a Foe it shall not be his hap,
And peace shall lull him in her flowry lap;
Yet shall he live in strife, and at his dore   85
Devouring war shall never cease to roare;
Yea it shall be his natural property
To harbour those that are at enmity.
What power, what force, what mighty spell, if not
Your learned hands, can loose this Gordian knot?   90

The next Quantity *and* Quality, *spake in Prose, then* Relation *was call'd by his Name.*

Rivers arise; whether thou be the Son
Of utmost *Tweed*, or *Oose*, or gulphie *Dun*,
Or *Trent*, who like some earth-born Giant spreads
His thirty Armes along the indented Meads,
Or sullen *Mole* that runneth underneath,   95
Or *Severn* swift, guilty of Maidens death,
Or Rockie *Avon*, or of Sedgie *Lee*,
Or Coaly *Tine*, or ancient hallowd *Dee*,
Or *Humber* loud that keeps the *Scythians* Name,
Or *Medway* smooth, or Royal Towred *Thame*.   100

The rest was Prose.

THE PASSION

I

Erewhile of Music and Ethereal mirth,
Wherewith the stage of Air and Earth did ring,
And joyous news of heav'nly Infants birth,
My muse with Angels did divide to sing;
But headlong joy is ever on the wing, 5
  In Wintry solstice like the shortend light
Soon swallowd up in dark and long out-living night.

II

For now to sorrow must I tune my song,
And set my Harp to notes of saddest wo,
Which on our dearest Lord did sieze ere long, 10
Dangers and snares and wrongs, and worse than so,
Which he for us did freely undergo.
  Most perfet *Hero*, tri'd in heaviest plight
Of labours huge and hard, too hard for human wight.

III

He sovran Priest stooping his regal head 15
That dropd with odorous oil down his fair eyes,
Poor fleshly Tabernacle entered,
His starry front low-rooft beneath the skies;
O what a mask was there, what a disguise!
  Yet more; the stroke of death he must abide, 20
Then lies him meekly down fast by his Brethrens side.

IV

These latest scenes confine my roving verse,
To this Horizon is my *Phoebus* bound;
His Godlike acts, and his temptations fierce,
And former sufferings other where are found; 25
Loud ore the rest *Cremona's* Trump doth sound;
  Me softer airs befit, and softer strings
Of Lute, or Viol still, more apt for mournful things.

22 latest] latter *Ed. 1*
23 bound;] bound, *Edd. 1, 2*
24 acts,] acts; *Edd. 1, 2*

V

Befriend me Night best Patroness of grief,
Over the Pole thy thickest mantle throw,   30
And work my flatterd fancy to belief,
That Heav'n and Earth are colourd with my wo;
My sorrows are too dark for Day to know:
  The leaves should all be black wheron I write,
And letters where my tears have washt a wannish white.   35

VI

See see the Chariot, and those rushing wheels,
That whirld the Prophet up at *Chebar* flood,
My spirit som transporting *Cherub* feels,
To bear me where the Towrs of *Salem* stood,
Once glorious Towrs, now sunk in guiltless blood;   40
  There doth my soul in holy vision sit
In pensive trance, and anguish, and ecstatic fit.

VII

Mine eye hath found that sad Sepulchral rock
That was the Casket of Heav'ns richest store,
And here though grief my feeble hands up-lock,   45
Yet on the softend Quarry would I score
My plaining verse as lively as before;
  For sure so well instructed are my tears,
That they would fitly fall in orderd Characters.

VIII

Or should I thence hurried on viewless wing   50
Take up a weeping on the Mountains wilde,
The gentle neighbourhood of grove and spring
Would soon unbosom all thir Echoes milde,
And I (for grief is easily beguild)
  Might think th'infection of my sorrows loud   55
Had got a race of mourners on som pregnant cloud.

*This Subject the Author finding to be above the years he had,
when he wrote it, and nothing satisfi'd with what was
begun, left it unfinisht.*

ON TIME

Fly envious *Time*, till thou run out thy race,
Call on the lazy leaden-stepping hours,
Whose speed is but the heavy Plummets pace;
And glut thy self with what thy womb devours,
Which is no more than what is false and vain,   5
And merely mortal dross;
So little is our loss,
So little is thy gain.
For when as each thing bad thou hast entomb'd,
And last of all, thy greedy self consum'd,   10
Then long Eternity shall greet our bliss
With an individual kiss;
And Joy shall overtake us as a flood,
When every thing that is sincerely good
And perfetly divine,   15
With Truth, and Peace, and Love shall ever shine
About the supreme Throne
Of him, t'whose happy-making sight alone,
When once our heav'nly-guided soul shall clime,
Then all this Earthy grossness quit,   20
Attir'd with Stars, we shall for ever sit,
    Triumphing over Death, and Chance, and thee O Time.

UPON THE CIRCUMCISION

Ye flaming Powers, and winged Warriors bright,
That erst with Music, and triumphant song
First heard by happy watchful Shepherds ear,
So sweetly sung your Joy the Clouds along
Through the soft silence of the list'ning night;   5
Now mourn, and if sad share with us to bear
Your fiery essence can distill no tear,
Burn in your sighs, and borrow
Seas wept from our deep sorrow,
He who with all Heav'ns heraldry whilear   10
Enterd the world, now bleeds to give us ease;
Alas, how soon our sin
    Sore doth begin
    His Infancy to sease!

O more exceeding love or law more just?   15
Just law indeed, but more exceeding love!
For we by rightful doom remediless
Were lost in death, till he that dwelt above

High thron'd in secret bliss, for us frail dust
Emptied his glory, ev'n to nakedness; 20
And that great Cov'nant which we still transgress
Intirely satisfi'd,
And the full wrath beside
Of vengeful Justice bore for our excess,
And seals obedience first with wounding smart 25
This day, but O ere long
Huge pangs and strong
Will pierce more near his heart.

AT A SOLEMN MUSIC

Blest pair of *Sirens*, pledges of Heav'ns joy,
Sphear-born harmonious Sisters, Voice and Verse,
Wed your divine sounds, and mixt power employ
Dead things with inbreath'd sense able to pierce,
And to our high-rais'd phantasie present 5
That undisturbed Song of pure concent,
Ay sung before the saphire-coulourd throne
To him that sits thereon
With Saintly shout and solemn Jubily,
Where the bright Seraphim in burning row 10
Their loud up-lifted Angel trumpets blow,
And the Cherubic host in thousand quires
Touch their immortal Harps of golden wires,
With those just Spirits that wear victorious Palms,
Hymns devout and holy Psalms 15
Singing everlastingly;
That we on Earth with undiscording voice
May rightly answer that melodious noise;
As once we did, till disproportiond sin
Jarrd against natures chime, and with harsh din 20
Broke the fair music that all creatures made
To their great Lord, whose love their motion swayd
In perfet Diapason, whilst they stood
In first obedience, and their state of good.
O may we soon again renew that Song, 25
And keep in tune with Heav'n, till God ere long
To his celestial consort us unite,
To live with him, and sing in endless morn of light.

6 concent, *Tr. MS., Ed. 2*] content, *Ed. 1*

AN EPITAPH ON THE
MARCHIONESS OF *WINCHESTER*

This rich Marble doth enterr
The honourd Wife of *Winchester*,
A Vicounts daughter, an Earls heir,
Besides what her vertues fair
Added to her noble birth,   5
More than she could own from Earth.
Summers three times eight save one
She had told, alas too soon,
After so short time of breath,
To house with darkness, and with **death**.   10
Yet had the number of her days
Bin as complete as was her praise,
Nature and fate had had no strife
In giving limit to her life.
Her high birth, and her graces **sweet**,   15
Quickly found a lover meet;
The Virgin quire for her request
The God that sits at marriage feast;
He at their invoking came
But with a scarce-wel-lighted flame;   20
And in his Garland as he stood,
Ye might discern a Cypress bud.
Once had the early Matrons run
To greet her of a lovely son,
And now with second hope she goes,   25
And calls *Lucina* to her throes;
But whether by mischance or blame
Atropos for *Lucina* came;
And with remorseless cruelty,
Spoild at once both fruit and tree: 30
The hapless Babe before his birth
Had burial, yet not laid in earth,
And the languisht Mothers Womb
Was not long a living Tomb.
So have I seen som tender slip   35
Sav'd with care from Winters nip,
The pride of her carnation train,
Pluckt up by som unheedy swain,
Who onely thought to crop the flowr
New shot up from vernal showr;   40
But the fair blossom hangs the head
Side-ways as on a dying bed,

26 Throes;] throws; *Edd. 1, 2*

And those Pearls of dew she wears
Prove to be presaging tears
Which the sad morn had let fall   45
On her hast'ning funerall.
Gentle Lady may thy grave
Peace and quiet ever have;
After this thy travail sore
Sweet rest sieze thee evermore,   50
That to give the world encrease
Shortend hast thy own lives lease;
Here, besides the sorrowing
That thy noble House doth bring,
Here be tears of perfet moan   55
Weept for thee in *Helicon*,
And som Flowers, and som Bays,
For thy Herse to strew the ways,
Sent thee from the banks of *Came*,
Devoted to thy vertuous name;   60
Whilst thou bright Saint high sitst in glory,
Next her much like to thee in story,
That fair *Syrian* Shepherdess
Who after years of barrenness
The highly favour'd *Joseph* bore   65
To him that serv'd for her before,
And at her next birth, much like thee,
Through pangs fled to felicity,
Far within the bosom bright
Of blazing Majesty and Light,   70
There with thee, new welcom Saint,
Like fortunes may her soul acquaint,
With thee there clad in radiant sheen,
No Marchioness, but now a Queen.

49 travail *Ed. 1*] travel *Ed. 2*

SONG ON MAY MORNING

Now the bright morning Star, Days harbinger,
Comes dancing from the East, and leads with her
The Flowry *May*, who from her green lap throws
The yellow Cowslip and the pale Primrose.
   Hail bounteous *May* that dost inspire   5
   Mirth and youth and warm desire,
   Woods and Groves are of thy dressing,
   Hill and Dale doth boast thy blessing.
Thus we salute thee with our early Song,
And welcom thee, and wish thee long.   10

ON SHAKESPEAR. 1630

What needs my *Shakespear* for his honourd Bones
The labour of an age in piled Stones,
Or that his hallowd reliques should be hid
Under a Star-ypointing *Pyramid*?
Dear son of memory, great heir of Fame,   5
What needst thou such weak witness of thy name?
Thou in our wonder and astonishment
Hast built thy self a live-long Monument.
For whilst to th'shame of slow-endevoring art,
Thy easie numbers flow, and that each heart   10
Hath from the leaves of thy unvalu'd Book
Those Delphic lines with deep impression took,
Then thou our fancy of it self bereaving
Dost make us Marble with too much conceaving;
And so Sepulcherd in such pomp dost lie,   15
That Kings for such a Tomb would wish to die.

On Shakespear. *First printed 1632 in the second folio Shakespeare with these variants:* Title] An epitaph on the admirable dramaticke poet W. Shakespeare   1 needs] neede   6 weak] dull   8 live-long] lasting   10 heart] part   13 it] her

ON THE UNIVERSITY CARRIER
WHO SICKN'D IN THE TIME OF HIS VACANCY,
BEING FORBID TO GO TO LONDON
BY REASON OF THE PLAGUE

Here lies old *Hobson*, Death hath broke his girt,
And here alas, hath laid him in the dirt,
Or else the ways being foul, twenty to one,
He's here stuck in a slough, and overthrown.
'Twas such a shifter, that if truth were known,   5
Death was half glad when he had got him down;
For he had any time this ten years full,
Dodg'd with him, betwixt *Cambridge* and the Bull.
And surely, Death could never have prevaild,
Had not his weekly course of carriage faild;   10
But lately finding him so long at home,
And thinking now his journeys end was come,
And that he had tane up his latest Inn,
In the kind office of a Chamberlin
Shewd him his room where he must lodge that night,   15
Pulld off his Boots, and took away the light:
If any ask for him, it shall be sed,
Hobson has supt, and's newly gon to bed.

[On the University Carrier. *A manuscript version exists in the Folger Library; it was included in the jest book,* The Banquet of Jests, *1640, and also, together with its companion piece, in* Wit Restor'd, *1658*]

8 Dogg'd him 'twixt Cambridge and the London-Bull *1658*
14 In the kind office] In craftie likenes *MS.*

ANOTHER ON THE SAME

Here lieth one who did most truly prove,
That he could never die while he could move,
So hung his destiny never to rot
While he might still jogg on, and keep his trot,
Made of sphear-metal, never to decay   5
Untill his revolution was at stay.
Time numbers motion, yet (without a crime
'Gainst old truth) motion numberd out his time:
And like an Engin mov'd with wheel and waight,
His principles being ceast, he ended straight.   10
Rest that gives all men life, gave him his death,
And too much breathing put him out of breath;
Nor were it contradiction to affirm
Too long vacation hastend on his term.
Merely to drive the time away he sickend,   15
Fainted, and died, nor would with Ale be quickend;
Nay, quoth he, on his swooning bed outstretcht,
If I may not carry, sure I'le ne're be fetcht,
But vow though the cross Doctors all stood hearers,
For one Carrier put down to make six bearers.   20
Ease was his chief disease, and to judge right,
He di'd for heaviness that his Cart went light,
His leasure told him that his time was com,
And lack of load made his life burdensom,
That ev'n to his last breath (ther be that say't)   25
As he were prest to death, he cri'd more waight;
But had his doings lasted as they were,
He had bin an immortal Carrier.
Obedient to the Moon he spent his date
In course reciprocal, and had his fate   30
Linkt to the mutual flowing of the Seas,
Yet (strange to think) his wain was his increase.
His Letters are deliverd all and gon,
Only remains this superscription.

L'ALLEGRO

Hence loathed Melancholy
   Of *Cerberus* and blackest midnight born,
In *Stygian* Cave forlorn
   'Mongst horrid shapes, and shrieks, and sights unholy,
Find out som uncouth cell,   5
   Where brooding darkness spreads his jealous wings,
And the night-Raven sings;
   There under *Ebon* shades, and low-browd Rocks,
As ragged as thy Locks,
   In dark *Cimmerian* desert ever dwell.   10
But come thou Goddess fair and free,
In Heav'n ycleapt *Euphrosyne*,
And by men, heart-easing Mirth,
Whom lovely *Venus* at a birth
With two sister Graces more   15
To Ivy-crowned *Bacchus* bore;
Or whether (as som Sager sing)
The frolic Wind that breathes the Spring,
Zephir with *Aurora* playing,
As he met her once a Maying,   20
There on Beds of Violets blew,
And fresh-blown Roses washt in dew,
Fill'd her with thee a daughter fair,
So buxom, blithe, and debonair.
Haste thee nymph, and bring with thee   25
Jest and youthful Jollity,
Quips and Cranks, and wanton Wiles,
Nods and Becks, and Wreathed Smiles
Such as hang on *Hebe's* cheek,
And love to live in dimple sleek;   30
Sport that wrinkl'd Care derides,
And Laughter holding both his sides.
Come, and trip it as ye go
On the light fantastic toe,
And in thy right hand lead with thee   35
The Mountain Nymph, sweet Liberty;
And if I give thee honour due,
Mirth, admit me of thy crue
To live with her, and live with thee,
In unreproved pleasures free;   40
To hear the Lark begin his flight,
And singing startle the dull night
From his watch-towr in the skies,
Till the dappled dawn doth rise;

3 forlorn *Ed. 1*] forlorn. *Ed. 2*   33 ye *Ed. 1*] you *Ed. 2*

Then to come in spite of sorrow   45
And at my window bid good morrow,
Through the Sweet-Briar or the Vine
Or the twisted Eglantine.
While the Cock with lively din
Scatters the rear of darkness thin,   50
And to the stack or the Barn dore
Stoutly struts his Dames before,
Oft list'ning how the Hounds and horn
Cheerly rouse the slumbring morn,
From the side of som Hoar Hill,   55
Through the high wood echoing shrill.
Som time walking not unseen
By Hedge-row Elms, on Hillocks green,
Right against the Eastern gate,
Where the great Sun begins his state,   60
Rob'd in flames and Amber light,
The clouds in thousand Liveries dight,
While the Plowman near at hand
Whistles ore the Furrowd Land,
And the Milkmaid singeth blithe,   65
And the Mower whets his sithe,
And every Shepherd tells his tale
Under the Hawthorn in the dale.
Straight mine eye hath caught new pleasures
Whilst the Lantskip round it measures,   70
Russet Lawns, and Fallows Gray,
Where the nibling flocks do stray,
Mountains on whose barren brest
The labouring clouds do often rest;
Meddows trim with Daisies pide,   75
Shallow Brooks, and Rivers wide.
Towrs and Battlements it sees
Bosomd high in tufted Trees,
Where perhaps som beauty lies,
The Cynosure of neighbouring eyes.   80
Hard by, a Cottage chimney smokes
From betwixt two aged Okes,
Where *Corydon* and *Thyrsis* met
Are at their savoury dinner set
Of Herbs and other Country Messes,   85
Which the neat-handed *Phillis* dresses;
And then in haste her Bowr she leaves,
With *Thestylis* to bind the Sheaves;
Or if the earlier season lead
To the tannd Haycock in the Mead.   .   90

62 dight, *Ed. 2*] dight. *Ed. 1*
90 Mead.]Mead, *Edd. 1, 2*

Some times with secure delight
The up-land Hamlets will invite,
When the merry Bells ring round,
And the jocond rebecks sound
To many a youth, and many a maid,   95
Dancing in the Chequerd shade;
And young and old come forth to play
On a Sunshine Holyday,
Till the live-long day-light fail,
Then to the Spicy Nut-brown Ale,   100
With stories told of many a feat,
How *Faery Mab* the junkets eat,
She was pincht and pulld she sed,
And by the Friars Lanthorn led,
Tells how the drudging *Goblin* swet,   105
To ern his Cream-bowl duly set,
When in one night, ere glimpse of morn,
His shaddowy Flale hath thresht the Corn
That ten day-labourers could not end,
Then lies him down the Lubbar Fend,   110
And stretcht out all the Chimney's length
Basks at the fire his hairy strength;
And Crop-full out of dores he flings,
Ere the first Cock his Mattin rings.
Thus don the Tales, to bed they creep,   115
By whispering Winds soon lulld asleep.
Towred Cities please us then,
And the busie humm of men,
Where throngs of Knights and Barons bold
In weeds of Peace high triumphs hold,   120
With store of Ladies, whose bright eyes
Rain influence, and judge the prize
Of Wit or Arms, while both contend
To win her Grace whom all commend.
There let *Hymen* oft appear   125
In Saffron robe, with Taper clear,
And pomp, and feast, and revelry,
With mask, and antique Pageantry,
Such sights as youthful Poets dream
On Summer eves by haunted stream.   130
Then to the well-trod stage anon,
If *Jonsons* learned Sock be on,
Or sweetest *Shakespear* fancys childe
Warble his native Wood-notes wilde.
And ever against eating Cares   135
Lap me in soft *Lydian* Aires,

104 And by the *Ed. 2*] And he by *Ed. 1* led,] led *Edd. 1, 2*
110 Fend,] Fend. *Edd. 1, 2*
134 wilde.] wilde, *Edd. 1, 2*

Married to immortal verse
Such as the meeting soul may pierce
In notes, with many a winding bout
Of linked sweetness long drawn out,   140
With wanton heed and giddy cunning
The melting voice through mazes running;
Untwisting all the chains that ty
The hidden soul of harmony.
That *Orpheus* self may heave his head   145
From golden slumber on a bed
Of heap't *Elysian* flowrs, and hear
Such strains as would have won the ear
Of *Pluto*, to have quite set free
His half regaind *Eurydice*.   150
These delights, if thou canst give,
Mirth with thee, I mean to live.

IL PENSEROSO

Hence vain deluding joys,
    The brood of folly without father bred,
How little you bested,
    Or fill the fixed mind with all your toys;
Dwell in som idle brain,   5
    And fancies fond with gaudy shapes possess,
As thick and numberless
    As the gay motes that people the Sun Beams,
Or likest hovering dreams
    The fickle Pensioners of *Morpheus* train.   10
But hail thou Goddess, sage and holy,
Hail divinest Melancholy,
Whose Saintly visage is too bright
To hit the Sense of human sight;
And therefore to our weaker view   15
Ore laid with black staid Wisdoms hue.
Black, but such as in esteem
Prince *Memnons* sister might beseem,
Or that starrd *Ethiope* Queen that strove
To set her beautys praise above   20
The Sea Nymphs, and their powers offended.
Yet thou art higher far descended,
Thee bright-haird *Vesta* long of yore
To solitary *Saturn* bore;
His daughter she (in *Saturns* raign   25
Such mixture was not held a stain)
Oft in glimmering Bowrs and glades
He met her, and in secret shades
Of woody *Ida's* inmost grove,
While yet there was no fear of *Jove*.   30
Come pensive Nun, devout and pure,
Sober, stedfast, and demure,
All in a robe of darkest grain,
Flowing with majestic train,
And sable stole of *Cypress* Lawn   35
Over thy decent shoulders drawn.
Come, but keep thy wonted state,
With even step, and musing gate,
And looks commercing with the skies,
Thy rapt soul sitting in thine eyes: 40
There held in holy passion still,
Forget thy self to Marble, till
With a sad Leaden downward cast,
Thou fix them on the earth as fast.
And join with thee calm Peace and Quiet,   45

Spare Fast, that oft with gods doth diet,
And hears the Muses in a ring
Ay round about *Joves* Altar sing.
And add to these retired Leasure,
That in trim Gardens takes his pleasure; 50
But first, and chiefest, with thee bring
Him that yon soars on golden wing,
Guiding the fiery-wheeled throne,
The Cherub Contemplation,
And the mute Silence hist along, 55
'Less *Philomel* will deign a Song,
In her sweetest, saddest plight,
Smoothing the rugged brow of night,
While *Cynthia* checks her Dragon yoke
Gently ore th'accustomd Oke; 60
Sweet Bird that shunnst the noise of folly,
Most musical, most melancholy!
Thee Chauntress oft the Woods among,
I woo to hear thy Even-Song;
And missing thee, I walk unseen 65
On the dry smooth-shaven Green,
To behold the wandring Moon
Riding near her highest noon,
Like one that had bin led astray
Through the Heav'ns wide pathless way; 70
And oft, as if her head she bowd,
Stooping through a fleecy cloud.
Oft on a Plat of rising ground,
I hear the far-off *Curfeu* sound,
Over som wide-waterd shoar, 75
Swinging slow with sullen roar;
Or if the Air will not permit,
Som still removed place will fit,
Where glowing Embers through the room
Teach light to counterfeit a gloom, 80
Far from all resort of mirth,
Save the Cricket on the hearth,
Or the Belmans drowsie charm,
To bless the dores from nightly harm:
Or let my Lamp at midnight hour 85
Be seen in som high lonely Towr,
Where I may oft outwatch the *Bear*,
With thrice great *Hermes*, or unsphear
The spirit of *Plato* to unfold
What Worlds, or what vast Regions hold 90
Th'immortal mind that hath forsook
Her mansion in this fleshly nook:
And of those *Dæmons* that are found
In fire, air, flood, or under ground,

Whose power hath a true consent   95
With Planet or with Element.
Som time let Gorgeous Tragedy
In Scepterd Pall come sweeping by,
Presenting *Thebs*, or *Pelops* line,
Or the tale of *Troy* divine.   100
Or what (though rare) of later age
Ennobl'd hath the Buskind stage.
But, O sad Virgin, that thy power
Might raise *Musaeus* from his bower,
Or bid the soul of *Orpheus* sing   105
Such notes as warbled to the string
Drew Iron tears down *Pluto's* cheek,
And made Hell grant what Love did seek.
Or call up him that left half told
The story of *Cambuscan* bold,   110
Of *Camball*, and of *Algarsife*,
And who had *Canace* to wife,
That ownd the vertuous Ring and Glass,
And of the wondrous Horse of Brass,
On which the *Tartar* King did ride;   115
And if aught else, great *Bards* beside
In sage and solemn tunes have sung,
Of Tourneys and of Trophies hung;
Of Forests, and inchantments drear,
Where more is meant than meets the ear.   120
Thus Night oft see me in thy pale career,
Till civil-suited Morn appeer,
Not trickt and frounc't as she was wont
With the Attic Boy to hunt,
But Kercheft in a comely Cloud,   125
While rocking Winds are Piping loud,
Or usherd with a shower still
When the gust hath blown his fill,
Ending on the russling Leaves,
With minute drops from off the Eaves.   130
And when the Sun begins to fling
His flaring beams, me Goddess bring
To arched walks of twilight groves,
And shaddows brown that *Sylvan* loves
Of Pine or monumental Oke,   135
Where the rude Axe with heaved stroke
Was never heard the Nymphs to daunt,
Or fright them from their hallowd haunt.
There in close covert by som Brook,
Where no profaner eye may look,   140
Hide me from Days garish eie,
While the Bee with Honied thie,
That at her flowry work doth sing,

And the Waters murmuring
With such consort as they keep,   145
Entice the dewy-featherd Sleep;
And let som strange mysterious dream
Wave at his Wings in Airy stream,
Of lively portrature displayd,
Softly on my eye-lids laid.   150
And as I wake, sweet music breath
Above, about, or underneath,
Sent by som spirit to mortals good,
Or th'unseen Genius of the Wood.
But let my due feet never fail   155
To walk the studious Cloisters pale,
And love the high embowed Roof,
With antic Pillars massy proof,
And storied Windows richly dight,
Casting a dimm religious light;   160
There let the pealing Organ blow,
To the full voic't Quire below,
In Service high, and Anthems clear,
As may with sweetness, through mine ear,
Dissolve me into extasies,   165
And bring all Heav'n before mine eyes.
And may at last my weary age
Find out the peaceful hermitage,
The Hairy Gown and Mossy Cell,
Where I may sit and rightly spell   170
Of every Star that Heav'n doth shew,
And every Herb that sips the dew;
Till old experience do attain
To something like Prophetic strain.
These pleasures *Melancholy* give,   175
And I with thee will choose to live.

THE FIFTH ODE OF HORACE. *LIB. I*

Quis multa gracilis te puer in Rosa, *Rendred almost word for word without Rhyme according to the Latin Measure, as near as the Language will permit.*

What slender Youth bedewd with liquid odours
Courts thee on Roses in som pleasant Cave,
    Pyrrha for whom bind'st thou
    In wreaths thy golden Hair,
Plain in thy neatness?   O how oft shall he   5
On Faith and changed Gods complain: and Seas
    Rough with black winds and storms
    Unwonted shall admire:
Who now enjoys thee credulous, all Gold,
Who always vacant, always amiable   10
    Hopes thee; of flattering gales
    Unmindful.   Hapless they
To whom thou untri'd seemst fair.   Me in my vowd
Picture the sacred wall declares t' have hung
    My dank and dropping weeds   15
    To the stern God of Sea.

AD PYRRHAM. *ODE V*

Horatius ex Pyrrhæ illecebris tamquam e naufragio enataverat cujus amore irretitos affirmat esse miseros.

    Quis multâ gracilis te puer in rosâ
    Perfusus liquidis urget odoribus
        Grato, Pyrrha, sub antro?
            Cui flavam religas comam
    Simplex munditie?   Heu quoties fidem   5
    Mutatosque deos flebit, et aspera
        Nigris æquora ventis
            Emirabitur insolens,
    Qui nunc te fruitur credulus aureâ;
    Qui semper vacuam, semper amabilem   10
        Sperat, nescius auræ
            Fallacis.   miseri quibus
    Intentata nites.   me tabulâ sacer
    Votivâ paries indicat uvida
        Suspendisse potenti   15
            Vestimenta maris Deo.

ARCADES

Part of an Entertainment presented to the Countess Dowager of Darby at Harefield, by some Noble Persons of her Family, who appear on the Scene in Pastoral Habit, moving toward the seat of State with this Song.

1. SONG

Look Nymphs, and Shepherds look,
What sudden blaze of Majesty
Is that which we from hence descry
Too divine to be mistook:
   This this is she   5
To whom our vows and wishes bend,
Here our solemn search hath end.

Fame that her high worth to raise,
Seemd erst so lavish and profuse,
We may justly now accuse   10
Of detraction from her praise,
   Less than half we find exprest,
   Envy bid conceal the rest.

Mark what radiant state she spreds,
In circle round her shining throne,   15
Shooting her beams like silver threds,
This this is she alone,
   Sitting like a Goddess bright,
   In the center of her light.

Might she the wise *Latona* be,   20
Or the towred *Cybele*,
Mother of a hundred gods;
Juno dares not give her odds;
   Who had thought this clime had held
   A deity so unparaleld?   25

As they com forward, the genius of the Wood appears, and turning toward them, speaks.

Gen. Stay gentle Swains, for though in this disguise,
I see bright honour sparkle through your eyes;
Of famous *Arcady* ye are, and sprung
Of that renowned flood, so often sung,
Divine *Alpheus*, who by secret sluse   30
Stole under Seas to meet his *Arethuse*;

And ye the breathing Roses of the Wood,
Fair silver-buskind Nymphs as great and good,
I know this quest of yours and free intent
Was all in honour and devotion ment   35
To the great Mistress of yon princely shrine,
Whom with low reverence I adore as mine,
And with all helpful service will comply
To furder this nights glad solemnity;
And lead ye where ye may more near behold   40
What shallow-searching *Fame* hath left untold;
Which I full oft amidst these shades alone
Have sate to wonder at, and gaze upon:
For know by lot from *Jove* I am the powr
Of this fair Wood, and live in Oaken bowr,   45
To nurse the Saplings tall, and curl the grove
With Ringlets quaint, and wanton windings wove.
And all my Plants I save from nightly ill,
Of noisom winds, and blasting vapours chill.
And from the Boughs brush off the evil dew,   50
And heal the harms of thwarting thunder blew,
Or what the cross dire-looking Planet smites,
Or hurtful Worm with cankerd venom bites.
When Ev'ning gray doth rise, I fetch my round
Over the mount and all this hallowd ground,   55
And early ere the odorous breath of morn
Awakes the slumbring leaves, or tasseld horn
Shakes the high thicket, haste I all about,
Number my ranks, and visit every sprout
With puissant words, and murmurs made to bless;   60
But else in deep of night when drowsiness
Hath lockt up mortal sense, then listen I
To the celestial *Sirens* harmony,
That sit upon the nine enfolded Sphears,
And sing to those that hold the vital shears,   65
And turn the Adamantine spindle round,
On which the fate of gods and men is wound.
Such sweet compulsion doth in music ly,
To lull the daughters of *Necessity*,
And keep unsteddy Nature to her law,   70
And the low world in measurd motion draw
After the heavenly tune, which none can hear
Of human mould with gross unpurged ear;
And yet such music worthiest were to blaze
The peerless height of her immortal praise   75
Whose lustre leads us, and for her most fit,
If my inferior hand or voice could hit
Inimitable sounds; yet as we go,
What e're the skill of lesser gods can show,
I will assay, her worth to celebrate,   80

And so attend ye toward her glittering state;
Where ye may all that are of noble stemm
Approach, and kiss her sacred vestures hemm.

2. SONG

Ore the smooth enameld green
Where no print of step hath been,   85
    Follow me as I sing,
    And touch the warbl'd string.
Under the shady roof
Of branching Elm Star-proof,
    Follow me,   90
I will bring you where she sits
Clad in splendor as befits
    Her deity.
Such a rural Queen
All *Arcadia* hath not seen.   95

3. SONG

Nymphs and Shepherds dance no more
    By sandy *Ladons* Lillied banks,
On old *Lycaeus* or *Cyllene* hoar
    Trip no more in twilight ranks,
Though *Erymanth* your loss deplore   100
    A better soil shall give ye thanks.
From the stony *Mænalus*
Bring your Flocks, and live with us,
Here ye shall have greater grace,
To serve the Lady of this place.   105
    Though *Syrinx* your *Pans* Mistress were,
    Yet *Syrinx* well might wait on her.
        Such a rural Queen
    All *Arcadia* hath not seen.

LYCIDAS

In this Monody the Author bewails a learned Friend, unfortunately drown'd in his passage from Chester on the Irish Seas, 1637.   And by occasion foretells the ruine of our corrupted Clergie then in their height.

Yet once more, O ye Laurels, and once more
Ye Myrtles brown, with Ivy never sear,
I come to pluck your Berries harsh and crude,
And with forc't fingers rude
Shatter your leaves before the mellowing year.   5
Bitter constraint, and sad occasion dear,
Compells me to disturb your season due:
For *Lycidas* is dead, dead ere his prime,
Young *Lycidas*, and hath not left his peer:
Who would not sing for *Lycidas*? he knew   10
Himself to sing, and build the lofty rime.
He must not float upon his watry bear
Unwept, and welter to the parching wind,
Without the meed of som melodious tear.
  Begin then, Sisters of the sacred well   15
That from beneath the seat of *Jove* doth spring,
Begin, and somewhat loudly sweep the string:
Hence with denial vain, and coy excuse.
So may som gentle Muse
With lucky words favour my destind Urn,   20
And as he passes, turn
And bid fair peace be to my sable shroud.
For we were nurst upon the self-same hill,
Fed the same flock, by fountain, shade, and rill.
  Together both, ere the high Lawns appear'd   25
Under the opening eyelids of the morn,
We drove a-field, and both together heard
What time the Gray-fly winds her sultry horn,
Batt'ning our flocks with the fresh dews of night,
Oft till the Star that rose, at Ev'ning, bright   30
Toward Heav'ns descent had slop'd his westering wheel.
Mean while the Rural ditties were not mute,
Temperd to th'Oaten Flute,
Rough *Satyrs* danc'd, and *Fauns* with cloven heel
From the glad sound would not be absent long,   35
And old *Damaetas* lov'd to hear our song.
  But O the heavy change, now thou art gon,
Now thou art gon, and never must return!
Thee Shepherd, thee the Woods and desert Caves,

10 he knew *Edd.*] he well knew *Tr. MS., corr. copies of 1638 ed. Camb. Univ. Lib. and Brit. Mus.*

With wilde Thyme and the gadding Vine o'rgrown, 40
And all their echoes mourn.
The Willows and the Hazle Copses green
Shall now no more be seen
Fanning their joyous Leaves to thy soft lays.
As killing as the Canker to the Rose, 45
Or Taint-worm to the weanling Herds that graze,
Or Frost to Flowrs that their gay wardrope wear
When first the White-thorn blows;
Such, *Lycidas*, thy loss to Shepherds ear.
    Where were ye Nymphs when the remorseless deep 50
Clos'd ore the head of your lov'd *Lycidas*?
For neither were ye playing on the steep,
Where your old *Bards*, the famous *Druids* lie,
Nor on the shaggy top of *Mona* high,
Nor yet where *Deva* spreads her wizard stream: 55
Ay me, I fondly dream!
Had ye bin there—for what could that have don?
What could the Muse her self that *Orpheus* bore,
The Muse her self for her inchanting son
Whom Universal nature did lament, 60
When by the rout that made the hideous roar
His goary visage down the stream was sent,
Down the swift *Hebrus* to the *Lesbian* shore.
    Alas! What boots it with uncessant care
To tend the homely slighted Shepherds trade, 65
And strictly meditate the thankless Muse?
Were it not better don as others use,
To sport with *Amaryllis* in the shade,
Or with the tangles of *Neaera's* hair?
Fame is the spur that the clear spirit doth raise 70
(That last infirmity of Noble mind)
To scorn delights, and live laborious days;
But the fair Guerdon when we hope to find,
And think to burst out into sudden blaze,
Comes the blind *Fury* with th'abhorred shears, 75
And slits the thin-spun life. But not the praise,
Phoebus repli'd, and touchd my trembling ears;
Fame is no plant that grows on mortal soil,
Nor in the glistering foil
Set off to th'world, nor in broad rumour lies, 80
But lives and spreads aloft by those pure eyes,
And perfet witness of all-judging *Jove*;
As he pronounces lastly on each deed,
Of so much fame in Heav'n expect thy meed.
    O Fountain *Arethuse*, and thou honourd flood, 85
Smooth-sliding *Mincius*, crownd with vocal reeds,

47 wardrope *Tr. MS.*] wardrop *Edd. 1, 2*] wardrobe *1638*

That strain I heard was of a higher mood:
But now my Oat proceeds,
And listens to the Herald of the Sea
That came in *Neptunes* plea.   90
He askd the Waves, and askd the Fellon winds,
What hard mishap hath doomd this gentle swain?
And questiond every gust of rugged wings
That blows from off each beaked Promontory;
They knew not of his story,   95
And sage *Hippotades* their answer brings,
That not a blast was from his dungeon strayd,
The Air was calm, and on the level brine
Sleek *Panope* with all her sisters playd.
It was that fatal and perfidious Bark   100
Built in th'eclipse, and riggd with curses dark,
That sunk so low that sacred head of thine.
  Next *Camus*, reverend Sire, went footing slow,
His Mantle hairy, and his Bonnet sedge,
Inwrought with figures dim, and on the edge   105
Like to that sanguin flowr inscrib'd with woe.
Ah! Who hath reft (quoth he) my dearest pledge?
Last came, and last did go,
The Pilot of the *Galilean* lake,
Two massy Keys he bore of metals twain   110
(The Golden opes, the Iron shuts amain),
He shook his Miterd locks, and stern bespake:
How well could I have spar'd for thee, young swain,
Anow of such as for their bellies sake
Creep and intrude and climb into the fold?   115
Of other care they little reck'ning make,
Than how to scramble at the shearers feast,
And shove away the worthy bidden guests;
Blind mouthes! that scarce themselves know how to hold
A Sheep-hook, or have learnt aught else the least   120
That to the faithful Herdmans art belongs!
What recks it them? What need they? They are sped;
And when they list, their lean and flashy songs
Grate on their scrannel Pipes of wretched straw,
The hungry Sheep look up, and are not fed,   125
But swoln with wind, and the rank mist they draw,
Rot inwardly, and foul contagion spread:
Besides what the grim Wolf with privy paw
Daily devours apace, and nothing sed.
But that two-handed engin at the door,   130
Stands ready to smite once, and smite no more.
  Return *Alpheus*, the dread voice is past
That shrunk thy streams; Return *Sicilian* Muse,
And call the Vales, and bid them hither cast

120 learn't *Tr. MS.*] learn'd *Edd. 1, 2, 1638*

Their Bells, and Flowrets of a thousand hues. 135
Ye valleys low where the milde whispers use
Of shades and wanton winds and gushing brooks,
On whose fresh lap the swart Star sparely looks,
Throw hither all your quaint enameld eyes,
That on the green terf suck the honied showrs, 140
And purple all the ground with vernal flowrs.
Bring the rathe Primrose that forsaken dies,
The tufted Crow-toe, and pale Gessamine,
The white Pink, and the Pansie freak't with jet,
The glowing Violet, 145
The Musk-rose, and the well attir'd Woodbine,
With Cowslips wan that hang the pensive hed,
And every flowr that sad embroidery wears:
Bid *Amarantus* all his beauty shed,
And Daffadillies fill their cups with tears, 150
To strew the Laureat Herse where *Lycid* lies.
For so to interpose a little ease,
Let our frail thoughts dally with false surmise.
Ay me! Whilst thee the shores and sounding Seas
Wash far away, where e're thy bones are hurld, 155
Whether beyond the stormy *Hebrides*,
Where thou perhaps under the whelming tide
Visitst the bottom of the monstrous world;
Or whether thou to our moist vows deni'd,
Sleepst by the fable of *Bellerus* old, 160
Where the great vision of the guarded Mount
Looks toward *Namancos* and *Bayona's* hold;
Look homeward Angel now, and melt with ruth.
And, Q ye *Dolphins*, waft the hapless youth.
    Weep no more, woeful Shepherds weep no more, 165
For *Lycidas* your sorrow is not dead,
Sunk though he be beneath the watry floore,
So sinks the day-star in the Ocean bed,
And yet anon repairs his drooping head,
And tricks his beams, and with new spangl'd Ore 170
Flames in the forhead of the morning sky:
So *Lycidas* sunk low, but mounted high
Through the dear might of him that walkd the waves;
Where other groves, and other streams along,
With *Nectar* pure his oozy Locks he laves. 175
And hears the unexpressive nuptial Song,
In the blest Kingdoms meek of joy and love.
There entertain him all the Saints above
In solemn troops and sweet Societies
That sing, and singing in their glory move, 180
And wipe the tears for ever from his eyes.

149 Amarantus *Ed. 2*] Amaranthus *Ed. 1*
157 whelming *Edd 1, 2*] humming *Tr. MS., 1638*

Now *Lycidas* the Shepherds weep no more;
Hence forth thou art the Genius of the shore
In thy large recompense, and shalt be good
To all that wander in that perilous flood. 185
   Thus sang the uncouth Swain to th'oaks and rills
While the still morn went out with Sandals gray;
He touchd the tender stops of various Quills,
With eager thought warbling his *Doric* lay:
And now the Sun had stretcht out all the hills, 190
And now was dropt into the Western bay;
At last he rose, and twitchd his Mantle blew:
Tomorrow to fresh Woods and Pastures new.

A MASK

A MASKE

PRESENTED

At Ludlow Castle,

1 6 3 4 :

On *Michaelmasse night*, *before the*
RIGHT HONORABLE,

IOHN *Earle of Bridgewater*, *Vicount* BRACKLY,
Lord Præ*ſident of* WALES, And one of
HIS MAIESTIES moſt honorable
Privie Counſell.

Eheu quid volui miſero mihi ! floribus auſtrum
Perditus ————

LONDON

Printed for HYMPHREY ROBINSON,
at the ſigne of the *Three Pidgeons* in
Pauls Church-yard. 1 6 3 7.

[1] To the Right Honourable, John Lord Vicount Bracly, **Son** and Heir apparent to the Earl of *Bridgewater, etc.*

My Lord,

   This Poem, *which receiv'd its first occasion of Birth from your Self, and others of your Noble Family, and much honour from your own Person in the performance, now returns again to make a finall Dedication of it self to you.   Although not openly acknowledg'd by the Author, yet it is a legitimate off-spring, so lovely, and so much desired, that the often Copying of it hath tir'd my Pen to give my severall friends satisfaction, and brought me to a necessity of producing it to the publike view; and now to offer it up in all rightfull devotion to those fair Hopes, and rare Endowments of your much-promising Youth, which give a full assurance, to all that know you, of a future excellence.   Live sweet Lord to be the honour of your Name, and receive this as your own, from the hands of him, who hath by many favours been long oblig'd to your most honour'd Parents, and as in this representation your attendant* Thyrsis, *so now in all reall expression*

Your faithfull, and most humble Servant

H. Lawes.

[1] The Copy of a Letter writt'n by Sir Henry Wootton, to the Author, upon the following Poem.

From the Colledge, this 13. of April, 1638.

Sir,

   It was a special favour, when you lately bestowed upon me here, the taste of your acquaintance, though no longer then to make me know that I wanted time to value it, and to enjoy it rightly; and in truth, if I could then have imagined your farther stay in these parts, which I understood afterwards by Mr *H.* I would have been bold in our vulgar phrase to mend my draught (for you left me with an extreme thirst) and to have begged your conversation again, joyntly with your said learned Friend, at a poor meal or two, that we might have banded together som good Authors of the antient time: Among which, I observed you to have been familiar.

Since your going, you have charg'd me with new Obligations, both for a very kinde Letter from you dated the sixth of this Month, and for a dainty peece of entertainment which came therwith. Wherin I should much commend the Tragical part, if the Lyrical did not ravish me with a certain Dorique delicacy in your Songs and Odes, wherunto I must plainly confess to have seen yet nothing parallel in our Language: *Ipsa mollities*. But I must not omit to tell you, that I now onely owe you thanks for intimating unto me (how modestly soever) the true Artificer. For the work it self I had view'd som good while before, with singular delight, having receiv'd it from our common Friend Mr *R*. in the very close of the late *R*'s Poems, Printed at *Oxford*, wherunto it was added (as I now suppose) that the Accessory might help out the Principal, according to the Art of *Stationers*, and to leave the Reader *Con la bocca dolce*.

Now Sir, concerning your travels, wherin I may chalenge a little more priviledge of Discours with you; I suppose you will not blanch *Paris* in your way; therfore I have been bold to trouble you with a few lines to Mr *M. B.* whom you shall easily find attending the young Lord *S.* as his Governour, and you may surely receive from him good directions for the shaping of your farther journey into *Italy*, where he did reside by my choice som time for the King, after mine own recess from *Venice*.

I should think that your best Line will be thorow the whole length of *France* to *Marseilles*, and thence by Sea to *Genoa*, whence the passage into *Tuscany* is as Diurnal as a *Gravesend* Barge: I hasten as you do to *Florence*, or *Siena*, the rather to tell you a short story from the interest you have given me in your safety.

At *Siena* I was tabled in the House of one *Alberto Scipioni*, an old *Roman* Courtier in dangerous times, having bin Steward to the *Duca di Pagliano*, who with all his Family were strangled, save this onely man that escap'd by foresight of the Tempest: With him I had often much chat of those affairs; Into which he took pleasure to look back from his Native Harbour; and at my departure toward *Rome* (which had been the center of his experience) I had wonn confidence enough to beg his advice, how I might carry my self securely there, without offence of others, or of mine own conscience. *Signor Arrigo mio* (sayes he) *I pensieri stretti, & il viso sciolto* will go safely over the whole World: Of which *Delphian* Oracle (for so I have found it) your judgement doth need no commentary; and therfore (Sir) I will commit you with it to the best of all securities, Gods dear love, remaining

> Your Friend as much at command
> as any of longer date,
> *Henry Wootton.*

Postscript

Sir, *I have expressly sent this my Foot-boy to prevent your departure without som acknowledgement from me of the receipt of your obliging Letter, having myself through som busines, I know not how, neglected the ordinary conveyance. In any part where I shall understand you fixed, I shall be glad, and diligent to entertain you with Home-Novelties; even for som fomentation of our friendship, too soon interrupted in the Cradle.*

THE PERSONS

The attendant Spirit afterwards in the habit of *Thyrsis*.
Comus with his crew.
The Lady.
1. Brother.
2. Brother.
Sabrina the Nymph.

The chief persons which presented, were

The Lord *Bracly*,
Mr *Thomas Egerton* his Brother,
The Lady *Alice Egerton*.

A MASK
PRESENTED
AT *LUDLOW* CASTLE
1634. etc.

The first Scene discovers a wilde Wood.

The attendant Spirit descends or enters.

Before the starry threshold of *Joves* Court
My mansion is, where those immortal shapes
Of bright aëreal Spirits live insphear'd
In Regions milde of calm and serene Air,
Above the smoke and stirr of this dim spot   5
Which men call Earth, and with low-thoughted care
Confin'd and pesterd in this pin-fold here
Strive to keep up a frail and Feaverish being
Unmindful of the crown that Vertue gives
After this mortal change, to her true Servants   10
Amongst the enthron'd gods on Sainted seats.
Yet som there be that by due steps aspire
To lay their just hands on that Golden Key
That opes the Palace of Eternity:
To such my errand is, and but for such   15
I would not soil these pure Ambrosial weeds
With the rank vapours of this Sin-worn mould.
   But to my task.   *Neptune* besides the sway
Of every salt Flood, and each ebbing Stream,
Took in by lot 'twixt high and nether *Jove*   20
Imperial rule of all the Sea-girt Iles
That like to rich and various gemms inlay
The unadorned bosom of the Deep,
Which he to grace his tributary gods
By course commits to several goverment,   25
And gives them leave to wear their Saphire crowns,
And wield their little tridents; but this Ile
The greatest, and the best of all the main
He quarters to his blue-haird deities;
And all this tract that fronts the falling Sun   30
A noble Peer of mickle trust and power
Has in his charge, with temperd awe to guide
An old and haughty Nation proud in Arms:
Where his fair off-spring nurst in Princely lore
Are coming to attend their Fathers state   35
And new-entrusted Scepter; but their way
Lies through the perplext paths of this drear Wood,

The nodding horror of whose shady brows
Threats the forlorn and wandring Passinger.
And here their tender age might suffer peril,   40
But that by quick command from Sovran *Jove*
I was dispatcht for their defence and guard;
And listen why, for I will tell ye now
What never yet was heard in Tale or Song
From old or modern Bard in Hall or Bowr.   45
   Bacchus that first from out the purple Grape
Crushd the sweet poison of mis-used Wine,
After the *Tuscan* Mariners transformd
Coasting the *Tyrrhene* shore, as the winds listed,
On *Circes* Iland fell (who knows not *Circe*   50
The daughter of the Sun? whose charmed Cup
Whoever tasted, lost his upright shape,
And downward fell into a grovling Swine);
This Nymph that gaz'd upon his clustring locks,
With Ivy berries wreath'd, and his blithe youth,   55
Had by him, ere he parted thence, a Son
Much like his Father, but his Mother more,
Whom therefore she brought up and *Comus* nam'd,
Who ripe and frolic of his full grown age,
Roving the *Celtic* and *Iberian* fields,   60
At last betakes him to this ominous Wood,
And in thick shelter of black shades imbowrd
Excells his Mother at her mighty Art,
Offring to every weary Traveller
His orient Liquor in a Crystal Glass,   65
To quench the drouth of *Phoebus*, which as they taste
(For most do taste through fond intemperat thirst)
Soon as the Potion works, their human count'nance,
Th' express resemblance of the gods, is chang'd
Into som brutish form of Wolf or Bear,   70
Or Ounce or Tiger, Hog or bearded Goat,
All other parts remaining as they were,
And they, so perfet is their misery,
Not once perceive their foul disfigurement,
But boast themselves more comely than before   75
And all their friends and native home forget
To roul with pleasure in a sensual stie.
Therefore when any favourd of high *Jove*
Chances to pass through this adventrous glade,
Swift as the Sparkle of a glancing Star   80
I shoot from Heav'n to give him safe convoy,
As now I do: But first I must put off
These my skie robes spun out of *Iris* Wooff,
And take the Weeds and likeness of a Swain,

43 ye *Ed. I*] you *Tr. MS., Ed. 2*

That to the service of this house belongs,   85
Who with his soft Pipe and smooth-dittied Song
Well knows to still the wilde winds when they roar
And hush the waving Woods; nor of less faith,
And in this office of his Mountain watch
Likeliest and nearest to the present aid   90
Of this occasion.   But I hear the tread
Of hateful steps, I must be viewless now.

Comus enters with a Charming Rod in one hand, his Glass in the other, with him a rout of Monsters, headed like sundry sorts of wilde Beasts, but otherwise like Men and Women, their Apparel glistring, they come in making a riotous and unruly noise, with Torches in their hands.

   Comus.   The Star that bids the Shepherd fold
Now the top of Heav'n doth hold,
And the gilded Car of Day   95
His glowing Axle doth allay
In the steep *Atlantic* stream,
And the slope Sun his upward beam
Shoots against the dusky Pole,
Pacing toward the other gole   100
Of his Chamber in the East.
Mean while welcom Joy and Feast,
Midnight shout and revelry,
Tipsie dance and Jollity.
Braid your Locks with rosie Twine   105
Dropping odours, dropping Wine.
Rigor now is gon to bed,
And Advice with scrupulous head,
Strict Age and sour Severity
With their grave Saws in slumber ly.   110
We that are of purer fire
Imitate the Starry Quire,
Who in their nightly watchful Sphears
Lead in swift round the Months and Years.
The Sounds and Seas with all their finny drove   115
Now to the Moon in wavering Morrice move,
And on the Tawny Sands and Shelves
Trip the pert Fairies and the dapper Elves;
By dimpl'd Brook and Fountain brim
The Wood-Nymphs deckt with Daisies trim   120
Their merry wakes and pastimes keep:
What hath night to do with sleep?
Night hath better sweets to prove,
Venus now wakes, and wakens Love.
Come let us our rites begin,   125
'Tis onely day-light that makes Sin
Which these dun shades will ne're report.
Hail Goddess of Nocturnal sport

Dark veild *Cotytto*, t' whom the secret flame
Of midnight Torches burns; mysterious Dame   130
That ne're art calld but when the Dragon woom
Of Stygian darkness spets her thickest gloom
And makes one blot of all the air,
Stay thy cloudy Ebon chair,
Wherin thou rid'st with *Hecat'*, and befriend   135
Us thy vowd Priests, till utmost end
Of all thy dues be done, and none left out,
Ere the blabbing Eastern scout,
The nice Morn on th' *Indian* steep
From her cabind loop-hole peep,   140
And to the tell-tale Sun discry
Our conceal'd Solemnity.
Come, knit hands, and beat the ground
In a light fantastic round.

The Measure.

Break off, break off, I feel the different pace   145
Of som chaste footing near about this ground.
Run to your shrouds, within these Brakes and Trees,
Our number may affright: Som Virgin sure
(For so I can distinguish by mine Art)
Benighted in these Woods.   Now to my charms   150
And to my wily trains, I shall ere long
Be well stockt with as fair a herd as graz'd
About my Mother *Circe*.   Thus I hurl
My dazling Spells into the spungy air,
Of power to cheat the eye with blear illusion   155
And give it false presentments, lest the place
And my quaint habits breed astonishment,
And put the Damsel to suspicious flight,
Which must not be, for that's against my course;
I under fair pretence of friendly ends,   160
And well plac't words of glozing courtesie
Baited with reasons not unplausible
Wind me into the easie-hearted man,
And hug him into snares.   When once her eye
Hath met the vertue of this Magic dust,   165
I shall appear som harmless Villager
And hearken, if I may her buisness hear.
But here she comes, I fairly step aside.

After line 165, Ed. 1 reads
          Whom thrift keeps up about his Country gear,
          But here she comes, I fairly step aside
          And hearken, if I may, her busines here.
*Ed. 2 omits the first line and transposes the other two : Errata Ed. 2 directs to
omit comma after* may, *and to read* hear *for* here. *From line 167 Ed. 2 and
the present text number one line less than Ed. 1.*

The Lady enters.

This way the noise was, if mine ear be true,
My best guide now; me thought it was the sound   170
Of Riot, and ill manag'd Merriment,
Such as the jocond Flute or gamesom Pipe
Stirs up among the loose unletterd Hinds,
When for their teeming Flocks and granges full
In wanton dance they praise the bounteous *Pan*,   175
And thank the gods amiss.   I should be loath
To meet the rudeness and swilld insolence
Of such late Wassailers; yet O where else
Shall I inform my unacquainted feet
In the blind mazes of this tangl'd Wood?   180
My Brothers when they saw me wearied out
With this long way, resolving here to lodge
Under the spreading favour of these Pines,
Stepd as they sed to the next Thicket side
To bring me Berries, or such cooling fruit   185
As the kind hospitable Woods provide.
They left me then, when the gray-hooded Ev'n
Like a sad Votarist in Palmers weed
Rose from the hindmost wheels of *Phoebus* wain.
But where they are, and why they came not back,   190
Is now the labour of my thoughts, 'tis likeliest
They had ingag'd their wandring steps too far,
And envious darkness, ere they could return,
Had stole them from me, else, O thievish Night
Why shouldst thou, but for som fellonious end,   195
In thy dark Lantern thus close up the Stars,
That nature hung in Heav'n, and filld their Lamps
With everlasting oil, to give due light
To the misled and lonely Traveller?
This is the place, as well as I may guess,   200
Whence even now the tumult of loud Mirth
Was rife, and perfet in my list'ning ear,
Yet naught but single darkness do I find.
What might this be?   A thousand fantasies
Begin to throng into my memory   205
Of calling shapes, and beckning shaddows dire,
And airy tongues that syllable mens names
On Sands and Shores and desert Wildernesses.
These thoughts may startle well, but not astound
The vertuous mind, that ever walks attended   210
By a strong siding champion Conscience. . . .
O welcom pure-ey'd Faith, white-handed Hope,
Thou hovering Angel girt with golden wings,
And thou unblemisht form of Chastity,

I see ye visibly, and now believe   215
That he, the Supreme good, t' whom all things ill
Are but as slavish officers of vengeance,
Would send a glistring Guardian if need were
To keep my life and honour unassaild.
Was I deceiv'd, or did a sable cloud   220
Turn forth her silver lining on the night?
I did not err, there does a sable cloud
Turn forth her silver lining on the night,
And casts a gleam over this tufted Grove.
I cannot hallow to my Brothers, but   225
Such noise as I can make to be heard fardest
I'le venter, for my new enlivend spirits
Prompt me; and they perhaps are not far off.

SONG

Sweet Echo, sweetest Nymph that liv'st unseen
    Within thy airy shell   230
      By slow Meanders margent green,
And in the violet imbroiderd vale
    Where the love-lorn Nightingale
Nightly to thee her sad Song mourneth well,
Canst thou not tell me of a gentle Pair   235
    That likest thy Narcissus are?
      O if thou have
    Hid them in som flowry Cave,
      Tell me but where
Sweet Queen of Parly, Daughter of the Sphear: 240
  So mayst thou be translated to the skies,
And give resounding grace to all Heav'ns Harmonies.

Com. Can any mortal mixture of Earths mould
Breathe such Divine inchanting ravishment?
Sure somthing holy lodges in that brest,   245
And with these raptures moves the vocal air
To testifie his hidden residence;
How sweetly did they float upon the wings
Of silence, through the empty-vaulted night
At every fall smoothing the Raven downe   250
Of darkness till it smil'd: I have oft heard
My mother Circe with the Sirens three,
Amidst the flowry-kirtl'd Naiades
Culling their potent herbs and baleful drugs,
Who as they sung, would take the prisond soul   255

---

226 fardest *Tr. MS., 1637*] farthest *Edd. 1, 2*
242 And give resounding grace *Edd. 1, 2, 1637*] And give a counterpoint
Tr. MS., cancelled
251 it *Edd. 1, 2*] She *Tr. MS., 1637*

And lap it in *Elysium*, *Scylla* wept
And chid her barking waves into attention,
And fell *Charybdis* murmurd soft applause:
Yet they in pleasing slumber lulld the sense
And in sweet madness robd it of it self,   260
But such a sacred and home-felt delight,
Such sober certainty of waking bliss
I never heard till now.   I'le speak to her
And she shall be my Queen.   Hail forren wonder
Whom certain these rough shades did never breed   265
Unless the Goddess that in rural shrine
Dwellst here with *Pan* or *Silvan*, by blest Song
Forbidding every bleak unkindly Fog
To touch the prosperous growth of this tall Wood.
   La. Nay gentle Shepherd ill is lost that praise   270
That is addrest to unattending Ears,
Not any boast of skill, but extreme shift
How to regain my severd company
Compelld me to awake the courteous Echo
To give me answer from her mossie Couch.   275
   Co. What chance good Lady hath bereft you thus?
   La. Dim darkness, and this leavie Labyrinth.
   Co. Could that divide you from near-ushering guides?
   La. They left me weary on a grassie terf.
   Co. By falsehood, or discourtesie, or why?   280
   La. To seek i'th valley som cool friendly Spring.
   Co. And left your fair side all unguarded Lady?
   La. They were but twain, and purposd quick return.
   Co. Perhaps fore-stalling night prevented them.
   La. How easie my misfortune is to hit!   285
   Co. Imports their loss, beside the present need?
   La. No less than if I should my brothers lose.
   Co. Were they of manly prime, or youthful bloom?
   La. As smooth as *Hebe's* their unrazord lips.
   Co. Two such I saw, what time the labourd Ox   290
In his loose traces from the furrow came,
And the swinkt hedger at his Supper sate;
I saw them under a green mantling vine
That crawls along the side of yon small hill,
Plucking ripe clusters from the tender shoots,   295
Their port was more than human, as they stood;
I took it for a faëry vision
Of som gay creatures of the element
That in the colours of the Rainbow live
And play i'th plighted clouds.   I was awe-strook,   300
And as I passd, I worshippd; if those you seek
It were a journey like the path to Heav'n,
To help you find them.   *La.* Gentle villager
What readiest way would bring me to that place?

Co. Due west it rises from this shrubby point.   305
La. To find out that, good Shepherd, I suppose,
In such a scant allowance of Star-light,
Would overtask the best Land-Pilots art,
Without the sure guess of well-practiz'd feet.
    Co. I know each lane and every alley green,   310
Dingle or bushy dell of this wilde Wood,
And every bosky bourn from side to side
My daily walks and ancient neighbourhood,
And if your stray attendance be yet lodg'd
Or shroud within these limits, I shall know   315
Ere morrow wake, or the low-roosted lark
From her thatcht pallat rouse; if otherwise
I can conduct you Lady to a low
But loyal cottage, where you may be safe
Till furder quest.   *La.* Shepherd I take thy word,   320
And trust thy honest offerd courtesie,
Which oft is sooner found in lowly sheds
With smoky rafters, than in tapstry Halls
And Courts of Princes, where it first was nam'd,
And yet is most pretended: In a place   325
Less warranted than this, or less secure
I cannot be, that I should fear to change it.
Eye me blest Providence, and square my trial
To my proportiond strength.   Shepherd lead on.—

The Two Brothers.

Eld. Bro. Unmuffle ye faint stars, and thou fair Moon
That wontst to love the travellers benizon   331
Stoop thy pale visage through an amber cloud
And disinherit *Chaos*, that reigns here
In double night of darkness and of shades;
Or if your influence be quite dammd up   335
With black usurping mists, som gentle taper
Though a rush Candle from the wicker hole
Of som clay habitation visit us
With thy long leveld rule of streaming light,
And thou shalt be our star of *Arcady*   340
Or *Tyrian* Cynosure.   *2. Bro.* Or if our eyes
Be barrd that happiness, might we but hear
The folded flocks pennd in their watl'd cotes,
Or sound of pastoral reed with oaten stops,
Or whistle from the Lodge, or Village Cock   345
Count the night watches to his feathery Dames,
'Twould be som solace yet, som little cheering
In this close dungeon of innumerous boughs.

320 furder *Tr. MS.*] further *Edd. 1, 2*

But O that hapless virgin our lost sister
Where may she wander now, whither betake her   350
From the chill dew, amongst rude burrs and thistles?
Perhaps som cold bank is her boulster now
Or 'gainst the rugged bark of som broad Elm
Leans her unpillowd head fraught with sad fears;
What if in wild amazement and affright,   355
Or while we speak within the direful grasp
Of Savage hunger or of Savage heat?
   Eld. Bro. Peace Brother, be not over-exquisite
To cast the fashion of uncertain evils;
For grant they be so, while they rest unknown   360
What need a man forestall his date of grief
And run to meet what he would most avoid?
Or if they be but false alarms of Fear,
How bitter is such self-delusion!
I do not think my sister so to seek   365
Or so unprincipl'd in vertues book
And the sweet peace that goodness bosoms ever,
As that the single want of light and noise
(Not being in danger, as I trust she is not)
Could stir the constant mood of her calm thoughts   370
And put them into mis-becoming plight.
Vertue could see to do what vertue would
By her own radiant light, though Sun and Moon
Were in the flat Sea sunk.   And Wisdoms self
Oft seeks to sweet retired Solitude,   375
Where with her best nurse Contemplation
She plumes her feathers, and lets grow her wings
That in the various bussle of resort
Were all to ruffl'd, and somtimes impaird.
He that has light within his own clear breast   380
May sit i'th center and enjoy bright day,
But he that hides a dark soul and foul thoughts
Benighted walks under the mid-day Sun;
Himself is his own dungeon.
   2. Bro. 'Tis most true
That musing meditation most affects   385
The pensive secrecy of desert cell,
Far from the cheerful haunt of men and herds,
And sits as safe as in a Senat house;
For who would rob a Hermit of his Weeds,
His few Books, or his Beads, or Maple Dish,   390
Or do his gray hairs any violence?
But beauty like the fair Hesperian Tree
Laden with blooming gold, had need the guard
Of dragon watch with uninchanted eye,
To save her blossoms and defend her fruit   395
From the rash hand of bold Incontinence.

You may as well spred out the unsunnd heaps
Of Misers treasure by an outlaws den,
And tell me it is safe, as bid me hope
Danger will wink on Opportunity,   400
And let a single helpless maiden pass
Uninjurd in this wilde surrounding waste.
Of night or loneliness it recks me not,
I fear the dread events that dog them both,
Lest som ill greeting touch attempt the person   405
Of our unowned sister.
    Eld. Bro. I do not, Brother,
Inferr, as if I thought my sisters state
Secure without all doubt or controversie:
Yet where an equal poise of hope and fear
Does arbitrate th'event, my nature is   410
That I encline to hope, rather than fear,
And gladly banish squint suspicion.
My sister is not so defenceless left
As you imagine, she has a hidden strength
Which you remember not.
    2. *Bro.* What hidden strength,   415
Unless the strength of Heav'n, if you mean that?
    Eld. Bro. I mean that too, but yet a hidden strength
Which if Heav'n gave it, may be termd her own:
'Tis chastity, my brother, chastity:
She that has that, is clad in complete steel,   420
And like a quiverd Nymph with Arrows keen
May trace huge Forests and unharbourd Heaths,
Infamous Hills and sandy perilous wildes,
Where through the sacred rays of Chastity
No savage fierce, Bandite or Mountaneer   425
Will dare to soil her Virgin purity;
Yea there, where very desolation dwells
By grots and caverns shaggd with horrid shades,
She may pass on with unblencht majesty,
Be it not don in pride or in presumption.   430
Som say no evil thing that walks by night
In fog or fire, by lake or moorish fen,
Blue meager Hag, or stubborn unlaid ghost
That breaks his magic chains at *curfeu* time,
No goblin, or swart faëry of the mine,   435
Hath hurtful power ore true Virginity.
Do ye believe me yet, or shall I call
Antiquity from the old Schools of *Greece*
To testifie the arms of Chastity?
Hence had the huntress *Dian* her dread bow   440
Fair silver-shafted Queen for ever chaste,
Wherwith she tam'd the brinded lioness
And spotted mountain pard, but set at naught

The frivolous bolt of *Cupid*, gods and men
Fear'd her stern frown, and she was queen o'th' Woods.
What was that snaky-headed *Gorgon* shield   446
That wise *Minerva* wore, unconquerd Virgin,
Wherewith she freez'd her foes to congeal'd stone,
But rigid looks of Chaste austerity,
And noble grace that dashd brute violence   450
With sudden adoration, and blank awe?
So dear to Heav'n is Saintly chastity,
That when a soul is found sincerely so,
A thousand liveried Angels lacky her,
Driving far off each thing of sin and guilt,   455
And in clear dream and solemn vision
Tell her of things that no gross ear can hear,
Till oft converse with heav'nly habitants
Begin to cast a beam on th'outward shape,
The unpolluted temple of the mind,   460
And turns it by degrees to the souls essence,
Till all be made immortal: but when lust
By unchaste looks, loose gestures, and foul talk,
But most by lewd and lavish act of sin,
Lets in defilement to the inward parts,   465
The soul grows clotted by contagion,
Imbodies and imbrutes, till she quite lose
The divine property of her first being.
Such are those thick and gloomy shaddows damp
Oft seen in Charnel vaults and Sepulchers   470
Lingering and sitting by a new made grave,
As loath to leave the Body that it lov'd,
And linkt it self by carnal sensualty
To a degenerate and degraded state,
    2. *Bro.* How charming is divine Philosophy!   475
Not harsh and crabbed as dull fools suppose,
But musical as is *Apollo's* lute,
And a perpetual feast of nectard sweets
Where no crude surfet reigns.   *Eld. Bro.* List, list, I hear
Som far off hallow break the silent Air.   480
    2. *Bro.* Me thought so too; what should it be?
    Eld. Bro. For certain
Either som one like us night-founderd here,
Or else som neighbour Wood-man, or at worst
Som roving Robber calling to his fellows.
    2. *Bro.* Heav'n keep my sister, agen agen and near, 485
Best draw, and stand upon our guard.
    Eld. Bro. I'le hallow;
If he be friendly he comes well, if not,
Defence is a good cause, and Heav'n be for us.

448 stone,] stone? *Edd. 1, 2*   451 aw?] aw. *Edd. 1, 2*
   473 sensualty *Tr. MS., Ed. 1*] sensuality, *1637, Ed. 2*

The attendant Spirit habited like a Shepherd.

That hallow I should know, what are you? speak;
Come not too near, you fall on iron stakes else.   490
   Spir. What voice is that? my young Lord? speak agen.
   2. *Bro.* O brother, 'tis my fathers Shepherd sure.
   Eld. Bro. Thyrsis? Whose artful strains have oft delayd
The hudling brook to hear his madrigal
And sweetend every muskrose of the dale,   495
How cam'st thou here good Swain? hath any Ram
Slipt from the fold, or young Kid lost his dam,
Or straggling Wether the pent flock forsook?
How couldst thou find this dark sequesterd nook?
   Spir. O my lov'd Masters heir, and his next joy,   500
I came not here on such a trivial toy
As a strayd Ewe, or to persue the stealth
Of pilfering Wolf, not all the fleecy wealth
That doth enrich these Downs is worth a thought
To this my errand, and the care it brought.   505
But O my Virgin Lady, where is she?
How chance she is not in your company?
   Eld. Bro. To tell thee sadly Shepherd, without blame
Or our neglect, we lost her as we came.
   Spir. Ay me unhappy, then my fears are true.   510
   Eld. Bro. What fears good *Thyrsis?* Prethee briefly shew.
   Spir. I'le tell ye; 'tis not vain or fabulous
(Though so esteemd by shallow ignorance)
What the sage Poets, taught by th' heav'nly Muse,
Storied of old in high immortal verse   515
Of dire *Chimeras* and inchanted Iles,
And rifted Rocks whose entrance leads to Hell,
For such there be, but unbelief is blind.
   Within the navil of this hideous Wood,
Immur'd in cypress shades a Sorcerer dwells,   520
Of *Bacchus* and of *Circe* born, great *Comus,*
Deep skilld in all his mothers witcheries,
And here to every thirsty wanderer
By sly enticement gives his baneful cup,
With many murmurs mixt, whose pleasing poison   525
The visage quite transforms of him that drinks,
And the inglorious likeness of a beast
Fixes instead, unmoulding reasons mintage
Characterd in the face; this have I learnt
Tending my flocks hard by i'th' hilly crofts   530
That brow this bottom glade, whence night by night
He and his monstrous rout are heard to howl

492 fathers *Tr. MS.*] father *Edd. 1, 2*

Like stabl'd wolves, or tigers at their prey,
Doing abhorred rites to *Hecate*
In their obscured haunts of inmost bowrs;   535
Yet have they many baits and guileful spells
T'inveigle and invite th'unwary sense
Of them that pass unweeting by the way.
This evening late, by then the chewing flocks
Had tane their supper on the savoury Herb   540
Of Knot-grass dew-besprent, and were in fold,
I sate me down to watch upon a bank
With Ivy canopied, and interwove
With flaunting Hony-suckle, and began
Wrapt in a pleasing fit of melancholy   545
To meditate my rural minstrelsie
Till fancy had her fill, but ere a close
The wonted roar was up amidst the Woods,
And filld the Air with barbarous dissonance;
At which I ceas'd, and listend them a while,   550
Till an unusual stop of sudden silence
Gave respit to the drowsie frighted steeds
That draw the litter of close-curtaind sleep.
At last a soft and solemn breathing sound
Rose like a steam of rich distilld perfumes   555
And stole upon the Air, that even Silence
Was took ere she was ware, and wishd she might
Deny her nature, and be never more
Still to be so displac't.   I was all ear,
And took in strains that might create a soul   560
Under the ribs of Death, but O ere long
Too well I did perceive it was the voice
Of my most honourd Lady, your dear sister.
Amaz'd I stood, harrowd with grief and fear,
And O poor hapless Nightingale thought I,   565
How sweet thou singst, how near the deadly snare!
Then down the Lawns I ran with headlong haste
Through paths and turnings often trod by day,
Till guided by mine ear I found the place
Where that damnd wizard hid in sly disguise   570
(For so by certain signes I knew) had met
Already, ere my best speed could prevent,
The aidless innocent Lady his wisht prey,
Who gently askd if he had seen such two,
Supposing him som neighbour villager;   575
Longer I durst not stay, but soon I guessd
Ye were the two she meant; with that I sprung
Into swift flight, till I had found you here;
But furder know I not. 2. *Bro.* O night and shades,
How are ye joind with hell in triple knot   580
Against th'unarmed weakness of one Virgin

Alone, and helpless!   Is this the confidence
You gave me Brother?   *Eld. Bro.* Yes, and keep it still,
Lean on it safely, not a period
Shall be unsaid for me: against the threats   585
Of malice or of sorcery, or that power
Which erring men call Chance, this I hold firm,
Vertue may be assaild but never hurt,
Surpriz'd by unjust force but not enthralld,
Yea even that which mischief meant most harm   590
Shall in the happy trial prove most glory.
But evil on it self shall back recoil
And mix no more with goodness, when at last
Gatherd like scum and settl'd to it self
It shall be in eternal restless change   595
Self-fed, and self-consum'd; if this fail,
The pillard firmament is rottenness,
And earths base built on stubble.   But come let's on.
Against th'opposing will and arm of Heav'n
May never this just sword be lifted up,   600
But for that damnd Magician, let him be girt
With all the griesly legions that troop
Under the sooty flag of *Acheron*,
Harpies and *Hydras*, or all the monstrous forms
'Twixt *Africa* and *Inde*, I'le find him out   605
And force him to restore his purchase back,
Or drag him by the curls to a foul death,
Curst as his life.
     Spir. Alas good ventrous youth,
I love thy courage yet, and bold Emprise,
But here thy sword can do thee little stead;   610
Farr other arms and other weapons must
Be those that quell the might of hellish charms;
He with his bare wand can unthred thy joints
And crumble all thy sinews.
     Eld. Bro. Why prethee Shepherd
How durst thou then thy self approach so near   615
As to make this Relation?
     Spir. Care and utmost shifts
How to secure the Lady from surprisal
Brought to my mind a certain Shepherd Lad
Of small regard to see to, yet well skilld
In every vertuous plant and healing herb   620
That spreads her verdant leaf to th'morning ray;
He lov'd me well, and oft would beg me sing,
Which when I did, he on the tender grass
Would sit, and hearken even to extasie,
And in requital ope his leathern scrip   . 625

604 forms *Edd. 1, 2*] buggs *MS.*] bugs *1637*

And shew me simples of a thousand names
Telling their strange and vigorous faculties;
Amongst the rest a small unsightly root,
But of divine effect, he culld me out;
The leaf was darkish, and had prickles on it,   630
But in another Country, as he said,
Bore a bright golden flowr, but not in this soil:
Unknown, and like esteemd, and the dull swain
Treads on it daily with his clouted shoon,
And yet more med'cinal is it than that *Moly*   635
That *Hermes* once to wise *Ulysses* gave;
He calld it *Haemony*, and gave it me,
And bad me keep it as of sovran use
'Gainst all inchantments, mildew blast, or damp,
Or gastly furies apparition;   640
I purs'd it up, but little reck'ning made
Till now that this extremity compelld,
But now I find it true; for by this means
I knew the foul inchanter though disguis'd,
Enterd the very lime-twigs of his spells,   645
And yet came off: if you have this about you
(As I will give you when we go) you may
Boldly assault the necromancers hall;
Where if he be, with dauntless hardihood
And brandisht blade rush on him, break his glass   650
And shed the lushious liquor on the ground,
But sieze his wand, though he and his curst crew
Fierce signe of battel make and menace high,
Or like the sons of *Vulcan* vomit smoke,
Yet will they soon retire, if he but shrink.   655
    Eld. Bro. *Thyrsis* lead on apace, I'le follow thee,
And som good angel bear a shield before us.

*The Scene changes to a stately Palace, set out with all manner of deliciousness;
soft Music, Tables spred with all dainties. Comus appears with his rabble,
and the Lady set in an inchanted Chair, to whom he offers his Glass,
which she puts by, and goes about to rise.*

    Comus. Nay Lady sit; if I but wave this wand,
Your nerves are all chaind up in Alablaster,
And you a statue; or as *Daphne* was   660
Root-bound, that fled *Apollo*.
    La. Fool do not boast,
Thou canst not touch the freedom of my minde
With all thy charms, although this corporal rinde
Thou hast immanacl'd, while Heav'n sees good.
    Co. Why are you vext Lady? why do you frown?   665
Here dwell no frowns, nor anger, from these gates
Sorrow flies far: See here be all the pleasures

That fancy can beget on youthful thoughts,
When the fresh blood grows lively and returns
Brisk as the *April* buds in Primrose-season.   670
And first behold this cordial Julep here
That flames and dances in his crystal bounds
With spirits of baum and fragrant Syrops mixt.
Not that *Nepenthes* which the wife of *Thone*
In *Egypt* gave to *Jove*-born *Helena*   675
Is of such power to stir up joy as this,
To life so friendly or so cool to thirst.
Why should you be so cruel to your self,
And to those dainty limbs which nature lent
For gentle usage and soft delicacy?   680
But you invert the cov'nants of her trust,
And harshly deal like an ill borrower
With that which you receiv'd on other terms,
Scorning the unexempt condition
By which all mortal frailty must subsist,   685
Refreshment after toil, ease after pain,
That have been tir'd all day without repast,
And timely rest have wanted; but fair Virgin
This will restore all soon.
     La. 'Twill not false traitor,
'Twill not restore the truth and honesty   690
That thou hast banisht from thy tongue with lies;
Was this the cottage and the safe abode
Thou told'st me of? What grim aspects are these,
These ugly-headed Monsters? Mercy guard me!
Hence with thy brewd inchantments, foul deceiver;   695
Hast thou betrayd my credulous innocence
With visord falsehood and base forgery,
And wouldst thou seek again to trap me here
With lickerish baits fit to ensnare a brute?
Were it a draft for *Juno* when she banquets,   700
I would not taste thy treasonous offer; none
But such as are good men can give good things,
And that which is not good, is not delicious
To a well-govern'd and wise appetite,
     Co. O foolishness of men! that lend their ears   705
To those budge Doctors of the *Stoic* Furr,
And fetch their precepts from the *Cynic* Tub,
Praising the lean and sallow Abstinence.
Wherefore did Nature pour her bounties forth
With such a full and unwithdrawing hand,   710
Covering the earth with odours, fruits and flocks,
Thronging the Seas with spawn innumerable,
But all to please and sate the curious taste?
And set to work millions of spinning Worms,
That in their green shops weave the smooth-haird silk

To deck her Sons, and that no corner might 716
Be vacant of her plenty, in her own loins
She hutchd th'all-worship ore and precious gems
To store her children with; if all the world
Should in a pet of temperance feed on Pulse, 720
Drink the clear stream, and nothing wear but Freize,
Th'all-giver would be unthankt, would be unprais'd,
Not half his riches known and yet despis'd,
And we should serve him as a grudging maister,
As a penurious niggard of his wealth, 725
And live like Natures bastards, not her sons,
Who would be quite surcharg'd with her own weight,
And strangl'd with her waste fertility;
Th'earth cumberd, and the wingd air darkt with plumes,
The herds would over-multitude their Lords, 730
The Sea o'erfraught would swell, and th'unsought diamonds
Would so emblaze the forhead of the Deep
And so bestudd with Stars, that they below
Would grow inur'd to light, and come at last
To gaze upon the Sun with shameless brows. 735
List Lady be not coy, and be not cosend
With that same vaunted name Virginity;
Beauty is natures coin, must not be hoarded
But must be currant, and the good thereof
Consists in mutual and partaken bliss, 740
Unsavoury in th'injoyment of it self;
If you let slip time, like a neglected rose
It withers on the stalk with languisht head.
Beauty is natures brag, and must be shown
In courts, at feasts, and high solemnities 745
Where most may wonder at the workmanship;
It is for homely features to keep home,
They had their name thence; coarse complexions
And cheeks of sorry grain will serve to ply
The sampler and to tease the huswifes wooll. 750
What need a vermeil-tinctur'd lip for that,
Love-darting eyes or tresses like the Morn?
There was another meaning in these gifts;
Think what, and be adviz'd, you are but young yet.

    La. I had not thought to have unlockt my lips 755
In this unhallowd air, but that this Jugler
Would think to charm my judgement, as mine eyes,
Obtruding false rules pranckt in reasons garb.
I hate when vice can bolt her arguments,
And vertue has no tongue to check her pride: 760
Impostor do not charge most innocent nature,
As if she would her children should be riotous

724 maister *Tr. MS.*] master *Edd. 1, 2*

With her abundance; she good cateress
Means her provision only to the good
That live according to her sober laws   765
And holy dictate of spare Temperance:
If every just man that now pines with want
Had but a moderat and beseeming share
Of that which lewdly-pamperd Luxury
Now heaps upon som few with vast excess,   770
Natures full blessings would be well dispenst
In unsuperfluous ev'n proportion,
And she no whit encumberd with her store;
And then the giver would be better thankt,
His praise due paid, for swinish gluttony   775
Ne're looks to Heav'n amidst his gorgeous feast,
But with besotted base ingratitude
Cramms, and blasphemes his feeder.   Shall I go on?
Or have I said anough?   To him that dares
Arm his profane tongue with contemptuous words   780
Against the Sun-clad power of Chastity,
Fain would I something say, yet to what end?
Thou hast nor Ear nor Soul to apprehend
The sublime notion and high mystery
That must be utterd to unfold the sage   785
And serious doctrine of Virginity,
And thou art worthy that thou shouldst not know
More happiness than this thy present lot.
Enjoy your dear Wit and gay Rhetoric
That hath so well been taught her dazling fence,   790
Thou art not fit to hear thy self convinc't;
Yet should I try, the uncontroled worth
Of this pure cause would kindle my rapt spirits
To such a flame of sacred vehemence,
That dumb things would be mov'd to sympathize,   795
And the brute Earth would lend her nerves and shake
Till all thy magic structures rear'd so high
Were shatterd into heaps ore thy false head.
    Co. She fables not, I feel that I do fear
Her words set off by som superior power;   800
And though not mortal, yet a cold shuddring dew
Dips me all ore, as when the wrath of *Jove*
Speaks thunder and the chains of *Erebus*
To som of *Saturns* crew.   I must dissemble,
And try her yet more strongly.   Come, no more,   805
This is mere moral babble, and direct
Against the canon laws of our foundation;
I must not suffer this, yet 'tis but the lees
And setlings of a melancholy blood;

779 anough *1645*] anow 1673

But this will cure all straight, one sip of this   810
Will bathe the drooping spirits in delight
Beyond the bliss of dreams.   Be wise, and taste. . . .

The Brothers *rush in with Swords drawn, wrest his Glass out of his hand, and*
break it against the ground; his rout make sign of resistance, but are all
driven in; The attendant Spirit comes in.

   Spir. What, have you let the false Enchanter scape?
O ye mistook, ye should have snatcht his wand
And bound him fast; without his rod reverst,   815
And backward mutters of disseevering power,
We cannot free the Lady that sits here
In stony fetters fixt, and motionless;
Yet stay, be not disturbd, now I bethink me,
Som other means I have that may be us'd,   820
Which once of *Melibaeus* old I learnd,
The soothest Shepherd that e're pip'd on plains.
   There is a gentle Nymph not far from hence
That with moist curb sways the smooth Severn stream,
Sabrina is her name, a Virgin pure;   825
Whilome she was the daughter of *Locrine*,
That had the Scepter from his father *Brute*.
She guiltless damsel, flying the mad persuit
Of her enraged stepdam *Guendolen*,
Commended her fair innocence to the flood   830
That stayd her flight with his cross-flowing course;
The water Nymphs that in the bottom playd
Held up their pearled wrists and took her in,
Bearing her straight to aged *Nereus* Hall,
Who pitteous of her woes rear'd her lank head   835
And gave her to his daughters to imbathe
In nectard lavers strewd with Asphodil,
And through the porch and inlet of each sense
Dropd in Ambrosial Oils till she reviv'd,
And underwent a quick immortal change   840
Made Goddess of the River; still she retains
Her maiden gentleness, and oft at Eve
Visits the herds along the twilight meddows,
Helping all urchin blasts and ill luck signes
That the shrewd medling Elfe delights to make,   845
Which she with precious viold liquors heals.
For which the Shepherds at their festivals
Carrol her goodness loud in rustic lays,
And throw sweet garland wreaths into her stream
Of pansies, pinks, and gaudy Daffadils.   850
And, as the old Swain said, she can unlock

    820 that *Tr. MS.*] which *Edd. 1, 2*
    828 She *Ed. 1*] The *Ed. 2*

The clasping charm, and thaw the numming spell,
If she be right invok't in warbled Song,
For maidenhood she loves, and will be swift
To aid a Virgin, such as was her self,   855
In hard besetting need; this will I try
And add the power of som adjuring verse.

SONG

Sabrina fair
   Listen where thou art sitting
Under the glassie, cool, translucent wave,   860
   In twisted braids of Lillies knitting
The loose train of thy amber-dropping hair,
   Listen for dear honours sake,
   Goddess of the silver lake,
          Listen and save.   865

Listen and appear to us
In name of great *Oceanus*,
By th'earth-shaking *Neptunes* mace,
And *Tethys* grave majestic pace,
By hoary *Nereus* wrinkl'd look,   870
And the *Carpathian* wizards hook,
By scaly *Tritons* winding shell,
And old sooth-saying *Glaucus* spell,
By *Leucothea's* lovely hands,
And her son that rules the strands,   875
By *Thetis* tinsel-slipperd feet
And the Songs of *Sirens* sweet,
By dead *Parthenope's* dear tomb,
And fair *Ligea's* golden comb,
Wherwith she sits on diamond rocks   880
Sleeking her soft alluring locks,
By all the *Nymphs* that nightly dance
Upon thy streams with wily glance,
Rise, rise, and heave thy rosie head
From thy coral-paven bed,   885
And bridle in thy headlong wave
Till thou our summons answerd have.
          Listen and save.

   Sabrina rises, attended by water-Nymphs, and sings.

   By the rushy-fringed bank,
Where grows the Willow and the Osier dank,   890
   My sliding Chariot stays,
Thick set with Agat, and the azurn sheen
Of Turkis blue, and Emrauld green
   That in the channel strays,

Whilst from off the waters fleet 895
Thus I set my printless feet
Ore the Cowslips Velvet head,
   That bends not as I tread,
Gentle swain at thy request
   I am here. 900

   Spir. Goddess dear
We implore thy powerful hand
To undo the charmed band
Of true Virgin here distrest,
Through the force and through the wile 905
Of unblest inchanter vile.
   Sab. Shepherd 'tis my office best
To help insnared chastity;
Brightest Lady look on me,
Thus I sprinkle on thy brest 910
Drops that from my fountain pure
I have kept of precious cure,
Thrice upon thy fingers tip,
Thrice upon thy rubied lip,
Next this marble venomd seat 915
Smear'd with gumms of glutenous heat
I touch with chaste palms moist and cold,
Now the spell hath lost his hold;
And I must haste ere morning hour
To wait in *Amphitrite's* bowr. 920

Sabrina *descends, and the* Lady *rises out of her seat.*

   Spir. Virgin, daughter of *Locrine*
Sprung of old *Anchises* line
May thy brimmed waves for this
Their full tribute never miss
From a thousand petty rills 925
That tumble down the snowy hills:
Summer drouth or singed air
Never scorch thy tresses fair,
Nor wet *Octobers* torrent flood
Thy molten crystal fill with mudd, 930
May thy billows roul ashore
The beryl and the golden ore,
May thy lofty head be crownd
With many a towr and terrace round,
And here and there thy banks upon 935
With Groves of myrrh and cinnamon.

Come Lady while Heaven lends us grace,
Let us fly this cursed place,
Lest the Sorcerer us intice

With som other new device.   940
Not a waste or needless sound
Till we come to holier ground,
I shall be your faithful guide
Through this gloomy covert wide,
And not many furlongs thence   945
Is your Fathers residence,
Where this night are met in state
Many a friend to gratulate
His wisht presence, and beside
All the Swains that there abide   950
With Jiggs and rural dance resort,
We shall catch them at their sport,
And our sudden coming there
Will double all their mirth and chere;
Come let us haste, the Stars grow high,   955
But night sits monarch yet in the mid sky.

The Scene changes, presenting Ludlow *Town and the Presidents Castle, then com in Country-Dancers, after them the attendant Spirit, with the two Brothers and the Lady.*

SONG

Spir. Back Shepherds, back, anough your play,
Till next Sun-shine holiday,
Here be without duck or nod
Other trippings to be trod   960
Of lighter toes, and such Court guise
As Mercury *did first devise*
With the mincing Dryades
On the Lawns and on the Leas.

This second Song presents them to their father and mother.

Noble Lord, and Lady bright,   965
I have brought ye new delight,
Here behold so goodly grown
Three fair branches of your own,
Heav'n hath timely tri'd their youth,
Their faith, their patience, and their truth,   970
And sent them here through hard assays
With a crown of deathless Praise,
    To triumph in victorious dance
Ore sensual Folly and Intemperance.

The dances ended, the Spirit Epiloguizes.

Spir. To the Ocean now I fly,   975
And those happy climes that ly

955 grow *Edd. 1, 2, Tr. MS. corr.*] are *1637, Tr. MS. orig., Br. MS.*

Where day never shuts his eye,
Up in the broad fields of the sky:
There I suck the liquid air
All amidst the Gardens fair   980
Of *Hesperus*, and his daughters three
That sing about the golden tree:
Along the crisped shades and bowrs
Revels the spruce and jocond Spring,
The Graces and the rosie-bosomd Hours   985
Thither all their bounties bring,
There eternal Summer dwells,
And West winds with musky wing
About the cedar'n alleys fling
Nard and *Cassia's* baumy smells.   990
Iris there with humid bow
Waters the odorous banks that blow
Flowers of more mingl'd hew
Than her purfl'd scarf can shew,
And drenches with *Elysian* dew   995
(List mortals if your ears be true)
Beds of *Hyacinth* and Roses
Where young *Adonis* oft reposes,
Waxing well of his deep wound
In slumber soft, and on the ground   1000
Sadly sits th' *Assyrian* Queen;
But far above in spangl'd sheen
Celestial *Cupid* her fam'd son advanc't
Holds his dear *Psyche* sweet intranc't
After her wandring labours long,   1005
Till free consent the gods among
Make her his eternal Bride,
And from her fair unspotted side
Two blissful twins are to be born,
Youth and Joy; so *Jove* hath sworn.   1010
    But now my task is smoothly don,
I can fly or I can run
Quickly to the green earths end,
Where the bowd welkin slow doth bend,
And from thence can soar as soon   1015
To the corners of the Moon.
    Mortals that would follow me,
Love vertue, she alone is free,
She can teach ye how to clime
Higher than the Spheary chime;   1020
Or if Vertue feeble were,
Heav'n it self would stoop to her.

SONNETS

I

O Nightingale, that on yon bloomy Spray
    Warbl'st at Eve, when all the Woods are still,
    Thou with fresh hope the Lovers heart dost fill,
    While the jolly hours lead on propitious *May*,
Thy liquid notes that close the eye of Day,   5
    First heard before the shallow Cuckoo's bill,
    Portend success in love; O if *Joves* will
    Have linkt that amorous power to thy soft lay,
Now timely sing, ere the rude Bird of Hate
    Foretell my hopeless doom in som Grove ny: 10
    As thou from year to year hast sung too late
For my relief; yet hadst no reason why:
    Whether the Muse or Love call thee his mate,
    Both them I serve, and of their train am I.

II

Donna leggiadra il cui bel nome honora
    L'herbosa val di Rheno, e il nobil varco,
    Ben è colui d'ogni valore scarco
    Qual tuo spirto gentil non innamora,
Che dolcemente mostrasi di fuora   5
    De' suoi atti soavi giamai parco,
    E i don' che son d'Amor saette ed arco,
    Là onde l'alta tua virtù s'infiora.
Quando tu vaga parli, o lieta canti
    Che mover possa duro alpestre legno,   10
    Guardi ciascun a gli occhi ed a gli orecchi
L'entrata, chi di te si truova indegno;
    Gratia sola di sù gli vaglia, inanti
Che'l disio amoroso al cuor s'invecchi.

III

Qual in colle aspro, a l'imbrunir di sera
    L'avvezza giovinetta pastorella
    Va bagnando l'herbetta strana e bella
    Che mal si spande a disusata spera
Fuor di sua natía alma primavera,   5

Così Amor meco insù la lingua snella
Desta il fior novo di strania favella,
Mentre io di te, vezzosamente altera,
Canto, dal mio buon popol non inteso,
   E'l bel Tamigi cangio col bel Arno.   10
   Amor lo volse, ed io a l'altrui peso
Seppi ch'Amor cosa mai volse indarno.
   Deh! foss'il mio cuor lento e'l duro seno
   A chi pianta dal ciel sì buon terreno.

CANZONE

Ridonsi donne e giovani amorosi
M'accostandosi attorno, e, Perche scrivi,
Perche tu scrivi in lingua ignota e strana
Verseggiando d'amor, e come t'osi?
Dinne, se la tua speme sia mai vana   5
E de' pensieri lo miglior t'arrivi;
Così mi van burlando, Altri rivi,
Altri lidi t'aspettan, ed altre onde
Nelle cui verdi sponde
Spuntati ad hor ad hor a la tua chioma   10
L'immortal guiderdon d'eterne frondi:
Perche alle spalle tue soverchia soma?
   Canzon dirotti, e tu per me rispondi,
Dice mia Donna, e'l suo dir è il mio cuore,
Questa è lingua di cui si vanta Amore.   15

IV

Diodati, e te'l dirò con maraviglia,
   Quel ritroso io ch'Amor spreggiar soléa
   E de' suoi lacci spesso mi ridéa
   Già caddi, ov'huom dabben talhor s'impiglia.
Nè treccie d'oro nè guancia vermiglia   5
   M'abbaglian sì, ma sotto nova idea
   Pellegrina bellezza che'l cuor bea,
   Portamenti alti honesti, e nelle ciglia
Quel sereno fulgor d'amabil nero,
   Parole adorne di lingua più d'una,   10
   E'l cantar che di mezzo l'hemispero
Traviar ben può la faticosa Luna,
   E degli occhi suoi avventa sì gran fuoco
   Che l'incerar gli orecchi mi fia poco.

V

Per certo i bei vostr'occhi, Donna mia,
　Esser non può che non sian lo mio sole,
　Sì mi percuoton forte, come ei suole
　Per l'arene di Libia chi s'invia,
Mentre un caldo vapor (nè senti' pria)   5
　Da quel lato si spinge ove mi duole,
　Che forse amanti nelle lor parole
　Chiaman sospir; io non so che si sia:
Parte rinchiusa e turbida si cela
　Scossomi il petto, e poi n'uscendo poco   10
　Quivi d'attorno o s'agghiaccia o s'ingiela;
Ma quanto a gli occhi giunge a trovar loco
　Tutte le notti a me suol far piovose
　Finchè mia Alba rivien colma di rose.

VI

Giovane, piano, e semplicetto amante
　Poi che fuggir me stesso in dubbio sono,
　Madonna a voi del mio cuor l'humil dono
　Farò divoto; io certo a prove tante
L'hebbi fedele, intrepido, costante,   5
　Di pensieri leggiadro, accorto, e buono;
　Quando rugge il gran mondo, e scocca il tuono,
　S'arma di se, e d'intero diamante,
Tanto del forse e d'invidia sicuro,
　Di timori e speranze al popol use   10
　Quanto d'ingegno e d'alto valor vago,
E di cetra sonora e delle Muse:
　Sol troverete in tal parte men duro
　Ove Amor mise l'insanabil ago.

VII

How soon hath Time the suttle thief of youth
　Stolne on his wing my three and twentith yeer!
　My hasting dayes flie on with full career,
　But my late spring no bud or blossom shewth.
Perhaps my semblance might deceive the truth,   5
　That I to manhood am arriv'd so near,
　And inward ripeness doth much less appear,
　That som more timely-happy spirits indu'th.
Yet be it less or more, or soon or slow,
　It shall be still in strictest measure ev'n   10
　To that same lot, however mean or high,
Toward which Time leads me, and the will of Heav'n;
　All is, if I have grace to use it so,
　As ever in my great task-Masters eye.

VIII

Captain or Colonel, or Knight in Arms,
    Whose chance on these defenceless dores may sease,
    If deed of honour did thee ever please,
    Guard them, and him within protect from harms;
He can requite thee, for he knows the charms   5
    That call Fame on such gentle acts as these,
    And he can spread thy Name ore Lands and Seas,
    What ever clime the Suns bright circle warms.
Lift not thy spear against the Muses Bowr,
    The great *Emathian* Conqueror bid spare   10
    The house of *Pindarus*, when Temple and Towr
Went to the ground: And the repeated air
    Of sad *Electra's* Poet had the power
    To save th' *Athenian* Walls from ruin bare.

IX

Lady that in the prime of earliest youth
    Wisely hath shunnd the broad way and the green,
    And with those few art eminently seen
    That labour up the Hill of heav'nly Truth,
The better part with *Mary* and with *Ruth*   5
    Chosen thou hast, and they that overween,
    And at thy growing vertues fret their spleen,
    No anger find in thee, but pitty and ruth.
Thy care is fixt and zealously attends
    To fill thy odorous Lamp with deeds of light,   10
    And Hope that reaps not shame.   Therefore be sure
Thou, when the Bridegroom with his feastful friends
    Passes to bliss at the mid hour of night,
    Hast gaind thy entrance, Virgin wise and pure.

X

Daughter to that good Earl, once President
    Of *Englands* Counsel and her Treasury,
    Who liv'd in both, unstain'd with gold or fee,
    And left them both, more in himself content,
Till the sad breaking of that Parlament   5
    Broke him, as that dishonest victory
    At *Chaeronéa*, fatal to liberty
    Killd with report that Old man eloquent:

VIII Tr. MS. supplies title, *When the assault was intended to the city.*
3 If ever deed of honour did thee please *Ed. 1*
IX 5 with *Ruth*] the *Ruth Ed. 1*
X Tr. MS. supplies title, *To the Lady Margaret Ley*

Though later born, than to have known the dayes
  Wherin your Father flourishd, yet by you   10
  Madam, me thinks I see him living yet;
So well your words his noble vertues praise,
  That all both judge you to relate them true,
  And to possess them, Honourd *Margaret*.

XI

A Book was writ of late calld *Tetrachordon*;
  And woven close, both matter, form and stile;
  The Subject new: it walkd the Town a while,
  Numbring good intellects; now seldom por'd on.
Cries the stall-reader, bless us! what a word on   5
  A title page is this! and some in file
  Stand spelling false, while one might walk to Mile-
End Green.   Why is it harder Sirs than Gordon,
Colkitto, or Macdonnel, or Galasp?
  Those rugged names to our like mouths grow sleek   10
  That would have made *Quintilian* stare and gasp.
Thy age, like ours, O Soul of Sir *John Cheek*,
  Hated not Learning worse than Toad or Asp;
  When thou taughtst *Cambridge* and King *Edward* Greek.

XII.   *On the same*

I did but prompt the age to quit their cloggs
  By the known rules of ancient libertie,
  When straight a barbarous noise environs me
  Of Owls and Cuckoos, Asses, Apes and Doggs.
As when those Hinds that were transformd to Froggs   5
  Raild at *Latona's* twin-born progenie
  Which after held the Sun and Moon in fee.
  But this is got by casting Pearl to Hoggs;
That bawl for freedom in their senseless mood,
  And still revolt when truth would set them free.   10
  Licence they mean when they cry libertie;
For who loves that, must first be wise and good;
  But from that mark how far they rove we see
  For all this waste of wealth, and loss of blood.

On the new forcers of Conscience under the
Long PARLAMENT

XIII

Because you have thrown off your Prelat Lord,
  And with stiff Vows renounc't his Liturgie
  To seize the widowd whore Pluralitie
  From them whose sin ye envi'd, not abhorrd,

Tr. MS. supplies title to Sonn. XI and XII, *On the detraction which followed
upon my writing certain treatises*

Dare ye for this adjure the Civil Sword   5
   To force our Consciences that Christ set free,
   And ride us with a classic Hierarchy
   Taught ye by mere *A. S.* and *Rotherford*?
Men whose Life, Learning, Faith and pure intent
   Would have been held in high esteem with *Paul*   10
   Must now be nam'd and printed Hereticks
     By shallow *Edwards* and Scotch what d'ye call:
But we do hope to find out all your tricks,
   Your plots and packings worse than those of *Trent*,
          That so the Parlament   15
May with their wholsom and preventive Shears
Clip your Phylacteries, though bauk your Ears,
            And succour our just Fears,
When they shall read this clearly in your charge
New Presbyter is but *Old Priest* writ Large.   20

To Mr H. Lawes, *on his Aires*

XIV

Harry whose tuneful and well measurd Song
   First taught our English Music how to span
   Words with just note and accent, not to scan
   With *Midas* Ears, committing short and long;
Thy worth and skill exempts thee from the throng,   5
   With praise anough for Envy to look wan;
   To after age thou shalt be writ the man
   That with smooth aire couldst humor best our tongue.
Thou honourst Verse, and Verse must send her wing
   To honour thee, the Priest of *Phoebus* Quire   10
   That tun'st their happiest lines in Hymn or Story.
Dante shall give Fame leave to set thee higher
   Than his *Casella*, whom he woo'd to sing
   Met in the milder shades of Purgatory.

XV

When Faith and Love, which parted from thee never,
   Had ripend thy just soul to dwell with God,
   Meekly thou didst resign this earthy load
   Of Death, calld Life; which us from Life doth sever.
Thy Works and Alms and all thy good Endevor   5
   Stayd not behind, nor in the grave were trod,
   But as Faith pointed with her golden rod
   Followd thee up to joy and bliss for ever.

XIV 9 send] lend *Tr. MS.*
XV *Tr. MS.* supplies title, *On the religious memorie of Mrs Catharine
Thomason my christian freind deceas'd 16 Decem. 1646*

Love led them on; and Faith who knew them best
   Thy hand-maids, clad them ore with purple beams   10
And azure wings, that up they flew so drest,
And spake the truth of thee on glorious Theams
   Before the Judge, who thenceforth bid thee rest
And drink thy fill of pure immortal streams.

On the Lord Gen. Fairfax at the seige of Colchester

XVI

Fairfax, whose name in arms through Europe rings
   Filling each mouth with envy or with praise,
   And all her jealous monarchs with amaze
   And rumors loud, that daunt remotest kings,
Thy firm unshaken vertue ever brings   5
   Victory home, though new rebellions raise
   Thir Hydra heads, and the false North displaies
   Her broken league, to imp thir serpent wings,
O yet a nobler task awaits thy hand;
   For what can Warr but endless warr still breed,   10
   Till Truth and Right from Violence be freed,
And Public Faith clear'd from the shameful brand
   Of Public Fraud.   In vain doth Valour bleed
While Avarice and Rapine share the land.

To the Lord Generall Cromwell May 1652
On the proposalls of certaine ministers at the Committee for Propagation of the Gospell.

XVII

Cromwell, our chief of men, who through a cloud
   Not of warr onely, but detractions rude,
   Guided by faith and matchless Fortitude
   To peace and truth thy glorious way hast ploughd,
And on the neck of crowned Fortune proud   5
   Hast rear'd Gods Trophies, and his work persu'd,
   While Darwen stream with blood of Scotts imbru'd,
   And Dunbarr field resounds thy praises loud,
And Worsters laureat wreath; yet much remaines
   To conquer still; peace hath her victories   10
   No less renownd than warr; new foes arise

[Sonn. XVI and XVII are in the Trinity MS. but were first printed in
1694 in the *Letters of State*, edited by Edward Phillips.   The present text
is based on the MS.]

XV 12 spake *Tr. MS.*] speak *Ed. 2.*   On *Ed. 2, fair copy Tr. MS.*] in *first 2
drafts Tr. MS.*

Threatning to bind our soules with secular chaines:
  Helpe us to save free Conscience from the paw
  Of hireling wolves whose Gospel is thir maw.

To Sr Henry Vane *the younger*

XVIII

Vane, young in years, but in sage counsel old,
  Than whom a better Senator ne're held
  The helm of *Rome*, when gowns not arms repelld
  The fierce *Epeirot* and the *African* bold,
Whether to settle peace, or to unfold   5
  The drift of hollow states, hard to be spelld,
  Then to advise how warr may best, upheld,
  Move by her two maine nerves, Iron and Gold
In all her equipage; besides to know
  Both spiritual powr and civil, what each meanes   10
  What severs each thou'hast learnt, which few have don.
The bounds of either sword to thee wee ow.
  Therfore on thy firme hand religion leanes
  In peace, and reckons thee her eldest son.

On the late Massacher *in* Piemont

XIX

Avenge O Lord thy slaughterd Saints, whose bones
  Lie scatterd on the Alpine mountains cold,
  Ev'n them who kept thy truth so pure of old
  When all our Fathers worshipd Stocks and Stones,
Forget not: in thy book record thir groans   5
  Who were thy Sheep and in thir ancient Fold
  Slain by the bloody *Piemontese* that roll'd
  Mother with Infant down the Rocks. Thir moans
The Vales redoubl'd to the Hills, and they
  To Heav'n. Thir martyrd blood and ashes sow   10
  Ore all th'*Italian* fields where still doth sway
The triple Tyrant: that from these may grow
  A hunderd-fold, who having learnt thy way
  Early may fly the *Babylonian* woe.

XX

When I consider how my light is spent,
  Ere half my days, in this dark world and wide,
  And that one Talent which is death to hide
  Lodg'd with me useless, though my Soul more bent

[Sonn. XVIII is in the Trinity MS.; it was first printed anonymously in 1662, and again in 1694 in the *Letters of State*. The present text is based on the MS.]

To serve therewith my Maker, and present   5
   My true account, lest he returning chide,
   Doth God exact day-labour, light deni'd,
   I fondly ask; But patience to prevent
That murmur, soon replies, God doth not need
   Either mans work or his own gifts, who best   10
   Bear his milde yoke, they serve him best, his State
Is Kingly.   Thousands at his bidding speed
   And post o'r Land and Ocean without rest:
   They also serve who only stand and waite.

XXI

Lawrence of vertuous Father vertuous Son,
   Now that the Fields are dank, and ways are mire,
   Where shall we sometimes meet, and by the fire
   Help waste a sullen day; what may be won
From the hard Season gaining: time will run   5
   On smoother, till *Favonius* re-inspire
   The frozen earth; and clothe in fresh attire
   The Lillie and Rose, that neither sowd nor spun.
What neat repast shall feast us, light and choice,
   Of Attic taste, with Wine, whence we may rise   10
   To hear the Lute well toucht, or artful voice
Warble immortal Notes and *Tuscan* Aire?
   He who of those delights can judge, and spare
   To interpose them oft, is not unwise.

XXII

Cyriack, whose Grandsire on the Royal Bench
   Of *Brittish Themis*, with no mean applause
   Pronounc'd and in his volumes taught our Laws,
   Which others at thir Barr so often wrench:
Today deep thoughts resolve with me to drench   5
   In mirth, that after no repenting draws;
   Let *Euclid* rest and *Archimedes* pause,
   And what the *Swede* intends, and what the *French*.
To measure life, learn thou betimes, and know
   Toward solid good what leads the nearest way;   10
   For other things mild Heav'n a time ordains,
And disapproves that care, though wise in show,
   That with superfluous burden loads the day,
   And when God sends a cheerful hour, refrains.

To Mr Cyriack Skinner *upon his Blindness*

XXIII

Cyriack, this three years day these eyes, though clear
 To outward view of blemish or of spot,
 Bereft of light thir seeing have forgot,
 Nor to thir idle orbs doth sight appear
Of Sun or Moon or Starr throughout the year,   5
 Or man or woman. Yet I argue not
 Against heav'ns hand or will, nor bate a jot
 Of heart or hope; but still bear up and steer
Right onward. What supports me, dost thou ask?
 The conscience, Friend, to have lost them overpli'd 10
 In libertys defence, my noble task,
Of which all *Europe* talks from side to side.
 This thought might lead me through the worlds vain mask
 Content though blind, had I no better guide.

XXIV

Methought I saw my late espoused Saint
 Brought to me like *Alcestis* from the grave,
 Whom *Joves* great Son to her glad Husband gave,
 Rescu'd from death by force though pale and faint.
Mine as whom washt from spot of child-bed taint 5
 Purification in the old Law did save,
 And such as yet once more I trust to have
 Full sight of her in Heav'n without restraint,
Came vested all in white, pure as her mind:
 Her face was veild, yet to my fancied sight   10
 Love, sweetness, goodness in her person shin'd
So clear, as in no face with more delight.
 But O as to embrace me she enclin'd
 I wak'd, she fled, and day brought back my night.

[Sonn. XXIII is in the Trinity MS. but was first printed in 1694 in the
Letters of State. The present text is based on the MS.]

PSALMS

PSAL. I.   *Done into Verse, 1653*

Bless'd is the man who hath not walkt astray
In counsel of the wicked, and ith'way
Of sinners hath not stood, and in the seat
Of scorners hath not sate.   But in the great
Jehovahs Law is ever his delight,   5
And in his Law he studies day and night.
He shall be as a tree which planted grows
By watry streams, and in his season knows
To yield his fruit, and his leaf shall not fall,
And what he takes in hand shall prosper all.   10
Not so the wicked, but as chaff which fannd
The wind drives, so the wicked shall not stand
In judgment, or abide their trial then,
Nor sinners in th'assembly of just men.
For the Lord knows th'upright way of the just,   15
And the way of bad men to ruin must.

PSAL. II.   *Done Aug.* 8. 1653.   *Terzetti*

Why do the Gentiles tumult, and the Nations
  Muse a vain thing? the Kings of th'earth upstand
  With power, and Princes in thir Congregations
Lay deep thir plots together through each Land,
  Against the Lord and his Messiah dear.   5
  Let us break off, say they, by strength of hand
Thir bonds, and cast from us, no more to wear,
  Thir twisted cords: hee who in Heav'n doth dwell
  Shall laugh, the Lord shall scoff them, then severe
Speak to them in his wrauth, and in his fell   10
  And fierce ire trouble them; but I saith hee
  Anointed have my King (though ye rebell)
On Sion my holi' hill.   A firm decree
  I will declare; the Lord to me hath sayd
  Thou art my Son, I have begotten thee   15
This day; ask of me, and the grant is made;
  As thy possession I on thee bestow
  Th'Heathen, and as thy conquest to be swayd
Earths utmost bounds: them shalt thou bring full low
  With Iron Scepter bruis'd, and them disperse   20
  Like to a potters vessel shiverd so.

And now be wise at length ye Kings averse,
  Be taught ye Judges of the earth; with fear
Jehovah serve, and let your joy converse
With trembling; kiss the Son lest he appear   25
  In anger and ye perish in the way
  If once his wrath take fire like fuel sere.
Happy all those who have in him thir stay.

PSAL. III.   *Aug.* 9. 1653
When he fled from Absalom

Lord how many are my foes!
  How many those
That in arms against me rise!
  Many are they
That of my life distrustfully thus say,   5
No help for him in God there lies.
But thou Lord art my shield, my glory,
      Thee through my story
    Th' exalter of my head I count;
      Aloud I cri'd   10
Unto Jehovah, he full soon repli'd
And heard me from his holy mount.
I lay and slept, I wak'd again,
      For my sustain
    Was the Lord.   Of many millions   15
      The populous rout
I fear not though incamping round about
They pitch against me thir Pavillions.
Rise Lord, save me my God; for thou
      Hast smote ere now   20
    On the cheek-bone all my foes,
      Of men abhorrd
Hast broke the teeth.   This help was from the Lord;
Thy blessing on thy people flows.

PSAL. IV.   *Aug.* 10. 1653

Answer me when I call
God of my righteousness;
In straits and in distress
Thou didst me disinthrall
And set at large; now spare,   5
  Now pitty me, and hear my earnest pray'r!
Great ones how long will ye
My glory have in scorn,
How long be thus forborne

Still to love vanity,   10
To love, to seek, to prize
  Things false and vain and nothing else but lies?
Yet know the Lord hath chose
Chose to himself apart
The good and meek of heart   15
(For whom to chuse he knows);
Jehovah from on high
  Will hear my voice what time to him I crie.
Be awd, and do not sin,
Speak to your hearts alone,   20
Upon your beds, each one,
And be at peace within.
Offer the offerings just
  Of righteousness, and in Jehovah trust.
Many there be that say   25
Who yet will shew us good?
Talking like this worlds brood;
But Lord, thus let me pray,
On us lift up the light
  Lift up the favour of thy count'nance bright.   30
Into my heart more joy
And gladness thou hast put
Than when a year of glut
Thir stores doth over-cloy,
And from thir plenteous grounds   35
  With vast increase thir corn and wine abounds.
In peace at once will I
Both lay me down and sleep,
For thou alone dost keep
Me safe where ere I lie;   40
As in a rocky Cell
  Thou Lord alone in safety mak'st me dwell.

PSAL. V.   *Aug* 12. 1653

Jehovah to my words give ear,
  My meditation waigh,
The voice of my complaining hear
My King and God; for unto thee I pray.
Jehovah thou my early voice   5
  Shalt in the morning hear,
I'th'morning I to thee with choice
Will rank my Prayers, and watch till thou appear.
For thou art not a God that takes
  In wickedness delight,   10
Evil with thee no biding makes,
Fools or mad men stand not within thy sight.

All workers of iniquity
   Thou hat'st and them unblest
Thou wilt destroy that speak a ly: 15
The bloodi' and guileful man God doth detest.
   But I will in thy mercies dear,
      Thy numerous mercies go
Into thy house; I in thy fear
Will towards thy holy temple worship low.   20
   Lord lead me in thy righteousness,
      Lead me because of those
That do observe if I transgress;
Set thy ways right before, where my step goes.
   For in his faltring mouth unstable   25
      No word is firm or sooth;
Thir inside, troubles miserable;
An open grave thir throat, thir tongue they smooth.
   God, find them guilty, let them fall
      By thir own counsels quelld;   30
Push them in thir rebellions all
Still on: for against thee they have rebelld.
   Then all who trust in thee shall bring
      Thir joy, while thou from blame
Defendst them; they shall ever sing   35
And shall triumph in thee, who love thy name.
   For thou Jehovah wilt be found
      To bless the just man still,
As with a shield thou wilt surround
Him with thy lasting favour and good will.   40

PSAL. VI. *Aug.* 13. 1653

Lord in thine anger do not reprehend me
   Nor in thy hot displeasure me correct;
Pity me Lord for I am much deject
   Am very weak and faint; heal and amend me,
For all my bones, that even with anguish ake,   5
   Are troubl'd, yea my soul is troubl'd sore;
And thou O Lord how long? turn Lord, restore
   My soul, O save me for thy goodness sake,
For in death no remembrance is of thee;
   Who in the grave can celebrate thy praise?   10
Wearied I am with sighing out my days,
   Nightly my Couch I make a kind of Sea;
My Bed I water with my tears; mine Eye
   Through grief consumes, is waxen old and dark
I'th' midst of all mine enemies that mark.   15
   Depart all yee that work iniquitie;

Depart from me, for the voice of my weeping
    The Lord hath heard, the Lord hath heard my pray'r,
My supplication with acceptance fair
    The Lord will own, and have me in his keeping.   20
Mine enemies shall all be blank and dasht
    With much confusion; then grow red with shame;
They shall return in haste the way they came
    And in a moment shall be quite abasht.

PSAL. VII.   *Aug.* 14. 1653

Upon the words of Chush *the* Benjamite
against him.

Lord my God to thee I flie,
Save me and secure me under
Thy protection while I crie,
Lest as a Lion (and no wonder)
He haste to tear my Soul asunder,   5
Tearing and no rescue nigh.

Lord my God, if I have thought
Or done this, if wickedness
Be in my hands, if I have wrought
Ill to him that meant me peace,   10
Or to him have renderd less,
And not freed my foe for naught;

Let th'enemy pursue my soul
And overtake it, let him tread
My life down to the earth and roul   15
In the dust my glory dead,
In the dust and there outspread
Lodge it with dishonour foul.

Rise Jehovah in thine ire,
Rouse thy self amidst the rage   20
Of my foes that urge like fire;
And wake for me, their furi' assuage;
Judgment here thou didst ingage
And command which I desire.

So th' assemblies of each Nation   25
Will surround thee, seeking right,
Thence to thy glorious habitation
Return on high and in thir sight.
Jehovah judgeth most upright
All people from the worlds foundation.   30

Judge me Lord, be judge in this
According to my righteousness
And the innocence which is
Upon me: cause at length to cease
Of evil men the wickedness   35
And their power that do amiss.

But the just establish fast,
Since thou art the just God that tries
Hearts and reins.   On God is cast
My defence, and in him lies,   40
In him who both just and wise
Saves th' upright of Heart at last.

God is a just Judge and severe,
And God is every day offended;
If th' unjust will not forbear,   45
His Sword he whets, his Bow hath bended
Already, and for him intended
The tools of death, that waits him near.

(His arrows purposely made he
For them that persecute.)   Behold   50
   He travels big with vanitie,
Trouble he hath conceiv'd of old
As in a womb, and from that mould
Hath at length brought forth a Lie.

He diggd a pit, and delv'd it deep,   55
And fell into the pit he made;
His mischief that due course doth keep,
Turns on his head, and his ill trade
Of violence will undelayd
Fall on his crown with ruin steep.   60

Then will I Jehovahs praise
According to his justice raise,
And sing the Name and Deitie
Of Jehovah the most high.

PSAL. VIII.   Aug. 14. 1653

O Jehovah our Lord how wondrous great
   And glorious is thy name through all the earth!
So as above the Heav'ns thy praise to set
   Out of the tender mouths of latest bearth,

Out of the mouths of babes and sucklings thou   5
  Hast founded strength because of all thy foes,
To stint th'enemy, and slack th'avengers brow
  That bends his rage thy providence to oppose.

When I behold thy Heavens, thy Fingers art,
  The Moon and Starrs which thou so bright hast set 10
In the pure firmament, then saith my heart,
  O what is man that thou remembrest yet,

And thinkst upon him? or of man begot
  That him thou visitst and of him art found?
Scarce to be less than Gods, thou mad'st his lot,   15
  With honour and with state thou hast him crownd.

Ore the works of thy hand thou mad'st him Lord,
  Thou hast put all under his lordly feet,
All Flocks and Herds, by thy commanding word,
  All beasts that in the field or forrest meet,   20

Fowl of the Heavens, and Fish that through the wet
  Sea-paths in shoals do slide, and know no dearth.
O Jehovah our Lord how wondrous great
  And glorious is thy name through all the earth!

April, 1648.   J. M.

*Nine of the Psalms done into Metre, wherein all but what is in a
different Character, are the very words of the
Text, translated from the Original.*

PSAL. LXXX

1 Thou Shepherd that dost Israel *keep*
    Give ear *in time of need,*
  Who leadest like a flock of sheep
    Thy loved Josephs seed,
  That sitst between the Cherubes *bright*   5
    Between thir wings outspred,
  Shine forth, *and from thy cloud give light,*
    And on our foes thy dread.
2 In Ephraims view and Benjamins,
    And in Manasse's sight   10
  Awake * thy strength, come, and *be seen*   * Gnorera
    To save us *by thy might.*

3 Turn us again, *thy grace divine*
    To us O God *voutsafe;*
  Cause thou thy face on us to shine   15
    And then we shall be safe.
4 Lord God of Hosts, how long wilt thou,
    How long wilt thou declare
  Thy * smoking wrauth, *and angry brow*   * *Gnashanta*
    Against thy peoples prayr.   20
5 Thou feedst them with the bread of tears,
    Thir bread with tears they eat,
  And mak'st them * largely drink the tears   * *Shalish*
    Wherwith thir cheeks are wet.
6 A strife thou mak'st us *and a prey*   25
    To every neighbour foe,
  Among themselves they * laugh, they * play, * *Jilgnagu*
    And * flouts at us they throw.
7 Return us, *and thy grace divine*
    O God of Hosts *voutsafe;*   30
  Cause thou thy face on us to shine,
    And then we shall be safe.
8 A Vine from Aegypt thou hast brought
    Thy free love made it thine,
  And drov'st out Nations *proud and haut*   35
    To plant this *lovely* Vine.
9 Thou didst prepare for it a place
    And root it deep and fast
  That it *began to grow apace,*
    And filld the land *at last.*   40
10 With her *green* shade *that* coverd *all,*
    The Hills were *overspread,*
  Her Bows as *high as* Cedars tall
    Advanc'd thir lofty head.
11 Her branches *on the western side*   45
    Down to the Sea she sent,
  And *upward* to that river *wide*
    Her other branches *went.*
12 Why hast thou laid her Hedges low
    And broken down her Fence,   50
  That all may pluck her, as they go,
    With rudest violence?
13 The *tusked* Boar out of the wood
    Up turns it by the roots,
  Wild Beasts there browse, and make thir food   55
    Her Grapes and tender Shoots.
14 Return now, God of Hosts, look down
    From Heav'n, thy Seat divine,
  Behold *us, but without a frown,*
    And visit this *thy* Vine.   60
15 Visit this Vine, which thy right hand

　　　Hath set, and planted *long*,
　　And the young branch, that for thy self
　　　Thou hast made firm and strong.
16 But now it is consum'd with fire,　　　　　　　65
　　And cut *with Axes* down,
　　They perish at thy dreadful ire,
　　　At thy rebuke and frown.
17 Upon the man of thy right hand
　　　Let thy *good* hand be *laid*,　　　　　　　70
　　Upon the Son of Man, whom thou
　　　Strong for thyself hast made.
18 So shall we not go back from thee
　　　To ways of sin and shame,
　　Quicken us thou, then *gladly* wee　　　　　　75
　　　Shall call upon thy Name.
　　Return us, *and thy grace divine*
　　　Lord God of Hosts *voutsafe*;
　　Cause thou thy face on us to shine,
　　　And then we shall be safe.　　　　　　　　　80

PSAL. LXXXI

1 To God our strength sing loud, *and clear*,
　　　Sing loud to God *our King*,
　　To Jacobs God, *that all may hear*
　　　Loud acclamations ring.
2 Prepare a Hymn, prepare a Song　　　　　　　5
　　　The Timbrel hither bring,
　　The *cheerful* Psaltry bring along
　　　And Harp *with* pleasant *string*.
3 Blow, *as is wont*, in the new Moon
　　　With Trumpets *lofty sound*,　　　　　　　10
　　Th' appointed time, the day wheron
　　　Our solemn Feast *comes round*.
4 This was a Statute *giv'n of old*
　　　For Israel *to observe*,
　　A Law of Jacobs God *to hold*　　　　　　　15
　　　From whence they might not swerve.
5 This he a Testimony ordaind
　　　In Joseph, *not to change*,
　　When as he passd through Aegypt land;
　　　The Tongue I heard, was strange.　　　　　20
6 From burden *and from slavish toile*
　　　I set his shoulder free;
　　His hands from pots *and mirie soile*
　　　Deliverd were *by me*.
7 When trouble did thee sore assail,　　　　　　25
　　　On me then didst thou call,

And I to free thee *did not fail,*
   And led thee out of thrall.
I answerd thee in * thunder deep   * *Besether ragnam*
   With clouds encompast round;   30
I tri'd thee at the water *steep*
   Of Meriba *renownd.*

8 Hear O my people, *hearken well,*
   I testifie to thee
   Thou ancient flock of Israel,   35
   If thou wilt list to me,

9 Through out the land of thy abode
   No alien God shall be
   Nor shalt thou to a forren God
   In honour bend thy knee.   40

10 I am the Lord thy God which brought
   Thee out of Aegypt land;
   Ask large anough, and I, *besought,*
   Will grant thy full demand.

11 And yet my people would not *hear,*   45
   Nor hearken to my voice;
   And Israel *whom I lov'd so dear*
   Mislik'd me for his choice.

12 Then did I leave them to thir will
   And to thir wandring mind;   50
   Thir own conceits they followd still
   Thir own devices blind.

13 O that my people would *be wise*
   To serve me *all thir days,*
   And O that Israel would *advise*   55
   To walk my *righteous* ways.

14 Then would I soon bring down thir foes
   That now so proudly rise,
   And turn my hand against *all those*
   That are thir enemies.   60

15 Who hate the Lord should *then be fain*
   To bow to him and bend,
   But *they, His people,* should *remain,*
   Thir time should have no end.

16 And he would feed them *from the shock*   65
   With flour of finest wheat,
   And satisfie them from the rock
   With Honey *for thir Meat.*

PSAL. LXXXII

1 God in the * great * assembly stands   * *Bagnadath-el*
   Of Kings and lordly States,
   Among the gods † on both his hands   † *Bekereb*
   He judges and debates.

2 How long will ye * pervert the right   * *Tishphetu gnavel* 5
    With * judgment false and wrong
    Favouring the wicked *by your might*,
      Who thence grow bold and strong?
3 * Regard the * weak and fatherless   * *Shiphtu-dal*
    * Dispatch the * poor mans cause,   10
    And † raise the man in deep distress
    By † just and equal Laws.   † *Hatzdiku*
4 Defend the poor and desolate,
    And rescue from the hands
    Of wicked men the low estate   15
    Of him *that help demands.*
5 They know not nor will understand,
    In darkness they walk on,
    The Earths foundations all are * mov'd   * *Jimmotu*
    And * out of order gon.   20
6 I said that ye were Gods, yea all
    The Sons of God most high,
7 But ye shall die like men, and fall
    As other Princes *die.*
8 Rise God, * judge thou the earth *in might*,   25
    This *wicked* earth * redress,   * *Shiphta*
    For thou art he who shalt by right
    The Nations all possess.

PSAL. LXXXIII

1 Be not thou silent, *now at length*
    O God hold not thy peace,
    Sit not thou still O God of *strength*;
    We cry, and do not cease.
2 For lo thy *furious* foes *now* * swell   5
    And * storm outrageously,   * *Jehemajun*
    And they that hate thee *proud and fell*
    Exalt thir heads full high.
3 Against thy people they † contrive   † *Jagnarimu*
    † Thir Plots and Counsels deep,   † *Sod* 10
    * Them to ensnare they chiefly strive   * *Jithjagnatsu gnal*
    * Whom thou dost hide and keep.   * *Tsephuneca*
4 Come let us cut them off say they,
    Till they no Nation be,
    That Israels name for ever may   15
    Be lost in memory.
5 For they consult † with all thir might,   † *Lev jachdau*
    And all as one in mind
    Themselves against thee they unite
    And in firm union bind.   20

6 The tents of Edom, and the brood
    Of *scornful* Ishmaël,
Moab, with them of Hagars blood
    That in the Desert dwell,
7 Gebal and Ammon *there conspire,*   25
    And *hateful* Amalec,
The Philistims, and they of Tyre
    Whose bounds the Sea doth check.
8 With them *great* Asshur also bands
    And doth confirm the knot,   30
All these have lent thir. armed hands,
    To aid the Sons of Lot.
9 Do to them as to Midian *bold*
    That wasted all the Coast,
To Sisera, and as *is told*   35
    Thou didst to Jabins *hoast,*
When at the brook of Kishon *old*
    They were repulst and slain,
10 At Endor quite cut off, and rowld
    As dung upon the plain.   40
11 As Zeb and Oreb evil sped
    So let their Princes speed,
As Zeba and Zalmunna *bled*
    So let their Princes *bleed.*
12 *For they amidst thir pride* have said   45
    By right now shall we seize
Gods houses, and *will now invade*
    † Thir stately Palaces.   † *Neoth Elohim bears both*
13 My God, oh make them as a wheel,
    No quiet let them find,   50
Giddy and *restless* let *them reel*
    Like stubble from the wind.
14 As *when* an *aged* wood takes fire
    Which on a sudden strays,
The *greedy* flame runs higher and higher   55
    Till all the mountains blaze,
15 So with thy whirlwind them persue,
    And with thy tempest chase;
16 * And till they * yield thee honour due,   * *They seek thy*
    Lord fill with shame thir face.   *Name.* Heb. 60
17 Asham'd and troubl'd let them be,
    Troubl'd and sham'd for ever,
Ever confounded, and so die
    With shame, *and scape it never.*
18 Then shall they know that thou whose **name**   65
    Jehovah is alone,
Art the most high, *and thou the same*
    Ore all the earth *art one.*

PSAL. LXXXIV

1 How lovely are thy dwellings fair!
   O Lord of Hosts, how dear
The *pleasant* Tabernacles are!
   Where thou dost dwell so near.

2 My Soul doth long and almost die   5
   Thy Courts O Lord to see,
My heart and flesh aloud do crie,
   O living God, for thee.

3 There ev'n the Sparrow *freed from wrong*
   Hath found a house of *rest*,   10
The Swallow there, to lay her young
   Hath built her *brooding* nest,
Ev'n *by* thy Altars Lord of Hoasts
   They find thir safe abode,
And home they fly from round the Coasts   15
   T'ward thee, My King, my God.

4 Happy, who in thy house reside
   Where thee they ever praise,

5 Happy, whose strength in thee doth bide,
   And in thir hearts thy ways.   20

6 They pass through Baca's *thirstie* Vale,
   That dry and barren ground,
As through a fruitful watry Dale
   Where Springs and Showrs abound.

7 They journey on from strength to strength   25
   With joy and gladsom cheer
Till all before *our* God *at lengtl*
   In Sion do appear.

8 Lord God of Hosts hear *now* my prayer
   O Jacobs God give ear,   30

9 Thou God our shield look on the face
   Of thy anointed *dear*.

10 For one day in thy Courts *to be*
   Is better *and more blest*
Than *in the joys of Vanity*   35
   A thousand days *at best*.
I in the temple of my God
   Had rather keep a dore,
Than dwell in Tents *and rich abode*
   With Sin *for evermore*.   40

11 For God the Lord, both Sun and Shield,
   Gives grace and glory *bright*,
No good from them shall be withheld
   Whose ways are just and right.

12 Lord *God* of Hosts *that reignst on high,*   45
    That man is *truly* blest
Who *only* on thee doth relie
    And in thee only rest.

PSAL. LXXXV

1 Thy Land to favour graciously
    Thou hast not Lord been slack,
Thou hast from *hard* Captivity
    Returned Jacob back.
2 Th' iniquity thou didst forgive   5
    That wrought thy people woe,
And all thir Sin, *that did thee grieve*
    Hast hid *where none shall know.*
3 Thine anger all thou hadst remov'd,
    And *calmly* didst return   10
From thy † fierce wrauth which we had prov'd   † Heb.
    Far worse than fire to burn.   *The burning heat of thy wrath*
4 God of our saving health and peace,
    Turn us, and us restore,
Thine indignation cause to cease   15
    Toward us, *and chide no more.*
5 Wilt thou be angry without end,
    For ever angry thus
Wilt thou thy frowning ire extend
    From age to age on us?   20
6 Wilt thou not * turn, and *hear our voice*   * Heb. *Turn*
    And us again * revive,   *to quicken us*
That so thy people may rejoice
    By thee preserv'd alive.
7 Cause us to see thy goodness Lord,   25
    To us thy mercy shew,
Thy saving health to us afford
    And life in us renew.
8 *And now* what God the Lord will speak
    I will *go straight and* hear,   30
For to his people he speaks peace
    And to his Saints *full dear,*
To his dear Saints he will speak peace,
    But let them never more
Return to folly, *but surcease*   35
    To trespass as before.
9 Surely to such as do him fear
    Salvation is at hand
And glory shall *ere long appear*   40
    To dwell within our Land.

10 Mercy and Truth *that long were misst*
    Now *joyfully* are met,
  Sweet Peace and Righteousness have kist
    And hand in hand are set.

11 Truth from the earth *like to a flowr*   45
    Shall bud and blossom *then,*
  And Justice from her heav'nly bowr
    Look down *on mortal men.*

12 The Lord will also then bestow
    Whatever thing is good;   50
  Our Land shall forth in plenty throw
    Her fruits *to be our food.*

13 Before him Righteousness shall go
    His Royal Harbinger;
  Then * will hee come, and not be slow,   * Heb. *He* 55
    His footsteps cannot err.   *will set his*
                                              steps to the
                                              way

PSAL. LXXXVI

1 Thy *gracious* ear, O Lord, encline,
    O hear me *I thee pray,*
  For I am poor, and almost pine
    With need, *and sad decay.*

2 Preserve my soul, for † I have trod   † Heb. *I am* 5
    Thy ways, and love the just,   *good, loving,*
  Save thou thy servant O my God   *a doer of good*
    Who *still* in thee doth trust.   *and holy things*

3 Pity me Lord, for daily thee
    I call; 4 O make rejoice   10
  Thy Servants Soul; for Lord to thee
    I lift my soul *and voice.*

5 For thou art good, thou Lord art prone
    To pardon, thou to all
  Art full of mercy, thou *alone*   15
    To them that on thee call.

6 Unto my supplication Lord
    Give ear, and to the cry
  Of my *incessant* prayers afford
    Thy hearing graciously.   20

7 I in the day of my distress
    Will call on thee *for aid*;
  For thou wilt *grant me free access*
    And answer, *what I prayd.*

8 Like thee among the gods is none   25
    O Lord, nor any works
  Of all that other gods have done
    Like to thy *glorious* works.

9 The Nations all whom thou hast made
  Shall come, *and all shall frame*   30
 To bow them low before thee Lord,
  And glorifie thy name.
10 For great thou art, and wonders great
  By thy strong hand are done,
 Thou *in thy everlasting Seat*   35
  Remainest God alone.
11 Teach me O Lord thy way *most right*,
  I in thy truth will bide,
 To fear thy name my heart unite
  So shall it never slide.   40
12 Thee will I praise O Lord my God
  Thee honour, and adore
 With my whole heart, and blaze abroad
  Thy name for ever more.
13 For great thy mercy is toward me, 45
  And thou hast freed my Soul
 Ev'n from the lowest Hell set free,
  From deepest darkness foul.
14 O God the proud against me rise
  And violent men are met   50
 To seek my life, and in thir eyes
  No fear of thee have set,
15 But thou Lord art the God most mild
  Readiest thy grace to shew,
 Slow to be angry, and *art styl'd*   55
  Most merciful, most true.
16 O turn to me *thy face at length*,
  And me have mercy on,
 Unto thy servant give thy strength,
  And save thy handmaids Son.   60
17 Some sign of good to me afford,
  And let my foes *then* see
 And be asham'd, because thou Lord
  Dost help and comfort me.

PSAL. LXXXVII

1 Among the holy Mountains *high*
  Is his foundation fast,
 There Seated in his Sanctuary,
  His Temple there is plac't.
2 Sions *fair* Gates the Lord loves more 5
  Than all the dwellings *faire*
 Of Jacobs *Land, though there be store,*
  And all within his care.

3 City of God, most glorious things
    Of thee *abroad* are spoke;   10
4 I mention Egypt, *where proud Kings*
    Did our forefathers yoke,
  I mention Babel to my friends,
    Philistia *full of scorn,*
  And Tyre with Ethiops *utmost ends,*   15
    Lo this man there was born:
5 But *twice that praise shall in our ear*
    Be said of Sion *last,*
  This and this man was born in her,
    High God shall fix her fast.   20
6 The Lord shall write it in a Scroul
    That ne're shall be out-worn
  When he the Nations doth enroul,
    That this man there was born.
7 Both they who sing and they who dance   25
    With sacred Songs are there,
  In thee *fresh brooks and soft streams glance*
    And all my fountains *clear.*

PSAL. LXXXVIII

1 Lord God that dost me save and keep,
    All day to thee I cry;
  And all night long before thee *weep*
    Before thee *prostrate lie.*
2 Into thy presence let my prayer   5
    With sighs devout ascend,
  And to my cries, that *ceaseless are,*
    Thine ear with favour bend.
3 For cloyd with woes and trouble store
    Surcharg'd my Soul doth lie,   10
  My life *at deaths uncheerful dore*
    Unto the grave draws nigh.
4 Reckond I am with them that pass
    Down to the *dismal* pit;
  I am a * man, but weak alas   * Heb. *A man*   15
    And for that name unfit.   *without manly*
                             strength
5 From life discharg'd and parted quite
    Among the dead *to sleep,*
  And like the slain *in bloody fight*
    That in the grave lie *deep,*
                                      20
  Whom thou rememberest no more,
    Dost never more regard;
  Them from thy hand deliverd ore
    Deaths hideous house hath barrd.

6 Thou in the lowest pit *profound*   25
    Hast set me *all forlorn*,
Where thickest darkness *hovers round*,
    In horrid deeps *to mourn*.

7 Thy wrauth *from which no shelter saves*
    Full sore doth press on me;   30
  * Thou break'st upon me all thy waves,   * The Heb.
  * And all thy waves break me.   *bears both*

8 Thou dost my friends from me estrange,
    And mak'st me odious,
Mee to them odious, *for they change*,   35
    And I here pent up thus.

9 Through sorrow and affliction great
    Mine eye grows dim and dead;
Lord all the day I thee entreat,
    My hands to thee I spread.   40

10 Wilt thou do wonders on the dead,
    Shall the deceas'd arise
And praise thee *from thir loathsom bed*
    With pale and hollow eyes?

11 Shall they thy loving kindness tell   45
    On whom the grave *hath hold*,
Or they *who* in perdition *dwell*
    Thy faithfulness *unfold?*

12 In darkness can thy mighty *hand*
    Or wondrous acts be known,   50
Thy justice in the *gloomy* land
    Of *dark* oblivion?

13 But I to thee O Lord do cry
    Ere yet my life be spent,
And *up to thee* my prayer *doth hie*   55
    Each morn, and thee prevent.

14 Why wilt thou Lord my soul forsake,
    And hide thy face from me,
15 That am already bruis'd, and † shake   † Heb. *Prae*
    With terror sent from thee;   *Concussione*   60
Bruis'd, and afflicted and *so low*
    As ready to expire,
While I thy terrors undergo
    Astonisht with thine ire.

16 Thy fierce wrauth over me doth flow,   65
    Thy threatnings cut me through;
17 All day they round about me go,
    Like waves they me persue.

18 Lover and friend thou hast remov'd
    And severd from me far.   70
They *fly me now* whom I have lov'd,
    And as in darkness are.

LATIN POEMS

Hæc quæ sequuntur de Authore testimonia, tametsi ipse intelligebat non tam de se quam supra se esse dicta, eo quod præclaro ingenio viri, nec non amici ita fere solent laudare, ut omnia suis potius virtutibus, quam veritati congruentia nimis cupide affingant, noluit tamen horum egregiam in se voluntatem non esse notam; Cum alii præsertim ut id faceret magnopere suaderent. Dum enim nimiæ laudis invidiam totis ab se viribus amolitur, sibique quod plus æquo est non attributum esse mavult, judicium interim hominum cordatorum atque illustrium quin summo sibi honori ducat, negare non potest.

Joannes Baptista Mansus, Marchio
Villensis Neapolitanus ad Joannem
Miltonium Anglum

Ut mens, forma, decor, facies, mos, si pietas sic,
Non Anglus, verùm herclè Angelus ipse fores.

Ad Joannem Miltonem Anglum triplici
poeseos laurea coronandum Græca nimirum,
Latina, atque Hetrusca, Epigramma
Joannis Salsilli Romani

Cede Meles, cedat depressa Mincius urna;
Sebetus Tassum desinat usque loqui;
At Thamesis victor cunctis ferat altior undas,
Nam per te, Milto, par tribus unus erit.

Ad Joannem Miltonum

Græcia Mæonidem, jactet sibi Roma Moronem,
Anglia Miltonum jactat utrique parem.
                                    Selvaggi.

104

Al Signor Gio. Miltoni Nobile Inglese

ODE

Ergimi all' Etra ò Clio
Perche di stelle intreccierò corona
Non più del Biondo Dio
La Fronde eterna in Pindo, e in Elicona,
Diensi a merto maggior, maggiori i fregi,   5
A celeste virtù celesti pregi.

Non può del tempo edace
Rimaner preda eterno alto valore,
Non può l'oblio rapace
Furar dalle memorie eccelso onore,   10
Su l'arco di mia cetra un dardo forte
Virtù m'adatti, e ferirò la Morte.

Del Ocean profondo
Cinta dagli ampi gorghi Anglia risiede
Separata dal mondo,   15
Però che il suo valor l'umano eccede:
Questa feconda sà produrre Eroi,
Ch'hanno a ragion del sovr'uman tra noi.

Alla virtù sbandita
Danno nei petti lor fido ricetto,   20
Quella gli è sol gradita,
Perche in lei san trovar gioia e diletto;
Ridillo tu, Giovanni, e mostra in tanto
Con tua vera virtù, vero il mio Canto.

Lungi dal Patrio lido   25
Spinse Zeusi l'industre ardente brama,
Ch'udio d'Helena il grido
Con aurea tromba rimbombar la fama,
E per poterla effigiare al paro
Dalle più belle Idee trasse il più raro.   30

Così l'Ape Ingegnosa
Trae con industria il suo liquor pregiato
Dal giglio e dalla rosa,
E quanti vaghi fiori ornano il prato;
Formano un dolce suon diverse Corde,   35
Fan varie voci melodia concorde.

30 più raro] priù *Edd. 1, 2*

Di bella gloria amante
Milton dal Ciel natío per varie parti
Le peregrine piante
Volgesti a ricercar scienze ed arti;   40
Del Gallo regnator vedesti i Regni,
E dell'Italia ancor gl'Eroi più degni.

Fabro quasi divino,
Sol virtù rintracciando, il tuo pensiero
Vide in ogni confino   45
Chi di nobil valor calca il sentiero;
L'ottimo dal miglior dopo scegliea
Per fabbricar d'ogni virtù l'Idea.

Quanti nacquero in Flora
O in lei del parlar Tosco appreser l'arte,   50
La cui memoria onora
Il mondo fatta eterna in dotte carte,
Volesti ricercar per tuo tesoro,
E parlasti con lor nell'opre loro.

Nell'altera Babelle   55
Per te il parlar confuse Giove in vano,
Che per varie favelle
Di se stessa trofeo cadde su'l piano:
Ch'ode oltr'all' Anglia il suo più degno Idioma
Spagna, Francia, Toscana, e Grecia e Roma.   60

I più profondi arcani
Ch'occulta la Natura e in cielo e in terra
Ch'a Ingegni sovrumani
Troppo avara tal'hor gli chiude, e serra,
Chiaramente conosci, e giungi al fine   65
Della moral virtude al gran confine.

Non batta il Tempo l'ale,
Fermisi immoto, e in un ferminsi gl'anni,
Che di virtù immortale
Scorron di troppo ingiuriosi ai danni;   70
Chè s'opre degne di Poema e storia
Furon già, l'hai presenti alla memoria.

Dammi tua dolce Cetra
Se vuoi ch'io dica del tuo dolce canto,
Ch'inalzandoti all' Etra   75
Di farti huomo celeste ottiene il vanto,
Il Tamigi il dirà che gl' è concesso
Per te suo cigno pareggiar Permesso.

66 moral *Edd. 1, 2*] mortal *conj. Purves*
71 e *Ed. 2*] o *Ed. 1*

Io che in riva del Arno
Tento spiegar tuo merto alto e preclaro   80
So che fatico indarno,
E ad ammirar, non a lodarlo imparo;
Freno dunque la lingua, e ascolto il core
Che ti prende a lodar con lo stupore.

Del sig. Antonio Francini gentilhuomo Fiorentino.

JOANNI MILTONI

LONDINIENSI

Juveni Patria, virtutibus eximio,

Viro qui multa peregrinatione, studio cuncta, orbis terrarum loca perspexit, ut novus Ulysses omnia ubique ab omnibus apprehenderet.

Polyglotto, in cujus ore linguæ jam deperditæ sic reviviscunt, ut idiomata omnia sint in ejus laudibus infacunda; Et jure ea percallet ut admirationes et plausus populorum ab propria sapientia excitatos, intelligat.

Illi, cujus animi dotes corporisque, sensus ad admirationem commovent, et per ipsam motum cuique auferunt; cujus opera ad plausus hortantur, sed venustate[1] vocem laudatoribus adimunt.

Cui in Memoria totus Orbis: In Intellectu Sapientia: In voluntate ardor gloriæ: In ore Eloquentia: Harmonicos Cælestium Sphærarum sonitus Astronomia Duce audienti; Characteres mirabilium naturæ per quos Dei magnitudo describitur magistra Philosophia legenti; Antiquitatum latebras, vetustatis excidia, eruditionis ambages, comite assidua autorum Lectione,

Exquirenti, restauranti, percurrenti.
At cur nitor in arduum?

Illi in cujus virtutibus evulgandis ora Famæ non sufficiant, nec hominum stupor in laudandis satis est, Reverentiæ et amoris ergo hoc ejus meritis debitum admirationis tributum offert Carolus Datus Patricius Florentinus,

Tanto homini servus, tantæ virtutis amator.

---

[1] venustate *Ed. 2*] vastitate *Ed. 1*

ELEGIARUM

Liber Primus

Elegia prima ad *Carolum Diodatum*

Tandem, chare, tuæ mihi pervenere tabellæ,
　　Pertulit et voces nuncia charta tuas,
Pertulit occiduâ Devæ Cestrensis ab orâ
　　Vergivium prono quà petit amne salum.
Multùm crede juvat terras aluisse remotas　　　　5
　　Pectus amans nostri, tamque fidele caput,
Quòdque mihi lepidum tellus longinqua sodalem
　　Debet, at unde brevi reddere jussa velit.
Me tenet urbs refluâ quam Thamesis alluit undâ,
　　Meque nec invitum patria dulcis habet.　　　　10
Jam nec arundiferum mihi cura revisere Camum,
　　Nec dudum vetiti me laris angit amor.
Nuda nec arva placent, umbrasque negantia molles,
　　Quàm male Phœbicolis convenit ille locus!
Nec duri libet usque minas perferre magistri　　　15
　　Cæteraque ingenio non subeunda meo.
Si sit hoc exilium patrios adiisse penates,
　　Et vacuum curis otia grata sequi,
Non ego vel profugi nomen sortemve recuso,
　　Lætus et exilii conditione fruor.　　　　20
O utinam vates nunquam graviora tulisset
　　Ille Tomitano flebilis exul agro;
Non tunc Jonio quicquam cessisset Homer
　　Neve foret victo laus tibi prima, Maro.
Tempora nam licet hîc placidis dare libera Musis,　25
　　Et totum rapiunt me mea vita libri.
Excipit hinc fessum sinuosi pompa theatri,
　　Et vocat ad plausus garrula scena suos.
Seu catus auditur senior, seu prodigus hæres,
　　Seu procus, aut positâ casside miles adest,　　30
Sive decennali fœcundus lite patronus
　　Detonat inculto barbara verba foro;
Sæpe vafer gnato succurrit servus amanti,
　　Et nasum rigidi fallit ubique Patris;
Sæpe novos illic virgo mirata calores　　　　35
　　Quid sit amor nescit, dum quoque nescit, amat.
Sive cruentatum furiosa Tragœdia sceptrum
　　Quassat, et effusis crinibus ora rotat,
Et dolet, et specto, juvat et spectasse dolendo,

Interdum et lacrymis dulcis amaror inest: 40
Seu puer infelix indelibata reliquit
   Gaudia, et abrupto flendus amore cadit,
Seu ferus e tenebris iterat Styga criminis ultor
   Conscia funereo pectora torre movens,
Seu mæret Pelopeia domus, seu nobilis Ili,   45
   Aut luit incestos aula Creontis avos.
Sed neque sub tecto semper nec in urbe latemus,
   Irrita nec nobis tempora veris eunt.
Nos quoque lucus habet vicinâ consitus ulmo
   Atque suburbani nobilis umbra loci.   50
Sæpius hic, blandas spirantia sidera flammas,
   Virgineos videas præteriisse choros.
Ah quoties dignæ stupui miracula formæ
   Quæ possit senium vel reparare Jovis;
Ah quoties vidi superantia lumina gemmas,   55
   Atque faces quotquot volvit uterque polus;
Collaque bis vivi Pelopis quæ brachia vincant,
   Quæque fluit puro nectare tincta via,
Et decus eximium frontis, tremulosque capillos,
   Aurea quæ fallax retia tendit Amor;   60
Pellacesque genas, ad quas hyacinthina sordet
   Purpura, et ipse tui floris, Adoni, rubor.
Cedite laudatæ toties Heroides olim,
   Et quæcunque vagum cepit amica Jovem.
Cedite Achæmeniæ turritâ fronte puellæ,   65
   Et quot Susa colunt, Memnoniamque Ninon.
Vos etiam Danaæ fasces submittite Nymphæ,
   Et vos Iliacæ, Romuleæque nurus.
Nec Pompeianas Tarpëia Musa columnas
   Jactet, et Ausoniis plena theatra stolis.   70
Gloria Virginibus debetur prima Britannis,
   Extera sat tibi sit fœmina posse sequi.
Tuque urbs Dardaniis Londinum structa colonis
   Turrigerum latè conspicienda caput,
Tu nimium felix intra tua mœnia claudis   75
   Quicquid formosi pendulus orbis habet.
Non tibi tot cælo scintillant astra sereno
   Endymioneæ turba ministra deæ,
Quot tibi conspicuæ formáque auróque puellæ
   Per medias radiant turba videnda vias.   80
Creditur huc geminis venisse invecta columbis
   Alma pharetrigero milite cincta Venus,
Huic Cnidon, et riguas Simoentis flumine valles,
   Huic Paphon, et roseam posthabitura Cypron.
Ast ego, dum pueri sinit indulgentia cæci,   85
   Mœnia quàm subitò linquere fausta paro;
Et vitare procul malefidæ infamia Circes
   Atria, divini Molyos usus ope.

Stat quoque juncosas Cami remeare paludes,
  Atque iterum raucæ murmur adire Scholæ.   90
Interea fidi parvum cape munus amici,
  Paucaque in alternos verba coacta modos.

Elegia secunda, Anno ætatis 17

In obitum Præconis Academici Cantabrigiensis

Te, qui conspicuus baculo fulgente solebas
  Palladium toties ore ciere gregem,
Ultima præconum præconem te quoque sæva
  Mors rapit, officio nec favet ipsa suo.
Candidiora licet fuerint tibi tempora plumis   5
  Sub quibus accipimus delituisse Jovem,
O dignus tamen Hæmonio juvenescere succo,
  Dignus in Æsonios vivere posse dies,
Dignus quem Stygiis medicâ revocaret ab undis
  Arte Coronides, sæpe rogante dea.   10
Tu si jussus eras acies accire togatas,
  Et celer a Phœbo nuntius ire tuo,
Talis in Iliacâ stabat Cyllenius aula
  Alipes, æthereâ missus ab arca Patris,
Talis et Eurybates ante ora furentis Achillei   15
  Rettulit Atridæ jussa severa ducis.
Magna sepulchrorum regina, satelles Averni
  Sæva nimis Musis, Palladi sæva nimis,
Quin illos rapias qui pondus inutile terræ
  Turba quidem est telis ista petenda tuis.   20
Vestibus hunc igitur pullis, Academia, luge,
  Et madeant lachrymis nigra feretra tuis.
Fundat et ipsa modos querebunda Elegëia tristes,
  Personet et totis nænia mœsta scholis.

Elegia tertia, Anno ætatis 17

In obitum Præsulis Wintoniensis

Mœstus eram, et tacitus nullo comitante sedebam,
  Hærebantque animo tristia plura meo,
Protinus en subiit funestæ cladis Imago
  Fecit in Angliaco quam Libitina solo;
Dum procerum ingressa est splendentes marmore turres 5
  Dira sepulchrali Mors metuenda face,
Pulsavitque auro gravidos et jaspide muros,
  Nec metuit satrapum sternere falce greges.
Tunc memini clarique ducis fratrisque verendi

Intempestivis ossa cremata rogis; 10
Et memini Heroum quos vidit ad æthera raptos,
   Flevit et amissos Belgia tota duces.
At te præcipuè luxi, dignissime præsul,
   Wintoniæque olim gloria magna tuæ;
Delicui fletu, et tristi sic ore querebar: 15
   Mors fera Tartareo diva secunda Jovi,
Nonne satis quod sylva tuas persentiat iras,
   Et quod in herbosos jus tibi detur agros,
Quodque afflata tuo marcescant lilia tabo,
   Et crocus, et pulchræ Cypridi sacra rosa, 20
Nec sinis ut semper fluvio contermina quercus
   Miretur lapsus prætereuntis aquæ?
Et tibi succumbit liquido quæ plurima cœlo
   Evehitur pennis quamlibet augur avis,
Et quæ mille nigris errant animalia sylvis, 25
   Et quod alunt mutum Proteos antra pecus.
Invida, tanta tibi cum sit concessa potestas,
   Quid juvat humanâ tingere cæde manus?
Nobileque in pectus certas acuisse sagittas,
   Semideamque animam sede fugâsse suâ? 30
Talia dum lacrymans alto sub pectore volvo,
   Roscidus occiduis Hesperus exit aquis,
Et Tartessiaco submerserat æquore currum
   Phœbus, ab Eöo littore mensus iter.
Nec mora, membra cavo posui refovenda cubili, 35
   Condiderant oculos noxque soporque meos,
Cum mihi visus eram lato spatiarier agro,
   Heu nequit ingenium visa referre meum.
Illic puniceâ radiabant omnia luce,
   Ut matutino cum juga sole rubent. 40
Ac veluti cum pandit opes Thaumantia proles,
   Vestitu nituit multicolore solum.
Non dea tam variis ornavit floribus hortos
   Alcinoi, Zephyro Chloris amata levi.
Flumina vernantes lambunt argentea campos, 45
   Ditior Hesperio flavet arena Tago.
Serpit odoriferas per opes levis aura Favoni,
   Aura sub innumeris humida nata rosis.
Talis in extremis terræ Gangetidis oris
   Luciferi regis fingitur esse domus. 50
Ipse racemiferis dum densas vitibus umbras
   Et pellucentes miror ubique locos,
Ecce mihi subitò Præsul Wintonius astat,
   Sidereum nitido fulsit in ore jubar;
Vestis ad auratos defluxit candida talos, 55
   Infula divinum cinxerat alba caput.
Dumque senex tali incedit venerandus amictu,
   Intremuit læto florea terra sono;

Agmina gemmatis plaudunt cælestia pennis,
    Pura triumphali personat æthra tubâ.   60
Quisque novum amplexu comitem cantuque salutat,
    Hosque aliquis placido misit ab ore sonos:
Nate veni, et patrii cape gaudia regni,
    Semper ab hinc duro, nate, labore vaca.
Dixit, et aligeræ tetigerunt nablia turmæ,   65
    At mihi cum tenebris aurea pulsa quies.
Flebam turbatos Cephaleiâ pellice somnos,
    Talia contingant somnia sæpe mihi.

Elegia quarta.   Anno ætatis 18

Ad Thomam Junium præceptorem suum apud
mercatores Anglicos Hamburgæ agentes
Pastoris munere fungentem

Curre per immensum subitò, mea littera, pontum,
    I, pete Teutonicos læve per æquor agros,
Segnes rumpe moras, et nil, precor, obstet eunti,
    Et festinantis nil remoretur iter.
Ipse ego Sicanio frænantem carcere ventos   5
    Æolon, et virides sollicitabo Deos,
Cæruleamque suis comitatam Dorida Nymphis,
    Ut tibi dent placidam per sua regna viam.
At tu, si poteris, celeres tibi sume jugales,
    Vecta quibus Colchis fugit ab ore viri,   10
Aut queis Triptolemus Scythicas devenit in oras
    Gratus Eleusinâ missus ab urbe puer.
Atque ubi Germanas flavere videbis arenas
    Ditis ad Hamburgæ mœnia flecte gradum,
Dicitur occiso quæ ducere nomen ab Hamâ,   15
    Cimbrica quem fertur clava dedisse neci.
Vivit ibi antiquâ clarus pietatis honore
    Præsul Christicolas pascere doctus oves;
Ille quidem est animæ plusquam pars altera nostræ,
    Dimidio vitæ vivere cogor ego.   20
Hei mihi quot pelagi, quot montes interjecti
    Me faciunt aliâ parte carere mei!
Charior ille mihi quàm tu, doctissime Graiûm,
    Cliniadi, pronepos qui Telamonis erat,
Quámque Stagirites generoso magnus alumno,   25
    Quem peperit Libyco Chaonis alma Jovi.
Qualis Amyntorides, qualis Philyrëius Heros
    Myrmidonum regi, talis et ille mihi.
Primus ego Aonios illo præeunte recessus

Lustrabam et bifidi sacra vireta jugi,   30
Pieriosque hausi latices, Clioque favente,
   Castalio sparsi læta ter ora mero.
Flammeus at signum ter viderat arietis Æthon
   Induxitque auro lanea terga novo,
Bisque novo terram sparsisti, Chlori, senilem   35
   Gramine, bisque tuas abstulit Auster opes;
Necdum ejus licuit mihi lumina pascere vultu,
   Aut linguæ dulces aure bibisse sonos.
Vade igitur, cursuque Eurum præverte sonorum,
   Quàm sit opus monitis res docet, ipsa vides.   40
Invenies dulci cum conjuge fortè sedentem,
   Mulcentem gremio pignora chara suo,
Forsitan aut veterum prælarga volumina patrum
   Versantem aut veri biblia sacra Dei,
Cælestive animas saturantem rore tenellas,   45
   Grande salutiferæ religionis opus.
Utque solet, multam sit dicere cura salutem,
   Dicere quam decuit, si modo adesset, herum.
Hæc quoque paulum oculos in humum defixa modestos,
   Verba verecundo sis memor ore loqui: 50
Hæc tibi, si teneris vacat inter prælia Musis
   Mittit ab Angliaco littore fida manus.
Accipe sinceram, quamvis sit sera, salutem;
   Fiat et hoc ipso gratior illa tibi.
Sera quidem, sed vera fuit, quam castra recepit   55
   Icaris a lento Penelopeia viro.
Ast ego quid volui manifestum tollere crimen,
   Ipse quod ex omni parte levare nequit?
Arguitur tardus meritò, noxamque fatetur,
   Et pudet officium deseruisse suum.   60
Tu modò da veniam fasso, veniamque roganti,
   Crimina diminui, quæ patuere, solent.
Non ferus in pavidos rictus diducit hiantes,
   Vulnifico pronos nec rapit ungue leo;
Sæpe sarissiferi crudelia pectora Thracis   65
   Supplicis ad mœstas delicuere preces;
Extensæque manus avertunt fulminis ictus,
   Placat et iratos hostia parva Deos.
Jamque diu scripsisse tibi fuit impetus illi,
   Neve moras ultra ducere passus Amor: 70
Nam vaga Fama refert, heu nuntia vera malorum!
   In tibi finitimis bella tumere locis,
Teque tuàmque urbem truculento milite cingi,
   Et jam Saxonicos arma parasse duces.
Te circum latè campos populatur Enyo,   75
   Et sata carne virûm jam cruor arva rigat.
Germanisque suum concessit Thracia Martem,
   Illuc Odrysios Mars pater egit equos.

Perpetuóque comans jam deflorescit oliva,
    Fugit et ærisonam Diva perosa tubam,   80
Fugit io terris, et jam non ultima Virgo
    Creditur ad superas justa volasse domos.
Te tamen intereà belli circumsonat horror,
    Vivis et ignoto solus inópsque solo;
Et, tibi quam patrii non exhibuere penates   85
    Sede peregrinâ quæris egenus opem.
Patria dura parens, et saxis sævior albis
    Spumea quæ pulsat littoris unda tui,
Siccine te decet innocuos exponere fœtus;
    Siccine in externam ferrea cogis humum,   90
Et sinis ut terris quærant alimenta remotis
    Quos tibi prospiciens miserat ipse Deus,
Et qui læta ferunt de cælo nuntia, quique
    Quæ via post cineres ducat ad astra docent?
Digna quidem Stygiis quæ vivas clausa tenebris,   95
    Æternâque animæ digna perire fame!
Haud aliter vates terræ Thesbitidis olim
    Pressit inassueto devia tesqua pede,
Desertasque Arabum salebras, dum regis Achabi
    Effugit atque tuas, Sidoni dira, manus.   100
Talis et, horrisono laceratus membra flagello,
    Paulus ad Æmathiâ pellitur urbe Cilix;
Piscosæque ipsum Gergessæ civis Jesum
    Finibus ingratus jussit abire suis.
At tu sume animos, nec spes cadat anxia curis   105
    Nec tua concutiat decolor ossa metus.
Sis etenim quamvis fulgentibus obsitus armis,
    Intententque tibi millia tela necem,
At nullis vel inerme latus violabitur armis,
    Deque tuo cuspis nulla cruore bibet.   110
Namque eris ipse Dei radiante sub ægide tutus,
    Ille tibi custos, et pugil ille tibi;
Ille Sionææ qui tot sub mœnibus arcis
    Assyrios fudit nocte silente viros;
Inque fugam vertit quos in Samaritidas oras   115
    Misit ab antiquis prisca Damascus agris,
Terruit et densas pavido rege cohortes,
    Aere dum vacuo buccina clara sonat,
Cornea pulvereum dum verberat ungula campum,
    Currus arenosam dum quatit actus humum,   120
Auditurque hinnitus equorum ad bella ruentûm,
    Et strepitus ferri, murmuraque alta virûm.
Et tu (quod superest miseris) sperare memento,
    Et tua magnanimo pectore vince mala.
Nec dubites quandoque frui melioribus annis,   125
    Atque iterum patrios posse videre lares.

Elegia quinta, Anno ætatis 20

In adventum veris

In se perpetuo Tempus revolubile gyro
    Jam revocat Zephyros vere tepente novos.
Induiturque brevem Tellus reparata juventam,
    Jamque soluta gelu dulce virescit humus.
Fallor? an et nobis redeunt in carmina vires,   5
    Ingeniumque mihi munere veris adest?
Munere veris adest, iterumque vigescit ab illo
    (Quis putet?) atque aliquod jam sibi poscit opus.
Castalis ante oculos, bifidumque cacumen oberrat,
    Et mihi Pyrenen somnia nocte ferunt.   10
Concitaque arcano fervent mihi pectora motu,
    Et furor et sonitus me sacer intùs agit.
Delius ipse venit, video Penëide lauro
    Implicitos crines, Delius ipse venit.
Jam mihi mens liquidi raptatur in ardua cœli,   15
    Perque vagas nubes corpore liber eo.
Perque umbras, perque antra feror penetralia vatum,
    Et mihi fana patent interiora Deûm.
Intuiturque animus toto quid agatur Olympo,
    Nec fugiunt oculos Tartara cæca meos.   20
Quid tam grande sonat distento spiritus ore?
    Quid parit hæc rabies, quid sacer iste furor?
Ver mihi, quod dedit ingenium, cantabitur illo;
    Profuerint isto reddita dona modo.
Jam, Philomela, tuos foliis adoperta novellis   25
    Instituis modulos, dum silet omne nemus.
Urbe ego, tu sylvâ simul incipiamus utrique,
    Et simul adventum veris uterque canat.
Veris io rediere vices, celebremus honores
    Veris, et hoc subeat Musa perennis opus.   30
Jam sol Æthiopas fugiens Tithoniaque arva
    Flectit ad Arctoäs aurea lora plagas.
Est breve noctis iter, brevis est mora noctis opacæ
    Horrida cum tenebris exulat illa suis.
Jamque Lycaonius plaustrum cæleste Boötes   35
    Non longâ sequitur fessus ut ante viâ,
Nunc etiam solitas circum Jovis atria toto
    Excubias agitant sidera rara polo:
Nam dolus et cædes et vis cum nocte recessit,
    Neve Giganteum Dii timuere scelus.   40
Forte aliquis scopuli recubans in vertice pastor,
    Roscida cum primo sole rubescit humus,
Hac, ait, hac certè caruisti nocte puellâ,
    Phœbe, tuâ, celeres quæ retineret equos.

Læta suas repetit sylvas, pharetramque resumit   45
  Cynthia, luciferas ut videt alta rotas,
Et tenues ponens radios gaudere videtur
  Officium fieri tam breve fratris ope.
Desere, Phœbus ait, thalamos Aurora seniles,
  Quid juvat effœto procubuisse toro?   50
Te manet Æolides viridi venator in herba,
  Surge, tuos ignes altus Hymettus habet.
Flava verecundo dea crimen in ore fatetur,
  Et matutinos ociùs urget equos.
Exuit invisam Tellus rediviva senectam,   55
  Et cupit amplexus Phœbe subire tuos;
Et cupit, et digna est, quid enim formosius illâ,
  Pandit ut omniferos luxuriosa sinus,
Atque Arabum spirat messes, et ab ore venusto
  Mitia cum Paphiis fundit amoma rosis?   60
Ecce coronatur sacro frons ardua luco,
  Cingit ut Idæam pinea turris Opim;
Et vario madidos intexit flore capillos,
  Floribus et visa est posse placere suis.
Floribus effusos ut erat redimita capillos   65
  Tænario placuit diva Sicana Deo.
Aspice Phœbe tibi faciles hortantur amores,
  Mellitasque movent flamina verna preces.
Cinnameâ Zephyrus leve plaudit odorifer alâ,
  Blanditiasque tibi ferre videntur aves.   70
Nec sine dote tuos temeraria quærit amores
  Terra, nec optatos poscit egena toros;
Alma salutiferum medicos tibi gramen in usus
  Præbet, et hinc titulos adjuvat ipsa tuos.
Quòd si te pretium, si te fulgentia tangunt   75
  Munera (muneribus sæpe coemptus Amor)
Illa tibi ostentat quascunque sub æquore vasto
  Et superinjectis montibus abdit opes.
Ah quoties cum tu clivoso fessus Olympo
  In vespertinas præcipitaris aquas,   80
Cur te, inquit, cursu languentem Phœbe diurno
  Hesperiis recipit cærula mater aquis?
Quid tibi cum Tethy? Quid cum Tartesside lymphâ?
  Dia quid immundo perluis ora salo?
Frigora Phœbe meâ melius captabis in umbrâ,   85
  Huc ades, ardentes imbue rore comas.
Mollior egelidâ veniet tibi somnus in herbâ,
  Huc ades, et gremio lumina pone meo.
Quáque jaces circum mulcebit lene susurrans
  Aura per humentes corpora fusa rosas.   90
Nec me (crede mihi) terrent Semelëia fata,
  Nec Phäetontéo fumidus axis equo;

Cum tu Phœbe tuo sapientius uteris igni,
  Huc ades et gremio lumina pone meo.
Sic Tellus lasciva suos suspirat amores;   95
  Matris in exemplum cætera turba ruunt.
Nunc etenim toto currit vagus orbe Cupido,
  Languentesque fovet solis ab igne faces.
Insonuere novis lethalia cornua nervis,
  Triste micant ferro tela corusca novo.   100
Jamque vel invictam tentat superâsse Dianam,
  Quæque sedet sacro Vesta pudica foco.
Ipsa senescentem reparat Venus annua formam,
  Atque iterum tepido creditur orta mari.
Marmoreas juvenes clamant *Hymenæe* per urbes,   105
  Litus *io Hymen* et cava saxa sonant.
Cultior ille venit tunicâque decentior aptâ,
  Puniceum redolet vestis odora crocum.
Egrediturque frequens ad amœni gaudia veris
  Virgineos auro cincta puella sinus;   110
Votum est cuique suum, votum est tamen omnibus unum,
  Ut sibi quem cupiat det Cytherea virum.
Nunc quoque septenâ modulatur arundine pastor,
  Et sua quæ jungat carmina Phyllis habet.
Navita nocturno placat sua sidera cantu,   115
  Delphinasque leves ad vada summa vocat.
Jupiter ispe alto cum conjuge ludit Olympo,
  Convocat et famulos ad sua festa Deos.
Nunc etiam Satyri, cum sera crepuscula surgunt,
  Pervolitant celeri florea rura choro,   120
Sylvanusque suâ Cyparissi fronde revinctus,
  Semicaperque Deus, semideusque caper.
Quæque sub arboribus Dryades latuere vetustis
  Per juga, per solos expatiantur agros.
Per sata luxuriat fruticetaque Mænalius Pan,   125
  Vix Cybele mater, vix sibi tuta Ceres;
Atque aliquam cupidus prædatur Oreada Faunus,
  Consulit in trepidos dum sibi Nympha pedes,
Jamque latet, latitansque cupit malè tecta videri,
  Et fugit, et fugiens pervelit ispa capi.   130
Dii quoque non dubitant cælo præponere sylvas,
  Et sua quisque sibi numina lucus habet.
Et sua quisque diu sibi numina lucus habeto,
  Nec vos arboreâ dii, precor, ite domo.
Te referant miseris te Jupiter aurea terris   135
  Sæcla, quid ad nimbos aspera tela redis?
Tu saltem lentè rapidos age Phœbe jugales
  Quà potes, et sensim tempora veris eant.
Brumaque productas tardè ferat hispida noctes,
  Ingruat et nostro serior umbra polo.   140

110 Virgineos *Ed. 3*] Virgineas *Edd. 1, 2*

Elegia sexta

Ad Carolum Diodatum ruri commorantem

*Qui cum idibus Decemb. scripsisset, et sua carmina excusari postulasset si
solito minus essent bona, quòd inter lautitias quibus erat ab amicis exceptus,
haud satis felicem operam Musis dare se posse affirmabat, hunc habuit responsum.*

Mitto tibi sanam non pleno ventre salutem,
   Quâ tu distento fortè carere potes.
At tua quid nostram prolectat Musa camœnam,
   Nec sinit optatas posse sequi tenebras?
Carmine scire velis quàm te redamemque colamque?   5
   Crede mihi vix hoc carmine scire queas,
Nam neque noster amor modulis includitur arctis,
   Nec venit ad claudos integer ipse pedes.
Quàm bene solennes epulas, hilaremque Decembrim
   Festaque cælifugam quæ coluere Deum,   10
Deliciasque refers, hiberni gaudia ruris,
   Haustaque per lepidos Gallica musta focos.
Quid quereris refugam vino dapibusque poesin?
   Carmen amat Bacchum, Carmina Bacchus amat.
Nec puduit Phœbum virides gestâsse corymbos,   15
   Atque hederam lauro præposuisse suæ.
Sæpiùs Aoniis clamavit collibus Euœ
   Mista Thyoneo turba novena choro.
Naso Corallæis mala carmina misit ab agris:
   Non illic epulæ, non sata vitis erat.   20
Quid nisi vina, rosasque racemiferumque Lyæum
   Cantavit brevibus Tëia Musa modis?
Pindaricosque inflat numeros Teumesius Euan,
   Et redolet sumptum pagina quæque merum,
Dum gravis everso currus crepat axe supinus,   25
   Et volat Eleo pulvere fuscus eques.
Quadrimoque madens Lyricen Romanus Iaccho
   Dulcè canit Glyceran, flavicomamque Chloen.
Jam quoque lauta tibi generoso mensa paratu
   Mentis alit vires, ingeniumque fovet.   30
Massica fœcundam despumant pocula venam,
   Fundis et ex ipso condita metra cado.
Addimus his artes, fusumque per intima Phœbum
   Corda; favent uni Bacchus, Apollo, Ceres.
Scilicet haud mirum tam dulcia carmina per te   35
   Numine composito tres peperisse Deos.
Nunc quoque Thressa tibi cælato barbitos auro
   Insonat argutâ molliter icta manu;
Auditurque chelys suspensa tapetia circum,
   Virgineos tremulâ quæ regat arte pedes.   40
Illa tuas saltem teneant spectacula Musas,
   Et revocent quantum crapula pellit iners.

Crede mihi dum psallit ebur, comitataque plectrum
   Implet odoratos festa chorea tholos,
Percipies tacitum per pectora serpere Phœbum,   45
   Quale repentinus permeat ossa calor,
Perque puellares oculos digitumque sonantem
   Irruet in totos lapsa Thalia sinus.
Namque Elegia levis multorum cura deorum est,
   Et vocat ad numeros quemlibet illa suos;   50
Liber adest elegis, Eratoque, Ceresque, Venusque,
   Et cum purpureâ matre tenellus Amor.
Talibus inde licent convivia larga poetis,
   Sæpiùs et veteri commaduisse mero.
At qui bella refert, et adultó sub Jove cælum,   55
   Heroasque pios, semideosque duces,
Et nunc sancta canit superûm consulta deorum,
   Nunc latrata fero regna profunda cane,
Ille quidem parcè Samii pro more magistri
   Vivat, et innocuos præbeat herba cibos;   60
Stet prope fagineo pellucida lympha catillo,
   Sobriaque e puro pocula fonte bibat.
Additur huic scelerisque vacans et casta juventus,
   Et rigidi mores, et sine labe manus;
Qualis veste nitens sacrâ et lustralibus undis   65
   Surgis ad infensos agur iture Deos.
Hoc ritu vixisse ferunt post rapta sagacem
   Lumina Tiresian, Ogygiumque Linon,
Et lare devoto profugum Calchanta, senemque
   Orpheon edomitis sola per antra feris;   70
Sic dapis exiguus, sic rivi potor Homerus
   Dulichium vexit per freta longa virum,
Et per monstrificam Perseiæ Phœbados aulam,
   Et vada fœmineis insidiosa sonis,
Perque tuas rex ime domos, ubi sanguine nigro   75
   Dicitur umbrarum detinuisse greges.
Diis etenim sacer est vates, divûmque sacerdos,
   Spirat et occultum pectus et ora Jovem.
At tu si quid agam scitabere (si modò saltem
   Esse putas tanti noscere siquid agam)   80
Paciferum canimus cælesti semine regem,
   Faustaque sacratis sæcula pacta libris,
Vagitumque Dei, et stabulantem paupere tecto
   Qui suprema suo cum patre regna colit;
Stelliparumque polum, modulantesque æthere turmas, 85
   Et subitò elisos ad sua fana Deos.
Dona quidem dedimus Christi natalibus illa,
   Illa sub auroram lux mihi prima tulit.
Te quoque pressa manent patriis meditata cicutis,
   Tu mihi, cui recitem, judicis instar eris.   90

Elegia septima, Anno ætatis
undevigesimo

Nondum blanda tuas leges Amathusia nôram,
    Et Paphio vacuum pectus ab igne fuit.
Sæpe cupidineas, puerilia tela, sagittas,
    Atque tuum sprevi maxime numen, Amor.
Tu puer imbelles, dixi, transfige columbas,   5
    Conveniunt tenero mollia bella duci,
Aut de passeribus tumidos age, parve, triumphos,
    Hæc sunt militiæ digna trophæa tuæ:
In genus humanum quid inania dirigis arma?
    Non valet in fortes ista pharetra viros.   10
Non tulit hoc Cyprius (neque enim Deus ullus ad iras
    Promptior) et duplici jam ferus igne calet.
Ver erat, et summæ radians per culmina villæ
    Attulerat primam lux tibi Maie diem:
At mihi adhuc refugam quærebant lumina noctem   15
    Nec matutinum sustinuere jubar.
Astat Amor lecto, pictis Amor impiger alis:
    Prodidit astantem mota pharetra Deum,
Prodidit et facies, et dulce minantis ocelli,
    Et quicquid puero dignum et Amore fuit.   20
Talis in æterno juvenis Sigeius Olympo
    Miscet amatori pocula plena Jovi;
Aut qui formosas pellexit ad oscula nymphas
    Thiodamantæus Naiade raptus Hylas.
Addideratque iras, sed et has decuisse putares,   25
    Addideratque truces, nec sine felle, minas.
Et miser exemplo sapuisses tutiùs, inquit,
    Nunc mea quid possit dextera testis eris.
Inter et expertos vires numerabere nostras,
    Et faciam vero per tua damna fidem.   30
Ipse ego, si nescis, strato Pythone superbum
    Edomui Phœbum, cessit et ille mihi;
Et quoties meminit Penëidos, ipse fatetur
    Certiùs et graviùs tela nocere mea.
Me nequit adductum curvare peritiùs arcum,   35
    Qui post terga solet vincere Parthus eques.
Cydoniusque mihi cedit venator, et ille
    Inscius uxori qui necis author erat.
Est etiam nobis ingens quoque victus Orion,
    Herculeæque manus, Herculeusque comes.   40
Jupiter ipse licet sua fulmina torqueat in me,
    Hærebunt lateri spicula nostra Jovis.
Cætera quæ dubitas meliùs mea tela docebunt,
    Et tua non leviter corda petenda mihi.
Nec te stulle tuæ poterunt defendere Musæ,   45
    Nec tibi Phœbæus porriget anguis opem.

Dixit, et aurato quatiens mucrone sagittam,
  Evolat in tepidos Cypridos ille sinus.
At mihi risuro tonuit ferus ore minaci,
  Et mihi de puero non metus ullus erat.   50
Et modò quà nostri spatiantur in urbe Quirites
  Et modò villarum proxima rura placent.
Turba frequens, faciéque simillima turba dearum
  Splendida per medias itque reditque vias.
Auctaque luce dies gemino fulgore coruscat,   55
  Fallor? an et radios hinc quoque Phœbus habet?
Hæc ego non fugi spectacula grata severus,
  Impetus et quò me fert juvenilis agor.
Lumina luminibus malè providus obvia misi,
  Neve oculos potui continuisse meos.   60
Unam fortè aliis supereminuisse notabam,
  Principium nostri lux erat illa mali.
Sic Venus optaret mortalibus ipsa videri,
  Sic regina Deûm conspicienda fuit.
Hanc memor objecit nobis malus ille Cupido,   65
  Solus et hos nobis texuit antè dolos.
Nec procul ipse vafer latuit, multæque sagittæ,
  Et facis a tergo grande pependit onus.
Nec mora, nunc ciliis hæsit, nunc virginis ori,
  Insilit hinc labiis, insidet inde genis: 70
Et quascunque agilis partes jaculator oberrat,
  Hei mihi, mille locis pectus inerme ferit.
Protinùs insoliti subierunt corda furores,
  Uror amans intùs, flammaque totus eram.
Interea misero quæ jam mihi sola placebat,   75
  Ablata est oculis non reditura meis.
Ast ego progredior tacitè querebundus, et excors,
  Et dubius volui sæpe referre pedem.
Findor, et hæc remanet, sequitur pars altera votum,
  Raptaque tam subitò gaudia flere juvat.   80
Sic dolet amissum proles Junonia cælum,
  Inter Lemniacos præcipitata focos;
Talis et abreptum solem respexit ad Orcum
  Vectus ab attonitis Amphiaraus equis.
Quid faciam infelix, et luctu victus? amores   85
  Nec licet inceptos ponere, neve sequi.
O utinam spectare semel mihi detur amatos
  Vultus, et coràm tristia verba loqui!
Forsitan et duro non est adamante creata,
  Fortè nec ad nostras surdeat illa preces.   90
Crede mihi nullus sic infeliciter arsit,
  Ponar in exemplo primus et unus ego.
Parce precor teneri cum sis Deus ales amoris,
  Pugnent officio nec tua facta tuo.

50 erat, *Ed. 2*] erat. *Ed. 1*

Jam tuus O certè est mihi formidabilis arcus,   95
  Nate deâ, jaculis nec minus igne potens:
Et tua fumabunt nostris altaria donis,
  Solus et in Superis tu mihi summus eris.
Deme meos tandem, verùm nec deme furores,
  Nescio cur, miser est suaviter omnis amans: 100
Tu modò da facilis, posthæc mea siqua futura est,
  Cuspis amaturos figat ut una duos.

Hæc ego mente olim lævâ studioque supino
  Nequitiæ posui vana trophæa meæ.
Scilicet abreptum sic me malus impulit error,
  Indocilisque ætas prava magistra fuit.
Donec Socraticos umbrosa Academia rivos   5
  Præbuit, admissum dedocuitque jugum.
Protinùs extinctis ex illo tempore flammis,
  Cincta rigent multo pectora nostra gelu.
Unde suis frigus metuit puer ipse Sagittis,
  Et Diomedeam vim timet ipsa Venus.   10

In Proditionem Bombardicam

Cum simul in regem nuper satrapasque Britannos
  Ausus es infandum perfide Fauxe nefas,
Fallor? an et mitis voluisti ex parte videri,
  Et pensare malâ cum pietate scelus?
Scilicet hos alti missurus ad atria cæli,   5
  Sulphureo curru flammivolisque rotis:
Qualiter ille feris caput inviolabile Parcis
  Liquit Iördanios turbine raptus agros.

In eandem

Siccine tentâsti cælo donâsse Iäcobum
  Quæ septemgemino Bellua monte lates?
Ni meliora tuum poterit dare munera numen,
  Parce precor donis insidiosa tuis.
Ille quidem sine te consortia serus adivit   5
  Astra, nec inferni pulveris usus ope.
Sic potiùs fœdos in cælum pelle cucullos,
  Et quot habet brutos Roma profana Deos.
Namque hac aut aliâ nisi quemque adjuveris arte,
  Crede mihi cæli vix bene scandet iter.   10

In eandem

Purgatorem animæ derisit Iäcobus ignem,
   Et sine quo superûm non adeunda domus.
Frenduit hoc trinâ monstrum Latiale coronâ
   Movit et horrificùm cornua dena minax.
Et nec inultus ait, temnes mea sacra, Britanne,   5
Supplicium spretâ relligione dabis;
Et si stelligeras unquam penetraveris arces,
   Non nisi per flammas triste patebit iter.
O quàm funesto cecinisti proxima vero,
   Verbaque ponderibus vix caritura suis!   10
Nam prope Tartareo sublime rotatus ab igni
   Ibat ad ætureas umbra perusta plagas.

In eandem

Quem modò Roma suis devoverat impia diris,
   Et Styge damnarat Tænarioque sinu,
Hunc vice mutatâ jam tollere gestit ad astra,
   Et cupit ad superos evehere usque Deos.

In inventorem Bombardæ

Iapetionidem laudavit cæca vetustas,
   Qui tulit ætheream solis ab axe facem;
At mihi major erit qui lurida creditur arma
   Et trifidum fulmen surripuisse Jovi.

Ad Leonoram Romæ canentem

Angelus unicuique suus (sic credite gentes)
   Obtigit æthereis ales ab ordinibus.
Quid mirum Leonora tibi si gloria major?
   Nam tua præsentem vox sonat ipsa Deum.
Aut Deus, aut vacui certè mens tertia cæli   5
   Per tua secretò guttura serpit agens;
Serpit agens, facilisque docet mortalia corda
   Sensim immortali assuescere posse sono.
Quòd si cuncta quidem Deus est, per cunctaque fusus,
   In te unâ loquitur, cætera mutus habet.   10

Ad eandem

Altera Torquatum cepit Leonora poetam,
　　Cujus ab insano cessit amore furens.
Ah miser ille tuo quanto feliciùs ævo
　　Perditus, et propter te Leonora foret!
Et te Pieriâ sensisset voce canentem　　　　　　　　5
　　Aurea maternæ fila movere lyræ;
Quamvis Dircæo torsisset lumina Pentheo
　　Sævior, aut totus desipuisset iners,
Tu tamen errantes cæcâ vertigine sensus
　　Voce eadem poteras composuisse tuâ;　　　　　　10
Et poteras ægro spirans sub corde quietem
　　Flexanimo cantu restituisse sibi.

Ad eandem

Credula quid liquidam Sirena Neapoli jactas,
　　Claraque Parthenopes fana Achelöiados,
Littoreamque tuâ defunctam Naiada ripâ
　　Corpora Chalcidico sacra dedisse rogo?
Ille quidem vivitque, et amœnâ Tibridis undâ　　　5
　　Mutavit rauci murmura Pausilipi.
Illic Romulidûm studiis ornata secundis,
　　Atque homines cantu detinet atque Deos.

Apologus de Rustico et Hero

Rusticus ex malo sapidissima poma quotannis
　　Legit, et urbano lecta dedit Domino:
Hic incredibili fructûs dulcedine captus
　　Malum ipsam in proprias transtulit areolas.
Hactenùs illa ferax, sed longo debilis ævo,　　　　5
　　Mota solo assueto, protinùs aret iners.
Quod tandem ut patuit Domino, spe lusus inani,
　　Damnavit celeres in sua damna manus;
Atque ait, Heu quantò satius fuit illa Coloni
　　(Parva licet) grato dona tulisse animo!　　　　　10
Possem ego avaritiam frænare, gulamque voracem:
　　Nunc periere mihi et fœtus et ipse parens.

[*Apologus de Rustico et Hero* was added in 1673.]

Elegiarum Finis

SYLVARUM LIBER

Anno ætatis 16. In obitum Procancellarii medici.

Parere Fati discite legibus,
Manusque Parcæ jam date supplices,
    Qui pendulum telluris orbem
      Iäpeti colitis nepotes.
Vos si relicto mors vaga Tænaro   5
Semel vocârit flebilis, heu moræ
    Tentantur incassùm dolique;
      Per tenebras Stygis ire certum est.
Si destinatam pellere dextera
Mortem valeret, non ferus Hercules   10
    Nessi venenatus cruore
      Æmathiâ jacuisset Oetâ;
Nec fraude turpi Palladis invidæ
Vidisset occisum Ilion Hectora, aut
    Quem larva Pelidis peremit   15
      Ense Locro, Jove lacrymante.
Si triste Fatum verba Hecatëia
Fugare possint, Telegoni parens
    Vixisset infamis, potentique
      Ægiali soror usa virgâ.   20
Numenque trinum fallere si queant
Artes medentûm, ignotaque gramina,
    Non gnarus herbarum Machaon
      Eurypyli cecidisset hastâ;
Læsisset et nec te Philyreie   25
Sagitta Echidnæ perlita sanguine;
    Nec tela te fulmenque avitum,
      Cæse puer genitricis alvo.
Tuque O alumno major Apolline,
Gentis togatæ cui regimen datum,   30
    Frondosa quem nunc Cirrha luget,
      Et mediis Helicon in undis,
Jam præfuisses Palladio gregi
Lætus superstes, nec sine gloria,
    Nec puppe lustrasses Charontis   35
      Horribiles barathri recessus.
At fila rupit Persephone tua
Irata, cum te viderit artibus
    Succoque pollenti tot atris
      Faucibus eripuisse Mortis.   40

29 Apolline] Apollinis *Warton conj.*

Colende Præses, membra precor tua
Molli quiescant cespite, et ex tuo
   Crescant rosæ calthæque busto,
     Purpureoque hyacinthus ore.
Sit mite de te judicium Æaci,   45
Subrideatque Ætnæa Proserpina,
   Interque felices perennis
     Elysio spatiere campo.

In quintum Novembris, Anno ætatis 17

Jam pius extremâ veniens Iäcobus ab arcto
Teucrigenas populos, latèque patentia regna
Albionum tenuit, jamque inviolabile fœdus
Sceptra Caledoniis conjunxerat Anglica Scotis:
Pacificusque novo felix divesque sedebat   5
In solio, occultique doli securus et hostis:
Cum ferus ignifluo regnans Acheronte tyrannus,
Eumenidum pater, æthereo vagus exul Olympo,
Fortè per immensum terrarum erraverat orbem,
Dinumerans sceleris socios vernasque fideles,   10
Participes regni post funera mœsta futuros;
Hic tempestates medio ciet aëre diras,
Illic unanimes odium struit inter amicos,
Armat et invictas in mutua viscera gentes,
Regnaque oliviferâ vertit florentia pace;   15
Et quoscunque videt puræ virtutis amantes,
Hos cupit adjicere imperio, fraudumque magister
Tentat inaccessum sceleri corrumpere pectus,
Insidiasque locat tacitas, cassesque latentes
Tendit, ut incautos rapiat, ceu Caspia Tigris   20
Insequitur trepidam deserta per avia prædam
Nocte sub illuni et somno nictantibus astris.
Talibus infestat populos Summanus et urbes
Cinctus cæruleæ fumanti turbine flammæ.
Jamque fluentisonis albentia rupibus arva   25
Apparent, et terra Deo dilecta marino,
Cui nomen dederat quondam Neptunia proles
Amphitryoniaden qui non dubitavit atrocem
Æquore tranato furiali poscere bello,
Ante expugnatæ crudelia sæcula Troiæ.   30
   At simul hanc opibusque et festâ pace beatam
Aspicit, et pingues donis Cerealibus agros,
Quodque magis doluit, venerantem numina veri
Sancta Dei populum, tandem suspiria rupit

46 Ætnæa] Ennæa H. W. Garrod conj.
20 ceu Warton] seu Edd. 1, 2

Tartareos ignes et luridum olentia sulphur;   35
Qualia Trinacriâ trux ab Jove clausus in Ætnâ
Efflat tabifico monstrosus ab ore Tiphœus.
Ignescunt oculi, stridetque adamantinus ordo
Dentis, ut armorum fragor, ictaque cuspide cuspis.
Atque pererrato solum hoc lacrymabile mundo   40
Inveni, dixit, gens hæc mihi sola rebellis,
Contemtrixque jugi, nostrâque potentior arte.
Illa tamen, mea si quicquam tentamina possunt,
Non feret hoc impune diu, non ibit inulta.
Hactenus; et piceis liquido natat aëre pennis;   45
Quà volat, adversi præcursant agmine venti,
Densantur nubes, et crebra tonitrua fulgent.
    Jamque pruinosas velox superaverat Alpes,
Et tenet Ausoniæ fines; à parte sinistrâ
Nimbifer Appenninus erat, priscique Sabini,   50
Dextra veneficiis infamis Hetruria, nec non
Te furtiva Tibris Thetidi videt oscula dantem;
Hinc Mavortigenæ consistit in arce Quirini.
Reddiderant dubiam jam sera crepuscula lucem,
Cum circumgreditur totam Tricoronifer urbem,   55
Panificosque Deos portat, scapulisque virorum
Evehitur, præeunt summisso poplite reges,
Et mendicantûm series longissima fratrum;
Cereaque in manibus gestant funalia cæci,
Cimmeriis nati in tenebris, vitamque trahentes.   60
Templa dein multis subeunt lucentia tædis
(Vesper erat sacer iste Petro) fremitusque canentûm
Sæpe tholos implet vacuos, et inane locorum.
Qualiter exululat Bromius, Bromiique caterva,
Orgia cantantes in Echionio Aracyntho,   65
Dum tremit attonitus vitreis Asopus in undis,
Et procul ipse cavâ responsat rupe Cithæron.
    His igitur tandem solenni more peractis,
Nox senis amplexus Erebi taciturna reliquit,
Præcipitesque impellit equos stimulante flagello,   70
Captum oculis Typhlonta, Melanchætemque ferocem,
Atque Acherontæo prognatam patre Siopen
Torpidam, et hirsutis horrentem Phrica capillis.
Interea regum domitor, Phlegetontius hæres,
Ingreditur thalamos (neque enim secretus adulter   75
Producit steriles molli sine pellice noctes);
At vix compositos somnus claudebat ocellos,
Cum niger umbrarum dominus, rectorque silentûm,
Prædatorque hominum falsâ sub imagine tectus
Astitit; assumptis micuerunt tempora canis,   80
Barba sinus promissa tegit, cineracea longo

44 inulta.] inulta, *Edd. 1, 2*

Syrmate verrit humum vestis, pendetque cucullus
Vertice de raso, et ne quicquam desit ad artes,
Cannabeo lumbos constrinxit fune salaces,
Tarda fenestratis figens vestigia calceis.   85
Talis, uti fama est, vastâ Franciscus eremo
Tetra vagabatur solus per lustra ferarum,
Sylvestrique tulit genti pia verba salutis
Impius, atque lupos domuit, Lybicosque leones.

     Subdolus at tali Serpens velatus amictu   90
Solvit in has fallax ora execrantia voces:
Dormis nate?   Etiamne tuos sopor opprimit artus?
Immemor O fidei, pecorumque oblite tuorum!
Dum cathedram venerande tuam diademaque triplex
Ridet Hyperboreo gens barbara nata sub axe   95
Dumque pharetrati spernunt tua jura Britanni:
Surge, age, surge piger, Latius quem Cæsar adorat,
Cui reserata patet convexi janua cæli,
Turgentes animos et fastus frange procaces,
Sacrilegique sciant tua quid maledictio possit   100
Et quid Apostolicæ possit custodia clavis;
Et memor Hesperiæ disjectam ulciscere classem,
Mersaque Iberorum lato vexilla profundo,
Sanctorumque cruci tot corpora fixa probrosæ,
Thermodoonteâ nuper regnante puellâ.   105
At tu si tenero mavis torpescere lecto
Crescentesque negas hosti contundere vires,
Tyrrhenum implebit numeroso milite Pontum,
Signaque Aventino ponet fulgentia colle:
Relliquias veterum franget, flammisque cremabit,   110
Sacraque calcabit pedibus tua colla profanis,
Cujus gaudebant soleis dare basia reges.
Nec tamen hunc bellis et aperto Marte lacesses,
Irritus ille labor, tu callidus utere fraude;
Quælibet hæreticis disponere retia fas est.   115
Jamque ad consilium extremis rex magnus ab oris
Patricios vocat, et procerum de stirpe creatos,
Grandævosque patres trabeâ canisque verendos;
Hos tu membratim poteris conspergere in auras,
Atque dare in cineres, nitrati pulveris igne   120
Ædibus injecto, quà convenere, sub imis.
Protinùs ipse igitur quoscunque habet Anglia fidos
Propositi factique mone; quisquamne tuorum
Audebit summi non jussa facessere Papæ?
Perculsosque metu subito casumque stupentes   125
Invadat vel Gallus atrox vel sævus Iberus.
Sæcula sic illic tandem Mariana redibunt,
Tuque in belligeros iterum dominaberis Anglos.
Et nequid timeas, divos divasque secundas
Accipe, quotque tuis celebrantur numina fastis.   130

Dixit et adscitos ponens malefidus amictus
Fugit ad infandam, regnum illætabile, Lethen.

 Jam rosea Eoas pandens Tithonia portas
Vestit inauratas redeunti lumine terras;
Mœstaque adhuc nigri deplorans funera nati 135
Irrigat ambrosiis montana cacumina guttis;
Cum somnos pepulit stellatæ janitor aulæ
Nocturnos visus et somnia grata revolvens.

 Est locus æternâ septus caligine noctis,
Vasta ruinosi quondam fundamina tecti, 140
Nunc torvi spelunca Phoni Prodotæque bilinguis
Effera quos uno peperit Discordia partu.
Hic inter cæmenta jacent præruptaque saxa
Ossa inhumata virûm et trajecta cadavera ferro;
Hic Dolus intortis semper sedet ater ocellis, 145
Jurgiaque, et stimulis armata Calumnia fauces,
Et Furor, atque viæ moriendi mille videntur,
Et Timor, exanguisque locum circumvolat Horror,
Perpetuoque leves per muta silentia Manes,
Exululat tellus et sanguine conscia stagnat. 150
Ipsi etiam pavidi latitant penetralibus antri
Et Phonos et Prodotes, nulloque sequente per antrum
Antrum horrens, scopulosum, atrum feralibus umbris,
Diffugiunt sontes, et retrò lumina vortunt.
Hos pugiles Romæ per sæcula longa fideles 155
Evocat antistes Babylonius, atque ita fatur:
Finibus occiduis circumfusum incolit æquor
Gens exosa mihi; prudens Natura negavit
Indignam penitùs nostro conjungere mundo:
Illuc, sic jubeo, celeri contendite gressu, 160
Tartareoque leves difflentur pulvere in auras
Et rex et pariter satrapæ, scelerata propago:
Et quotquot fidei caluere cupidine veræ
Consilii socios adhibete operisque ministros.
Finierat, rigidi cupidè paruere gemelli. 165

 Interea longo flectens curvamine cælos
Despicit æthereâ Dominus qui fulgurat arce,
Vanaque perversæ ridet conamina turbæ,
Atque sui causam populi volet ipse tueri.

 Esse ferunt spatium, quà distat ab Aside terrâ 170
Fertilis Europe, et spectat Mareotidas undas;
Hic turris posita est Titanidos ardua Famæ
Ærea, lata, sonans, rutilis vicinior astris
Quàm superimpositum vel Athos vel Pelion Ossæ.
Mille fores aditusque patent, totidemque fenestræ, 175
Amplaque per tenues translucent atria muros,
Excitat hic varios plebs agglomerata susurros;

143 præruptaque *Ed. 2*] semifractaque *Ed. 1*
149, 150 Manes, Exululat *Ed. 2 Errata*] Manes Exululant, *Ed. 1*

Qualiter instrepitant circum mulctralia bombis
Agmina muscarum, aut texto per ovilia junco,
Dum Canis æstivum cæli petit ardua culmen.   180
Ipsa quidem summâ sedet ultrix matris in arce,
Auribus innumeris cinctum caput eminet olli,
Queis sonitum exiguum trahit, atque levissima captat
Murmura, ab extremis patuli confinibus orbis.
Nec tot Aristoride servator inique juvencæ   185
Isidos, immiti volvebas lumina vultu,
Lumina non unquam tacito nutantia somno,
Lumina subjectas latè spectantia terras.
Istis illa solet loca luce carentia sæpe
Perlustrare, etiam radianti impervia soli;   190
Millenisque loquax auditaque visaque linguis
Cuilibet effundit temeraria, veraque mendax
Nunc minuit, modò confictis sermonibus auget.
Sed tamen a nostro meruisti carmine laudes
Fama, bonum quo non aliud veracius ullum,   195
Nobis digna cani, nec te memorâsse pigebit
Carmine tam longo; servati scilicet Angli
Officiis vaga diva tuis, tibi reddimus æqua.
Te Deus æternos motu qui temperat ignes,
Fulmine præmisso alloquitur, terrâque tremente: 200
Fama siles? an te latet impia Papistarum
Conjurata cohors in meque meosque Britannos,
Et nova sceptrigero cædes meditata Iäcobo?
Nec plura, illa statim sensit mandata Tonantis,
Et satis antè fugax stridentes induit alas,   205
Induit et variis exilia corpora plumis;
Dextra tubam gestat Temesæo ex ære sonoram.
Nec mora, jam pennis cedentes remigat auras,
Atque parum est cursu celeres prævertere nubes,
Jam ventos, jam solis equos post terga reliquit: 210
Et primò Angliacas solito de more per urbes
Ambiguas voces incertaque murmura spargit,
Mox arguta dolos et detestabile vulgat
Proditionis opus, nec non facta horrida dictu,
Authoresque addit sceleris, nec garrula cæcis   215
Insidiis loca structa silet; stupuere relatis,
Et pariter juvenes, pariter tremuere puellæ,
Effœtique senes pariter, tantæque ruinæ
Sensus ad ætatem subitò penetraverat omnem.
Attamen interea populi miserescit ab alto   220
Æthereus Pater, et crudelibus obstitit ausis
Papicolûm; capti pœnas raptantur ad acres;
At pia thura Deo et grati solvuntur honores;
Compita læta focis genialibus omnia fumant;
Turba choros juvenilis agit: Quintoque Novembris   225
Nulla Dies toto occurrit celebratior anno.

Anno ætatis 17.   In obitum Præsulis Eliensis

Adhuc madentes rore squalebant genæ,
  Et sicca nondum lumina
Adhuc liquentis imbre turgebant salis,
  Quem nuper effudi pius,
Dum mœsta charo justa persolvi rogo   5
  Wintoniensis præsulis.
Cum centilinguis Fama (proh semper mali
  Cladisque vera nuntia)
Spargit per urbes divitis Britanniæ,
  Populosque Neptuno satos,   10
Cessisse Morti et ferreis Sororibus
  Te generis humani decus,
Qui rex sacrorum illâ fuisti in insulâ
  Quæ nomen Anguillæ tenet.
Tunc inquietum pectus irâ protinùs   15
  Ebulliebat fervidâ,
Tumulis potentem sæpe devovens deam:
  Nec vota Naso in Ibida
Concepit alto diriora pectore,
  Graiusque vates parciùs   20
Turpem Lycambis execratus est dolum,
  Sponsamque Neobolen suam.
At ecce diras ipse dum fundo graves,
  Et imprecor neci necem,
Audisse tales videor attonitus sonos   25
  Leni, sub aurâ, flamine:
Cæcos furores pone, pone vitream
  Bilemque et irritas minas:
Quid temerè violas non nocenda numina,
  Subitòque ad iras percita?   30
Non est, ut arbitraris elusus miser,
  Mors atra Noctis filia,
Erebóve patre creta, sive Erinnye,
  Vastóve nata sub Chao:
Ast illa cælo missa stellato, Dei   35
  Messes ubique colligit;
Animasque mole carneâ reconditas
  In lucem et auras evocat:
Ut cum fugaces excitant Horæ diem
  Themidos Jovisque filiæ;   40
Et sempiterni ducit ad vultus patris;
  At justa raptat impios
Sub regna furvi luctuosa Tartari
  Sedesque subterraneas.
Hanc ut vocantem lætus audivi, citò   45
  Fœdum reliqui carcerem,

Volatilesque faustus inter milites
  Ad astra sublimis feror:
Vates ut olim raptus ad cælum senex
  Auriga currus ignei;   50
Non me Boötis terruere lucidi
  Sarraca tarda frigore, aut
Formidolosi Scorpionis brachia,
  Non ensis Orion tuus.
Prætervolavi fulgidi solis globum,   55
  Longèque sub pedibus deam
Vidi triformem, dum coercebat suos
  Frænis dracones aureis.
Erraticorum siderum per ordines,
  Per lacteas vehor plagas,   60
Velocitatem sæpe miratus novam,
  Donec nitentes ad fores
Ventum est Olympi, et regiam Crystallinam, et
  Stratum smaragdis Atrium.
Sed hic tacebo, nam quis effari queat   65
  Oriundus humano patre
Amœnitates illius loci? mihi
  Sat est in æternum frui.

Naturam non pati senium

Heu quàm perpetuis erroribus acta fatiscit
Avia mens hominum, tenebrisque immersa profundis
Œdipodioniam volvit sub pectore noctem!
Quæ vesana suis metiri facta deorum
Audet, et incisas leges adamante perenni   5
Assimilare suis, nulloque solubile sæclo
Consilium fati peritûris alligat horis.
  Ergone marcescet sulcantibus obsita rugis
Naturæ facies, et rerum publica mater
Omniparum contracta uterum sterilescet ab ævo? 10
Et se fassa senem malè certis passibus ibit
Sidereum tremebunda caput? num tetra vetustas
Annorumque æterna fames, squalorque situsque
Sidera vexabunt? an et insatiabile Tempus
Esuriet Cælum, rapietque in viscera patrem? 15
Heu, potuitne suas imprudens Jupiter arces
Hoc contra munîsse nefas, et Temporis isto
Exemisse malo, gyrosque dedisse perennes?
Ergo erit ut quandoque sono dilapsa tremendo
Convexi tabulata ruant, atque obvius ictu 20
Stridat uterque polus, superâque ut Olympius aulâ
Decidat, horribilisque retectâ Gorgone Pallas.

Qualis in Ægæam proles Junonia Lemnon
Deturbata sacro cecidit de limine cæli.
Tu quoque Phœbe tui casus imitabere nati   25
Præcipiti curru, subitâque ferere ruinâ
Pronus, et extinctâ fumabit lampade Nereus,
Et dabit attonito feralia sibila ponto.
Tunc etiam aërei divulsis sedibus Hæmi
Dissultabit apex, imoque allisa barathro   30
Terrebunt Stygium dejecta Ceraunia Ditem
In superos quibus usus erat fraternaque bella.
    At Pater omnipotens fundatis fortius astris
Consuluit rerum summæ, certoque peregit
Pondere Fatorum lances, atque ordine summo   35
Singula perpetuum jussit servare tenorem.
Volvitur hinc lapsu mundi rota prima diurno;
Raptat et ambitos sociâ vertigine cælos.
Tardior haud solito Saturnus, et acer ut olim
Fulmineùm rutilat cristatâ casside Mavors.   40
Floridus æternùm Phœbus juvenile coruscat,
Nec fovet effœtas loca per declivia terras
Devexo temone Deus; sed semper amicâ
Luce potens eadem currit per signa rotarum.
Surgit odoratis pariter formosus ab Indis   45
Æthereum pecus albenti qui cogit Olympo
Manè vocans et serus agens in pascua cæli,
Temporis et gemino dispertit regna colore.
Fulget, obitque vices alterno Delia cornu,
Cæruleumque ignem paribus complectitur ulnis.   50
Nec variant elementa fidem, solitoque fragore
Lurida perculsas jaculantur fulmina rupes.
Nec per inane furit leviori murmure Corus,
Stringit et armiferos æquali horrore Gelonos
Trux Aquilo, spiratque hiemem, nimbosque volutat. 55
Utque solet, Siculi diverberat ima Pelori
Rex maris, et raucâ circumstrepit æquora conchâ
Oceani Tubicen, nec vastâ mole minorem
Ægæona ferunt dorso Balearica cete.
Sed neque Terra tibi sæcli vigor ille vetusti   60
Priscus abest, servatque suum Narcissus odorem,
Et puer ille suum tenet et puer ille decorem
Phœbe tuusque et Cypri tuus, nec ditior olim
Terra datum sceleri celavit montibus aurum
Conscia, vel sub aquis gemmas.   Sic denique in ævum 65
Ibit cunctarum series justissima rerum,
Donec flamma orbem populabitur ultima, latè
Circumplexa polos et vasti culmina cæli;
Ingentique rogo flagrabit machina mundi.

De Idea Platonica quemadmodum
Aristoteles intellexit

Dicite sacrorum præsides nemorum deæ,
Tuque O noveni perbeata numinis
Memoria mater, quæque in immenso procul
Antro recumbis otiosa Æternitas,
Monumenta servans et ratas leges Jovis,   5
Cælique fastos atque ephemeridas Deûm,
Quis ille primus cujus ex imagine
Natura solers finxit humanum genus,
Æternus, incorruptus, æquævus polo,
Unusque et universus, exemplar Dei?   10
Haud ille Palladis gemellus innubæ
Interna proles insidet menti Jovis;
Sed quamlibet natura sit communior,
Tamen seorsus extat ad morem unius,
Et, mira, certo stringitur spatio loci;   15
Seu sempiternus ille siderum comes
Cæli pererrat ordines decemplicis,
Citimumve terris incolit Lunæ globum:
Sive inter animas corpus adituras sedens
Obliviosas torpet ad Lethes aquas: 20
Sive in remotâ fortè terrarum plagâ
Incedit ingens hominis archetypus gigas,
Et diis tremendus erigit celsum caput
Atlante major portitore siderum.
Non cui profundum cæcitas lumen dedit   25
Dircæus augur vidit hunc alto sinu;
Non hunc silenti nocte Plëiones nepos
Vatum sagaci præpes ostendit choro;
Non hunc sacerdos novit Assyrius, licet
Longos vetusti commemoret atavos Nini,   30
Priscumque Belon, inclytumque Osiridem.
Non ille trino gloriosus nomine
Ter magnus Hermes (ut sit arcani sciens)
Talem reliquit Isidis cultoribus.
At tu perenne ruris Academi decus   35
(Hæc monstra si tu primus induxti scholis)
Jam jam poetas urbis exules tuæ
Revocabis, ipse fabulator maximus,
Aut institutor ipse migrabis foras.

Ad Patrem

Nunc mea Pierios cupiam per pectora fontes
Irriguas torquere vias, totumque per ora
Volvere laxatum gemino de vertice rivum;
Ut tenues oblita sonos audacibus alis
Surgat in officium venerandi Musa parentis.   5
Hoc utcunque tibi gratum pater optime carmen
Exiguum meditatur opus, nec novimus ipse
Aptiùs a nobis quæ possint munera donis
Respondere tuis, quamvis nec maxima possint
Respondere tuis, nedum ut par gratia donis   10
Esse queat vacuis quæ redditur arida verbis.
Sed tamen hæc nostros ostendit pagina census,
Et quod habemus opum chartâ numeravimus istâ,
Quæ mihi sunt nullæ, nisi quas dedit aurea Clio
Quas mihi semoto somni peperere sub antro,   15
Et nemoris laureta sacri Parnassides umbræ.
  Nec tu vatis opus divinum despice carmen,
Quo nihil æthereos ortus et semina cæli,
Nil magis humanam commendat origine mentem,
Sancta Prometheæ retinens vestigia flammæ.   20
Carmen amant Superi, tremebundaque Tartara carmen
Ima ciere valet, divosque ligare profundos,
Et triplici duros Manes adamante coercet.
Carmine sepositi retegunt arcana futuri
Phœbades, et tremulæ pallentes ora Sibyllæ;   25
Carmina sacrificus sollennes pangit ad aras
Aurea seu sternit motantem cornua taurum,
Seu cum fata sagax fumantibus abdita fibris
Consulit et tepidis Parcam scrutatur in extis.
Nos etiam patrium tunc cum repetemus Olympum,   30
Æternæque moræ stabunt immobilis ævi,
Ibimus auratis per cæli templa coronis,
Dulcia suaviloquo sociantes carmina plectro,
Astra quibus geminique poli convexa sonabunt.
Spiritus et rapidos qui circinat igneus orbes,   35
Nunc quoque sidereis intercinit ipse choreis
Immortale melos et inenarrabile carmen;
Torrida dum rutilus compescit sibila Serpens,
Demissoque ferox gladio mansuescit Orion;
Stellarum nec sentit onus Maurusius Atlas.   40
Carmina regales epulas ornare solebant,
Cum nondum luxus, vastæque immensa vorago
Nota gulæ, et modico spumabat cœna Lyæo.
Tum de more sedens festa ad convivia vates
Æsculeâ intonsos redimitus ab arbore crines,   45
Heroumque actus imitandaque gesta canebat,

Et Chaos, et positi latè fundamina Mundi,
Reptantesque Deos, et alentes numina glandes,
Et nondum Ætneo quæsitum fulmen ab antro.
Denique quid vocis modulamen inane juvabit,   50
Verborum sensusque vacans, numerique loquacis?
Silvestres decet iste choros, non Orphea cantus,
Qui tenuit fluvios et quercubus addidit aures
Carmine, non citharâ, simulacraque functa canendo
Compulit in lacrymas; habet has a carmine laudes.   55
    Nec tu perge precor sacras contemnere Musas,
Nec vanas inopesque puta, quarum ipse peritus
Munere mille sonos numeros componis ad aptos,
Millibus et vocem modulis variare canoram
Doctus, Arionii meritò sis nominis hæres.   60
Nunc tibi quid mirum, si me genuisse poëtam
Contigerit, charo si tam propè sanguine juncti
Cognatas artes studiumque affine sequamur?
Ipse volens Phœbus se dispertire duobus,
Altera dona mihi, dedit altera dona parenti,   65
Dividuumque Deum genitorque puerque tenemus.
    Tu tamen ut simules teneras odisse Camœnas,
Non odisse reor, neque enim, pater, ire jubebas
Quà via lata patet, quà pronior area lucri,
Certaque condendi fulget spes aurea nummi: 70
Nec rapis ad leges, malè custoditaque gentis
Jura, nec insulsis damnas clamoribus aures.
Sed magis excultam cupiens ditescere mentem,
Me procul urbano strepitu, secessibus altis
Abductum, Aoniæ jucunda per otia ripæ   75
Phœbæo lateri comitem sinis ire beatum.
Officium chari taceo commune parentis,
Me poscunt majora; tuo pater optime sumptu
Cum mihi Romuleæ patuit facundia linguæ
Et Latii veneres, et quæ Jovis ora decebant   80
Grandia magniloquis elata vocabula Graiis,
Addere suasisti quos jactat Gallia flores,
Et quam degeneri novus Italus ore loquelam
Fundit, barbaricos testatus voce tumultus,
Quæque Palæstinus loquitur mysteria vates.   85
Denique quicquid habet cælum, subjectaque cælo,
Terra parens, terræque et cælo interfluus aër,
Quicquid et unda tegit, pontique agitabile marmor,
Per te nôsse licet, per te, si nôsse libebit.
Dimotâque venit spectanda scientia nube,   90
Nudaque conspicuos inclinat ad oscula vultus,
Ni fugisse velim, ni sit libâsse molestum.
    I nunc, confer opes quisquis malesanus avitas
Austriaci gazas Perüanaque regna præoptas.
Quæ potuit majora pater tribuisse, vel ipse   95

Jupiter, excepto, donâsset ut omnia, cælo?
Non potiora dedit, quamvis et tuta fuissent,
Publica qui juveni commisit lumina nato,
Atque Hyperionios currus, et fræna diei,
Et circum undantem radiatâ luce tiaram.   100
Ergo ego jam doctæ pars quamlibet ima catervæ
Victrices hederas inter laurosque sedebo,
Jamque nec obscurus populo miscebor inerti,
Vitabuntque oculos vestigia nostra profanos.
Este procul vigiles Curæ, procul este Querelæ,   105
Invidiæque acies transverso tortilis hirquo,
Sæva nec anguiferos extende Calumnia rictus;
In me triste nihil fœdissima turba potestis,
Nec vestri sum juris ego; securaque tutus
Pectora vipereo gradiar sublimis ab ictu.   110
   At tibi, chare pater, postquam non æqua merenti
Posse referre datur, nec dona rependere factis,
Sit memorâsse satis, repetitaque munera grato
Percensere animo, fidæque reponere menti.
   Et vos, O nostri, juvenilia carmina, lusus,   115
Si modò perpetuos sperare audebitis annos,
Et domini superesse rogo, lucemque tueri,
Nec spisso rapient oblivia nigra sub Orco,
Forsitan has laudes, decantatumque parentis
Nomen, ad exemplum, sero servabitis ævo.   120

Psalm 114

Ἰσραὴλ ὅτε παῖδες, ὅτ᾽ ἀγλαὰ φῦλ᾽ Ἰακώβου
Αἰγύπτιον λίπε δῆμον, ἀπεχθέα, βαρβαρόφωνον,
Δὴ τότε μοῦνον ἔην ὅσιον γένος υἷες Ἰούδα·
Εν δὲ θεὸς λαοῖσι μέγα κρείων βασίλευεν.
Εἶδε, καὶ ἐντροπάδην φύγαδ᾽ ἐρρώησε θάλασσα   5
Κύματι εἰλυμένη ῥοθίῳ, ὁ δ᾽ ἄρ᾽ ἐστυφελίχθη
Ἱρὸς Ἰορδάνης ποτὶ ἀργυροειδέα πηγὴν.
Ἐκ δ᾽ ὄρεα σκαρθμοῖσιν ἀπειρέσια κλονέοντο,
Ὡς κριοὶ σφριγόωντες ἐϋτραφερῷ ἐν ἀλωῇ.
Βαιότεραι δ᾽ ἅμα πᾶσαι ἀνασκίρτησαν ἐρίπναι,   10
Οἷα παραὶ σύριγγι φίλῃ ὑπὸ μητέρι ἄρνες.
Τίπτε σύ γ᾽ αἰνὰ θάλασσα πέλωρ φύγαδ᾽ ἐρρώησας;
Κύματι εἰλυμένη ῥοθίῳ; τί δ᾽ ἄρ᾽ ἐστυφελίχθης
Ἱρὸς Ἰορδάνη ποτὶ ἀργυροειδέα πηγὴν;
Τίπτ᾽ ὄρεα σκαρθμοῖσιν ἀπειρέσια κλονέεσθε   15
Ὡς κριοὶ σφριγόωντες ἐϋτραφερῷ ἐν ἀλωῇ;
Βαιοτέραι τί δ᾽ ἄρ᾽ ὕμμες ἀνασκιρτήσατ᾽ ἐρίπναι,
Οἷα παραὶ σύριγγι φίλῃ ὑπὸ μητέρι ἄρνες;
Σείεο γαῖα τρέουσα θεὸν μεγάλ᾽ ἐκκτυπέοντα,
Γαῖα θεὸν τρείουσ᾽ ὕπατον σέβας Ἰσσακίδαο   20
Ὅς τε καὶ ἐκ σπιλάδων ποταμοὺς χέε μορμύροντας,
Κρήνην᾽ ἀέναον πέτρης ἀπὸ δακρυοέσσης.

*Philosophus ad regem quendam qui eum ignotum et insontem inter
reos forte captum inscius damnaverat,* τὴν ἐπὶ θανάτῳ
πορευόμενος, *hæc subito misit.*

'Ω ἄνα εἰ ὀλέσῃς με τὸν ἔννομον, οὐδέ τιν' ἀνδρῶν
Δεινὸν ὅλως δράσαντα, σοφώτατον ἴσθι κάρηνον
'Ρηϊδίως ἀφέλοιο, τὸ δ' ὕστερον αὖθι νοήσεις,
Μαψιδίως δ' ἄρ ἔπειτα τεον πρὸς θυμὸν ὀδύρῃ
Τοιόνδ' ἐκ πόλιος περιώνυμον ἄλκαρ ὀλέσσας.

In Effigiei ejus Sculptorem

'Αμαθεῖ γεγράφθαι χειρὶ τήνδε μὲν εἰκόνα
Φαίης τάχ' ἄν, πρὸς εἶδος αὐτοφυὲς βλέπων·
Τὸν δ' ἐκτυπωτὸν οὐκ ἐπιγνόντες, φίλοι,
Γελᾶτε φαύλου δυσμίμημα ζωγράφου.

Ad Salsillum poetam Romanum ægrotantem

Scazontes

O Musa gressum quæ volens trahis claudum,
Vulcanioque tarda gaudes incessu,
Nec sentis illud in loco minus gratum
Quàm cùm decentes flava Dëiope suras
Alternat aureum ante Junonis lectum,   5
Adesdum et hæc s'is verba pauca Salsillo
Refer, Camœna nostra cui tantum est cordi,
Quamque ille magnis prætulit immeritò divis.
Hæc ergo alumnus ille Londini Milto,
Diebus hisce qui suum linquens nidum   10
Polique tractum (pessimus ubi ventorum,
Insanientis impotensque pulmonis
Pernix anhela sub Jove exercet flabra)
Venit feraces Itali soli ad glebas,
Visum superbâ cognitas urbes famâ   15
Virosque doctæque indolem juventutis,
Tibi optat idem hic fausta multa, Salsille,
Habitumque fesso corpori penitus sanum;
Cui nunc profunda bilis infestat renes,
Præcordiisque fixa damnosum spirat.   20
Nec id pepercit impia quòd tu Romano
Tam cultus ore Lesbium condis melos.
O dulce divûm munus, O salus Hebes
Germana! Tuque Phœbe morborum terror

4 Μαψ ἄντως δ' ἄρ' ἔπειτα χρόνῳ μάλα πολλὸν ὀδύρῃ *Ed. 1*
5 τοιόνδ' *Burney*] τοιόν δ' *Edd. 1, 2*] πόλιος *Ed. 2*] πόλεως *Ed. 1*

Pythone cæso, sive tu magis Pæan   25
Libenter audis, hic tuus sacerdos est.
Querceta Fauni, vosque rore vinoso
Colles benigni, mitis Evandri sedes,
Siquid salubre vallibus frondet vestris,
Levamen ægro ferte certatim vati.   30
Sic ille charis redditus rursùm Musis
Vicina dulci prata mulcebit cantu.
Ipse inter atros emirabitur lucos
Numa, ubi beatum degit otium æternum,
Suam reclivis semper Ægeriam spectans.   35
Tumidusque et ipse Tibris hinc delinitus
Spei favebit annuæ colonorum:
Nec in sepulchris ibit obsessum reges
Nimiùm sinistro laxus irruens loro:
Sed fræna melius temperabit undarum,   40
Adusque curvi salsa regna Portumni.

Mansus

*Joannes Baptista Mansus Marchio Villensis vir ingenii laude, tum literarum
studio, nec non et bellicâ virtute apud Italos clarus in primis est. Ad quem
Torquati Tassi dialogus extat de Amicitiâ scriptus; erat enim Tassi amicissimus;
ab quo etiam inter Campaniæ principes celebratur, in illo poemate cui titulus
Gerusalemme conquistata, lib. 20.*

> Fra cavalier magnanimi, è cortesi
> Risplende il Manso———

*Is authorem Neapoli commorantem summâ benevolentiâ prosecutus est, multa-
que ei detulit humanitatis officia. Ad hunc itaque hospes ille antequam ab eâ
urbe discederet, ut ne ingratum se ostenderet, hoc carmen misit.*

Hæc quoque Manse tuæ meditantur carmina laudi
Pierides, tibi Manse choro notissime Phœbi,
Quandoquidem ille alium haud æquo est dignatus honore,
Post Galli cineres et Mecænatis Hetrusci.
Tu quoque, si nostræ tantùm valet aura Camœnæ,   5
Victrices hederas inter laurosque sedebis.
Te pridem magno felix concordia Tasso
Junxit, et æternis inscripsit nomina chartis,
Mox tibi dulciloquum non inscia Musa Marinum
Tradidit; ille tuum dici se gaudet alumnum   10
Dum canit Assyrios divûm prolixus amores,
Mollis et Ausonias stupefecit carmine nymphas.
Ille itidem moriens tibi soli debita vates
Ossa tibi soli, supremaque vota reliquit:
Nec manes pietas tua chara fefellit amici,   15
Vidimus arridentem operoso ex ære poetam.
Nec satis hoc visum est in utrumque, et nec pia cessant
Officia in tumulo, cupis integros rapere Orco,

Quà potes, atque avidas Parcarum eludere leges:
Amborum genus, et variâ sub sorte peractam   20
Describis vitam, moresque, et dona Minervæ;
Æmulus illius Mycalen qui natus ad altam
Rettulit Æolii vitam facundus Homeri.
Ergo ego te Cliûs et magni nomine Phœbi,
Manse pater, jubeo longum salvere per ævum   25
Missus Hyperboreo juvenis peregrinus ab axe.
Nec tu longinquam bonus aspernabere Musam,
Quæ nuper gelidâ vix enutrita sub Arcto
Imprudens Italas ausa est volitare per urbes.
Nos etiam in nostro modulantes flumine cygnos   30
Credimus obscuras noctis sensisse per umbras,
Quà Thamesis latè puris argenteus urnis
Oceani glaucos perfundit gurgite crines.
Quin et in has quondam pervenit Tityrus oras.
Sed neque nos genus incultum, nec inutile Phœbo   35
Quà plaga septeno mundi sulcata Trione
Brumalem patitur longâ sub nocte Boöten.
Nos etiam colimus Phœbum, nos munera Phœbo
Flaventes spicas, et lutea mala canistris,
Halantemque crocum (perhibet nisi vana vetustas)   40
Misimus, et lectus Druidum de gente choreas.
(Gens Druides antiqua sacris operata deorum
Heroum laudes imitandaque gesta canebant;)
Hinc quoties festo cingunt altaria cantu
Delo in herbosâ Graiæ de more puellæ   45
Carminibus lætis memorant Corineïda Loxo,
Fatidicamque Upin, cum flavicomâ Hecaërge
Nuda Caledonio variatas pectora fuco.
Fortunate senex, ergo quacunque per orbem
Torquati decus et nomen celebrabitur ingens,   50
Claraque perpetui succrescet fama Marini,
Tu quoque in ora frequens venies plausumque virorum,
Et parili carpes iter immortale volatu.
Dicetur tum sponte tuos habitâsse penates
Cynthius, et famulas venisse ad limina Musas: 55
At non sponte domum tamen idem et regis adivit
Rura Pheretiadæ cælo fugitivus Apollo;
Ille licet magnum Alciden susceperat hospes;
Tantùm ubi clamosos placuit vitare bubulcos,
Nobile mansueti cessit Chironis in antrum,   60
Irriguos inter saltus frondosaque tecta
Peneium prope rivum: ibi sæpe sub ilice nigrâ
Ad citharæ strepitum, blandâ prece victus amici,
Exilii duros lenibat voce labores.
Tum neque ripa suo, barathro nec fixa sub imo   65
Saxa stetere loco, nutat Trachinia rupes
Nec sentit solitas, immania pondera, silvas,

Emotæque suis properant de collibus orni,
Mulcenturque novo maculosi carmine lynces.
Diis dilecte senex, te Jupiter æquus oportet   70
Nascentem, et miti lustrarit lumine Phœbus,
Atlantisque nepos; neque enim nisi charus ab ortu
Diis superis poterit magno favisse poetae.
Hinc longæva tibi lento sub flore senectus
Vernat, et Æsonios lucratur vivida fusos,   75
Nondum deciduos servans tibi frontis honores,
Ingeniumque vigens, et adultum mentis acumen.
O mihi si mea sors talem concedat amicum
Phœbæos decorâsse viros qui tam bene nôrit,
Siquando indigenas revocabo in carmina reges,   80
Arturumque etiam sub terris bella moventem;
Aut dicam invictæ sociali fœdere mensæ
Magnanimos Heroas, et (O modò spiritus adsit)
Frangam Saxonicas Britonum sub Marte phalanges.
Tandem ubi non tacitæ permensus tempora vitæ,   85
Annorumque satur cineri sua jura relinquam,
Ille mihi lecto madidis astaret ocellis,
Astanti sat erit si dicam, sim tibi curæ;
Ille meos artus liventi morte solutos
Curaret parvâ componi molliter urnâ.   90
Forsitan et nostros ducat de marmore vultus,
Nectens aut Paphiâ myrti aut Parnasside lauri
Fronde comas, at ego securâ pace quiescam.
Tum quoque, si qua fides, si præmia certa bonorum,
Ipse ego cælicolûm semotus in æthera divûm,   95
Quò labor et mens pura vehunt atque ignea virtus,
Secreti hæc aliquâ mundi de parte videbo
(Quantum fata sinunt) et totâ mente serenùm
Ridens purpureo suffundar lumine vultus
Et simul æthereo plaudam mihi lætus Olympo.   100

Epitaphium
DAMONIS

Argumentum

Thyrsis et Damon ejusdem viciniæ Pastores, eadem studia sequuti a
pueritiâ amici erant, ut qui plurimum. Thyrsis animi causâ profectus peregrè
de obitu Damonis nuncium accepit. Domum postea reversus, et rem ita esse
comperto, se, suamque solitudinem hoc carmine deplorat. Damonis autem
sub personâ hic intelligitur Carolus Deodatus ex urbe Hetruriæ Luca paterno
genere oriundus, cætera Anglus; ingenio, doctrina, clarissimisque cæteris
virtutibus, dum viveret, juvenis egregius.

Himerides nymphæ (nam vos et Daphnin et Hylan,
Et plorata diu meministis fata Bionis)
Dicite Sicelicum Thamesina per oppida carmen:

Quas miser effudit voces, quæ murmura Thyrsis,
Et quibus assiduis exercuit antra querelis, 5
Fluminaque, fontesque vagos, nemorumque recessus,
Dum sibi præreptum queritur Damona, neque altam
Luctibus exemit noctem, loca sola pererrans.
Et jam bis viridi surgebat culmus aristâ,
Et totidem flavas numerabant horrea messes, 10
Ex quo summa dies tulerat Damona sub umbras,
Nec dum aderat Thyrsis; pastorem scilicet illum
Dulcis amor Musæ Thuscâ retinebat in urbe.
Ast ubi mens expleta domum pecorisque relicti
Cura vocat, simul assuetâ seditque sub ulmo, 15
Tum verò amissum tum denique sentit amicum,
Cœpit et immensum sic exonerare dolorem.
 Ite domum impasti, domino jam non vacat, agni.
Hei mihi! quæ terris, quæ dicam numina cælo,
Postquam te immiti rapuerunt funere Damon; 20
Siccine nos linquis, tua sic sine nomine virtus
Ibit, et obscuris numero sociabitur umbris?
At non ille, animas virgâ qui dividit aureâ,
Ista velit, dignumque tui te ducat in agmen,
Ignavumque procul pecus arceat omne silentûm. 25
 Ite domum impasti, domino jam non vacat, agni.
Quicquid erit, certè nisi me lupus antè videbit
Indeplorato non comminuere sepulchro,
Constabitque tuus tibi honos, longùmque vigebit
Inter pastores, illi tibi vota secundo 30
Solvere post Daphnin, post Daphnin dicere laudes
Gaudebunt, dum rura Pales, dum Faunus amabit:
Si quid id est, priscamque fidem coluisse, piúmque,
Palladiasque artes, sociumque habuisse canorum.
 Ite domum impasti, domino jam non vacat, agni. 35
Hæc tibi certa manent, tibi erunt hæc præmia Damon;
At mihi quid tandem fiet modò? quis mihi fidus
Hærebit lateri comes, ut tu sæpe solebas
Frigoribus duris, et per loca fœta pruinis,
Aut rapido sub sole, siti morientibus herbis? 40
Sive opus in magnos fuit eminùs ire leones
Aut avidos terrere lupos præsepibus altis;
Quis fando sopire diem cantuque solebit?
 Ite domum impasti, domino jam non vacat, agni.
Pectora cui credam? quis me lenire docebit 45
Mordaces curas, quis longam fallere noctem
Dulcibus alloquiis, grato cum sibilat igni
Molle pirum et nucibus strepitat focus, at malus Auster
Miscet cuncta foris et desuper intonat ulmo?
 Ite domum impasti, domino jam non vacat, agni. 50
Aut æstate, dies medio dum vertitur axe,
Cum Pan æsculeâ somnum capit abditus umbrâ,

Et repetunt sub aquis sibi nota sedilia nymphæ,
Pastoresque latent, stertit sub sepe colonus,
Quis mihi blanditiasque tuas, quis tum mihi risus,   55
Cecropiosque sales referet, cultosque lepores?
    Ite domum impasti, domino jam non vacat, agni.
At jam solus agros, jam pascua solus oberro,
Sicubi ramosæ densantur vallibus umbræ,
Hic serum expecto, supra caput imber et Eurus   60
Triste sonant, fractæque agitata crepuscula silvæ.
    Ite domum impasti, domino jam non vacat, agni.
Heu quàm culta mihi priùs arva procacibus herbis
Involvuntur, et ipsa situ seges alta fatiscit!
Innuba neglecto marcescit et uva racemo,   65
Nec myrteta juvant; ovium quoque tædet, at illæ
Mœrent, inque suum convertunt ora magistrum.
    Ite domum impasti, domino jam non vacat, agni.
Tityrus ad corylos vocat, Alphesibœus ad ornos,
Ad salices Aegon, ad flumina pulcher Amyntas,   70
Hic gelidi fontes, hic illita gramina musco,
Hic Zephyri, hic placidas interstrepit arbutus undas;
Ista canunt surdo, frutices ego nactus abibam.
    Ite domum impasti, domino jam non vacat, agni.
Mopsus ad hæc, nam me redeuntem fortè notârat   75
(Et callebat avium linguas et sidera Mopsus),
Thyrsi quid hoc? dixit, quæ te coquit improba bilis?
Aut te perdit amor, aut te malè fascinat astrum;
Saturni grave sæpe fuit pastoribus astrum,
Intimaque obliquo figit præcordia plumbo.   80
    Ite domum impasti, domino jam non vacat, agni.
Mirantur nymphæ, et quid te Thyrsi futurum est?
Quid tibi vis? aiunt, non hæc solet esse juventæ
Nubila frons oculique truces vultusque severi,
Illa choros lususque leves et semper amorem   85
Jure petit; bis ille miser qui serus amavit.
    Ite domum impasti, domino jam non vacat, agni.
Venit Hyas, Dryopeque, et filia Baucidis Aegle
Docta modos citharæque sciens sed perdita fastu,
Venit Idumanii Chloris vicina fluenti;   90
Nil me blanditiæ, nil me solantia verba,
Nil me si quid adest movet, aut spes ulla futuri.
    Ite domum impasti, domino jam non vacat, agni.
Hei mihi quam similes ludunt per prata juvenci,
Omnes unanimi secum sibi lege sodales!   95
Nec magis hunc alio quisquam secernit amicum
De grege; sic densi veniunt ad pabula thoes,
Inque vicem hirsuti paribus junguntur onagri;
Lex eadem pelagi, deserto in littore Proteus
Agmina Phocarum numerat; vilisque volucrum   100

        82 quid te] quid de te *conj. H. W. Garrod*

Passer habet semper quicum sit et omnia circum
Farra libens volitet, serò sua tecta revisens,
Quem si fors letho objecit, seu milvus adunco
Fata tulit rostro seu stravit arundine fossor,
Protinùs ille alium socio petit inde volatu.   105
Nos durum genus, et diris exercita fatis
Gens homines aliena animis, et pectore discors,
Vix sibi quisque parem de millibus invenit unum,
Aut si sors dederit tandem non aspera votis,
Illum inopina dies, quâ non speraveris horâ,   110
Surripit, æternum linquens in sæcula damnum.
    Ite domum impasti, domino jam non vacat, agni.
Heu quis me ignotas traxit vagus error in oras
Ire per aëreas rupes Alpemque nivosam!
Ecquid erat tanti Romam vidisse sepultam?   115
Quamvis illa foret qualem dum viseret olim
Tityrus ipse suas et oves et rura reliquit;
Ut te tam dulci possem caruisse sodale,
Possem tot maria alta, tot interponere montes,
Tot sylvas, tot saxa tibi, fluviosque sonantes.   120
Ah certè extremùm licuisset tangere dextram,
Et bene compositos placidè morientis ocellos,
Et dixisse vale, nostri memor ibis ad astra.
    Ite domum impasti, domino jam non vacat, agni.
Quamquam etiam vestri nunquam meminisse pigebit   125
Pastores Thusci, Musis operata juventus,
Hic Charis, atque Lepos; et Thuscus tu quoque Damon,
Antiquâ genus unde petis Lucumonis ab urbe.
O ego quantus eram, gelidi cum stratus ad Arni
Murmura, populeumque nemus, quà mollior herba,   130
Carpere nunc violas, nunc summas carpere myrtos,
Et potui Lycidæ certantem audire Menalcam.
Ipse etiam tentare ausus sum, nec puto multùm
Displicui, nam sunt et apud me munera vestra
Fiscellæ, calathique et cerea vincla cicutæ;   135
Quin et nostra suas docuerunt nomina fagos
Et Datis et Francinus, erant et vocibus ambo
Et studiis noti, Lydorum sanguinis ambo.
    Ite domum impasti, domino jam non vacat, agni.
Hæc mihi tum læto dictabat roscida luna,   140
Dum solus teneros claudebam cratibus hœdos.
Ah quoties dixi, cum te cinis ater habebat,
Nunc canit, aut lepori nunc tendit retia Damon,
Vimina nunc texit varios sibi quod sit in usus;
Et quæ tum facili sperabam mente futura   145
Arripui voto levis, et præsentia finxi:
Heus bone numquid agis? nisi te quid fortè retardat
Imus et argutâ paulùm recubamus in umbrâ,

137 Datis *Edd. 1, 2*] Datus *conj Garrod*

Aut ad aquas Colni, aut ubi jugera Cassibelauni?
Tu mihi percurres medicos, tua gramina, succos,   150
Helleborumque, humilesque crocos, foliumque hyacinthi,
Quasque habet ista palus herbas, artesque medentûm.
Ah pereant herbæ, pereant artesque medentûm,
Gramina postquam ipsi nil profecere magistro.
Ipse etiam, nam nescio quid mihi grande sonabat   155
Fistula, ab undecimâ jam lux est altera nocte,
Et tum fortè novis admôram labra cicutis,
Dissiluere tamen ruptâ compage, nec ultra
Ferre graves potuere sonos; dubito quoque ne sim
Turgidulus, tamen et referam, vos cedite silvæ.   160
    Ite domum impasti, domino jam non vacat, agni.
Ipse ego Dardanias Rutupina per æquora puppes
Dicam, et Pandrasidos regnum vetus Inogeniæ,
Brennumque Arviragumque duces, priscumque Belinum,
Et tandem Armoricos Britonum sub lege colonos;   165
Tum gravidam Arturo fatali fraude Iögernen;
Mendaces vultus, assumptaque Gorlöis arma,
Merlini dolus.   O mihi tum si vita supersit,
Tu procul annosâ pendebis fistula pinu
Multùm oblita mihi, aut patriis mutata camœnis   170
Brittonicum strides; quid enim? omnia non licet uni,
Non sperâsse uni licet omnia; mî satis ampla
Merces, et mihi grande decus (sim ignotus in ævum
Tum licet, externo penitusque inglorius orbi)
Si me flava comas legat Usa, et potor Alauni,   175
Vorticibusque frequens Abra, et nemus omne Treantæ,
Et Thamesis meus ante omnes, et fusca metallis
Tamara, et extremis me discant Orcades undis.
    Ite domum impasti, domino jam non vacat, agni.
Hæc tibi servabam lentâ sub cortice lauri,   180
Hæc et plura simul; tum quæ mihi pocula Mansus,
Mansus Chalcidicæ non ultima gloria ripæ,
Bina dedit, mirum artis opus, mirandus et ipse,
Et circum gemino cælaverat argumento:
In medio Rubri Maris unda et odoriferum ver,   185
Littora longa Arabum et sudantes balsama silvæ,
Has inter Phœnix divina avis, unica terris
Cæruleùm fulgens diversicoloribus alis
Auroram vitreis surgentem respicit undis.
Parte aliâ polus omnipatens et magnus Olympus;   190
Quis putet? hic quoque Amor, pictæque in nube pharetræ,
Arma corusca, faces, et spicula tincta pyropo;
Nec tenues animas pectusque ignobile vulgi
Hinc ferit, at circum flammantia lumina torquens
Semper in erectum spargit sua tela per orbes   195
Impiger, et pronos nunquam collimat ad ictus;
Hinc mentes ardere sacræ formæque deorum.

Tu quoque in his, nec me fallit spes lubrica Damon,
Tu quoque in his certè es, nam quò tua dulcis abiret
Sanctaque simplicitas, nam quò tua candida virtus?   200
Nec te Lethæo fas quæsivisse sub Orco,
Nec tibi conveniunt lacrymæ, nec flebimus ultra,
Ite procul lacrymæ, purum colit æthera Damon,
Æthera purus habet, pluvium pede reppulit arcum;
Heroumque animas inter, divosque perennes,   205
Æthereos haurit latices et gaudia potat
Ore sacro.   Quin tu cæli post jura recepta
Dexter ades, placidusque fave quicunque vocaris,
Seu tu noster eris Damon, sive æquior audis
Diodotus, quo te divino nomine cuncti   210
Cælicolæ nôrint, sylvisque vocabere Damon.
Quòd tibi purpureus pudor et sine labe juventus
Grata fuit, quòd nulla tori libata voluptas,
En etiam tibi virginei servantur honores;
Ipse caput nitidum cinctus rutilante coronâ,   215
Lætaque frondentis gestans umbracula palmæ,
Æternùm perages immortales hymenæos;
Cantus ubi choreisque furit lyra mista beatis,
Festa Sionæo bacchantur et Orgia thyrso.

Jan. 23. 1646

Ad *Joannem Rousium* Oxoniensis Academiæ Bibliothecarium

*De libro Poematum amisso, quem ille sibi denuo mitti postulabat, ut cum aliis
nostris in Bibliothecâ publicâ reponeret, Ode.*

Strophe 1

Gemelle cultu simplici gaudens liber,
Fronde licet geminâ,
Munditiéque nitens non operosâ,
Quam manus attulit
Juvenilis olim,   5
Sedula tamen haud nimii Poetæ;
Dum vagus Ausonias nunc per umbras
Nunc Britannica per vireta lusit
Insons populi, barbitóque devius
Indulsit patrio, mox itidem pectine Daunio   10
Longinquum intonuit melos
Vicinis, et humum vix tetigit pede;

[*Ad Joannem Rousium* was added in 1673]

2 Fronde *Ed. 2, MS. Bodl.*] Fronte *conj. Warton*
6 Sedula . . . nimii *Ed. 2, MS. Bodl.*] Seduli . . . nimis *conj. Garrod*

Antistrophe

Quis te, parve liber, quis te fratribus
Subduxit reliquis dolo?
Cum tu missus ab urbe, 15
Docto jugiter obsecrante amico,
Illustre tendebas iter
Thamesis ad incunabula
Cærulei patris,
Fontes ubi limpidi 20
Aonidum, thyasusque sacer
Orbi notus per immensos
Temporum lapsus redeunte cælo,
Celeberque futurus in ævum;

Strophe 2

Modò quis deus aut editus deo 25
Pristinam gentis miseratus indolem
(Si satis noxas luimus priores
Mollique luxu degener otium)
Tollat nefandos civium tumultus,
Almaque revocet studia sanctus 30
Et relegatas sine sede Musas
Jam penè totis finibus Angligenûm;
Immundasque volucres
Unguibus imminentes
Figat Apollineâ pharetrâ, 35
Phinéamque abigat pestem procul anme Pegaséo?

Antistrophe

Quin tu, libelle, nuntii licet malâ
Fide vel oscitantiâ
Semel erraveris agmine fratrum,
Seu quis te teneat specus, 40
Seu qua te latebra, forsan unde vili
Callo teréris institoris insulsi,
Lætare felix; en iterum tibi
Spes nova fulget posse profundam
Fugere Lethen, vehique Superam 45
In Jovis aulam remige pennâ;

Strophe 3

Nam te Roüsius sui
Optat peculî, numeróque justo
Sibi pollicitum queritur abesse,
Rogatque venias ille cujus inclyta 50

Sunt data virûm monumenta curæ:
Téque adytis etiam sacris
Voluit reponi quibus et ipse præsidet
Æternorum operum custos fidelis,
Quæstorque gazæ nobilioris   55
Quàm cui præfuit Iön
Clarus Erechtheides,
Opulenta dei per templa parentis,
Fulvosque tripodas, donaque Delphica,
Iön Actæâ genitus Creusâ.   60

Antistrophe

Ergo tu visere lucos
Musarum ibis amœnos,
Diamque Phœbi rursus ibis in domum
Oxoniâ quam valle colit
Delo posthabitâ   65
Bifidóque Parnassi jugo:
Ibis honestus,
Postquam egregiam tu quoque sortem
Nactus abis, dextri prece sollicitatus amici.
Illic legéris inter alta nomina   70
Authorum, Graiæ simul et Latinæ
Antiqua gentis lumina et verum decus.

Epodos

Vos tandem haud vacui mei labores,
Quicquid hoc sterile fudit ingenium,
Jam serò placidam sperare jubeo   75
Perfunctam invidiâ requiem, sedesque beatas
Quas bonus Hermes
Et tutela dabit solers Roüsi,
Quò neque lingua procax vulgi penetrabit, atque longè
Turba legentûm prava facesset;   80
At ultimi nepotes
Et cordatior ætas
Judicia rebus æquiora forsitan
Adhibebit integro sinu.
Tum livore sepulto   85
Si quid meremur sana posteritas sciet
Roüsio favente.

Ode tribus constat Strophis totidemque Antistrophis unâ demum epodo
clausis, quas, tametsi omnes nec versuum numero nec certis ubique colis
exactè respondeant, itâ tamen secuimus, commodè legendi potius quam ad
antiquos concinendi modos rationem spectantes. Alioquin hoc genus rectius
fortasse dici monostrophicum debuerat. Metre partim sunt κατὰ σχέσιν,
partim ἀπολελυμένα. Phaleucia quæ sunt, spondæum tertio loco bis ad-
mittunt, quod idem in secundo loco Catullus ad libitum fecit.

PARADISE LOST

Paradiſe loſt.

A
POEM
Written in
TEN BOOKS
By *JOHN MILTON.*

Licenſed and Entred according
to Order.

LONDON
Printed, and are to be ſold by *Peter Parker*
under *Creed* Church neer *Aldgate* ; And by
Robert Boulter at the *Turks Head* in *Biſhopſgate-ſtreet* ;
And *Matthias Walker*, under St. *Dunſtons* Church
in *Fleet-ſtreet*, 1667.

Paradise Lost.

A POEM

IN TWELVE BOOKS.

The Author
JOHN MILTON.

The Second Edition
Revised and Augmented by the
same Author.

LONDON,
Printed by *S. Simmons* next door to the
Golden Lion in *Aldersgate-street,* 1674.

COMMENDATORY POEMS

In
Paradisum Amissam
Summi Poetæ
Johannis Miltoni

Qui legis Amissam Paradisum, grandia magni
  Carmina Miltoni, quid nisi cuncta legis?
Res cunctas, & cunctarum primordia rerum,
  Et fata, & fines continet iste liber.
Intima panduntur magni penetralia mundi,
  Scribitur & toto quicquid in Orbe latet.
Terræque, tractusque maris, cœlumque profundum
  Sulphureumque Erebi flammivomumque specus.
Quæque colunt terras, Pontumque & Tartara cæca,
  Quæque colunt summi lucida regna Poli.
Et quodcunque ullis conclusum est finibus usquam,
  Et sine fine Chaos, & sine fine Deus;
Et sine fine magis, si quid magis est sine fine,
  In Christo erga homines conciliatus amor.
Hæc qui speraret quis crederet esse futurum?
  Et tamen hæc hodie terra Britanna legit.
O quantos in bella Duces! quæ protulit arma!
  Quæ canit, et quanta prælia dira tuba.
Cœlestes acies! atque in certamine Cœlum!
  Et quæ Cœlestes pugna deceret agros!
Quantus in ætheriis tollit se Lucifer armis!
  Atque ipso graditur vix Michaele minor!
Quantis, & quam funestis concurritur iris
  Dum ferus hic stellas protegit, ille rapit!
Dum vulsos Montes ceu Tela reciproca torquent,
  Et non mortali desuper igne pluunt:
Stat dubius cui se parti concedat Olympus,
  Et metuit pugnæ non superesse suæ.
At simul in cœlis Messiæ insignia fulgent,
  Et currus animes, armaque digna Deo,
Horrendumque rotæ strident, & sæva rotarum
  Erumpunt torvis fulgura luminibus,
Et flammæ vibrant, & vera tonitrua rauco
  Admistis flammis insonuere Polo:
Excidit attonitis mens omnis, & impetus omnis
  Et cassis dextris irrita Tela cadunt.

Ad pænas fugiunt, & ceu foret Orcus asylum
  Infernis certant condere se tenebris.
Cedite Romani *scriptores, cedite* Graii
  Et quos fama recens vel celebravit anus.
Hæc quicunque leget tantum cecinisse putabit
  Mæonidem ranus. Virgilium culices.

S. B.,[1] M.D.

ON
PARADISE LOST

When I beheld the Poet blind, yet bold,
In slender Book, his vast Design unfold,
Messiah Crown'd, Gods Reconcil'd Decree,
Rebelling Angels, the Forbidden Tree,
Heav'n, Hell, Earth, Chaos, All; the Argument
Held me a while misdoubting his Intent,
That he would ruine (for I saw him strong)
The sacred Truths to Fable and old Song
(So *Sampson* groap'd the Temples Posts in spight)
The World o'rewhelming to revenge his sight.
  Yet as I read, soon growing less severe,
I lik'd his Project, the success did fear;
Through that wide Field how he his way should find
O're which lame Faith leads Understanding blind;
Lest he perplex'd the things he would explain,
And what was easie he should render vain.
  Or if a Work so infinite he spann'd,
Jealous I was that some less skilful hand
(Such as disquiet always what is well,
And by ill imitating would excell)
Might hence presume the whole Creations day
To change in Scenes, and show it in a Play.
  Pardon me, Mighty Poet, nor despise
My causeless, yet not impious, surmise.
But I am now convinc'd, and none will dare
Within thy Labours to pretend a share.
Thou hast not miss'd one thought that could be fit,
And all that was improper dost omit:
So that no room is here for Writers left,
But to detect their Ignorance or Theft.
  That Majesty which through thy Work doth **Reign**
Draws the Devout, deterring the Profane.
And things divine thou treatst of in such state
As them preserves, and thee, inviolate.

---

[1] *S. B.*] Probably Samuel Barrow

At once delight and horrour on us seise,
Thou singst with so much gravity and ease;
And above humane flight dost soar aloft
With Plume so strong, so equal, and so soft.
The Bird nam'd from that Paradise you sing
So never flaggs, but always keeps on Wing.
  Where couldst thou words of such a compass find?
Whence furnish such a vast expence of mind?
Just Heav'n thee like *Tiresias* to requite
Rewards with Prophesie thy loss of sight.
  Well mightst thou scorn thy Readers to allure
With tinkling Rhime, of thy own sense secure;
While the *Town-Bayes* writes all the while and spells,
And like a Pack-horse tires without his Bells:
Their Fancies like our Bushy-points appear,
The Poets tag them, we for fashion wear.
I too transported by the Mode offend,
And while I meant to Praise thee must Commend.
Thy Verse created like thy Theme sublime,
In Number, Weight, and Measure, needs not Rhime.

                                        A. M.[1]

---

[1] *A. M.*] Andrew Marvell
These two commendatory poems were added in the second edition.

THE PRINTER
TO THE READER

Courteous Reader, there was no Argument at first intended to the Book, but for the satisfaction of many that have desired it, I have procur'd it, and withall a reason of that which stumbled many others, why the Poem Rimes not.

S. Simmons.

THE VERSE

The measure is *English* Heroic Verse without Rime, as that of *Homer* in *Greek*, and *Virgil* in *Latin*; Rime being no necessary Adjunct or true Ornament of Poem or good Verse, in longer Works especially, but the Invention of a barbarous Age, to set off wretched matter and lame Meeter; grac't indeed since by the use of some famous modern Poets, carried away by Custom, but much to thir own vexation, hindrance, and constraint to express many things otherwise, and for the most part worse then else they would have exprest them.   Not without cause therefore some both *Italian* and *Spanish* Poets of prime note have rejected Rime both in longer and shorter Works, as have also long since our best *English* Tragedies, as a thing of it self, to all judicious eares, triveal and of no true musical delight; which consists only in apt Numbers, fit quantity of Syllables, and the sense variously drawn out from one Verse into another, not in the jingling sound of like endings, a fault avoyded by the learned Ancients both in Poetry and all good Oratory.   This neglect then of Rime so little is to be taken for a defect, though it may seem so perhaps to vulgar Readers, that it rather is to be esteem'd an example set, the first in *English*, of ancient liberty recover'd to Heroic Poem from the troublesom and modern bondage of Rimeing.

ERRATA

Lib. 1. vers. 25. for *th'Eternal,* read *Eternal.*
Lib. 1. v. 409. for *Heronaim,* r. *Horonaim.*
Lib. 1. v. 760. for *hundreds* r. *hunderds.*
Lib. 2. v. 414. for *we* r. *wee.*
Lib. 2. v. 881. for *great* r. *grate.*
Lib. 3. v. 760. for *with* r. *in.*
Lib. 5. v. 193. for *breath* r. *breathe.*
Lib. 5. v. 598. for *whoseop* r. *whose top.*
Lib. 5. v. 656. for *more Heaven* r. *more in Heaven.*
Lib. 6. v. 184. for *blessed* r. *blest.*
Lib. 6. v. 215. for *sounder* r. *so under.*
Lib. 10. v. 575. for *lost* r. *last.*

Other literal faults the Reader of himself may Correct.

[The Printer to the Reader, *followed by* The Argument, The Verse, *and* Errata *first appear in copies with the fourth title of the first edition, 1668.* The Printer to the Reader *is omitted from copies with the sixth title-page. In the second edition only* The Verse *remains of this pre-liminary matter,* The Argument *being distributed through the books of the poem, and the* Errata *being corrected in the text, except for ii. 414.*]

PARADISE LOST

BOOK I

THE ARGUMENT

This first Book proposes first in brief the whole Subject, *Mans disobedience,
and the loss thereupon of Paradise wherein he was plac't:* Then touches *the
prime cause of his fall, the Serpent, or rather* Satan *in the Serpent; who revolt-
ing from God, and drawing to his side many Legions of Angels, was by the
command of God driven out of Heaven with all his Crew into the great Deep.*
Which action past over, the Poem hasts into the midst of things, presenting
Satan *with his Angels now fallen into Hell,* describ'd here, *not in the Center*
(for Heaven and Earth may be suppos'd as yet not made, certainly not yet
accurst) *but in a place of utter darknesse, fitliest call'd* Chaos: Here Satan *with
his Angels lying on the burning Lake, thunder-struck and astonisht, after a
certain space recovers, as from confusion, calls up him who next in Order and
Dignity lay by him; they confer of thir miserable fall.* Satan *awakens all his
Legions, who lay till then in the same manner confounded; They rise, thir
Numbers, array of Battel, thir chief Leaders nam'd, according to the Idols
known afterwards in* Canaan *and the Countries adjoining.* To these Satan
directs his Speech, comforts them with hope yet of regaining Heaven, but tells
them lastly of a new World and new kind of Creature to be created, according to
an ancient Prophesie or report in Heaven; for that Angels were long before
this visible Creation, was the opinion of many ancient Fathers. *To find out
the truth of this Prophesie, and what to determin thereon he refers to a full
Councell. What his Associates thence attempt.* Pandemonium *the Palace of*
Satan *rises, suddenly built out of the Deep: The infernal Peers there sit in
Counsell.*

  Of Mans First Disobedience, and the Fruit
 Of that Forbidden Tree, whose mortal taste
 Brought Death into the World, and all our woe,
 With loss of *Eden,* till one greater Man
 Restore us, and regain the blissful Seat,   5
 Sing Heav'nly Muse, that on the secret top
 Of *Oreb,* or of *Sinai,* didst inspire
 That Shepherd, who first taught the chosen Seed,
 In the Beginning how the Heav'ns and Earth
 Rose out of *Chaos:* Or if *Sion* Hill   10
 Delight thee more, and *Siloa's* Brook that flowd
 Fast by the Oracle of God; I thence
 Invoke thy aid to my adventrous Song,
 That with no middle flight intends to soar

Above th' *Aonian* Mount, while it persues   15
Things unattempted yet in Prose or Rime.
And chiefly Thou O Spirit, that dost preferr
Before all Temples th' upright heart and pure,
Instruct me, for Thou knowst; Thou from the first
Wast present, and with mighty wings outspred   20
Dove-like satst brooding on the vast Abyss
And mad'st it pregnant: What in me is dark
Illumin, what is low raise and support;
That to the highth of this great Argument
I may assert Eternal Providence,   25
And justifie the wayes of God to men.
     Say first, for Heav'n hides nothing from thy view
Nor the deep Tract of Hell, say first what cause
Mov'd our Grand Parents in that happy State,
Favour'd of Heav'n so highly, to fall off   30
From thir Creator, and transgress his Will
For one restraint, Lords of the World besides?
Who first seduc'd them to that foul revolt?
Th' infernal Serpent; he it was, whose guile
Stird up with Envy and Revenge, deceiv'd   35
The Mother of Mankind, what time his Pride
Had cast him out from Heav'n, with all his Host
Of Rebel Angels, by whose aid aspiring
To set himself in Glory above his Peers,
He trusted to have equald the most High,   40
If he oppos'd; and with ambitious aim
Against the Throne and Monarchy of God
Rais'd impious War in Heav'n and Battel proud
With vain attempt.   Him the Almighty Power
Hurld headlong flaming from th' Ethereal Skie   45
With hideous ruin and combustion down
To bottomless perdition, there to dwell
In Adamantine Chains and penal Fire,
Who durst defie th' Omnipotent to Arms.
Nine times the Space that measures Day and Night   50
To mortal men, hee with his horrid crew
Lay vanquisht, rouling in the fiery Gulf
Confounded though immortal: But his doom
Reserv'd him to more wrauth; for now the thought
Both of lost happiness and lasting pain   55
Torments him; round he throws his baleful eyes
That witnessd huge affliction and dismay
Mixt with obdurat pride and stedfast hate:
At once as far as Angels kenn he views
The dismal Situation waste and wild;   60
A Dungeon horrible, on all sides round
As one great Furnace flam'd, yet from those flames
No light, but rather darkness visible

Serv'd onely to discover sights of woe,
Regions of sorrow, doleful shades, where peace   65
And rest can never dwell, hope never comes
That comes to all; but torture without end
Still urges, and a fiery Deluge, fed
With ever-burning Sulphur unconsum'd:
Such place Eternal Justice had prepar'd   70
For those rebellious, here thir Pris'n ordaind
In utter darkness, and thir portion set
As far remov'd from God and light of Heav'n
As from the Center thrice to th' utmost Pole.
O how unlike the place from whence they fell!   75
There the companions of his fall, orewhelmd
With Floods and Whirlwinds of tempestuous fire,
He soon discerns, and weltring by his side
One next himself in power, and next in crime,
Long after known in *Palestine*, and nam'd   80
Beëlzebub.   To whom th' Arch-Enemy,
And thence in Heav'n called *Satan*, with bold words
Breaking the horrid silence thus began.

  If thou beest he; But O how fall'n! how chang'd
From him, who in the happy Realms of Light   85
Cloth'd with transcendent brightness didst outshine
Myriads though bright: If he whom mutual league,
United thoughts and counsels, equal hope,
And hazard in the Glorious Enterprize,
Joind with me once, now misery hath joind   90
In equal ruin: into what Pit thou seest
From what highth fall'n, so much the stronger prov'd
Hee with his Thunder: and till then who knew
The force of those dire Arms? yet not for those
Nor what the Potent Victor in his rage   95
Can else inflict do I repent or change,
Though chang'd in outward lustre, that fixt mind
And high disdain, from sense of injurd merit,
That with the mightiest rais'd me to contend,
And to the fierce contention brought along   100
Innumerable force of Spirits armd
That durst dislike his reign, and mee preferring,
His utmost power with adverse power oppos'd
In dubious Battel on the Plains of Heav'n,
And shook his throne.   What though the field be lost?
All is not lost; th'unconquerable Will,   106
And study of revenge, immortal hate,
And courage never to submit or yield:
And what is else not to be overcome?
That Glory never shall his wrauth or might   110

71 those *Edd. 1, 2*] these *MS.*

Extort from me.   To bow and sue for grace
With suppliant knee, and deifie his power
Who from the terror of this Arm so late
Doubted his Empire, that were low indeed,
That were an ignominy and shame beneath   115
This downfall; since by Fate the strength of Gods
And this Empyreal substance cannot fail,
Since through experience of this great event
In Arms not worse, in foresight much advanc't,
We may with more successful hope resolve   120
To wage by force or guile eternal Warr
Irreconcileable, to our grand Foe,
Who now triumphs, and in th' excess of joy
Sole reigning holds the Tyranny of Heav'n.
   So spake th' Apostat Angel, though in pain,   125
Vaunting aloud, but rackt with deep despair:
And him thus answerd soon his bold Compeer.
   O Prince, O Chief of many Throned Powers,
That led th' imbatteld Seraphim to Warr
Under thy conduct, and in dreadful deeds   130
Fearless, endangerd Heav'ns perpetual King;
And put to proof his high Supremacy,
Whether upheld by strength, or Chance, or Fate;
Too well I see and rue the dire event,
That with sad overthrow and foul defeat   135
Hath lost us Heav'n, and all this mighty Host
In horrible destruction laid thus low,
As far as Gods and Heav'nly Essences
Can Perish: for the mind and spirit remains
Invincible, and vigor soon returns,   140
Though all our Glory extinct, and happy state
Here swallowd up in endless misery.
But what if hee our Conqueror (whom I now
Of force believe Almighty, since no less
Than such could have orepow'rd such force as ours) 145
Have left us this our spirit and strength entire
Strongly to suffer and support our pains,
That we may so suffice his vengeful ire
Or do him mightier service as his thralls
By right of Warr, what e're his buisness be   150
Here in the heart of Hell to work in Fire,
Or do his Errands in the gloomy Deep;
What can it then avail though yet we feel
Strength undiminisht, or eternal being
To undergo eternal punishment?   155
Whereto with speedy words th' Arch-fiend repli'd.
   Fall'n Cherube, to be weak is miserable
Doing or Suffering: but of this be sure,
To do aught good never will be our task,

But ever to do ill our sole delight,   160
As being the contrary to his high will
Whom we resist.   If then his Providence
Out of our evil seek to bring forth good,
Our labour must be to pervert that end,
And out of good still to find means of evil;   165
Which oft times may succeed, so as perhaps
Shall grieve him, if I fail not, and disturb
His inmost counsels from thir destind aim.
But see the angry Victor hath recalld
His Ministers of vengeance and persuit   170
Back to the Gates of Heav'n: the Sulphurous Hail
Shot after us in storm, oreblown hath laid
The fiery Surge, that from the Precipice
Of Heav'n receiv'd us falling, and the Thunder,
Wingd with red Lightning and impetuous rage,   175
Perhaps hath spent his shafts, and ceases now
To bellow through the vast and boundless Deep.
Let us not slip th' occasion, whether scorn
Or satiat fury yield it from our Foe.
Seest thou yon dreary Plain, forlorn and wild,   180
The seat of desolation, void of light,
Save what the glimmering of these livid flames
Casts pale and dreadful?   Thither let us tend
From off the tossing of these fiery waves,
There rest, if any rest can harbour there,   185
And reassembling our afflicted Powers
Consult how we may henceforth most offend
Our Enemy, our own loss how repair,
How overcome this dire Calamity,
What reinforcement we may gain from Hope,   190
If not what resolution from despair.
    Thus *Satan* talking to his nearest Mate
With Head up-lift above the wave, and Eyes
That sparkling blaz'd, his other Parts besides
Prone on the Flood extended long and large   195
Lay floating many a rood, in bulk as huge
As whom the Fables name of monstrous size,
Titanian or *Earth-born*, that warrd on *Jove*,
Briarios or *Typhon*, whom the Den
By ancient *Tarsus* held, or that Sea-beast   200
Leviathan, which God of all his works
Created hugest that swim th' Ocean stream:
Him haply slumbring on the *Norway* foam
The Pilot of som small night-founderd Skiff,
Deeming som Iland, oft, as Sea-men tell,   205
With fixed Anchor in his scaly rinde
Moors by his side under the Lee, while Night
Invests the Sea, and wished Morn delays:

So stretcht out huge in length the Arch-fiend lay
Chaind on the burning Lake, nor ever thence   210
Had ris'n or heav'd his head, but that the will
And high permission of all-ruling Heaven
Left him at large to his own dark designs,
That with reiterated crimes he might
Heap on himself damnation, while he sought   215
Evil to others, and enrag'd might see
How all his malice serv'd but to bring forth
Infinit goodness, grace and mercy shewn
On Man by him seduc't, but on himselfe
Treble confusion, wrauth and vengeance pourd.   220
Forthwith upright he rears from off the Pool
His mighty Stature; on each hand the flames
Driv'n backward slope thir pointing spires, and rould
In billows, leave i' th' midst a horrid Vale.
Then with expanded wings he steers his flight   225
Aloft, incumbent on the dusky Air
That felt unusual weight, till on dry Land
He lights, if it were Land that ever burnd
With solid, as the Lake with liquid fire;
And such appear'd in hue, as when the force   230
Of subterranean wind transports a Hill
Torn from *Pelorus*, or the shatterd side
Of thundring *Ætna*, whose combustible
And feweld entrails thence conceiving Fire,
Sublim'd with Mineral fury, aid the Winds,   235
And leave a singed bottom all involv'd
With stench and smoke: Such resting found the sole
Of unblest feet.   Him followd his next Mate,
Both glorying to have scap't the *Stygian* flood
As Gods, and by thir own recoverd strength,   240
Not by the sufferance of supernal Power.
  Is this the Region, this the Soil, the Clime,
Said then the lost Arch-Angel, this the seat
That we must change for Heav'n, this mournful gloom
For that celestial light?   Be it so, since he   245
Who now is Sovran can dispose and bid
What shall be right: fardest from him is best
Whom reason hath equald, force hath made supream
Above his equals.   Farewel happy Fields
Where Joy for ever dwells: Hail horrors, hail   250
Infernal World, and thou profoundest Hell
Receive thy new Possessor: One who brings
A mind not to be chang'd by Place or Time.
The mind is its own place, and in it self
Can make a Heav'n of Hell, a Hell of Heav'n.   255
What matter where, if I be still the same,
And what I should be, all but less than he

Whom Thunder hath made greater?   Here at least
We shall be free; th' Almighty hath not built
Here for his envy, will not drive us hence: 260
Here we may reign secure, and in my choice
To reign is worth ambition though in Hell:
Better to reign in Hell, than serve in Heav'n.
But wherefore let we then our faithful friends,
Th' associates and copartners of our loss   265
Lie thus astonisht on th' oblivious Pool,
And call them not to share with us their part
In this unhappy Mansion, or once more
With rallied Arms to try what may be yet
Regaind in Heav'n, or what more lost in Hell?   270
    So *Satan* spake, and him *Beëlzebub*
Thus answerd.   Leader of those Armies bright,
Which but th' Omnipotent none could have foild,
If once they hear that voice, thir liveliest pledge
Of hope in fears and dangers, heard so oft   275
In worst extreams, and on the perilous edge
Of battel when it rag'd, in all assaults
Thir surest signal, they will soon resume
New courage and revive, though now they lie
Groveling and prostrate on yon Lake of Fire,   280
As we erewhile, astounded and amaz'd,
No wonder, fall'n such a pernicious highth.
    He scarce had ceas't when the superior Fiend
Was moving toward the shore; his ponderous shield
Ethereal temper, massy, large and round,   285
Behind him cast; the broad circumference
Hung on his shoulders like the Moon, whose Orb
Through Optic Glass the *Tuscan* Artist views
At Ev'ning from the top of *Fesole*,
Or in *Valdarno*, to descry new Lands,   290
Rivers or Mountains in her spotty Globe.
His Spear, to equal which the tallest Pine
Hewn on *Norwegian* hills, to be the Mast
Of som great Ammiral, were but a wand,
He walkd with to support uneasie steps   295
Over the burning Marle, not like those steps
On Heavens Azure, and the torrid Clime
Smote on him sore besides, vaulted with Fire;
Nathless he so endur'd, till on the Beach
Of that inflamed Sea, he stood and calld   300
His Legions, Angel Forms, who lay intranc't
Thick as Autumnal Leaves that strow the Brooks
In *Vallombrosa*, where th' *Etrurian* shades
High overarcht imbowr; or scatterd sedge
Afloat, when with fierce Winds *Orion* armd   305
Hath vext the Red-Sea Coast, whose waves orethrew

Busiris and his *Memphian* Chivalrie,
While with perfidious hatred they persu'd
The Sojourners of *Goshen*, who beheld
From the safe shore thir floating Carcasses   310
And broken Chariot Wheels: so thick bestrown
Abject and lost lay these, covering the Flood,
Under amazement of thir hideous change.
He calld so loud, that all the hollow Deep
Of Hell resounded.   Princes, Potentates,   315
Warriors, the Flowr of Heav'n, once yours, now lost,
If such astonishment as this can sieze
Eternal spirits; or have ye chos'n this place
After the toil of Battel to repose
Your wearied vertue, for the ease you find   320
To slumber here, as in the Vales of Heav'n?
Or in this abject posture have ye sworn
To adore the Conqueror? who now beholds
Cherube and Seraph rouling in the Flood
With scatterd Arms and Ensigns, till anon   325
His swift persuers from Heav'n Gates discern
Th' advantage, and decending tread us down
Thus drooping, or with linked Thunderbolts
Transfix us to the bottom of this Gulf.
Awake, arise, or be for ever fall'n.   330
   They heard, and were abasht, and up they sprung
Upon the wing, as when men wont to watch
On duty, sleeping found by whom they dread,
Rouse and bestir themselves ere well awake.
Nor did they not perceive the evil plight   335
In which they were, or the fierce pains not feel;
Yet to thir Generals Voice they soon obeyd
Innumerable.   As when the potent Rod
Of *Amrams* Son in *Egypts* evil day
Wav'd round the Coast, up calld a pitchy cloud   340
Of *Locusts*, warping on the Eastern Wind,
That ore the Realm of impious *Pharaoh* hung
Like Night, and darkend all the Land of *Nile*:
So numberless were those bad Angels seen
Hovering on wing under the Cope of Hell   345
'Twixt upper, nether, and surrounding Fires;
Till, as a signal giv'n, th' uplifted Spear
Of thir great Sultan waving to direct
Thir course, in even ballance down they light
On the firm brimstone, and fill all the Plain;   350
A multitude, like which the populous North
Pourd never from her frozen loins, to pass
Rhene or the *Danaw*, when her barbarous Sons

314 Deep] deeps *MS.*

Came like a Deluge on the South, and spred
Beneath *Gibraltar* to the *Lybian* sands.   355
Forthwith from every Squadron and each Band
The Heads and Leaders thither haste where stood
Thir great Commander; Godlike shapes and forms
Excelling human, Princely Dignities,
And Powers that erst in Heaven sat on Thrones;   360
Though of thir Names in heav'nly Records now
Be no memorial, blotted out and ras'd
By thir Rebellion, from the Books of Life.
Nor had they yet among the Sons of *Eve*
Got them new Names, till wandring ore the Earth,   365
Through Gods high sufferance for the trial of man,
By falsities and lies the greatest part
Of Mankind they corrupted to forsake
God thir Creator, and th' invisible
Glory of him, that made them, to transform   370
Oft to the Image of a Brute, adornd
With gay Religions full of Pomp and Gold,
And Devils to adore for Deities:
Then were they known to men by various Names,
And various Idols through the Heathen World.   375
Say, Muse, thir Names then known, who first, who last,
Rous'd from the slumber on that fiery Couch,
At thir great Emperors call, as next in worth
Came singly where he stood on the bare strand,
While the promiscuous crowd stood yet aloof.   380
The chief were those who from the Pit of Hell
Roaming to seek thir prey on earth, durst fix
Thir Seats long after next the Seat of God,
Thir Altars by his Altar, Gods ador'd
Among the Nations round, and durst abide   385
Jehovah thundring out of *Sion*, thron'd
Between the Cherubim; yea, often plac'd
Within his Sanctuary it self thir Shrines,
Abominations; and with cursed things
His holy Rites and solemn Feasts profan'd,   390
And with thir darkness durst affront his light.
First *Moloch*, horrid King besmear'd with blood
Of human sacrifice, and parents tears,
Though for the noise of Drums and Timbrels loud
Thir childrens cries unheard, that passd through fire   395
To his grim Idol.   Him the *Ammonite*
Worshipd in *Rabba* and her watry Plain,
In *Argob* and in *Basan*, to the stream
Of utmost *Arnon*.   Nor content with such
Audacious neighbourhood, the wisest heart   400
Of *Solomon* he led by fraud to build
His Temple right against the Temple of God

On that opprobrious Hill, and made his Grove
The pleasant Vally of *Hinnom*, *Tophet* thence
And black *Gehenna* calld, the Type of Hell.   405
Next *Chemos*, th' obscene dread of *Moabs* Sons,
From *Aroer* to *Nebo*, and the wild
Of Southmost *Abarim*; in *Hesebon*
And *Horonaim*, *Seons* Realm, beyond
The flowry Dale of *Sibma* clad with Vines,   410
And *Eleale* to th' *Asphaltic* Pool.
Peor his other Name, when he entic'd
Israel in *Sittim* on thir march from *Nile*
To do him wanton rites, which cost them woe.
Yet thence his lustful Orgies he enlarg'd   415
Ev'n to that Hill of scandal, by the Grove
Of *Moloch* homicide, lust hard by hate;
Till good *Josiah* drove them thence to Hell.
With these came they, who from the bordring flood
Of old *Euphrates* to the Brook that parts   420
Egypt from *Syrian* ground, had general Names
Of *Baälim* and *Ashtaroth*, those male,
These Feminine.   For Spirits when they please
Can either Sex assume, or both; so soft
And uncompounded is thir Essence pure,   425
Not ti'd or manacl'd with joint or limb,
Nor founded on the brittle strength of bones,
Like cumbrous flesh; but in what shape they choose
Dilated or condenst, bright or obscure,
Can execute thir aerie purposes,   430
And works of love or enmity fulfill.
For those the Race of *Israel* oft forsook
Thir living strength, and unfrequented left
His righteous Altar, bowing lowly down
To bestial Gods; for which thir heads as low   435
Bowd down in Battel, sunk before the Spear
Of despicable foes.   With these in troop
Came *Astoreth*, whom the *Phœnicians* calld
Astarte, Queen of Heav'n, with crescent Horns;
To whose bright Image nightly by the Moon   440
Sidonian Virgins paid thir Vows and Songs,
In *Sion* also not unsung, where stood
Her Temple on th' offensive Mountain, built
By that uxorious King, whose heart though large,
Beguil'd by fair Idolatresses, fell   445
To Idols foul.   *Thammuz* came next behind,
Whose annual wound in *Lebanon* allur'd
The *Syrian* Damsels to lament his fate
In amorous ditties all a Summers day,
While smooth *Adonis* from his native Rock   450
Ran purple to the Sea, suppos'd with blood

Of *Thammuz* yearly wounded: the Love-tale
Infected *Sions* daughters with like heat,
Whose wanton passions in the sacred Porch
Ezekiel saw, when by the Vision led   455
His eye surveyd the dark Idolatries
Of alienated *Judah*.   Next came one
Who mournd in earnest, when the Captive Ark
Maimd his brute Image, head and hands lopt off
In his own Temple, on the grunsel edge,   460
Where he fell flat, and sham'd his Worshippers:
Dagon his Name, Sea Monster, upward Man
And downward Fish: yet had his Temple high
Rear'd in *Azotus*; dreaded through the Coast
Of *Palestine*, in *Gath* and *Ascalon*,   465
And *Accaron* and *Gaza's* frontier bounds.
Him followd *Rimmon*, whose delightful Seat
Was fair *Damascus*, on the fertil Banks
Of *Abbana* and *Pharphar*, lucid streams.
He also against the house of God was bold: 470
A Leper once he lost and gaind a King,
Ahaz his sottish Conqueror, whom he drew
Gods Altar to disparage and displace
For one of *Syrian* mode, whereon to burn
His odious offrings, and adore the Gods   475
Whom he had vanquisht.   After these appear'd
A crew who under Names of old Renown,
Osiris, Isis, Orus and thir Train
With monstrous shapes and sorceries abus'd
Fanatic *Egypt* and her Priests, to seek   480
Thir wandring Gods disguis'd in brutish forms
Rather than human.   Nor did *Israel* scape
Th' infection when thir borrowd Gold compos'd
The Calf in *Oreb*: and the Rebel King
Doubl'd that sin in *Bethel* and in *Dan*,   485
Lik'ning his Maker to the Grazed Ox,
Jehovah, who in one Night when he passd
From *Egypt* marching, equald with one stroke
Both her first born and all her bleating Gods.
Belial came last, than whom a Spirit more lewd   490
Fell not from Heaven, or more gross to love
Vice for it self: To him no Temple stood
Or Altar smok'd; yet who more oft than hee
In Temples and at Altars, when the Priest
Turns Atheist, as did *Ely's* Sons, who filld   495
With lust and violence the house of God.
In Courts and Palaces he also Reigns
And in luxurious Cities, where the noise
Of riot ascends above thir loftiest Towrs,
And injury and outrage: And when Night   500

Darkens the Streets, then wander forth the Sons
Of *Belial*, flown with insolence and wine.
Witness the Streets of *Sodom*, and that night
In *Gibeah*, when the hospitable dore
Expos'd a Matron to avoid worse rape.   505
These were the prime in order and in might;
The rest were long to tell, though far renownd,
Th' *Ionian* Gods, of *Javans* Issue held
Gods, yet confest later than Heav'n and Earth
Thir boasted Parents; *Titan* Heav'ns first born   510
With his enormous brood, and birthright seiz'd
By younger *Saturn*, he from mightier *Jove*
His own and *Rhea's* Son like measure found;
So *Jove* usurping reignd: these first in *Crete*
And *Ida* known, thence on the Snowy top   515
Of cold *Olympus* rul'd the middle Air
Thir highest Heav'n; or on the *Delphian* Cliff,
Or in *Dodona*, and through all the bounds
Of *Doric* Land; or who with *Saturn* old
Fled over *Adria* to th' *Hesperian* Fields,   520
And ore the *Celtic* roamd the utmost Iles.
All these and more came flocking; but with looks
Down cast and damp, yet such wherein appear'd
Obscure som glimpse of joy, t'have found thir chief
Not in despair, t'have found themselves not lost   525
In loss it self; which on his count'nance cast
Like doubtful hue: but he his wonted pride
Soon recollecting, with high words, that bore
Semblance of worth, not substance, gently rais'd
Thir fainted courage, and dispelld thir fears.   530
Then straight commands that at the warlike sound
Of Trumpets loud and Clarions be uprear'd
His mighty Standard; that proud honour claimd
Azazel as his right, a Cherube tall:
Who forthwith from the glittering Staff unfurld   535
Th' Imperial Ensign, which full high advanc't
Shon like a Meteor streaming to the Wind
With Gemms and Golden lustre rich imblaz'd,
Seraphic arms and Trophies: all the while
Sonorous mettal blowing Martial sounds: 540
At which the universal Host upsent
A shout that tore Hells Concave, and beyond
Frighted the Reign of *Chaos* and old *Night*.
All in a moment through the gloom were seen
Ten thousand Banners rise into the Air   545
With Orient Colours waving; with them rose

504–5 the hospitable dore   Expos'd a Matron to avoid *Ed. 2*]
    hospitable Dores   Yielded thir Matrons to prevent *Ed. I*
530 fainted *MS., Ed. 1*] fanting *Ed. 2*

A Forrest huge of Spears; and thronging Helms
Appear'd, and serried Shields in thick array
Of depth immeasurable: Anon they move
In perfet *Phalanx* to the *Dorian* mood   550
Of Flutes and soft Recorders; such as rais'd
To highth of noblest temper Heroes old
Arming to Battel, and in stead of rage
Deliberat valour breath'd, firm and unmov'd
With dread of death to flight or foul retreat,   555
Nor wanting power to mitigate and swage
With solemn touches, troubl'd thoughts, and chase
Anguish and doubt and fear and sorrow and pain
From mortal or immortal minds.   Thus they
Breathing united force with fixed thought   560
Mov'd on in silence to soft Pipes that charmd
Thir painful steps ore the burnt soil; and now
Advanc't in view they stand, a horrid Front
Of dreadful length and dazling Arms, in guise
Of Warriers old with orderd Spear and Shield,   565
Awaiting what command thir mighty Chief
Had to impose: Hee through the armed Files
Darts his experienc't eye, and soon traverse
The whole Battalion views, thir order due,
Thir visages and stature as of Gods,   570
Thir number last he summs.   And now his heart
Distends with pride, and hardning in his strength
Glories: For never since created man,
Met such imbodied force, as nam'd with these
Could merit more than that small infantry   575
Warrd on by Cranes: though all the Giant brood
Of *Phlegra* with th' Heroic Race were joind
That fought at *Theb's* and *Ilium*, on each side
Mixt with auxiliar Gods; and what resounds
In Fable or Romance of *Uthers* Son   580
Begirt with *Brittish* and *Armoric* Knights;
And all who since, Baptiz'd or Infidel
Jousted in *Aspramont* or *Montalban*,
Damasco, or *Marocco*, or *Trebisond*,
Or whom *Biserta* sent from *Afric* shore   585
When *Charlemain* with all his Peerage fell
By *Fontarabbia*.   Thus far these beyond
Compare of mortal prowess, yet observ'd
Thir dread Commander: he above the rest
In shape and gesture proudly eminent   590
Stood like a Tower; his form had yet not lost
All her Original brightness, nor appear'd
Less than Arch-Angel ruind, and th' excess
Of Glory obscur'd: As when the Sun new ris'n
Looks through the Horizontal misty Air   595

Shorn of his Beams, or from behind the Moon
In dim Eclipse disastrous twilight sheds
On half the Nations, and with fear of change
Perplexes Monarchs.   Darkend so, yet shon
Above them all th' Arch-Angel: but his face   600
Deep scars of Thunder had intrencht, and care
Sat on his faded cheek, but under Brows
Of dauntless courage, and considerat Pride
Waiting revenge: cruel his eye, but cast
Signes of remorse and passion to behold   605
The fellows of his crime, the followers rather
(Far other once beheld in bliss) condemnd
For ever now to have thir lot in pain,
Millions of Spirits for his fault amerc't
Of Heav'n, and from Eternal Splendors flung   610
For his revolt, yet faithful how they stood,
Thir Glory witherd.   As when Heavens Fire
Hath scath'd the Forrest Oaks or Mountain Pines,
With singed top thir stately growth though bare
Stands on the blasted Heath.   He now prepar'd   615
To speak; whereat thir doubl'd Ranks they bend
From Wing to Wing, and half enclose him round
With all his Peers: attention held them mute.
Thrice he assayd, and thrice in spite of scorn,
Tears such as Angels weep, burst forth: at last   620
Words interwove with sighs found out thir way.
   O Myriads of immortal Spirits, O Powers
Matchless, but with th' Almighty, and that strife
Was not inglorious, though th' event was dire,
As this place testifies, and this dire change   625
Hateful to utter: but what power of mind
Foreseeing or presaging, from the Depth
Of knowledge past or present, could have fear'd
How such united force of Gods, how such
As stood like these, could ever know repulse?   630
For who can yet believe, though after loss,
That all these puissant Legions, whose exile
Hath emptied Heav'n, shall faile to re-ascend
Self-rais'd, and repossess thir native seat?
For mee be witness all the Host of Heav'n,   635
If counsels different, or danger shunned
By me, have lost our hopes.   But he who reigns
Monarch in Heav'n, till then as one secure
Sat on his Throne, upheld by old repute,
Consent or custom, and his Regal State   640
Put forth at full, but still his strength conceal'd,
Which tempted our attempt, and wrought our fall.

603 courage] valour *MS.*

Henceforth his might we know, and know our own
So as not either to provoke, or dread
New warr, provok't; our better part remains   645
To work in close design, by fraud or guile
What force effected not: that he no less
At length from us may find, who overcomes
By force, hath overcome but half his foe.
Space may produce new Worlds; whereof so rife   650
There went a fame in Heav'n that he ere long
Intended to create, and therein plant
A generation, whom his choice regard
Should favour equal to the Sons of Heaven:
Thither, if but to prie, shall be perhaps   655
Our first eruption, thither or elsewhere:
For this Infernal Pit shall never hold
Celestial Spirits in Bondage, nor th' Abysse
Long under darkness cover.   But these thoughts
Full Counsel must mature: Peace is despaird,   660
For who can think Submission?   Warr then, Warr
Open or understood must be resolv'd.
      He spake: and to confirm his words, out-flew
Millions of flaming swords, drawn from the thighs
Of mighty Cherubim; the sudden blaze   665
Far round illumind hell: highly they rag'd
Against the Highest, and fierce with grasped Arms
Clashd on thir sounding shields the din of war,
Hurling defiance toward the Vault of Heav'n.
      There stood a Hill not far whose griesly top   670
Belchd fire and rouling smoke; the rest entire
Shon with a glossie scurff, undoubted sign
That in his womb was hid metallic Ore,
The work of Sulphur.   Thither wingd with speed
A numerous Brigad hastend.   As when bands   675
Of Pioners with Spade and Pickaxe armd
Forerun the Royal Camp, to trench a Field
Or cast a Rampart.   *Mammon* led them on,
Mammon, the least erected Spirit that fell
From Heav'n, for ev'n in Heav'n his looks and thoughts
Were always downward bent, admiring more   681
The riches of Heav'ns pavement, trodden Gold
Than aught divine or holy else enjoyd
In vision beatific: by him first
Men also, and by his suggestion taught,   685
Ransackd the Center, and with impious hands
Rifl'd the bowels of thir mother Earth
For Treasures better hid.   Soon had his crew
Opend into the Hill a spacious wound
And diggd out ribs of Gold.   Let none admire   690
That riches grow in Hell; that soil may best

Deserve the precious bane.   And here let those
Who boast in mortal things, and wondring tell
Of *Babel*, and the works of *Memphian* Kings,
Learn how thir greatest Monuments of Fame,   695
And Strength and Art are easily outdone
By Spirits reprobate, and in an hour
What in an age they with incessant toile
And hands innumerable scarce perform.
Nigh on the Plain in many cells prepar'd,   700
That underneath had veins of liquid fire
Sluc't from the Lake, a second multitude
With wondrous Art found out the massie Ore,
Severing each kind, and scummd the Bullion dross:
A third as soon had formd within the ground   705
A various mould, and from the boiling cells
By strange conveyance filld each hollow nook,
As in an Organ from one blast of wind
To many a row of Pipes the sound-board breathes.
Anon out of the earth a Fabric huge   710
Rose like an Exhalation, with the sound
Of Dulcet Symphonies and voices sweet,
Built like a Temple, where *Pilasters* round
Were set, and Doric pillars overlaid
With Golden Architrave; nor did there want   715
Cornice or Freeze, with bossy Sculptures grav'n,
The Roof was fretted Gold.   Not *Babilon*,
Nor great *Alcairo* such magnificence
Equald in all thir glories, to inshrine
Belus or *Serapis* thir Gods, or seat   720
Thir Kings, when *Egypt* with *Assyria* strove
In wealth and luxurie.   Th' ascending pile
Stood fixt her stately highth, and straight the dores
Op'ning thir brazen folds discover wide
Within, her ample spaces, ore the smooth   725
And level pavement: from the arched roof
Pendant by suttle Magic many a row
Of Starry Lamps and blazing Cressets fed
With *Naphtha* and *Asphaltus* yielded light
As from a sky.   The hasty multitude   730
Admiring enterd, and the work some praise
And some the Architect: his hand was known
In Heav'n by many a Towred structure high,
Where Scepterd Angels held thir residence,
And sat as Princes, whom the supreme King   735
Exalted to such power, and gave to rule,
Each in his Hierarchie, the Orders bright.
Nor was his name unheard or unador'd

703 found out *Ed. 2*] founded *MS.*, *Ed. 1*

In ancient *Greece*; and in *Ausonian* land
Men calld him *Mulciber*; and how he fell   740
From Heav'n, they fabl'd, thrown by angry *Jove*
Sheer o'er the Crystal Battlements: from Morn
To Noon he fell, from Noon to dewy Eve,
A Summers day; and with the setting Sun
Dropd from the Zenith like a falling Star,   745
On *Lemnos* th' *Ægæan* Ile: thus they relate,
Erring; for he with this rebellious rout
Fell long before; nor aught availd him now
To have built in Heav'n high Towrs; nor did he scape
By all his Engins, but was headlong sent   750
With his industrious crew to build in Hell.
Mean while the winged Haralds by command
Of Sovran power, with awful Ceremony
And Trumpets sound throughout the Host proclaim
A solemn Councel forthwith to be held   755
At *Pandæmonium*, the high Capital
Of *Satan* and his Peers: thir summons calld
From every Band and squared Regiment
By place or choice the worthiest; they anon
With hundreds and with thousands trooping came   760
Attended: all access was throngd, the Gates
And Porches wide, but chief the spacious Hall
(Though like a coverd field, where Champions bold
Wont ride in armd, and at the Soldans chair
Defi'd the best of *Panim* chivalry   765
To mortal combat or career with Lance)
Thick swarmd, both on the ground and in the air,
Brusht with the hiss of russling wings.   As Bees
In spring time, when the Sun with *Taurus* rides,
Pour forth thir populous youth about the Hive   770
In clusters; they among fresh dews and flowers
Flie to and fro, or on the smoothed Plank,
The suburb of thir Straw-built Cittadel,
New rubd with Baum, expatiate and conferr
Thir State affairs.   So thick the aerie crowd   775
Swarmd and were straitend; till the Signal giv'n,
Behold a wonder! they but now who seemd
In bigness to surpass Earths Giant Sons
Now less than smallest Dwarfs, in narrow room
Throng numberless, like that Pigmean Race   780
Beyond the *Indian* Mount, or Faerie Elves
Whose midnight Revels by a Forrest side
Or Fountain some belated Peasant sees,
Or dreams he sees, while over-head the Moon
Sits Arbitress, and nearer to the Earth   785

756 Capital *Edd. 1, 2*] Capitoll *corr. to* Capitall *MS.*]

Wheels her pale course, they on thir mirth and dance
Intent, with jocond Music charm his ear;
At once with joy and fear his heart rebounds.
Thus incorporeal Spirits to smallest forms
Reduc'd thir shapes immense, and were at large,   790
Though without number still amidst the Hall
Of that infernal Court.   But far within
And in thir own dimensions like themselves
The great Seraphic Lords and Cherubim
In close recess and secret conclave sat   795
A thousand Demi-Gods on golden seats,
Frequent and full.   After short silence then
And summons read, the great consult began.

The End of the First Book

BOOK II

THE ARGUMENT

The Consultation begun, Satan *debates whether another Battel be to be hazarded for the recovery of Heaven: some advise it, others dissuade: A third proposal is prefer'd, mention'd before by* Satan, *to search the truth of that Prophesie or Tradition in Heaven concerning another world, and another kind of creature equal or not much inferiour to themselves, about this time to be created: Thir doubt who shall be sent on this difficult search:* Satan *thir chief undertakes alone the voyage, is honourd and applauded. The Councel thus ended, the rest betake them several wayes and to several imployments, as thir inclinations lead them, to entertain the time till Satan return. He passes on his Journey to Hell Gates, finds them shut, and who sat there to guard them, by whom at length they are op'nd, and discover to him the great Gulf between Hell and Heaven; with what difficulty he passes through, directed by* Chaos, *the Power of that place, to the sight of this new World which he sought.*

High on a Throne of Royal State, which far
Outshon the wealth of *Ormus* and of *Ind,*
Or where the gorgeous East with richest hand
Showrs on her Kings *Barbaric* Pearl and Gold,
Satan exalted sat, by merit rais'd   5
To that bad eminence; and from despair
Thus high uplifted beyond hope, aspires
Beyond thus high, insatiat to persue
Vain Warr with Heav'n, and by success untaught
His proud imaginations thus displayd.   10
    Powers and Dominions, Deities of Heav'n,
For since no deep within her gulf can hold
Immortal vigor, though opprest and fall'n,
I give not Heav'n for lost. From this descent
Celestial Vertues rising, will appear   15
More glorious and more dread than from no fall,
And trust themselves to fear no second fate:
Mee though just right and the fixt Laws of Heav'n
Did first create your Leader, next free choice,
With what besides, in Counsel or in Fight,   20
Hath bin achiev'd of merit, yet this loss
Thus farr at least recoverd, hath much more
Establisht in a safe unenvied Throne
Yielded with full consent. The happier state
In Heav'n, which follows dignity, might draw   25
Envy from each inferior; but who here

Argument l. 6 shall] should *1669*
177

Will envy whom the highest place exposes
Formost to stand against the Thunderers aime
Your bulwark, and condemns to greatest share
Of endless pain? where there is then no good   30
For which to strive, no strife can grow up there
From Faction; for none sure will claim in hell
Precedence, none, whose portion is so small
Of present pain, that with ambitious mind
Will covet more.   With this advantage then   35
To union, and firm Faith, and firm accord,
More than can be in Heav'n, we now return
To claim our just inheritance of old,
Surer to prosper than prosperity
Could have assur'd us; and by what best way,   40
Whether of open Warr or covert guile,
We now debate; who can advise, may speak.
   He ceas'd, and next him *Moloc*, Scepterd King
Stood up, the strongest and the fiercest Spirit
That fought in Heav'n; now fiercer by despair: 45
His trust was with th' Eternal to be deemed
Equal in strength, and rather than be less
Car'd not to be at all; with that care lost
Went all his fear: of God, or Hell, or worse
He reckd not, and these words thereafter spake.   50
   My sentence is for open Warr: Of Wiles,
More unexpert, I boast not: them let those
Contrive who need, or when they need, not now,
For while they sit contriving, shall the rest,
Millions that stand in Arms, and longing wait   55
The Signal to ascend, sit lingring here
Heav'ns fugitives, and for thir dwelling place
Accept this dark opprobrious Den of shame,
The Prison of his Tyranny who Reigns
By our delay? no, let us rather choose   60
Armd with Hell flames and fury all at once
O'er Heav'ns high Towrs to force resistless way,
Turning our Tortures into horrid Arms
Against the Torturer; when to meet the noise
Of his Almighty Engin he shall hear   65
Infernal Thunder, and for Lightning see
Black fire and horror shot with equal rage
Among his Angels; and his Throne it self
Mixt with *Tartarean* Sulphur, and strange fire,
His own invented Torments.   But perhaps   70
The way seems difficult and steep to scale
With upright wing against a higher foe.
Let such bethink them, if the sleepy drench
Of that forgetful Lake benumm not still,
That in our proper motion we ascend   75

Up to our native seat: descent and fall
To us is adverse.   Who but felt of late
When the fierce Foe hung on our broken Rear
Insulting, and persu'd us through the Deep,
With what compulsion and laborious flight   80
We sunk thus low? Th' ascent is easie then;
Th' event is fear'd; should we again provoke
Our stronger, som worse way his wrauth may find
To our destruction: if there be in Hell
Fear to be worse destroyd: what can be worse   85
Than to dwell here, driv'n out from bliss, condemnd
In this abhorred Deep to utter woe;
Where pain of unextinguishable fire
Must exercise us without hope of end
The Vassals of his anger, when the Scourge   90
Inexorably, and the torturing houre
Calls us to Penance?   More destroyd than thus
We should be quite abolisht and expire.
What fear we then? what doubt we to incense
His utmost ire? which to the highth enrag'd,   95
Will either quite consume us, and reduce
To nothing this essential, happier farr
Than miserable to have eternal being:
Or if our substance be indeed Divine,
And cannot cease to be, we are at worst   100
On this side nothing; and by proof we feel
Our power sufficient to disturb his Heav'n,
And with perpetual inroads to Alarm,
Though inaccessible, his fatal Throne:
Which if not Victory is yet Revenge.   105
    He ended frowning, and his look denounc'd
Desperat revenge, and Battel dangerous
To less than Gods.   On th' other side up rose
Belial, in act more graceful and humane;
A fairer person lost not Heav'n; he seemd   110
For dignity compos'd and high exploit:
But all was false and hollow; though his Tongue
Dropd Manna, and could make the worse appear
The better reason, to perplex and dash
Maturest Counsels: for his thoughts were low;   115
To vice industrious, but to Nobler deeds
Timorous and slothful: yet he pleas'd the ear,
And with persuasive accent thus began.
    I should be much for open Warr, O Peers,
As not behind in hate; if what was urg'd   120
Main reason to persuade immediat Warr,
Did not dissuade me most, and seem to cast
Ominous conjecture on the whole success:
When he who most excells in fact of Arms,

In what he counsels and in what excells   125
Mistrustful, grounds his courage on despair
And utter dissolution, as the scope
Of all his aim, after som dire revenge.
First, what Revenge? the Towrs of Heav'n are filld
With Armed watch, that render all access   130
Impregnable; oft on the bordering Deep
Encamp thir Legions, or with obscure wing
Scout farr and wide into the Realm of *Night*,
Scorning surprize.   Or could we break our way
By force, and at our heels all Hell should rise   135
With blackest Insurrection, to confound
Heav'ns purest Light, yet our great Enemie
All incorruptible would on his Throne
Sit unpolluted, and th' Ethereal mould
Incapable of stain would soon expell   140
Her mischief, and purge off the baser fire
Victorious.   Thus repulst, our final hope
Is flat despair: we must exasperate
Th' Almighty Victor to spend all his rage,
And that must end us, that must be our cure,   145
To be no more; sad cure; for who would lose,
Though full of pain, this intellectual being,
Those thoughts that wander through Eternity,
To perish rather, swallowd up and lost
In the wide womb of uncreated night,   150
Devoid of sense and motion? and who knows,
Let this be good, whether our angry Foe
Can give it, or will ever? how he can
Is doubtful; that he never will is sure.
Will he, so wise, let loose at once his ire,   155
Belike through impotence, or unaware,
To give his Enemies thir wish, and end
Them in his anger, whom his anger saves
To punish endless? wherefore cease we then?
Say they who counsel Warr, we are decreed,   160
Reserv'd and destind to Eternal woe;
Whatever doing, what can we suffer more,
What can we suffer worse? is this then worst,
Thus sitting, thus consulting, thus in Arms?
What when we fled amain, persu'd and strook   165
With Heav'ns afflicting Thunder, and besought
The Deep to shelter us? this Hell then seemd
A refuge from those wounds: or when we lay
Chaind on the burning Lake? that sure was worse.
What if the breath that kindl'd those grim fires   170
Awak't should blow them into sev'nfold rage
And plunge us in the flames? or from above
Should intermitted vengeance arm again

His red right hand to plague us? what if all
Her stores were opend and this Firmament   175
Of Hell should spout her Cataracts of Fire,
Impendent horrors, threatning hideous fall
One day upon our heads? while we perhaps
Designing or exhorting glorious Warr,
Caught in a fierie Tempest shall be hurld   180
Each on his rock transfixt, the sport and prey
Of racking whirlwinds, or for ever sunk
Under yon boiling Ocean, wrapt in Chains;
There to converse with everlasting groans,
Unrespited, unpittied, unpriev'd,   185
Ages of hopeless end; this would be worse.
Warr therefore, open or conceal'd, alike
My voice dissuades; for what can force or guile
With him, or who deceive his mind, whose eye
Views all things at one view? he from Heav'ns highth 190
All these our motions vain, sees and derides;
Not more Almighty to resist our might
Than wise to frustrate all our plots and wiles.
Shall we then live thus vile, the Race of Heav'n
Thus trampl'd, thus expelld to suffer here   195
Chains and these Torments? better these than worse
By my advice; since Fate inevitable
Subdues us, and Omnipotent Decree,
The Victors will.   To suffer, as to do,
Our strength is equal, nor the Law unjust   200
That so ordains: this was at first resolv'd,
If we were wise, against so great a foe
Contending, and so doubtful what might fall.
I laugh, when those who at the Spear are bold
And vent'rous, if that fail them, shrink and fear   205
What yet they know must follow, to endure
Exile or ignominy or bonds or pain,
The sentence of thir Conqueror: This is now
Our doom; which if we can sustain and bear,
Our Supreme Foe in time may much remit   210
His anger, and perhaps thus farr remov'd
Not mind us not offending, satisfi'd
With what is punisht; whence these raging fires
Will slacken, if his breath stir not thir flames.
Our purer essence then will overcome   215
Thir noxious vapour, or enur'd not feel,
Or chang'd at length, and to the place conformd
In temper and in nature, will receive
Familiar the fierce heat, and void of pain;
This horror will grow mild, this darkness light,   220
Besides what hope the never-ending flight
Of future days may bring, what chance, what change

Worth waiting, since our present lot appears
For happy though but ill, for ill not worst,
If we procure not to our selves more woe,   225
    Thus *Belial* with words cloth'd in reasons garb
Counseld ignoble ease, and peaceful sloath,
Not peace: and after him thus *Mammon* spake.
    Either to disinthrone the King of Heav'n
We warr, if warr be best, or to regain   230
Our own right lost: him to unthrone we then
May hope, when everlasting Fate shall yield
To fickle Chance, and *Chaos* judge the strife:
The former vain to hope argues as vain
The latter: for what place can be for us   235
Within Heav'ns bound, unless Heav'ns Lord supream
We overpower?   Suppose he should relent
And publish Grace to all, on promise made
Of new Subjection; with what eyes could we
Stand in his presence humble, and receive   240
Strict Laws impos'd, to celebrate his Throne
With warbl'd Hymns, and to his Godhead sing
Forc't Halleluiahs; while he Lordly sits
Our envied Sovran, and his Altar breathes
Ambrosial Odours and Ambrosial Flowers,   245
Our servile offerings.   This must be our task
In Heav'n, this our delight; how wearisom
Eternity so spent in worship paid
To whom we hate.   Let us not then persue
By force impossible, by leave obtain   250
Unacceptable, though in Heav'n, our state
Of splendid vassalage, but rather seek
Our own good from our selves, and from our own
Live to our selves, though in this vast recess,
Free, and to none accountable, preferring   255
Hard liberty before the easie yoke
Of servile Pomp.   Our greatness will appear
Then most conspicuous, when great things of small,
Useful of hurtful, prosperous of adverse
We can create, and in what place so e're   260
Thrive under evil, and work ease out of pain
Through labour and endurance.   This deep world
Of darkness do we dread?   How oft amidst
Thick clouds and dark doth Heav'ns all-ruling Sire
Choose to reside, his Glory unobscur'd,   265
And with the Majesty of darkness round
Covers his Throne; from whence deep thunders roar
Must'ring thir rage, and Heav'n resembles Hell?
As he our Darkness, cannot we his Light
Imitate when we please?   This Desert soile   270
Wants not her hidden lustre, Gemms and Gold;

Nor want we skill or art, from whence to raise
Magnificence; and what can Heav'n shew more?
Our torments also may in length of time
Become our Elements, these piercing Fires   275
As soft as now severe, our temper chang'd
Into their temper; which must needs remove
The sensible of pain.   All things invite
To peaceful Counsels, and the settl'd State
Of order, how in safety best we may   280
Compose our present evils, with regard
Of what we are and were, dismissing quite
All thoughts of warr: ye have what I advise.

   He scarce had finisht, when such murmur filld
Th' Assembly, as when hollow Rocks retain   285
The sound of blustring winds, which all night long
Had rous'd the Sea, now with hoarse cadence lull
Sea-faring men orewatcht, whose Bark by chance
Or Pinnace anchors in a craggy Bay
After the Tempest: Such applause was heard   290
As *Mammon* ended, and his Sentence pleas'd,
Advising peace: for such another Field
They dreaded worse than Hell: so much the fear
Of Thunder and the Sword of *Michaël*
Wrought still within them; and no less desire   295
To found this nether Empire, which might rise
By pollicy, and long process of time,
In emulation opposite to Heav'n.
Which when *Beëlzebub* perceiv'd, than whom,
Satan except, none higher sat, with grave   300
Aspect he rose, and in his rising seemd
A Pillar of State; deep on his Front engraven
Deliberation sat and public care;
And Princely counsel in his face yet shon,
Majestic though in ruin: sage he stood   305
With *Atlantean* shoulders fit to bear
The weight of mightiest Monarchies; his look
Drew audience and attention still as Night
Or Summers Noon-tide air, while thus he spake.

   Thrones and Imperial Powers, offspring of Heav'n, 310
Ethereal Vertues; or these Titles now
Must we renounce, and changing style be calld
Princes of Hell? for so the popular vote
Inclines, here to continue, and build up here
A growing Empire; doubtless; while we dream,   315
And know not that the King of Heav'n hath doomd
This place our dungeon, not our safe retreat
Beyond his Potent arm, to live exempt

282 were *Ed. 2*] where *Ed. 1*

From Heav'ns high jurisdiction in new League,
Banded against his Throne, but to remain   320
In strictest bondage, though thus far remov'd,
Under th' inevitable curb, reserv'd
His captive multitude: For he, be sure,
In highth or depth, still first and last will Reign
Sole King, and of his Kingdom lose no part   325
By our revolt, but over Hell extend
His Empire, and with Iron Scepter rule
Us here, as with his Golden those in Heav'n.
What sit we then projecting Peace and Warr?
Warr hath determind us, and foild with loss   330
Irreparable; terms of peace yet none
Voutsaf't or sought; for what peace will be giv'n
To us enslav'd, but custody severe,
And stripes, and arbitrary punishment
Inflicted? and what peace can we return,   335
But to our power hostility and hate,
Untam'd reluctance, and revenge though slow,
Yet ever plotting how the Conqueror least
May reap his conquest, and may least rejoice
In doing what we most in suffering feel?   340
Nor will occasion want, nor shall we need
With dangerous expedition to invade
Heav'n, whose high walls fear no assault or siege,
Or ambush from the Deep.   What if we find
Som easier enterprize?   There is a place   345
(If ancient and prophetic fame in Heav'n
Err not) another World, the happy seat
Of som new Race calld *Man*, about this time
To be created like to us, though less
In power and excellence, but favour'd more   350
Of him who rules above; so was his will
Pronounc't among the Gods, and by an Oath,
That shook Heav'ns whole circumference, confirmd.
Thither let us bend all our thoughts, to learn
What creatures there inhabit, of what mould   355
Or substance, how endu'd, and what thir Power,
And where thir weakness, how attempted best,
By force or suttlety: Though Heav'n be shut,
And Heav'ns high Arbitrator sit secure
In his own strength, this place may lie expos'd   360
The utmost border of his Kingdom, left
To their defence who hold it: here perhaps
Som advantagious act may be achiev'd
By sudden onset, either with Hell fire
To waste his whole Creation, or possess   365
All as our own, and drive as we were driven,
The punie habitants, or if not drive,

Seduce them to our Party, that thir God
May prove thir foe, and with repenting hand
Abolish his own works.   This would surpass   370
Common revenge, and interrupt his joy
In our Confusion, and our Joy upraise
In his disturbance; when his darling Sons
Hurld headlong to partake with us, shall curse
Thir frail Original, and faded bliss,   375
Faded so soon.   Advise if this be worth
Attempting, or to sit in darkness here
Hatching vain Empires.   Thus *Beëlzebub*
Pleaded his devilish Counsel, first devis'd
By *Satan*, and in part propos'd: for whence,   380
But from the Author of all ill could Spring
So deep a malice, to confound the race
Of mankind in one root, and Earth with Hell
To mingle and involve, done all to spite
The great Creator?   But thir spite still serves   385
His glory to augment.   The bold design
Pleas'd highly those infernal States, and joy
Sparkl'd in all thir eyes; with full assent
They vote: whereat his speech he thus renews.

    Well have ye judg'd, well ended long debate,   390
Synod of Gods, and like to what ye are,
Great things resolv'd; which from the lowest deep
Will once more lift us up, in spite of Fate,
Nearer our ancient Seat; perhaps in view
Of those bright confines, whence with neighbouring Arms
And opportune excursion we may chance   396
Re-enter Heav'n; or else in some mild Zone
Dwell not unvisited of Heav'ns fair Light
Secure, and at the brightning Orient beam
Purge off this gloom; the soft delicious Air,   400
To heal the scarr of these corrosive Fires
Shall breathe her baum.   But first whom shall we send
In search of this new world, whom shall we find
Sufficient? who shall tempt with wandring feet
The dark unbottomd infinite Abyss   405
And through the palpable obscure find out
His uncouth way, or spread his aerie flight
Upborne with indefatigable wings
Over the vast abrupt, ere he arrive
The happy Ile; what strength, what art can then   410
Suffice, or what evasion·bear him safe
Through the strict Senteries and Stations thick
Of Angels watching round?   Here he had need
All circumspection, and wee now no less

375 Original *Ed. 2*] Originals *Ed. 1*   414 wee *Errata Ed. 1*] we *Ed. 2*

Choice in our suffrage; for on whom we send,   415
The weight of all and our last hope relies.
   This said, he sat; and expectation held
His look suspence, awaiting who appear'd
To second, or oppose, or undertake
The perilous attempt: but all sat mute,   420
Pondering the danger with deep thoughts; and each
In others count'nance read his own dismay
Astonisht: none among the choice and prime
Of those Heav'n-warring Champions could be found
So hardie as to proffer or accept   425
Alone the dreadful voyage; till at last
Satan, whom now transcendent glory rais'd
Above his fellows, with Monarchal pride
Conscious of highest worth, unmov'd thus spake.
   O Progeny of Heav'n, Empyreal Thrones,   430
With reason hath deep silence and demurr
Seiz'd us, though undismayd: long is the way
And hard, that out of Hell leads up to light;
Our prison strong, this huge convex of Fire,
Outrageous to devour, immures us round   435
Ninefold, and gates of burning Adamant
Barrd over us prohibit all egress.
These past, if any pass, the void profound
Of unessential Night receives him next
Wide gaping, and with utter loss of being   440
Threatens him, plung'd in that abortive gulf.
If thence he scape into what ever World
Or unknown Region, what remains him less
Than unknown dangers and as hard escape.
But I should ill become this Throne, O Peers,   445
And this Imperial Sovranty, adornd
With splendor, armd with power, if aught propos'd
And judg'd of public moment, in the shape
Of difficulty or danger could deterr
Mee from attempting. Wherefore do I assume   450
These Royalties, and not refuse to Reign,
Refusing to accept as great a share
Of hazard as of honour, due alike
To him who Reigns, and so much to him due
Of hazard more, as he above the rest   455
High honour'd sits? Goe therfore mighty Powers,
Terror of Heav'n, though fall'n; intend at home,
While here shall be our home, what best may ease
The present misery, and render Hell
More tollerable; if there be cure or charm   460
To respit or deceive, or slack the pain
Of this ill Mansion: intermit no watch

450 Mee *Ed. 2, State* 2] Me *Ed. I, Ed. II, State 1*

Against a wakeful Foe, while I abroad
Through all the Coasts of dark destruction seek
Deliverance for us all: this enterprize   465
None shall partake with me.   Thus saying rose
The Monarch, and prevented all reply,
Prudent, lest from his resolution rais'd
Others among the chief might offer now
(Certain to be refus'd) what erst they fear'd;   470
And so refus'd might in opinion stand
His rivals, winning cheap the high repute
Which he through hazard huge must earn.   But they
Dreaded not more th' adventure than his voice
Forbidding; and at once with him they rose;   475
Thir rising all at once was as the sound
Of Thunder heard remote.   Towards him they bend
With awful reverence prone; and as a God
Extoll him equal to the highest in Heav'n:
Nor faild they to express how much they prais'd,   480
That for the general safety he despis'd
His own: for neither do the Spirits damnd
Lose all thir vertue; lest bad men should boast
Thir specious deeds on earth, which glory excites,
Or close ambition varnisht o'er with zeal.   485
Thus they thir doubtful consultations dark
Ended rejoicing in thir matchless Chief:
As when from mountain tops the dusky clouds
Ascending, while the North wind sleeps, o'erspread
Heav'ns cheerful face, the louring Element   490
Scowls o'er the darkend lantskip Snow or showr;
If chance the radiant Sun with farewel sweet
Extend his ev'ning beam, the fields revive,
The birds thir notes renew, and bleating herds
Attest thir joy, that hill and valley rings.   495
O shame to men!   Devil with Devil damnd
Firm concord holds, men onely disagree
Of·Creatures rational, though under hope
Of heav'nly Grace: and God proclaiming peace,
Yet live in hatred, enmitie, and strife   500
Among themselves, and levie cruel warrs,
Wasting the Earth, each other to destroy:
As if (which might induce us to accord)
Man had not hellish foes anow besides,
That day and night for his destruction wait.   505
    The *Stygian* Councel thus dissolv'd; and forth
In order came the grand infernal Peers,
Midst came thir mighty Paramount, and seemd
Alone th' Antagonist of Heav'n, nor less
Than Hells dread Emperor with pomp Supream,   510
And God-like imitated State; him round

A Globe of fierie Seraphim inclos'd
With bright imblazonrie, and horrent Arms.
Then of thir Session ended they bid cry
With Trumpets regal sound the great result: 515
Toward the four winds four speedy Cherubim
Put to thir mouths the sounding Alchymie
By Haralds voice explain'd: the hollow Abyss
Heard farr and wide, and all the host of Hell
With deafning shout, return'd them loud acclaim.   520
Thence more at ease thir minds and somwhat rais'd
By false presumptuous hope, the ranged Powers
Disband, and wandring, each his several way
Persues, as inclination or sad choice
Leads him perplext, where he may likeliest find   525
Truce to his restless thoughts, and entertain
The irksom hours, till his great Chief return.
Part on the Plain, or in the Air sublime
Upon the wing, or in swift race contend,
As at th' *Olympian* Games or *Pythian* fields;   530
Part curb thir fierie Steeds, or shun the Goal
With rapid wheels, or fronted Brigads form.
As when to warn proud Cities warr appears
Wag'd in the troubl'd Skie, and Armies rush
To Battel in the Clouds, before each Van   535
Prick forth the Aerie Knights, and couch thir spears
Till thickest Legions close; with feats of Arms
From either end of Heav'n the welkin burns.
Others with vast *Typhœan* rage more fell
Rend up both Rocks and Hills, and ride the Air   540
In whirlwind; Hell scarce holds the wild uproar.
As when *Alcides* from *Œchalia* Crownd
With conquest, felt th' envenomd robe, and tore
Through pain up by the roots *Thessalian* Pines,
And *Lichas* from the top of *Œta* threw   545
Into th' *Euboic* Sea.   Others more mild,
Retreated in a silent valley, sing
With notes Angelical to many a Harp
Thir own Heroic deeds and hapless fall
By doom of Battel; and complain that Fate   550
Free Vertue should enthrall to Force or Chance.
Thir Song was partial, but the harmony
(What could it less when Spirits immortal sing?)
Suspended Hell, and took with ravishment
The thronging audience.   In discourse more sweet   555
(For Eloquence the Soul, Song charms the Sense,)
Others apart sat on a Hill retir'd,
In thoughts more elevate, and reasond high

527 his *Ed. 1*] this *Ed. 2*

Of Providence, Foreknowledge, Will, and Fate,
Fixt Fate, free Will, Foreknowledge absolute,   560
And found no end, in wandring mazes lost.
Of good and evil much they argu'd then,
Of happiness and final misery,
Passion and Apathie, and glory and shame,
Vain wisdom all, and false Philosophie: 565
Yet with a pleasing sorcerie could charm
Pain for a while or anguish, and excite
Fallacious hope, or arm th' obdured brest
With stubborn patience as with triple steel.
Another part in Squadrons and gross Bands,   570
On bold adventure to discover wide
That dismal world, if any Clime perhaps
Might yield them easier habitation, bend
Four ways thir flying March, along the Banks
Of four infernal Rivers that disgorge   575
Into the burning Lake thir baleful streams:
Abhorred *Styx* the flood of deadly hate,
Sad *Acheron* of sorrow, black and deep;
Cocytus, nam'd of lamentation loud
Heard on the rueful stream; fierce *Phlegeton*   580
Whose waves of torrent fire inflame with rage.
Farr off from these a slow and silent stream,
Lethe the River of Oblivion roules
Her watrie Labyrinth, whereof who drinks,
Forthwith his former state and being forgets,   585
Forgets both joy and grief, pleasure and pain.
Beyond this flood a frozen Continent
Lies dark and wild, beat with perpetual storms
Of Whirlwind and dire Hail, which on firm land
Thaws not, but gathers heap, and ruin seems   590
Of ancient pile; all else deep snow and ice,
A gulf profound as that *Serbonian* Bog
Betwixt *Damiata* and mount *Casius* old,
Where Armies whole have sunk: the parching Air
Burns frore, and cold performs th' effect of Fire.   595
Thither by harpy-footed Furies hal'd,
At certain revolutions all the damnd
Are brought: and feel by turns the bitter change
Of fierce extreams, extreams by change more fierce,
From Beds of raging Fire to starve in Ice   600
Thir soft Ethereal warmth, and there to pine
Immovable, infixt, and frozen round,
Periods of time, thence hurried back to fire.
They ferry over this *Lethean* Sound
Both to and fro, thir sorrow to augment,   605
And wish and struggle, as they pass, to reach
The tempting stream, with one small drop to lose

In sweet forgetfulness all pain and woe,
All in one moment, and so near the brink;
But Fate withstands, and to oppose th' attempt   610
Medusa with *Gorgonian* terror guards
The Ford, and of it self the water flies
All taste of living wight, as once it fled
The lip of *Tantalus*.   Thus roving on
In confus'd march forlorn, th' adventrous Bands   615
With shuddring horror pale, and eyes agast
Viewd first thir lamentable lot, and found
No rest: through many a dark and drearie Vale
They passd, and many a Region dolorous,
Ore many a Frozen, many a Fierie Alp,   620
Rocks, Caves, Lakes, Fens, Bogs, Dens, and shades of death,
A Universe of death, which God by curse
Created evil, for evil only good,
Where all life dies, death lives, and nature breeds,
Perverse, all monstrous, all prodigious things,   625
Abominable, inutterable, and worse
Than Fables yet have feignd, or fear conceiv'd,
Gorgons and *Hydras*, and *Chimeras* dire.
    Mean while the Adversary of God and Man,
Satan with thoughts inflam'd of highest design,   630
Puts on swift wings, and toward the Gates of Hell
Explores his solitary flight; somtimes
He scours the right hand coast, somtimes the left,
Now shaves with level wing the Deep, then soares
Up to the fiery concave touring high.   635
As when farr off at Sea a Fleet descri'd
Hangs in the Clouds, by *Æquinoctial* Winds
Close sailing from *Bengala*, or the Iles
Of *Ternate* and *Tidore*, whence Merchants bring
Thir spicie Drugs: they on the Trading Flood   640
Through the wide *Ethiopian* to the Cape
Ply stemming nightly toward the Pole.   So seemd
Farr off the flying Fiend: at last appear
Hell bounds high reaching to the horrid Roof,
And thrice threefold the Gates; three folds were Brass,
Three Iron, three of Adamantine Rock,   646
Impenetrable, impal'd with circling fire,
Yet unconsum'd.   Before the Gates there sat
On either side a formidable shape;
The one seemd Woman to the waist, and fair,   650
But ended foul in many a scaly fold
Voluminous and vast, a Serpent armd
With mortal sting: about her middle round
A cry of Hell Hounds never ceasing barkd

With wide *Cerberean* mouths full loud, and rung   655
A hideous Peal; yet, when they list, would creep,
If aught disturbd thir noise, into her womb,
And kennel there, yet there still barkd and howld
Within unseen.   Farr less abhorrd than these
Vexd *Scylla* bathing in the Sea that parts   660
Calabria from the hoarse *Trinacrian* shore:
Nor uglier follow the Night-Hag, when calld
In secret, riding through the Air she comes
Lur'd with the smell of infant blood, to dance
With *Lapland* Witches, while the labouring Moon   665
Eclipses at thir charms.   The other shape,
If shape it might be calld that shape had none
Distinguishable in member, joint or limb,
Or substance might be calld that shaddow seemd,
For each seemd either; black it stood as Night,   670
Fierce as ten Furies, terrible as Hell,
And shook a dreadful Dart; what seemd his head
The likeness of a Kingly Crown had on.
Satan was now at hand, and from his seat
The Monster moving onward came as fast,   675
With horrid strides, Hell trembled as he strode.
Th' undaunted Fiend what this might be admir'd,
Admir'd, not fear'd; God and his Son except,
Created thing naught valu'd he nor shunnd;
And with disdainful look thus first began.   680

   Whence and what art thou, execrable shape,
That dar'st, though grim and terrible, advance
Thy miscreated Front athwart my way
To yonder Gates? through them I mean to pass,
That be assur'd, without leave askt of thee: 685
Retire, or taste thy folly, and learn by proof,
Hell-born, not to contend with Spirits of Heav'n.
   To whom the Goblin full of wrauth repli'd.
Art thou that Traitor Angel, art thou hee
Who first broke peace in Heav'n and Faith, till then   690
Unbroken, and in proud rebellious Arms
Drew after him the third part of Heav'ns Sons
Conjur'd against the Highest, for which both Thou
And they outcast from God, are here condemnd
To waste Eternal days in woe and pain?   695
And reckonst thou thy self with Spirits of Heav'n,
Hell-doomd, and breath'st defiance here and scorn,
Where I reign King, and to enrage thee more,
Thy King and Lord?   Back to thy punishment,
False fugitive, and to thy speed add wings,   700
Lest with a whip of Scorpions I persue
Thy lingring, or with one stroke of this Dart
Strange horror seize thee, and pangs unfelt before.

So spake the grieslie Terror, and in shape,
So speaking and so threatning, grew tenfold   705
More dreadful and deform: on th' other side
Incenst with indignation *Satan* stood
Unterrifi'd, and like a Comet burnd,
That fires the length of *Ophiucus* huge
In th' Artic Sky, and from his horrid hair   710
Shakes Pestilence and Warr.   Each at the Head
Leveld his deadly aim; thir fatal hands
No second stroke intend, and such a frown
Each cast at th' other, as when two black Clouds
With Heav'ns Artillery fraught, come rattling on   715
Over the *Caspian*, then stand front to front
Hov'ring a space, till Winds the signal blow
To join thir dark Encounter in mid air:
So frownd the mighty Combatants, that Hell
Grew darker at thir frown, so matcht they stood;   720
For never but once more was either like
To meet so great a foe: and now great deeds
Had been achiev'd, whereof all Hell had rung,
Had not the Snakie Sorceress that sat
Fast by Hell Gate, and kept the fatal Key,   725
Ris'n, and with hideous outcry rusht between.
   O Father, what intends thy hand, she cri'd,
Against thy only Son?   What fury O Son,
Possesses thee to bend that mortal Dart
Against thy Fathers head? and knowst for whom?   730
For him who sits above and laughs the while
At thee ordaind his drudge, to execute
What e're his wrauth, which he calls Justice, bids,
His wrauth which one day will destroy ye both.
   She spake, and at her words the hellish Pest   735
Forbore, then these to her *Satan* returnd:
   So strange thy outcry, and thy words so strange
Thou interposest, that my sudden hand
Prevented spares to tell thee yet by deeds
What it intends; till first I know of thee,   740
What thing thou art, thus double-formd, and why
In this infernal Vale first met thou callst
Me Father, and that Fantasm callst my Son?
I know thee not, nor ever saw till now
Sight more detestable than him and thee.   745
   T' whom thus the Portress of Hell Gate repli'd;
Hast thou forgot me then, and do I seem
Now in thine eye so foul, once deemd so fair
In Heav'n, when at th' Assembly, and in sight
Of all the Seraphim with thee combin'd   750
In bold conspiracy against Heav'ns King,
All on a sudden miserable pain

Surpris'd thee, dim thine eyes, and dizzie swumm
In darkness, while thy head flames thick and fast
Threw forth, till on the left side op'ning wide,   755
Likest to thee in shape and count'nance bright,
Then shining heav'nly fair, a Goddess armd
Out of thy head I sprung: amazement seiz'd
All th' Host of Heav'n; back they recoild afraid
At first, and calld me *Sin*, and for a Sign   760
Portentous held me; but familiar grown,
I pleas'd, and with attractive graces won
The most averse, thee chiefly, who full oft
Thy self in me thy perfet image viewing
Becam'st enamourd, and such joy thou tookst   765
With me in secret, that my womb conceiv'd
A growing burden.   Mean while Warr arose,
And fields were fought in Heav'n; wherein remaind
(For what could else) to our Almighty Foe
Clear Victory, to our part loss and rout   770
Through all the Empyrean: down they fell
Driv'n headlong from the Pitch of Heaven, down
Into this Deep, and in the general fall
I also; at which time this powerful Key
Into my hand was giv'n, with charge to keep   775
These Gates for ever shut, which none can pass
Without my op'ning.   Pensive here I sat
Alone, but long I sat not, till my womb
Pregnant by thee, and now excessive grown
Prodigious motion felt and rueful throes.   780
At last this odious offspring whom thou seest
Thine own begotten, breaking violent way
Tore through my entrails, that with fear and pain
Distorted, all my nether shape thus grew
Transformd: but he my inbred enemie   785
Forth issu'd, brandishing his fatal Dart
Made to destroy: I fled, and cri'd out *Death*;
Hell trembl'd at the hideous Name, and sigh'd
From all her Caves, and back resounded *Death*.
I fled, but he persu'd (though more, it seems,   790
Inflam'd with lust than rage) and swifter far,
Mee overtook his mother all dismayd,
And in embraces forcible and foule
Ingendring with me, of that rape begot
These yelling Monsters that with ceaseless cry   795
Surround me, as thou sawst, hourly conceiv'd
And hourly born, with sorrow infinite
To me, for when they list into the womb
That bred them they return, and howle and gnaw
My Bowels, thir repast; then bursting forth   800
Afresh with conscious terrors vex me round,

That rest or intermission none I find.
Before mine eyes in opposition sits
Grim *Death* my Son and foe, who sets them on,
And me his Parent would full soon devour   805
For want of other prey, but that he knows
His end with mine involv'd; and knows that I
Should prove a bitter Morsel, and his bane,
Whenever that shall be; so Fate pronounc'd.
But thou O Father, I forewarn thee, shun   810
His deadly arrow; neither vainly hope
To be invulnerable in those bright Arms,
Though temperd heav'nly, for that mortal dint,
Save he who reigns above, none can resist.
   She finishd, and the suttle Fiend his lore   815
Soon learnd, now milder, and thus answerd smooth.
Dear Daughter, since thou claimst me for thy Sire,
And my fair Son here showst me, the dear pledge
Of dalliance had with thee in Heav'n, and joys
Then sweet, now sad to mention, through dire change 820
Befall'n us unforeseen, unthought of, know
I come no enemie, but to set free
From out this dark and dismal house of pain
Both him and thee, and all the heav'nly Host
Of Spirits that in our just pretences armd   825
Fell with us from on high: from them I go
This uncouth errand sole, and one for all
My self expose, with lonely steps to tread
Th' unfounded Deep, and through the void immense
To search with wandring quest a place foretold   830
Should be, and, by concurring signs, ere now
Created vast and round, a place of bliss
In the Purlieus of Heav'n, and therein plac't
A race of upstart Creatures, to supply
Perhaps our vacant room, though more remov'd,   835
Lest Heav'n surcharg'd with potent multitude
Might hap to move new broils: Be this or aught
Than this more secret now design'd, I haste
To know, and this once known, shall soon return,
And bring ye to the place where Thou and Death   840
Shall dwell at ease, and up and down unseen
Wing silently the buxom Air, imbaumd
With odours: there ye shall be fed and filld
Immeasurably, all things shall be your prey.
He ceas'd, for both seemd highly pleas'd, and Death 845
Grinnd horrible a gastly smile, to hear
His famin should be filld, and blest his mawe
Destind to that good hour: no less rejoic'd
His mother bad, and thus bespake her Sire.
   The key of this infernal Pit by due,   850

And by command of Heav'ns all-powerful King
I keep, by him forbidden to unlock
These Adamantine Gates; against all force
Death ready stands to interpose his dart,
Fearless to be o'ermatcht by living might.   855
But what ow I to his commands above
Who hates me, and hath hither thrust me down
Into this gloom of *Tartarus* profound,
To sit in hateful Office here confin'd,
Inhabitant of Heav'n, and heav'nlie-born,   860
Here is perpetual agonie and pain,
With terrors and with clamors compast round
Of mine own brood, that on my bowels feed:
Thou art my Father, thou my Author, thou
My being gav'st me; whom should I obey   865
But thee, whom follow? thou wilt bring me soon
To that new world of light and bliss, among
The Gods who live at ease, where I shall Reign
At thy right hand voluptuous, as beseems
Thy daughter and thy darling, without end.   870
    Thus saying, from her side the fatal Key,
Sad instrument of all our woe, she took;
And towards the Gate rouling her bestial train,
Forthwith the huge Porcullis high up drew,
Which but her self not all the *Stygian* Powers   875
Could once have mov'd; then in the key-hole turns
Th' intricat wards, and every Bolt and Bar
Of massie Iron or sollid Rock with ease
Unfastens: on a sudden open flie
With impetuous recoil and jarring sound   880
Th' infernal dores, and on thir hinges grate
Harsh Thunder, that the lowest bottom shook
Of *Erebus*.   She opend, but to shut
Excell'd her power; the Gates wide open stood,
That with extended wings a Bannerd Host   885
Under spred Ensigns marching might pass through
With Horse and Chariots rankt in loose array;
So wide they stood, and like a Furnace mouth
Cast forth redounding smoke and ruddy flame.
Before thir eyes in sudden view appear   890
The secrets of the hoarie Deep, a dark
Illimitable Ocean without bound,
Without dimension, where length, bredth, and highth
And time and place are lost; where eldest *Night*
And *Chaos*, Ancestors of Nature, hold   895
Eternal Anarchie, amidst the noise
Of endless Warrs, and by confusion stand.
For hot, cold, moist, and dry, four Champions fierce
Strive here for Maistrie, and to Battel bring

Thir embryon Atoms; they around the flag   900
Of each his faction, in thir several Clanns,
Light-armd or heavy, sharp, smooth, swift or slow,
Swarm populous, unnumberd as the Sands
Of *Barca* or *Cyrene*'s torrid soil,
Levied to side with warring Winds, and poise   905
Thir lighter wings. To whom these most adhere
Hee rules a moment: *Chaos* Umpire sits,
And by decision more imbroiles the fray
By which he Reigns: next him high Arbiter
Chance governs all. Into this wilde Abyss,   910
The Womb of nature and perhaps her Grave,
Of neither Sea, nor Shore, nor Air, nor Fire,
But all these in thir pregnant causes mixt
Confus'dly, and which thus must ever fight,
Unless th' Almighty Maker them ordain   915
His dark materials to create more Worlds,
Into this wild Abyss the warie Fiend
Stood on the brink of Hell and lookd a while,
Pondering his Voyage; for no narrow frith
He had to cross. Nor was his ear less peal'd   920
With noises loud and ruinous (to compare
Great things with small) than when *Bellona* storms,
With all her battering Engins bent to rase
Som Capital City; or less than if this frame
Of Heav'n were falling, and these Elements   925
In mutinie had from her Axle torn
The stedfast Earth. At last his Sail-broad Vanns
He spreads for flight, and in the surging smoke
Uplifted spurns the ground, thence many a League
As in a cloudy Chair ascending rides   930
Audacious, but that seat soon failing, meets
A vast vacuitie: all unawares
Fluttering his pennons vain plumb down he drops
Ten thousand fadom deep, and to this hour
Down had been falling, had not by ill chance   935
The strong rebuff of som tumultuous cloud
Instinct with Fire and Nitre hurried him
As many miles aloft: that furie stayd,
Quencht in a Boggie *Syrtis*, neither Sea
Nor good dry Land: nigh founderd on he fares,   940
Treading the crude consistence, half on foot,
Half flying; behoves him now both Oar and Sail.
As when a Gryfon through the Wilderness
With winged course o'er Hill or moarie Dale,
Persues the *Arimaspian*, who by stelth   945
Had from his wakeful custody purloind
The guarded Gold: So eagerly the Fiend
O'er bog or steep, through strait, rough, dense or rare,

With head, hands, wings or feet persues his way,
And swims or sinks, or wades, or creeps, or flies: 950
At length a universal hubbub wilde
Of stunning sounds and voices all confus'd
Borne through the hollow dark assaults his ear
With loudest vehemence: thither he plies,
Undaunted to meet there what ever Power   955
Or Spirit of the nethermost Abyss
Might in that noise reside, of whom to ask
Which way the nearest coast of darkness lies
Bordering on light; when straight behold the Throne
Of *Chaos*, and his dark Pavilion spred   960
Wide on the wasteful Deep; with him Enthron'd
Sat Sable-vested *Night*, eldest of things,
The consort of his Reign; and by them stood
Orcus and *Ades*, and the dreaded name
Of *Demogorgon*; *Rumor* next and *Chance*,   965
And *Tumult* and *Confusion* all imbroild,
And *Discord* with a thousand various mouths.
    T' whom *Satan* turning boldly, thus.   Ye Powers
And Spirits of this nethermost Abyss,
Chaos and *ancient Night*, I come no Spie,   970
With purpose to explore or to disturb
The secrets of your Realm, but by constraint
Wandring this darksom Desert, as my way
Lies through your spacious Empire up to light,
Alone, and without guide, half lost, I seek   975
What readiest path leads where your gloomie bounds
Confine with Heav'n; or if som other place
From your Dominion won, th' Ethereal King
Possesses lately, thither to arrive
I travel this profound, direct my course;   980
Directed, no mean recompense it brings
To your behoof, if I that Region lost,
All usurpation thence expelld, reduce
To her original darkness and your sway
(Which is my present journey) and once more   985
Erect the Standard there of *ancient Night*;
Yours be th' advantage all, mine the revenge.
    Thus *Satan*; and him thus the Anarch old
With faultring speech and visage incompos'd
Answer'd.   I know thee, stranger, who thou art,   990
That mighty leading Angel, who of late
Made head against Heav'ns King, though overthrown.
I saw and heard, for such a numerous Host
Fled not in silence through the frighted Deep
With ruin upon ruin, rout on rout,   995
Confusion worse confounded; and Heav'n Gates
Pourd out by millions her victorious Bands

Persuing.   I upon my Frontiers here
Keep residence; if all I can will serve
That little which is left so to defend,   1000
Encroacht on still through our intestin broiles
Weaking the Scepter of old *Night*: first Hell
Your dungeon stretching far and wide beneath;
Now lately Heaven and Earth, another World
Hung o'er my Realm, linkt in a golden Chain   1005
To that side Heav'n from whence your Legions fell:
If that way be your walk, you have not farr;
So much the nearer danger; goe and speed;
Havoc and spoil and ruin are my gain.

    He ceas'd; and *Satan* stayd not to reply,   1010
But glad that now his Sea should find a shore,
With fresh alacritie and force renewd
Springs upward like a Pyramid of fire
Into the wild expanse, and through the shock
Of fighting Elements, on all sides round   1015
Environd wins his way; harder beset
And more endangerd, than when *Argo* passd
Through *Bosporus* betwixt the justling Rocks:
Or when *Ulysses* on the Larbord shunnd
Charybdis, and by th' other whirlpool steerd.   1020
So he with difficulty and labour hard
Mov'd on, with difficulty and labour he;
But hee once past, soon after when Man fell,
Strange alteration! Sin and Death amain
Following his track, such was the will of Heav'n,   1025
Pav'd after him a broad and beaten way
Over the dark Abyss, whose boiling Gulf
Tamely endur'd a Bridge of wondrous length
From Hell continu'd reaching th' utmost Orb
Of this frail World; by which the Spirits perverse   1030
With easie intercourse pass to and fro
To tempt or punish mortals, except whom
God and good Angels guard by special grace.
But now at last the sacred influence
Of light appears, and from the walls of Heav'n   1035
Shoots farr into the bosom of dim Night
A glimmering dawn; here Nature first begins
Her fardest verge, and *Chaos* to retire
As from her outmost works a broken foe
With tumult less and with less hostile din,   1040
That *Satan* with less toil, and now with ease
Wafts on the calmer wave by dubious light
And like a weather-beaten Vessel holds
Gladly the Port, though Shrouds and Tackle torn;
Or in the emptier waste, resembling Air,   1045
Weighs his spred wings, at leasure to behold

Farr off th' Empyreal Heav'n, extended wide
In circuit, undetermind square or round,
With Opal Towrs and Battlements adornd
Of living Saphire, once his native Seat;   1050
And fast by hanging in a golden Chain
This pendant world, in bigness as a Starr
Of smallest Magnitude close by the Moon.
Thither full fraught with mischievous revenge,
Accurst, and in a cursed hour he hies.   1055

The End of the Second Book

BOOK III

THE ARGUMENT

God *sitting on his Throne sees Satan flying towards this World, then newly created; shews him to the Son who sat on his right hand; foretells the success of Satan in perverting mankind; clears his own Justice and Wisdom from all imputation, having created Man free and able enough to have withstood his Tempter; yet declares his purpose of grace towards him, in regard he fell not of his own malice, as did Satan, but by him seduc't. The Son of God renders praises to his Father for the manifestation of his gracious purpose towards Man; but God again declares, that Grace cannot be extended towards Man without the satisfaction of divine Justice; Man hath offended the majesty of God by aspiring to Godhead, and therefore with all his Progeny devoted to death, must dye, unless some one can be found sufficient to answer for his offence, and undergo his Punishment. The Son of God freely offers himself a Ransome for Man: the Father accepts him, ordains his incarnation, pronounces his exaltation above all Names in Heaven and Earth; commands all the Angels to adore him; they obey, and hymning to thir Harps in full Quire, celebrate the Father and the Son. Mean while Satan alights upon the bare convex of this Worlds outermost Orb; where wandring he first finds a place since call'd The Limbo of Vanity; what persons and things fly up thither; thence comes to the Gate of Heaven, describ'd ascending by stairs, and the waters above the Firmament that flow about it: His passage thence to the Orb of the Sun; he finds there Uriel the Regent of that Orb, but first changes himself into the shape of a meaner Angel; and pretending a zealous desire to behold the new Creation and Man whom God had plac't here, inquires of him the place of his habitation, and is directed; alights first on Mount* Niphates.

Hail holy Light, offspring of Heav'n first-born,
Or of th' Eternal Coeternal beam
May I express thee unblam'd? since God is Light,
And never but in unapproached Light
Dwelt from Eternitie, dwelt then in thee,   5
Bright effluence of bright essence increate.
Or hear'st thou rather pure Ethereal stream,
Whose Fountain who shall tell? before the Sun,
Before the Heav'ns thou wert, and at the voice
Of God, as with a Mantle didst invest   10
The rising world of waters dark and deep,
Won from the void and formless infinite.
Thee I revisit now with bolder wing,
Escap't the *Stygian* Pool, though long detaind
In that obscure sojourn, while in my flight   15
Through utter and through middle darkness borne
With other notes than to th' *Orphean* Lyre
I sung of *Chaos* and *Eternal Night*,
Taught by the heav'nly Muse to venture down
The dark descent, and up to reascend,   20
Though hard and rare: thee I revisit safe,

And feel thy sovran vital Lamp; but thou
Revisitst not these eyes, that roul in vain
To find thy piercing ray, and find no dawn;
So thick a drop serene hath quencht thir Orbs,   25
Or dim suffusion veild.   Yet not the more
Cease I to wander where the Muses haunt
Clear Spring, or shadie Grove, or Sunnie Hill,
Smit with the love of sacred song; but chief
Thee *Sion* and the flowrie Brooks beneath   30
That wash thy hallowd feet, and warbling flow,
Nightly I visit: nor somtimes forget
Those other two equald with me in Fate,
So were I equald with them in renown,
Blind *Thamyris* and blind *Mæonides*,   35
And *Tiresias* and *Phineus* Prophets old.
Then feed on thoughts, that voluntarie move
Harmonious numbers; as the wakeful Bird
Sings darkling, and in shadiest Covert hid
Tunes her nocturnal Note.   Thus with the Year   40
Seasons return, but not to me returns
Day, or the sweet approach of Ev'n or Morn,
Or sight of vernal bloom, or Summers Rose,
Or flocks, or herds, or human face divine;
But cloud in stead, and ever-during dark   45
Surrounds me, from the cheerful ways of men
Cut off, and for the Book of knowledge fair
Presented with a Universal blanc
Of Natures works to mee expung'd and ras'd,
And wisdom at one entrance quite shut out.   50
So much the rather thou Celestial Light
Shine inward, and the mind through all her powers
Irradiate, there plant eyes, all mist from thence
Purge and disperse, that I may see and tell
Of things invisible to mortal sight.   55
  Now had th' Almighty Father from above,
From the pure Empyrean where he sits
High Thron'd above all highth, bent down his eye,
His own works and their works at once to view:
About him all the Sanctities of Heaven   60
Stood thick as Starrs, and from his sight receiv'd
Beatitude past utterance; on his right
The radiant image of his Glory sat
His onely Son: On Earth he first beheld
Our two first Parents, yet the onely two   65
Of mankind, in the happie Garden plac't,
Reaping immortal fruits of joy and love,
Uninterrupted joy, unrivald love
In blissful solitude; he then surveyd
Hell and the Gulf between, and *Satan* there   70

Coasting the wall of Heav'n on this side Night
In the dun Air sublime, and ready now
To stoop with wearied wings and willing feet
On the bare outside of this World, that seemd
Firm land imbosomd without Firmament,   75
Uncertain which, in Ocean or in Air.
Him God beholding from his prospect high,
Wherein past, present, future he beholds,
Thus to his onely Son foreseeing spake.

Onely begotten Son, seest thou what rage   80
Transports our adversarie, whom no bounds
Prescrib'd, no barrs of Hell, nor all the chains
Heap't on him there, nor yet the main Abyss
Wide interrupt can hold; so bent he seems
On desperate revenge, that shall redound   85
Upon his own rebellious head.   And now
Through all restraint broke loose he wings his way
Not farr off Heav'n, in the Precincts of light,
Directly towards the new created World,
And Man there plac't, with purpose to assay   90
If him by force he can destroy, or worse,
By som false guile pervert; and shall pervert;
For man will hark'n to his glozing lies,
And easily transgress the sole Command,
Sole pledge of his obedience: So will fall   95
Hee and his faithless Progenie: whose fault?
Whose but his own? ingrate, he had of mee
All he could have; I made him just and right,
Sufficient to have stood, though free to fall.
Such I created all th' Ethereal Powers   100
And Spirits, both them who stood and them who faild;
Freely they stood who stood, and fell who fell.
Not free, what proof could they have giv'n sincere
Of true allegiance, constant Faith or Love,
Where only what they needs must do, appear'd,   105
Not what they would? what praise could they receive?
What pleasure I from such obedience paid,
When Will and Reason (Reason also is choice)
Useless and vain, of freedom both despoild,
Made passive both, had serv'd necessitie,   110
Not mee.   They therefore as to right belongd,
So were created, nor can justly accuse
Thir maker, or thir making, or thir Fate;
As if Predestination over-rul'd
Thir will, dispos'd by absolute Decree   115
Or high foreknowledge; they themselves decreed
Thir own revolt, not I: if I foreknew,
Foreknowledge had no influence on their fault,
Which had no less prov'd certain unforeknown.

So without least impulse or shaddow of Fate,   120
Or aught by me immutablie foreseen,
They trespass, Authors to themselves in all
Both what they judge and what they choose; for so
I formd them free, and free they must remain,
Till they enthrall themselves: I else must change   125
Thir nature, and revoke the high Decree
Unchangeable, Eternal, which ordaind
Thir freedom; they themselves ordaind thir fall.
The first sort by thir own suggestion fell
Self-tempted, self-deprav'd: Man falls deceiv'd   130
By th' other first: Man therefore shall find grace,
The other none: in Mercy and Justice both,
Through Heav'n and Earth, so shall my glorie excell,
But Mercy first and last shall brightest shine.

   Thus while God spake, ambrosial fragrance filld   135
All Heav'n, and in the blessed Spirits elect
Sense of new joy ineffable diffus'd:
Beyond compare the Son of God was seen
Most glorious, in him all his Father shon
Substantially exprest, and in his face   140
Divine compassion visibly appear'd,
Love without end, and without measure Grace,
Which uttering thus hee to his Father spake.

   O Father, gracious was that word which clos'd
Thy sovran sentence, that Man should find grace;   145
For which both Heav'n and Earth shall high extoll
Thy praises, with th' innumerable sound
Of Hymns and sacred Songs, wherewith thy Throne
Encompast shall resound thee ever blest.
For should Man finally be lost, should Man   150
Thy creature late so lov'd, thy youngest Son
Fall circumvented thus by fraud, though joind
With his own folly? that be from thee farr,
That farr be from thee, Father, who art Judge
Of all things made, and judgest only right.   155
Or shall the Adversarie thus obtain
His end, and frustrate thine, shall he fulfill
His malice, and thy goodness bring to naught,
Or proud return though to his heavier doom,
Yet with revenge accomplisht and to Hell   160
Draw after him the whole Race of mankind,
By him corrupted? or wilt thou thy self
Abolish thy Creation, and unmake,
For him, what for thy glorie thou hast made?
So should thy goodness and thy greatness both   165
Be questiond and blaspheam'd without defence.

   To whom the great Creator thus repli'd.
O Son, in whom my Soul hath chief delight,

Son of my bosom, Son who art alone
My word, my wisdom, and effectual might,   170
All hast thou spoken as my thoughts are, all
As my Eternal purpose hath decreed:
Man shall not quite be lost, but sav'd who will,
Yet not of will in him, but grace in mee
Freely voutsaf't; once more I will renew   175
His lapsed powers, though forfeit and enthralld
By sin to foul exorbitant desires;
Upheld by me, yet once more he shall stand
On even ground against his mortal foe,
By me upheld, that he may know how frail   180
His fall'n condition is, and to mee owe
All his deliv'rance, and to none but me.
Some I have chosen of peculiar grace
Elect above the rest; so is my will:
The rest shall hear me call, and oft be warnd   185
Thir sinful state, and to appease betimes
Th' incensed Deitie, while offerd grace
Invites; for I will clear thir senses dark,
What may suffice, and soften stonie hearts
To pray, repent, and bring obedience due.   190
To prayer, repentance, and obedience due,
Though but endevord with sincere intent,
Mine ear shall not be slow, mine eye not shut.
And I will place within them as a guide
My Umpire *Conscience*, whom if they will hear,   195
Light after light well us'd they shall attain,
And to the end persisting, safe arrive.
This my long sufferance and my day of grace
They who neglect and scorn, shall never taste;
But hard be hardend, blind be blinded more,   200
That they may stumble on, and deeper fall;
And none but such from mercy I exclude.
But yet all is not don; Man disobeying,
Disloyal breaks his fealtie, and sinns
Against the high Supremacie of Heav'n,   205
Affecting God-head, and so losing all,
To expiate his Treason hath naught left,
But to destruction sacred and devote,
Hee with his whole posteritie must die,
Die hee or Justice must; unless for him   210
Som other able, and as willing, pay
The rigid satisfaction, death for death.
Say Heav'nly Powers, where shall we find such love,
Which of ye will be mortal to redeem
Mans mortal crime, and just th' unjust to save,   215
Dwells in all Heaven charitie so dear?
    He askd, but all the Heav'nly Quire stood mute,

And silence was in Heav'n: on mans behalf
Patron or Intercessor none appear'd,
Much less that durst upon his own head draw　　220
The deadly forfeiture, and ransom set.
And now without redemption all mankind
Must have bin lost, adjudg'd to Death and Hell
By doom severe, had not the Son of God,
In whom the fulness dwells of love divine,　　225
His dearest mediation thus renewd.

   Father, thy word is past, man shall find grace;
And shall grace not find means, that finds her way,
The speediest of thy winged messengers,
To visit all thy creatures, and to all　　230
Comes unprevented, unimplor'd, unsought,
Happie for man, so coming; he her aid
Can never seek, once dead in sins and lost;
Attonement for himself or offering meet,
Indebted and undon, hath none to bring:　　235
Behold mee then, mee for him, life for life
I offer, on mee let thine anger fall;
Account mee man; I for his sake will leave
Thy bosom, and this glorie next to thee
Freely put off, and for him lastly die　　240
Well pleas'd, on me let Death wreck all his rage;
Under his gloomie power I shall not long
Lie vanquisht; thou hast giv'n me to possess
Life in my self for ever, by thee I live,
Though now to Death I yield, and am his due　　245
All that of me can die, yet that debt paid,
Thou wilt not leave me in the loathsom grave
His prey, nor suffer my unspotted Soul
For ever with corruption there to dwell;
But I shall rise Victorious, and subdue　　250
My Vanquisher, spoild of his vanted spoil;
Death his deaths wound shall then receive, and stoop
Inglorious, of his mortal sting disarmd.
I through the ample Air in Triumph high
Shall lead Hell Captive maugre Hell, and show　　255
The Powers of darkness bound.　Thou at the sight
Pleas'd, out of Heaven shalt look down and smile,
While by thee rais'd I ruin all my Foes,
Death last, and with his Carcass glut the Grave:
Then with the multitude of my redeemd　　260
Shall enter Heaven long absent, and return,
Father, to see thy face, wherein no cloud
Of anger shall remain, but peace assur'd,
And reconcilement; wrauth shall be no more
Thenceforth, but in thy presence Joy entire.　　265
   His words here ended, but his meek aspect

Silent yet spake, and breath'd immortal love
To mortal men, above which only shon
Filial obedience: as a sacrifice
Glad to be offerd, he attends the will   270
Of his great Father.   Admiration seiz'd
All Heav'n, what this might mean, and whither tend
Wondring; but soon th' Almighty thus repli'd:
    O thou in Heav'n and Earth the only peace
Found out for mankind under wrauth, O thou   275
My sole complacence! well thou knowst how dear
To me are all my works, nor Man the least
Though last created, that for him I spare
Thee from my bosom and right hand, to save,
By losing thee a while, the whole Race lost.   280
Thou therefore whom thou only canst redeem,
Thir Nature also to thy Nature join;
And be thy self Man among men on Earth,
Made flesh, when time shall be, of Virgin seed,
By wondrous birth: Be thou in *Adams* room   285
The Head of all mankind, though *Adams* Son.
As in him perish all men, so in thee
As from a second root shall be restor'd,
As many as are restor'd, without thee none.
His crime makes guiltie all his Sons, thy merit   290
Imputed shall absolve them who renounce
Thir own both righteous and unrighteous deeds,
And live in thee transplanted, and from thee
Receive new life.   So Man, as is most just,
Shall satisfie for Man, be judg'd and die,   295
And dying rise, and rising with him raise
His Brethren, ransomd with his own dear life.
So Heav'nly love shall outdoo Hellish hate,
Giving to death, and dying to redeem,
So dearly to redeem what Hellish hate   300
So easily destroyd, and still destroyes
In those who, when they may, accept not grace.
Nor shalt thou by descending to assume
Mans Nature, lessen or degrade thine own.
Because thou hast, though Thron'd in highest bliss   305
Equal to God, and equally enjoying
God-like fruition, quitted all to save
A World from utter loss, and hast been found
By Merit more than Birthright Son of God,
Found worthiest to be so by being Good,   310
Farr more than Great or High; because in thee
Love hath abounded more than Glory abounds,
Therefore thy Humiliation shall exalt
With thee thy Manhood also to this Throne;
Here shalt thou sit incarnate, here shalt Reign   315

Both God and Man, Son both of God and Man,
Anointed universal King; all Power
I give thee, reign for ever, and assume
Thy Merits; under thee as Head Supream
Thrones, Princedoms, Powers, Dominions I reduce: 320
All knees to thee shall bow, of them that bide
In Heav'n, or Earth, or under Earth in Hell;
When thou attended gloriously from Heav'n
Shalt in the Skie appear, and from thee send
The summoning Arch-Angels to proclaim   325
Thy dread Tribunal: forthwith from all Winds
The living, and forthwith the cited dead
Of all past Ages to the general Doom
Shall hasten, such a peal shall rouse thir sleep.
Then all thy Saints assembl'd, thou shalt judge   330
Bad men and Angels, they arraignd shall sink
Beneath thy Sentence; Hell, her numbers full,
Thenceforth shall be for ever shut.   Mean while
The World shall burn, and from her ashes spring
New Heav'n and Earth, wherein the just shall dwell   335
And after all thir tribulations long
See golden days, fruitful of golden deeds,
With Joy and Love triumphing, and fair Truth.
Then thou thy regal Scepter shalt lay by,
For regal Scepter then no more shall need,   340
God shall be All in All.   But all ye Gods
Adore him, who to compass all this dies,
Adore the Son, and honour him as mee.
   No sooner had th' Almighty ceas't, but all
The multitude of Angels with a shout   345
Loud as from numbers without number, sweet
As from blest voices, uttering joy, Heav'n rung
With Jubilee, and loud Hosannas filld
Th' eternal Regions: lowly reverent
Towards either Throne they bow, and to the ground   350
With solemn adoration down they cast
Thir Crowns inwove with Amarant and Gold,
Immortal Amarant, a Flowr which once
In Paradise, fast by the Tree of Life
Began to bloom, but soon for mans offence   355
To Heav'n remov'd where first it grew, there grows,
And flowrs aloft shading the Fount of Life,
And where the river of Bliss through midst of Heav'n
Rouls o'er *Elisian* Flowrs her Amber stream;
With these that never fade the Spirits Elect   360
Binde thir resplendent locks inwreath'd with beams,
Now in loose Garlands thick thrown off, the bright
Pavement that like a Sea of Jasper shon
Impurpl'd with Celestial Roses smil'd.

Then Crownd again thir golden Harps they took,   365
Harps ever tun'd, that glittering by thir side
Like Quivers hung, and with Præamble sweet
Of charming symphonie they introduce
Thir sacred Song, and waken raptures high;
No voice exempt, no voice but well could join   370
Melodious part, such concord is in Heav'n.
　　Thee Father first they sung Omnipotent,
Immutable, Immortal, Infinite,
Eternal King; thee Author of all being,
Fountain of Light, thy self invisible   375
Amidst the glorious brightness where thou sitst
Thron'd inaccessible, but when thou shad'st
The full blaze of thy beams, and through a cloud
Drawn round about thee like a radiant Shrine,
Dark with excessive bright thy skirts appear,   380
Yet dazle Heav'n, that brightest Seraphim
Approach not, but with both wings veil thir eyes.
Thee next they sang of all Creation first,
Begotten Son, Divine Similitude,
In whose conspicuous count'nance, without cloud   385
Made visible, th' Almighty Father shines,
Whom else no Creature can behold; on thee
Imprest th' effulgence of his Glorie abides,
Transfus'd on thee his ample Spirit rests.
Hee heav'n of Heavens and all the Powers therein   390
By thee created, and by thee threw down
Th' aspiring Dominations: thou that day
Thy Fathers dreadful Thunder didst not spare,
Nor stop thy flaming Chariot wheels, that shook
Heav'ns everlasting Frame, while o'er the necks   395
Thou drov'st of warring Angels disarrayd.
Back from persuit thy Powers with loud acclaime
Thee only extolld, Son of thy Fathers might,
To execute fierce vengeance on his foes,
Not so on Man; him through their malice fall'n,   400
Father of Mercie and Grace, thou didst not doom
So strictly, but much more to pittie encline:
No sooner did thy dear and onely Son
Perceive thee purpos'd not to doom frail Man
So strictly, but much more to pittie enclin'd,   405
He, to appease thy wrauth, and end the strife
Of Mercy and Justice in thy face discernd,
Regardless of the Bliss wherein he sat
Second to thee, offerd himself to die
For mans offence.　O unexampl'd love,   410
Love no where to be found less than Divine!
Hail Son of God, Saviour of Men, thy Name
Shall be the copious matter of my Song

Henceforth, and never shall my Harp thy praise
Forget, nor from thy Fathers praise disjoin.   415
    Thus they in Heav'n, above the starry Sphear,
Thir happie hours in joy and hymning spent.
Mean while upon the firm opacous Globe
Of this round World, whose first convex divides
The luminous inferior Orbs, enclos'd   420
From *Chaos* and th' inroad of Darkness old,
Satan alighted walks: a Globe farr off
It seemd, now seems a boundless Continent
Dark, waste, and wild, under the frown of Night
Starless expos'd, and ever-threatning storms   425
Of *Chaos* blustring round, inclement skie;
Save on that side which from the wall of Heav'n
Though distant farr som small reflection gains
Of glimmering air less vext with tempest loud:
Here walkd the Fiend at large in spacious field.   430
As when a Vultur on *Imaus* bred,
Whose snowie ridge the roving *Tartar* bounds,
Dislodging from a Region scarce of prey
To gorge the flesh of Lambs or yeanling Kids
On Hills where Flocks are fed, flies toward the Springs
Of *Ganges* or *Hydaspes*, *Indian* streams;   436
But in his way lights on the barren Plains
Of *Sericana*, where *Chineses* drive
With Sails and Wind thir canie Waggons light:
So on this windie Sea of Land, the Fiend   440
Walkd up and down alone bent on his prey,
Alone, for other Creature in this place
Living or liveless to be found was none,
None yet, but store hereafter from the earth
Up hither like Aëreal vapours flew   445
Of all things transitorie and vain, when Sin
With vanity had filld the works of men:
Both all things vain, and all who in vain things
Built thir fond hopes of Glorie or lasting fame,
Or happiness in this or th' other life;   450
All who have thir reward on Earth, the fruits
Of painful Superstition and blind Zeal,
Naught seeking but the praise of men, here find
Fit retribution, emptie as thir deeds;
All th' unaccomplisht works of Natures hand,   455
Abortive, monstrous or unkindly mixt,
Dissolv'd on earth, fleet hither, and in vain,
Till final dissolution, wander here,
Not in the neighbouring Moon, as some have dream'd;
Those argent Fields more likely habitants,   460
Translated Saints, or middle Spirits hold
Betwixt th' Angelical and Human kind:

Hither of ill-joind Sons and Daughters born
First from the ancient World those Giants came
With many a vain exploit, though then renownd: 465
The builders next of *Babel* on the Plain
Of *Sennaär*, and still with vain designe
New *Babels*, had they wherewithall, would build:
Others came single; he who to be deemd
A God, leap'd fondly into *Ætna* flames   470
Empedocles, and hee who to enjoy
Plato's Elysium, leap'd into the Sea,
Cleombrotus, and many more too long,
Embryoes and Idiots, Eremits and Friers
White, Black and Grey, with all thir trumperie.   475
Here Pilgrims roam, that strayd so farr to seek
In *Golgotha* him dead, who lives in Heav'n;
And they who to be sure of Paradise
Dying put on the weeds of *Dominic*,
Or in *Franciscan* think to pass disguis'd;   480
They pass the Planets sev'n, and pass the fixt,
And that Crystallin Sphear whose ballance weighs
The Trepidation talkt, and that first mov'd;
And now Saint *Peter* at Heav'ns Wicket seems
To wait them with his Keys, and now at foot   485
Of Heav'ns ascent they lift thir Feet, when loe
A violent cross wind from either Coast
Blows them transverse ten thousand Leagues awry
Into the devious Air; then might ye see
Cowls, Hoods and Habits with thir wearers tost   490
And flutterd into Raggs, then Reliques, Beads,
Indulgences, Dispenses, Pardons, Bulls,
The sport of Winds: all these upwhirld aloft
Fly ore the backside of the World farr off
Into a *Limbo* large and broad, since calld   495
The Paradise of Fools, to few unknown
Long after, now unpeopl'd and untrod;
All this dark Globe the Fiend found as he passd,
And long he wanderd, till at last a gleam
Of dawning light turnd thither-ward in haste   500
His traveld steps; farr distant he descries
Ascending by degrees magnificent
Up to the wall of Heav'n a Structure high,
At top whereof, but farr more rich appear'd
The work as of a Kingly Palace Gate   505
With Frontispice of Diamond and Gold
Imbellisht, thick with sparkling orient Gemms
The Portal shon, inimitable on Earth
By Model, or by shading Pencil drawn.
The Stairs were such as whereon *Jacob* saw   510
Angels ascending and descending, bands

Of Guardians bright, when he from *Esau* fled
To *Padan-Aram* in the field of *Luz*,
Dreaming by night under the open Skie,
And waking cri'd, This is the Gate of Heav'n.   515
Each Stair mysteriously was meant, nor stood
There always, but drawn up to Heav'n somtimes
Viewless, and underneath a bright Sea flowd
Of Jasper, or of liquid Pearl, whereon
Who after came from Earth, sailing arriv'd,   520
Wafted by Angels, or flew o'er the Lake
Rapt in a Chariot drawn by fiery Steeds.
The Stairs were then let down, whether to dare
The Fiend by easie ascent, or aggravate
His sad exclusion from the dores of Bliss.   525
Direct against which opend from beneath,
Just o'er the blissful seat of Paradise,
A passage down to th' Earth, a passage wide,
Wider by farr than that of after-times
Over Mount *Sion* and, though that were large,   530
Over the *Promis'd Land* to God so dear,
By which, to visit oft those happy Tribes,
On high behests his Angels to and fro
Passd frequent, and his eye with choice regard
From *Paneas* the fount of *Jordans* flood   535
To *Bëersaba*, where the *Holy Land*
Borders on *Egypt* and th'*Arabian* shore;
So wide the op'ning seemd, where bounds were set
To darkness, such as bound the Ocean wave.
Satan from hence now on the lower stair   540
That scal'd by steps of Gold to Heav'n Gate
Looks down with wonder at the sudden view
Of all this World at once.   As when a Scout
Through dark and desert ways with peril gone
All night; at last by break of cheerful dawn   545
Obtains the brow of some high-climbing Hill,
Which to his eye discovers unaware
The goodly prospect of som forren land
First-seen, or some renownd Metropolis
With glistering Spires and Pinnacles adornd,   550
Which now the Rising Sun gilds with his beams.
Such wonder seiz'd, though after Heaven seen,
The Spirit malign, but much more envy seiz'd
At sight of all this World beheld so fair.
Round he surveys, and well might, where he stood   555
So high above the circling Canopie
Of Nights extended shade; from Eastern Point
Of *Libra* to the fleecie Starr that bears
Andromeda farr off *Atlantic* Seas
Beyond th' *Horizon*; then from Pole to Pole   560

He views in bredth, and without longer pause
Down right into the Worlds first Region throws
His flight precipitant, and windes with ease
Through the pure marble Air his oblique way
Amongst innumerable Starrs, that shon   565
Stars distant, but nigh hand seemd other Worlds,
Or other Worlds they seemd or happy Iles,
Like those *Hesperian* Gardens fam'd of old,
Fortunat Fields, and Groves and flowrie Vales,
Thrice happy Iles, but who dwelt happy there   570
He stayd not to enquire: above them all
The golden Sun in splendor likest Heaven
Allur'd his eye: Thither his course he bends
Through the calm Firmament; but up or down,
By center or eccentric, hard to tell,   575
Or Longitude, where the great Luminarie
Aloof the vulgar Constellations thick,
That from his Lordly eye keep distance due,
Dispenses Light from farr; they as they move
Thir Starry dance in numbers that compute   580
Days, months, and years, towards his all-cheering Lamp
Turn swift thir various motions, or are turnd
By his Magnetic beam, that gently warms
The Universe, and to each inward part
With gentle penetration, though unseen,   585
Shoots invisible vertue ev'n to the Deep:
So wondrously was set his Station bright.
There lands the Fiend, a spot like which perhaps
Astronomer in the Suns lucent Orbe
Through his glaz'd Optic Tube yet never saw.   590
The place he found beyond expression bright,
Compar'd with aught on Earth, Mettal or Stone;
Not all parts like, but all alike informd
With radiant light, as glowing Iron with fire;
If mettal, part seemd Gold, part Silver clear;   595
If stone, Carbuncle most or Chrysolite.
Rubie or Topaz, to the Twelve that shon
In *Aarons* Brest-plate, and a stone besides
Imagind rather oft than elsewhere seen,
That stone, or like to that which here below   600
Philosophers in vain so long have sought,
In vain, though by thir powerful Art they binde
Volatil *Hermes*, and call up unbound
In various shapes old *Proteus* from the Sea,
Draind through a Limbec to his Native form.   605
What wonder then if fields and regions here
Breathe forth *Elixir* pure, and Rivers run

586 ev'n] even *Edd. 1, 2*   592 Mettal *Tickel*] Medal *Edd. 1-6*

Potable Gold, when with one vertuous touch
Th' Arch-chimic Sun so farr from us remote
Produces with Terrestrial Humor mixt   610
Here in the dark so many precious things
Of colour glorious and effect so rare?
Here matter new to gaze the Devil met
Undazl'd, farr and wide his eye commands,
For sight no obstacle found here, nor shade,   615
But all Sun-shine, as when his Beams at Noon
Culminate from th' Æquator, as they now
Shot upward still direct, whence no way round
Shaddow from body opaque can fall, and th' Air,
No where so clear, sharpend his visual ray   620
To objects distant farr, whereby he soon
Saw within kenn a glorious Angel stand,
The same whom John saw also in the Sun:
His back was turnd, but not his brightness hid;
Of beaming sunnie Rays, a golden tiar   625
Circl'd his Head, nor less his Locks behind
Illustrious on his Shoulders fledge with wings
Lay waving round; on som great charge imployd
He seemd, or fixt in cogitation deep.
Glad was the Spirit impure; as now in hope   630
To find who might direct his wandring flight
To Paradise the happie seat of Man,
His journeys end and our beginning woe.
But first he casts to change his proper shape,
Which else might work him danger or delay: 635
And now a stripling Cherube he appears,
Not of the prime, yet such as in his face
Youth smil'd Celestial, and to every Limb
Sutable grace diffus'd, so well he feignd;
Under a Coronet his flowing hair   640
In curls on either cheek playd, wings he wore
Of many a coulour'd plume sprinkl'd with Gold,
His habit fit for speed succinct, and held
Before his decent steps a Silver wand.
He drew not nigh unheard; the Angel bright,   645
Ere he drew nigh, his radiant visage turnd,
Admonisht by his ear, and straight was known
Th' Arch-Angel Uriel, one of the sev'n
Who in Gods presence, nearest to his Throne
Stand ready at command, and are his Eyes   650
That run through all the Heav'ns, or down to th' Earth
Bear his swift errands over moist and dry,
O'er Sea and Land; him Satan thus accosts.
　　Uriel, for thou of those sev'n Spirits that stand
In sight of Gods high Throne, gloriously bright,   655
The first art wont his great authentic will

Interpreter through highest Heav'n to bring,
Where all his Sons thy Embassie attend;
And here art likeliest by supream decree
Like honour to obtain, and as his Eye   660
To visit oft this new Creation round;
Unspeakable desire to see, and know
All these his wondrous works, but chiefly **Man**,
His chief delight and favour, him for whom
All these his works so wondrous he ordaind,   665
Hath brought me from the Quires of Cherubim
Alone thus wandring. Brightest Seraph tell
In which of all these shining Orbes hath Man
His fixed seat, or fixed seat hath none,
But all these shining Orbes his choice to dwell;   670
That I may find him, and with secret gaze
Or open admiration him behold
On whom the great Creator hath bestowd
Worlds, and on whom hath all these graces **pourd**;
That both in him and all things, as is meet,   675
The Universal Maker we may praise;
Who justly hath driv'n out his Rebel Foes
To deepest Hell, and to repair that loss
Created this new happie Race of Men
To serve him better: wise are all his ways.   680
   So spake the false dissembler unperceiv'd;
For neither Man nor Angel can discern
Hypocrisie, the onely evil that walks
Invisible, except to God alone,
By his permissive will, through Heav'n and Earth: 685
And oft though wisdom wake, suspicion sleeps
At wisdoms Gate, and to simplicitie
Resigns her charge, while goodness thinks no ill
Where no ill seems: Which now for once beguil'd
Uriel, though Regent of the Sun, and held   690
The sharpest sighted Spirit of all in Heav'n;
Who to the fraudulent Impostor foule
In his uprightness answer thus returnd.
Faire Angel, thy desire which tends to know
The works of God, thereby to glorifie   695
The great Work-Maister, leads to no excess
That reaches blame, but rather merits praise
The more it seems excess, that led thee hither
From thy Empyreal Mansion thus alone,
To witness with thine eyes what some perhaps   700
Contented with report heare onely in Heav'n:
For wonderful indeed are all his works,
Pleasant to know, and worthiest to be all
Had in remembrance always with delight;
But what created mind can comprehend   705

Thir number, or the wisdom infinite
That brought them forth, but hid thir causes deep.
I saw when at his Word the formless Mass,
This worlds material mould, came to a heap:
Confusion heard his voice, and wilde uproar   710
Stood rul'd, stood vast infinitude confin'd;
Till at his second bidding darkness fled,
Light shon, and order from disorder sprung:
Swift to thir several Quarters hasted then
The cumbrous Elements, Earth, Flood, Air, Fire,   715
And this Ethereal quintessence of Heav'n
Flew upward, spirited with various forms,
That rould orbicular, and turnd to Starrs
Numberless, as thou seest, and how they move;
Each had his place appointed, each his course,   720
The rest in circuit walles this Universe.
Look downward on that Globe whose hither side
With light from hence, though but reflected, shines;
That place is Earth the seat of Man, that light
His day, which else as th' other Hemisphere   725
Night would invade, but there the neighbouring Moon
(So call that opposite fair Starr) her aide
Timely interposes, and her monthly round
Still ending, still renewing through mid Heav'n,
With borrowd light her countenance triform   730
Hence fills and empties to enlighten the Earth,
And in her pale dominion checks the night.
That spot to which I point is *Paradise*,
Adams abode, those loftie shades his Bowr.
Thy way thou canst not miss, me mine requires.   735
    Thus said, he turnd, and *Satan* bowing low,
As to superior Spirits is wont in Heav'n,
Where honour due and reverence none neglects,
Took leave, and toward the coast of Earth beneath,
Down from th' Ecliptic, sped with hop't success,   740
Throws his steep flight in many an Aerie wheel,
Nor stayd, till on *Niphates* top he lights.

731 the Earth *Ed. 1 state 2*] th' Earth *Ed. 1 state 1, Ed. 2*

The End of the Third Book

BOOK IV

THE ARGUMENT

Satan *now in prospect of Eden, and nigh the place where he must now attempt the bold enterprize which he undertook alone against God and Man, falls into many doubts with himself, and many passions, fear, envy, and despare; but at length confirms himself in evil, journeys on to Paradise, whose outward prospect and scituation is described, overleaps the bounds, sits in the shape of a Cormorant on the Tree of life, as highest in the Garden to look about him. The Garden describ'd; Satans first sight of Adam and Eve; his wonder at thir excellent form and happy state, but with resolution to work thir fall; overhears thir discourse, thence gathers that the Tree of knowledge was forbidden them to eat of, under penalty of death; and thereon intends to found his temptation, by seducing them to transgress: then leaves them a while, to know further of thir state by some other means. Mean while Uriel descending on a Sun-beam warns Gabriel, who had in charge the Gate of Paradise, that some evil spirit had escap'd the Deep, and past at Noon by his Sphere in the shape of a good Angel down to Paradise, discovered after by his furious gestures in the Mount. Gabriel promises to find him ere morning. Night coming on, Adam and Eve discourse of going to thir rest: thir Bower describ'd; thir Evening worship. Gabriel drawing forth his Bands of Night-watch to walk the round of Paradise, appoints two strong Angels to Adams Bower, least the evill spirit should be there doing some harm to Adam or Eve sleeping; there they find him at the ear of Eve, tempting her in a dream, and bring him, though unwilling, to Gabriel; by whom question'd, he scornfully answers, prepares resistance, but hinder'd by a Sign from Heaven, flies out of Paradise.*

O for that warning voice, which he who saw
Th' *Apocalyps*, heard cry in Heaven aloud,
Then when the Dragon, put to second rout,
Came furious down to be reveng'd on men,
Woe to th' inhabitants on Earth! that now,   5
While time was, our first Parents had bin warnd
The coming of thir secret foe, and scap't
Haply so scap't his mortal snare; for now
Satan, now first inflam'd with rage, came down,
The Tempter ere th' Accuser of Mankind   10
To wreck on innocent frail man his loss
Of that first Battel, and his flight to Hell:
Yet not rejoicing in his speed, though bold,
Far off and fearless, nor with cause to boast,
Begins his dire attempt, which nigh the birth   15
Now rouling, boils in his tumultuous brest,
And like a devilish Engin back recoils
Upon himself; horror and doubt distract
His troubl'd thoughts, and from the bottom stirr
The Hell within him, for within him Hell   20

216

He brings, and round about him, nor from Hell
One step no more than from himself can fly
By change of place: Now conscience wakes despair
That slumberd, wakes the bitter memorie
Of what he was, what is, and what must be　　　25
Worse; of worse deeds worse sufferings must ensue.
Sometimes towards *Eden* which now in his view
Lay pleasant, his griev'd look he fixes sad,
Sometimes towards Heav'n and the full-blazing Sun,
Which now sat high in his Meridian Towr:　　　30
Then much revolving, thus in sighs began.
　　O thou that with surpassing Glory crownd,
Lookst from thy sole Dominion like the God
Of this new World; at whose sight all the Starrs
Hide thir diminisht heads; to thee I call,　　　35
But with no friendly voice, and add thy name
O Sun, to tell thee how I hate thy beams
That bring to my remembrance from what state
I fell, how glorious once above thy Sphear;
Till Pride and worse Ambition threw me down,　　　40
Warring in Heav'n against Heav'ns matchless King:
Ah wherefore! he deserv'd no such return
From me, whom he created what I was
In that bright eminence, and with his good
Upbraided none; nor was his service hard.　　　45
What could be less than to afford him praise,
The easiest recompense, and pay him thanks,
How due! yet all his good prov'd ill in me,
And wrought but malice; lifted up so high
I sdeind subjection, and thought one step higher　　　50
Would set me highest, and in a moment quit
The debt immense of endless gratitude,
So burthensome still paying, still to ow;
Forgetful what from him I still receiv'd,
And understood not that a grateful mind　　　55
By owing owes not, but still pays, at once
Indebted and discharg'd; what burden then?
O had his powerful Destiny ordaind
Me som inferior Angel, I had stood
Then happie; no unbounded hope had rais'd　　　60
Ambition.　Yet why not? som other Power
As great might have aspir'd, and me though mean
Drawn to his part; but other Powers as great
Fell not, but stand unshaken, from within
Or from without, to all temptations armd.　　　65
Hadst thou the same free Will and Power to stand?
Thou hadst: whom hast thou then or what to accuse,
But Heav'ns free Love dealt equally to all?
Be then his Love accurst, since love or hate,

To me alike, it deals eternal woe.   70
Nay curst be thou; since against his thy will
Chose freely what it now so justly rues.
Me miserable! which way shall I flie
Infinite wrauth, and infinite despair?
Which way I flie is Hell; my self am Hell;   75
And in the lowest deep a lower deep
Still threatning to devour me opens wide,
To which the Hell I suffer seems a Heav'n.
O then at last relent: is there no place
Left for Repentance, none for Pardon left?   80
None left but by submission; and that word
Disdain forbids me, and my dread of shame
Among the Spirits beneath, whom I seduc'd
With other promises and other vaunts
Than to submit, boasting I could subdue   85
Th' Omnipotent.   Ay me, they little know
How dearly I abide that boast so vain,
Under what torments inwardly I groan:
While they adore me on the Throne of Hell,
With Diadem and Scepter high advanc't   90
The lower still I fall, onely Supream
In miserie; such joy Ambition finds.
But say I could repent and could obtaine
By Act of Grace my former state; how soon
Would highth recall high thoughts, how soon unsay   95
What feignd submission swore: ease would recant
Vows made in pain, as violent and void.
For never can true reconcilement grow
Where wounds of deadly hate have pierc't so deep:
Which would but lead me to a worse relapse,   100
And heavier fall: so should I purchase deare
Short intermission bought with double smart.
This knows my punisher; therefore as farr
From granting hee, as I from begging peace:
All hope excluded thus, behold in stead   105
Of us out-cast, exil'd, his new delight,
Mankind created, and for him this World.
So farewel Hope, and with Hope farewel Fear,
Farewel Remorse: all Good to me is lost;
Evil be thou my Good; by thee at least   110
Divided Empire with Heav'ns King I hold
By thee, and more than half perhaps will reign;
As Man ere long, and this new World shall know.
    Thus while he spake, each passion dimmd his face
Thrice chang'd with pale, ire, envie and despair,   115
Which marrd his borrowd visage, and betrayd
Him counterfet, if any eye beheld.
For heav'nly mindes from such distempers foule

Are ever clear.   Whereof hee soon aware,
Each perturbation smooth'd with outward calm,   120
Artificer of fraud; and was the first
That practis'd falsehood under saintly shew,
Deep malice to conceal, coucht with revenge:
Yet not anough had practis'd to deceive
Uriel once warnd; whose eye persu'd him down   125
The way he went, and on th' *Assyrian* mount
Saw him disfigurd, more than could befall
Spirit of happie sort: his gestures fierce
He markd and mad demeanour, then alone,
As he suppos'd, all unobserv'd, unseen.   130
So on he fares, and to the border comes
Of *Eden*, where delicious Paradise,
Now nearer, Crowns with her enclosure green,
As with a rural mound the champain head
Of a steep wilderness, whose hairie sides   135
With thicket overgrown, grottesque and wild,
Access deni'd; and over head up grew
Insuperable highth of loftiest shade,
Cedar and Pine and Firr and branching Palm,
A Silvan Scene, and as the ranks ascend   140
Shade above shade, a woodie Theatre
Of stateliest view.   Yet higher than thir tops
The verdurous wall of Paradise up sprung:
Which to our general Sire gave prospect large
Into his nether Empire neighbouring round.   145
And higher than that Wall a circling row
Of goodliest Trees loaden with fairest Fruit,
Blossoms and Fruits at once of golden hue
Appear'd, with gay enameld colours mixt:
On which the Sun more glad impressd his beams   150
Than in fair Ev'ning Cloud, or humid Bow,
When God hath showrd the earth; so lovely seemd
That Lantskip: And of pure now purer aire
Meets his approach, and to the heart inspires
Vernal delight and joy, able to drive   155
All sadness but despair: now gentle gales
Fanning thir odoriferous wings dispense
Native perfumes, and whisper whence they stole
Those baumie spoils.   As when to them who sail
Beyond the *Cape of Hope*, and now are past   160
Mozambic, off at Sea North-East winds blow
Sabean Odours from the spicie shore
Of *Arabie* the blest, with such delay
Well pleas'd they slack thir course, and many a League
Cheerd with the grateful smell old Ocean smiles.   165
So entertaind those odorous sweets the Fiend
Who came thir bane, though with them better pleas'd

Than *Asmodeus* with the fishie fume,
That drove him, though enamourd, from the Spouse
Of *Tobits* Son, and with a vengeance sent   170
From *Media* post to *Egypt*, there fast bound.
   Now to th' ascent of that steep savage Hill
Satan had journied on, pensive and slow;
But further way found none, so thick entwin'd,
As one continu'd brake, the undergrowth   175
Of shrubs and tangling bushes had perplext
All path of Man or Beast that passd that way: ·
One Gate there only was, and that lookd East
On th' other side: which when th' Arch-fellon saw
Due entrance he disdaind, and in contempt   180
At one slight bound high overleap'd all bound
Of Hill or highest Wall, and sheer within
Lights on his feet.   As when a prowling Wolf,
Whom hunger drives to seek new haunt for prey,
Watching where Shepherds pen thir Flocks at Eve   185
In hurdl'd Cotes amid the field secure,
Leaps ore the fence with ease into the Fold:
Or as a Thief bent to unhoard the cash
Of som rich Burgher, whose substantial dores,
Cross-barrd and bolted fast, fear no assault,   190
In at the window climbs, or ore the tiles;
So clomb this first grand Thief into Gods Fold:
So since into his Church lewd Hirelings climb.
Thence up he flew, and on the Tree of Life,
The middle Tree and highest there that grew,   195
Sat like a Cormorant; yet not true Life
Thereby regaind, but sat devising Death
To them who liv'd; nor on the vertue thought
Of that life-giving Plant, but only us'd
For prospect, what well us'd had bin the pledge   200
Of immortalitie.   So little knows
Any, but God alone, to value right
The good before him, but perverts best things
To worst abuse, or to thir meanest use.
Beneath him with new wonder now he views   205
To all delight of human sense expos'd
In narrow room Natures whole wealth, yea more,
A Heav'n on Earth: for blissful Paradise
Of God the Garden was, by him in th' East
Of *Eden* planted; *Eden* stretchd her Line   210
From *Auran* Eastward to the Royal Towrs
Of Great *Seleucia*, built by *Grecian* Kings,
Or where the Sons of *Eden* long before
Dwelt in *Telassar*: in this pleasant soile
His farr more pleasant Garden God ordaind;   215
Out of the fertil ground he caus'd to grow

All Trees of noblest kind for sight, smell, taste;
And all amid them stood the Tree of Life,
High eminent, blooming Ambrosial Fruit
Of vegetable Gold; and next to Life   220
Our Death the Tree of Knowledge grew fast by,
Knowledge of Good bought dear by knowing ill.
Southward through *Eden* went a River large,
Nor chang'd his course, but through the shaggie hill
Passd underneath ingulft, for God had thrown   225
That Mountain as his Garden mould high rais'd
Upon the rapid current, which through veins
Of porous Earth with kindly thirst up drawn,
Rose a fresh Fountain, and with many a rill
Waterd the Garden; thence united fell   230
Down the steep glade, and met the nether Flood,
Which from his darksom passage now appears,
And now divided into four main Streams
Runs diverse, wandring many a famous Realm
And Country whereof here needs no account,   235
But rather to tell how, if Art could tell,
How from that Saphire Fount the crisped Brooks,
Rouling on Orient Pearl and sands of Gold,
With mazie error under pendant shades
Ran Nectar, visiting each plant, and fed   240
Flowrs worthy of Paradise which not nice Art
In Beds and curious Knots, but Nature boon
Pourd forth profuse on Hill and Dale and Plain,
Both where the morning Sun first warmly smote
The open field, and where the unpierc't shade   245
Imbrownd the noontide Bowrs: Thus was this place,
A happy rural seat of various view;
Groves whose rich Trees wept odorous Gumms and Baum,
Others whose fruit burnish't with Golden Rinde
Hung amiable, *Hesperian* Fables true,   250
If true, here only, and of delicious taste:
Betwixt them Lawns or level Downs, and Flocks
Grazing the tender herb, were interpos'd,
Or palmie hillock, or the flowrie lap
Of som irriguous Valley spred her store,   255
Flowrs of all hue, and without Thorn the Rose:
Another side, umbrageous Grots and Caves
Of cool recess, ore which the mantling Vine
Lays forth her purple Grape, and gently creeps
Luxuriant; mean while murmuring waters fall   260
Down the slope hills, disperst or in a Lake,
That to the fringed Bank with Myrtle crownd
Her crystal mirror holds, unite thir streams.
The Birds thir quire apply; airs, vernal airs,
Breathing the smell of field and grove, attune   265

The trembling leaves, while Universal *Pan*
Knit with the *Graces* and the *Hours* in dance
Led on th' Eternal Spring.   Not that fair field
Of *Enna*, where *Proserpin* gathring flowrs
Her self a fairer Flowre by gloomie *Dis*   270
Was gatherd, which cost *Ceres* all that pain
To seek her through the world; nor that sweet Grove
Of *Daphne* by *Orontes*, and th' inspir'd
Castalian Spring, might with this Paradise
Of *Eden* strive; nor that *Nyseian* Ile   275
Girt with the River *Triton*, where old *Cham*,
Whom Gentiles *Ammon* call and *Libyan Jove*,
Hid *Amalthea* and her Florid Son
Young *Bacchus* from his Stepdame *Rhea's* eye;
Nor where *Abassin* Kings thir issue Guard,   280
Mount *Amara*, though this by some suppos'd
True Paradise under the *Ethiop* Line
By *Nilus* head, enclos'd with shining Rock,
A whole days journey high, but wide remote
From this *Assyrian* Garden, where the Fiend   285
Saw undelighted all delight, all kind
Of living Creatures new to sight and strange:
Two of far nobler shape erect and tall,
Godlike erect, with native Honour clad
In naked Majestie seemd Lords of all,   290
And worthie seemd, for in thir looks Divine
The image of thir glorious Maker shon,
Truth, Wisdom, Sanctitude severe and pure,
Severe, but in true filial freedom plac't;
Whence true autoritie in men; though both   295
Not equal, as thir sex not equal seemd;
For contemplation hee and valour formd,
For softness shee and sweet attractive Grace,
Hee for God only, shee for God in him:
His fair large Front and Eye sublime declar'd   300
Absolute rule; and Hyacinthin Locks
Round from his parted forelock manly hung
Clustring, but not beneath his shoulders broad:
Shee as a veil down to the slender waist
Her unadorned golden tresses wore   305
Dissheveld, but in wanton ringlets wav'd
As the Vine curls her tendrils, which impli'd
Subjection, but requir'd with gentle sway,
And by her yielded, by him best receiv'd,
Yielded with coy submission, modest pride,   310
And sweet reluctant amorous delay.
Nor those mysterious parts were then conceal'd,
Then was not guiltie shame, dishonest shame
Of Natures works: honor dishonorable,

Sin-bred, how have ye troubl'd all mankind   315
With shews instead, mere shews of seeming pure,
And banisht from mans life his happiest life,
Simplicitie and spotless innocence.
So passd they naked on, nor shunnd the sight
Of God or Angel, for they thought no ill: 320
So hand in hand they passd, the lovliest pair
That ever since in loves imbraces met,
Adam the goodliest man of men since born
His Sons, the fairest of her Daughters *Eve*.
Under a tuft of shade that on a green   325
Stood whispering soft, by a fresh Fountain side
They sat them down, and after no more toil
Of thir sweet Gardning labour than suffic'd
To recommend cool *Zephyr*, and made ease
More easie, wholsom thirst and appetite   330
More grateful, to thir Supper Fruits they fell,
Nectarine Fruits which the compliant boughes
Yielded them, side-long as they sat recline
On the soft downie Bank damaskt with flowrs:
The savourie pulp they chew, and in the rinde   335
Still as they thirsted scoop the brimming stream;
Nor gentle purpose, nor endearing smiles
Wanted, nor youthful dalliance as beseems
Fair couple, linkt in happie nuptial League,
Alone as they.   About them frisking playd   340
All Beasts of th' Earth, since wild, and of all chase
In Wood or Wilderness, Forrest or Den;
Sporting the Lion rampd, and in his paw
Dandl'd the Kid; Bears, Tigers, Ounces, Pards
Gambold before them, th' unwieldy Elephant   345
To make them mirth us'd all his might, and wreath'd
His Lithe Proboscis; close the Serpent sly
Insinuating, wove with Gordian twine
His breaded train, and of his fatal guile
Gave proof unheeded; others on the grass   350
Coucht, and now filld with pasture gazing sat,
Or Bedward ruminating: for the Sun
Declin'd was hasting now with prone career
To th' Ocean Iles, and in th' ascending Scale
Of Heav'n the Starrs that usher Ev'ning rose: 355
When *Satan* still in gaze, as first he stood,
Scarce thus at length faild speech recoverd sad.
    O Hell! what doe mine eyes with grief behold,
Into our room of bliss thus high advanc't
Creatures of other mould, earth-born perhaps,   360
Not Spirits, yet to heav'nly Spirits bright
Little inferior; whom my thoughts persue
With wonder, and could love, so lively shines

In them Divine resemblance, and such grace
The hand that formd them on thir shape hath pourd.   365
Ah gentle pair, ye little think how nigh
Your change approaches, when all these delights
Will vanish and deliver ye to woé,
More woe, the more your taste is now of joy;
Happie, but for so happie ill secur'd   370
Long to continue, and this high seat your Heav'n
Ill fenc't for Heav'n to keep out such a foe
As now is enterd; yet no purpos'd foe
To you whom I could pittie thus forlorne
Though I unpittied: League with you I seek,   375
And mutual amitie so strait, so close,
That I with you must dwell, or you with me
Henceforth; my dwelling haply may not please
Like this fair Paradise, your sense, yet such
Accept your Makers work: he gave it me,   380
Which I as freely give; Hell shall unfold,
To entertain you two, her widest Gates,
And send forth all her Kings; there will be room,
Not like these narrow limits, to receive
Your numerous offspring; if no better place,   385
Thank him who puts me loath to this revenge
On you who wrong me not for him who wrongd.
And should I at your harmless innocence
Melt, as I do, yet public reason just,
Honour and Empire with revenge enlarg'd,   390
By conquering this new World, compells me now
To do what else though damnd I should abhorr.
    So spake the Fiend, and with necessitie,
The Tyrants plea, excus'd his devilish deeds.
Then from his loftie stand on that high Tree   395
Down he alights among the sportful Herd
Of those fourfooted kinds, himself now one,
Now other, as thir shape serv'd best his end
Nearer to view his prey, and unespi'd
To mark what of thir state he more might learn   400
By word or action markt: about them round
A Lion now he stalkes with fierie glare,
Then as a Tiger, who by chance hath spi'd
In some Purlieu two gentle Fawns at play,
Straight couches close, then rising changes oft   405
His couchant watch, as one who chose his ground
Whence rushing he might surest seize them both
Grip't in each paw: when *Adam* first of men
To first of women *Eve* thus moving speech,
Turnd him all eare to hear new utterance flow.   410
    Sole partner and sole part of all these joys,
Dearer thy self than all; needs must the Power

That made us, and for us this ample World
Be infinitly good, and of his good
As liberal and free as infinite,   415
That rais'd us from the dust and plac'd us here
In all this happiness, who at his hand
Have nothing merited, nor can performe
Aught whereof hee hath need, hee who requires
From us no other service than to keep   420
This one, this easie charge, of all the Trees
In Paradise that beare delicious fruit
So various, not to taste that onely Tree
Of Knowledge, planted by the Tree of Life,
So near grows Death to Life, what e're Death is,   425
Som dreadful thing no doubt; for well thou knowst
God hath pronounc't it death to taste that Tree,
The only sign of our obedience left
Among so many signes of power and rule
Conferrd upon us, and Dominion giv'n   430
Over all other Creatures that possess
Earth, Air, and Sea.   Then let us not think hard
One easie prohibition, who enjoy
Free leave so large to all things else, and choice
Unlimited of manifold delights: 435
But let us ever praise him, and extoll
His bountie, following our delightfull task
To prune these growing Plants, and tend these Flowrs,
Which were it toilsom, yet with thee were sweet.
    To whom thus *Eve* repli'd.   O thou for whom   440
And from whom I was formd flesh of thy flesh,
And without whom am to no end, my Guide
And Head, what thou hast said is just and right.
For wee to him indeed all praises owe
And daily thanks, I chiefly who enjoy   445
So farr the happier Lot, enjoying thee
Praeeminent by so much odds, while thou
Like consort to thy self canst no where find.
That day I oft remember, when from sleep
I first awak'd, and found my self repos'd   450
Under a shade of flowrs, much wondring where
And what I was, whence thither brought, and how.
Not distant far from thence a murmuring sound
Of waters issu'd from a Cave and spred
Into a liquid Plain, then stood unmov'd   455
Pure as th' expanse of Heav'n; I thither went
With unexperienc't thought, and laid me downe
On the green bank, to look into the clear
Smooth Lake, that to me seemd another Skie.

451 of *Ed. 2*] on *Ed. 1*

As I bent down to look, just opposite,   460
A Shape within the watry gleam appear'd
Bending to look on me, I started back,
It started back, but pleas'd I soon returnd,
Pleas'd it returnd as soon with answering looks
Of sympathie and love; there I had fixt   465
Mine eyes till now, and pin'd with vain desire,
Had not a voice thus warnd me, What thou seest,
What there thou seest fair Creature is thy self,
With thee it came and goes: but follow me,
And I will bring thee where no shaddow stays   470
Thy coming, and thy soft imbraces, hee
Whose image thou art, him thou shalt enjoy
Inseparablie thine, to him shalt beare
Multitudes like thy self, and thence be calld
Mother of human Race: what could I doe   475
But follow straight, invisibly thus led?
Till I espi'd thee, fair indeed and tall,
Under a Platan, yet methought less fair,
Less winning soft, less amiablie mild,
Than that smooth watry image; back I turnd,   480
Thou following crie'dst aloud, Return fair *Eve*,
Whom fli'st thou? whom thou fli'st, of him thou art,
His flesh, his bone; to give thee being I lent
Out of my side to thee, nearest my heart
Substantial Life, to have thee by my side   485
Henceforth an individual solace dear;
Part of my Soul I seek thee, and thee claim
My other half: with that thy gentle hand
Seiz'd mine, I yielded, and from that time see
How beauty is excelld by manly grace   490
And wisdom, which alone is truly fair.
     So spake our general Mother, and with eyes
Of conjugal attraction unreprov'd,
And meek surrender, half imbracing lean'd
On our first Father, half her swelling Brest   495
Naked met his under the flowing Gold
Of her loose tresses hid: hee in delight
Both of her Beauty and submissive Charms
Smil'd with superior Love, as *Jupiter*
On *Juno* smiles, when he impregns the Clouds   500
That shed *May* Flowers; and pressd her Matron lip
With kisses pure: aside the Devil turnd
For envie, yet with jealous leer maligne
Ey'd them askance, and to himself thus plaind.
     Sight hateful, sight tormenting! thus these two   505
Imparadis't in one anothers arms
The happier *Eden*, shall enjoy thir fill
Of bliss on bliss, while I to Hell am thrust,

Where neither joy nor love, but fierce desire,
Among our other torments not the least,			510
Still unfulfilld with pain of longing pines;
Yet let me not forget what I have gaind
From thir own mouths; all is not theirs it seems:
One fatal Tree there stands of Knowledge calld,
Forbidden them to taste: Knowledge forbidd'n?		515
Suspicious, reasonless.   Why should thir Lord
Envie them that? can it be sin to know,
Can it be death? and do they onely stand
By Ignorance, is that thir happie state,
The proof of thir obedience and thir faith?		520
O fair foundation laid whereon to build
Thir ruin!   Hence I will excite thir minds
With more desire to know, and to reject
Envious commands, invented with design
To keep them low whom knowledge might exalt		525
Equal with Gods; aspiring to be such,
They taste and die: what likelier can ensue?
But first with narrow search I must walk round
This Garden, and no corner leave unspi'd;
A chance but chance may lead where I may meet		530
Som wandring Spirit of Heav'n, by Fountain side
Or in thick shade retir'd, from him to draw
What furder would be learnt.   Live while ye may,
Yet happie pair; enjoy, till I return,
Short pleasures, for long woes are to succeed.		535
	So saying, his proud step he scornful turnd,
But with sly circumspection, and began
Through wood, through waste, ore hill, ore dale his roam.
Mean while in utmost Longitude, where Heav'n
With Earth and Ocean meets, the setting Sun		540
Slowly descending, and with right aspect
Against the eastern Gate of Paradise
Leveld his ev'ning Rays: it was a Rock
Of Alablaster, pil'd up to the Clouds,
Conspicuous farr, winding with one ascent		545
Accessible from Earth, one entrance high;
The rest was craggie cliff, that overhung
Still as it rose, impossible to climb.
Betwixt these rockie Pillars *Gabriel* sat
Chief of th' Angelic Guards, awaiting night;		550
About him exercis'd Heroic Games
Th' unarmed Youth of Heav'n, but nigh at hand
Celestial Armourie, Shields, Helms and Spears
Hung high with Diamond flaming, and with Gold.
Thither came *Uriel*, gliding through the Even		555
On a Sun beam, swift as a shooting Starr
In *Autumn* thwarts the night, when vapours fir'd

Impress the Air, and shews the Mariner
From what point of his Compass to beware
Impetuous winds: he thus began in haste.   560
   Gabriel, to thee thy course by Lot hath giv'n
Charge and strict watch that to this happie Place
No evil thing approach or enter in;
This day at highth of Noon came to my Sphear
A Spirit, zealous, as he seemd, to know   565
More of th' Almightys works, and chiefly Man
Gods latest Image: I describ'd his way
Bent all on speed, and markd his Aerie Gait;
But in the Mount that lies from *Eden* North,
Where he first lighted, soon discernd his looks   570
Alien from Heav'n, with passions foul obscur'd:
Mine eye persu'd him still, but under shade
Lost sight of him; one of the banisht crew
I fear, hath ventur'd from the Deep, to raise
New troubles; him thy care must be to find.   575
   To whom the winged Warrior thus returnd:
Uriel, no wonder if thy perfet sight,
Amid the Suns bright circle where thou sitst.
See farr and wide: in at this Gate none pass
The vigilance here plac't, but such as come   580
Well known from Heav'n; and since Meridian hour
No Creature thence: if Spirit of other sort,
So minded, have o'erleapt these earthie bounds
On purpose, hard thou knowst it to exclude
Spiritual substance with corporeal barr.   585
But if within the circuit of these walks
In whatsoever shape he lurk, of whom
Thou tellst, by morrow dawning I shall know
   So promis'd hee, and *Uriel* to his charge
Returnd on that bright beam, whose point now rais'd   590
Bore him slope downward to the Sun now fall'n
Beneath th' *Azores*; whether the prime Orb,
Incredible how swift, had thither rould
Diurnal, or this less volubil Earth
By shorter flight to th' East, had left him there   595
Arraying with reflected Purple and Gold
The Clouds that on his Western Throne attend:
Now came still Ev'ning on, and Twilight gray
Had in her sober Liverie all things clad;
Silence accompanied, for Beast and Bird,   600
They to thir grassie Couch, these to thir Nests
Were slunk, all but the wakeful Nightingale;
Shee all night long her amorous descant sung;
Silence was pleas'd: now glowd the Firmament

---

592 whether *Ticknell 1719*] whither (alternative form of 'whether') *Edd. 1, 2.*
603 Shee] She *Edd. 1, 2.*

With living Saphirs: *Hesperus* that led　　　605
The starrie Host, rode brightest, till the Moon
Rising in clouded Majestie, at length
Apparent Queen unveild her peerless light,
And o'er the dark her Silver Mantle threw.
　　When *Adam* thus to *Eve*: Fair Consort, th' hour　　610
Of night, and all things now retir'd to rest
Mind us of like repose, since God hath set
Labour and rest, as day and night to men
Successive, and the timely dew of sleep
Now falling with soft slumbrous weight inclines　　615
Our eye-lids; other Creatures all day long
Rove idle unimployd, and less need rest;
Man hath his daily work of body or mind
Appointed, which declares his Dignitie,
And the regard of Heav'n on all his ways;　　620
While other Animals unactive range,
And of thir doings God takes no account.
To morrow ere fresh Morning streak the East
With first approach of light, we must be ris'n,
And at our pleasant labour, to reform　　625
Yon flowrie Arbors, yonder Allies green,
Our walk at noon, with branches overgrown,
That mock our scant manuring, and require
More hands than ours to lop thir wanton growth:
Those Blossoms also, and those dropping Gumms,　　630
That lie bestrowne unsightly and unsmooth,
Ask riddance, if we mean to tread with ease;
Mean while, as Nature wills, Night bids us rest.
　　To whom thus *Eve* with perfet beauty adornd.
My Author and Disposer, what thou bidst　　635
Unargu'd I obey; so God ordains,
God is thy Law; thou mine: to know no more
Is womans happiest knowledge and her praise.
With thee conversing I forget all time,
All seasons and thir change, all please alike.　　640
Sweet is the breath of morn, her rising sweet,
With charm of earliest Birds; pleasant the Sun
When first on this delightful Land he spreads
His orient Beams, on herb, tree, fruit, and flowr,
Glistring with dew; fragrant the fertil earth　　645
After soft showers; and sweet the coming on
Of grateful Ev'ning mild, then silent Night
With this her solemn Bird and this fair Moon,
And these the Gemms of Heav'n, her starrie train:
But neither breath of Morn when she ascends　　650
With charm of earliest Birds, nor rising Sun
On this delightful land, nor herb, fruit, flowr,
Glistring with dew, nor fragrance after showers,

Nor grateful Ev'ning mild, nor silent Night
With this her solemn Bird, nor walk by Moon,   655
Or glittering Starr-light without thee is sweet.
But wherfore all night long shine these, for whom
This glorious sight, when sleep hath shut all eyes?
    To whom our general Ancestor repli'd.
Daughter of God and Man, accomplisht *Eve*,   660
Those have thir course to finish, round the Earth,
By morrow Ev'ning, and from Land to Land
In order, though to Nations yet unborn,
Ministring light prepar'd, they set and rise;
Lest total darkness should by Night regain   665
Her old possession, and extinguish life
In Nature and all things, which these soft fires
Not only enlighten, but with kindly heat
Of various influence foment and warm,
Temper or nourish, or in part shed down   670
Thir stellar vertue on all kinds that grow
On Earth, made hereby apter to receive
Perfection from the Suns more potent Ray.
These then, though unbeheld in deep of night,
Shine not in vain, nor think, though men were none,   675
That Heav'n would want spectators, God want praise;
Millions of spiritual Creatures walk the Earth
Unseen, both when we wake, and when we sleep:
All these with ceaseless praise his works behold
Both day and night: how often from the steep   680
Of echoing Hill or Thicket have we heard
Celestial voices to the midnight air,
Sole, or responsive each to others note
Singing thir great Creator: oft in bands
While they keep watch, or nightly rounding walk   685
With Heav'nly touch of instrumental sounds
In full harmonic number joind, thir songs
Divide the night, and lift our thoughts to Heaven.
    Thus talking hand in hand alone they passd
On to thir blissful Bower; it was a place   690
Chos'n by the sovran Planter, when he fram'd
All things to mans delightful use; the roof
Of thickest covert was inwoven shade
Laurel and Mirtle, and what higher grew
Of firm and fragrant leaf; on either side   695
Acanthus, and each odorous bushie shrub
Fenc'd up the verdant wall; each beauteous flowr,
Iris all hues, Roses and Gessamin
Rear'd high thir flourisht heads between, and wrought
Mosaic; underfoot the Violet,   700
Crocus and Hyacinth, with rich inlay
Broiderd the ground, more colourd than with stone

Of costliest Emblem: other Creature here
Beast, Bird, Insect or Worm durst enter none;
Such was thir awe of Man.   In shadier Bower   705
More sacred and sequesterd, though but feignd,
Pan or *Silvanus* never slept, nor Nymph
Nor *Faunus* haunted.   Here in close recess
With Flowers, Garlands, and sweet-smelling Herbs
Espoused *Eve* deckd first her nuptial Bed,   710
And heav'nly Quires the Hymenæan sung,
What day the genial Angel to our Sire
Brought her in naked beauty more adornd,
More lovely than *Pandora*, whom the Gods
Endowd with all thir gifts, and O too like   715
In sad event, when to th'unwiser Son
Of *Japhet* brought by *Hermes*, she ensnar'd
Mankind with her faire looks, to be aveng'd
On him who had stole *Joves* authentic fire.

     Thus at thir shadie Lodge arriv'd, both stood   720
Both turnd, and under open Skie ador'd
The God that made both Skie, Air, Earth and Heav'n
Which they beheld, the Moons resplendent Globe
And starrie Pole: Thou also mad'st the Night,
Maker Omnipotent, and thou the Day,   725
Which we in our appointed work imployd
Have finisht happie in our mutual help
And mutual love, the Crown of all our bliss
Ordaind by thee, and this delicious place
For us too large, where thy abundance wants   730
Partakers, and uncropt falls to the ground.
But thou hast promis'd from us two a Race
To fill the Earth, who shall with us extoll
Thy goodness infinite, both when we wake,
And when we seek, as now, thy gift of sleep.   735
     This said unaminous, and other Rites
Observing none, but adoration pure
Which God likes best, into thir inmost bower
Handed they went; and eas'd the putting off
These troublesom disguises which wee wear,   740
Straight side by side were laid, nor turnd I weene
Adam from his fair Spouse, nor *Eve* the Rites
Mysterious of connubial Love refus'd:
Whatever Hypocrites austerely talk
Of puritie and place and innocence,   745
Defaming as impure what God declares
Pure, and commands to som, leaves free to all.
Our Maker bids increase, who bids abstain
But our Destroyer, foe to God and Man?
Haile wedded Love, mysterious Law, true source   750
Of human offspring, sole proprietie,

In Paradise of all things common else.
By thee adulterous lust was driv'n from men
Among the bestial herds to range, by thee
Founded in Reason, Loyal, Just and Pure,   755
Relations dear, and all the Charities
Of Father, Son, and Brother first were known.
Farr be it, that I should write thee sin or blame,
Or think thee unbefitting holiest place,
Perpetual Fountain of Domestic sweets,   760
Whose bed is undefil'd and chaste pronounc't,
Present or past, as Saints and Patriarchs us'd.
Here Love his golden shafts imploys, here lights
His constant Lamp, and waves his purple wings,
Reigns here and revels; not in the bought smile   765
Of Harlots, loveless, joyless, unindear'd,
Casual fruition, nor in Court Amours
Mixt Dance or wanton Mask, or Midnight Bal,
Or Serenate which the starv'd Lover sings
To his proud fair, best quitted with disdain.   770
These lulld by Nightingales imbracing slept,
And on thir naked limbs the flowrie roof
Showrd Roses, which the Morn repaird.   Sleep on,
Blest pair; and O yet happiest if ye seek
No happier state, and know to know no more.   775
   Now had night measurd with her shaddowie Cone
Half way up Hill this vast Sublunar Vault,
And from thir Ivorie Port the Cherubim
Forth issuing at th' accustomd hour stood armd
To thir night watches in warlike Parade,   780
When *Gabriel* to his next in power thus spake.
   Uzziel, half these draw off, and coast the South
With strictest watch; these other wheel the North,
Our circuit meets full West.   As flame they part
Half wheeling to the Shield, half to the Spear.   785
From these, two strong and suttle Spirits he calld
That near him stood, and gave them thus in charge.
   Ithuriel and *Zephon*, with wingd speed
Search through this Garden, leave unsearcht no nook,
But chiefly where those two fair Creatures Lodge,   790
Now laid perhaps asleep secure of harm.
This Ev'ning from the Suns decline arriv'd
Who tells of som infernal Spirit seen
Hitherward bent (who could have thought?) escap't
The barrs of Hell, on errand bad no doubt: 795
Such where ye find, seize fast, and hither bring.
   So saying, on he led his radiant Files,
Dazling the Moon; these to the Bowr direct
In search of whom they sought: him there they found
Squat like a Toad, close at the ear of *Eve*;   800

Assaying by his Devilish art to reach
The Organs of her Fancie, and with them forge
Illusions as he list, Fantasms and Dreams,
Or if, inspiring venom, he might taint
Th' animal spirits that from pure blood arise   805
Like gentle breaths from Rivers pure, thence raise
At least distemperd, discontented thoughts,
Vain hopes, vain aims, inordinate desires
Blown up with high conceits ingendring pride.
Him thus intent *Ithuriel* with his Spear   810
Touchd lightly; for no falsehood can endure
Touch of Celestial temper, but returns
Of force to its own likeness: up he starts
Discoverd and surpriz'd.   As when a spark
Lights on a heap of nitrous Powder, laid   815
Fit for the Tun som Magazin to store
Against a rumord Warr, the Smuttie grain
With sudden blaze diffus'd, inflames the Air:
So started up in his own shape the Fiend.
Back stepd those two fair Angels half amaz'd   820
So sudden to behold the grieslie King;
Yet thus, unmov'd with fear, accost him soon.
     Which of those rebel Spirits adjudg'd to Hell
Comst thou, escap't thy prison, and transformd,
Why satst thou like an enemie in waite   825
Here watching at the head of these that sleep?
     Know ye not then said *Satan*, filld with scorn
Know ye not mee? ye knew me once no mate
For you, there sitting where ye durst not soar;
Not to know mee argues your selves unknown,   830
The lowest of your throng; or if ye know,
Why ask ye, and superfluous begin
Your message, like to end as much in vain?
To whom thus *Zephon*, answering scorn with scorn.
Think not, revolted Spirit, thy shape the same,   835
Or undiminisht brightness, to be known
As when thou stoodst in Heav'n upright and pure;
That Glorie then, when thou no more wast good,
Departed from thee, and thou resembl'st now
Thy sin and place of doom obscure and foul.   840
But come, for thou, be sure, shalt give account
To him who sent us, whose charge is to keep
This place inviolable, and these from harm.
     So spake the Cherube, and his grave rebuke
Severe in youthful beautie, added grace   845
Invincible: abasht the Devil stood,
And felt how awful goodness is, and saw
Vertue in her shape how lovely, saw, and pin'd
His loss; but chiefly to find here observ'd

His lustre visibly impair'd; yet seemd   850
Undaunted.   If I must contend, said he,
Best with the best, the Sender not the sent,
Or all at once; more glorie will be wonn,
Or less be lost.   Thy fear, said *Zephon* bold,
Will save us trial what the least can doe   855
Single against thee wicked, and thence weak.
   The Fiend repli'd not, overcome with rage;
But like a proud Steed reind, went haughtie on,
Chaumping his iron curb: to strive or flie
He held it vain; awe from above had quelld   860
His heart, not else dismayd.   Now drew they nigh
The western Point, where those half-rounding guards
Just met, and closing stood in squadron joind
Awaiting next command.   To whom thir Chief
Gabriel from the Front thus calld aloud.   865
   O friends, I hear the tread of nimble feet
Hasting this way, and now by glimpse discern
Ithuriel and *Zephon* through the shade,
And with them comes a third of Regal port,
But faded splendor wan; who by his gait   870
And fierce demeanour seems the Prince of Hell,
Not likely to part hence without contest;
Stand firm, for in his look defiance lours.
   He scarce had ended, when those two approachd
And brief related whom they brought, where found,   875
How busied, in what form and posture couch't.
   To whom with stern regard thus *Gabriel* spake.
Why hast thou *Satan* broke the bounds prescrib'd
To thy transgressions, and disturbd the charge
Of others, who approve not to transgress   880
By thy example, but have power and right
To question thy bold entrance on this place;
Imployd it seems to violate sleep, and those
Whose dwelling God hath planted here in bliss?
   To whom thus *Satan*, with contemptuous brow.   885
Gabriel, thou hadst in Heav'n th' esteem of wise,
And such I held thee; but this question askt
Puts me in doubt.   Lives there who loves his pain?
Who would not, finding way, break loose from Hell,
Though thither doomd?   Thou wouldst thy self, no doubt,
And boldly venture to whatever place   891
Fardest from pain, where thou mightst hope to change
Torment with ease, and soonest recompense
Dole with delight, which in this place I sought;
To thee no reason; who knowst only good,   895
But evil hast not tri'd: and wilt object
His will who bound us? let him surer barr
His Iron Gates, if he intends our stay

In that dark durance: thus much what was askt.
The rest is true, they found me where they say;　　900
But that implies not violence or harm.
　　Thus hee in scorn.　The warlike Angel mov'd,
Disdainfully half smiling thus repli'd.
O loss of one in Heav'n to judge of wise,
Since *Satan* fell, whom follie overthrew,　　905
And now returns him from his prison scap't,
Gravely in doubt whether to hold them wise
Or not, who ask what boldness brought him hither
Unlicenc't from his bounds in Hell prescrib'd;
So wise he judges it to fly from pain　　910
However, and to scape his punishment.
So judge thou still, presumptuous, till the wrauth,
Which thou incurrst by flying, meet thy flight
Sev'nfold, and scourge that wisdom back to Hell,
Which taught thee yet no better, that no pain　　915
Can equal anger infinite provok't.
But wherefore thou alone? wherefore with thee
Came not all Hell broke loose? is pain to them
Less pain, less to be fled, or thou than they
Less hardie to endure? courageous Chief,　　920
The first in flight from pain, hadst thou alleg'd
To thy deserted host this cause of flight,
Thou surely hadst not come sole fugitive.
　　To which the Fiend thus answerd frowning stern.
Not that I less endure, or shrink from pain,　　925
Insulting Angel, well thou knowst I stood
Thy fiercest, when in Battel to thy aide
The blasting vollied Thunder made all speed
And seconded thy else not dreaded Spear.
But still thy words at random, as before,　　930
Argue thy inexperience what behooves
From hard assayes and ill successes past
A faithful Leader, not to hazard all
Through ways of danger by himself untri'd.
I therefore, I alone first undertook　　935
To wing the desolate Abyss, and spie
This new created World, whereof in Hell
Fame is not silent, here in hope to finde
Better abode, and my afflicted Powers
To settle here on Earth, or in mid Air;　　940
Though for possession put to try once more
What thou and thy gay Legions dare against;
Whose easier buisness were to serve thir Lord
High up in Heav'n, with songs to hymn his Throne,
And practis'd distances to cringe, not fight.　　945

928 The *Ed. 1*] Thy *Ed. 2*

   To whom the warrior Angel soon repli'd.
To say and straight unsay, pretending first
Wise to flie pain, professing next the Spie,
Argues no Leader but a liar trac't,
Satan, and couldst thou faithful add?   O name,   950
O sacred name of faithfulness profan'd!
Faithful to whom? to thy rebellious crew?
Armie of Fiends, fit body to fit head;
Was this your discipline and faith ingag'd,
Your military obedience, to dissolve   955
Allegeance to th' acknowledg'd Power supream?
And thou sly hypocrite, who now wouldst seem
Patron of libertie, who more than thou
Once fawnd, and cring'd, and servilly ador'd
Heav'ns awful Monarch? wherefore but in hope   960
To dispossess him, and thy self to reign?
But mark what I arreed thee now, avant;
Flie thither whence thou fledst: if from this hour
Within these hallowd limits thou appear,
Back to th' infernal pit I drag thee chaind,   965
And Seale thee so, as henceforth not to scorne
The facil gates of Hell too slightly barrd.
   So threatend hee, but *Satan* to no threats
Gave heed, but waxing more in rage repli'd.
   Then when I am thy captive talk of chains,   970
Proud limitarie Cherube, but ere then
Farr heavier load thy self expect to feel
From my prevailing arm, though Heavens King
Ride on thy wings, and thou with thy Compeers,
Us'd to the yoke, drawst his triumphant wheels   975
In progress through the road of Heav'n Star-pav'd.
   While thus he spake, th' Angelic Squadron bright
Turnd fierie red, sharpning in mooned horns
Thir Phalanx, and began to hemm him round
With ported Spears, as thick as when a field   980
Of *Ceres* ripe for harvest waving bends
Her bearded Grove of ears, which way the wind
Swayes them; the careful Plowman doubting stands
Lest on the threshing floore his hopeful sheaves
Prove chaff.   On th' other side *Satan* alarmd   985
Collecting all his might dilated stood,
Like *Teneriff* or *Atlas* unremov'd:
His stature reach'd the Skie, and on his Crest
Sat horror Plum'd; nor wanted in his grasp
What seemd both Spear and Shield: now dreadful deeds
Might have ensu'd, nor onely Paradise   991
In this commotion, but the Starrie Cope
Of Heav'n perhaps, or all the Elements
At least had gon to wrack, disturbd and torne

With violence of this conflict, had not soon　　　995
Th' Eternal to prevent such horrid fray
Hung forth in Heav'n his golden Scales, yet seen
Betwixt *Astrea* and the *Scorpion* sign,
Wherein all things created first he weighd,
The pendulous round Earth with ballanc't Aire　　　1000
In counterpoise, now ponders all events,
Battels and Realms: in these he put two weights
The sequel each of parting and of fight;
The latter quick up flew, and kickd the beam;
Which *Gabriel* spying, thus bespake the Fiend.　　　1005
　　Satan I know thy strength, and thou knowst mine,
Neither our own but giv'n; what follie then
To boast what Arms can do, since thine no more
Than Heav'n permits, nor mine, though doubl'd now
To trample thee as mire: for proof look up,　　　1010
And read thy Lot in yon celestial Sign
Where thou art weighd, and shown how light, how weak,
If thou resist.　The Fiend lookd up and knew
His mounted scale aloft: nor more; but fled
Murmuring, and with him fled the shades of night.　　　1015

The End of the Fourth Book

BOOK V

THE ARGUMENT

Morning approacht, Eve *relates to* Adam *her troublesome dream; he likes it not, yet comforts her: They come forth to thir day labours: Their Morning Hymn at the Door of their Bower. God to render Man inexcusable sends* Raphael *to admonish him of his obedience, of his free estate, of his enemy near at hand; who he is, and why his enemy, and whatever else may avail* Adam *to know.* Raphael *comes down to Paradise, his appearance describ'd, his coming discernd by* Adam *afar off sitting at the door of his Bower; he goes out to meet him, brings him to his lodge, entertains him with the choycest fruits of Paradise got together by* Eve; *their discourse at Table:* Raphael *performs his message, minds* Adam *of his state and of his enemy; relates at* Adams *request who that enemy is, and how he came to be so, beginning from his first revolt in Heaven, and the occasion thereof; how he drew his Legions after him to the parts of the North, and there incited them to rebel with him, perswading all but only* Abdiel *a Seraph, who in Argument diswades and opposes him, then forsakes him.*

Now Morn her rosie steps in th' Eastern Clime
Advancing, sowd the Earth with Orient Pearl,
When *Adam* wak'd, so customd, for his sleep
Was Aerie light, from pure digestion bred,
And temperat vapours bland, which th' only sound   5
Of leaves and fuming rills, *Aurora's* fan,
Lightly dispersd, and the shrill Mattin Song
Of Birds on every bough; so much the more
His wonder was to find unwaken'd *Eve*
With Tresses discompos'd, and glowing Cheek,   10
As through unquiet rest: hee on his side
Leaning half-rais'd, with looks of cordial Love
Hung over her enamourd, and beheld
Beautie, which whether waking or asleep,
Shot forth peculiar Graces; then with voice   15
Milde as when *Zephyrus* on *Flora* breathes,
Her hand soft touching, whisperd thus.   Awake
My fairest, my espous'd, my latest found,
Heav'ns last best gift, my ever new delight,
Awake, the morning shines, and the fresh field   20
Calls us, we lose the prime, to mark how spring
Our tended Plants, how blows the Citron Grove,
What drops the Myrrh, and what the baumie Reed,

How Nature paints her colours, how the Bee
Sits on the Bloom extracting liquid sweet.   25
   Such whispering wak'd her, but with startl'd eye
On *Adam*, whom imbracing, thus she spake.
   O Sole in whom my thoughts find all repose,
My Glorie, my Perfection, glad I see
Thy face, and Morn returnd, for I this Night,   30
Such night till this I never passd, have dream'd,
If dream'd, not as I oft am wont, of thee,
Works of day past, or morrows next design,
But of offence and trouble, which my mind
Knew never till this irksom night; methought   35
Close at mine ear one calld me forth to walk
With gentle voice, I thought it thine; it said,
Why sleepst thou *Eve*? now is the pleasant time,
The cool, the silent, save where silence yields
To the night-warbling Bird, that now awake   40
Tunes sweetest his love-labord song; now reigns
Full Orbd the Moon, and with more pleasing light
Shaddowie sets off the face of things; in vain,
If none regard; Heav'n wakes with all his eyes,
Whom to behold but thee, Natures desire,   45
In whose sight all things joy, with ravishment
Attracted by thy beauty still to gaze.
I rose as at thy call, but found thee not;
To find thee I directed then my walk;
And on, methought, alone I passd through ways   50
That brought me on a sudden to the Tree
Of interdicted Knowledge: fair it seemd,
Much fairer to my Fancie than by day:
And as I wondring lookd, beside it stood
One shap'd and wingd like one of those from Heav'n   55
By us oft seen; his dewie locks distilld
Ambrosia; on that Tree he also gaz'd;
And O fair Plant, said he, with fruit surcharg'd,
Deigns none to ease thy load and taste thy sweet,
Nor God, nor Man; is Knowledge so despis'd?   60
Or envie or what reserve forbids to taste?
Forbid who will, none shall from me withhold
Longer thy offerd good, why else set here?
This said he paus'd not, but with ventrous Arme
He pluckd, he tasted; mee damp horror chilld   65
At such bold words voucht with a deed so bold:
But he thus overjoyd, O Fruit Divine,
Sweet of thy self, but much more sweet thus cropt,
Forbidden here, it seems, as onely fit
For Gods, yet able to make Gods of Men: 70
And why not Gods of Men, since good, the more
Communicated, more abundant grows,

The Author not impaird, but honourd more?
Here, happie Creature, fair Angelic *Eve*,
Partake thou also; happie though thou art, 75
Happier thou mayst be, worthier canst not be:
Taste this, and be henceforth among the Gods
Thy self a Goddess, not to Earth confin'd,
But sometimes in the Air, as wee, somtimes
Ascend to Heav'n, by merit thine, and see 80
What life the Gods live there, and such live thou.
So saying, he drew nigh, and to me held,
Ev'n to my mouth of that same fruit held part
Which he had pluckt; the pleasant savourie smell
So quickend appetite, that I, methought, 85
Could not but taste. Forthwith up to the Clouds
With him I flew, and underneath beheld
The Earth outstretcht immense, a prospect wide
And various; wondring at my flight and change
To this high exaltation: suddenly 90
My Guide was gon, and I, me thought, sunk down,
And fell asleep; but O how glad I wak'd
To find this but a dream! Thus *Eve* her Night
Related, and thus *Adam* answerd sad.

Best Image of my self and dearer half, 95
The trouble of thy thoughts this night in sleep
Affects me equally; nor can I like
This uncouth dream, of evil sprung I fear;
Yet evil whence? in thee can harbour none,
Created pure. But know that in the Soul 100
Are many lesser Faculties that serve
Reason as chief; among these Fancie next
Her office holds; of all external things,
Which the five watchful Senses represent,
She forms Imaginations, Aerie shapes, 105
Which Reason joining or disjoining, frames
All what we affirm or what deny, and call
Our knowledge or opinion; then retires
Into her privat Cell when Nature rests.
Oft in her absence mimic Fancie wakes 110
To imitate her; but misjoining shapes,
Wilde work produces oft, and most in dreams,
Ill matching words and deeds long past or late.
Som such resemblances methinks I find
Of our last Ev'nings talk, in this thy dream, 115
But with addition strange; yet be not sad.
Evil into the mind of God or Man
May come and go, so unapprov'd, and leave
No spot or blame behind: Which gives me hope
That what in sleep thou didst abhorr to dream, 120
Waking thou never wilt consent to do.

Be not disheartend then, nor cloud those looks
That wont to be more cheerful and serene
Then when fair Morning first smiles on the World,
And let us to our fresh imployments rise   125
Among the Groves, the Fountains, and the Flowrs
That open now thir choicest bosomd smells
Reserv'd from night, and kept for thee in store.
    So cheerd he his fair Spouse, and she was cheerd,
But silently a gentle tear let fall   130
From either eye, and wip'd them with her hair;
Two other precious drops that ready stood,
Each in thir crystal sluce, hee ere they fell
Kissd as the gracious signs of sweet remorse
And pious awe, that fear'd t'have offended.   135
    So all was clear'd, and to the Field they haste.
But first from under shadie arborous roof,
Soon as they forth were come to open sight
Of day-spring and the Sun, who scarce up risen,
With wheels yet hov'ring ore the Ocean brim,   140
Shot paralel to the Earth his dewie ray,
Discovering in wide Lantskip all the East
Of Paradise and *Edens* happie Plains,
Lowly they bowd adoring, and began
Thir Orisons, each Morning duly paid   145
In various style, for neither various style
Nor holy rapture wanted they to praise
Thir Maker, in fit strains pronounc't or sung
Unmeditated, such prompt eloquence
Flowd from thir lips, in Prose or numerous Verse,   150
More tuneable than needed Lute or Harp
To add more sweetness, and they thus began.
    These are thy glorious works, Parent of good,
Almightie, thine this universal Frame,
Thus wondrous fair; thy self how wondrous then!   155
Unspeakable, who sitst above these Heavens
To us invisible or dimly seen
In these thy lowest works, yet these declare
Thy goodness beyond thought, and Power Divine:
Speak yee who best can tell, ye Sons of light,   160
Angels, for yee behold him, and with songs
And choral symphonies, Day without Night,
Circle his Throne rejoicing, yee in Heav'n,
On Earth join all ye Creatures to extoll
Him first, him last, him midst, and without end.   165
Fairest of Starrs, last in the train of Night,
If better thou belong not to the dawn,
Sure pledge of day, that crownst the smiling Morn
With thy bright Circlet, praise him in thy Spheare
While day arises, that sweet hour of Prime.   170

Thou Sun, of this great World both Eye and Soul,
Acknowledge him thy Greater, sound his praise
In thy eternal course, both when thou climb'st,
And when high Noon hast gaind, and when thou fallst.
Moon, that now meetst the orient Sun, now fli'st   175
With the fixt Starrs, fixt in thir Orb that flies,
And yee five other wandring Fires that move
In mystic Dance not without Song, resound
His praise, who out of Darkness calld up Light.
Air, and ye Elements the eldest birth   180
Of Natures Womb, that in quaternion run
Perpetual Circle, multiform; and mix
And nourish all things, let your ceaseless change
Varie to our great Maker still new praise.
Ye Mists and Exhalations that now rise   185
From Hill or steaming Lake, duskie or grey,
Till the Sun paint your fleecie skirts with Gold,
In honour to the Worlds great Author rise,
Whether to deck with Clouds th' uncolourd skie,
Or wet the thirstie Earth with falling showers,   190
Rising or falling still advance his praise.
His praise ye Winds, that from four Quarters blow,
Breathe soft or loud; and wave your tops, ye Pines,
With every Plant, in sign of Worship wave.
Fountains and yee that warble, as ye flow,   195
Melodious murmurs, warbling tune his praise.
Join voices all ye living Souls, ye Birds,
That singing up to Heaven Gate ascend,
Bear on your wings and in your notes his praise;
Yee that in Waters glide, and yee that walk   200
The Earth, and stately tread, or lowly creep;
Witness if I be silent, Morn or Even,
To Hill or Valley, Fountain or fresh shade
Made vocal by my Song, and taught his praise.
Hail universal Lord, be bounteous still   205
To give us onely good; and if the night
Have gatherd aught of evil or conceal'd,
Disperse it, as now light dispells the dark.
  So prayd they innocent, and to thir thoughts
Firm peace recoverd soon and wonted calm.   210
On to thir mornings rural work they haste
Among sweet dews and flowrs; where any row
Of Fruit-trees overwoodie reach'd too farr
Thir pamperd boughs, and needed hands to check
Fruitless imbraces: or they led the Vine   215
To wed her Elm; she spous'd about him twines
Her marriageable arms, and with her brings
Her dowr th' adopted Clusters, to adorn
His barren leaves.   Them thus imployd beheld

With pittie Heav'ns high King, and to him calld   220
Raphael, the sociable Spirit, that deignd
To travel with *Tobias*, and secur'd
His marriage with the sev'ntimes-wedded Maid.
  Raphael, said he, thou hear'st what stir on Earth
Satan from Hell scap't through the darksom Gulf   225
Hath rais'd in Paradise, and how disturbd
This night the human pair, how he designes
In them at once to ruin all mankind.
Goe therefore, half this day as friend with friend
Converse with *Adam*, in what Bowr or shade   230
Thou find'st him from the heat of Noon retir'd,
To respit his day-labour with repast
Or with repose; and such discourse bring on,
As may advise him of his happie state,
Happiness in his power left free to will,   235
Left to his own free Will, his Will though free
Yet mutable; whence warn him to beware
He swerve not too secure: tell him withall
His danger, and from whom, what enemie
Late fall'n himself from Heav'n, is plotting now   240
The fall of others from like state of bliss;
By violence, no, for that shall be withstood,
But by deceit and lies; this let him know,
Lest wilfully transgressing he pretend
Surprisal, unadmonisht, unforewarnd.   245
  So spake th' Eternal Father, and fulfilld
All Justice: nor delayd the winged Saint
After his charge receiv'd; but from among
Thousand Celestial Ardors, where he stood
Veild with his gorgeous wings, up springing light   250
Flew through the midst of Heav'n; th' angelic Quires
On each hand parting, to his speed gave way
Through all th' Empyreal road; till at the Gate
Of Heav'n arriv'd, the gate self-opend wide
On golden Hinges turning, as by work   255
Divine the sovran Architect had fram'd.
From hence, no cloud or, to obstruct his sight,
Starr interpos'd, however small he sees,
Not unconform to other shining Globes,
Earth and the Gard'n of God, with Cedars crownd   260
Above all Hills.   As when by night the Glass
Of *Galileo*, less assur'd, observes
Imagind Lands and Regions in the Moon:
Of Pilot from amidst the *Cyclades*
Delos or *Samos* first appearing kenns   265
A cloudy spot.   Down thither prone in flight
He speeds, and through the vast Ethereal Skie
Sails between worlds and worlds, with steddie wing

Now on the polar winds, then with quick Fann
Winnows the buxom Air; till within soare   270
Of Touring Eagles, to all the Fowls he seems
A *Phœnix*, gaz'd by all, as that sole Bird
When to enshrine his reliques in the Suns
Bright Temple, to *Egyptian Theb's* he flies.
At once on th' Eastern cliff of Paradise   275
He lights, and to his proper shape returns
A Seraph wingd; six wings he wore, to shade
His lineaments Divine; the pair that clad
Each shoulder broad, came mantling ore his brest
With regal Ornament; the middle pair   280
Girt like a Starrie Zone his waist, and round
Skirted his loins and thighes with downie Gold
And colours dipt in Heav'n; the third his feet
Shaddowd from either heele with featherd maile
Skie-tinctur'd grain.   Like *Maia's* son he stood,   285
And shook his Plumes, that Heav'nly fragrance filld
The circuit wide.   Straight knew him all the Bands
Of Angels under watch; and to his state,
And to his message high in honour rise;
For on som message high they guessd him bound.   290
Thir glittering Tents he passd, and now is come
Into the blissful field, through Groves of Myrrh,
And flowring Odours, Cassia, Nard and Baum;
A Wilderness of sweets; for Nature here
Wantond as in her prime, and playd at will   295
Her Virgin Fancies, pouring forth more sweet,
Wilde above rule or art; enormous bliss.
Him through the spicie Forrest onward come
Adam discernd, as in the dore he sat
Of his cool Bowre, while now the mounted Sun   300
Shot down direct his fervid Rays, to warme
Earths inmost womb, more warmth than *Adam* needs:
And *Eve* within, due at her hour prepar'd
For dinner savourie fruits, of taste to please
True appetite, and not disrelish thirst   305
Of nectarous draughts between, from milkie stream,
Berrie or Grape: to whom thus *Adam* calld.
     Haste hither *Eve*, and worth thy sight behold
Eastward among those Trees, what glorious shape
Comes this way moving; seems another Morn   310
Ris'n on mid-noon; som great behest from Heav'n
To us perhaps he brings, and will voutsafe
This day to be our Guest.   But go with speed,
And what thy stores contain, bring forth and poure
Abundance, fit to honour and receive   315
Our Heav'nly stranger; well we may afford
Our givers thir own gifts, and large bestow

From large bestowd, where Nature multiplies
Her fertil growth, and by disburd'ning grows
More fruitful, which instructs us not to spare.   320
    To whom thus *Eve*.   *Adam*, earths hallowd mould,
Of God inspir'd, small store will serve, where store,
All seasons, ripe for use hangs on the stalk;
Save what by frugal storing firmness gains
To nourish, and superfluous moist consumes: 325
But I will haste and from each bough and brake,
Each Plant and juiciest Gourd will pluck such choice
To entertain our Angel guest, as hee
Beholding shall confess that here on Earth
God hath dispenst his bounties as in Heav'n.   330
    So saying, with dispatchful looks in haste
She turns, on hospitable thoughts intent
What choice to choose for delicacie best,
What order, so contriv'd as not to mix
Tastes, not well joind, inelegant, but bring   335
Taste after taste upheld with kindliest change,
Bestirs her then, and from each tender stalk
Whatever Earth all-bearing Mother yields
In *India* East or West, or middle shore
In *Pontus* or the *Punic* Coast, or where   340
Alcinous reignd, fruit of all kinds, in coat,
Rough or smooth rin'd, or bearded husk, or shell
She gathers, Tribute large, and on the board
Heaps with unsparing hand; for drink the Grape
She crushes, inoffensive moust, and meathes   345
From many a berrie, and from sweet kernels prest
She tempers dulcet creams, nor these to hold
Wants her fit vessels pure; then strews the ground
With Rose and Odours from the shrub unfum'd.
Mean while our Primitive great Sire, to meet   350
His god-like Guest, walks forth, without more train
Accompanied than with his own complete
Perfections, in himself was all his state,
More solemn than the tedious pomp that waits
On Princes, when thir rich Retinue long   355
Of Horses led and Grooms besmear'd with Gold
Dazles the crowd, and sets them all agape.
Nearer his presence *Adam* though not awd,
Yet with submiss approach and reverence meek,
As to a superior Nature, bowing low,   360
    Thus said.   Native of Heav'n, for other place
None can than Heav'n such glorious shape contain;
Since by descending from the Thrones above,
Those happie places thou hast deignd a while

To want, and honour these, voutsafe with us   365
Two onely, who yet by sovran gift possess
This spacious ground, in yonder shadie Bowr
To rest, and what the Garden choicest bears
To sit and taste, till this meridian heat
Be over, and the Sun more cool decline.   370
    Whom thus th'Angelic Vertue answerd mild.
Adam, I therefore came, nor art thou such
Created, or such place hast here to dwell,
As may not oft invite, though Spirits of Heav'n
To visit thee; lead on then where thy Bowr   375
O'ershades; for these mid-hours, till Ev'ning rise
I have at will.   So to the Silvan Lodge
They came, that like *Pomona*'s Arbour smil'd
With flowrets deckt and fragrant smells; but *Eve*
Undeckt, save with her self more lovely fair   380
Than Wood-Nymph, or the fairest Goddess feignd
Of three that in Mount *Ida* naked strove,
Stood to entertain her guest from Heav'n; no veile
Shee needed, Vertue-proof, no thought infirme
Alterd her cheek.   On whom the Angel *Haile*   385
Bestowd, the holy salutation us'd
Long after to blest *Marie*, second *Eve*.
    Haile Mother of Mankind, whose fruitful Womb
Shall fill the World more numerous with thy Sons
Than with these various fruits the Trees of God   390
Have heap't this Table.   Rais'd of grassie terf
Thir Table was, and mossie seats had round,
And on her ample Square from side to side
All *Autumn* pil'd, though *Spring* and *Autumn* here
Danc'd hand in hand.   A while discourse they hold; 395
No fear lest Dinner cool; when thus began
Our Author.   Heav'nly stranger, please to taste
These bounties which our Nourisher, from whom
All perfet good unmeasurd out, descends,
To us for food and for delight hath caus'd   400
The Earth to yield; unsavourie food perhaps
To spiritual Natures; only this I know,
That one Celestial Father gives to all.
    To whom the Angel.   Therefore what he gives
(Whose praise be ever sung) to man in part   405
Spiritual, may of purest Spirits be found
No ingrateful food: and food alike those pure
Intelligential substances require
As doth your Rational; and both contain
Within them every lower facultie   410
Of sense, whereby they hear, see, smell, touch, taste,
Tasting concoct, digest, assimilate,
And corporeal to incorporeal turn.

For know, whatever was created, needs
To be sustaind and fed; of Elements   415
The grosser feeds the purer, Earth the Sea,
Earth and the Sea feed Air, the Air those Fires
Ethereal, and as lowest first the Moon;
Whence in her visage round those spots, unpurg'd
Vapours not yet into her substance turnd.   420
Nor doth the Moon no nourishment exhale
From her moist Continent to higher Orbs.
The Sun that light imparts to all, receives
From all his alimental recompense
In humid exhalations, and at Even   425
Sups with the Ocean: though in Heav'n the Trees
Of life ambrosial fruitage bear, and vines
Yield Nectar, though from off the boughs each Morn
We brush mellifluous Dews, and find the ground
Coverd with pearly grain: yet God hath here   430
Varied his bounty so with new delights,
As may compare with Heav'n; and to taste
Think not I shall be nice.   So down they sat,
And to thir viands fell, nor seemingly
The Angel, nor in mist, the common gloss   435
Of Theologians, but with keen dispatch
Of real hunger, and concoctive heat
To transubstantiate; what redounds, transpires
Through Spirits with ease; nor wonder; if by fire
Of sooty coal th'Empiric Alchimist   440
Can turn, or holds it possible to turn
Mettals of drossiest Ore to perfet Gold
As from the Mine.   Mean while at Table *Eve*
Ministerd naked, and thir flowing cups
With pleasant liquors crownd: O innocence   445
Deserving Paradise! if ever, then,
Then had the Sons of God excuse to have bin
Enamourd at that sight; but in those hearts
Love unlibidinous reignd, nor jealousie
Was understood, the injur'd Lovers Hell.   450
    Thus when with meats and drinks they had suffic't
Not burdend Nature, sudden mind arose
In *Adam*, not to let th' occasion pass
Giv'n him by this great Conference to know
Of things above his World, and of thir being   455
Who dwell in Heav'n, whose excellence he saw
Transcend his own so farr, whose radiant forms
Divine effulgence, whose high Power so far
Exceeded human, and his wary speech
Thus to th' Empyreal Minister he fram'd.   460
    Inhabitant with God, now know I well
Thy favour, in this honour don to man,

Under whose lowly roof thou hast voutsaf't
To enter, and these earthly fruits to taste,
Food not of Angels, yet accepted so,   465
As that more willingly thou couldst not seem
At Heav'ns high feasts to have fed: yet what **compare?**
    To whom the winged Hierarch repli'd.
O *Adam*, one Almightie is, from whom
All things proceed, and up to him return,   470
If not deprav'd from good, created all
Such to perfection, one first matter all,
Indu'd with various forms, various degrees
Of substance, and in things that live, of life;
But more refin'd, more spiritous and pure,   475
As nearer to him plac't or nearer tending
Each in thir several active Sphears assignd,
Till body up to spirit work, in bounds
Proportiond to each kind.   So from the root
Springs lighter the green stalk, from thence the leaves 480
More aerie, last the bright consummat flowre
Spirits odorous breathes: flowrs and thir fruit
Mans nourishment, by gradual scale sublim'd
To vital Spirits aspire, to animal,
To intellectual, give both life and sense,   485
Fancie and understanding, whence the Soule
Reason receives, and reason is her being,
Discursive or Intuitive; discourse
Is oftest yours, the latter most is ours,
Differing but in degree, of kind the same.   490
Wonder not then, what God for you saw good
If I refuse not, but convert, as you,
To proper substance; time may come when men
With Angels may participate, and find
No inconvenient Diet, nor too light Fare: 495
And from these corporal nutriments perhaps
Your bodies may at last turn all to Spirit,
Improv'd by tract of time, and wingd ascend
Ethereal, as wee, or may at choice
Here or in Heav'nly Paradises dwell;   500
If ye be found obedient, and retain
Unalterably firm his love entire
Whose progenie you are.   Mean while enjoy
Your fill what happiness this happie state
Can comprehend, incapable of more.   505
    To whom the Patriarch of mankind repli'd.
O favourable spirit, propitious guest,
Well hast thou taught the way that might direct
Our knowledge, and the scale of Nature set
From center to circumference, whereon   510
In contemplation of created things

By steps we may ascend to God.   But say,
What meant that caution joind, *if ye be found
Obedient?* can we want obedience then
To him, or possibly his love desert   515
Who formd us from the dust, and plac'd us here
Full to the utmost measure of what bliss
Human desires can seek or apprehend?
    To whom the Angel.   Son of Heav'n and Earth,
Attend: That thou art happie, ow to God;   520
That thou continu'st such, owe to thy self,
That is, to thy obedience; therein stand.
This was that caution giv'n thee; be advis'd.
God made thee perfet, not immutable;
And good he made thee, but to persevere   525
He left it in thy power, ordaind thy will
By nature free, not over-rul'd by Fate
Inextricable, or strict Necessity;
Our voluntarie service he requires,
Not our necessitated, such with him   530
Findes no acceptance, nor can find, for how
Can hearts, not free, be tri'd whether they serve
Willing or no, who will but what they must
By Destinie, and can no other choose?
My self and all th' Angelic Host that stand   535
In sight of God enthon'd, our happie state
Hold, as you yours, while our obedience holds;
On other surety none; freely we serve
Because wee freely love, as in our will
To love or not; in this we stand or fall: 540
And som are fall'n, to disobedience fall'n,
And so from Heav'n to deepest Hell; O fall
From what high state of bliss into what woe!
    To whom our great Progenitor.   Thy words
Attentive, and with more delighted eare   545
Divine instructer, I have heard, than when
Cherubic Songs by night from neighbouring Hills
Aëreal Music send: nor knew I not
To be both will and deed created free;
Yet that we never shall forget to love   550
Our maker, and obey him whose command
Single, is yet so just, my constant thoughts
Assur'd me, and still assure: though what thou tellst
Hath past in Heav'n, som doubt within me move,
But more desire to hear, if thou consent,   555
The full relation, which must needs be strange,
Worthy of Sacred silence to be heard;
And we have yet large day, for scarce the Sun
Hath finisht half his journey, and scarce begins
His other half in the great Zone of Heav'n.   560

Thus *Adam* made request, and *Raphaël*
After short pause assenting, thus began.
   High matter thou injoinst me, O prime of men,
Sad task and hard, for how shall I relate
To human sense th' invisible exploits   565
Of warring Spirits; how without remorse
The ruin of so many glorious once
And perfet while they stood; how last unfold
The secrets of another world, perhaps
Not lawful to reveal? yet for thy good   570
This is dispenst, and what surmounts the reach
Of human sense, I shall delineate so,
By lik'ning spiritual to corporeal forms,
As may express them best, though what if Earth
Be but the shaddow of Heav'n, and things therein   575
Each to other like, more than on Earth is thought?
   As yet this World was not, and *Chaos* wilde
Reignd where these Heav'ns now roul, where Earth now rests
Upon her Center pois'd, when on a day
(For Time, though in Eternitie, appli'd   580
To motion, measures all things durable
By present, past, and future) on such day
As Heav'ns great Year brings forth, th' Empyreal Host
Of Angels by Imperial summons calld,
Innumerable before th' Almighty Throne   585
Forthwith from all the ends of Heav'n appear'd
Under thir Hierarchs in orders bright:
Ten thousand thousand Ensigns high advanc't,
Standards and Gonfalons twixt Van and Reare
Streame in the Air, and for distinction serve   590
Of Hierarchies, of Orders, and Degrees;
Or in thir glittering Tissues bear imblaz'd
Holy Memorials, acts of Zeal and Love
Recorded eminent.   Thus when in Orbs
Of circuit inexpressible they stood,   595
Orb within Orb, the Father infinite,
By whom in bliss imbosomd sat the Son,
Amidst as from a flaming Mount, whose top
Brightness had made invisible, thus spake.
   Hear all ye Angels, Progenie of Light,   600
Thrones, Dominations, Princedoms, Vertues, Powers,
Hear my Decree, which unrevok't shall stand.
This day I have begot whom I declare
My onely Son, and on this holy Hill
Him have anointed, whom ye now behold   605
At my right hand; your Head I him appoint;
And by my Self have sworn to him shall bow

573 corporeal *Ed. 4*] corporal *Edd. 1–3*

All knees in Heav'n, and shall confess him Lord:
Under his great Vice-gerent Reign abide
United as one individual Soule   610
For ever happie: him who disobeyes
Mee disobeys, breaks union, and that day
Cast out from God and blessed vision, falls
Into utter darkness, deep ingulft, his place
Ordaind without redemption, without end.   615
  So spake th' Omnipotent, and with his words
All seemd well pleas'd, all seemd, but were not all.
That day, as other solemn days, they spent
In song and dance about the sacred Hill,
Mystical dance, which yonder starrie Spheare   620
Of Planets and of fixt in all her Wheeles
Resembles nearest, mazes intricate,
Eccentric, intervolv'd, yet regular
Then most, when most irregular they seem:
And in thir motions harmonie Divine   625
So smooths her charming tones, that Gods own eare
Listens delighted. Ev'ning now approachd
(For wee have also our Ev'ning and our Morn,
Wee ours for change delectable, not need)
Forthwith from dance to sweet repast they turn   630
Desirous; all in Circles as they stood,
Tables are set, and on a sudden pil'd
With Angels Food, and rubied Nectar flows
In Pearl, in Diamond, and massie Gold,
Fruit of delicious Vines, the growth of Heav'n.   635
On flowrs repos'd, and with fresh flowrets crownd,
They eat, they drink, and in communion sweet
Quaff immortalitie and joy, secure
Of surfet where full measure onely bounds
Excess, before th' all bounteous King, who showrd   640
With copious hand, rejoicing in thir joy.
Now when ambrosial Night with Clouds exhal'd
From that high mount of God, whence light and shade
Spring both, the face of brightest Heav'n had chang'd
To grateful Twilight (for Night comes not there   645
In darker veil) and roseat Dews dispos'd
All but th'unsleeping eyes of God to rest,
Wide over all the Plain, and wider farr
Than all this globous Earth in Plain outspred,
(Such are the Courts of God) th' Angelic throng   650
Disperst in Bands and Files thir Camp extend
By living Streams among the Trees of Life,
Pavilions numberless, and sudden rear'd,

636–40 They eat, they drink, and with refection sweet
          Are fill'd, before th' all-bounteous King, who showrd *Ed. 1*

Celestial Tabernacles, where they slept
Fannd with cool Winds, save those who in thir course 655
Melodious Hymns about the sovran Throne
Alternate all night long: but not so wak'd
Satan, so call him now, his former name
Is heard no more in Heav'n; hee of the first,
If not the first Arch-Angel, great in Power,   660
In favour and præeminence, yet fraught
With envie against the Son of God, that day
Honourd by his great Father, and proclaimd
Messiah King anointed, could not beare
Through pride that sight, and thought himself impaird.
Deep malice thence conceiving and disdain,   666
Soon as midnight brought on the duskie houre
Friendliest to sleep and silence, he resolv'd
With all his Legions to dislodge, and leave
Unworshipt, unobeyd the Throne supream   670
Contemptuous, and his next subordinate
Awak'ning, thus to him in secret spake.
     Sleepst thou Companion dear, what sleep can close
Thy eye-lids? and remembrest what Decree
Of yesterday, so late hath past the lips   675
Of Heav'ns Almightie.   Thou to me thy thoughts
Wast wont, I mine to thee was wont to impart;
Both waking we were one; how then can now
Thy sleep dissent? new Laws thou seest impos'd;
New Laws from him who reigns, new minds may raise
In us who serve, new Counsels, to debate   681
What doubtful may ensue: more in this place
To utter is not safe.   Assemble thou
Of all those Myriads which we lead the chief;
Tell them that by command, ere yet dim Night   685
Her shaddowie Cloud withdraws, I am to haste,
And all who under me thir Banners wave,
Homeward with flying march where we possess
The Quarters of the North, there to prepare
Fit entertainment to receive our King   690
The great *Messiah*, and his new commands,
Who speedily through all the Hierarchies
Intends to pass triumphant, and give Laws.
     So spake the false Arch-Angel, and infus'd
Bad influence into th' unwarie brest   695
Of his Associate; hee together calls,
Or several one by one, the Regent Powers,
Under him Regent, tells, as he was taught,
That the most High commanding, now ere Night,
Now ere dim Night had disincumberd Heav'n,   700
The great Hierarchal Standard was to move;
Tells the suggested cause, and casts between

Ambiguous words and jealousies, to sound
Or taint integritie; but all obeyd
The wonted signal, and superior voice   705
Of thir great Potentate; for great indeed
His name, and high was his degree in Heav'n;
His count'nance, as the Morning Starr that guides
The starrie flock, allur'd them, and with lies
Drew after him the third part of Heav'ns Host: 710
Mean while th' Eternal eye, whose sight discerns
Abstrusest thoughts, from forth his holy Mount
And from within the golden Lamps that burne
Nightly before him, saw without thir light
Rebellion rising, saw in whom, how spred   715
Among the sons of Morn, what multitudes
Were banded to oppose his high Decree;
And smiling to his onely Son thus said.

Son, thou in whom my glory I behold
In full resplendence, Heir of all my might,   720
Nearly it now concernes us to be sure
Of our Omnipotence, and with what Arms
We mean to hold what anciently we claim
Of Deitie or Empire, such a foe
Is rising, who intends to erect his Throne   725
Equal to ours, throughout the spacious North;
Nor so content, hath in his thought to try
In battel, what our Power is, or our right.
Let us advise, and to this hazard draw
With speed what force is left, and all imploy   730
In our defence, lest unawares we lose
This our high place, our Sanctuarie, our Hill.

To whom the Son with calm aspect and clear
Light'ning Divine, ineffable, serene,
Made answer.   Mightie Father, thou thy foes   735
Justly hast in derision, and secure
Laughst at thir vain designes and tumults vain,
Matter to mee of Glory, whom thir hate
Illustrates, when they see all Regal Power
Giv'n me to quell thir pride, and in event   740
Know whether I be dextrous to subdue
Thy Rebels, or be found the worst in Heav'n.

So spake the Son, but *Satan* with his Powers
Far was advanc't on winged speed, an Host
Innumerable as the Starrs of Night,   745
Or Starrs of Morning, Dew-drops, which the Sun
Impearls on every leaf and every flower.
Regions they passd, the mightie Regencies
Of Seraphim and Potentates and Thrones
In thir triple Degrees, Regions to which   750
All thy Dominion, *Adam*, is no more

Than what this Garden is to all the Earth,
And all the Sea, from one entire globose
Stretcht into Longitude; which having past
At length into the limits of the North   755
They came, and *Satan* to his Royal seate
High on a Hill, far blazing, as a Mount
Rais'd on a Mount, with Pyramids and Towrs
From Diamond Quarries hewn and Rocks of Gold,
The Palace of great *Lucifer*, (so call   760
That Structure in the Dialect of men
Interpreted) which not long after, he
Affecting all equality with God,
In imitation of that Mount whereon
Messiah was declar'd in sight of Heav'n,   765
The Mountain of the Congregation calld;
For thither he assembl'd all his Train,
Pretending so commanded to consult
About the great reception of thir King,
Thither to come, and with calumnious Art   770
Of counterfeted truth thus held thir ears.
    Thrones, Dominations, Princedoms, Vertues, Powers,
If these magnific Titles yet remain
Not merely titular, since by Decree
Another now hath to himself ingross't   775
All Power, and us eclipst under the name
Of King anointed, for whom all this haste
Of midnight march, and hurried meeting here,
This onely to consult how we may best
With what may be devis'd of honours new   780
Receive him coming to receive from us
Knee-tribute yet unpaid, prostration vile,
Too much to one, but double how endur'd,
To one and to his image now proclaimd?
But what if better counsels might erect   785
Our minds and teach us to cast off this Yoke?
Will ye submit your necks, and choose to bend
The supple knee? ye will not, if I trust
To know ye right, or if ye know your selves
Natives and Sons of Heav'n possest before   790
By none, and if not equal all, yet free,
Equally free; for Orders and Degrees
Jarr not with liberty, but well consist.
Who can in reason then or right assume
Monarchie over such as live by right   795
His equals, if in power and splendor less,
In freedom equal? or can introduce
Law and Edict on us, who without law
Erre not, much less for this to be our Lord,
And look for adoration to th' abuse   800

Of those Imperial Titles which assert
Our being ordaind to govern, not to serve?
   Thus farr his bold discourse without controule
Had audience, when among the Seraphim
Abdiel, than whom none with more zeale ador'd   805
The Deitie, and divine commands obeyd,
Stood up, and in a flame of zeale severe
The current of his fury thus oppos'd,
   O argument blasphemous, false and proud!
Words which no eare ever to hear in Heav'n   810
Expected, least of all from thee, ingrate
In place thy self so high above thy Peers.
Canst thou with impious obloquie condemne
The just Decree of God, pronounc't and sworn,
That to his only Son by right endu'd   815
With Regal Scepter, every Soul in Heav'n
Shall bend the knee, and in that honour due
Confess him rightful King? unjust thou sayst
Flatly unjust, to bind with Laws the free,
And equal over equals to let Reign,   820
One over all with unsucceeded power.
Shalt thou give Law to God, shalt thou dispute
With him the points of libertie, who made
Thee what thou art, and formd the Pow'rs of Heav'n
Such as he pleas'd, and circumscrib'd thir being? 825
Yet by experience taught we know how good,
And of our good, and of our dignitie
How provident he is, how farr from thought
To make us less, bent rather to exalt
Our happie state under one Head more near   830
United.   But to grant it thee unjust,
That equal over equals Monarch Reign:
Thy self though great and glorious dost thou count,
Or all Angelic Nature joind in one,
Equal to him begotten Son, by whom   835
As by his Word the mighty Father made
All things, ev'n thee, and all the Spirits of Heav'n
By him created in thir bright degrees,
Crownd them with Glory, and to thir Glory nam'd
Thrones, Dominations, Princedoms, Vertues, Powers, 840
Essential Powers, nor by his Reign obscur'd,
But more illustrious made, since he the Head
One of our number thus reduc't becomes,
His Laws our Laws, all honour to him done
Returns our own.   Cease then this impious rage,   845
And tempt not these; but hasten to appease
Th' incensed Father, and th' incensed Son,
While Pardon may be found in time besought.
   So spake the fervent Angel, but his zeale

None seconded, as out of season judg'd,   850
Or singular and rash, whereat rejoic'd
Th' Apostat, and more haughty thus repli'd.
That we were formd then sayst thou? and the work
Of secondarie hands, by task transferrd
From Father to his Son? strange point and new!   855
Doctrin which we would know whence learnt: who saw
When this creation was? rememberst thou
Thy making, while the Maker gave thee being?
We know no time when we were not as now;
Know none before us, self-begot, self-rais'd   860
By our own quick'ning power, when fatal course
Had circl'd his full Orb, the birth mature
Of this our native Heav'n, Ethereal Sons.
Our puissance is our own, our own right hand
Shall teach us highest deeds, by proof to try   865
Who is our equal: then thou shalt behold
Whether by supplication we intend
Address, and to begirt th' Almighty Throne
Beseeching or besieging.   This report,
These tidings carrie to th' anointed King;   870
And fly, ere evil intercept thy flight.
     He said, and as the sound of waters deep
Hoarse murmur echo'd to his words applause
Through the infinite Host, nor less for that
The flaming Seraph fearless, though alone   875
Encompast round with foes, thus answerd bold.
     O alienate from God, O spirit accurst,
Forsaken of all good; I see thy fall
Determind, and thy hapless crew involv'd
In this perfidious fraud, contagion spred   880
Both of thy crime and punishment: henceforth
No more be troubl'd how to quit the yoke
Of Gods *Messiah*; those indulgent Laws
Will not now be voutsaf't, other Decrees
Against thee are gon forth without recall;   885
That Golden Scepter which thou didst reject
Is now an Iron Rod to bruise and breake
Thy disobedience.   Well thou didst advise,
Yet not for thy advice or threats I fly
These wicked Tents devoted, lest the wrauth   890
Impendent, raging into sudden flame
Distinguish not: for soon expect to feel
His Thunder on thy head, devouring fire.
Then who created thee lamenting learn,
When who can uncreate thee thou shalt know.   895
     So spake the Seraph *Abdiel* faithful found,
Among the faithless, faithful only hee;

889 advice *Ed. 4*] advise *Edd. 1, 2, 3*

Among innumerable false, unmov'd,
Unshaken, unseduc't, unterrifi'd
His Loyaltie he kept, his Love, his Zeal;   900
Nor number, nor example with him wrought
To swerve from truth, or change his constant mind
Though single.   From amidst them forth he passd,
Long way through hostile scorn, which he sustaind
Superior, nor of violence fear'd aught;   905
And with retorted scorn his back he turnd
On those proud Towrs to swift destruction doomd.

The End of the Fifth Book

BOOK VI

THE ARGUMENT

Raphael *continues to relate how* Michael *and* Gabriel *were sent forth to battel against* Satan *and his Angels. The first Fight describ'd :* Satan *and his Powers retire under Night : He calls a Councel, invents devilish Engines, which in the second dayes Fight put* Michael *and his Angels to some disorder ; But they at length pulling up Mountains overwhelm'd both the force and Machins of* Satan *: Yet the Tumult not so ending, God on the third day sends* Messiah *his Son, for whom he had reserv'd the glory of that Victory : Hee in the Power of his Father coming to the place, and causing all his Legions to stand still on either side, with his Chariot and Thunder driving into the midst of his Enemies, pursues them unable to resist towards the wall of Heaven ; which opening, they leap down with horrour and confusion into the place of punishment prepar'd for them in the Deep :* Messiah *returns with triumph to his Father.*

All night the dreadless Angel unpersu'd
Through Heav'ns wide Champain held his way, till Morn,
Wak't by the circling Hours, with rosie hand
Unbarrd the gates of Light.   There is a Cave
Within the Mount of God, fast by his Throne,   5
Where light and darkness in perpetual round
Lodge and dislodge by turns, which makes through Heav'n
Grateful vicissitude, like Day and Night;
Light issues forth, and at the other dore
Obsequious darkness enters, till her hour   10
To veil the Heav'n, though darkness there might well
Seem twilight here; and now went forth the Morn
Such as in highest Heav'n, arrayd in Gold
Empyreal, from before her vanishd Night,
Shot through with orient Beams: when all the Plaine   15
Coverd with thick embatteld Squadrons bright,
Chariots and flaming Arms, and fierie Steeds
Reflecting blaze on blaze, first met his view:
Warr he perceiv'd, warr in procinct, and found
Already known what he for news had thought   20
To have reported: gladly then he mixt
Among those friendly Powers who him receiv'd
With joy and acclamations loud, that one
That of so many Myriads fall'n, yet one
Returnd not lost: On to the sacred hill   25
They led him high applauded, and present
Before the seat supream; from whence a voice
From midst a Golden Cloud thus milde was heard.
    Servant of God, well done, well hast thou fought
The better fight, who single hast maintaind   30

258

Against revolted multitudes the Cause
Of Truth, in word mightier than they in Arms;
And for the testimonie of Truth hast borne
Universal reproach, far worse to bear
Than violence: for this was all thy care   35
To stand approv'd in sight of God, though Worlds
Judg'd thee perverse: the easier conquest now
Remains thee, aided by this host of friends,
Back on thy foes more glorious to return
Than scornd thou didst depart, and to subdue   40
By force, who reason for thir Law refuse,
Right reason for thir Law, and for thir King
Messiah, who by right of merit Reigns.
Goe *Michael* of Celestial Armies Prince,
And thou in Military prowess next   45
Gabriel, lead forth to Battel these my Sons
Invincible, lead forth my armed Saints
By Thousands and by Millions rang'd for fight;
Equal in number to that Godless crew
Rebellious, them with Fire and hostile Arms   50
Fearless assault, and to the brow of Heav'n
Persuing drive them out from God and bliss,
Into thir place of punishment, the Gulf
Of *Tartarus*, which ready opens wide
His fiery *Chaos* to receive thir fall.   55
    So spake the Sovran voice, and Clouds began
To darken all the Hill, and smoke to roul
In duskie wreathes, reluctant flames, the sign
Of wrauth awak't: nor with less dread the loud
Ethereal Trumpet from on high gan blow: 60
At which command the Powers Militant,
That stood for Heav'n, in mighty Quadrate joind
Of Union irresistible, mov'd on
In silence thir bright Legions, to the sound
Of instrumental Harmonie that breath'd   65
Heroic Ardor to adventrous deeds
Under thir God-like Leaders, in the Cause
Of God and his *Messiah*. On they move
Indissolubly firm; nor obvious Hill,
Nor strait'ning Vale, nor Wood, nor Stream divides   70
Thir perfet ranks; for high above the ground
Thir march was, and the passive Air upbore
Thir nimble tread, as when the total kind
Of Birds in orderly array on wing
Came summond over *Eden* to receive   75
Thir names of thee; so over many a tract
Of Heav'n they marchd, and many a Province wide
Tenfold the length of this terrene: at last
Farr in th' Horizon to the North appear'd

From skirt to skirt a fierie Region, stretcht   80
In battailous aspect, and nearer view
Bristl'd with upright beams innumerable
Of rigid Spears, and Helmets throngd, and Shields
Various, with boastful Argument portrayd,
The banded Powers of *Satan* hasting on   85
With furious expedition; for they weend
That self same day by fight or by surprize
To win the Mount of God, and on his Throne
To set the envier of his State, the proud
Aspirer, but thir thoughts prov'd fond and vaine   90
In the mid way: though strange to us it seemd
At first, that Angel should with Angel warr,
And in fierce hosting meet, who wont to meet
So oft in Festivals of joy and love
Unanimous, as sons of one great Sire   95
Hymning th' Eternal Father: but the shout
Of Battel now began, and rushing sound
Of onset ended soon each milder thought.
High in the midst exalted as a God
Th' Apostat in his Sun-bright Chariot sate   100
Idol of Majestie Divine, enclos'd
With Flaming Cherubim, and golden Shields;
Then lighted from his gorgeous Throne, for now
'Twixt Host and Host but narrow space was left,
A dreadful intervall, and Front to Front   105
Presented stood in terrible array
Of hideous length: before the cloudie Van,
On the rough edge of battel ere it joind,
Satan with vast and haughtie strides advanc't
Came towring, armd in Adamant and Gold;   110
Abdiel that sight endur'd not, where he stood
Among the mightiest, bent on highest deeds,
And thus his own undaunted heart explores.

  O Heav'n! that such resemblance of the Highest
Should yet remain, where faith and realtie   115
Remain not; wherefore should not strength and might
There fail where Vertue fails, or weakest prove
Where boldest; though to sight unconquerable?
His puissance, trusting in th' Almightys aid
I mean to try, whose Reason I have tri'd   120
Unsound and false; nor is it aught but just,
That he who in debate of Truth hath won,
Should win in Arms, in both disputes alike
Victor; though brutish that contest and foul,
When Reason hath to deal with force, yet so   125
Most reason is that Reason overcome.
  So pondering, and from his armed Peers
Forth stepping opposite, half way he met

His daring foe, at this prevention more
Incenst, and thus securely him defi'd.　　　　　130
　　Proud, art thou met? thy hope was to have reach't
The highth of thy aspiring unoppos'd,
The Throne of God unguarded, and his side
Abandond at the terror of thy Power
Or potent tongue; fool, not to think how vain　　135
Against th' Omnipotent to rise in Arms;
Who out of smallest things could without end
Have rais'd incessant Armies to defeat
Thy folly; or with solitarie hand
Reaching beyond all limit, at one blow　　　　140
Unaided could have finisht thee, and whelmd
Thy Legions under darkness; but thou seest
All are not of thy Train; there be who Faith
Prefer, and Pietie to God, though then
To thee not visible, when I alone　　　　　　145
Seemd in thy World erroneous to dissent
From all: my Sect thou seest, now learn too late
How few somtimes may know, when thousands err.
　　Whom the grand Foe with scornful eye askance
Thus answerd.　Ill for thee, but in wisht houre　150
Of my revenge, first sought for thou returnst
From flight, seditious Angel, to receive
Thy merited reward, the first assay
Of this right hand provok't, since first that tongue
Inspir'd with contradiction durst oppose　　　155
A third part of the Gods, in Synod met
Thir Deities to assert, who while they feel
Vigor Divine within them, can allow
Omnipotence to none.　But well thou comst
Before thy fellows, ambitious to win　　　　160
From me som Plume, that thy success may show
Destruction to the rest: this pause between
(Unanswerd lest thou boast) to let thee know;
At first I thought that Libertie and Heav'n
To heav'nly Soules had bin all one; but now　　165
I see that most through sloath had rather serve,
Ministring Spirits, traind up in Feast and Song;
Such hast thou armd, the Minstrelsie of Heav'n,
Servilitie with freedom to contend,
As both thir deeds compar'd this day shall prove.　170
　　To whom in brief thus *Abdiel* stern repli'd.
Apostat, still thou errst, nor end wilt find
Of erring, from the path of truth remote:
Unjustly thou deprav'st it with the name
Of *Servitude* to serve whom God ordains　　　175
Or Nature; God and Nature bid the same,
When he who rules is worthiest, and excells

Them whom he governs.   This is servitude,
To serve th' unwise, or him who hath rebelld
Against his worthier, as thine now serve thee,   180
Thy self not free, but to thy self enthralld;
Yet lewdly dar'st our ministring upbraid.
Reign thou in Hell thy Kingdom, let mee serve
In Heav'n God ever blest, and his Divine
Behests obey, worthiest to be obeyd,   185
Yet Chains in Hell, not Realms expect: mean while
From mee returnd, as erst thou saidst, from flight,
This greeting on thy impious Crest receive.
    So saying, a noble stroke he lifted high,
Which hung not, but so swift with tempest fell   190
On the proud Crest of *Satan*, that no sight,
Nor motion of swift thought, less could his Shield
Such ruin intercept: ten paces huge
He back recoild; the tenth on bended knee
His massie Spear upstayd; as if on Earth   195
Winds under ground or waters forcing way
Sidelong, had pusht a Mountain from his seat
Half sunk with all his Pines.   Amazement seiz'd
The Rebel Thrones, but greater rage to see
Thus foild thir mightiest, ours joy filld, and shout,   200
Presage of Victorie and fierce desire
Of Battel: whereat *Michaël* bid sound
Th' Arch-angel trumpet; through the vast of Heav'n
It sounded, and the faithful Armies rung
Hosanna to the Highest: nor stood at gaze   205
The adverse Legions, nor less hideous joind
The horrid shock: now storming furie rose,
And clamor such as heard in Heav'n till now
Was never, Arms on Armour clashing brayd
Horrible discord, and the madding Wheeles   210
Of brazen Chariots rag'd; dire was the noise
Of conflict; over head the dismal hiss
Of fiery Darts in flaming vollies flew,
And flying vaulted either Host with fire.
So under fierie Cope together rushd   215
Both Battels main, with ruinous assault
And inextinguishable rage; all Heav'n
Resounded, and had Earth bin then, all Earth
Had to her Center shook.   What wonder? when
Millions of fierce encountring Angels fought   220
On either side, the least of whom could wield
These Elements, and arm him with the force
Of all thir Regions: how much more of Power
Armie against Armie numberless to raise
Dreadful combustion warring, and disturb,   225
Though not destroy, thir happie Native seat;

Had not th' Eternal King Omnipotent
From his strong hold of Heav'n high over-rul'd
And limited thir might; though numberd such
As each divided Legion might have seemd   230
A numerous Host, in strength each armed hand
A Legion; led in fight, yet Leader seemd
Each Warrior single as in Chief, expert
When to advance, or stand, or turn the sway
Of Battel, open when, and when to close   235
The ridges of grim Warr; no thought of flight,
None of retreat, no unbecoming deed
That argu'd fear; each on himself reli'd,
As onely in his arm the moment lay
Of victorie; deeds of eternal fame   240
Were don, but infinite: for wide was spred
That Warr and various: somtimes on firm ground
A standing fight, then soaring on main wing
Tormented all the Air; all Air seemd then
Conflicting Fire: long time in even scale   245
The Battel hung; till *Satan*, who that day
Prodigious power had shewn, and met in Armes
No equal, ranging through the dire attack
Of fighting Seraphim confus'd, at length
Saw where the Sword of *Michael* smote, and felld 250
Squadrons at once, with huge two-handed sway
Brandisht aloft the horrid edge came down
Wide wasting; such destruction to withstand
He hasted, and oppos'd the rockie Orb
Of tenfold Adamant, his ample Shield   255
A vast circumference: At his approach
The great Arch-Angel from his warlike toil
Surceas'd, and glad as hoping here to end
Intestin War in Heav'n, th'Arch-foe subdu'd
Or Captive dragd in Chains, with hostile frown   260
And visage all enflam'd first thus began.
   Author of evil, unknown till thy revolt,
Unnam'd in Heav'n, now plenteous, as thou seest
These Acts of hateful strife, hateful to all,
Though heaviest by just measure on thy self   265
And thy adherents: how hast thou disturbd
Heav'ns blessed peace, and into Nature brought
Miserie, uncreated till the crime
Of thy Rebellion! how hast thou instilld
Thy malice into thousands, once upright   270
And faithful, now prov'd false! But think not here
To trouble Holy Rest; Heav'n casts thee out
From all her Confines. Heav'n the seat of bliss
Brooks not the works of violence and Warr.
Hence then, and evil go with thee along   275

Thy offspring, to the place of evil, Hell,
Thou and thy wicked crew; there mingle broils,
Ere this avenging Sword begin thy doom,
Or som more sudden vengeance wingd from God
Precipitate thee with augmented pain.   280
    So spake the Prince of Angels; to whom thus
The Adversarie.   Nor think thou with wind
Of airie threats to aw whom yet with deeds
Thou canst not.   Hast thou turnd the least of these
To flight, or if to fall, but that they rise   285
Unvanquisht, easier to transact with mee
That thou shouldst hope, imperious, and with threats
To chase me hence? erre not that so shall end
The strife which thou callst evil, but wee style
The strife of Glorie: which we mean to win,   290
Or turn this Heav'n it self into the Hell
Thou fablest, here however to dwell free,
If not to reign: mean while thy utmost force,
And join him nam'd *Almightie* to thy aid,
I flie not, but have sought thee farr and nigh.   295
    They ended parle, and both addressd for fight
Unspeakable; for who, though with the tongue
Of Angels, can relate, or to what things
Liken on Earth conspicuous, that may lift
Human imagination to such highth   300
Of Godlike Power: for likest Gods they seemd,
Stood they or mov'd, in stature, motion, armes
Fit to decide the Empire of great Heav'n.
Now wav'd thir fierie Swords, and in the Air
Made horrid Circles; two broad Suns thir Shields   305
Blaz'd opposite, while expectation stood
In horror; from each hand with speed retir'd
Where erst was thickest fight, th' Angelic throng,
And left large field, unsafe within the wind
Of such commotion, such as to set forth   310
Great things by small, If Natures concord broke,
Among the Constellations warr were sprung,
Two Planets rushing from aspect malign
Of fiercest opposition in mid Skie,
Should combat, and thir jarring Sphears confound.   315
Together both with next to Almightie Arme
Uplifted imminent, one stroke they aimd
That might determin, and not need repeat,
As not of power, at once; nor odds appear'd
In might or swift prevention; but the sword   320
Of *Michael* from the Armorie of God
Was giv'n him temperd so, that neither keen
Nor solid might resist that edge: it met
The sword of *Satan* with steep force to smite

Descending, and in half cut sheer, nor stayd,   325
But with swift wheele reverse, deep entring shar'd
All his right side; then *Satan* first knew pain,
And writh'd him to and fro convolv'd; so sore
The griding sword with discontinuous wound
Passd through him, but th' Ethereal substance clos'd   330
Not long divisible, and from the gash
A stream of Nectarous humor issuing flowd
Sanguin, such as Celestial Spirits may bleed,
And all his Armour staind erewhile so bright.
Forthwith on all sides to his aide was run   335
By Angels many and strong, who interpos'd
Defence, while others bore him on thir Shields
Back to his Chariot, where it stood retir'd
From off the files of warr; there they him laid
Gnashing for anguish and despite and shame   340
To find himself not matchless, and his pride
Humbl'd by such rebuke, so farr beneath
His confidence to equal God in power.
Yet soon he heal'd; for Spirits that live throughout
Vital in every part, not as frail man   345
In Entrails, Heart or Head, Liver or Reins,
Cannot but by annihilating die;
Nor in thir liquid texture mortal wound
Receive, no more than can the fluid Air:
All Heart they live, all Head, all Eye, all Ear,   350
All Intellect, all Sense, and as they please
They Limb themselves, and colour, shape or size
Assume, as likes them best, condense or rare.
  Mean while in other parts like deeds deserv'd
Memorial, where the might of *Gabriel* fought,   355
And with fierce Ensignes pierc'd the deep array
Of *Moloc* furious King, who him defi'd,
And at his Chariot wheeles to drag him bound
Threatend, nor from the Holie One of Heav'n
Refraind his tongue blasphemous; but anon   360
Down cloven to the waist, with shatterd Arms
And uncouth pain fled bellowing.   On each wing
Uriel and *Raphaël* his vaunting foe,
Though huge, and in a Rock of Diamond Armd,
Vanquishd *Adramelec* and *Asmadai*,   365
Two potent Thrones, that to be less than Gods
Disdaind, but meaner thoughts learnd in thir flight,
Mangl'd with gastly wounds through Plate and Mail.
Nor stood unmindful *Abdiel* to annoy
The Atheist crew, but with redoubl'd blow   370
Ariel and *Arioc*, and the violence
Of *Ramiel* scorcht and blasted overthrew.
I might relate of thousands, and thir names

Eternize here on Earth; but those elect
Angels contented with thir fame in Heav'n   375
Seek not the praise of men: the other sort
In might though wondrous and in Acts of Warr,
Nor of Renown less eager, yet by doome,
Canceld from Heav'n and sacred memorie,
Nameless in dark oblivion let them dwell.   380
For strength from Truth divided and from Just,
Illaudable, naught merits but dispraise
And ignominie, yet to glorie aspires
Vain glorious, and through infamie seeks fame:
Therefore Eternal silence be thir doom.   385
    And now thir Mightiest quelld, the battel swerv'd,
With many an inroad gor'd; deformed rout
Enterd, and foul disorder; all the ground
With shiverd armour strown, and on a heap
Chariot and Charioter lay overturnd   390
And fierie foaming Steeds; what stood, recoild
O'erwearied, through the faint Satanic Host
Defensive scarce, or with pale fear surpris'd,
Then first with fear surpris'd and sense of paine
Fled ignominious, to such evil brought   395
By sin of disobedience, till that hour
Not liable to fear or flight or pain.
Far otherwise th' inviolable Saints
In Cubic Phalanx firm advanc'd entire,
Invulnerable, impenitrably armd: 400
Such high advantages thir innocence
Gave them above thir foes, not to have sinnd,
Not to have disobeyd; in fight they stood
Unwearied, unobnoxious to be paind
By wound, though from thir place by violence mov'd. 405
    Now Night her course began, and over Heav'n
Inducing darkness, grateful truce impos'd,
And silence on the odious dinn of Warr:
Under her Cloudie covert both retir'd.
Victor and Vanquisht: on the foughten field   410
Michaël and his Angels prevalent
Encamping, plac'd in Guard thir Watches round,
Cherubic waving fires: on th' other part
Satan with his rebellious disappear'd,
Far in the dark dislodg'd, and void of rest,   415
His Potentates to Councel calld by night;
And in the midst thus undismayd began.
    O now in danger tri'd, now known in Armes
Not to be overpowerd, Companions dear,
Found worthy not of Libertie alone,   420
Too mean pretence, but what we more affect,
Honour, Dominion, Glorie, and renown,

Who have sustaind one day in doubtful fight
(And if one day, why not Eternal days?)
What Heavens Lord had powerfullest to send   425
Against us from about his Throne, and judg'd
Sufficient to subdue us to his will,
But proves not so: then fallible, it seems,
Of future we may deem him, though till now
Omniscient thought.   True is, less firmly armd,   430
Some disadvantage we endur'd and pain,
Till now not known, but known as soon contemnd,
Since now we find this our Empyreal form
Incapable of mortal injurie
Imperishable, and though peirc't with wound,   435
Soon closing, and by native vigor heal'd.
Of evil then so small as easie think
The remedie; perhaps more valid Arms,
Weapons more violent, when next we meet,
May serve to better us, and worse our foes,   440
Or equal what between us made the odds,
In Nature none: if other hidden cause
Left them Superior, while we can preserve
Unhurt our minds, and understanding sound,
Due search and consultation will disclose.   445
   He sat; and in th' assembly next upstood
Nisroc, of Principalities the prime;
As one he stood escap't from cruel fight,
Sore toild, his riven Armes to havoc hewn,
And cloudie in aspect thus answering spake.   450
Deliverer from new Lords, leader to free
Enjoyment of our right as Gods; yet hard
For Gods, and too unequal work we find
Against unequal armes to fight in pain,
Against unpaind, impassive; from which evil   455
Ruin must needs ensue; for what availes
Valour or strength, though matchless, quelld with pain
Which all subdues, and makes remiss the hands
Of Mightiest.   Sense of pleasure we may well
Spare out of life perhaps, and not repine,   460
But live content, which is the calmest life:
But pain is perfet miserie, the worst
Of evils, and excessive, overturnes
All patience.   He who therefore can invent
With what more forcible we may offend   465
Our yet unwounded Enemies, or arm
Our selves with like defence, to me deserves
No less than for deliverance what we ow.
   Whereto with look compos'd *Satan* repli'd.
Not uninvented that, which thou aright   470
Believ'st so main to our success, I bring;

Which of us who beholds the bright surface
Of this Ethereous mould whereon we stand,
This continent of spacious Heav'n, adornd
With Plant, Fruit, Flowr Ambrosial, Gemms and Gold,
Whose Eye so superficially surveys   476
These things, as not to mind from whence they grow
Deep under ground, materials dark and crude,
Of spiritous and fierie spume, till toucht
With Heav'ns ray, and temperd they shoot forth   480
So beauteous, op'ning to the ambient light.
These in thir dark Nativitie the Deep
Shall yield us pregnant with infernal flame,
Which into hollow Engins long and round
Thick-rammd, at th' other bore with touch of fire   485
Dilated and infuriat shall send forth
From far with thundring noise among our foes
Such implements of mischief as shall dash
To pieces and orewhelm whatever stands
Adverse, that they shall fear we have disarmd   490
The Thunderer of his only dreaded bolt.
Nor long shall be our labour, yet ere dawne
Effect shall end our wish.   Mean while revive;
Abandon fear; to strength and counsel joind
Think nothing hard, much less to be despaird.   495
He ended, and his words thir drooping cheer
Enlightend, and thir languisht hope reviv'd.
Th' invention all admir'd, and each, how hee
To be th' inventer missd, so easie it seemd
Once found, which yet unfound most would have thought
Impossible: yet haply of thy Race   501
In future days, if Malice should abound,
Some one intent on mischief, or inspir'd
With dev'lish machination might devise
Like instrument to plague the Sons of men   505
For sin, on warr and mutual slaughter bent.
Forthwith from Councel to the work they flew,
None arguing stood, innumerable hands
Were ready, in a moment up they turnd
Wide the Celestial soil, and saw beneath   510
Th' originals of Nature in thir crude
Conception; Sulphurous and Nitrous Foam
They found, they mingl'd, and with suttle Art
Concocted and adusted they reduc'd
To blackest grain, and into store conveyd: 515
Part hidden veins diggd up (nor hath this Earth
Entrails unlike) of Mineral and Stone,
Whereof to found thir Engins and thir Balls

484 hollow] hallow *Edd. 1, 2*

Of missive ruin; part incentive reed
Provide, pernicious with one touch to fire.   520
So all ere day-spring, under conscious Night
Secret they finishd, and in order set,
With silent circumspection unespi'd.
Now when fair Morn Orient in Heav'n appear'd
Up rose the Victor Angels, and to Arms   525
The mattin Trumpet Sung: in Arms they stood
Of Golden Panoplie, refulgent Host,
Soon banded; others from the dawning Hills
Lookd round, and Scouts each Coast light-armed scour
Each quarter, to descrie the distant foe,   530
Where lodg'd, or whither fled, or if for fight,
In motion or in alt: him soon they met
Under spred Ensignes moving nigh, in slow
But firm Battalion; back with speediest Sail
Zophiel, of Cherubim the swiftest wing,   535
Came flying, and in mid Aire aloud thus cri'd.
   Arme, Warriors, Arme for fight, the foe at hand,
Whom fled we thought, will save us long persuit
This day, fear not his flight; so thick a Cloud
He comes, and settl'd in his face I see   540
Sad resolution and secure: let each
His Adamantine coat gird well, and each
Fit well his Helm, gripe fast his orbed Shield,
Borne ev'n or high, for this day will pour down,
If I conjecture aught, no drizling showr,   545
But ratling storm of Arrows barbd with fire.
So warnd he them aware themselves, and soon
In order, quit of all impediment;
Instant without disturb they took Alarm,
And onward move Embatteld; when behold   550
Not distant far with heavie pace the Foe
Approaching gross and huge; in hollow Cube
Training his devilish Enginrie, impal'd
On every side with shaddowing Squadrons Deep,
To hide the fraud.   At interview both stood   555
A while, but suddenly at head appear'd
Satan: And thus was heard Commanding loud.
   Vanguard, to Right and Left the Front unfold;
That all may see who hate us, how we seek
Peace and composure, and with open brest   560
Stand readie to receive them, if they like
Our overture, and turn not back perverse;
But that I doubt; however witness Heaven,
Heav'n witness thou anon, while we discharge
Freely our part: yee who appointed stand   565
Doe as you have in charge, and briefly touch
What we propound, and loud that all may hear.

       So scoffing in ambiguous words, he scarce
Had ended; when to Right and Left the Front
Divided, and to either Flank retir'd.   570
Which to our eyes discoverd new and strange
A triple-mounted row of Pillars laid
On Wheels (for like to Pillars most they seemd
Or hollowd bodies made of Oak or Firr
With branches lopt, in Wood or Mountain felld)   575
Brass, Iron, Stonie mould, had not thir mouthes
With hideous orifice gap't on us wide,
Portending hollow truce; at each behind
A Seraph stood, and in his hand a Reed
Stood waving tipt with fire; while we suspense,   580
Collected stood within our thoughts amus'd,
Not long, for sudden all at once thir Reeds
Put forth, and to a narrow vent appli'd
With nicest touch.   Immediat in a flame,
But soon obscur'd with smoke, all Heav'n appear'd,   585
From those deep-throated Engins belcht, whose roar
Emboweld with outragious noise the Air,
And all her entrails tore, disgorging foule
Thir devilish glut, chaind Thunderbolts and Hail
Of Iron Globes, which on the Victor Host   590
Leveld, with such impetuous furie smote,
That whom they hit, none on thir feet might stand,
Though standing else as Rocks, but down they fell
By thousands, Angel on Arch-Angel rould;
The sooner for thir Arms, unarmd they might   595
Have easily as Spirits evaded swift
By quick contraction or remove; but now
Foule dissipation followd and forc't rout;
Nor serv'd it to relax thir serried files.
What should they do? if on they rushd, repulse   600
Repeated, and indecent overthrow
Doubl'd, would render them yet more despis'd,
And to thir foes a laughter; for in view
Stood rankt of Seraphim another row
In posture to displode thir second tire   605
Of Thunder: back defeated to return
They worse abhorrd.   *Satan* beheld thir plight,
And to his Mates thus in derision calld.

       O Friends, why come not on these Victors proud?
Erewhile they fierce were coming, and when wee   610
To entertain them fair with open Front
And Brest (what could we more?) propounded terms
Of composition, straight they chang'd thir minds,
Flew off, and into strange vagaries fell,
As they would dance, yet for a dance they seemd   615
Somewhat extravagant and wild, perhaps

For joy of offerd peace: but I suppose
If our proposals once again were heard
We should compell them to a quick result.
    To whom thus *Belial* in like gamesom mood.   620
Leader, the terms we sent were terms of weight,
Of hard contents, and full of force urg'd home,
Such as we might perceive amus'd them all,
And stumbl'd many: who receives them right
Had need from head to foot well understand;   625
Not understood, this gift they have besides,
They shew us when our foes walk not upright.
    So they among themselves in pleasant veine
Stood scoffing, highthend in thir thoughts beyond
All doubt of Victorie, eternal might   630
To match with thir inventions they presum'd
So easie, and of his Thunder made a scorn,
And all his Host derided, while they stood
A while in trouble; but they stood not long,
Rage prompted them at length, and found them **arms** 635
Against such hellish mischief fit to oppose.
Forthwith (behold the excellence, the power
Which God hath in his mighty Angels plac't)
Thir Arms away they threw, and to the Hills
(For Earth hath this variety from Heav'n   640
Of pleasure situate in Hill and Dale)
Light as the Lightning glimpse they ran, they flew,
From thir foundations loosning to and fro
They pluckd the seated Hills with all thir load,
Rocks, Waters, Woods, and by the shaggie tops   645
Up lifting bore them in thir hands: Amaze,
Be sure, and terror seiz'd the rebel Host,
When coming towards them so dread they saw
The bottom of the Mountains upward turnd,
Till on those cursed Engins triple-row   650
They saw them whelmd, and all thir confidence
Under the weight of Mountains buried deep,
Themselves invaded next, and on thir heads
Main Promontories flung, which in the Air
Came shaddowing, and oppressd whole Legions armd, 655
Thir armour helpd thir harm, crusht in and bruis'd
Into thir substance pent, which wrought them pain
Implacable, and many a dolorous groan,
Long struggling underneath, ere they could winde
Out of such prison, though Spirits of purest light,   660
Purest at first, now gross by sinning grown.
The rest in imitation to like Arms
Betook them, and the neighbouring Hills **uptore;**
So Hills amid the Air encounterd Hills
Hurld to and fro with jaculation dire,   665

That under ground they fought in dismal shade:
Infernal noise; Warr seemd a civil Game
To this uproar; horrid confusion heap't
Upon confusion rose: and now all Heav'n
Had gone to wrack, with ruin overspred,   670
Had not th' Almightie Father where he sits
Shrin'd in his Sanctuarie of Heav'n secure,
Consulting on the sum of things, foreseen
This tumult, and permitted all, advis'd:
That his great purpose he might so fulfill,   675
To honour his Anointed Son aveng'd
Upon his enemies, and to declare
All power on him transferrd: whence to his Son
Th' Assessor of his Throne he thus began.

    Effulgence of my Glorie, Son belov'd,   680
Son in whose face invisible is beheld
Visibly, what by Deitie I am,
And in whose hand what by Decree I do,
Second Omnipotence, two dayes are past,
Two dayes as we compute the dayes of Heav'n,   685
Since *Michael* and his Powers went forth to tame
These disobedient; sore hath been thir fight,
As likeliest was, when two such Foes met armd;
For to themselves I left them, and thou knowst
Equal in their Creation they were formd,   690
Save what sin hath impaird, which yet hath wrought
Insensibly, for I suspend thir doom;
Whence in perpetual fight they needs must last
Endless, and no solution will be found:
Warr wearied hath performd what Warr can do,   695
And to disorderd rage let loose the reins,
With Mountains as with Weapons armd, which makes
Wild work in Heav'n, and dangerous to the main.
Two days are therefore past, the third is thine;
For thee I have ordaind it, and thus farr   700
Have sufferd, that the Glorie may be thine
Of ending this great Warr, since none but Thou
Can end it.   Into thee such Vertue and Grace
Immense I have transfus'd, that all may know
In Heav'n and Hell thy Power above compare,   705
And this perverse Commotion governd thus
To manifest thee worthiest to be Heir
Of all things, to be Heir and to be King
By Sacred Unction, thy deserved right.
Goe then thou Mightiest in thy Fathers might,   710
Ascend my Chariot, guide the rapid Wheels

That shake Heav'ns basis, bring forth all my Warr,
My Bow and Thunder, my Almightie Arms
Gird on, and Sword upon thy puissant Thigh;
Persue these sons of Darkness, drive them out   715
From all Heav'ns bounds into the utter Deep:
There let them learn, as likes them, to despise
God and *Messiah* his anointed King.
   He said, and on his Son with Rays direct
Shon full: he all his Father full exprest   720
Ineffably into his face receiv'd,
And thus the filial Godhead answering spake.
   O Father, O Supream of heav'nly Thrones,
First, Highest, Holiest, Best, thou always seekst
To glorifie thy Son, I always thee,   725
As is most just; this I my Glorie account,
My exaltation, and my whole delight,
That thou in me well pleas'd declar'st thy will
Fulfilld, which to fulfill is all my bliss.
Scepter and Power, thy giving, I assume,   730
And gladlier shall resign, when in the end
Thou shalt be All in All, and I in thee
For ever, and in mee all whom thou lov'st:
But whom thou hat'st, I hate, and can put on
Thy terrors, as I put thy mildness on,   735
Image of thee in all things; and shall soon,
Armd with thy might, rid heav'n of these rebelld,
To thir prepar'd ill Mansion driven down
To chains of darkness, and th' undying Worm,
That from thy just obedience could revolt,   740
Whom to obey is happiness entire.
Then shall thy Saints unmixt, and from th' impure
Farr separate, circling thy holy Mount
Unfained *Halleluiahs* to thee sing,
Hymns of high praise, and I among them chief.   745
So said, hee ore his Scepter bowing, rose
From the right hand of Glorie where he sate,
And the third sacred Morn began to shine
Dawning through Heav'n: forth rushd with whirlwind sound
The Chariot of Paternal Deitie,   750
Flashing thick flames, Wheele within Wheel undrawn,
It self instinct with Spirit, but convoyd
By four Cherubic shapes, four Faces each
Had wondrous, as with Starrs thir bodies all
And Wings were set with Eyes, with Eyes the Wheels   755
Of Beril, and careering Fires between;
Over thir heads a crystal Firmament,
Whereon a Saphir Throne, inlaid with pure
Amber, and colours of the showrie Arch.
Hee in Celestial Panoplie all armd   760

Of radiant *Urim*, work divinely wrought,
Ascended, at his right hand Victorie
Sate Eagle-wingd, beside him hung his Bow
And Quiver with three-bolted Thunder stor'd,
And from about him fierce Effusion rould   765
Of smoke and bickering flame, and sparkles dire;
Attended with ten thousand thousand Saints,
He onward came, farr off his coming shon,
And twentie thousand (I thir number heard)
Chariots of God, half on each hand were seen: 770
Hee on the wings of Cherube rode sublime
On the Crystallin Skie, in Saphir Thron'd.
Illustrious farr and wide, but by his own
First seen, them unexpected joy surpriz'd,
When the great Ensign of *Messiah* blaz'd   775
Aloft by Angels borne, his Sign in Heav'n:
Under whose conduct *Michael* soon reduc'd
His Armie, circumfus'd on either Wing,
Under thir Head imbodied all in one.
Before him Power Divine his way prepar'd;   780
At his command th' uprooted Hills retir'd
Each to his place, they heard his voice and went
Obsequious, Heav'n his wonted face renewd,
And with fresh Flowrets Hill and Valley smil'd.
This saw his hapless Foes but stood obdur'd,   785
And to rebellious fight rallied thir Powers
Insensate, hope conceiving from despair.
In heav'nly Spirits could such perverseness dwell?
But to convince the proud what Signs avail,
Or Wonders move th' obdurat to relent?   790
They hardend more by what might most reclaim,
Grieving to see his Glorie, at the sight
Took envie, and aspiring to his highth,
Stood reimbatteld fierce, by force or fraud
Weening to prosper, and at length prevail   795
Against God and *Messiah*, or to fall
In universal ruin last, and now
To final Battel drew, disdaining flight
Or faint retreat; when the great Son of God
To all his Host on either hand thus spake.   800
    Stand still in bright array ye Saints, here stand
Ye Angels armd, this day from Battel rest;
Faithful hath been your warfare, and of God
Accepted, fearless in his righteous Cause,
And as ye have receiv'd, so have ye don   805
Invincibly; but of this cursed crew
The punishment to other hand belongs,
Vengeance is his, or whose he sole appoints;
Number to this days work is not ordaind

Nor multitude, stand only and behold   810
Gods indignation on these Godless pourd
By mee, not you but mee they have despis'd,
Yet envied; against mee is all thir rage,
Because the Father, t'whom in Heav'n supream
Kingdom and Power and Glorie appertains,   815
Hath honourd me according to his will.
Therefore to mee thir doom he hath assign'd;
That they may have thir wish, to trie with mee
In Battel which the stronger proves, they all,
Or I alone against them, since by strength   820
They measure all, of other excellence
Not emulous, nor care who them excells;
Nor other strife with them do I voutsafe.
    So spake the Son, and into terror chang'd
His count'nance too severe to be beheld   825
And full of wrauth bent on his Enemies.
At once the Four spred out thir Starrie wings
With dreadful shade contiguous, and the Orbes
Of his fierce Chariot rould, as with the sound
Of torrent Floods or of a numerous Host.   830
Hee on his impious Foes right onward drove,
Gloomie as Night; under his burning Wheeles
The stedfast Empyrean shook throughout,
All but the Throne it self of God.   Full soon
Among them he arriv'd; in his right hand   835
Grasping ten thousand Thunders, which he sent
Before him, such as in thir Souls infixd
Plagues; they astonisht all resistance lost,
All courage; down thir idle weapons dropd;
O'er Shields and Helms, and helmed heads he rode   840
Of Thrones and mighty Seraphim prostrate,
That wishd the Mountains now might be again
Thrown on them as a shelter from his ire.
Nor less on either side tempestuous fell
His arrows, from the fourfold-visag'd Four   845
Distinct with eyes, and from the living Wheels
Distinct alike with multitude of eyes,
One Spirit in them rul'd, and every eye
Glar'd lightning, and shot forth pernicious fire
Among th' accurst, that witherd all thir strength,   850
And of thir wonted vigor left them draind,
Exhausted, spiritless, afflicted, fall'n.
Yet half his strength he put not forth, but checkd
His Thunder in mid Vollie, for he meant
Not to destroy, but root them out of Heav'n: 855
The overthrown he rais'd, and as a Herd
Of Goats or timorous flock together throngd
Drove them before him Thunder-struck, persu'd

With terrors and with furies to the bounds
And Crystal wall of Heav'n, which op'ning wide   860
Rould inward, and a spacious Gap disclos'd
Into the wasteful Deep; the monstrous sight
Strook them with horror backward, but far worse
Urg'd them behind; headlong themselves they threw
Down from the verge of Heav'n, Eternal wrauth   865
Burnd after them to the bottomless pit.
    Hell heard th' unsufferable noise, Hell saw
Heav'n ruining from Heav'n and would have fled
Affrighted; but strict Fate had cast too deep
Her dark foundations, and too fast had bound.   870
Nine days they fell; confounded *Chaos* roard,
And felt tenfold confusion in thir fall
Through his wilde Anarchie, so huge a rout
Incumberd him with ruin: Hell at last
Yawning receiv'd them whole, and on them clos'd,   875
Hell thir fit habitation fraught with fire
Unquenchable, the house of woe and pain.
Disburdend Heav'n rejoic'd, and soon repaird
Her mural breach, returning whence it rould.
Sole Victor from th' expulsion of his Foes   880
Messiah his triumphal Chariot turnd:
To meet him all his Saints, who silent stood
Eye witnesses of his Almightie Acts,
With Jubilie advanc'd; and as they went,
Shaded with branching Palm, each order bright   885
Sung Triumph, and him sung Victorious King,
Son, Heir, and Lord, to him Dominion giv'n,
Worthiest to Reign: he celebrated rode
Triumphant through mid Heav'n, into the Courts
And Temple of his mightie Father Thron'd   890
On high; who into Glorie him receiv'd,
Where now he sits at the right hand of bliss.
    Thus measuring things in Heav'n by things on Earth
At thy request, and that thou mayst beware
By what is past, to thee I have reveal'd   895
What might have else to human Race bin hid;
The discord which befell, and Warr in Heav'n
Among th' Angelic Powers, and the deep fall
Of those too high aspiring, who rebelld
With *Satan*, hee who envies now thy state,   900
Who now is plotting how he may seduce
Thee also from obedience, that with him
Bereav'd of happiness thou mayst partake
His punishment, Eternal miserie;
Which would be all his solace and revenge,   905
As a despite don against the most High,
Thee once to gaine Companion of his woe.

But listen not to his Temptations, warne
Thy weaker; let it profit thee t'have heard
By terrible Example the reward   910
Of disobedience; firm they might have stood,
Yet fell; remember, and fear to transgress.

The End of the Sixth Book

BOOK VII

THE ARGUMENT

Raphael at the request of Adam relates how and wherefore this world was first created; that God, after the expelling of Satan and his Angels out of Heaven, declar'd his pleasure to create another World and other Creatures to dwell therein; sends his Son with Glory and attendance of Angels to perform the work of Creation in six dayes: the Angels celebrate with Hymns the performance thereof, and his reascention into Heaven.

Descend from Heav'n *Urania*, by that name
If rightly thou art calld, whose Voice divine
Following, above th' *Olympian* Hill I soar,
Above the flight of *Pegasean* wing.
The meaning, not the Name I call: for thou   5
Nor of the Muses nine, nor on the top
Of old *Olympus* dwellst, but Heav'nlie born,
Before the Hills appear'd, or Fountain flowd,
Thou with Eternal wisdom didst converse,
Wisdom thy Sister, and with her didst play   10
In presence of th' Almightie Father, pleas'd
With thy Celestial Song.   Up led by thee
Into the Heav'n of Heav'ns I have presum'd,
An Earthlie Guest, and drawn Empyreal Air,
Thy tempring; with like safetie guided down   15
Return me to my Native Element:
Lest from this flying Steed unreind, (as once
Bellerophon, though from a lower Clime)
Dismounted, on th' *Aleian* Field I fall
Erroneous there to wander and forlorn.   20
Half yet remains unsung, but narrower bound
Within the visible Diurnal Sphear;
Standing on Earth, not rapt above the Pole,
More safe I Sing with mortal voice, unchang'd
To hoarse or mute, though fall'n on evil days,   25
On evil days though fall'n, and evil tongues;
In darkness, and with dangers compast round,
And solitude; yet not alone, while thou
Visitst my slumbers Nightly, or when Morn
Purples the East: still govern thou my Song,   30
Urania, and fit audience find, though few.
But drive farr off the barbarous dissonance
of *Bacchus* and his revellers, the Race
Of that wilde Rout that tore the *Thracian* Bard
In *Rhodope*, where Woods and Rocks had Eares   35

To rapture, till the savage clamor drownd
Both Harp and Voice; nor could the Muse defend
Her Son.   So fail not thou, who thee implores:
For thou art Heav'nlie, shee an empty dream.
    Say Goddess, what ensu'd when *Raphaël*,   40
The affable Arch-Angel, had forewarnd
Adam by dire example to beware
Apostasie, by what befell in Heav'n
To those Apostats, lest the like befall
In Paradise to *Adam* or his Race,   45
Charg'd not to touch the interdicted Tree,
If they transgress, and slight that sole command,
So easily obeyd amid the choice
Of all tastes else to please thir appetite,
Though wandring.   He with his consorted *Eve*   50
The storie heard attentive, and was filld
With admiration, and deep muse to hear
Of things so high and strange, things to thir thought
So unimaginable as hate in Heav'n,
And Warr so near the Peace of God in bliss   55
With such confusion: but the evil soon
Driv'n back redounded as a flood on those
From whom it sprung, impossible to mix
With Blessedness.   Whence *Adam* soon repeal'd
The doubts that in his heart arose: and now   60
Led on, yet sinless, with desire to know
What nearer might concern him, how this World
Of Heav'n and Earth conspicuous first began,
When, and whereof created, for what cause,
What within *Eden* or without was don   65
Before his memorie, as one whose drouth
Yet scarce allayd still eyes the current stream,
Whose liquid murmur heard new thirst excites,
Proceeded thus to ask his Heav'nly Guest.
    Great things, and full of wonder in our ears,   70
Farr differing from this World, thou hast reveal'd
Divine Interpreter, by favour sent
Down from the Empyrean to forewarn
Us timely of what might else have bin our loss,
Unknown, which human knowledge could not reach: 75
For which to th'infinitly Good we ow
Immortal thanks, and his admonishment
Receive with solemn purpose to observe
Immutably his sovran will, the end
Of what we are.   But since thou hast voutsaf't   80
Gently for our instruction to impart
Things above Earthly thought, which yet concernd
Our knowing, as to highest wisdom seemd,
Deign to descend now lower, and relate

What may no less perhaps avail us known,   85
How first began this Heav'n which we behold
Distant so high, with moving Fires adornd
Innumerable, and this which yields or fills
All space, the ambient Aire wide interfus'd
Imbracing round this florid Earth, what cause   90
Mov'd the Creator in his holy Rest
Through all Eternitie so late to build
In *Chaos*, and the work begun, how soon
Absolv'd, if unforbid thou mayst unfold
What we, not to explore the secrets aske   95
Of his Eternal Empire, but the more
To magnifie his works, the more we know.
And the great Light of Day yet wants to run
Much of his Race though steep, suspense in Heav'n
Held by thy voice, thy potent voice he hears,   100
And longer will delay to hear thee tell
His Generation, and the rising Birth
Of Nature from the unapparent Deep:
Or if the Starr of Ev'ning and the Moon
Haste to thy audience, Night with her will bring   105
Silence, and Sleep listning to thee will watch,
Or we can bid his absence, till thy Song
End, and dismiss thee ere the Morning shine.
     Thus *Adam* his illustrious Guest besought:
And thus the Godlike Angel answerd mild.   110
This also thy request with caution askt
Obtain: though to recount Almightie works
What words or tongue of Seraph can suffice,
Or heart of man suffice to comprehend?
Yet what thou canst attain, which best may serve   115
To glorifie the Maker, and inferr
Thee also happier, shall not be withheld
Thy hearing, such Commission from above
I have receiv'd, to answer thy desire
Of knowledge within bounds; beyond abstain   120
To ask, nor let thine own inventions hope
Things not reveal'd, which th' invisible King,
Onely Omniscient, hath supprest in Night,
To none communicable in Earth or Heaven:
Anough is left besides to search and know.   125
But Knowledge is as food, and needs no less
Her Temperance over Appetite, to know
In measure what the mind may well contain,
Oppresses else with Surfet, and soon turnes
Wisdom to Folly, as Nourishment to Wind.   130
     Know then, that after *Lucifer* from Heav'n
(So call him, brighter once amidst the Host
Of Angels, than that Starr the Starrs among)

Fell with his flaming Legions through the Deep
Into his place, and the great Son returnd   135
Victorious with his Saints, th' Omnipotent
Eternal Father from his Throne beheld
Thir multitude, and to his Son thus spake.
 At least our envious Foe hath faild, who thought
All like himself rebellious, by whose aid   140
This inaccessible high strength, the seat
Of Deitie supream, us dispossest,
He trusted to have seiz'd, and into fraud
Drew many, whom thir place knows here no more;
Yet farr the greater part have kept, I see,   145
Thir station, Heav'n yet populous retaines
Number sufficient to possess her Realmes
Though wide, and this high Temple to frequent
With Ministeries due and solemn Rites:
But lest his heart exalt him in the harm   150
Already don, to have dispeopl'd Heav'n,
My damage fondly deemd, I can repair
That detriment, if such it be to lose
Self-lost, and in a moment will create
Another World, out of one man a Race   155
Of men innumerable, there to dwell,
Not here, till by degrees of merit rais'd
They open to themselves at length the way
Up hither, under long obedience tri'd,
And Earth be chang'd to Heavn, and Heav'n to Earth,
One Kingdom, Joy and Union without end.   161
Mean while inhabit lax, ye Powers of Heav'n;
And thou my Word, begotten Son, by thee
This I perform, speak thou, and be it don:
My overshadowing Spirit and might with thee   165
I send along, ride forth, and bid the Deep
Within appointed bounds be Heav'n and Earth,
Boundless the Deep, because I am who fill
Infinitude, nor vacuous the space.
Though I uncircumscrib'd my self retire,   170
And put not forth my goodness, which is free
To act or not, Necessitie and Chance
Approach not mee, and what I will is Fate.
 So spake th' Almightie, and to what he spake
His Word, the Filial Godhead, gave effect.   175
Immediat are the Acts of God, more swift
Than time or motion, but to human ears
Cannot without process of speech be told,
So told as earthly notion can receive.
Great triumph and rejoicing was in Heav'n   180
When such was heard declar'd the Almightys will;
Glorie they sung to the most High, good will

To future men, and in thir dwellings peace:
Glorie to him whose just avenging ire
Had driven out th' ungodly from his sight   185
And th' habitations of the just; to him
Glorie and praise, whose wisdom had ordaind
Good out of evil to create, in stead
Of Spirits maligne a better Race to bring
Into thir vacant room, and thence diffuse   190
His good to Worlds and Ages infinite.
So sang the Hierarchies: Mean while the Son
On his great Expedition now appear'd,
Girt with Omnipotence, with Radiance crownd
Of Majestie Divine, Sapience and Love   195
Immense, and all his Father in him shon.
About his Chariot numberless were pourd
Cherube and Seraph, Potentates and Thrones,
And Vertues, winged Spirits, and Chariots wingd,
From th'Armoury of God, where stand of old   200
Myriads between two brazen Mountains lodg'd
Against a solemn day, harnest at hand,
Celestial Equipage; and now came forth
Spontaneous, for within them Spirit liv'd,
Attendant on thir Lord: Heav'n opend wide   205
Her ever during Gates, Harmonious sound
On golden Hinges moving, to let forth
The King of Glorie in his powerful Word
And Spirit coming to create new Worlds.
On heav'nly ground they stood, and from the shore   210
They viewd the vast immeasurable Abyss
Outrageous as a Sea, dark, wasteful, wild,
Up from the bottom turnd by furious winds
And surging waves, as Mountains to assault
Heav'ns highth, and with the Center mix the Pole.   215
   Silence, ye troubl'd waves, and thou Deep, peace,
Said then th' Omnific Word, your discord end:
   Nor stayd, but on the Wings of Cherubim
Uplifted, in Paternal Glorie rode
Farr into *Chaos*, and the World unborn;   220
For *Chaos* heard his voice: him all his Traine
Followd in bright procession to behold
Creation, and the wonders of his might.
Then stayd the fervid Wheels, and in his hand
He took the golden Compasses, prepar'd   225
In Gods Eternal store, to circumscribe
This Universe, and all created things:
One foot he centerd, and the other turnd
Round through the vast profunditie obscure.
And said, thus farr extend, thus farr thy bounds,   230
This be thy just Circumference, O World.

Thus God the Heav'n created, thus the Earth,
Matter unformd and void: Darkness profound
Coverd th' Abyss: but on the watrie Calm
His brooding wings the Spirit of God outspred,   235
And vital vertue infus'd, and vital warmth
Throughout the fluid Mass, but downward purg'd
The black tartareous cold Infernal dregs
Adverse to life: then founded, then conglob'd
Like things to like, the rest to several place   240
Disparted, and between spun out the Air,
And Earth self-ballanc't on her Center hung.
   Let ther be Light, said God, and forthwith Light
Ethereal, first of things, quintessence pure
Sprung from the Deep, and from her Native East   245
To journie through the airie gloom began,
Sphear'd in a radiant Cloud, for yet the Sun
Was not; shee in a cloudie Tabernacle
Sojournd the while.   God saw the Light was good;
And light from darkness by the Hemisphere   250
Divided: Light the Day, and Darkness Night
He nam'd.   Thus was the first Day Ev'n and Morn:
Nor passd uncelebrated, nor unsung
By the Celestial Quires, when Orient Light
Exhaling first from Darkness they beheld;   255
Birth-day of Heav'n and Earth; with joy and shout
The hollow Universal Orb they filld,
And touchd thir Golden Harps, and hymning prais'd
God and his works, Creator him they sung,
Both when first Ev'ning was, and when first Morn.   260
   Again God said, let ther be Firmament
Amid the Waters, and let it divide
The Waters from the Waters: and God made
The Firmament, expanse of liquid, pure,
Transparent, Elemental Air, diffus'd   265
In circuit to the uttermost convex
Of this great Round: partition firm and sure,
The Waters underneath from those above
Dividing: for as Earth, so he the World
Built on circumfluous Waters calm, in wide   270
Crystallin Ocean, and the loud misrule
Of *Chaos* farr remov'd, lest fierce extreams
Contiguous might distemper the whole frame:
And Heav'n he nam'd the Firmament: So Ev'n
And Morning *Chorus* sung the second Day.   275
   The Earth was formd, but in the Womb as yet
Of Waters, Embryon immature involv'd,
Appear'd not: over all the face of Earth
Main Ocean flowd, not idle, but with warm
Prolific humour soft'ning all her Globe,   280

Fermented the great Mother to conceive,
Satiate with genial moisture, when God said
Be gatherd now ye Waters under Heav'n
Into one place, and let dry Land appear.
Immediatly the Mountains huge appear   285
Emergent, and thir broad bare backs upheave
Into the Clouds, thir tops ascend the Skie:
So high as heav'd the tumid Hills, so low
Down sunk a hollow bottom broad and deep,
Capacious bed of Waters: thither they   290
Hasted with glad precipitance, uprould
As drops on dust conglobing from the drie;
Part rise in crystal Wall or ridge direct,
For haste; such flight the great command impressd
On the swift floods: as Armies at the call   295
Of Trumpet (for of Armies thou hast heard)
Troop to thir Standard, so the watrie throng,
Wave rouling after Wave, where way they found,
If steep, with torrent rapture, if through Plain,
Soft-ebbing; nor withstood them Rock or Hill,   300
But they, or under ground or circuit wide
With Serpent error wandring, found thir way,
And on the washie Oose deep Channels wore;
Easie, ere God had bid the ground be drie,
All but within those banks, where Rivers now   305
Stream, and perpetual draw thir humid train.
The dry Land, Earth, and the great receptacle
Of congregated Waters he calld Seas:
And saw that it was good, and said, Let th' Earth
Put forth the verdant Grass, Herb yielding Seed,   310
And Fruit Tree yielding Fruit after her kind;
Whose Seed is in her self upon the Earth.
He scarce had said, when the bare Earth, till then
Desert and bare, unsightly, unadornd,
Brought forth the tender Grass, whose verdure clad   315
Her Universal Face with pleasant green,
Then Herbs of every leaf, that sudden flowrd
Op'ning thir various colours, and made gay
Her bosom smelling sweet: and these scarce blown,
Forth flourishd thick the clustring Vine, forth crept   320
The swelling Gourd, up stood the cornie Reed
Embatteld in her field: and th'humble Shrub,
And Bush with frizl'd hair implicit: last
Rose as in Dance the stately Trees, and spred
Thir branches hung with copious Fruit; or gemmd   325
Thir blossoms: with high woods the hills were crownd,

321 swelling *Bentley conj.*] smelling *Edd. 1, 2*
322 and *Ed. 2*] add *Ed. 1*

With tufts the vallies and each fountain side,
With borders long the Rivers.   That Earth now
Seemd like to Heav'n, a seat where Gods might dwell,
Or wander with delight, and love to haunt   330
Her sacred shades: though God had yet not raind
Upon the Earth, and man to till the ground
None was, but from the Earth a dewie Mist
Went up and waterd all the ground, and each
Plant of the field, which ere it was in th' Earth   335
God made, and every Herb, before it grew
On the green stemm; God saw that it was good.
So Ev'n and Morn recorded the Third Day.

     Again th' Almightie spake: Let ther be Lights
High in th' expanse of Heaven to divide   340
The Day from Night; and let them be for Signs,
For Seasons, and for Days and circling Years,
And let them be for Lights as I ordaine
Thir Office in the Firmament of Heav'n
To give Light on the Earth; and it was so.   345
And God made two great Lights, great for **thir use**
To Man, the greater to have rule by Day,
The less by Night altern: and made the Starrs,
And set them in the Firmament of Heav'n
T'illuminate the Earth, and rule the Day   350
In thir vicissitude, and rule the Night,
And Light from Darkness to divide.   God saw,
Surveying his great Work, that it was good:
For of Celestial Bodies first the Sun
A mightie Sphear he fram'd, unlightsom first,   355
Though of Ethereal Mould: then formd the Moon
Globose, and everie magnitude of Starrs,
And sowd with Starrs the Heav'n thick as a field:
Of Light by farr the greater part he took,
Transplanted from her cloudie Shrine, and plac'd   360
In the Suns Orb, made porous to receive
And drink the liquid Light, firm to retain
Her gatherd beams, great Palace now of Light.
Hither as to thir Fountain other Starrs
Repairing, in thir golden Urns draw Light,   365
And hence the Morning Planet gilds her horns;
By tincture or reflection they augment
Thir small peculiar, though from human sight
So farr remote, with diminution seen.
First in his East the glorious Lamp was seen,   370
Regent of Day, and all th' Horizon round
Invested with bright Rays, jocond to run
His Longitude through Heav'ns high road: the gray

366 her *Ed. 2*] his *Ed. 1*

Dawn, and the *Pleiades* before him danc'd
Shedding sweet influence: less bright the Moon,   375
But opposite in leveld West was set
His mirror, with full face borrowing her Light
From him, for other light she needed none
In that aspect, and still that distance keeps
Till night, then in the East her turn she shines,   380
Revolv'd on Heav'ns great Axle, and her Reign
With thousand lesser Lights dividual holds,
With thousand thousand Starrs, that then appear'd
Spangling the Hemisphere: then first adornd
With thir bright Luminaries that Set and Rose,   385
Glad Ev'ning and glad Morn crownd the fourth day.
    And God said, let the Waters generate
Reptil with Spawn abundant, living Soul:
And let Fowl flie above the Earth, with wings
Displayd on th'open Firmament of Heav'n.   390
And God created the great Whales, and each
Soul living, each that crept, which plenteously
The waters generated by thir kinds,
And every Bird of wing after his kind;
And saw that it was good, and blessd them, saying,   395
Be fruitful, multiply, and in the Seas
And Lakes and running Streams the waters fill;
And let the Fowle be multipli'd on th'Earth.
Forthwith the Sounds and Seas, each Creek and Bay
With Frie innumerable swarm, and Shoals   400
Of Fish that with thir Finns and shining Scales
Glide under the green Wave, in Sculls that oft
Bank the mid Sea: part single or with mate
Graze the Sea weed thir pasture, and through Groves
Of Coral stray, or sporting with quick glance   405
Show to the Sun thir wav'd coats dropt with Gold,
Or in thir Pearlie shells at ease, attend
Moist nutriment, or under Rocks thir food
In jointed Armour watch: on smooth the Seal
And bended Dolphins play: part huge of bulk   410
Wallowing unwieldie, enormous in thir Gait
Tempest the Ocean: there Leviathan
Hugest of living Creatures, on the Deep
Stretcht like a Promontorie sleeps or swimms,
And seems a moving Land, and at his Gills   415
Draws in, and at his Trunk spouts out a Sea.
Mean while the tepid Caves, and Fens and shores
Thir Brood as numerous hatch, from th'Egg that soon
Bursting with kindly rupture forth disclos'd
Thir callow young, but featherd soon and fledge   420
They summd thir Penns, and soaring th' air sublime
With clang despis'd the ground, under a cloud

In prospect; there the Eagle and the Stork
On Cliffs and Cedar tops thir Eyries build:
Part loosely wing the Region, part more wise   425
In common, rang'd in figure wedge thir way,
Intelligent of seasons, and set forth
Thir Aerie Caravan high over Seas
Flying, and over Lands with mutual wing
Easing thir flight; so steers the prudent Crane   430
Her annual Voyage, borne on Winds; the Aire
Floats, as they pass, fannd with unnumberd plumes:
From Branch to Branch the smaller Birds with song
Solac'd the Woods, and spred thir painted wings
Till Ev'n, nor then the solemn Nightingal   435
Ceas'd warbling, but all night tun'd her soft lays:
Others on Silver Lakes and Rivers Bath'd
Thir downie Brest; the Swan with Arched neck
Between her white wings mantling proudly, Rows
Her state with Oarie feet: yet oft they quit   440
The Dank, and rising on stiff Pennons, tour
The mid Aëreal Skie: Others on ground
Walkd firm; the crested Cock whose clarion sounds
The silent hours, and th' other whose gay Train
Adorns him, coulourd with the Florid hue   445
Of Rainbows and Starrie Eyes.   The Waters thus
With Fish replenisht, and the Air with Fowl,
Ev'ning and Morn solemniz'd the Fift day.
    The Sixt, and of Creation last arose
With Ev'ning Harps and Mattin, when God said,   450
Let th' Earth bring forth Soul living in her kind,
Cattel and Creeping things, and Beast of th' Earth,
Each in their kind.   The Earth obeyd, and straight
Op'ning her fertil Woomb teemd at a Birth
Innumerous living Creatures, perfet forms,   455
Limbd and full grown: out of the ground up rose
As from his Laire the wild Beast where he wonns
In Forrest wild, in Thicket, Brake or Den;
Among the Trees in Pairs they rose, they walkd:
The Cattel in the Fields and Meddows green: 460
Those rare and solitarie, these in flocks
Pasturing at once, and in broad Herds upsprung.
The grassie Clods now Calv'd, now half appear'd
The Tawnie Lion, pawing to get free
His hinder parts, then springs as broke from Bonds,   465
And Rampant shakes his Brinded mane; the Ounce,
The Libbard and the Tiger, as the Moale
Rising, the crumbl'd Earth above them threw
In Hillocks; the swift Stag from under ground

451 Soul *Bentley conj.*] Fowle *Ed. 1* Foul *Ed. 2*

Bore up his branching head: scarce from his mould   470
Behemoth biggest born of Earth upheav'd
His vastness: Fleec't the Flocks and bleating rose,
As Plants: ambiguous between Sea and Land
The River Horse and scalie Crocodile.
At once came forth whatever creeps the ground,   475
Insect or Worm; those wav'd thir limber fans
For wings, and smallest Lineaments exact
In all the Liveries deckt of Summers pride
With spots of Gold and Purple, azure and green:
These as a line thir long dimension drew,   480
Streaking the ground with sinuous trace; not all
Minims of Nature; some of Serpent kinde
Wondrous in length and corpulence involv'd
Thir Snakie folds, and added wings.   First crept
The Parsimonious Emmet, provident   485
Of future, in small room large heart enclos'd,
Pattern of just equalitie perhaps
Hereafter, joind in her popular Tribes
Of Commonaltie: swarming next appear'd
The Femal Bee that feeds her Husband Drone   490
Deliciously, and builds her waxen Cells
With Honey stor'd: the rest are numberless,
And thou thir Natures knowst, and gav'st them Names,
Needless to thee repeated; nor unknown
The Serpent suttl'st Beast of all the field,   495
Of huge extent somtimes, with brazen Eyes
And hairie Mane terrific, though to thee
Not noxious, but obedient at thy call.
Now Heav'n in all her Glorie shon, and rould
Her motions, as the great first-Movers hand   500
First wheeld thir course; Earth in her rich attire
Consummat lovely smil'd; Air, Water, Earth,
By Fowl, Fish, Beast, was flown, was swum, was walkt
Frequent; and of the Sixt day yet remaind;
There wanted yet the Master work, the end   505
Of all yet don; a Creature who not prone
And Brute as other Creatures, but endu'd
With Sanctitie of Reason, might erect
His Stature, and upright with Front serene
Govern the rest, self-knowing, and from thence   510
Magnanimous to correspond with Heav'n,
But grateful to acknowledge whence his good
Descends, thither with heart and voice and eyes
Directed in Devotion, to adore
And worship God Supream, who made him chief   515
Of all his works: therefore th'Omnipotent
Eternal Father (For where is not hee
Present) thus to his Son audibly spake.

Let us make now Man in our image, Man
In our similitude, and let them rule   520
Over the Fish and Fowle of Sea and Air,
Beast of the Field, and over all the Earth,
And every creeping thing that creeps the ground.
This said, he formd thee, *Adam*, thee O Man,
Dust of the ground, and in thy nostrils breath'd   525
The breath of Life; in his own Image hee
Created thee, in the Image of God
Express, and thou becam'st a living Soul.
Male he created thee, but thy consort
Femal for Race; then blessd Mankind, and said,   530
Be fruitful, multiplie, and fill the Earth,
Subdue it, and throughout Dominion hold
Over Fish of the Sea, and Fowl of the Air,
And every living thing that moves on th'Earth.
Wherever thus created, for no place   535
Is yet distinct by name, thence, as thou knowst
He brought thee into this delicious Grove,
This Garden, planted with the Trees of God,
Delectable both to behold and taste;
And freely all thir pleasant fruit for food   540
Gave thee, all sorts are here that all th' Earth yields,
Varietie without end; but of the Tree
Which tasted works knowledge of Good and Evil,
Thou mayst not; in the day thou eat'st, thou di'st;
Death is the penaltie impos'd, beware,   545
And govern well thy appetite, lest sin
Surprise thee, and her black attendant Death.
Here finishd hee, and all that he had made
Viewd, and behold all was entirely good;
So Ev'n and Morn accomplishd the Sixt day: 550
Yet not till the Creator from his work
Desisting, though unwearied, up returnd
Up to the Heav'n of Heav'ns his high abode,
Thence to behold this new created World
Th' addition of his Empire, how it shewd   555
In prospect from his Throne, how good, how fair,
Answering his great Idea.   Up he rode
Followd with acclamation and the sound
Symphonious of ten thousand Harpes that tun'd
Angelic harmonies: the Earth, the Aire   560
Resounded, (thou rememberst for thou heardst)
The Heav'ns and all the Constellations rung,
The Planets in thir station list'ning stood,
While the bright Pomp ascended jubilant.
Open, ye everlasting Gates, they sung,   565

563 station *Ed. 2*] stations *Ed. 1*

Open, ye Heav'ns, your living dores; let in
The Great Creator from his work returnd
Magnificent, his Six days work, a World;
Open, and henceforth oft; for God will deign
To visit oft the dwellings of just Men   570
Delighted, and with frequent intercourse
Thither will send his winged Messengers
On errands of supernal Grace.   So sung
The glorious Train ascending: He through Heav'n,
That opend wide her blazing Portals, led   575
To Gods Eternal house direct the way,
A broad and ample road, whose dust is Gold
And pavement Starrs, as Starrs to thee appear,
Seen in the Galaxie, that Milkie way
Which nightly as a circling Zone thou seest   580
Powderd with Starrs.   And now on Earth the Sev'nth
Ev'ning arose in *Eden*, for the Sun
Was set, and twilight from the East came on,
Forerunning Night; when at the holy mount
Of Heav'ns high-seated top, th' Imperial Throne   585
Of Godhead, fixt for ever firm and sure,
The Filial Power arriv'd, and sate him down
With his great Father, for hee also went
Invisible, yet stayd (such priviledge
Hath Omnipresence) and the work ordaind,   590
Author and end of all things, and from work
Now resting, blessd and hallowd the Sev'nth day,
As resting on that day from all his work,
But not in silence holy kept; the Harp
Had work and rested not, the solemn Pipe   595
And Dulcimer, all Organs of sweet stop,
All sounds on Fret by String or Golden Wire
Temperd soft Tunings, intermixt with Voice
Choral or Unison: of incense Clouds
Fuming from Golden Censers hid the Mount.   600
Creation and the Six days acts they sung:
Great are thy works, *Jehovah*, infinite
Thy power; what thought can measure thee or tongue
Relate thee; greater now in thy return
Than from the Giant Angels; thee that day   605
Thy Thunders magnifi'd; but to create
Is greater than created to destroy.
Who can impair thee, mighty King, or bound
Thy Empire? easily the proud attempt
Of Spirits apostat and thir Counsels vain   610
Thou hast repelld, while impiously they thought
Thee to diminish, and from thee withdraw
The number of thy worshippers.   Who seeks
To lessen thee, against his purpose serves

To manifest the more thy might: his evil   615
Thou usest, and from thence creat'st more good.
Witness this new-made World, another Heav'n
From Heaven Gate not farr, founded in view
On the clear *Hyaline*, the Glassie Sea;
Of amplitude almost immense, with Starrs   620
Numerous, and every Starr perhaps a World
Of destind habitation; but thou knowst
Thir seasons: among these the seat of men,
Earth with her nether Ocean circumfus'd,
Thir pleasant dwelling place.   Thrice happie men,   625
And sons of men, whom God hath thus advanc't,
Created in his Image, there to dwell
And worship him, and in reward to rule
Over his Works, on Earth, in Sea, or Air,
And multiply a Race of Worshippers   630
Holy and just: thrice happie if they know
Thir happiness, and persevere upright.
   So sung they, and the Empyrean rung,
With *Halleluiahs*: Thus was Sabbath kept.
And thy request think now fulfilld, that askd   635
How first this World and face of things began,
And what before thy memorie was don
From the beginning, that posteritie
Informd by thee might know; if else thou seekst
Aught, not surpassing human measure, say.   640

The End of the Seventh Book

BOOK VIII

THE ARGUMENT

Adam inquires concerning celestial Motions, is doubtfully answer'd, and exhorted to search rather things more worthy of knowledg: Adam assents, and still desirous to detain Raphael, relates to him what he remember'd since his own Creation, his placing in Paradise, his talk with God concerning solitude and fit society, his first meeting and Nuptials with Eve, his discourse with the Angel thereupon; who after admonitions repeated departs.

 The Angel ended, and in *Adams* Ear
So Charming left his voice, that he a while
Thought him still speaking, still stood fixt **to hear;**
Then as new wak't thus gratefully repli'd.
What thanks sufficient, or what recompense   5
Equal have I to render thee, Divine
Historian, who thus largely hast allayd
The thirst I had of knowledge, and voutsaf't
This friendly condescension to relate
Things else by me unsearchable, now heard   10
With wonder, but delight, and, as is due,
With glorie attributed to the high
Creator; something yet of doubt remains,
Which onely thy solution can resolve.
When I behold this goodly Frame, this World   15
Of Heav'n and Earth consisting, and compute
Thir magnitudes, this Earth a spot, a grain,
An Atom, with the Firmament compar'd
And all her numberd Starrs, that seem to roule
Spaces incomprehensible (for such   20
Thir distance argues and thir swift return
Diurnal) merely to officiate light
Round this opacous Earth, this punctual spot,
One day and night; in all thir vast survey
Useless besides: reasoning I oft admire,   25
How Nature wise and frugal could commit
Such disproportions, with superfluous hand
So many nobler Bodies to create,
Greater so manifold to this one use,
For aught appears, and on thir Orbs impose 30
Such restless revolution day by day

1–4 These lines were added in Ed. 2, when Book VII was divided into two at line 640. Line 641 Ed. I reads: 'To whom thus *Adam* gratefully repli'd.'

Repeated, while the sedentarie Earth,
That better might with farr less compass move,
Serv'd by more noble than her self, attains
Her end without least motion, and receives   35
As Tribute such a sumless journey brought
Of incorporeal speed, her warmth and light;
Speed, to describe whose swiftness Number fails.
    So spake our Sire, and by his count'nance seemd
Entring on studious thoughts abstruse, which *Eve*   40
Perceiving where she sat retir'd in sight,
With lowliness Majestic from her seat,
And Grace that won who saw to wish her stay,
Rose, and went forth among her Fruits and Flowrs,
To visit how they prosperd, bud and bloom,   45
Her Nurserie; they at her coming sprung
And toucht by her fair tendance gladlier grew.
Yet went she not, as not with such discourse
Delighted, or not capable her ear
Of what was high: such pleasure she reserv'd   50
Adam relating, she sole Auditress;
Her Husband the Relater she preferrd
Before the Angel, and of him to ask
Chose rather; hee she knew would intermix
Grateful digressions, and solve high dispute   55
With conjugal Caresses, from his Lip
Not Words alone pleas'd her.   O when meet now
Such pairs, in Love and mutual Honour joind?
With Goddess-like demeanour forth she went;
Not unattended, for on her as Queen   60
A pomp of winning Graces waited still,
And from about her shot Darts of desire
Into all Eyes to wish her still in sight.
And *Raphael* now to *Adams* doubt propos'd
Benevolent and facil thus repli'd.   65
    To ask or search I blame thee not, for Heav'n
Is as the Book of God before thee set,
Wherein to read his wondrous Works, and learn
His Seasons, Hours or Dayes or Months or Years:
This to attain, whether Heav'n move to Earth,   70
Imports not, if thou reckon right, the rest
From Man or Angel the great Architect
Did wisely to conceal, and not divulge
His secrets to be scannd by them who ought
Rather admire; or if they list to try   75
Conjecture, he his Fabric of the Heav'ns
Hath left to thir disputes, perhaps to move
His laughter at thir quaint Opinions wide
Hereafter, when they come to model Heav'n
And calculate the Starrs, how they will wield   80

The mightie frame, how build, unbuild, contrive
To save appearances, how gird the Sphear
With Centric and Eccentric scribl'd ore,
Cycle and Epicycle, Orb in Orb:
Alreadie by thy reasoning this I guess,   85
Who art to lead thy offspring, and supposest
That bodies bright and greater should not serve
The less not bright, nor Heav'n such journies run,
Earth sitting still, when she alone receives
The benefit: consider first, that Great   90
Or Bright inferrs not Excellence: the Earth
Though, in comparison of Heav'n, so small,
Nor glistering, may of solid good contain
More plenty than the Sun that barren shines,
Whose vertue on it self works no effect,   95
But in the fruitful Earth; there first receiv'd
His beams, unactive else, thir vigor find.
Yet not to Earth are those bright Luminaries
Officious, but to thee Earths habitant.
And for the Heav'ns wide Circuit, let it speak   100
The Makers high magnificence, who built
So spacious, and his Line stretchd out so farr;
That Man may know he dwells not in his own;
An Edifice too large for him to fill,
Lodg'd in a small partition, and the rest   105
Ordaind for uses to his Lord best known.
The swiftness of those Circles attribute,
Though numberless, to his Omnipotence,
That to corporeal substances could adde
Speed almost Spiritual; mee thou thinkst not slow,   110
Who since the Morning hour set out from Heav'n
Where God resides, and ere mid-day arriv'd
In *Eden*, distance inexpressible
By Numbers that have name.   But this I urge,
Admitting Motion in the Heav'ns, to shew   115
Invalid that which thee to doubt it mov'd;
Not that I so affirm, though so it seem
To thee who hast thy dwelling here on Earth.
God to remove his wayes from human sense,
Plac'd Heav'n from Earth so farr, that earthly sight,   120
If it presume, might err in things too high,
And no advantage gain.   What if the Sun
Be Center to the World, and other Starrs
By his attractive vertue and thir own
Incited, dance about him various rounds?   125
Thir wandring course now high, now low, then hid,
Progressive, retrograde, or standing still,
In six thou seest, and what if sev'nth to these
The Planet Earth, so stedfast though she seem,

Insensibly three different Motions move?   130
Which else to several Sphears thou must ascribe,
Mov'd contrarie with thwart obliquities,
Or save the Sun his labour, and that swift
Nocturnal and Diurnal rhomb suppos'd,
Invisible else above all Starrs, the Wheel   135
Of Day and Night; which needs not thy belief,
If Earth industrious of her self fetch Day
Travelling East, and with her part averse
From the Suns beam meet Night, her other part
Still luminous by his ray.   What if that light   140
Sent from her through the wide transpicuous air,
To the terrestrial Moon be as a Starr
Enlightning her by Day, as she by Night
This Earth? reciprocal, if Land be there,
Fields and Inhabitants: Her spots thou seest   145
As Clouds, and Clouds may rain, and Rain produce
Fruits in her softend Soil, for some to eate
Allotted there; and other Suns perhaps
With thir attendant Moons thou wilt descrie
Communicating Male and Femal Light,   150
Which two great Sexes animate the World,
Stor'd in each Orb perhaps with some that live.
For such vast room in Nature unpossest
By living Soul, desert and desolate,
Onely to shine, yet scarce to contribute   155
Each Orb a glimpse of Light, conveyd so farr
Down to this habitable, which returnes
Light back to them, is obvious to dispute.
But whether thus these things, or whether not,
Whether the Sun predominant in Heav'n   160
Rise on the Earth, or Earth rise on the Sun,
Hee from the East his flaming road begin,
Or Shee from West her silent course advance
With inoffensive pace that spinning sleeps
On her soft Axle, while she paces ev'n   165
And bears thee soft with the smooth Air along,
Solicit not thy thoughts with matters hid,
Leave them to God above, him serve and fear;
Of other Creatures, as him pleases best,
Wherever plac't, let him dispose: joy thou   170
In what he gives to thee, this Paradise
And thy fair *Eve*; Heav'n is for thee too high
To know what passes there; be lowlie wise:
Think onely what concernes thee and thy being;
Dream not of other Worlds, what Creatures there   175
Live, in what state, condition or degree,
Contented that thus farr hath been reveal'd
Not of Earth onely but of highest Heav'n.

To whom thus *Adam* clear'd of doubt, repli'd.
How fully hast thou satisfi'd me, pure   180
Intelligence of Heav'n, Angel serene,
And freed from intricacies, taught to live
The easiest way, nor with perplexing thoughts
To interrupt the sweet of Life, from which
God hath bid dwell farr off all anxious cares,   185
And not molest us, unless we our selves
Seek them with wandring thoughts, and notions vain.
But apt the Mind or Fancie is to rove
Uncheckt, and of her roving is no end;
Till warnd, or by experience taught, she learne   190
That not to know at large of things remote
From use, obscure and suttle, but to know
That which before us lies in daily life,
Is the prime Wisdom; what is more, is fume,
Or emptiness, or fond impertinence,   195
And renders us in things that most concerne
Unpractis'd, unprepar'd, and still to seek.
Therefore from this high pitch let us descend
A lower flight, and speak of things at hand
Useful, whence haply mention may arise   200
Of somthing not unseasonable to ask
By sufferance, and thy wonted favour deignd.
Thee I have heard relating what was done
Ere my remembrance: now hear mee relate
My Storie, which perhaps thou hast not heard;   205
And Day is yet not spent; till then thou seest
How suttly to detaine thee I devise,
Inviting thee to hear while I relate,
Fond, were it not in hope of thy reply:
For while I sit with thee, I seem in Heav'n,   210
And sweeter thy discourse is to my eare
Than Fruits of Palm-tree pleasantest to thirst
And hunger both, from labour, at the hour
Of sweet repast; they satiate, and soon fill,
Though pleasant, but thy words with Grace Divine   215
Imbu'd, bring to thir sweetness no satietie.
    To whom thus *Raphael* answerd heav'nly meek.
Nor are thy lips ungraceful, Sire of men,
Nor tongue ineloquent; for God on thee
Abundantly his gifts hath also pour'd   220
Inward and outward both, his image fair:
Speaking or mute all comliness and grace
Attends thee, and each word, each motion forms.
Nor less think wee in Heav'n of thee on Earth
Than of our fellow servant, and inquire   225
Gladly into the wayes of God with Man:
For God we see hath honourd thee, and set

On Man his Equal Love: say therefore on;
For I that Day was absent, as befell,
Bound on a voyage uncouth and obscure,   230
Farr on excursion toward the Gates of Hell;
Squar'd in full Legion (such command we had)
To see that none thence issu'd forth a spie
Or enemie, while God was in his work,
Lest hee incenst at such eruption bold,   235
Destruction with Creation might have mixt.
Not that they durst without his leave attempt,
But us he sends upon his high behests
For state, as Sovran King, and to enure
Our prompt obedience.   Fast we found, fast shut   240
The dismal Gates, and barricado'd strong;
But long ere our approaching heard within
Noise, other than the sound of Dance or Song,
Torment and loud lament and furious rage.
Glad we returnd up to the coasts of Light   245
Ere Sabbath Ev'ning: so we had in charge.
But thy relation now; for I attend,
Pleas'd with thy words no less than thou with mine.
    So spake the Godlike Power, and thus our Sire.
For Man to tell how human Life began   250
Is hard; for who himself beginning knew?
Desire with thee still longer to converse
Induc'd me.   As new wak't from soundest sleep
Soft on the flowrie herb I found me laid
In Baumie Sweat, which with his Beams the Sun   255
Soon dri'd, and on the reeking moisture fed.
Straight toward Heav'n my wondring Eyes I turnd,
And gaz'd a while the ample Skie, till rais'd
By quick instinctive motion up I sprung,
As thitherward endevoring, and upright   260
Stood on my feet; about me round I saw
Hill, Dale, and shadie Woods, and sunnie Plains,
And liquid Lapse of murmuring Streams; by these,
Creatures that liv'd, and mov'd, and walkd, or flew,
Birds on the branches warbling; all things smil'd,   265
With fragrance and with joy my heart oreflowd.
My self I then perus'd, and Limb by Limb
Surveyd, and sometimes went, and sometimes ran
With supple joints, as lively vigor led:
But who I was, or where, or from what cause,   270
Knew not; to speak I tri'd, and forthwith spake,
My Tongue obeyd and readily could name
What e're I saw.   Thou Sun, said I, fair Light,
And thou enlightend Earth, so fresh and gay,

269 as *Ed. 1*] and *Ed. 2*

Ye Hills and Dales, ye Rivers, Woods and Plains,   275
And ye that live and move, fair Creatures, tell,
Tell, if ye saw, how came I thus, how here?
Not of my self; by some great Maker then,
In goodness and in power præeminent;
Tell me, how may I know him, how adore,   280
From whom I have that thus I move and live,
And feel that I am happier than I know.
While thus I calld, and strayd I knew not whither,
From where I first drew Air, and first beheld
This happie Light, when answer none returnd,   285
On a green shadie Bank profuse of Flowrs
Pensive I sate me down; there gentle sleep
First found me, and soft oppression seiz'd
My drowsed sense, untroubl'd, though I thought
I then was passing to my former state   290
Insensible, and forthwith to dissolve:
When suddenly stood at my Head a dream,
Whose inward apparition gently mov'd
My fancy to believe I yet had being,
And liv'd: One came, methought, of shape Divine,   295
And said, Thy Mansion wants thee *Adam*, rise,
First Man, of Men innumerable ordaind
First Father, calld by thee I come thy Guide
To the Garden of bliss, thy seat prepar'd.
So saying, by the hand he took me rais'd,   300
And over Fields and Waters, as in Aire
Smooth sliding without step, last led me up
A woodie Mountain; whose high top was plain,
A Circuit wide, enclos'd, with goodliest Trees
Planted, with Walks and Bowers, that what I saw   305
Of Earth before scarce pleasant seemd.   Each Tree
Loaden with fairest Fruit that hung to th'Eye
Tempting, stirrd in me sudden appetite
To pluck and eat; whereat I wak'd, and found
Before mine Eyes all real, as the dream   310
Had lively shaddowd: Here had new begun
My wandring, had not hee who was my Guide
Up hither, from among the Trees appear'd,
Presence Divine.   Rejoicing, but with awe
In adoration at his feet I fell   315
Submiss: he rear'd me, and Whom thou soughtst I am,
Said mildly, Author of all this thou seest
Above or round about thee or beneath.
This Paradise I give thee, count it thine
To Till and keep, and of the Fruit to eat: 320
Of every Tree that in the Garden growes
Eate freely with glad heart; fear here no dearth:
But of the Tree whose operation brings

Knowledge of good and ill, which I have set
The Pledge of thy Obedience and thy Faith,   325
Amid the Garden by the Tree of Life,
Remember what I warn thee, shun to taste,
And shun the bitter consequence: for know,
The day thou eat'st thereof, my sole command
Transgrest, inevitably thou shalt die;   330
From that day mortal, and this happie State
Shalt lose, expelld from hence into a World
Of woe and sorrow.   Sternly he pronounc'd
The rigid interdiction, which resounds
Yet dreadful in mine ear, though in my choice   335
Not to incurr; but soon his clear aspect
Returnd and gracious purpose thus renewd.
Not onely these fair bounds, but all the Earth
To thee and to thy Race I give; as Lords
Possess it, and all things that therein live,   340
Or live in Sea or Air, Beast, Fish and Fowl.
In sign whereof each Bird and Beast behold
After thir kinds; I bring them to receive
From thee thir Names, and pay thee fealtie
With low subjection; understand the same   345
Of Fish within thir watry residence,
Not hither summond, since they cannot change
Thir Element to draw the thinner Air.
As thus he spake, each Bird and Beast behold
Approaching two and two, These cowring low   350
With blandishment, each Bird stoopt on his wing.
I nam'd them, as they passd, and understood
Thir Nature, with such knowledge God endu'd
My sudden apprehension: but in these
I found not what me thought I wanted still;   355
And to the Heav'nly vision thus presum'd.

O by what Name, for thou above all these,
Above mankind, or aught than mankind higher,
Surpassest farr my naming, how may I
Adore thee, Author of this Universe   360
And all this good to man, for whose well being
So amply, and with hands so liberal
Thou hast provided all things: but with mee
I see not who partakes.   In solitude
What happiness, who can enjoy alone,   365
Or all enjoying, what contentment find?
Thus I presumptuous; and the vision bright,
As with a smile more brightend, thus repli'd.

What callst thou solitude? is not the Earth
With various living creatures, and the Aire   370
Replenisht, and all these at thy command
To come and play before thee, knowst thou not

Thir language and thir ways? they also know,
And reason not contemptibly; with these
Find pastime, and bear rule; thy Realm is large.   375
So spake the Universal Lord, and seemd
So ordering.   I with leave of speech implor'd
And humble deprecation thus repli'd.
    Let not my words offend thee, Heav'nly Power,
My Maker, be propitious while I speak.   380
Hast thou not made me here thy substitute,
And these inferior farr beneath me set?
Among unequals what societie
Can sort, what harmonie or true delight?
Which must be mutual, in proportion due   385
Giv'n and receiv'd; but in disparitie
The one intense, the other still remiss
Cannot well suit with either, but soon prove
Tedious alike: Of fellowship I speak
Such as I seek, fit to participate   390
All rational delight, wherein the brute
Cannot be human consort; they rejoice
Each with thir kind, Lion with Lioness;
So fitly them in pairs thou hast combin'd;
Much less can Bird with Beast, or Fish with Fowle   395
So well converse, nor with the Ox the Ape;
Worse then can Man with Beast, and least of all.
    Whereto th' Almighty answerd, not displeas'd.
A nice and suttle happiness I see
Thou to thy self proposest, in the choice   400
Of thy Associates *Adam*, and wilt taste
No pleasure, though in pleasure, solitarie.
What thinkst thou then of mee, and this my State,
Seem I to thee sufficiently possest
Of happiness, or not? who am alone   405
From all Eternitie, for none I know
Second to me or like, equal much less.
How have I then with whom to hold converse
Save with the Creatures which I made, and those
To me inferior, infinite descents   410
Beneath what other Creatures are to thee?
    He ceas'd, I lowly answerd.   To attain
The highth and depth of thy Eternal wayes
All human thoughts come short, Supream of things;
Thou in thy self art perfet, and in thee   415
Is no deficience found; not so is Man,
But in degree, the cause of his desire
By conversation with his like to help,
Or solace his defects.   No need that thou
Shouldst propagate, already infinite;   420
And through all numbers absolute, though One;

But Man by number is to manifest
His single imperfection, and beget
Like of his like, his Image multipli'd,
In unitie defective, which requires   425
Collateral love, and dearest amitie.
Thou in thy secresie although alone,
Best with thy self accompanied, seekst not
Social communication, yet so pleas'd
Canst raise thy Creature to what highth thou wilt   430
Of Union or Communion, deifi'd;
I by conversing cannot these erect
From prone, nor in thir wayes complacence find.
Thus I emboldend spake, and freedom us'd
Permissive, and acceptance found, which gaind   435
This answer from the gracious voice Divine.

    Thus farr to try thee *Adam*, I was pleas'd,
And finde thee knowing not of Beasts alone,
Which thou hast rightly nam'd, but of thy self,
Expressing well the spirit within thee free,   440
My Image, not imparted to the Brute,
Whose fellowship therefore unmeet for thee
Good reason was thou freely shouldst dislike,
And be so minded still; I, ere thou spak'st,
Knew it not good for Man to be alone,   445
And no such companie as then thou sawst
Intended thee, for trial onely brought,
To see how thou couldst judge of fit and meet:
What next I bring shall please thee, be assur'd,
Thy likeness, thy fit help, thy other self,   450
Thy wish exactly to thy hearts desire.

    Hee ended, or I heard no more, for now
My earthly by his Heav'nly overpowerd,
Which it had long stood under, straind to the highth
In that celestial Colloquie sublime,   455
As with an object that excells the sense,
Dazl'd and spent, sunk down, and sought repair
Of sleep, which instantly fell on me, calld
By Nature as in aid, and clos'd mine eyes.
Mine eyes he clos'd, but open left the Cell   460
Of Fancie my internal sight, by which
Abstract as in a trance methought I saw,
Though sleeping, where I lay, and saw the shape
Still glorious before whom awake I stood;
Who stooping opend my left side, and took   465
From thence a Rib, with cordial spirits warm,
And Life-blood streaming fresh; wide was the wound,
But suddenly with flesh filld up and heal'd:
The Rib he formd and fashiond with his hands;
Under his forming hands a Creature grew,   470

Manlike, but different Sex, so lovely faire
That what seemd fair in all the World, seemd now
Mean, or in her summd up, in her containd
And in her looks, which from that time infus'd
Sweetness into my heart, unfelt before,   475
And into all things from her Air inspir'd
The spirit of love and amorous delight.
Shee disappear'd, and left me dark, I wak'd
To find her, or for ever to deplore
Her loss, and other pleasures all abjure: 480
When out of hope, behold her, not farr off,
Such as I saw her in my dream, adornd
With what all Earth or Heaven could bestow
To make her amiable: On she came,
Led by her Heav'nly Maker, though unseen,   485
And guided by his voice, nor uninformd
Of nuptial Sanctitie and marriage Rites;
Grace was in all her steps, Heav'n in her Eye,
In every gesture dignitie and love.
I overjoyd could not forbear aloud.   490
    This turn hath made amends; thou hast fulfilld
Thy words, Creator bounteous and benign,
Giver of all things fair, but fairest this
Of all thy gifts, nor enviest.   I now see
Bone of my Bone, Flesh of my Flesh, my Self   495
Before me; Woman is her Name, of Man
Extracted; for this cause he shall forgoe
Father and Mother, and to his Wife adhere;
And they shall be one Flesh, one Heart, one Soul.
    She heard me thus, and though divinely brought,   500
Yet Innocence and Virgin Modestie,
Her vertue and the conscience of her worth,
That would be woo'd, and not unsought be won,
Not obvious, not obtrusive, but retir'd,
The more desirable, or to say all,   505
Nature her self, though pure of sinful thought,
Wrought in her so, that seeing me, she turnd;
I followd her, she what was Honour knew,
And with obsequious Majestie approv'd
My pleaded reason.   To the Nuptial Bowre   510
I led her blushing like the Morn: all Heav'n,
And happie Constellations on that houre
Shed thir selectest influence; the Earth
Gave sign of gratulation, and each Hill;
Joyous the Birds; fresh Gales and gentle Aires   515
Whisperd it to the Woods, and from thir wings
Flung Rose, flung Odours from the spicie Shrub,
Disporting, till the amorous Bird of Night
Sung Spousal, and bid haste the Ev'ning Starr

On his Hill top, to light the bridal Lamp.　　520
Thus I have told thee all my State, and brought
My Storie to the sum of earthly bliss
Which I enjoy, and must confess to find
In all things else delight indeed, but such
As us'd or not, works in the mind no change　　525
Nor vehement desire, these delicacies
I mean of Taste, Sight, Smell, Herbs, Fruits and Flowrs,
Walks, and the melodie of Birds; but here
Farr otherwise, transported I behold,
Transported touch; here passion first I felt,　　530
Commotion strange, in all enjoyments else
Superior and unmov'd, here onely weake
Against the charm of Beautys powerful glance.
Or Nature faild in me, and left som part
Not proof anough such Object to sustain,　　535
Or from my side subducting, took perhaps
More than anough; at least on her bestowd
Too much of Ornament, in outward shew
Elaborate, of inward less exact.
For well I understand in the prime end　　540
Of Nature her th'inferior, in the mind
And inward Faculties, which most excell,
In outward also her resembling less
His Image who made both, and less expressing
The character of that Dominion giv'n　　545
O'er other Creatures; yet when I approach
Her loveliness, so absolute she seems
And in her self complete, so well to know
Her own, that what she wills to do or say
Seems wisest, vertuousest, discreetest, best;　　550
All higher knowledge in her presence falls
Degraded, Wisdom in discourse with her
Loses discount'nanc't, and like folly shews;
Autority and Reason on her wait,
As one intended first, not after made　　555
Occasionally; and to consummat all,
Greatness of mind and nobleness thir seat
Build in her loveliest, and create an awe
About her, as a guard Angelic plac't.
To whom the Angel with contracted brow.　　560
　Accuse not Nature, she hath don her part;
Do thou but thine, and be not diffident
Of Wisdom, she deserts thee not, if thou
Dismiss not her, when most thou needst her nigh,
By attributing overmuch to things　　565
Less excellent, as thou thy self perceiv'st.
For what admir'st thou, what transports thee so,
An outside? fair no doubt, and worthy well

Thy cherishing, thy honouring, and thy love,
Not thy subjection: weigh with her thy self;   570
Then value: Oft times nothing profits more
Than self-esteem, grounded on just and right
Well manag'd; of that skill the more thou knowst,
The more she will acknowledge thee her Head,
And to realities yield all her shows;   575
Made so adorn for thy delight the more,
So awful, that with honour thou mayst love
Thy mate, who sees when thou art seen least wise.
But if the sense of touch whereby mankind
Is propagated seem such dear delight   580
Beyond all other, think the same voutsaf't
To Cattel and each Beast; which would not be
To them made common and divulg'd, if aught
Therein enjoyd were worthy to subdue
The Soul of Man, or passion in him move.   585
What higher in her societie thou find'st
Attractive, human, rational, love still;
In loving thou dost well, in passion not,
Wherein true Love consists not; love refines
The thoughts, and heart enlarges, hath his seat   590
In Reason, and is judicious, is the scale
By which to heav'nly Love thou mayst ascend,
Not sunk in carnal pleasure, for which cause
Among the Beasts no Mate for thee was found.
    To whom thus half abasht *Adam* repli'd.   595
Neither her out-side formd so fair, nor aught
In procreation common to all kinds
(Though higher of the genial Bed by far,
And with mysterious reverence I deem)
So much delights me as those graceful acts,   600
Those thousand decencies that daily flow
From all her words and actions, mixt with Love
And sweet compliance, which declare unfeignd
Union of Mind, or in us both one Soul:
Harmonie to behold in wedded pair   605
More grateful than harmonious sound to th'ear.
Yet these subject not; I to thee disclose
What inward thence I feel, not therefore foild,
Who meet with various objects, from the sense
Variously representing; yet still free   610
Approve the best, and follow what I approve.
To love thou blam'st me not, for love thou sayst
Leads up to Heav'n, is both the way and guide;
Bear with me then, if lawful what I ask:
Love not the heav'nly Spirits, and how thir Love   615
Express they, by looks onely, or do they mix
Irradiance, virtual or immediat touch?

To whom the Angel with a smile that glowd
Celestial rosie red, Loves proper hue,
Answerd.   Let it suffice thee that thou knowst   620
Us happie, and without Love no happiness.
Whatever pure thou in the body enjoyst
(And pure thou wert created) we enjoy
In eminence, and obstacle find none
Of membrane, joint or limb, exclusive barrs: 625
Easier than Air with Air, if Spirits embrace,
Total they mix, Union of Pure with Pure
Desiring; nor restraind conveyance need
As Flesh to mix with Flesh, or Soul with Soul.
But I can now no more; the parting Sun   630
Beyond the Earths green Cape and verdant Iles
Hesperean sets, my Signal to depart.
Be strong, live happie, and love, but first of all
Him whom to love is to obey, and keep
His great command; take heed lest Passion sway   635
Thy Judgement to do aught, which else free Will
Would not admit; thine and of all thy Sons
The weal or woe in thee is plac't; beware.
I in thy persevering shall rejoice,
And all the Blest: stand fast; to stand or fall   640
Free in thine own Arbitrement it lies.
Perfet within, no outward aid require;
And all temptation to transgress repell.
So saying, he arose; whom *Adam* thus
Followd with benediction.   Since to part,   645
Goe heav'nly Guest, Ethereal Messenger,
Sent from whose sovran goodness I adore.
Gentle to me and affable hath been
Thy condescension, and shall be honourd ever
With grateful Memorie: thou to mankind   650
Be good and friendly still, and oft return.
So parted they, the Angel up to Heav'n
From the thick shade, and *Adam* to his Bowr.

The End of the Eighth Book

BOOK IX

THE ARGUMENT

Satan having compast the Earth, with meditated guile returns as a mist by Night into Paradise, enters into the Serpent sleeping. Adam and Eve in the Morning go forth to thir labours, which Eve proposes to divide in several places, each labouring apart: Adam consents not, alledging the danger, lest that Enemy, of whom they were forewarn'd, should attempt her found alone: Eve loath to be thought not circumspect or firm enough, urges her going apart, the rather desirous to make tryal of her strength; Adam at last yields: The Serpent finds her alone; his subtle approach, first gazing, then speaking, with much flattery extolling Eve above all other Creatures. Eve wondring to hear the Serpent speak, asks how he attain'd to human speech and such understanding not till now; the Serpent answers, that by tasting of a certain Tree in the Garden he attain'd both to Speech and Reason, till then void of both: Eve requires him to bring her to that Tree, and finds it to be the Tree of Knowledge forbidden: The Serpent now grown bolder, with many wiles and arguments induces her at length to eat; she pleas'd with the taste deliberates awhile whether to impart thereof to Adam or not, at last brings him of the Fruit, relates what persuaded her to eat thereof: Adam at first amaz'd, but perceiving her lost, resolves through vehemence of love to perish with her; and extenuating the trespass, eats also of the Fruit: The effects thereof in them both; they seek to cover thir nakedness; then fall to variance and accusation of one another.

No more of talk where God or Angel Guest
With man, as with his Friend, familiar us'd
To sit indulgent, and with him partake
Rural repast, permitting him the while
Venial discourse unblam'd: I now must change   5
Those Notes to Tragic; foul distrust, and breach
Disloyal on the part of Man, revolt,
And disobedience: On the part of Heav'n
Now alienated, distance and distaste,
Anger and just rebuke, and judgement giv'n,   10
That brought into this World a world of woe,
Sinne and her shaddow Death, and Miserie
Deaths Harbinger: Sad task, yet argument
Not less but more Heroic than the wrauth
Of stern *Achilles* on his Foe persu'd   15
Thrice Fugitive about *Troy* Wall; or rage
Of *Turnus* for *Lavinia* disespous'd,
Or *Neptune*'s ire or *Juno*'s, that so long
Perplexd the *Greek* and *Cytherea*'s Son;
If answerable style I can obtain   20
Of my Celestial Patroness, who deigns
Her nightly visitation unimplor'd,
And dictates to me slumbering, or inspires

Easie my unpremeditated Verse:
Since first this Subject for Heroic Song   25
Pleas'd me long choosing, and beginning late;
Not sedulous by Nature to indite
Warrs, hitherto the onely Argument
Heroic deemd, chief maistrie to dissect
With long and tedious havoc fabl'd Knights   30
In Battels feignd; the better fortitude
Of Patience and Heroic Martyrdom
Unsung; or to describe Races and Games,
Or tilting Furniture, emblazond Shields,
Impreses quaint, Caparisons and Steeds;   35
Bases and tinsel Trappings, gorgious Knights
At Joust and Tournament; then marshald Feast
Serv'd up in Hall with Sewers, and Seneshals;
The skill of Artifice or Office mean,
Not that which justly gives Heroic name   40
To Person or to Poem.   Mee of these
Nor skilld nor studious, higher Argument
Remains, sufficient of it self to raise
That name, unless an age too late, or cold
Climat, or Years damp my intended wing   45
Deprest, and much they may, if all be mine,
Not Hers who brings it nightly to my Ear.
     The Sun was sunk, and after him the Starr
Of *Hesperus*, whose Office is to bring
Twilight upon the Earth, short Arbiter   50
Twixt Day and Night, and now from end to end
Nights Hemisphere had veild th'Horizon round:
When *Satan* who late fled before the threats
Of *Gabriel* out of *Eden*, now improv'd
In meditated fraud and malice, bent   55
On Mans destruction, maugre what might hap
Of heavier on himself, fearless returnd.
By Night he fled, and at Midnight returnd
From compassing the Earth, cautious of day,
Since *Uriel* Regent of the Sun descri'd   60
His entrance, and forewarnd the Cherubim
That kept thir watch; thence full of anguish driv'n,
The space of sev'n continu'd Nights he rode
With darkness, thrice the Equinoctial Line
He circl'd, four times crossd the Carr of Night   65
From Pole to Pole, traversing each Colure;
On th'eighth returnd, and on the Coast averse
From entrance or Cherubic Watch, by stelth
Found unsuspected way.   There was a place,
Now not, though Sin, not Time, first wrought the change,
Where *Tigris* at the foot of Paradise   71
Into a Gulf shot under ground, till part

Rose up a Fountain by the Tree of Life;
In with the River sunk, and with it rose
Satan involv'd in rising Mist, then sought   75
Where to lie hid; Sea he had searcht and Land
From *Eden* over *Pontus*, and the Pool
Mæotis, up beyond the River *Ob*;
Downward as farr Antartic; and in length
West from *Orontes* to the Ocean barrd   80
At *Darien*, thence to the Land where flowes
Ganges and *Indus*: thus the Orb he roamd
With narrow search; and with inspection deep
Considerd every Creature, which of all
Most opportune might serve his Wiles, and found   85
The Serpent suttlest Beast of all the Field.
Him after long debate, irresolute
Of thoughts revolv'd, his final sentence chose
Fit Vessel, fittest Imp of fraud, in whom
To enter, and his dark suggestions hide   90
From sharpest sight: for in the wilie Snake,
Whatever sleights none would suspicious mark,
As from his wit and native suttletie
Proceeding, which in other Beasts observ'd
Doubt might beget of Diabolic pow'r   95
Active within beyond the sense of brute.
Thus he resolv'd, but first from inward griefe
His bursting passion into plaints thus pourd:
     O Earth, how like to Heav'n, if not preferrd
More justly, Seat worthier of Gods, as built   100
With second thoughts, reforming what was old!
For what God after better worse would build?
Terrestrial Heav'n, danc't round by other Heav'ns
That shine, yet bear thir bright officious Lamps,
Light above Light, for thee alone, as seems,   105
In thee concentring all thir precious beams
Of sacred influence: As God in Heav'n
Is Center, yet extends to all, so thou
Centring receiv'st from all those Orbs; in thee,
Not in themselves, all thir known vertue appears   110
Productive in Herb, Plant, and nobler birth
Of Creatures animate with gradual life
Of Growth, Sense, Reason, all summd up in Man.
With what delight could I have walkt thee round
If I could joy in aught, sweet interchange   115
Of Hill and Vallie, Rivers, Woods and Plains,
Now Land, now Sea, and Shores with Forrest crownd,
Rocks, Dens and Caves; but I in none of these
Find place or refuge; and the more I see
Pleasures about me, so much more I feel   120
Torment within me, as from the hateful siege

Of contraries; all good to me becomes
Bane, and in Heav'n much worse would be my state.
But neither here seek I, no nor in Heav'n
To dwell, unless by maistring Heav'ns Supream;   125
Nor hope to be my self less miserable
By what I seek, but others to make such
As I, though thereby worse to me redound:
For onely in destroying I find ease
To my relentless thoughts; and him destroyd,   130
Or won to what may work his utter loss,
For whom all this was made, all this will soon
Follow, as to him linkt in weal or wo,
In woe then; that destruction wide may range:
To mee shall be the glorie sole among   135
Th'infernal Powers, in one day to have marrd
What he *Almightie* styl'd, six Nights and Days
Continu'd making, and who knows how long
Before had bin contriving, though perhaps
Not longer than since I in one Night freed   140
From servitude inglorious welnigh half
Th' Angelic Name, and thinner left the throng
Of his adorers: hee to be aveng'd,
And to repaire his numbers thus impaird,
Whether such vertue spent of old now faild   145
More Angels to Create, if they at least
Are his Created, or to spite us more,
Determin'd to advance into our room
A Creature formd of Earth, and him endow,
Exalted from so base original,   150
With Heav'nly spoils, our spoils: What he decreed
He effected; Man he made, and for him built
Magnificent this World, and Earth his seat,
Him Lord pronounc'd, and, O indignitie!
Subjected to his service Angel wings,   155
And flaming Ministers to watch and tend
Thir earthy Charge: Of these the vigilance
I dread, and to elude, thus wrapt in mist
Of midnight vapour glide obscure, and prie
In every Bush and Brake, where hap may find   160
The Serpent sleeping, in whose mazie folds
To hide me, and the dark intent I bring.
O foul descent! that I who erst contended
With Gods to sit the highest, am now constraind
Into a Beast, and mixt with bestial slime,   165
This essence to incarnate and imbrute,
That to the highth of Dietie aspir'd;
But what will not Ambition and Revenge
Descend to? who aspires must down as low
As high he soard, obnoxious first or last   170

To basest things.   Revenge, at first though sweet,
Bitter ere long back on it self recoils;
Let it; I reck not, so it light well aimd,
Since higher I fall short, on him who next
Provokes my envie, this new Favorite   175
Of Heav'n, this Man of Clay, Son of despite,
Whom us the more to spite his Maker rais'd
From dust: spite then with spite is best repaid.
   So saying, through each Thicket Dank or Drie,
Like a black mist low creeping, he held on   180
His midnight search, where soonest he might find
The Serpent: him fast sleeping soon he found
In Labyrinth of many a round self-rould,
His head the midst, well stor'd with suttle wiles:
Not yet in horrid Shade or dismal Den,   185
Nor nocent yet, but on the grassie Herbe
Fearless unfear'd he slept: in at his Mouth
The Devil enterd, and his brutal sense,
In heart or head, possessing soon inspir'd
With act intelligential; but his sleep   190
Disturbd not, waiting close th' approach of Morn.
Now whenas sacred Light began to dawn
In *Eden* on the humid Flowrs, that breath'd
Thir morning Incense, when all things that breathe
From th' Earths great Altar send up silent praise   195
To the Creator, and his Nostrils fill
With grateful Smell, forth came the human pair
And joind thir vocal Worship to the Quire
Of Creatures wanting voice; that don, partake
The season, prime for sweetest Scents and Airs: 200
Then commune how that day they best may ply
Thir growing work: for much thir work outgrew
The hands dispatch of two Gardning so wide.
And *Eve* first to her Husband thus began.
   Adam, well may we labour still to dress   205
This Garden, still to tend Plant, Herb and Flowr,
Our pleasant task enjoind, but till more hands
Aid us, the work under our labour grows,
Luxurious by restraint; what we by daye
Lop overgrown, or prune, or prop, or bind,   210
One night or two with wanton growth derides
Tending to wild.   Thou therefore now advise
Or hear what to my minde first thoughts present,
Let us divide our labours, thou where choice
Leads thee, or where most needs, whether to wind   215
The Woodbine round this Arbour, or direct
The clasping Ivie where to climb, while I

In yonder Spring of Roses intermixt
With Myrtle, find what to redress till Noon:
For while so near each other thus all day   220
Our task we choose, what wonder if so near
Looks intervene and smiles, or object new
Casual discourse draw on, which intermits
Our days work brought to little, though begun
Early, and th' hour of Supper comes unearnd.   225
    To whom mild answer *Adam* thus returnd.
Sole *Eve*, Associat sole, to me beyond
Compare above all living Creatures dear,
Well hast thou motion'd, well thy thoughts imployd
How we might best fulfill the work which here   230
God hath assign'd us, nor of me shalt pass
Unprais'd: for nothing lovelier can be found
In Woman, than to studie household good,
And good workes in her Husband to promote.
Yet not so strictly hath our Lord impos'd   235
Labour, as to debarr us when we need
Refreshment, whether food or talk between,
Food of the mind or this sweet intercourse
Of looks and smiles, for smiles from Reason flow,
To brute deni'd, and are of Love the food,   240
Love not the lowest end of human life.
For not to irksom toil, but to delight
He made us, and delight to Reason joind.
These paths and Bowers doubt not but our joint hands
Will keep from Wilderness with ease, as wide   245
As we need walk, till younger hands ere long
Assist us: But if much converse perhaps
Thee satiate, to short absence I could yield.
For solitude somtimes is best societie,
And short retirement urges sweet return.   250
But other doubt possesses me, lest harm
Befall thee severd from me; for thou knowst
What hath bin warnd us, what malicious Foe
Envying our happiness, and of his own
Despairing, seeks to work us woe and shame   255
By sly assault; and somewhere nigh at hand
Watches, no doubt, with greedy hope to find
His wish and best advantage, us asunder,
Hopeless to circumvent us joind, where each
To other speedie aide might lend at need;   260
Whether his first designe be to withdraw
Our fealtie from God, or to disturb
Conjugal Love, than which perhaps no bliss
Enjoyd by us excites his envie more;
Or this, or worse, leave not the faithful side   265
That gave thee being, stil shades thee and protects.

The Wife, where danger or dishonour lurks,
Safest and seemliest by her Husband stays,
Who guards her, or with her the worst endures.
    To whom the Virgin Majestie of *Eve*,   270
As one who loves, and som unkindness meets,
With sweet austere composure thus repli'd.
    Offspring of Heav'n and Earth, and all Earths Lord,
That such an Enemie we have, who seeks
Our ruin, both by thee informd I learn,   275
And from the parting Angel over-heard
As in a shadie nook I stood behind,
Just then returnd at shut of Ev'ning Flowrs.
But that thou shouldst my firmness therfore doubt
To God or thee, because we have a foe   280
May tempt it, I expected not to hear.
His violence thou fear'st not, being such
As wee, not capable of death or pain,
Can either not receive, or can repell.
His fraud is then thy fear, which plain inferrs   285
Thy equal fear that my firm Faith and Love
Can by his fraud be shaken or seduc't;
Thoughts, which how found they harbour in thy brest
Adam, misthought of her to thee so dear?
    To whom with healing words *Adam* repli'd.   290
Daughter of God and Man, immortal *Eve*,
For such thou art, from sin and blame entire:
Not diffident of thee do I dissuade
Thy absence from my sight, but to avoid
Th' attempt it self, intended by our Foe.   295
For hee who tempts, though in vain, at least asperses
The tempted with dishonour foul, suppos'd
Not incorruptible of Faith, not prooff
Against temptation; thou thy self with scorn
And anger wouldst resent the offerd wrong,   300
Though ineffectual found: misdeem not then,
If such affront I labour to avert
From thee alone, which on us both at once
The Enemie, though bold, will hardly dare,
Or daring, first on mee th' assault shall light.   305
Nor thou his malice and false guile contemn;
Suttle he needs must be, who could seduce
Angels; nor think superfluous others aid.
I from the influence of thy looks receive
Access in every Vertue, in thy sight   310
More wise, more watchful, stronger, if need were
Of outward strength; while shame, thou looking on,
Shame to be overcome or over-reacht
Would utmost vigor raise, and rais'd unite.
Why shouldst not thou like sense within thee feel   315

When I am present, and thy trial choose
With me, best witness of thy Vertue tri'd?
  So spake domestic *Adam* in his care
And Matrimonial Love; but *Eve*, who thought
Less attributed to her Faith sincere,   320
Thus her reply with accent sweet renewd.
  If this be our condition, thus to dwell
In narrow circuit straitend by a Foe,
Suttle or violent, we not endu'd
Single with like defence, wherever met,   325
How are we happie, still in fear of harm?
But harm precedes not sin: onely our Foe
Tempting affronts us with his foul esteem
Of our integritie: his foul esteeme
Sticks no dishonor on our Front, but turnes   330
Foule on himself; then wherefore shunnd or fear'd
By us? who rather double honour gaine
From his surmise prov'd false, find peace within,
Favour from Heav'n, our witness from th' event.
And what is Faith, Love, Vertue unassayd   335
Alone, without exterior help sustaind?
Let us not then suspect our happie State
Left so imperfet by the Maker wise,
As not secure to single or combin'd:
Fraile is our happiness, if this be so,   340
And *Eden* were no *Eden* thus expos'd.
  To whom thus *Adam* fervently repli'd.
O Woman, best are all things as the will
Of God ordaind them, his creating hand
Nothing imperfet or deficient left   345
Of all that he Created, much less Man,
Or aught that might his happie State secure,
Secure from outward force; within himself
The danger lies, yet lies within his power:
Against his will he can receive no harm.   350
But God left free the Will, for what obeyes
Reason, is free, and Reason he made right
But bid her well beware, and still erect,
Lest by som faire appearing good surpris'd
She dictate false, and misinform the Will   355
To do what God expressly hath forbid.
Not then mistrust, but tender love enjoins,
That I should mind thee oft, and mind thou me.
Firm we subsist, yet possible to swerve,
Since Reason not impossibly may meet   360
Som specious object by the Foe subornd,
And fall into deception unaware,
Not keeping strictest watch, as she was warnd.
Seek not temptation then, which to avoide

353 beware *Edd. 1, 2*] be ware *conj.* Richardson.

Were better, and most likelie if from mee   365
Thou sever not: Trial will come unsought.
Wouldst thou approve thy constancie, approve
First thy obedience; th' other who can know,
Not seeing thee attempted, who attest?
But if thou think, trial unsought may find   370
Us both securer than thus warnd thou seemst,
Go; for thy stay, not free, absents thee more;
Goe in thy native innocence, relie
On what thou hast of vertue, summon all,
For God towards thee hath don his part, do thine.   375
     So spake the Patriarch of Mankind, but *Eve*
Persisted, yet submiss, though last, repli'd.
     With thy permission then, and thus forewarnd
Chiefly by what thy own last reasoning words
Touchd only, that our trial, when least sought,   380
May find us both perhaps farr less prepar'd,
The willinger I go, nor much expect
A Foe so proud will first the weaker seek;
So bent, the more shall shame him his repulse.
Thus saying, from her Husbands hand her hand   385
Soft she withdrew, and like a Wood-Nymph light
Oread or *Dryad*, or of *Delia*'s Train,
Betook her to the Groves, but *Delia*'s self
In gait surpassd and Goddess-like deport,
Though not as shee with Bow and Quiver armd,   390
But with such Gardning Tools as Art yet rude
Guiltless of fire had formd, or Angels brought.
To *Pales*, or *Pomona*, thus adornd,
Likest she seemd, *Pomona* when she fled
Vertumnus, or to *Ceres* in her Prime,   395
Yet Virgin of *Proserpina* from *Jove*.
Her long with ardent look his Eye persu'd
Delighted, but desiring more her stay.
Oft he to her his charge of quick returne
Repeated, shee to him as oft engag'd   400
To be returnd by Noon amid the Bowr,
And all things in best order to invite
Noontide repast, or Afternoons repose.
O much deceiv'd, much failing, hapless *Eve*,
Of thy presum'd return! event perverse!   405
Thou never from that houre in Paradise
Foundst either sweet repast or sound repose;
Such ambush hid among sweet Flowrs and Shades
Waited with hellish rancour imminent
To intercept thy way, or send thee back   410
Despoild of Innocence, of Faith, of Bliss.

---

394 Likest *Ed. 1*] Likeliest *Ed. 2*

For now, and since first break of dawne the Fiend,
Mere Serpent in appearance, forth was come,
And on his Quest, where likeliest he might finde
The onely two of Mankind, but in them   415
The whole included Race, his purposd prey.
In Bowr and Field he sought, where any tuft
Of Grove or Garden-Plot more pleasant lay,
Thir tendance or Plantation for delight,
By Fountain or by shadie Rivulet   420
He sought them both, but wishd his hap might find
Eve separate; he wishd, but not with hope
Of what so seldom chanc'd, when to his wish,
Beyond his hope, *Eve* separate he spies,
Veild in a Cloud of Fragrance, where she stood,   425
Half spi'd, so thick the Roses bushing round
About her glowd, oft stooping to support
Each Flowr of slender stalk, whose head though gay
Carnation, Purple, Azure, or spect with Gold,
Hung drooping unsustaind, them she upstayes   430
Gently with Mirtle band, mindless the while,
Her self, though fairest unsupported Flowr,
From her best prop so farr, and storm so nigh.
Nearer he drew, and many a walk travers'd
Of stateliest Covert, Cedar, Pine or Palm,   435
Then voluble and bold, now hid, now seen
Among thick-woven Arborets and Flowrs
Imborderd on each Bank, the hand of *Eve*:
Spot more delicious than those Gardens feignd
Or of reviv'd *Adonis*, or renownd   440
Alcinous, host of old *Laertes* Son,
Or that, not Mystic, where the Sapient King
Held dalliance with his faire *Egyptian* Spouse.
Much hee the Place admir'd, the Person more.
As one who long in populous City pent,   445
Where Houses thick and Sewers annoy the Air,
Forth issuing on a Summers Morn to breathe
Among the pleasant Villages and Farms
Adjoind, from each thing met conceives delight,
The smell of Grain, or tedded Grass or Kine   450
Or Dairie, each rural sight, each rural sound;
If chance with Nymphlike step fair Virgin pass,
What pleasing seemd, for her now pleases more,
She most, and in her looks summs all Delight.
Such Pleasure took the Serpent to behold   455
This Flowrie Plat, the sweet recess of *Eve*
Thus earlie, thus alone; her Heav'nly form
Angelic, but more soft and Feminine,
Her graceful Innocence, her every Air
Of gesture or least action overawd   460

His Malice, and with rapine sweet bereav'd
His fierceness of the fierce intent it brought:
That space the Evil one abstracted stood
From his own evil, and for the time remaind
Stupidly good, of enmitie disarmd,   465
Of guile, of hate, of envie, of revenge;
But the hot Hell that always in him burnes,
Though in mid Heav'n, soon ended his delight,
And tortures him now more, the more he sees
Of pleasure not for him ordaind: then soon   470
Fierce hate he recollects, and all his thoughts
Of mischief, gratulating, thus excites.
   Thoughts, whither have ye led me, with what sweet
Compulsion thus transported to forget
What hither brought us, hate, not love, nor hope   475
Of Paradise for Hell, hope here to taste
Of pleasure, but all pleasure to destroy;
Save what is in destroying, other joy
To me is lost.   Then let me not let pass
Occasion which now smiles, behold alone   480
The Woman, opportune to all attempts;
Her Husband, for I view far round, not nigh,
Whose higher intellectual more I shun,
And strength, of courage haughtie and of limb
Heroic built, though of terrestrial mould,   485
Foe not informidable, exempt from wound,
I not; so much hath Hell debas'd, and pain
Infeebl'd me, to what I was in Heav'n.
Shee fair, divinely fair, fit Love for Gods,
Not terrible, though terror be in Love   490
And beautie, not approacht by stronger hate,
Hate stronger, under shew of Love well feignd,
The way which to her ruin now I tend.
   So spake the Enemie of Mankind, enclos'd
In Serpent, Inmate bad, and toward *Eve*   495
Addressd his way, not with indented wave
Prone on the ground, as since, but on his rear,
Circular base of rising folds, that towrd
Fold above fold a surging Maze, his Head
Crested aloft, and Carbuncle his Eyes;   500
With burnisht Neck of verdant Gold, erect
Amidst his circling Spires, that on the grasse
Floated redundant: pleasing was his shape
And lovely, never since of Serpent kinde
Lovelier, not those that in *Illyria* chang'd   505
Hermione and *Cadmus*, or the God
In *Epidaurus*; nor to which transformd
Ammonian Jove, or *Capitoline* was seen,
Hee with *Olympias*, this with her who bore

Scipio the highth of *Rome*.   With tract oblique   510
At first, as one who sought access, but fear'd
To interrupt, side-long he works his way.
As when a Ship by skilful Steersman wrought
Nigh Rivers mouth or Foreland, where the Wind
Veers oft, as oft so steers, and shifts her Sail;   515
So varied hee, and of his tortuous Traine
Curld many a wanton wreath in sight of *Eve*,
To lure her Eye; shee busied heard the sound
Of russling Leaves, but minded not, as us'd
To such disport before her through the Field,   520
From every Beast, more duteous at her call
Than at *Circean* call the Herd disguis'd.
Hee bolder now, uncalld before her stood;
But as in gaze admiring: Oft he bowd
His turret Crest, and sleek enameld Neck,   525
Fawning, and lickd the ground whereon she trod.
His gentle dumb expression turnd at length
The Eye of *Eve* to mark his play; he glad
Of her attention gaind, with Serpent Tongue
Organic, or impulse of vocal Air,   530
His fraudulent temptation thus began.
    Wonder not, sovran Mistress, if perhaps
Thou canst, who art sole Wonder, much less arm
Thy looks, the Heav'n of mildness, with disdain,
Displeas'd that I approach thee thus, and gaze   535
Insatiat, I thus single, nor have fear'd
Thy awful brow, more awful thus retir'd.
Fairest resemblance of thy Maker fair,
Thee all things living gaze on, all things thine
By gift, and thy Celestial Beautie adore   540
With ravishment beheld, there best beheld
Where universally admir'd; but here
In this enclosure wild, these Beasts among,
Beholders rude, and shallow to discerne
Half what in thee is fair, one man except,   545
Who sees thee? (and what is one?) who shouldst be
    seen
A Goddess among Gods, ador'd and serv'd
By Angels numberless, thy daily Train.
    So gloz'd the Tempter, and his Proem tun'd;
Into the Heart of *Eve* his words made way,   550
Though at the voice much marveling; at length
Not unamaz'd she thus in answer spake.
What may this mean?   Language of Man pronounc't
By Tongue of Brute, and human sense exprest?
The first at least of these I thought deni'd   555
To Beasts, whom God on thir Creation-Day
Created mute to all articulat sound;

The latter I demurr, for in thir looks
Much reason, and in thir actions oft appears.
Thee, Serpent, suttlest beast of all the field   560
I knew, but not with human voice endu'd;
Redouble then this miracle, and say
How cam'st thou speakable of mute, and how
To me so friendly grown above the rest
Of brutal kind, that daily are in sight?   565
Say, for such wonder claims attention due.
    To whom the guileful Tempter thus repli'd.
Empress of this fair World, resplendent *Eve*,
Easie to mee it is to tell thee all
What thou commandst, and right thou shouldst be obeyd:
I was at first as other Beasts that graze   571
The trodden Herb, of abject thoughts and low,
As was my food, nor aught but food discernd
Or Sex, and apprehended nothing high:
Till on a day roving the field, I chanc'd   575
A goodly Tree farr distant to behold
Loaden with fruit of fairest colours mixt,
Ruddie and Gold: I nearer drew to gaze;
When from the boughes a savourie odour blown,
Grateful to appetite, more pleas'd my sense   580
Than smell of sweetest Fenel, or the Teats
Of Ewe or Goat dropping with Milk at Ev'n,
Unsuckt of Lamb or Kid, that tend thir play.
To satisfie the sharp desire I had
Of tasting those fair Apples, I resolv'd   585
Not to deferr; hunger and thirst at once,
Powerful persuaders, quickend at the scent
Of that alluring fruit, urg'd me so keen.
About the mossie Trunk I wound me soon,
For high from ground the branches would require   590
Thy utmost reach or *Adams*: Round the Tree
All other Beasts that saw, with like desire
Longing and envying stood, but could not reach.
Amid the Tree now got, where plenty hung
Tempting so nigh, to pluck and eat my fill   595
I spar'd not, for such pleasure till that hour
At Feed or Fountain never had I found.
Sated at length, ere long I might perceive
Strange alteration in me, to degree
Of Reason in my inward powers, and Speech   600
Wanted not long, though to this shape retaind.
Thenceforth to Speculations high or deep
I turnd my thoughts, and with capacious mind
Considerd all things visible in Heav'n
Or Earth or Middle, all things fair and good;   605
But all that fair and good in thy Divine

Semblance, and in thy Beautys heav'nly Ray
United I beheld; no Fair to thine
Equivalent or second, which compelld
Mee thus, though importune perhaps, to come   610
And gaze, and worship thee of right declar'd
Sovran of Creatures, universal Dame.
   So talkd the spirited sly Snake; and *Eve*
Yet more amaz'd unwarie thus repli'd.
   Serpent, thy overpraising leaves in doubt   615
The vertue of that Fruit, in thee first prov'd:
But say, where grows the Tree, from hence how far?
For many are the Trees of God that grow
In Paradise, and various, yet unknown
To us, in such abundance lies our choice,   620
As leaves a greater store of Fruit untoucht,
Still hanging incorruptible, till men
Grow up to thir provision, and more hands
Help to disburden Nature of her Bearth.
   To whom the wilie Adder, blithe and glad.   625
Empress, the way is readie, and not long,
Beyond a row of Myrtles, on a Flat,
Fast by a Fountain, one small Thicket past
Of blowing Myrrh and Baum; if thou accept
My conduct, I can bring thee thither soon.   630
   Lead then, said *Eve*.   Hee leading swiftly rould
In tangles, and made intricate seem straight,
To mischief swift.   Hope elevates and joye
Brightens his Crest, as when a wandring Fire
Compact of unctuous vapour, which the Night   635
Condenses, and the cold invirons round,
Kindl'd through agitation to a Flame,
Which oft, they say, som evil Spirit attends
Hovering and blazing with delusive Light,
Misleads th' amaz'd Night-wanderer from his way   640
To Boggs and Mires, and oft through Pond or Pool,
There swallowd up and lost, from succour farr.
So glisterd the dire Snake, and into fraud
Led *Eve* our credulous Mother, to the Tree
Of prohibition, root of all our woe;   645
Which when she saw, thus to her guide she spake.
   Serpent, we might have spar'd our coming hither,
Fruitless to mee, though Fruit be here to excess,
The credit of whose vertue rest with thee,
Wondrous indeed, if cause of such effects.   650
But of this Tree we may not taste nor touch;
God so commanded, and left that Command
Sole Daughter of his voice; the rest, we live
Law to our selves, our Reason is our Law.
   To whom the Tempter guilefully repli'd.   655

Indeed? hath God then said that of the Fruit
Of all these Garden Trees ye shall not eat,
Yet Lords declar'd of all in Earth or Air?
  To whom thus *Eve* yet sinless. Of the Fruit
Of each Tree in the Garden we may eat,   660
But of the Fruit of this fair Tree amidst
The Garden, God hath said, Ye shall not eate
Thereof, nor shall ye touch it, lest ye die.
  She scarce had said, though brief, when now more bold
The Tempter, but with shew of Zeal and Love   665
To Man, and indignation at his wrong,
New part puts on, and as to passion mov'd
Fluctuats disturbd, yet comely, and in act
Rais'd, as of som great matter to begin.
As when of old som Orator renownd   670
In *Athens* or free *Rome*, where Eloquence
Flourishd, since mute, to som great cause addrest,
Stood in himself collected, while each part,
Motion, each act won audience ere the tongue,
Somtimes in highth began, as no delay   675
Of Preface brooking through his Zeal of Right.
So standing, moving, or to highth upgrown
The Tempter all impassiond thus began.
  O Sacred, Wise, and Wisdom-giving Plant,
Mother of Science, Now I feel thy Power   680
Within me clear, not onely to discerne
Things in thir Causes, but to trace the ways
Of highest Agents, deemd however wise.
Queen of this Universe, do not believe
Those rigid threats of Death; ye shall not Die: 685
How should ye? by the Fruit? it gives you Life
To Knowledge: By the Threatner? look on mee,
Mee who have toucht and tasted, yet both live,
And life more perfet have attaind than Fate
Meant mee, by ventring higher than my Lot.   690
Shall that be shut to Man, which to the Beast
Is open? or will God incense his ire
For such a petty Trespass, and not praise
Rather your dauntless vertue, whom the pain
Of Death denounc't, whatever thing Death be,   695
Deterrd not from achieving what might lead
To happier life, knowledge of Good and Evil;
Of good, how just? of evil, if what is evil
Be real, why not known, since easier shunnd?
God therefore cannot hurt ye, and be just;   700
Not just, not God; not fear'd then, nor obeyd:

687 To Knowledge: By the Threatner?] To Knowledge? By the Threatner,
Edd. 1, 2

Your feare it self of Death removes the fear.
Why then was this forbid? Why but to awe,
Why but to keep ye low and ignorant,
His worshippers; he knows that in the day   705
Ye Eate thereof, your Eyes that seem so clear,
Yet are but dim, shall perfetly be then
Opend and clear'd, and ye shall be as Gods,
Knowing both Good and Evil as they know.
That ye should be as Gods, since I as Man,   710
Internal Man, is but proportion meet,
I of brute human, yee of human Gods.
So ye shall die perhaps, by putting off
Human, to put on Gods, death to be wisht,
Though threatnd, which no worse than this can bring.
And what are Gods that Man may not become   716
As they, participating God-like food?
The Gods are first, and that advantage use
On the belief, that all from them proceeds;
I question it, for this fair Earth I see,   720
Warmd by the Sun, producing every kind,
Them nothing: If they all things, who enclos'd
Knowledge of Good and Evil in this Tree,
That whoso eats thereof forthwith attaines
Wisdom without their leave? and wherein lies   725
Th' offence, that Man should thus attain to know?
What can your knowledge hurt him, or this Tree
Impart against his will if all be his?
Or is it envie, and can envie dwell
In heav'nly brests? these, these and many more   730
Causes import your need of this fair Fruit.
Goddess humane, reach then, and freely taste.
    He ended, and his words replete with guile
Into her heart too easie entrance won:
Fixt on the Fruit she gaz'd, which to behold   735
Might tempt alone, and in her ears the sound
Yet rung of his persuasive words, impregnd
With Reason, to her seeming, and with Truth;
Meanwhile the hour of Noon drew on, and wak'd
An eager appetite, rais'd by the smell   740
So savourie of that Fruit, which with desire,
Inclinable now grown to touch or taste,
Solicited her longing eye; yet first
Pausing a while, thus to her self she mus'd.
    Great are thy Vertues, doubtless, best of Fruits,   745
Though kept from Man, and worthy to be admir'd,
Whose taste, too long forborne, at first assay
Gave elocution to the mute, and taught
Thy Tongue not made for Speech to speak thy praise:
Thy praise hee also who forbids thy use   750

Conceales not from us, naming thee the Tree
Of Knowledge, knowledge both of good and evil;
Forbids us then to taste, but his forbidding
Commends thee more, while it inferrs the good
By thee communicated, and our want: 755
For good unknown, sure is not had, or had
And yet unknown, is as not had at all.
In plain then, what forbids he but to know,
Forbids us good, forbids us to be wise?
Such prohibitions binde not.   But if Death   760
Binde us with after-bands, what profits then
Our inward freedom?   In the day we eate
Of this fair Fruit, our doom is, we shall die.
How dies the Serpent? hee hath eat'n and lives,
And knows, and speaks, and reasons, and discerns,   765
Irrational till then.   For us alone
Was death invented? or to us deni'd
This intellectual food, for beasts reserv'd?
For Beasts it seems: yet that one Beast which first
Hath tasted, envies not, but brings with joy   770
The good befall'n him, Author unsuspect,
Friendly to man, farr from deceit or guile.
What fear I then, rather what know to feare
Under this ignorance of Good and Evil,
Of God or Death, of Law or Penaltie?   775
Here grows the Cure of all, this Fruit Divine,
Faire to the Eye, inviting to the Taste,
Of vertue to make wise: what hinders then
To reach, and feed at once both Bodie and Mind?
   So saying, her rash hand in evil hour   780
Forth reaching to the Fruit, she pluckd, she eat:
Earth felt the wound, and Nature from her seate
Sighing through all her Works gave signs of woe,
That all was lost.   Back to the Thicket slunk
The guiltie Serpent, and well might, for *Eve*   785
Intent now wholly on her taste, naught else
Regarded, such delight till then, as seemd,
In Fruit she never tasted, whether true
Or fancied so, through expectation high
Of knowledge, nor was God-head from her thought.   790
Greedily she ingorg'd without restraint,
And knew not eating Death: Satiate at length,
And hightend as with Wine, jocond and boon,
Thus to her self she pleasingly began.
   O Sovran, vertuous, precious of all Trees   795
In Paradise, of operation blest
To Sapience, hitherto obscur'd, infam'd,
And thy fair Fruit let hang, as to no end
Created; but henceforth my early care,

Not without Song, each Morning, and due praise   800
Shall tend thee, and the fertil burden ease
Of thy full branches offerd free to all;
Till dieted by thee I grow mature
In knowledge, as the Gods who all things know;
Though others envie what they cannot give;   805
For had the gift bin theirs, it had not here
Thus grown.   Experience, next to thee I ow,
Best guide; not following thee, I had remaind
In ignorance, thou openst Wisdoms way,
And giv'st access, though secret she retire.   810
And I perhaps am secret; Heav'n is high,
High and remote to see from thence distinct
Each thing on Earth; and other care perhaps
May have diverted from continual watch
Our great Forbidder, safe with all his Spies   815
About him.   But to *Adam* in what sort
Shall I appear? shall I to him make known
As yet my change, and give him to partake
Full happiness with mee, or rather not,
But keep the odds of Knowledge in my power   820
Without Copartner? so to add what wants
In Femal Sex, the more to draw his Love,
And render me more equal, and perhaps,
A thing not undesireable, sometime
Superior; for inferior who is free?   825
This may be well: but what if God have seen
And Death ensue? then I shall be no more,
And *Adam* wedded to another *Eve*
Shall live with her enjoying, I extinct;
A death to think.   Confirmd then I resolve,   830
Adam shall share with me in bliss or woe:
So dear I love him, that with him all deaths
I could endure, without him live no life.
    So saying, from the Tree her step she turnd,
But first low Reverence don, as to the power   835
That dwelt within, whose presence had infus'd
Into the plant sciential sap, deriv'd
From Nectar, drink of Gods.   *Adam* the while
Waiting desirous her return, had wove
Of choicest Flowrs a Garland to adorn   840
Her Tresses, and her rural labours crown
As Reapers oft are wont thir Harvest Queen.
Great joy he promis'd to his thoughts, and new
Solace in her return, so long delayd;
Yet oft his heart, divine of somthing ill,   845
Misgave him; hee the faultring measure felt;
And forth to meet her went, the way she took
That Morn when first they parted; by the Tree

Of Knowledge he must pass, there he her met,
Scarce from the Tree returning; in her hand   850
A bough of fairest fruit that downie smil'd,
New gatherd, and ambrosial smell diffus'd.
To him she hasted, in her face Excuse
Came Prologue, and Apologie to prompt,
Which with bland words at will she thus addressd.   855
     Hast thou not wonderd, *Adam*, at my stay?
Thee I have misst, and thought it long, depriv'd
Thy presence, agonie of love till now
Not felt, nor shall be twice, for never more
Mean I to trie, what rash untri'd I sought,   860
The paine of absence from thy sight.   But strange
Hath bin the cause, and wonderful to hear:
This Tree is not as we are told, a Tree
Of danger tasted, nor to evil unknown
Op'ning the way, but of Divine effect   865
To open Eyes, and make them Gods who taste;
And hath bin tasted such: the Serpent wise,
Or not restraind as wee, or not obeying,
Hath eaten of the fruit, and is become,
Not dead, as we are threatend, but thenceforth   870
Endu'd with human voice and human sense,
Reasoning to admiration, and with mee
Persuasively hath so prevaild, that I
Have also tasted, and have also found
Th' effects to correspond, op'ner mine Eyes,   875
Dimm erst, dilated Spirits, ampler Heart,
And growing up to Godhead; which for thee
Chiefly I sought, without thee can despise.
For bliss, as thou hast part, to me is bliss,
Tedious, unshar'd with thee, and odious soon.   880
Thou therefore also taste, that equal Lot
May joine us, equal Joy, as equal Love;
Lest thou not tasting, different degree
Disjoine us, and I then too late renounce
Deitie for thee, when Fate will not permit.   885
     Thus *Eve* with Countnance blithe her storie told;
But in her Cheek distemper flushing glowd.
On th' other side, *Adam*, soon as he heard
The fatal Trespass don by *Eve*, amaz'd,
Astonied stood and Blank, while horror chill   890
Ran through his veins, and all his joints relaxd;
From his slack hand the Garland wreath'd for *Eve*
Down dropd, and all the faded Roses shed:
Speechless he stood and pale, till thus at length
First to himself he inward silence broke.   895

O fairest of Creation, last and best
Of all Gods works, Creature in whom excelld
Whatever can to sight or thought be formd,
Holy, divine, good, amiable, or sweet!
How art thou lost, how on a sudden lost,   900
Defac't, deflowrd, and now to Death devote?
Rather how hast thou yielded to transgress
The strict forbiddance, how to violate
The sacred Fruit forbidden! som cursed fraud
Of Enemie hath beguil'd thee, yet unknown,   905
And mee with thee hath ruind, for with thee
Certain my resolution is to Die;
How can I live without thee, how forgoe
Thy sweet Converse and Love so dearly joind,
To live again in these wilde Woods forlorn?   910
Should God create another *Eve*, and I
Another Rib afford, yet loss of thee
Would never from my heart; no no, I feel
The Link of Nature draw me: Flesh of Flesh,
Bone of my Bone thou art, and from thy State   915
Mine never shall be parted, bliss or woe.
    So having said, as one from sad dismay
Recomforted, and after thoughts disturbd
Submitting to what seemd remediless,
Thus in calm mood his Words to *Eve* he turnd.   920
    Bold deed thou hast presum'd, adventrous *Eve*,
And peril great provok't, who thus hath dar'd
Had it bin onely coveting to Eye
That sacred Fruit, sacred to abstinence,
Much more to taste it under bann to touch.   925
But past who can recall, or don undoe?
Not God Omnipotent, nor Fate, yet so
Perhaps thou shalt not Die, perhaps the Fact
Is not so hainous now, foretasted Fruit,
Profan'd first by the Serpent, by him first   930
Made common and unhallowd ere our taste;
Nor yet on him found deadly, he yet lives,
Lives, as thou saidst, and gaines to live as Man
Higher degree of Life, inducement strong
To us, as likely tasting to attain   935
Proportional ascent, which cannot be
But to be Gods, or Angels Demi-gods.
Nor can I think that God, Creator wise,
Though threatning, will in earnest so destroye
Us his prime Creatures, dignifi'd so high,   940
Set over all his Works, which in our Fall,
For us created, needs with us must fail,

922 hath *Ed. 2*] hast *Ed. 1*

Dependent made; so God shall uncreate,
Be frustrate, do, undo, and labour lose,
Not well conceiv'd of God, who though his Power   945
Creation could repeat, yet would be loath
Us to abolish, lest the Adversary
Triumph and say; Fickle their State whom God
Most Favors, who can please him long?   Mee first
He ruind, now Mankind; whom will he next?   950
Matter of scorn, not to be giv'n the Foe.
However I with thee have fixt my Lot,
Certain to undergo like doom; if Death
Consort with thee, Death is to mee as Life;
So forcible within my heart I feel   955
The Bond of Nature draw me to my own,
My own in thee, for what thou art is mine;
Our State cannot be severd, we are one,
One Flesh; to lose thee were to lose my self.

   So *Adam*, and thus *Eve* to him repli'd.   960
O glorious trial of exceeding Love,
Illustrious evidence, example high!
Ingaging me to emulate, but short
Of thy perfection, how shall I attaine
Adam, from whose deare side I boast me sprung,   965
And gladly of our Union hear thee speak,
One Heart, one Soul in both; whereof good prooff
This day affords, declaring thee resolv'd,
Rather than Death or aught than Death more dread
Shall separate us, linkt in Love so dear,   970
To undergo with mee one Guilt, one Crime,
If any be, of tasting this fair Fruit,
Whose vertue, for of good still good proceeds,
Direct or by occasion hath presented
This happie trial of thy Love, which else   975
So eminently never had bin known.
Were it I thought Death menac't would ensue
This my attempt, I would sustain alone
The worst, and not persuade thee, rather die
Deserted than oblige thee with a fact   980
Pernicious to thy Peace, chiefly assur'd
Remarkably so late of thy so true,
So faithful Love unequald; but I feel
Farr otherwise th' event, not Death, but Life
Augmented, opend Eyes, new Hopes, new Joys,   985
Taste so Divine, that what of sweet before
Hath toucht my sense, flat seems to this, and harsh.
On my experience *Adam*, freely taste,
And fear of Death deliver to the Winds.

   So saying, she embrac'd him, and for joye   990
Tenderly wept, much won that he his Love

Had so enobl'd, as of choice to incurr
Divine displeasure for her sake, or Death.
In recompense (for such compliance bad
Such recompense best merits) from the bough   995
She gave him of that fair enticing Fruit
With liberal hand: he scrupl'd not to eat
Against his better knowledge, not deceiv'd,
But fondly overcome with Femal charm.
Earth trembl'd from her entrails, as again   1000
In pangs, and Nature gave a second groan,
Skie lour'd, and muttering Thunder, som sad drops
Wept at completing of the mortal Sin
Original; while *Adam* took no thought,
Eating his fill, nor *Eve* to iterate   1005
Her former trespass fear'd, the more to soothe
Him with her lov'd societie, that now
As with new Wine intoxicated both
They swim in mirth, and fancie that they feel
Divinitie within them breeding wings   1010
Wherewith to scorn the Earth: but that false Fruit
Farr other operation first displayd,
Carnal desire enflaming, hee on *Eve*
Began to cast lascivious Eyes, she him
As wantonly repaid; in Lust they burne: 1015
Till *Adam* thus 'gan *Eve* to dalliance move.
     Eve, now I see thou art exact of taste
And elegant, of Sapience no small part,
Since to each meaning savour we apply,
And Palate call judicious; I the praise   1020
Yield thee, so well this day thou hast purveyd.
Much pleasure we have lost, while we abstain
From this delightful Fruit, nor known till now
True relish, tasting; if such pleasure be
In things to us forbidden, it might be wisht   1025
For this one Tree had bin forbidden ten.
But come, so well refresht, now let us play,
As meet is, after such delicious Fare;
For never did thy Beautie since the day
I saw thee first and wedded thee, adornd   1030
With all perfections, so enflame my sense
With ardor to enjoy thee, fairer now
Than ever, bountie of this vertuous Tree.
     So said he, and forbore not glance or toy
Of amorous intent, well understood   1035
Of *Eve*, whose Eye darted contagious Fire.
Her hand he seiz'd, and to a shadie bank
Thick overhead with verdant roof imbowrd
He led her nothing loath; Flowrs were the Couch,
Pansies and Violets and Asphodel   1040

And Hyacinth, Earths freshest softest lap.
There they thir fill of Love and Loves disport
Took largely, of thir mutual guilt the Seal,
The solace of thir sin, till dewie sleep
Oppressd them, wearied with thir amorous play.   1045
Soon as the force of that fallacious Fruit,
That with exhilerating vapour bland
About thir spirits had playd, and inmost powers
Made err, was now exhal'd, and grosser sleep
Bred of unkindly fumes, with conscious dreams   1050
Encumberd, now had left them, up they rose
As from unrest, and each the other viewing
Soon found thir Eyes how opend, and thir minds
How darkend; innocence, that as a veil
Had shaddowd them from knowing ill, was gon,   1055
Just confidence and native righteousness
And honour from about them, naked left
To guiltie Shame; hee coverd, but his Robe
Uncoverd more. So rose the *Danite* strong
Herculean Samson from the Harlot-lap   1060
Of *Philistean Dalilah*, and wak'd
Shorn of his strength, They destitute and bare
Of all thir vertue, silent, and in face
Confounded long they sate, as strucken mute,
Till *Adam*, though not less than *Eve* abasht,   1065
At length gave utterance to these words constraind.

     O *Eve*, in evil hour thou didst give ear
To that false Worm, of whomsoever taught
To counterfet Mans voice, true in our Fall,
False in our promis'd Rising; since our Eyes   1070
Opend we find indeed, and find we know
Both Good and Evil, Good lost, and Evil got,
Bad Fruit of Knowledge, if this be to know,
Which leaves us naked thus, of Honour void,
Of Innocence, of Faith, of Puritie,   1075
Our wonted Ornaments now soild and staind,
And in our Faces evident the signs
Of foul concupiscence; whence evil store;
Even shame, the last of evils; of the first
Be sure then. How shall I behold the face   1080
Henceforth of God or Angel, erst with joy
And rapture so oft beheld? those heav'nly shapes
Will dazle now this earthly, with thir blaze
Insufferably bright. O might I here
In solitude live savage, in som glade   1085
Obscur'd, where highest Woods impenetrable

1058 Shame; hee] shame hee *Edd. 1, 2*
1059 more. So *Ed. 1*] more, so *Ed. 2*

To Starr or Sun-light, spread thir umbrage broad
And brown as Ev'ning: Cover me ye Pines,
Ye Cedars, with innumerable boughes
Hide me, where I may never see them more.   1090
But let us now, as in bad plight, devise
What best may for the present serve to hide
The Parts of each from other, that seem most
To shame obnoxious, and unseemliest seen,
Som Tree whose broad smooth Leaves together sowd,
And girded on our loins, may cover round   1096
Those middle parts, that this new comer, Shame,
There sit not, and reproach us as unclean.
    So counseld hee, and both together went
Into the thickest Wood, there soon they chose   1100
The Figtree, not that kind for Fruit renownd,
But such as at this day to *Indians* known
In *Malabar* or *Decan* spreads her Armes
Braunching so broad and long, that in the ground
The bended Twigs take root, and Daughters grow   1105
About the Mother Tree, a Pillard shade
High overarcht, and echoing Walks between;
There oft the *Indian* Herdsman shunning heate
Shelters in cool, and tends his pasturing Herds
At Loopholes cut through thickest shade: Those Leaves
They gatherd, broad as *Amazonian* Targe,   1111
And with what skill they had, together sowd,
To gird thir waist, vain Covering if to hide
Thir guilt and dreaded shame; O how unlike
To that first naked Glorie.   Such of late   1115
Columbus found th' *American* so girt
With featherd Cincture, naked else and wilde
Among the Trees on Iles and woodie Shores.
Thus fenc't, and as they thought, thir shame in part
Coverd, but not at rest or ease of Mind,   1120
They sate them down to weep, nor onely Teares
Raind at thir Eyes, but high Winds worse within
Began to rise, high Passions, Anger, Hate,
Mistrust, Suspicion, Discord, and shook sore
Thir inward State of Mind, calm Region once   1125
And full of Peace, now tost and turbulent:
For Understanding rul'd not, and the Will
Heard not her lore, both in subjection now
To sensual Appetite, who from beneath
Usurping over sovran Reason claimd   1130
Superior sway: From thus distemperd brest
Adam, estrang'd in look and alterd style,
Speech intermitted thus to *Eve* renewd.
    Would thou hadst hearkend to my words, and stayd
With me, as I besought thee, when that strange   1135

Desire of wandring this unhappie Morn,
I know not whence possessd thee; we had then
Remaind still happie, not as now, despoild
Of all our good, sham'd, naked, miserable.
Let none henceforth seek needless cause to approve   1140
The Faith they ow; when earnestly they seek
Such proof, conclude, they then begin to fail.
    To whom soon mov'd with touch of blame thus *Eve*.
What words have past thy Lips, *Adam* severe,
Imput'st thou that to my default, or will   1145
Of wandring, as thou callst it, which who knows
But might as ill have happend thou being by,
Or to thy self perhaps: hadst thou bin there,
Or here th' attempt, thou couldst not have discernd
Fraud in the Serpent, speaking as he spake;   1150
No ground of enmitie between us known,
Why hee should mean me ill, or seek to harm.
Was I to have never parted from thy side?
As good have grown there still a liveless Rib.
Being as I am, why didst not thou the Head   1155
Command me absolutely not to go,
Going into such danger as thou saidst?
Too facil then thou didst not much gainsay,
Nay didst permit, approve, and fair dismiss.
Hadst thou bin firm and fixt in thy dissent,   1160
Neither had I transgrest, nor thou with mee.
    To whom then first incenst *Adam* repli'd.
Is this the Love, is this the recompense
Of mine to thee, ingrateful *Eve*, exprest
Immutable when thou wert lost, not I,   1165
Who might have liv'd and joyd immortal bliss,
Yet willingly chose rather Death with thee:
And am I now upbraided, as the cause
Of thy transgressing? not anough severe,
It seems, in thy restraint: what could I more?   1170
I warnd thee, I admonishd thee, foretold
The danger, and the lurking Enemie
That lay in wait; beyond this had bin force,
And force upon free Will hath here no place.
But confidence then bore thee on, secure   1175
Either to meet no danger or to finde
Matter of glorious trial; and perhaps
I also errd in overmuch admiring
What seemd in thee so perfet, that I thought
No devil durst attempt thee, but I rue   1180
That error now, which is become my crime,
And thou th' accuser. Thus it shall befall
Him who to worth in Women overtrusting
Lets her will rule; restraint she will not brook,

And left to her self, if evil thence ensue,   1185
Shee first his weak indulgence will accuse.
   Thus they in mutual accusation spent
The fruitless hours, but neither self-condemning,
And of thir vain contest appear'd no end.

The End of the Ninth Book

BOOK X

THE ARGUMENT

Mans *transgression known, the Guardian Angels forsake Paradise, and return up to Heaven to approve thir vigilance, and are approv'd, God declaring that The entrance of* Satan *could not be by them prevented. He sends his Son to judge the Transgressors, who descends and gives sentence accordingly; then in pity cloaths them both, and reascends. Sin and Death sitting till then at the Gates of Hell, by wondrous sympathie feeling the success of Satan in this new World, and the sin by Man there committed, resolve to sit no longer confin'd in Hell, but to follow Satan thir Sire up to the place of Man: To make the way easier from Hell to this World to and fro, they pave a broad Highway or Bridge over Chaos, according to the Track that Satan first made; then preparing for Earth, they meet him proud of his success returning to Hell; thir mutual gratulation. Satan arrives at* Pandemonium, *in full assembly relates with boasting his success against Man; instead of applause is entertained with a general hiss by all his audience, transform'd with himself also suddenly into Serpents, according to his doom giv'n in Paradise; then deluded with a shew of the forbidden Tree springing up before them, they greedily reaching to take of the Fruit, chew dust and bitter ashes. The proceedings of Sin and Death; God foretels the final Victory of his Son over them, and the renewing of all things; but for the present commands his Angels to make several alterations in the Heavens and Elements. Adam more and more perceiving his fall'n condition heavily bewailes, rejects the condolement of Eve; she persists and at length appeases him; then to evade the Curse likely to fall on thir Ofspring, proposes to Adam violent wayes, which he approves not, but conceiving better hope, puts her in mind of the late Promise made them, that her Seed should be aveng'd on the Serpent, and exhorts her with him to seek Peace of the offended Diety, by repentance and supplication.*

Meanwhile the heinous and despiteful act
Of *Satan* done in Paradise, and how
Hee in the Serpent had perverted *Eve*,
Her Husband shee, to taste the fatal fruit,
Was known in Heav'n; for what can scape the Eye   5
Of God All-seeing, or deceive his Heart
Omniscient, who in all things wise and just,
Hinderd not *Satan* to attempt the mind
Of Man, with strength entire and free Will armd,
Complete to have discoverd and repulst   10
Whatever wiles of Foe or seeming Friend.
For still they knew, and ought to have still rememberd
The high Injunction not to taste that Fruit,
Whoever tempted; which they not obeying,
Incurrd, what could they less, the penaltie,   15
And manifold in sin, deserv'd to fall.
Up into Heav'n from Paradise in haste
Th' Angelic Guards ascended, mute and sad

For Man, for of his state by this they knew,
Much wondring how the suttle Fiend had stolne   20
Entrance unseen.   Soon as th' unwelcom news
From Earth arriv'd at Heaven Gate, displeas'd
All were who heard, dim sadness did not spare
That time Celestial visages, yet mixt
With pittie, violated not thir bliss.   25
About the new-arriv'd, in multitudes
Th'ethereal People ran, to hear and know
How all befell: they towards the Throne Supream
Accountable made haste to make appear
With righteous plea, thir utmost vigilance,   30
And easily approv'd; when the most High
Eternal Father from his secret Cloud
Amidst, in Thunder utterd thus his voice.

    Assembl'd Angels, and ye Powers returnd
From unsuccessful charge, be not dismayd   35
Nor troubl'd at these tidings from the Earth,
Which your sincerest care could not prevent,
Foretold so lately what would come to pass,
When first this Tempter crossd the Gulf from Hell.
I told ye then he should prevail and speed   40
On his bad Errand, Man should be seduc't
And flatterd out of all, believing lies
Against his Maker; no Decree of mine
Concurring to necessitate his Fall,
Or touch with lightest moment of impulse   45
His free Will, to her own inclining left
In even scale.   But fall'n he is, and now
What rests but that the mortal Sentence pass
On his transgression, Death denounc't that day,
Which he presumes already vain and void,   50
Because not yet inflicted, as he fear'd,
By som immediat stroke; but soon shall find
Forbearance no acquittance ere day end.
Justice shall not return as bountie scornd.
But whom send I to judge them? whom but thee   55
Vicegerent Son, to thee I have transferrd
All Judgement, whether in Heav'n or Earth or Hell.
Easie it may be seen that I intend
Mercie colleague with Justice, sending thee
Mans Friend, his Mediator, his design'd   60
Both Ransom and Redeemer voluntarie,
And destind Man himself to judge Man fall'n.
    So spake the Father, and unfolding bright
Toward the right hand his Glorie, on the Son

32-3 Cloud Amidst,] Cloud, Amidst *Edd. 1, 2*
58 may *Ed. 1*] might *Ed. 2*

Blaz'd forth unclouded Deitie; he full   65
Resplendent all his Father manifest
Expressd, and thus divinely answerd mild.
   Father Eternal, thine is to decree,
Mine both in Heav'n and Earth to do thy will
Supream, that thou in mee thy Son belov'd   70
Mayst ever rest well pleas'd.   I go to judge
On Earth these thy transgressors, but thou knowst,
Whoever judg'd, the worst on mee must light,
When time shall be, for so I undertook
Before thee; and not repenting, this obtain   75
Of right, that I may mitigate thir doom
On me deriv'd, yet I shall temper so
Justice with Mercie, as may illustrate most
Them fully satisfi'd, and thee appease.
Attendance none shall need, nor Train, where none   80
Are to behold the Judgment, but the judg'd,
Those two; the third best absent is condemnd,
Convict by flight and Rebel to all Law:
Conviction to the Serpent none belongs.
   Thus saying, from his radiant Seat he rose   85
Of high collateral glorie: him Thrones and Powers,
Princedoms and Dominations ministrant
Accompanied to Heaven Gate, from whence
Eden and all the Coast in prospect lay.
Down he descended straight; the speed of Gods   90
Time counts not, though with swiftest minutes wingd.
Now was the Sun in Western cadence low
From Noon, and gentle Aires due at thir hour
To fan the Earth now wak'd, and usher in
The Ev'ning coole when he from wrauth more coole   95
Came the mild Judge and Intercessor both
To sentence Man: the voice of God they heard
Now walking in the Garden, by soft windes
Brought to thir Ears, while day declin'd, they heard
And from his presence hid themselves among   100
The thickest Trees, both Man and Wife, till God
Approaching, thus to *Adam* calld aloud.
   Where art thou *Adam*, wont with joy to meet
My coming seen far off? I miss thee here,
Not pleas'd, thus entertaind with solitude,   105
Where obvious dutie erewhile appear'd unsought:
Or come I less conspicuous, or what change
Absents thee, or what chance detains?   Come forth.
He came, and with him *Eve*, more loath, though first
To offend, discount'nanc't both, and discompos'd;   110
Love was not in thir looks, either to God
Or to each other, but apparent guilt
And shame and perturbation and despair,

Anger and obstinacie and hate and guile.
Whence *Adam* faultring long, thus answerd brief.　115
 I heard thee in the Garden, and of thy voice
Afraid, being naked, hid my self.　To whom
The gracious Judge without revile repli'd.
 My voice thou oft hast heard, and hast not fear'd,
But still rejoic't, how is it now become　120
So dreadful to thee? that thou art naked, who
Hath told thee? hast thou eaten of the Tree
Whereof I gave thee charge thou shouldst not eat?
 To whom thus *Adam* sore beset repli'd.
O Heav'n! in evil strait this day I stand　125
Before my Judge, either to undergo
My self the total Crime, or to accuse
My other self, the partner of my life;
Whose failing, while her Faith to me remains,
I should conceal, and not expose to blame　130
By my complaint; but strict necessitie
Subdues me, and calamitous constraint,
Lest on my head both sin and punishment,
However insupportable, be all
Devolv'd; though should I hold my peace, yet thou　135
Wouldst easily detect what I conceal.
This Woman whom thou mad'st to be my help,
And gav'st me as thy perfet gift, so good,
So fit, so acceptable, so Divine,
That from her hand I could suspect no ill,　140
And what she did, whatever in it self,
Her doing seemd to justifie the deed;
Shee gave me of the Tree, and I did eat.
 To whom the sovran Presence thus repli'd.
Was shee thy God, that her thou didst obey　145
Before his voice, or was shee made thy guide,
Superior, or but equal, that to her
Thou didst resigne thy Manhood, and the Place
Wherein God set thee above her, made of thee
And for thee, whose perfection farr excelld　150
Hers in all real dignitie?　Adornd
She was indeed, and lovely to attract
Thy Love, not thy Subjection, and her Gifts
Were such as under Goverment well seemd,
Unseemly to bear rule, which was thy part　155
And person, hadst thou known thy self aright.
 So having said, he thus to *Eve* in few:
Say Woman, what is this which thou hast don?
 To whom sad *Eve* with shame nigh overwhelmd,
Confessing soon, yet not before her Judge　160
Bold or loquacious, thus abasht repli'd.
 The Serpent me beguil'd and I did eat.

Which when the Lord God heard, without delay
To Judgement he proceeded on th' accus'd
Serpent though brute, unable to transferr   165
The Guilt on him who made him instrument
Of mischief, and polluted from the end
Of his Creation: justly then accurst,
As vitiated in Nature: more to know
Concernd not Man (since he no further knew)   170
Nor alterd his offence; yet God at last
To *Satan* first in sin his doom appli'd,
Though in mysterious terms, judg'd as then best:
And on the Serpent thus his curse let fall.

      Because thou hast done this, thou art accurst   175
Above all Cattel, each Beast of the Field;
Upon thy Belly groveling thou shalt go,
And dust shalt eate all the days of thy Life.
Between Thee and the Woman I will put
Enmitie, and between thine and her Seed;   180
Her Seed shall bruise thy head, thou bruise his heel.

      So spake this Oracle, then verifi'd
When *Jesus* son of *Mary* second *Eve*
Saw *Satan* fall like Lightning down from Heav'n,
Prince of the Air; then rising from his Grave   185
Spoild Principalities and Powers, triumphd
In open shew, and with ascension bright
Captivity led captive through the Air,
The Realm it self of Satan long usurpt,
Whom he shall tread at last under our feet;   190
Ev'n hee who now foretold his fatal bruise,
And to the Woman thus his Sentence turnd.

      Thy sorrow I will greatly multiplie
By thy Conception; Childern thou shalt bring
In sorrow forth, and to thy Husbands will   195
Thine shall submit, hee over thee shall rule.

      On *Adam* last thus judgement he pronounc'd.
Because thou hast hearkend to the voice of thy Wife,
And eaten of the Tree concerning which
I charg'd thee, saying: Thou shalt not eat thereof,   200
Curst is the ground for thy sake, thou in sorrow
Shalt eat thereof all the days of thy Life;
Thorns also and Thistles it shall bring thee forth
Unbid, and thou shalt eate th' Herb of the Field,
In the sweat of thy Face shalt thou eat Bread,   205
Till thou return unto the ground, for thou
Out of the ground wast taken: know thy Birth,
For dust thou art, and shalt to dust return.

      So judg'd he Man, both Judge and Saviour sent,

194 Childern *Ed. 1*] Children *Ed. 2*   204 the Field] th' Field *Edd. 1, 2*

And th' instant stroke of Death denounc't that day   210
Remov'd farr off; then pittying how they stood
Before him naked to the air, that now
Must suffer change, disdaind not to begin
Thenceforth the form of servant to assume,
As when he washd his servants feet, so now   215
As Father of his Familie he clad
Thir nakedness with Skins of Beasts, or slain
Or as the Snake with youthful Coat repaid;
And thought not much to clothe his Enemies:
Nor he thir outward onely with the Skins   220
Of Beasts, but inward nakedness, much more
Opprobrious, with his Robe of righteousness
Arraying coverd from his Fathers sight.
To him with swift ascent he up returnd,
Into his blissful bosom reassum'd   225
In glory as of old, to him appeas'd
All, though all-knowing, what had past with Man
Recounted, mixing intercession sweet.
Meanwhile ere thus was sinnd and judg'd on Earth,
Within the Gates of Hell sate Sin and Death,   230
In counterview within the Gates, that now
Stood open wide, belching outrageous flame
Farr into *Chaos*, since the Fiend passd through,
Sin op'ning, who thus now to Death began.
    O Son, why sit we here each other viewing   235
Idly, while *Satan* our great Author thrives
In other Worlds, and happier Seat provides
For us his offspring dear?   It cannot be
But that success attends him; if mishap,
Ere this he had returnd, with fury driv'n   240
By his Avengers, since no place like this
Can fit his punishment, or their revenge.
Methinks I feel new strength within me rise,
Wings growing, and Dominion giv'n me large
Beyond this Deep; whatever draws me on,   245
Or sympathie or som connatural force
Powerful at greatest distance to unite
With secret amity things of like kinde
By secretest conveyance.   Thou my Shade
Inseparable must with mee along: 250
For Death from Sin no power can separate.
But lest the difficultie of passing back
Staye his return perhaps over this Gulf
Impassable, impervious, let us try
Adventrous work, yet to thy power and mine   255
Not unagreeable, to found a path

Over this Maine from Hell to that new World
Where *Satan* now prevails, a Monument
Of merit high to all th' infernal Host,
Easing thir passage hence, for intercourse   260
Or transmigration, as thir lot shall lead.
Nor can I miss the way, so strongly drawn
By this new felt attraction and instinct.
    Whom thus the meager Shaddow answerd soon.
Goe whither Fate and inclination strong   265
Leads thee, I shall not lag behind, nor err
The way, thou leading, such a scent I draw
Of carnage, prey innumerable, and taste
The savour of Death from all things there that live:
Nor shall I to the work thou enterprisest   270
Be wanting, but afford thee equal aid.
    So saying, with delight he snuffd the smell
Of mortal change on Earth.   As when a flock
Of ravenous Fowl, though many a League remote,
Against the day of Battel, to a Field   275
Where Armies lie encampt, come flying, lur'd
With scent of living Carcasses design'd
For death, the following day, in bloodie fight.
So scented the grim Feature, and upturnd
His Nostril wide into the murkie Air,   280
Sagacious of his Quarry from so farr.
Then Both from out Hell Gates into the waste
Wide Anarchie of *Chaos* damp and dark
Flew diverse, and with Power (thir Power was great)
Hovering upon the Waters; what they met   285
Solid or slimie, as in raging Sea
Tost up and down, together crowded drove
From each side shoaling towards the mouth of Hell.
As when two Polar Winds blowing adverse
Upon the *Cronian* Sea, together drive   290
Mountains of Ice, that stop th' imagind way
Beyond *Petsora* Eastward, to the rich
Cathaian Coast.   The aggregated Soile
Death with his Mace petrific, cold and dry,
As with a Trident smote, and fixd as firm   295
As *Delos* floating once; the rest his look
Bound with *Gorgonian* rigor not to move,
And with *Asphaltic* slime; broad as the Gate,
Deep to the Roots of Hell the gatherd beach
They fastend, and the Mole immense wrought on   300
Over the foaming Deep high Archt, a Bridge
Of length prodigious joining to the Wall
Immoveable of this now fenceless World
Forfeit to Death; from hence a passage broad,
Smooth, easie, inoffensive down to Hell.   305

So, if great things to small may be compar'd,
Xerxes, the Libertie of *Greece* to yoke,
From *Susa* his *Memnonian* Palace high
Came to the Sea, and over *Hellespont*
Bridging his way, *Europe* with *Asia* joind,   310
And scourg'd with many a stroke th' indignant waves.
Now had they brought the work by wondrous Art
Pontifical, a ridge of pendent Rock
Over the vext Abyss, following the track
Of *Satan*, to the self same place where hee   315
First lighted from his Wing, and landed safe
From out of *Chaos* to the outside bare
Of this round World: with Pinns of Adamant
And chains they made all fast, too fast they made
And durable; and now in little space   320
The confines met of Empyrean Heav'n
And of this World, and on the left hand Hell
With long reach interpos'd; three sev'ral ways
In sight, to each of these three places led.
And now thir way to Earth they had descri'd,   325
To Paradise first tending, when behold
Satan in likeness of an Angel bright
Betwixt the *Centaure* and the *Scorpion* steering
His *Zenith*, while the Sun in *Aries* rose:
Disguis'd he came, but those his Childern dear   330
Thir Parent soon discernd, though in disguise.
Hee, after *Eve* seduc't, unminded slunk
Into the Wood fast by, and changing shape
To observe the sequel, saw his guileful act
By *Eve*, though all unweeting, seconded   335
Upon her Husband, saw thir shame that sought
Vain covertures; but when he saw descend
The Son of God to judge them, terrifi'd
Hee fled, not hoping to escape, but shun
The present, fearing guiltie what his wrauth   340
Might suddenly inflict; that past, returnd
By Night, and listning where the hapless Paire
Sate in thir sad discourse and various plaint,
Thence gatherd his own doom, which understood
Not instant, but of future time.   With joy   345
And tidings fraught, to Hell he now returnd,
And at the brink of Chaos, near the foot
Of this new wondrous Pontifice, unhop't
Met who to meet him came, his Offspring dear.
Great joy was at thir meeting, and at sight   350
Of that stupendious Bridge his joy encreas'd.
Long hee admiring stood, till Sin, his fair
Inchanting Daughter, thus the silence broke.
    O Parent, these are thy magnific deeds,

Thy Trophies, which thou viewst as not thine own,   355
Thou art thir Author and prime Architect:
For I no sooner in my Heart divin'd,
My Heart, which by a secret harmonie
Still moves with thine, joind in connexion sweet,
That thou on Earth hadst prosperd, which thy looks   360
Now also evidence, but straight I felt
Though distant from thee Worlds between, yet felt
That I must after thee with this thy Son;
Such fatal consequence unites us three:
Hell could no longer hold us in her bounds,   365
Nor this unvoyageable Gulf obscure
Detain from following thy illustrious track.
Thou hast achiev'd our libertie, confin'd
Within Hell Gates till now, thou us impow'rd
To fortifie thus farr, and overlay   370
With this portentous Bridge the dark Abyss.
Thine now is all this World, thy vertue hath won
What thy hands builded not, thy Wisdom gaind
With odds what Warr hath lost, and fully aveng'd
Our foil in Heav'n; here thou shalt Monarch reign,   375
There didst not; there let him still Victor sway,
As Battel hath adjudg'd, from this new World
Retiring, by his own doom alienated,
And henceforth Monarchie with thee divide
Of all things, parted by th' Empyreal bounds,   380
His Quadrature, from thy Orbicular World,
Or trie thee now more dang'rous to his Throne.
    Whom thus the Prince of Darkness answerd glad.
Fair Daughter, and thou Son and Grandchild both,
High proof ye now have giv'n to be the Race   385
Of *Satan* (for I glorie in the name,
Antagonist of Heav'ns Almightie King)
Amply have merited of me, of all
Th' infernal Empire, that so near Heav'ns dore
Triumphal with triumphal act have met,   390
Mine with this glorious Work, and made one Realme
Hell and this World, one Realm, one Continent,
Of easie thorough-fare.   Therefore while I
Descend through Darkness, on your Road with ease
To my associate Powers, them to acquaint   395
With these successes, and with them rejoice,
You two this way, among those numerous Orbs
All yours, right down to Paradise descend;
There dwell and Reign in bliss, thence on the Earth
Dominion exercise and in the Air,   400
Chiefly on Man, sole Lord of all declar'd,

397 these *Ed. 2*] those *Ed. 1*

Him first make sure your thrall, and lastly kill.
My Substitutes I send ye, and Create
Plenipotent on Earth, of matchless might
Issuing from mee: on your joint vigor now   405
My hold of this new Kingdom all depends,
Through Sin to Death expos'd by my exploit.
If your joint power prevail, th' affairs of Hell
No detriment need fear, goe and be strong.
  So saying he dismissd them, they with speed   410
Thir course through thickest Constellations held
Spreading thir bane; the blasted Starrs lookd wan,
And Planets, Planet-strook, real Eclipse
Then sufferd.   Th' other way *Satan* went down
The Causey to Hell Gate; on either side   415
Disparted *Chaos* overbuilt exclaimd,
And with rebounding surge the barrs assaild,
That scornd his indignation: through the Gate,
Wide open and unguarded, *Satan* passd,
And all about found desolate; for those   420
Appointed to sit there had left thir charge,
Flown to the upper World; the rest were all
Farr to th'inland retir'd, about the walls
Of *Pandæmonium*, Citie and proud seat
Of *Lucifer*, so by allusion calld,   425
Of that bright Starr to *Satan* paragond.
There kept thir Watch the Legions, while the Grand
In Council sate, solicitous what chance
Might intercept thir Emperor sent, so hee
Departing gave command, and they observ'd.   430
As when the *Tartar* from his *Russian* Foe
By *Astracan* over the Snowie Plains
Retires, or *Bactrian* Sophi from the horns
Of *Turkish* Crescent, leaves all waste beyond
The Realm of *Aladule*, in his retreat   435
To *Tauris* or *Casbeen*: So these the late
Heav'n-banisht Host left desert utmost Hell
Many a dark League, reduc't in careful Watch
Round thir Metropolis, and now expecting
Each hour thir great adventurer from the search   440
Of *Forren* Worlds: hee through the midst unmarkt,
In shew plebeian Angel militant
Of lowest order, passd; and from the dore
Of that *Plutonian* Hall, invisible
Ascended his high Throne, which under state   445
Of richest texture spred, at th' upper end
Was plac't in regal lustre.   Down a while
He sate, and round about him saw unseen:

408 prevail] prevaile *Ed. 1*] prevailes *Ed. 2*
440 thir] their *Edd. 1, 2*
441 hee] he *Edd. 1, 2*

At last as from a Cloud his fulgent head
And shape Starr-bright appear'd, or brighter, clad   450
With what permissive glory since his fall
Was left him, or false glitter: All amaz'd
At that so sudden blaze the *Stygian* throng
Bent thir aspect, and whom they wishd beheld,
Thir mighty Chief returnd: loud was th' acclaim: 455
Forth rushd in haste the great consulting Peers,
Rais'd from thir dark *Divan*, and with like joy
Congratulant approachd him, who with hand
Silence, and with these words attention won.
    Thrones, Dominations, Princedoms, Vertues, Powers,
For in possession such, not onely of right,   461
I call ye and declare ye now, returnd
Successful beyond hope, to lead ye forth
Triumphant out of this infernal Pit
Abominable, accurst, the house of woe,   465
And Dungeon of our Tyrant: Now possess,
As Lords, a spacious World, to our native Heaven
Little inferior, by my adventure hard
With peril great achiev'd.   Long were to tell
What I have don, what sufferd, with what paine   470
Voyag'd th' unreal, vast, unbounded Deep
Of horrible confusion, over which
By Sin and Death a broad way now is pav'd
To expedite your glorious march; but I
Toild out my uncouth passage, forc't to ride   475
Th' untractable Abyss, plung'd in the womb
Of unoriginal *Night* and *Chaos* wild,
That jealous of thir secrets fiercely oppos'd
My journey strange, with clamorous uproare
Protesting Fate supream; thence how I found   480
The new created World, which fame in Heav'n
Long had foretold, a Fabric wonderful
Of absolute perfection, therein Man
Plac't in a Paradise, by our exile
Made happie: Him by fraud I have seduc't   485
From his Creator, and the more to increase
Your wonder, with an Apple; he thereat
Offended, worth your laughter, hath giv'n up
Both his beloved Man and all his World,
To Sin and Death a prey, and so to us,   490
Without our hazard, labour or alarm,
To range in and to dwell, and over Man
To rule, as over all hee should have rul'd.
True is, mee also he hath judg'd, or rather
Mee not, but the brute Serpent in whose shape   495
Man I deceiv'd: that which to mee belongs
Is enmity, which he will put between

Mee and Mankind; I am to bruise his heel;
His Seed, when is not set, shall bruise my head:
A World who would not purchase with a bruise, 500
Or much more grievous pain?   Ye have th' account
Of my performance: What remains, ye Gods,
But up and enter now into full bliss.
    So having said, a while he stood, expecting
Thir universal shout and high applause 505
To fill his ear, when contrary he hears
On all sides, from innumerable tongues
A dismal universal hiss, the sound
Of public scorn; he wonderd, but not long
Had leasure, wondring at himself now more; 510
His Visage drawn he felt to sharp and spare,
His Arms clung to his Ribs, his Leggs entwining
Each other, till supplanted down he fell
A monstrous Serpent on his Belly prone,
Reluctant, but in vain, a greater power 515
Now rul'd him, punisht in the shape he sinnd,
According to his doom: he would have spoke,
But hiss for hiss returnd with forked tongue
To forked tongue, for now were all transformd
Alike, to Serpents all as accessories 520
To his bold Riot: dreadful was the din
Of hissing through the Hall, thick swarming now
With complicated monsters, head and tail,
Scorpion and Asp, and *Amphisbæna* dire,
Cerastes hornd, *Hydrus*, and *Ellops* drear, 525
And *Dipsas* (not so thick swarmd once the Soil
Bedropt with blood of *Gorgon*, or the Ile
Ophiusa) but still greatest hee the midst,
Now Dragon grown, larger than whom the Sun
Ingenderd in the *Pythian* Vale on slime, 530
Huge *Python*, and his Power no less he seemd
Above the rest still to retain; they all
Him followd issuing forth to th' open Field,
Where all yet left of that revolted Rout
Heav'n-fall'n, in station stood or just array, 535
Sublime with expectation when to see
In Triumph issuing forth thir glorious Chief;
They saw, but other sight instead, a crowd
Of ugly Serpents; horror on them fell,
And horrid sympathie; for what they saw 540
They felt themselves now changing; down thir arms,
Down fell both Spear and Shield, down they as fast,
And the dire hiss renewd, and the dire form
Catchd by Contagion, like in punishment,
As in thir crime.   Thus was th' applause they meant 545
Turnd to exploding hiss, triumph to shame

Cast on themselves from thir own mouths.   There stood
A Grove hard by, sprung up with this thir change,
His will who reigns above, to aggravate
Thir penance, laden with fair Fruit, like that   550
Which grew in Paradise, the bait of *Eve*
Us'd by the Tempter: on that prospect strange
Thir earnest eyes they fixd, imagining
For one forbidden Tree a multitude
Now ris'n, to work them furder woe or shame;   555
Yet parcht with scalding thirst and hunger fierce,
Though to delude them sent, could not abstain,
But on they rould in heaps, and up the Trees
Climbing, sat thicker than the snakie locks
That curld *Megæra*: greedily they pluckd   560
The Frutage fair to sight, like that which grew
Near that bituminous Lake where *Sodom* flam'd;
This more delusive, not the touch but taste
Deceiv'd; they fondly thinking to allay
Thir appetite with gust, instead of Fruit   565
Chewd bitter Ashes, which th' offended taste
With spattering noise rejected: oft they assayd,
Hunger and thirst constraining, drugd as oft,
With hatefullest disrelish writh'd thir jaws
With soot and cinders filld; so oft they fell   570
Into the same illusion, not as Man
Whom they triumphd once lapst.   Thus were they plagu'd
And worn with Famin, long and ceaseless hiss,
Till thir lost shape, permitted, they resum'd,
Yearly enjoind, som say, to undergo   575
This annual humbling certain numberd days,
To dash thir pride and joy for Man seduc't.
However some tradition they dispersd
Among the Heathen of thir purchase got,
And Fabl'd how the Serpent, whom they calld   580
Ophion with *Eurynome*, the wide-
Encroaching *Eve* perhaps, had first the rule
Of high *Olympus*, thence by *Saturn* driv'n
And *Ops*, ere yet *Dictæan Jove* was born.
Mean while in Paradise the hellish pair   585
Too soon arriv'd, *Sin* there in power before,
Once actual, now in body, and to dwell
Habitual habitant; behind her *Death*
Close following pace for pace, not mounted yet
On his pale Horse: to whom *Sin* thus began.   590
     Second of *Satan* sprung, all conquering *Death*,
What thinkst thou of our Empire now, though earnd
With travail difficult, not better farr
Than still at Hells dark threshold t'have sate watch,
Unnam'd, undreaded, and thy self half starv'd?   595

Whom thus the Sin-born Monster answerd soon.
To mee, who with eternal Famin pine,
Alike is Hell or Paradise or Heaven,
There best, where most with ravin I may meet;
Which here, though plenteous, all too little seems   600
To stuff this Maw, this vast unhide-bound Corps.
　　To whom th' incestuous Mother thus repli'd.
Thou therefore on these Herbs and Fruits and Flowrs
Feed first, on each Beast next, and Fish and Fowl,
No homely morsels, and whatever thing   605
The Sithe of Time mows down, devour unspar'd,
Till I in Man residing through the Race,
His thoughts, his looks, words, actions all infect,
And season him thy last and sweetest prey.
　　This said, they both betook them several ways.   610
Both to destroy, or unimmortal make
All kinds, and for destruction to mature
Sooner or later; which th' Almightie seeing,
From his transcendent Seat the Saints among,
To those bright Orders utterd thus his voice.   615
　　See with what heat these Dogs of Hell advance
To waste and havoc yonder World, which I
So fair and good created, and had still
Kept in that state, had not the folly of Man
Let in these wasteful Furies, who impute   620
Folly to mee, so doth the Prince of Hell
And his Adherents, that with so much ease
I suffer them to enter and possess
A place so heav'nly, and conniving seem
To gratifie my scornful Enemies,   625
That laugh, as if transported with som fit
Of Passion, I to them had quitted all,
At random yielded up to their misrule;
And know not that I calld and drew them thither
My Hell-hounds, to lick up the draff and filth   630
Which mans polluting Sin with taint hath shed
On what was pure, till crammd and gorg'd, nigh burst
With suckt and glutted offal, at one sling
Of thy victorious Arm, well-pleasing Son,
Both *Sin* and *Death*, and yawning *Grave* at last   635
Through *Chaos* hurld, obstruct the mouth of Hell
For ever, and seal up his ravenous Jaws.
Then Heav'n and Earth renewd shall be made pure
To sanctitie that shall receive no stain:
Till then the Curse pronounc't on both precedes.   640
　　He ended, and the heav'nly Audience loud
Sung *Halleluiah*, as the sound of Seas,
Through multitude that sung: Just are thy ways,
Righteous are thy Decrees on all thy Works;

Who can extenuate thee? Next, to the Son,   645
Destind restorer of Mankind, by whom
New Heav'n and Earth shall to the Ages rise,
Or down from Heav'n descend.   Such was thir song,
While the Creator calling forth by name
His mightie Angels gave them several charge,   650
As sorted best with present things.   The Sun
Had first his precept so to move, so shine,
As might affect the Earth with cold and heat
Scarce tollerable, and from the North to call
Decrepit Winter, from the South to bring   655
Solstitial summers heat.   To the blanc Moon
Her office they prescrib'd, to th' other five
Thir planetarie motions and aspects
In *Sextile*, *Square*, and *Trine*, and *Opposite*,
Of noxious efficacie, and when to join   660
In Synod unbenign, and taught the fixt
Thir influence malignant when to showr,
Which of them rising with the Sun, or falling,
Should prove tempestuous: To the Winds they set
Thir corners, when with bluster to confound   665
Sea, Air, and Shore, the Thunder when to roul
With terror through the dark Aëreal Hall.
Some say he bid his Angels turn askance
The Poles of Earth twice ten degrees and more
From the Suns Axle; they with labour pushd   670
Oblique the Centric Globe: Some say the Sun
Was bid turn Reines from th' Equinoctial Road
Like distant bredth to *Taurus* with the Sev'n
Atlantic Sisters, and the *Spartan* Twins
Up to the *Tropic* Crab; thence down amain   675
By *Leo* and the *Virgin* and the *Scales*,
As deep as *Capricorn*, to bring in change
Of Seasons to each Clime; else had the Spring
Perpetual smil'd on Earth with vernant Flowrs,
Equal in Days and Nights, except to those   680
Beyond the Polar Circles; to them Day
Had unbenighted shon, while the low Sun
To recompense his distance, in thir sight
Had rounded still th' Horizon, and not known
Or East or West, which had forbid the Snow   685
From cold *Estotiland*, and South as farr
Beneath *Magellan*.   At that tasted Fruit
The Sun, as from *Thyestean* Banquet, turnd
His course intended; else how had the World
Inhabited, though sinless, more than now   690
Avoided pinching cold and scorching heat?
These changes in the Heav'ns, though slow, produc'd
Like change on Sea and Land, sideral blast,

Vapour and Mist, and Exhalation hot,
Corrupt and Pestilent: Now from the North   695
Of *Norumbega* and the *Samoed* shore
Bursting thir brazen Dungeon, armd with ice
And snow and haile and stormie gust and flaw,
Boreas and *Cæcias* and *Argestes* loud
And *Thrascias* rend the Woods and Seas upturn; 700
With adverse blast upturns them from the South
Notus and *Afer* black with thundrous Clouds
From *Serraliona*; thwart of these as fierce
Forth rush the *Levant* and the *Ponent* Windes
Eurus and *Zephir* with thir lateral noise,   705
Sirocco and *Libecchio*.   Thus began
Outrage from liveless things; but Discord first
Daughter of Sin, among th' irrational,
Death introduc'd through fierce antipathie:
Beast now with Beast gan war, and Fowl with Fowl, 710
And Fish with Fish; to graze the Herb all leaving,
Devourd each other; nor stood much in awe
Of Man, but fled him, or with count'nance grim
Glar'd on him passing: these were from without
The growing miseries, which *Adam* saw   715
Alreadie in part, though hid in gloomiest shade,
To sorrow abandond, but worse felt within,
And in a troubl'd Sea of passion tost
Thus to disburden sought with sad complaint.

   O miserable of happie! is this the end   720
Of this new glorious World, and mee so late
The Glory of that Glory, who now becom
Accurst of blessed, hide me from the face
Of God, whom to behold was then my highth
Of happiness: yet well, if here would end   725
The miserie, I deserv'd it, and would beare
My own deservings; but this will not serve;
All that I eat or drink, or shall beget,
Is propagated curse.   O voice once heard
Delightfully, *Encrease and multiply*,   730
Now death to hear! for what can I encrease
Or multiplie, but curses on my head?
Who of all Ages to succeed, but feeling
The evil on him brought by me, will curse
My Head, Ill fare our Ancestor impure,   735
For this we may thank *Adam*; but his thanks
Shall be the execration; so besides
Mine own that bide upon me, all from mee
Shall with a fierce reflux on mee redound,
On mee as on thir natural center light   740
Heavie, though in thir place.   O fleeting joyes
Of Paradise, deare bought with lasting woes!

Did I request thee, Maker, from my Clay
To mould me Man, did I solicit thee
From darkness to promote me, or here place   745
In this delicious Garden? as my Will
Concurrd not to my being, it were but right
And equal to reduce me to my dust,
Desirous to resign and render back
All I receiv'd, unable to performe   750
Thy terms too hard, by which I was to hold
The good I sought not.   To the loss of that,
Sufficient penaltie, why hast thou added
The sense of endless woes? inexplicable
Thy Justice seems; yet to say truth, too late   755
I thus contest; then should have been refus'd
Those terms whatever, when they were propos'd:
Thou didst accept them; wilt thou enjoy the good,
Then cavil the conditions? and though God
Made thee without thy leave, what if thy Son   760
Prove disobedient, and reprov'd, retort,
Wherefore didst thou beget me? I sought it not:
Wouldst thou admit for his contempt of thee
That proud excuse? yet him not thy election
But Natural necessity begot.   765
God made thee of choice his own, and of his own
To serve him, thy reward was of his Grace,
Thy punishment then justly is at his Will.
Be it so, for I submit, his doom is fair,
That dust I am, and shall to dust return: 770
O welcom hour whenever! why delayes
His hand to execute what his Decree
Fixd on this day? why do I overlive,
Why am I mockt with death, and lengthend out
To deathless pain? how gladly would I meet   775
Mortalitie my sentence, and be Earth
Insensible, how glad would lay me down
As in my Mothers lap! there I should rest
And sleep secure; his dreadful voice no more
Would Thunder in my ears, no fear of worse   780
To mee and to my offspring would torment me
With cruel expectation.   Yet one doubt
Persues me still, lest all I cannot die,
Lest that pure breath of Life, the Spirit of Man
Which God inspir'd, cannot together perish   785
With this corporeal Clod; then in the Grave,
Or in som other dismal place, who knows
But I shall die a living Death? O thought
Horrid, if true! yet why? it was but breath
Of Life that sinnd; what dies but what had life   790
And sin? the Bodie properly hath neither.

All of me then shall die: let this appease
The doubt, since human reach no further knows.
For though the Lord of all be infinite,
Is his wrauth also? be it, Man is not so,   795
But mortal doomd.   How can he exercise
Wrauth without end on Man whom Death must end?
Can he make deathless Death? that were to make
Strange contradiction, which to God himself
Impossible is held, as Argument   800
Of weakness, not of Power.   Will he draw out,
For angers sake, finite to infinite
In punisht man, to satisfie his rigor
Satisfi'd never? that were to extend
His Sentence beyond dust and Natures Law,   805
By which all Causes else according still
To the reception of thir matter act,
Not to th' extent of thir own Sphear.   But say
That Death be not one stroke, as I suppos'd,
Bereaving sense, but endless miserie   810
From this day onward, which I feel begun
Both in me and without me, and so last
To perpetuitie; Ay me, that fear
Comes thundring back with dreadful revolution
On my defenceless head; both Death and I   815
Am found Eternal, and incorporate both,
Nor I on my part single, in mee all
Posteritie stands curst: Fair Patrimonie
That I must leave ye, Sons; O were I able
To waste it all my self, and leave ye none!   820
So disinherited how would ye bless
Mee now your Curse!   Ah, why should all mankind
For one mans fault thus guiltless be condemnd,
If guiltless?   But from me what can proceed,
But all corrupt, both Mind and Will deprav'd,   825
Not to doe only, but to will the same
With me? how can they then acquitted stand
In sight of God?   Him after all Disputes
Forc't I absolve: all my evasions vain
And reasonings, though through Mazes, lead me still 830
But to my own conviction: first and last
On mee, mee onely, as the source and spring
Of all corruption, all the blame lights due;
So might the wrauth.   Fond wish! couldst thou support
That burden heavier than the Earth to bear,   835
Than all the World much heavier, though divided
With that bad Woman?   Thus what thou desir'st,
And what thou fear'st, alike destroys all hope

822 Mee] Me *Edd. 1, 2*
827 they then *Ed. 2*] they *Ed. 1*

Of refuge, and concludes thee miserable
Beyond all past example and future,   840
To *Satan* only like both crime and doom.
O Conscience, into what Abyss of fears
And horrors hast thou driv'n me; out of which
I find no way, from deep to deeper plung'd!
　　Thus *Adam* to himself lamented loud   845
Through the still Night, not now, as ere man fell,
Wholsom and cool and mild, but with black Air
Accompanied, with damps and dreadful gloom,
Which to his evil Conscience represented
All things with double terror: On the Ground   850
Outstretcht he lay, on the cold ground, and oft
Curs'd his Creation, Death as oft accus'd
Of tardie execution, since denounc't
The day of his offence.　Why comes not Death,
Said he, with one thrice acceptable stroke   855
To end me?　Shall Truth fail to keep her word,
Justice Divine not hasten to be just?
But Death comes not at call, Justice Divine
Mends not her slowest pace for prayers or cries.
O Woods, O Fountains, Hillocks, Dales and Bowrs,   860
With other echo late I taught your Shades
To answer, and resound farr other Song.
Whom thus afflicted when sad *Eve* beheld,
Desolate where she sate, approaching nigh
Soft words to his fierce passion she assayd: 865
But her with stern regard he thus repelld.
　　Out of my sight, thou Serpent, that name best
Befits thee with him leagu'd, thy self as false
And hateful; nothing wants, but that thy shape,
Like his, and colour Serpentine may shew   870
Thy inward fraud, to warn all Creatures from thee
Henceforth; lest that too heav'nly form, pretended
To hellish falsehood, snare them.　But for thee
I had persisted happie, had not thy pride
And wandring vanitie, when least was safe,   875
Rejected my forewarning, and disdaind
Not to be trusted, longing to be seen
Though by the Devil himself, him overweening
To over-reach, but with the Serpent meeting
Foold and beguil'd, by him thou, I by thee,   880
To trust thee from my side, imagind wise,
Constant, mature, proof against all assaults,
And understood not all was but a shew
Rather than solid vertue, all but a Rib
Crooked by nature, bent, as now appears,   885
More to the part sinister from me drawn,
Well if thrown out, as supernumerarie

To my just number found.   O why did God,
Creator wise, that peopl'd highest Heav'n
With Spirits Masculine, create at last   890
This noveltie on Earth, this fair defect
Of Nature, and not fill the World at once
With Men as Angels without Feminine,
Or find som other way to generate
Mankind? this mischief had not then befall'n,   895
And more that shall befall, innumerable
Disturbances on Earth through Femal snares,
And strait conjunction with this Sex: for either
He never shall find out fit Mate, but such
As some misfortune brings him or mistake,   900
Or whom he wishes most shall seldom gain
Through her perverseness, but shall see her gaind
By a farr worse, or if she love, withheld
By Parents, or his happiest choice too late
Shall meet, already linkt and Wedlock-bound   905
To a fell Adversarie, his hate or shame:
Which infinite calamitie shall cause
To Human life, and household peace confound.
    He added not, and from her turnd, but *Eve*
Not so repulst, with Tears that ceas'd not flowing,   910
And tresses all disorderd, at his feet
Fell humble, and imbracing them, besought
His peace, and thus proceeded in her plaint.
    Forsake me not thus, *Adam*, witness Heav'n
What love sincere and reverence in my heart   915
I bear thee, and unweeting have offended,
Unhappilie deceiv'd; thy suppliant
I beg, and clasp thy knees; bereave me not,
Whereon I live, thy gentle looks, thy aid,
Thy counsel in this uttermost distress,   920
My onely strength and stay: forlorn of thee,
Whither shall I betake me, where subsist?
While yet we live, scarce one short hour perhaps,
Between us two let there be peace, both joining,
As joind in injuries, one enmitie   925
Against a Foe by doom express assign'd us,
That cruel Serpent: On mee exercise not
Thy hatred for this miserie befall'n,
On mee already lost, mee than thy self
More miserable; both have sinnd, but thou   930
Against God onely, I against God and thee,
And to the place of judgement will return,
There with my cries importune Heaven, that all
The sentence from thy head remov'd may light
On me, sole cause to thee of all this woe,   935
Mee mee onely just object of his ire.

927 mee] me *Edd. 1, 2*
929 mee] me *Edd. 1, 2*

She ended weeping, and her lowlie plight,
Immoveable till peace obtaind from fault
Acknowledg'd and deplor'd, in *Adam* wrought
Commiseration; soon his heart relented   940
Towards her, his life so late and sole delight,
Now at his feet submissive in distress,
Creature so faire his reconcilement seeking,
His counsel whom she had displeas'd, his aid;
As one disarmd, his anger all he lost,   945
And thus with peaceful words uprais'd her soon.

Unwarie, and too desirous, as before,
So now of what thou knowst not, who desir'st
The punishment all on thy self; alas,
Beare thine own first, ill able to sustaine   950
His full wrauth whose thou feelst as yet least part,
And my displeasure bear'st so ill.   If Prayers
Could alter high Decrees, I to that place
Would speed before thee, and be louder heard,
That on my head all might be visited,   955
Thy frailtie and infirmer Sex forgiv'n,
To me committed and by me expos'd.
But rise, let us no more contend, nor blame
Each other, blam'd anough elsewhere, but strive
In offices of Love, how we may light'n   960
Each others burden in our share of woe;
Since this days Death denounc't, if aught I see,
Will prove no sudden, but a slow-pac't evil,
A long days dying to augment our pain,
And to our Seed (O hapless Seed!) deriv'd.   965

To whom thus *Eve*, recovering heart, repli'd.
Adam, by sad experiment I know
How little weight my words with thee can find,
Found so erroneous, thence by just event
Found so unfortunate; nevertheless,   970
Restor'd by thee, vile as I am, to place
Of new acceptance, hopeful to regaine
Thy Love, the sole contentment of my heart
Living or dying, from thee I will not hide
What thoughts in my unquiet brest are ris'n,   975
Tending to som relief of our extreams,
Or end, though sharp and sad, yet tollerable,
As in our evils, and of easier choice.
If care of our descent perplex us most,
Which must be born to certain woe, devour   980
By Death at last, and miserable it is
To be to others cause of misery,
Our own begotten, and of our Loins to bring
Into this cursed World a woful Race,
That after wretched Life must be at last   985

Food for so foule a Monster, in thy power
It lies, yet ere Conception to prevent
The Race unblest, to being yet unbegot.
Childless thou art, Childless remain: So Death
Shall be deceiv'd his glut, and with us two   990
Be forc't to satisfie his Rav'nous Maw.
But if thou judge it hard and difficult,
Conversing, looking, loving, to abstain
From Loves due Rites, Nuptial imbraces sweet,
And with desire to languish without hope,   995
Before the present object languishing
With like desire, which would be miserie
And torment less than none of what we dread,
Then both our selves and Seed at once to free
From what we fear for both, let us make short,   1000
Let us seek Death, or he not found, supply
With our own hands his Office on our selves;
Why stand we longer shivering under fears
That shew no end but Death, and have the power,
Of many ways to die the shortest choosing,   1005
Destruction with destruction to destroy.
      She ended here, or vehement despaire
Broke off the rest; so much of Death her thoughts
Had entertaind, as di'd her Cheeks with pale.
But *Adam* with such counsel nothing swayd,   1010
To better hopes his more attentive minde
Labouring had rais'd, and thus to *Eve* repli'd.
      Eve, thy contempt of life and pleasure seems
To argue in thee somthing more sublime
And excellent than what thy minde contemns;   1015
But self-destruction therefore sought, refutes
That excellence thought in thee, and implies,
Not thy contempt, but anguish and regret
For loss of life and pleasure overlov'd.
Or if thou covet death as utmost end   1020
Of miserie, so thinking to evade
The penaltie pronounc't, doubt not but God
Hath wiselier armd his vengeful ire than so
To be forestalld; much more I fear lest Death
So snatcht will not exempt us from the pain   1025
We are by doom to pay; rather such acts
Of contumacie will provoke the highest
To make death in us live: Then let us seek
Som safer resolution, which methinks
I have in view, calling to mind with heede   1030
Part of our Sentence, that thy Seed shall bruise
The Serpents head; pitteous amends, unless
Be meant, whom I conjecture, our grand Foe
Satan, who in the Serpent hath contriv'd

Against us this deceit: to crush his head   1035
Would be revenge indeed; which will be lost
By death brought on our selves, or childless days
Resolv'd, as thou proposest; so our Foe
Shall scape his punishment ordaind, and wee
Instead shall double ours upon our heads.   1040
No more be mentiond then of violence
Against our selves, and wilful barrenness,
That cuts us off from hope, and savours onely
Rancor and pride, impatience and despite,
Reluctance against God and his just yoke   1045
Laid on our Necks.   Remember with what mild
And gracious temper he both heard and judg'd
Without wrauth or reviling; wee expected
Immediat dissolution, which we thought
Was meant by Death that day, when lo, to thee   1050
Pains onely in Child-bearing were foretold,
And bringing forth, soon recompens't with joy,
Fruit of thy Womb: On mee the Curse aslope
Glanc'd on the ground, with labour I must earn
My bread; what harm?   Idleness had bin worse;   1055
My labour will sustain me; and lest Cold
Or Heat should injure us, his timely care
Hath unbesought provided, and his hands
Cloth'd us unworthie, pittying while he judg'd;
How much more, if we pray him, will his ear   1060
Be open, and his heart to pittie incline,
And teach us furder by what means to shun
Th' inclement Seasons, Rain, Ice, Hail and Snow,
Which now the Skie with various Face begins
To shew us in this Mountain, while the Winds   1065
Blow moist and keen, shattering the graceful locks
Of these fair spreading Trees; which bids us seek
Som better shroud, som better warmth to cherish
Our Limbs benummd, ere this diurnal Starr
Leave cold the Night, how we his gatherd beams   1070
Reflected, may with matter sere foment,
Or by collision of two bodies grinde
The Air attrite to Fire, as late the Clouds
Justling or pusht with Winds rude in thir shock
Tine the slant Lightning, whose thwart flame driv'n down
Kindles the gummie bark of Firr or Pine,   1076
And sends a comfortable heat from farr,
Which might supplie the Sun: such Fire to use,
And what may else be remedie or cure
To evils which our own misdeeds have wrought,   1080
Hee will instruct us praying, and of Grace
Beseeching him, so as we need not fear
To pass commodiously this life, sustaind

By him with many comforts, till we end
In dust, our final rest and native home.   1085
What better can we do, than to the place
Repairing where he judg'd us, prostrate fall
Before him reverent, and there confess
Humbly our faults, and pardon beg, with teares
Watering the ground, and with our sighs the Air   1090
Frequenting, sent from hearts contrite, in sign
Of sorrow unfeignd, and humiliation meek.
Undoubtedly he will relent and turn
From his displeasure; in whose look serene,
When angry most he seemd and most severe,   109
What else but favour, grace, and mercie shon?
   So spake our Father penitent, nor *Eve*
Felt less remorse: they forthwith to the place
Repairing where he judg'd them, prostrate fell
Before him reverent, and both confessd   1100
Humbly thir faults, and pardon beggd, with teares
Watering the ground, and with thir sighs the Air
Frequenting, sent from hearts contrite, in sign
Of sorrow unfeignd, and humiliation meek.

The End of the Tenth Book

BOOK XI

THE ARGUMENT.

The Son of God presents to his Father the Prayers of our first Parents now repenting, and intercedes for them: God accepts them, but declares that they must no longer abide in Paradise; sends Michael with a Band of Cherubim to dispossess them; but first to reveal to Adam *future things:* Michaels *coming down.* Adam *shews to* Eve *certain ominous signs; he discerns* Michaels *approach, goes out to meet him: the Angel denounces thir departure.* Eve's *Lamentation.* Adam *pleads, but submits: The Angel leads him up to a high Hill, sets before him in vision what shall happ'n till the Flood.*

Thus they in lowliest plight repentant stood
Praying, for from the Mercie-seat above
Prevenient Grace descending had remov'd
The stonie from thir hearts, and made new flesh
Regenerat grow instead, that sighs now breath'd   5
Unutterable, which the Spirit of prayer
Inspir'd, and wingd for Heav'n with speedier flight
Than loudest Oratorie: yet thir port
Not of mean suiters, nor important less
Seemd thir Petition than when th' ancient Pair   10
In Fables old, less ancient yet then these,
Deucalion and chaste *Pyrrha*, to restore
The Race of Mankind drownd, before the Shrine
Of *Themis* stood devout.   To Heav'n thir prayers
Flew up, nor missd the way, by envious windes   15
Blown vagabond or frustrate: in they passd
Dimensionless through Heav'nly dores; then clad
With incense, where the Golden Altar fum'd,
By thir great Intercessor, came in sight
Before the Fathers Throne: Them the glad Son   20
Presenting thus, to intercede began.

See Father, what first fruits on Earth are sprung
From thy implanted Grace in Man, these Sighs
And Prayers, which in this Golden Censer, mixt
With Incense, I thy Priest before thee bring,   25
Fruits of more pleasing savour from thy seed
Sown with contrition in his heart, than those
Which his own hand manuring all the Trees
Of Paradise could have produc't, ere fall'n
From innocence.   Now therefore bend thine ear   30
To supplication, hear his sighs though mute;
Unskilful with what words to pray, let mee
Interpret for him, mee his Advocate
And propitiation, all his works on mee

356

Good or not good ingraft, my Merit those　　35
Shall perfet, and for these my Death shall pay.
Accept me, and in mee from these receive
The smell of peace toward Mankinde, let him live
Before thee reconcil'd, at least his dayes
Numberd, though sad, till Death, his doom (which I　　40
To mitigate thus plead, not to reverse)
To better life shall yield him, where with mee
All my redeemd may dwell in joy and bliss,
Made one with me as I with thee am one.
　　To whom the Father, without Cloud, serene.　　45
All thy request for Man, accepted Son,
Obtain, all thy request was my Decree:
But longer in that Paradise to dwell,
The Law I gave to Nature him forbids:
Those pure immortal Elements that know　　50
No gross, no unharmoneous mixture foul,
Eject him tainted now, and purge him off
As a distemper, gross to aire as gross,
And mortal food, as may dispose him best
For dissolution wrought by Sin, that first　　55
Distemperd all things, and of incorrupt
Corrupted.　I at first with two fair gifts
Created him endowd, with Happiness
And Immortalitie: that fondly lost,
This other serv'd but to eternize wo;　　60
Till I provided Death; so Death becomes
His final remedie, and after Life
Tri'd in sharp tribulation, and refin'd
By Faith and faithful works, to second Life,
Wak't in the renovation of the just,　　65
Resigns him up with Heav'n and Earth renewd.
But let us call to Synod all the Blest
Through Heav'ns wide bounds; from them I will not hide
My judgments, how with Mankind I proceed,
As how with peccant Angels late they saw;　　70
And in thir state, though firm, stood more confirmd.
　　He ended, and the Son gave signal high
To the bright Minister that watchd, hee blew
His Trumpet, heard in *Oreb* since perhaps
When God descended, and perhaps once more　　75
To sound at general Doom.　Th' Angelic blast
Filld all the Regions: from thir blissful Bowrs
Of *Amarantin* Shade, Fountain or Spring,
By the waters of Life, where ere they sate
In fellowships of joy, the Sons of Light　　80
Hasted, resorting to the Summons high,
And took thir Seats; till from his Throne supream
Th' Almighty thus pronounc'd his sovran Will.

O Sons, like one of us Man is become
To know both Good and Evil, since his taste   85
Of that defended Fruit; but let him boast
His knowledge of Good lost, and Evil got,
Happier, had it suffic't him to have known
Good by it self, and Evil not at all.
He sorrows now, repents, and prays contrite,   90
My motions in him, longer then they move,
His heart I know how variable and vain
Self-left.   Lest therefore his now bolder hand
Reach also of the Tree of Life, and eat,
And live for ever, dream at least to live   95
For ever, to remove him I decree,
And send him from the Garden forth to Till
The Ground whence he was taken, fitter soil.
    Michael, this my behest have thou in charge,
Take to thee from among the Cherubim   100
Thy choice of flaming Warriors, lest the Fiend
Or in behalf of Man or to invade
Vacant possession, som new trouble raise:
Haste thee, and from the Paradise of God
Without remorse drive out the sinful Pair,   105
From hallowd ground th' unholie, and denounce
To them and to thir Progenie from thence
Perpetual banishment.   Yet lest they faint
At the sad Sentence rigorously urg'd,
For I behold them softend and with tears   110
Bewailing thir excess, all terror hide.
If patiently thy bidding they obey,
Dismiss them not disconsolate; reveale
To *Adam* what shall come in future days,
As I shall thee enlighten, intermix   115
My Cov'nant in the Womans seed renewd;
So send them forth, though sorrowing, yet in peace:
And on the East side of the Garden place,
Where entrance up from *Eden* easiest climbs,
Cherubic watch, and of a Sword the flame   120
Wide waving, all approach farr off to fright,
And guard all passage to the Tree of Life:
Lest Paradise a receptacle prove
To Spirits foul, and all my Trees thir prey,
With whose stol'n Fruit Man once more to delude.   125
    He ceas'd; and th' Archangelic Power prepar'd
For swift descent, with him the Cohort bright
Of watchful Cherubim; four faces each
Had, like a double *Janus*, all thir shape
Spangl'd with eyes more numerous than those   130
Of *Argus*, and more wakeful than to drowse,
Charmd with *Arcadian* Pipe, the Pastoral Reed

Of *Hermes* or his opiate Rod. Mean while
To resalute the World with sacred Light
Leucothea wak'd, and with fresh dews imbaumd   135
The Earth, when *Adam* and first Matron *Eve*
Had ended now thir Orisons, and found
Strength added from above, new hope to spring
Out of despair, joy, but with fear yet linkt;
Which thus to *Eve* his welcome words renewd.   140
    Eve, easily may Faith admit, that all
The good which we enjoy, from Heav'n descends;
But that from us aught should ascend to Heav'n
So prevalent as to concerne the mind
Of God high-blest, or to incline his will,   145
Hard to belief may seem; yet this will Prayer,
Or one short sigh of human breath, up-borne
Ev'n to the Seat of God. For since I sought
By Prayer th' offended Deitie to appease,
Kneeld and before him humbl'd all my heart,   150
Methought I saw him placable and mild,
Bending his ear; persuasion in me grew
That I was heard with favour; peace returnd
Home to my brest, and to my memorie
His promise, that thy Seed shall bruise our Foe;   155
Which then not minded in dismay, yet now
Assures me that the bitterness of death
Is past, and we shall live. Whence Haile to thee,
Eve rightly calld, Mother of all Mankind,
Mother of all things living, since by thee   160
Man is to live, and all things live for Man.
    To whom thus *Eve* with sad demeanour meek.
Ill worthie I such title should belong
To me transgressor, who for thee ordaind
A help, became thy snare; to mee reproach   165
Rather belongs, distrust and all dispraise:
But infinite in pardon was my Judge,
That I who first brought Death on all, am grac't
The source of life; next favourable thou,
Who highly thus to entitle me voutsaf'st,   170
Farr other name deserving. But the Field
To labour calls us now with sweat impos'd,
Though after sleepless Night; for see the Morn
All unconcernd with our unrest, begins
Her rosie progress smiling; let us forth,   175
I never from thy side henceforth to stray,
Where're our days work lies, though now enjoind
Laborious, till day droop; while here we dwell,
What can be toilsom in these pleasant Walks?
Here let us live, though in fall'n state, content.   180
    So spake, so wishd much-humbl'd *Eve*, but Fate

Subscrib'd not; Nature first gave Signs, imprest
On Bird, Beast, Air; Aire suddenly eclips'd
After short blush of Morn; nigh in her sight
The Bird of *Jove*, stoopt from his aerie tour,   185
Two Birds of gayest plume before him drove:
Down from a Hill the Beast that reigns in Woods,
First hunter then, persu'd a gentle brace,
Goodliest of all the Forrest, Hart and Hind;
Direct to th' Eastern Gate was bent thir flight.   190
Adam observ'd, and with his Eye the chase
Persuing, not unmov'd to *Eve* thus spake.

  O *Eve*, som furder change awaits us nigh,
Which Heav'n by these mute signs in Nature shews
Forerunners of his purpose, or to warn   195
Us haply too secure of our discharge
From penaltie, because from death releast
Some days; how long, and what till then our life,
Who knows, or more than this, that we are dust,
And thither must return and be no more.   200
Why else this double object in our sight
Of flight persu'd in th' Air and o'er the ground
One way the self-same hour? why in the East
Darkness ere Days mid-course, and Morning light
More orient in yon Western Cloud that draws   205
O'er the blue Firmament a radiant white,
And slow descends, with somthing heav'nly fraught.

  He errd not, for by this the heav'nly Bands,
Down from a Skie of Jasper, lighted now
In Paradise, and on a Hill made alt,   210
A glorious Apparition, had not doubt
And carnal fear that day dimmd *Adams* eye.
Not that more glorious, when the Angels met
Jacob in *Mahanaim*, where he saw
The field Paviliond with his Guardians bright;   215
Nor that which on the flaming Mount appear'd
In *Dothan*, coverd with a Camp of Fire,
Against the *Syrian* King, who to surprize
One man, Assassin-like had levied Warr,
Warr unproclaimd.   The Princely Hierarch   220
In thir bright stand, there left his Powers to seize
Possession of the Garden; hee alone,
To find where *Adam* shelterd, took his way,
Not unperceiv'd of *Adam*, who to *Eve*,
While the great Visitant approachd, thus spake.   225

  Eve, now expect great tidings, which perhaps
Of us will soon determin, or impose
New Laws to be observ'd; for I descrie
From yonder blazing Cloud that veils the Hill
One of the heav'nly Host, and by his Gait   230

None of the meanest, some great Potentate
Or of the Thrones above, such Majestie
Invests him coming; yet not terrible,
That I should fear, nor sociably mild,
As *Raphaël*, that I should much confide,   235
But solemn and sublime, whom not to offend
With reverence I must meet, and thou retire.
He ended; and th' Arch-Angel soon drew nigh,
Not in his shape Celestial, but as Man
Clad to meet Man; over his lucid Arms   240
A militarie Vest of purple flowd
Livelier than *Melibæan*, or the grain
Of *Sarra*, worn by Kings and Heroes old
In time of Truce; *Iris* had dipt the wooff;
His starrie Helm unbuckl'd shewd him prime   245
In Manhood where Youth ended; by his side
As in a glistering *Zodiac* hung the Sword,
Satans dire dread, and in his hand the Spear.
Adam bowd low, hee Kingly from his State
Inclin'd not, but his coming thus declar'd.   250
   Adam, Heav'ns high behest no Preface needs:
Sufficient that thy Prayers are heard, and Death,
Then due by sentence when thou didst transgress,
Defeated of his seizure many dayes
Giv'n thee of Grace, wherein thou mayst repent,   255
And one bad act with many deeds well done
Mayst cover: well may then thy Lord appeas'd
Redeem thee quite from Deaths rapacious claim;
But longer in this Paradise to dwell
Permits not; to remove thee I am come,   260
And send thee from the Garden forth to till
The ground whence thou wast taken, fitter Soil.
   He added not, for *Adam* at the newes
Heart-strook with chilling gripe of sorrow stood,
That all his senses bound; *Eve*, who unseen   265
Yet all had heard, with audible lament
Discoverd soon the place of her retire.
   O unexpected stroke, worse than of Death!
Must I thus leave thee Paradise? thus leave
Thee Native Soil, these happie Walks and Shades,   270
Fit haunt of Gods? where I had hope to spend,
Quiet though sad, the respit of that day
That must be mortal to us both.   O flowrs,
That never will in other Climat grow,
My early visitation, and my last   275
At Ev'n, which I bred up with tender hand
From the first op'ning bud, and gave ye Names,
Who now shall reare ye to the Sun, or rank
Your Tribes, and water from th' ambrosial Fount?

Thee lastly nuptial Bowr, by mee adornd   280
With what to sight or smell was sweet; from thee
How shall I part, and whither wander down
Into a lower World, to this obscure
And wild, how shall we breathe in other Aire
Less pure, accustomd to immortal Fruits?   285
   Whom thus the Angel interrupted mild.
Lament not *Eve*, but patiently resigne
What justly thou hast lost; nor set thy heart,
Thus over-fond, on that which is not thine;
Thy going is not lonely, with thee goes   290
Thy Husband, him to follow thou art bound;
Where he abides, think there thy native soil.
   Adam by this from the cold sudden damp
Recovering, and his scatterd spirits returnd,
To *Michael* thus his humble words addressd.   295
   Celestial, whether among the Thrones, or nam'd
Of them the Highest, for such of shape may seem
Prince above Princes, gently hast thou told
Thy message, which might else in telling wound,
And in performing end us; what besides   300
Of sorrow and dejection and despair
Our frailtie can sustain, thy tidings bring,
Departure from this happy place, our sweet
Recess, and onely consolation left
Familiar to our eyes, all places else   305
Inhospitable appear and desolate,
Nor knowing us nor known: and if by prayer
Incessant I could hope to change the will
Of him who all things can, I would not cease
To wearie him with my assiduous cries: 310
But prayer against his absolute Decree
No more availes than breath against the wind,
Blown stifling back on him that breathes it forth:
Therefore to his great bidding I submit.
This most afflicts me, that departing hence,   315
As from his face I shall be hid, depriv'd
His blessed count'nance; here I could frequent,
With worship, place by place where he voutsaf'd
Presence Divine, and to my Sons relate:
On this Mount he appear'd, under this Tree   320
Stood visible, among these Pines his voice
I heard, here with him at this Fountain talkd:
So many grateful Altars I would reare
Of grassie Terf, and pile up every Stone
Of lustre from the brook, in memorie   325
Or monument to Ages, and thereon
Offer sweet smelling Gumms and Fruits and Flowrs:
In yonder nether World where shall I seek

His bright appearances, or footstep trace?
For though I fled him angrie, yet recalld   330
To life prolongd and promis'd Race, I now
Gladly behold though but his utmost skirts
Of glory, and farr off his steps adore.
　　To whom thus *Michael* with regard benign.
Adam, thou knowst Heav'n his, and all the Earth,   335
Not this Rock onely; his Omnipresence fills
Land, Sea, and Air, and every kind that lives,
Fomented by his virtual power and warmd:
All th' Earth he gave thee to possess and rule,
No despicable gift; surmise not then   340
His presence to these narrow bounds confin'd
Of Paradise or *Eden*: this had been
Perhaps thy Capital Seat, from whence had spred
All generations, and had hither come
From all the ends of th' Earth, to celebrate   345
And reverence thee thir great Progenitor.
But this præeminence thou hast lost, brought down
To dwell on even ground now with thy Sons:
Yet doubt not but in Vallie and in Plaine
God is as here, and will be found alike   350
Present, and of his presence many a signe
Still following thee, still compassing thee round
With goodness and paternal Love, his Face
Express, and of his steps the track Divine.
Which that thou mayst believe, and be confirmd   355
Ere thou from hence depart, know I am sent
To shew thee what shall come in future days
To thee and to thy Offspring; good with bad
Expect to hear, supernal Grace contending
With sinfulness of Men; thereby to learn   360
True patience, and to temper joy with fear
And pious sorrow, equally enur'd
By moderation either state to bear,
Prosperous or adverse: so shalt thou leade
Safest thy life, and best prepar'd endure   365
Thy mortal passage when it comes.　Ascend
This Hill; let *Eve* (for I have drencht her eyes)
Here sleep below while thou to foresight wak'st,
As once thou slepst, while shee to life was formd.
　　To whom thus *Adam* gratefully repli'd.   370
Ascend, I follow thee, safe Guide, the path
Thou lead'st me, and to the hand of Heav'n submit,
However chast'ning, to the evil turn
My obvious breast, arming to overcome
By suffering, and earne rest from labour won,   375
If so I may attain.　So both ascend
In the Visions of God: It was a Hill

Of Paradise the highest, from whose top
The Hemisphere of Earth in clearest Ken
Stretcht out to th' amplest reach of prospect lay.   380
Not higher that Hill nor wider looking round,
Whereon for different cause the Tempter set
Our second *Adam* in the Wilderness,
To shew him all Earths Kingdoms and thir Glory.
His Eye might there command wherever stood   385
City of old or modern Fame, the Seat
Of mightiest Empire, from the destind Walls
Of *Cambalu*, seat of *Cathaian Can*
And *Samarchand* by *Oxus*, *Temirs* Throne,
To *Paquin* of *Sinæan* Kings, and thence   390
To *Agra* and *Lahor* of great *Mogul*
Down to the golden *Chersonese*, or where
The *Persian* in *Ecbatan* sate, or since
In *Hispahan*, or where the *Russian Ksar*
In *Mosco*, or the Sultan in *Bizance*,   395
Turchestan-born; nor could his eye not ken
Th' Empire of *Negus* to his utmost Port
Ercoco and the less Maritim Kings
Mombaza, and *Quiloa*, and *Melind*,
And *Sofala* thought *Ophir*, to the Realm   400
Of *Congo*, and *Angola* fardest South;
Or thence from *Niger* Flood to *Atlas* Mount
The Kingdoms of *Almansor*, *Fez* and *Sus*,
Marocco and *Algiers*, and *Tremisen*;
On *Europe* thence, and where *Rome* was to sway   405
The World: in Spirit perhaps he also saw
Rich *Mexico* the seat of *Motezume*,
And *Cusco* in *Peru*, the richer seat
Of *Atabalipa*, and yet unspoild
Guiana, whose great Citie *Geryons* Sons   410
Call *El Dorado*: but to nobler sights
Michael from *Adams* eyes the Filme remov'd
Which that false Fruit that promis'd clearer sight
Had bred; then purg'd with Euphrasie and Rue
The visual Nerve, for he had much to see;   415
And from the Well of Life three drops instilld.
So deep the power of these Ingredients pierc'd,
Ev'n to the inmost seat of mental sight,
That *Adam* now enforc't to close his eyes
Sunk down and all his spirits became intranc't: 420
But him the gentle Angel by the hand
Soon rais'd, and his attention thus recalld.
   Adam, now ope thine eyes, and first behold

380 th' amplest] the amplest *Ed. 2*] amplest *Ed 1*
398 Maritim *Ed. 2*] Maritine *Ed. 1*

Th' effects which thy original crime hath wrought
In some to spring from thee, who never touchd   425
Th' excepted Tree, nor with the Snake conspir'd,
Nor sinnd thy sin, yet from that sin derive
Corruption to bring forth more violent deeds.
    His eyes he opend, and beheld a field,
Part arable and tilth, whereon were Sheaves   430
New reap't, the other part sheep-walks and folds;
Ith' midst an Altar as the Land-mark stood
Rustic, of grassie sord; thither anon
A sweatie Reaper from his Tillage brought
First Fruits, the green Eare and the yellow Sheaf,   435
Unculld, as came to hand; a Shepherd next
More meek came with the Firstlings of his Flock
Choicest and best; then sacrificing, laid
The Inwards and thir Fat, with Incense strewd,
On the cleft Wood, and all due Rites performd.   440
His Offring soon propitious Fire from Heav'n
Consum'd with nimble glance, and grateful steam;
The others not, for his was not sincere;
Whereat hee inlie rag'd, and as they talkd
Smote him into the Midriff with a stone   445
That beat out life; he fell, and deadly pale
Groand out his Soul with gushing blood effus'd.
Much at that sight was *Adam* in his heart
Dismayd, and thus in haste to th' Angel cri'd.
    O Teacher, some great mischief hath befall'n   450
To that meek man, who well had sacrific't;
Is Pietie thus and pure Devotion paid?
    T' whom *Michael* thus, hee also mov'd, repli'd.
These two are Brethren, *Adam,* and to come
Out of thy loins; th' unjust the just hath slain,   455
For envie that his Brothers Offering found
From Heav'n acceptance; but the bloodie Fact
Will be aveng'd, and th' others Faith approv'd
Lose no reward, though here thou see him die,
Rouling in dust and gore.   To which our Sire.   460
    Alas, both for the deed and for the cause!
But have I now seen Death?   Is this the way
I must return to native dust?   O sight
Of terror, foul and ugly to behold,
Horrid to think, how horrible to feel!   465
    To whom thus *Michaël.*   Death thou hast seen
In his first shape on man; but many shapes
Of Death, and many are the ways that lead
To his grim Cave, all dismal; yet to sense
More terrible at th' entrance than within.   470
Some, as thou sawst, by violent stroke shall die,
By Fire, Flood, Famin, by Intemperance more

In Meats and Drinks, which on the Earth shall bring
Diseases dire, of which a monstrous crew
Before thee shall appear; that thou mayst know   475
What miserie th' inabstinence of *Eve*
Shall bring on men.   Immediatly a place
Before his eyes appear'd, sad, noisom, dark,
A Lazar-house it seemd, wherein were laid
Numbers of all diseas'd, all maladies   480
Of gastly Spasm or racking torture, qualms
Of heart-sick Agonie, all feavorous kinds,
Convulsions, Epilepsies, fierce Catarrhs,
Intestin Stone and Ulcer, Colic pangs,
Dæmoniac Phrenzie, moping Melancholie   485
And Moon-struck madness, pining Atrophie,
Marasmus, and wide-wasting Pestilence,
Dropsies and Asthmas, and Joint-racking Rheums.
Dire was the tossing, deep the groans, despaire
Tended the sick busiest from Couch to Couch;   490
And over them triumphant Death his Dart
Shook, but delayd to strike, though oft invok't
With vows, as thir chief good, and final hope.
Sight so deform what heart of Rock could long
Drie-ey'd behold?   *Adam* could not, but wept,   495
Though not of Woman born; compassion quelld
His best of Man, and gave him up to tears
A space, till firmer thoughts restraind excess,
And scarce recovering words his plaint renewd.

   O miserable Mankind, to what fall   500
Degraded, to what wretched state reserv'd!
Better end here unborn.   Why is life giv'n
To be thus wrested from us? rather why
Obtruded on us thus? who, if we knew
What we receive, would either not accept   505
Life offerd or soon beg to lay it down,
Glad to be so dismisst in peace.   Can thus
Th' Image of God in man created once
So goodly and erect, though faultie since,
To such unsightly sufferings be debas't   510
Under inhuman pains?   Why should not Man,
Retaining still Divine similitude
In part, from such deformities be free,
And for his Makers Image sake exempt?

   Thir Makers Image, answerd *Michael*, then   515
Forsook them, when themselves they villifi'd
To serve ungovernd appetite, and took
His Image whom they serv'd, a brutish vice,
Inductive mainly to the sin of *Eve*.

485-7 *Added Ed.* 2

Therefore so abject is thir punishment,   520
Disfiguring not Gods likeness, but thir own,
Or if his likeness, by themselves defac't
While they pervert pure Natures healthful rules
To loathsom sickness, worthily, since they
Gods Image did not reverence in themselves.   525
    I yield it just, said *Adam*, and submit.
But is there yet no other way, besides
These painful passages, how we may come
To Death, and mix with our connatural dust?
    There is, said *Michael*, if thou well observe   530
The rule of not too much, by temperance taught
In what thou eat'st and drinkst, seeking from thence
Due nourishment, not gluttonous delight,
Till many years over thy head return:
So mayst thou live, till like ripe Fruit thou drop   535
Into thy Mothers lap, or be with ease
Gatherd, not harshly pluckt, for death mature:
This is old age; but then thou must outlive
Thy youth, thy strength, thy beauty, which will change
To witherd weak and gray; thy Senses then   540
Obtuse, all taste of pleasure must forgo,
To what thou hast, and for the Air of youth
Hopeful and cheerful, in thy blood will reign
A melancholly damp of cold and dry
To weigh thy spirits down, and last consume   545
The Baum of Life. To whom our Ancestor.
    Henceforth I flie not Death, nor would prolong
Life much, bent rather how I may be quit
Fairest and easiest of this cumbrous charge,
Which I must keep till my appointed day   550
Of rendring up, and patiently attend
My dissolution. *Michaël* repli'd,
    Nor love thy Life, nor hate; but what thou liv'st
Live well, how long or short permit to Heav'n:
And now prepare thee for another sight.   555
    He lookd and saw a spacious Plain, whereon
Were Tents of various hue; by some were herds
Of Cattel grazing: others, whence the sound
Of Instruments that made melodious chime
Was heard, of Harp and Organ; and who mov'd   560
Thir stops and chords was seen: his volant touch
Instinct through all proportions low and high
Fled and persu'd transverse the resonant fugue.
In other part stood one who at the Forge
Labouring, two massie clods of Iron and Brass   565
Had melted (whether found where casual fire

551-2 *Ed. 2*] Of rendering up. *Michael* to him repli'd. *Ed. 1*

Had wasted woods on Mountain or in Vale,
Down to the veins of Earth, thence gliding hot
To som Caves mouth, or whether washt by stream
From underground); the liquid Ore he draind   570
Into fit moulds prepar'd; from which he formd
First his own Tools; then, what might else be wrought
Fusil or grav'n in metal.   After these,
But on the hither side, a different sort
From the high neighbouring Hills, which was thir Seat,
Down to the Plain descended: by thir guise   576
Just men they seemd, and all thir study bent
To worship God aright, and know his works
Not hid, nor those things last which might preserve
Freedom and Peace to men: they on the Plain   580
Long had not walkt, when from the Tents behold
A Bevie of fair Women, richly gay
In Gems and wanton dress; to th' Harp they sung
Soft amorous Ditties, and in dance came on:
The Men though grave, ey'd them, and let thir eyes   585
Rove without rein, till in the amorous Net
Fast caught, they lik'd, and each his liking chose;
And now of love they treat till th' Ev'ning Star
Loves Harbinger appear'd; then all in heat
They light the Nuptial Torch, and bid invoke   590
Hymen, then first to marriage Rites invok't;
With Feast and Musick all the Tents resound.
Such happy interview and fair event
Of love and youth not lost, Songs, Garlands, Flowrs
And charming Symphonies attachd the heart   595
Of *Adam*, soon enclin'd to admit delight,
The bent of Nature; which he thus expressd.
     True op'ner of mine eyes, prime Angel blest,
Much better seems this Vision, and more hope
Of peaceful days portends, than those two past;   600
Those were of hate and death, or pain much worse,
Here Nature seems fulfilld in all her ends.
     To whom thus *Michael*.   Judge not what is best
By pleasure, though to Nature seeming meet,
Created, as thou art, to nobler end   605
Holie and pure, conformitie divine.
Those Tents thou sawst so pleasant, were the Tents
Of wickedness, wherein shall dwell his Race
Who slew his Brother; studious they appear
Of Arts that polish Life, Inventers rare,   610
Unmindful of thir Maker, though his Spirit
Taught them, but they his gifts acknowledg'd none.
Yet they a beauteous offspring shall beget;
For that fair femal Troop thou sawst, that seemd
Of Goddesses, so blithe, so smooth, so gay,   615

Yet empty of all good wherein consists
Womans domestic honour and chief praise;
Bred onely and completed to the taste
Of lustful appetence, to sing, to dance,
To dress, and troule the Tongue, and roule the Eye.　620
To these that sober Race of Men, whose lives
Religious titl'd them the Sons of God,
Shall yield up all thir vertue, all thir fame
Ignobly, to the traines and to the smiles
Of these fair Atheists, and now swim in joy　　625
(Erelong to swim at large) and laugh; for which
The world erelong a world of tears must weep.

　　To whom thus *Adam* of short joy bereft.
O pittie and shame, that they who to live well
Enterd so fair, should turn aside to tread　　630
Paths indirect, or in the mid way faint!
But still I see the tenor of Mans woe
Holds on the same, from Woman to begin.

　　From Mans effeminat slackness it begins,
Said th' Angel, who should better hold his place　635
By wisdom, and superior gifts receiv'd.
But now prepare thee for another Scene.

　　He lookd and saw wide Territorie spred
Before him, Towns, and rural works between,
Cities of Men with lofty Gates and Towrs,　　640
Concourse in Arms, fierce Faces threatning Warr,
Giants of mightie Bone, and bold emprise;
Part wield thir Arms, part curb the foaming Steed,
Single or in Array of Battel rang'd
Both Horse and Foot, nor idly mustring stood;　645
One way a Band select from forage drives
A herd of Beeves, fair Oxen and fair Kine
From a fat Meddow ground; or fleecy Flock,
Ewes and thir bleating Lambs over the Plain,
Thir Bootie; scarce with Life the Shepherds fly,　650
But call in aid, which makes a bloody Fray;
With cruel Tournament the Squadrons join;
Where Cattel pastur'd late, now scatterd lies
With Carcasses and Arms th' ensanguind Field
Deserted: Others to a Citie strong　　655
Lay Siege, encampt; by Batterie, Scale and Mine
Assaulting; others from the wall defend
With Dart and Jav'lin, Stones and sulphurous Fire;
On each hand slaughter and gigantic deeds.
In other part the scepterd Haralds call　　660
To Councel in the Citie Gates: anon
Grey-headed men and grave, with Warriors mixt,

Assemble, and Harangues are heard, but soon
In factious opposition, till at last
Of middle Age one rising, eminent   665
In wise deport, spake much of Right and Wrong,
Of Justice, of Religion, Truth and Peace,
And Judgement from above: him old and young
Exploded, and had seiz'd with violent hands,
Had not a Cloud descending snatcht him thence   670
Unseen amid the throng: so violence
Proceeded, and Oppression, and Sword-Law
Through all the Plain, and refuge none was found.
Adam was all in tears, and to his guide
Lamenting turnd full sad; O what are these,   675
Deaths Ministers, not Men, who thus deal Death
Inhumanly to men, and multiply
Ten thousandfold the sin of him who slew
His Brother; for of whom such massacher
Make they but of thir Brethren, men of men?   680
But who was that Just Man, whom had not Heav'n
Rescu'd, had in his Righteousness bin lost?
      To whom thus *Michael*.   These are the product
Of those ill-mated Marriages thou sawst;
Where good with bad were matcht, who of themselves
Abhorr to join; and by imprudence mixt   686
Produce prodigious Births of bodie or mind.
Such were these Giants, men of high renown;
For in those dayes Might onely shall be admir'd,
And Valour and Heroic Vertue calld;   690
To overcome in Battel, and subdue
Nations, and bring home spoils with infinite
Man-slaughter, shall be held the highest pitch
Of human Glorie, and for Glorie done
Of triumph, to be styl'd great Conquerors,   695
Patrons of Mankind, Gods, and Sons of Gods,
Destroyers rightlier calld and Plagues of men.
Thus Fame shall be achiev'd, renown on Earth,
And what most merits fame in silence hid.
But hee the sev'nth from thee, whom thou beheldst   700
The onely righteous in a World perverse,
And therefore hated, therefore so beset
With Foes for daring single to be just,
And utter odious Truth, that God would come
To judge them with his Saints: Him the most High   705
Rapt in a baumie Cloud with winged Steeds
Did, as thou sawst, receive, to walk with God
High in Salvation and the Climes of bliss,
Exempt from Death; to shew thee what reward
Awaits the good, the rest what punishment;   710
Which now direct thine eyes and soon behold.

He lookd, and saw the face of things quite chang'd;
The brazen Throat of Warr had ceas't to roar,
All now was turnd to jollitie and game,
To luxurie and riot, feast and dance,   715
Marrying or prostituting, as befell,
Rape or Adulterie, where passing faire
Allur'd them; thence from Cups to civil Broils.
At length a Reverend Sire among them came,
And of thir doings great dislike declar'd,   720
And testifi'd against thir ways; hee oft
Frequented thir Assemblies, whereso met,
Triumphs or Festivals, and to them preach'd
Conversion and Repentance, as to Souls
In Prison under Judgements imminent: 725
But all in vain: which when he saw, he ceas'd
Contending, and remov'd his Tents farr off;
Then from the Mountain hewing Timber tall,
Began to build a Vessel of huge bulk,
Measur'd by Cubit, length and bredth and highth,   730
Smear'd round with Pitch, and in the side a dore
Contriv'd, and of provisions laid in large
For Man and Beast: when loe a wonder strange!
Of every Beast, and Bird, and Insect small
Came sev'ns and pairs, and enterd in, as taught   735
Thir order; last the Sire, and his three Sons
With thir four Wives; and God made fast the dore.
Meanwhile the Southwind rose, and with black wings
Wide hovering, all the Clouds together drove
From under Heav'n; the Hills to thir supplie   740
Vapour and Exhalation dusk and moist
Sent up amain; and now the thickend Skie
Like a dark Ceiling stood; down rushd the Rain
Impetuous, and continu'd till the Earth
No more was seen; the floating Vessel swum   745
Uplifted; and secure with beaked prow
Rode tilting ore the Waves, all dwellings else
Flood overwhelmd, and them with all thir pomp
Deep under water rould; Sea coverd Sea,
Sea without shore; and in thir Palaces   750
Where luxurie late reignd, Sea-monsters whelpd
And stabl'd; of Mankind, so numerous late,
All left, in one small bottom swum imbarkt.
How didst thou grieve then, *Adam*, to behold
The end of all thy Offspring, end so sad,   755
Depopulation; thee another Flood,
Of tears and sorrow a Flood thee also drownd,
And sunk thee as thy Sons; till gently rear'd
By th' Angel, on thy feet thou stoodst at last,
Though comfortless, as when a Father mourns   760

His Childern, all in view destroyd at once;
And scarce to th' Angel utterdst thus thy plaint.
    O Visions ill foreseen! better had I
Liv'd ignorant of future, so had borne
My part of evil only, each days lot   765
Anough to bear; those now, that were dispenst
The burd'n of many Ages, on me light
At once, by my foreknowledge gaining Birth
Abortive, to torment me ere thir being,
With thought that they must be.   Let no man seek   770
Henceforth to be foretold what shall befall
Him or his Childern, evil he may be sure,
Which neither his foreknowing can prevent,
And hee the future evil shall no less
In apprehension than in substance feel   775
Grievous to bear: but that care now is past,
Man is not whom to warn: those few escap't
Famin and anguish will at last consume
Wandring that watrie Desert: I had hope
When violence was ceas't, and Warr on Earth,   780
All would have then gon well, peace would have crownd
With length of happy dayes the race of man;
But I was farr deceiv'd; for now I see
Peace to corrupt no less than Warr to waste.
How comes it thus? unfold, Celestial Guide,   785
And whether here the Race of man will end.
To whom thus *Michael.*   Those whom last thou sawst
In triumph and luxurious wealth, are they
First seen in acts of prowess eminent
And great exploits, but of true vertue void;   790
Who having spilt much blood, and don much waste
Subduing Nations, and achiev'd thereby
Fame in the World, high titles and rich prey,
Shall change thir course to pleasure, ease and sloth,
Surfet and lust, till wantonness and pride   795
Raise out of friendship hostil deeds in Peace.
The conquerd also and enslav'd by Warr
Shall with thir freedom lost all vertue lose
And fear of God, from whom thir pietie feignd
In sharp contest of Battel found no aid   800
Against invaders; therefore coold in zeale
Thenceforth shall practice how to live secure,
Worldlie or dissolute, on what thir Lords
Shall leave them to enjoy; for th' Earth shall beare
More than anough, that temperance may be tri'd: 805
So all shall turn degenerat, all deprav'd,
Justice and Temperance, Truth and Faith forgot;
One Man except, the onely Son of light
In a dark Age, against example good,

Against allurement, custom, and a World   810
Offended; fearless of reproach and scorn
Or violence, hee of thir wicked ways
Shall them admonish, and before them set
The paths of righteousness, how much more safe,
And full of peace, denouncing wrauth to come   815
On thir impenitence; and shall returne
Of them derided, but of God observ'd
The one just Man alive; by his command
Shall build a wondrous Ark, as thou beheldst,
To save himself and household from amidst   820
A World devote to universal wrack.
No sooner hee with them of Man and Beast
Select for life, shall in the Ark be lodg'd
And shelterd round, but all the Cataracts
Of Heav'n set open on the Earth shall poure   825
Raine day and night, all fountains of the Deep
Broke up, shall heave the Ocean to usurp
Beyond all bounds, till inundation rise
Above the highest Hills: then shall this Mount
Of Paradise by might of Waves be mov'd   830
Out of his place, pusht by the horned flood,
With all his verdure spoilt and Trees adrift
Down the great River to the op'ning Gulf,
And there take root an Iland salt and bare,
The haunt of Seals and Orcs, and Sea-mews clang;   835
To teach thee that God attributes to place
No sanctitie, if none be thither brought
By Men who there frequent or therein dwell.
And now what further shall ensue, behold.

    He lookd, and saw the Ark hull on the flood,   840
Which now abated, for the Clouds were fled,
Driv'n by a keen North-wind, that blowing drie
Wrinkl'd the face of Deluge, as decayd;
And the clear Sun on his wide watrie Glass
Gaz'd hot, and of the fresh Wave largely drew,   845
As after thirst, which made thir flowing shrink
From standing lake to tripping ebb, that stole
With soft foot towards the Deep, who now had stopt
His Sluces, as the Heav'n his windows shut.
The Ark no more now floats, but seems on ground   850
Fast on the top of som high mountain fixt.
And now the tops of Hills as Rocks appear;
With clamor thence the rapid Currents drive
Towards the retreating Sea thir furious tide.
Forthwith from out the Arke a Raven flies,   855
And after him, the surer messenger,
A Dove sent forth once and agen to spie
Green Tree or ground whereon his foot may light;

832 spoilt] Spoil'd *Edd. 1, 2*

The second time returning, in his Bill
An Olive leaf he brings, pacific sign: 860
Anon drie ground appears, and from his Ark
The ancient Sire descends with all his Train;
Then with uplifted hands and eyes devout,
Grateful to Heav'n, over his head beholds
A dewie Cloud, and in the Cloud a Bow   865
Conspicuous with three listed colours gay,
Betok'ning peace from God, and Cov'nant new.
Whereat the heart of *Adam* erst so sad
Greatly rejoic'd, and thus his joy broke forth.
    O thou who future things canst represent   870
As present, Heav'nly instructer, I revive
At this last sight, assur'd that Man shall live
With all the Creatures, and thir seed preserve.
Farr less I now lament for one whole World
Of wicked Sons destroyd, than I rejoice   875
For one Man found so perfet and so just,
That God voutsafes to raise another World
From him, and all his anger to forget.
But say, what mean those colourd streaks in Heav'n,
Distended as the Brow of God appeas'd,   880
Or serve they as a flowrie verge to bind
The fluid skirts of that same watrie Cloud,
Lest it again dissolve and showr the Earth?
    To whom th' Archangel.   Dextrously thou aimst;
So willingly doth God remit his Ire,   885
Though late repenting him of Man deprav'd,
Griev'd at his heart, when looking down he saw
The whole Earth filld with violence, and all flesh
Corrupting each thir way; yet those remov'd,
Such grace shall one just Man find in his sight,   890
That he relents, not to blot out mankind,
And makes a Cov'nant never to destroy
The Earth again by flood, nor let the Sea
Surpass his bounds, nor Rain to drown the World
With Man therein or Beast; but when he brings   895
Over the Earth a Cloud, will therein set
His triple-colour'd Bow, whereon to look
And call to mind his Cov'nant: Day and Night,
Seed time and Harvest, Heat and hoary Frost
Shall hold thir course, till fire purge all things new,   900
Both Heav'n and Earth, wherein the just shall dwell.

The End of the Eleventh Book

BOOK XII

THE ARGUMENT

The Angel Michael *continues from the Flood to relate what shall succeed; then, in the mention of* Abraham, *comes by degrees to explain, who that Seed of the Woman shall be, which was promised* Adam *and* Eve *in the Fall; his Incarnation, Death, Resurrection, and Ascention; the state of the Church till his second Coming.* Adam *greatly satisfied and recomforted by these Relations and Promises descends the Hill with* Michael; *wakens* Eve, *who all this while had slept, but with gentle dreams compos'd to quietness of mind and submission.* Michael *in either hand leads them out of Paradise, the fiery Sword waving behind them, and the Cherubim taking thir Stations to guard the Place.*

As one who in his journey baits at Noon,
Though bent on speed, so here th'Archangel paus'd
Betwixt the world destroyd and world restor'd,
If *Adam* aught perhaps might interpose;
Then with transition sweet new Speech resumes.   5
    Thus thou hast seen one World begin and end;
And Man as from a second stock proceed.
Much thou hast yet to see, but I perceive
Thy mortal sight to fail; objects divine
Must needs impaire and wearie human sense: 10
Henceforth what is to come I will relate,
Thou therefore give due audience, and attend.
This second source of Men, while yet but few,
And while the dread of judgement past remains
Fresh in thir minds, fearing the Deitie,   15
With some regard to what is just and right
Shall lead thir lives, and multiplie apace,
Labouring the soil, and reaping plenteous crop,
Corn, wine and oil; and from the herd or flock
Oft sacrificing Bullock, Lamb or Kid,   20
With large Wine-offerings pourd, and sacred Feast,
Shall spend thir dayes in joy unblam'd, and dwell
Long time in peace by Families and Tribes
Under paternal rule; till one shall rise
Of proud ambitious heart, who not content   25
With fair equalitie, fraternal state,
Will arrogate Dominion undeserv'd
Over his brethren, and quite dispossess
Concord and law of Nature from the Earth,

1-5 *added in Ed. 2 when Bk* x *of Ed. 1 was divided into Bks xi and xii*
1 baits] bates *Ed. 2*

Hunting (and Men not Beasts shall be his game)   30
With Warr and hostil snare such as refuse
Subjection to his Empire tyrannous:
A mightie Hunter thence he shall be styl'd
Before the Lord, as in despite of Heav'n,
Or from Heav'n claiming second Sovrantie;   35
And from Rebellion shall derive his name,
Though of Rebellion others he accuse.
Hee with a crew, whom like Ambition joins
With him or under him to tyrannize,
Marching from *Eden* towards the West, shall find   40
The Plain, wherein a black bituminous gurge ·
Boils out from under ground, the mouth of Hell;
Of Brick and of that stuff they cast to build
A Citie and Towr, whose top may reach to Heav'n;
And get themselves a name, lest far disperst   45
In forren Lands thir memorie be lost,
Regardless whether good or evil fame.
But God who oft descends to visit men
Unseen, and through thir habitations walks
To mark thir doings, them beholding soon,   50
Comes down to see thir Citie, ere the Tower
Obstruct Heav'n Towrs, and in derision sets
Upon thir Tongues a various Spirit to rase
Quite out thir Native Language, and instead
To sow a jangling noise of words unknown: 55
Forthwith a hideous gabble rises loud
Among the Builders; each to other calls
Not understood, till hoarse, and all in rage,
As mockt they storm; great laughter was in Heav'n
And looking down, to see the hubbub strange   60
And hear the din; thus was the building left
Ridiculous, and the work Confusion nam'd.
     Whereto thus *Adam* fatherly displeas'd.
O execrable Son so to aspire
Above his Brethren, to himself assuming   65
Autoritie usurpt, from God not giv'n:
He gave us onely over Beast, Fish, Fowl
Dominion absolute; that right we hold
By his donation; but Man over men
He made not Lord; such title to himself   70
Reserving, human left from human free.
But this Usurper his encroachment proud
Stayes not on Man; to God his Towr intends
Siege and defiance: Wretched man! what food
Will he convey up thither to sustain   75
Himself and his rash Armie, where thin Aire
Above the Clouds will pine his entrails gross,
And famish him of Breath, if not of Bread?

    To whom thus *Michael.*   Justly thou abhorrst
That Son, who on the quiet state of men   80
Such trouble brought, affecting to subdue
Rational Libertie; yet know withall,
Since thy original lapse, true Libertie
Is lost, which alwayes with right Reason dwells
Twinnd, and from her hath no dividual being: 85
Reason in man obscur'd, or not obeyd,
Immediatly inordinate desires
And upstart Passions catch the Goverment
From Reason, and to servitude reduce
Man till then free.   Therefore since hee permits   90
Within himself unworthie Powers to reign
Over free Reason, God in Judgement just
Subjects him from without to violent Lords;
Who oft as undeservedly enthrall
His outward freedom: Tyrannie must be,   95
Though to the Tyrant thereby no excuse.
Yet sometimes Nations will decline so low
From vertue, which is reason, that no wrong,
But Justice, and som fatal curse annext
Deprives them of thir outward libertie,   100
Thir inward lost: Witness th'irreverent Son
Of him who built the Ark, who for the shame
Done to his Father, heard this heavie curse,
Servant of Servants, on his vicious Race.
Thus will this latter, as the former World,   105
Still tend from bad to worse, till God at last
Wearied with thir iniquities, withdraw
His presence from among them, and avert
His holy Eyes; resolving from thenceforth
To leave them to thir own polluted wayes;   110
And one peculiar Nation to select
From all the rest, of whom to be invok't,
A Nation from one faithful man to spring:
Him on this side *Euphrates* yet residing,
Bred up in Idol-worship; O that men   115
(Canst thou believe?) should be so stupid grown,
While yet the Patriarch liv'd who scap'd the Flood,
As to forsake the living God, and fall
To worship thir own work in Wood and Stone
For Gods! yet him God the most High voutsafes   120
To call by Vision from his Fathers house,
His kindred and false Gods, into a Land
Which he will shew him, and from him will raise
A mightie Nation, and upon him showr
His benediction so, that in his Seed   125
All Nations shall be blest; he straight obeys,
Not knowing to what Land, yet firm believes:

I see him, but thou canst not, with what Faith
He leaves his Gods, his Friends, and native Soile
Ur of *Chaldæa*, passing now the Ford   130
To *Haran*, after him a cumbrous Train
Of Herds and Flocks, and numerous servitude;
Not wandring poor, but trusting all his wealth
With God, who calld him, in a land unknown.
Canaan he now attains, I see his Tents   135
Pitcht about *Sechem*, and the neighbouring Plain
Of *Moreh*; there by promise he receives
Gift to his Progenie of all that Land;
From *Hamath* Northward to the Desert South
(Things by thir names I call, though yet unnam'd)   140
From *Hermon* East to the great Western Sea,
Mount *Hermon*, yonder Sea, each place behold
In prospect, as I point them; on the shore
Mount *Carmel*; here the double-founted streame
Jordan, true limit Eastward; but his Sons   145
Shall dwell to *Senir*, that long ridge of Hills.
This ponder, that all Nations of the Earth
Shall in his Seed be blessed; by that Seed
Is meant thy great deliverer, who shall bruise
The Serpents head; whereof to thee anon   150
Plainlier shall be reveal'd.   This Patriarch blest,
Whom *faithful Abraham* due time shall call,
A Son, and of his Son a Grand-child leaves,
Like him in faith, in wisdom, and renown;
The Grandchild with twelve Sons increas't, departs   155
From *Canaan*, to a Land hereafter calld
Egypt, divided by the River *Nile*;
See where it flows, disgorging at sev'n mouthes
Into the Sea: to sojourn in that Land
He comes invited by a younger Son   160
In time of dearth, a Son whose worthy deeds
Raise him to be the second in that Realm
Of *Pharao*: there he dies, and leaves his Race
Growing into a Nation, and now grown
Suspected to a sequent King, who seeks   165
To stop thir overgrowth, as inmate guests
Too numerous; whence of guests he makes them slaves
Inhospitably, and kills thir infant Males:
Till by two brethren (those two brethren call
Moses and *Aaron*) sent from God to claim   170
His people from enthralment, they return
With glory and spoile back to thir promis'd Land.
But first the lawless Tyrant, who denies
To know thir God, or message to regard,
Must be compelld by Signs and Judgements dire;   175
To blood unshed the Rivers must be turnd,

Frogs, Lice and Flies must all his Palace fill
With loathd intrusion, and fill all the land;
His Cattel must of Rot and Murren die,
Botches and blaines must all his flesh imboss,   180
And all his people; Thunder mixt with Hail,
Haile mixt with fire must rend th' *Egyptian* Skie
And wheel on th' Earth, devouring where it rouls;
What it devours not, Herb or Fruit or Grain,
A darksom Cloud of Locusts swarming down   185
Must eat, and on the ground leave nothing green:
Darkness must overshadow all his bounds,
Palpable darkness, and blot out three days;
Last with one midnight stroke all the first-born
Of *Egypt* must lie dead.   Thus with ten wounds   190
The River-dragon tam'd at length submits
To let his sojourners depart, and oft
Humbles his stubborn heart, but still as Ice
More hardend after thaw, till in his rage
Persuing whom he late dismissd, the Sea   195
Swallows him with his Host, but them lets pass
As on drie land between two crystal walls,
Awd by the rod of *Moses* so to stand
Divided, till his rescu'd gain thir shore:
Such wondrous power God to his Saint will lend,   200
Though present in his Angel, who shall go
Before them in a Cloud, and Pillar of Fire,
By day a Cloud, by night a Pillar of Fire,
To guide them in thir journey, and remove
Behinde them, while th' obdurat King persues: 205
All night he will persue, but his approach
Darkness defends between till morning Watch;
Then through the Fiery Pillar and the Cloud
God looking forth will trouble all his Host
And craze thir Chariot wheels: when by command   210
Moses once more his potent Rod extends
Over the Sea; the Sea his Rod obeys;
On thir imbatteld ranks the Waves return,
And overwhelm thir Warr: the Race elect
Safe towards *Canaan* from the shore advance   215
Through the wilde Desert, not the readiest way,
Lest entring on the *Canaanite* alarmd
Warr terrifie them inexpert, and feare
Return them back to *Egypt*, choosing rather
Inglorious life with servitude; for life   220
To noble and ignoble is more sweet
Untraind in Arms, where rashness leads not on.
This also shall they gain by thir delay

191 The *Ed. 2*] This *Ed. 1*

In the wide Wilderness, there they shall found
Thir goverment, and thir great Senat choose   225
Through the twelve Tribes, to rule by Laws ordaind:
God from the Mount of *Sinai*, whose gray top
Shall tremble, he descending, will himself
In Thunder, Lightning and loud Trumpets sound
Ordain them Laws; part such as appertain   230
To civil Justice, part religious Rites
Of sacrifice, informing them, by types
And shaddows, of that destind Seed to bruise
The Serpent, by what means he shall achieve
Mankinds deliverance.   But the voice of God   235
To mortal eare is dreadful; they beseech
That *Moses* might report to them his will,
And terror cease; he grants what they besought,
Instructed that to God is no access
Without Mediator, whose high Office now   240
Moses in figure bears, to introduce
One greater of whose day he shall foretell,
And all the Prophets in thir Age the times
Of great *Messiah* shall sing.   Thus Laws and Rites
Establisht, such delight hath God in Men   245
Obedient to his will, that he voutsafes
Among them to set up his Tabernacle,
The holy One with mortal Men to dwell:
By his prescript a Sanctuary is fram'd
Of Cedar, overlaid with Gold, therein   250
An Ark, and in the Ark his Testimony,
The Records of his Cov'nant, over these
A Mercie-seat of Gold between the wings
Of two bright Cherubim; before him burn
Sev'n Lamps as in a Zodiac representing   255
The Heav'nly fires; over the Tent a Cloud
Shall rest by Day, a fiery gleam by Night,
Save when they journie, and at length they come,
Conducted by his Angel to the Land
Promis'd to *Abraham* and his Seed: the rest   260
Were long to tell, how many Battels fought,
How many Kings destroyd, and Kingdoms won,
Or how the Sun shall in mid Heav'n stand still
A day entire, and Nights due course adjourn,
Mans voice commanding, Sun in *Gibeon* stand,   265
And thou Moon in the vale of *Aialon*,
Till *Israel* overcome; so call the third
From *Abraham*, Son of *Isaac*, and from him
His whole descent, who thus shall *Canaan* win.
   Here *Adam* interpos'd.   O sent from Heav'n,   270

238 what they besought *Ed. 2*] them their desire *Ed. 1*

Enlightner of my darkness, gracious things
Thou hast reveal'd, those chiefly which concerne
Just *Abraham* and his Seed: now first I find
Mine eyes true op'ning, and my heart much eas'd,
Erewhile perplext with thoughts what would become   275
Of mee and all Mankind; but now I see
His day, in whom all Nations shall be blest,
Favour unmerited by me, who sought
Forbidden knowledge by forbidden means.
This yet I apprehend not, why to those   280
Among whom God will deigne to dwell on Earth
So many and so various Laws are giv'n;
So many Laws argue so many sins
Among them; how can God with such reside?
  To whom thus *Michael*. Doubt not but that sin   285
Will reign among them, as of thee begot;
And therefore was Law given them to evince
Thir natural pravitie, by stirring up
Sinn against Law to fight; that when they see
Law can discover sin, but not remove,   290
Save by those shaddowie expiations weak,
The blood of Bulls and Goats, they may conclude
Some blood more precious must be paid for Man,
Just for unjust, that in such righteousness
To them by Faith imputed, they may finde   295
Justification towards God, and peace
Of Conscience, which the Law by Ceremonies
Cannot appease, nor Man the moral part
Perform, and not performing cannot live.
So Law appears imperfet, and but giv'n   300
With purpose to resign them in full time
Up to a better Cov'nant, disciplind
From shaddowie Types to Truth, from Flesh to Spirit,
From imposition of strict Laws, to free
Acceptance of large Grace, from servil fear   305
To filial, works of Law to works of Faith.
And therefore shall not *Moses*, though of God
Highly belov'd, being but the Minister
Of Law, his people into *Canaan* lead;
But *Joshua* whom the Gentiles *Jesus* call,   310
His Name and Office bearing, who shall quell
The adversarie Serpent, and bring back
Through the Worlds wilderness long wanderd Man
Safe to eternal Paradise of rest.
Meanwhile they in thir earthly *Canaan* plac't   315
Long time shall dwell and prosper, but when sinns
National interrupt thir public peace,
Provoking God to raise them enemies:
From whom as oft he saves them penitent

By Judges first, then under Kings; of whom   320
The second, both for pietie renownd
And puissant deeds, a promise shall receive
Irrevocable, that his Regal Throne
For ever shall endure; the like shall sing
All Prophecie, That of the Royal Stock   325
Of *David* (so I name this King) shall rise
A Son, the Womans Seed to thee foretold,
Foretold to *Abraham*, as in whom shall trust
All Nations, and to Kings foretold, of Kings
The last, for of his Reign shall be no end.   330
But first a long succession must ensue,
And his next Son for Wealth and Wisdom fam'd,
The clouded Ark of God till then in Tents
Wandring, shall in a glorious Temple enshrine.
Such follow him, as shall be registerd   335
Part good, part bad, of bad the longer scrowl,
Whose foul Idolatries, and other faults
Heap't to the popular sum, will so incense
God, as to leave them, and expose thir Land,
Thir Citie, his Temple, and his holy Ark   340
With all his sacred things, a scorn and prey
To that proud Citie, whose high Walls thou sawst
Left in confusion, *Babylon* thence calld.
There in captivitie he lets them dwell
The space of sev'ntie years, then brings them back,   345
Remembring mercie, and his Cov'nant sworn
To *David*, stablisht as the days of Heav'n.
Returnd from *Babylon* by leave of Kings
Thir Lords, whom God dispos'd, the house of God
They first re-edifie, and for a while   350
In mean estate live moderate, till grown
In wealth and multitude, factious they grow;
But first among the Priests dissension springs,
Men who attend the Altar, and should most
Endevor Peace; thir strife pollution brings   355
Upon the Temple it self: at last they seize
The Scepter, and regard not *Davids* Sons,
Then lose it to a stranger, that the true
Anointed King *Messiah* might be born
Barrd of his right; yet at his Birth a Starr   360
Unseen before in Heav'n proclaims him come
And guides the Eastern Sages, who enquire
His place, to offer Incense, Myrrh and Gold;
His place of birth a solemn Angel tells
To simple Shepherds, keeping watch by night;   365
They gladly thither haste, and by a Quire
Of squadrond Angels hear his Carol sung.
A Virgin is his Mother, but his Sire

The Power of the most High; he shall ascend
The Throne hereditarie, and bound his Reign   370
With earths wide bounds, his glory with the Heav'ns.
   He ceas'd, discerning *Adam* with such joy
Surcharg'd, as had like grief bin dewd in tears,
Without the vent of words, which these he breath'd.
   O Prophet of glad tidings, finisher   375
Of utmost hope! now clear I understand
What oft my steddiest thoughts have searcht in vain,
Why our great expectation should be calld
The seed of Woman: Virgin Mother, Hail,
High in the love of Heav'n, yet from my Loins   380
Thou shalt proceed, and from thy Womb the Son
Of God most High; So God with man unites.
Needs must the Serpent now his capital bruise
Expect with mortal pain: say where and when
Thir fight, what stroke shall bruise the Victors heel.   385
   To whom thus *Michael*. Dream not of thir fight
As of a Duel, or the local wounds
Of head or heel: not therefore joins the Son
Manhood to God-head, with more strength to foil
Thy enemie; nor so is overcome   390
Satan, whose fall from Heav'n, a deadlier bruise,
Disabl'd not to give thee thy deaths wound:
Which hee, who comes thy Saviour, shall recure,
Not by destroying *Satan*, but his works
In thee and in thy Seed: nor can this be,   395
But by fulfilling that which thou didst want,
Obedience to the Law of God, impos'd
On penaltie of death, and suffering death,
The penaltie to thy transgression due,
And due to theirs which out of thine will grow: 400
So onely can high Justice rest appaid.
The Law of God exact he shall fulfill
Both by obedience and by love, though love
Alone fulfill the Law; thy punishment
He shall endure by coming in the Flesh   405
To a reproachful life and cursed death,
Proclaiming Life to all who shall believe
In his redemption, and that his obedience
Imputed becomes theirs by Faith, his merits
To save them, not thir own, though legal works.   410
For this he shall live hated, be blasphem'd,
Seiz'd on by force, judg'd, and to death condemnd,
A shameful and accurst, naild to the Cross
By his own Nation, slaine for bringing Life;
But to the Cross he nailes thy Enemies,   415
The Law that is against thee, and the sins
Of all mankind, with him there crucifi'd,

Never to hurt them more who rightly trust
In this his satisfaction; so he dies,
But soon revives, Death over him no power   420
Shall long usurp; ere the third dawning light
Return, the Starrs of Morn shall see him rise
Out of his grave, fresh as the dawning light,
Thy ransom paid, which Man from death redeems,
His death for Man, as many as offerd Life   425
Neglect not, and the benefit imbrace
By Faith not void of works: this God-like act
Annuls thy doom, the death thou shouldst have·di'd,
In sin for ever lost from life; this act
Shall bruise the head of *Satan*, crush his strength   430
Defeating Sin and Death, his two maine arms,
And fix farr deeper in his head thir stings
Than temporal death shall bruise the Victors heel,
Or theirs whom he redeems, a death like sleep,
A gentle wafting to immortal Life.   435
Nor after resurrection shall he staye
Longer on Earth than certain times to appear
To his Disciples, Men who in his Life
Still followd him; to them shall leave in charge
To teach all nations what of him they learnd   440
And his Salvation, them who shall believe
Baptizing in the profluent stream, the sign
Of washing them from guilt of sin to Life
Pure, and in mind prepar'd, if so befall,
For death, like that which the redeemer di'd.   445
All Nations they shall teach; for from that day
Not onely to the Sons of *Abrahams* Loins
Salvation shall be Preach't, but to the Sons
Of *Abrahams* Faith wherever through the world;
So in his seed all Nations shall be blest.   450
Then to the Heav'n of Heav'ns he shall ascend
With victory, triumphing through the aire
Over his foes and thine; there shall surprise
The Serpent, Prince of Air, and drag in Chains
Through all his realm, and there confounded leave;   455
Then enter into glory, and resume
His Seat at Gods right hand, exalted high
Above all names in Heav'n; and thence shall come,
When this Worlds dissolution shall be ripe,
With glory and power to judge both quick and dead,   460
To judge th' unfaithful dead, but to reward
His faithful, and receive them into bliss,
Whether in Heav'n or Earth, for then the Earth
Shall all be Paradise, far happier place
Than this of *Eden*, and far happier days.   465
    So spake th' Archangel *Michaël*, then paus'd,

As at the Worlds great period; and our Sire
Replete with joy and wonder thus repli'd.
　　O goodness infinite, goodness immense!
That all this good of evil shall produce,　　　　470
And evil turn to good; more wonderful
Than that which by creation first brought forth
Light out of darkness! full of doubt I stand,
Whether I should repent me now of sin
By mee done and occasiond, or rejoice　　　　475
Much more, that much more good thereof shall spring,
To God more glory, more good will to Men
From God, and over wrauth grace shall abound.
But say, if our deliverer up to Heav'n
Must reascend, what will betide the few　　　　480
His faithful, left among th' unfaithful herd,
The enemies of truth; who then shall guide
His people, who defend? will they not deale
Worse with his followers than with him they dealt?
　　Be sure they will, said th' Angel; but from Heav'n　　485
Hee to his own a Comforter will send,
The promise of the Father, who shall dwell
His Spirit within them, and the Law of Faith
Working through love, upon thir hearts shall write,
To guide them in all truth, and also arme　　　　490
With spiritual Armour, able to resist
Satans assaults, and quench his fierie darts,
What Man can doe against them, not afraid,
Though to the death, against such cruelties
With inward consolations recompenst,　　　　495
And oft supported so as shall amaze
Thir proudest persecuters: for the Spirit
Pourd first on his Apostles, whom he sends
To evangelize the Nations, then on all
Baptiz'd, shall them with wondrous gifts endue　　　500
To speak all Tongues, and do all Miracles,
As did thir Lord before them.　Thus they win
Great numbers of each Nation to receive
With joy the tidings brought from Heav'n: at length
Thir Ministry performd, and race well run,　　　505
Thir doctrine and thir story written left,
Thy die; but in thir room, as they forewarn,
Wolves shall succeed for teachers, grievous Wolves,
Who all the sacred mysteries of Heav'n
To thir own vile advantages shall turne　　　　510
Of lucre and ambition, and the truth
With superstitions and traditions taint,
Left onely in those written Records pure,
Though not but by the Spirit understood.
Then shall they seek to avail themselves of names,　　515

Places and titles, and with these to joine
Secular power, though feigning still to act
By spiritual, to themselves appropriating
The Spirit of God, promis'd alike and giv'n
To all Believers; and from that pretence,   520
Spiritual Lawes by carnal power shall force
On every conscience; Laws which none shall finde
Left them inrould, or what the Spirit within
Shall on the heart engrave.   What will they then
But force the Spirit of Grace it self, and bind   525
His consort Libertie; what, but unbuild
His living Temples, built by Faith to stand,
Thir own Faith not anothers: for on Earth
Who against Faith and Conscience can be heard
Infallible? yet many will presume: 530
Whence heavie persecution shall arise
On all who in the worship persevere
Of Spirit and Truth; the rest, farr greater part,
Will deem in outward Rites and specious formes
Religion satisfi'd; Truth shall retire   535
Bestuck with slandrous darts, and works of Faith
Rarely be found: so shall the World goe on,
To good malignant, to bad men benign,
Under her own weight groaning, till the day
Appear of respiration to the just,   540
And vengeance to the wicked, at return
Of him so lately promis'd to thy aid,
The Womans seed, obscurely then foretold,
Now amplier known thy Saviour and thy Lord,
Last in the Clouds from Heav'n to be reveal'd   545
In glory of the Father, to dissolve
Satan with his perverted World, then raise
From the conflagrant mass, purg'd and refin'd,
New Heav'ns, new Earth, Ages of endless date
Founded in righteousness and peace and love,   550
To bring forth fruits, Joy and eternal Bliss.
    He ended; and thus *Adam* last repli'd.
How soon hath thy prediction, Seer blest,
Measur'd this transient World, the Race of time,
Till time stand fixt: beyond is all abyss,   555
Eternitie, whose end no eye can reach.
Greatly instructed I shall hence depart,
Greatly in peace of thought, and have my fill
Of knowledge, what this vessel can contain;
Beyond which was my folly to aspire.   560
Henceforth I learn, that to obey is best,
And love with feare the onely God, to walk
As in his presence, ever to observe
His providence, and on him sole depend,

Merciful over all his works, with good   565
Still overcoming evil, and by small
Accomplishing great things, by things deemd weak
Subverting worldly strong, and worldly wise
By simple meek; that suffering for Truths sake
Is fortitude to highest victorie,   570
And to the faithful Death the Gate of Life;
Taught this by his example whom I now
Acknowledge my Redeemer ever blest.
    To whom thus also th' Angel last repl'd:
This having learnt, thou hast attaind the summ   575
Of wisdom; hope no higher, though all the Starrs
Thou knewst by name, and all th' ethereal Powers,
All secrets of the Deep, all Natures works,
Or works of God in Heav'n, Air, Earth or Sea,
And all the riches of this World enjoydst,   580
And all the rule, one Empire; only add
Deeds to thy knowledge answerable, add Faith,
Add Vertue, Patience, Temperance, add Love,
By name to come calld Charitie, the soul
Of all the rest: then wilt thou not be loath   585
To leave this Paradise, but shalt possess
A paradise within thee, happier farr.
Let us descend now therefore from this top
Of Speculation; for the hour precise
Exacts our parting hence; and see, the Guards,   590
By mee encampt on yonder Hill, expect
Thir motion, at whose Front a flaming Sword,
In signal of remove, waves fiercely round;
We may no longer stay: go waken *Eve*;
Her also I with gentle Dreams have calmd   595
Portending good, and all her spirits compos'd
To meek submission: thou at season fit
Let her with thee partake what thou hast heard,
Chiefly what may concern her Faith to know,
The great deliverance by her Seed to come   600
(For by the Womans Seed) on all Mankind.
That ye may live, which will be many days,
Both in one Faith unanimous though sad,
With cause for evils past, yet much more cheerd
With meditation on the happie end.   605
    He ended, and they both descend the Hill;
Descended, *Adam* to the Bowre where *Eve*
Lay sleeping ran before, but found her wak't;
And thus with words not sad she him receiv'd.
    Whence thou returnst, and whither wentst, I know; 610
For God is also in sleep, and Dreams advise,
Which he hath sent propitious, som great good
Presaging, since with sorrow and hearts distress

Wearied I fell asleep: but now lead on;
In mee is no delay; with thee to goe   615
Is to stay here; without thee here to staye
Is to go hence unwilling; thou to mee
Art all things under Heav'n, all places thou,
Who for my wilful crime art banisht hence.
This further consolation yet secure   620
I carry hence; though all by mee is lost,
Such favour I unworthie am voutsaf't,
By mee the Promis'd Seed shall all restore.
    So spake our Mother *Eve*, and *Adam* heard
Well pleas'd, but answerd not; for now too nigh   625
Th' Archangel stood, and from the other Hill
To thir fixt Station, all in bright array
The Cherubim descended; on the ground
Gliding meteorous, as Ev'ning Mist
Ris'n from a River o'er the marish glides,   630
And gathers ground fast at the Labourers heel
Homeward returning.   High in Front advanc't,
The brandisht Sword of God before them blaz'd
Fierce as a Comet; which with torrid heat,
And vapour as the *Libyan* Air adust,   635
Began to parch that temperat Clime; whereat
In either hand the hastning Angel caught
Our lingring Parents, and to th' Eastern Gate
Led them direct, and down the Cliff as fast
To the subjected Plain; then disappear'd.   640
They looking back, all th' Eastern side beheld
Of Paradise, so late thir happie seat,
Wav'd over by that flaming Brand, the Gate
With dreadful Faces throngd and fierie Arms:
Som natural tears they dropd, but wip'd them soon;   645
The World was all before them, where to choose
Thir place of rest, and Providence thir guide:
They hand in hand with wandring steps and slow,
Through *Eden* took their solitarie way.

The End

[Places where this text differs from Ed. 2 in emphatic and unemphatic
forms of the pronouns:

hee *for* he: i. 51, 93, 143, 567 (hee *MS. at all four*); iii, 143, 209; iv. 497, 902;
    v. 11, 659; vi. 746; x. 441, 493.
he *for* hee: ii. 1022; iii. 408; v. 224.
mee *for* me: i. 102 (mee *MS.*); iii. 174, x. 822, 927, 929.
Shee *for* She: iv. 603.
wee *for* we: ii. 414 (*errata, Ed. 1*).   we *for* wee: vii. 95.
thir *for* their: x. 440.]

PARADISE REGAIN'D

PARADISE REGAIN'D.

A POEM.

In IV *BOOKS*.

To which is added

SAMSON AGONISTES.

The Author
JOHN MILTON.

LONDON,

Printed by *J. M* for *John Starkey* at the
Mitre in *Fleetstreet*, near *Temple-Bar.*
MDCLXXI.

PARADISE REGAIN'D

BOOK I

I who erewhile the happy Garden sung,
By one mans disobedience lost, now sing
Recoverd Paradise to all mankind,
By one mans firm obedience fully tri'd
Through all temptation, and the Tempter foild   5
In all his wiles, defeated and repulst,
And *Eden* rais'd in the waste Wilderness.
   Thou Spirit who ledst this glorious Eremite
Into the Desert, his Victorious Field
Against the Spiritual Foe, and broughtst him thence   10
By proof th'undoubted Son of God, inspire,
As thou art wont, my prompted Song else mute,
And bear through highth or depth of natures bounds
With prosperous wing full summd to tell of deeds
Above Heroic, though in secret don,   15
And unrecorded left through many an Age,
Worthy t' have not remaind so long unsung.
   Now had the great Proclaimer with a voice
More awful than the sound of Trumpet, cri'd
Repentance, and Heavens Kingdom nigh at hand   20
To all Baptiz'd: to his great Baptism flockd
With awe the Regions round, and with them came
From *Nazareth* the Son of *Joseph* deemd
To the flood *Jordan*, came as then obscure,
Unmarkt, unknown; but him the Baptist soon   25
Descri'd, divinely warnd, and witness bore
As to his worthier, and would have resign'd
To him his Heav'nly Office, nor was long
His witness unconfirmd: on him baptiz'd
Heav'n opend, and in likeness of a Dove   30
The Spirit descended, while the Fathers voice
From Heav'n pronounc'd him his beloved Son.
That heard the Adversary, who roving still
About the world, at that assembly fam'd
Would not be last, and with the voice divine   35
Nigh Thunder-struck, th' exalted man, to whom
Such high attest was giv'n, a while surveyd

With wonder, then with envy fraught and rage
Flies to his place: nor rests, but in mid air
To Councel summons all his mighty Peers,   40
Within thick Clouds and dark tenfold involv'd,
A gloomy Consistory; and them amidst
With looks agast and sad he thus bespake.
　　O ancient Powers of Air and this wide World,
For much more willingly I mention Air,   45
This our old Conquest, than remember Hell
Our hated habitation; well ye know
How many Ages, as the years of men,
This Universe we have possest, and rul'd
In manner at our will th' affairs of Earth,   50
Since *Adam* and his facil consort *Eve*
Lost Paradise deceiv'd by me, though since
With dread attending when that fatal wound
Shall be inflicted by the Seed of *Eve*
Upon my head: long the decrees of Heav'n   55
Delay, for longest time to him is short;
And now too soon for us the circling hours
This dreaded time have compast, wherein we
Must bide the stroke of that long threatend wound,
At least if so we can, and by the head   60
Broken be not intended all our power
To be infring'd, our freedom and our being
In this fair Empire won of Earth and Air:
For this ill news I bring, the Womans seed
Destind to this, is late of woman born;   65
His birth to our just fear gave no small cause,
But his growth now to youths full flowr, displaying
All vertue, grace and wisdom to achieve
Things highest, greatest, multiplies my fear.
Before him a great Prophet, to proclaim   70
His coming, is sent Harbinger, who all
Invites, and in the Consecrated stream
Pretends to wash off sin, and fit them so
Purifi'd to receive him pure, or rather
To do him honour as thir King; all come,   75
And he himself among them was baptiz'd,
Not thence to be more pure, but to receive
The testimony of Heaven, that who he is
Thenceforth the Nations may not doubt; I saw
The Prophet do him reverence; on him rising   80
Out of the water, Heav'n above the Clouds
Unfold her Crystal Dores, thence on his head
A perfet Dove descend, what e're it meant,
And out of Heav'n the Sovran voice I heard,
This is my Son belov'd, in him am pleas'd.   85
His Mother then is mortal, but his Sire

Hee who obtains the Monarchy of Heav'n,
And what will he not doe t' advance his Son?
His first-begot we know, and sore have felt,
When his fierce thunder drove us to the Deep;   90
Who this is we must learn, for man he seems
In all his lineaments, though in his face
The glimpses of his Fathers glory shine.
Ye see our danger on the utmost edge
Of hazard, which admits no long debate,   95
But must with somthing sudden be oppos'd,
Not force, but well coucht fraud, well woven snares,
Ere in the head of Nations he appear
Thir King, thir Leader, and Supream on Earth.
I, when no other durst, sole undertook   100
The dismal expedition to find out
And ruin *Adam*, and th'exploit performd
Successfully; a calmer voyage now
Will waft me; and the way found prosperous once
Induces best to hope of like success.   105
     He ended, and his words impression left
Of much amazement to th' infernal Crew,
Distracted and surpriz'd with deep dismay
At these sad tidings; but no time was then
For long indulgence to thir fears or grief: 110
Unanimous they all commit the care
And management of this main enterprize
To him thir great Dictator, whose attempt
At first against mankind so well had thriv'd
In *Adams* overthrow, and led thir march   115
From Hells deep-vaulted Den to dwell in light,
Regents and Potentates, and Kings, yea gods
Of many a pleasant Realm and Province wide.
So to the Coast of *Jordan* he directs
His easie steps, girded with snaky wiles,   120
Where he might likeliest find this new-declar'd,
This Man of men, attested Son of God,
Temptation and all guile on him to try;
So to subvert whom he suspected rais'd
To end his Reign on Earth so long enjoyd: 125
But contrary unweeting he fulfilld
The purpos'd Counsel pre-ordaind and fixt
Of the most High, who in full frequence bright
Of Angels, thus to *Gabriel* smiling spake.
     Gabriel this day by proof thou shalt behold,   130
Thou and all Angels conversant on Earth
With man or mens affairs, how I begin
To verifie that solemn message late,

On which I sent thee to the Virgin pure
In *Galilee*, that she should bear a Son   135
Great in Renown, and calld the Son of God;
Then toldst her doubting how these things could be
To her a Virgin, that on her should come
The Holy Ghost, and the power of the Highest
O'er-shadow her: this man born and now up-grown,   140
To shew him worthy of his birth divine
And high prediction, henceforth I expose
To Satan; let him tempt and now assay
His utmost suttlety, because he boasts
And vaunts of his great cunning to the throng   145
Of his Apostasie; he might have learnt
Less over-weening, since he faild in *Job*,
Whose constant perseverance overcame
Whate're his cruel malice could invent.
He now shall know I can produce a man   150
Of femal Seed, far abler to resist
All his solicitations, and at length
All his vast force, and drive him back to Hell,
Winning by Conquest what the first man lost
By fallacy surpriz'd.   But first I mean   155
To exercise him in the Wilderness,
There he shall first lay down the rudiments
Of his great warfare, ere I send him forth
To conquer Sin and Death, the two grand foes,
By Humiliation and strong Sufferance: 160
His weakness shall o'ercome Satanic strength
And all the world, and mass of sinful flesh;
That all the Angels and Ethereal Powers,
They now, and men hereafter may discern,
From what consummat vertue I have chose,   165
This perfet Man, by merit calld my Son,
To earn Salvation for the Sons of men.
    So spake th' Eternal Father, and all Heaven
Admiring stood a space, then into Hymns
Burst forth, and in Celestial measures mov'd,   170
Circling the Throne and Singing, while the hand
Sung with the voice, and this the argument.
    Victory and Triumph to the Son of God
Now entring his great duel, not of arms,
But to vanquish by wisdom hellish wiles.   175
The Father knows the Son; therefore secure
Ventures his filial Vertue, though untri'd,
Against whate're may tempt, whate're seduce,
Allure or terrifie or undermine.
Be frustrate all ye stratagems of Hell,   180
And devilish machinations come to naught.
    So they in Heav'n thir Odes and Vigils tun'd:

Mean while the Son of God, who yet som days
Lodg'd in *Bethabara* where *John* baptiz'd,
Musing and much revolving in his brest,   185
How best the mighty work he might begin
Of Saviour to mankind, and which way first
Publish his God-like office now mature,
One day forth walkd alone, the Spirit leading
And his deep thoughts, the better to converse   190
With solitude, till far from track of men,
Thought following thought, and step by step led on,
He enterd now the bordering Desert wild,
And with dark shades and rocks environd round,
His holy Meditations thus persu'd.   195
   O what a multitude of thoughts at once
Awakend in me swarm, while I consider
What from within I feel my self, and hear
What from without comes often to my ears,
Ill sorting with my present state compar'd.   200
When I was yet a child, no childish play
To me was pleasing, all my mind was set
Serious to learn and know, and thence to do
What might be public good; my self I thought
Born to that end, born to promote all truth,   205
All righteous things: therefore above my years,
The Law of God I read, and found it sweet,
Made it my whole delight, and in it grew
To such perfection, that ere yet my age
Had measurd twice six years, at our great Feast   210
I went into the Temple, there to hear
The Teachers of our Law, and to propose
What might improve my knowledge or thir own;
And was admir'd by all: yet this not all
To which my Spirit aspir'd, victorious deeds   215
Flam'd in my heart, heroic acts, one while
To rescue *Israel* from the *Roman* yoke,
Thence to subdue and quell ore all the earth
Brute violence and proud Tyrannic power,
Till truth were freed, and equity restor'd: 220
Yet held it more humane, more heav'nly first
By winning words to conquer willing hearts,
And make persuasion do the work of fear;
At least to try, and teach the erring Soul
Not wilfully misdoing, but unware   225
Misled: the stubborn only to subdue.
These growing thoughts my Mother soon perceiving
By words at times cast forth, inly rejoic'd,
And said to me apart, High are thy thoughts

189 leading] leading; *1671*

O Son, but nourish them and let them soar   230
To what highth sacred vertue and true worth
Can raise them, though above example high;
By matchless Deeds express thy matchless Sire.
For know, thou art no Son of mortal man;
Though men esteem thee low of Parentage,   235
Thy Father is th' Eternal King, who rules
All Heav'n and Earth, Angels and Sons of men;
A messenger from God foretold thy birth
Conceiv'd in me a Virgin, he foretold
Thou shouldst be great and sit on *Davids* Throne,   240
And of thy Kingdom there should be no end.
At thy Nativity a glorious Quire
Of Angels in the fields of *Bethlehem* sung
To Shepherds watching at thir folds by night,
And told them the Messiah now was born,   245
Where they might see him; and to thee they came,
Directed to the Manger where thou layst,
For in the Inn was left no better room:
A Star not seen before, in Heav'n appearing
Guided the Wise Men thither from the East,   250
To honour thee with Incense, Myrrh, and Gold,
By whose bright course led on they found the place,
Affirming it thy Star new grav'n in Heaven,
By which they knew thee King of *Israel* born.
Just *Simeon* and Prophetic *Anna*, warnd   255
By Vision, found thee in the Temple, and spake
Before the Altar and the vested Priest
Like things of thee to all that present stood.
This having heard, straight I again revolv'd
The Law and Prophets, searching what was writ   260
Concerning the Messiah, to our Scribes
Known partly, and soon found of whom they spake
I am; this chiefly, that my way must lie
Through many a hard assay ev'n to the death,
Ere I the promis'd Kingdom can attain,   265
Or work Redemption for mankind, whose sins
Full weight must be transferrd upon my head.
Yet neither thus disheartend or dismayd,
The time prefixt I waited, when behold
The Baptist (of whose birth I oft had heard,   270
Not knew by sight) now come, who was to come
Before Messiah and his way prepare.
I as all others to his Baptism came,
Which I believ'd was from above; but hee
Straight knew me, and with loudest voice proclaimd   275
Mee him (for it was shewn him so from Heaven)

276 Mee] Me *1671*

Mee him whose Harbinger he was; and first
Refus'd on me his Baptism to conferr,
As much his greater, and was hardly won;
But as I rose out of the laving stream   280
Heav'n opend her eternal doors, from whence
The Spirit descended on me like a Dove;
And last the sum of all, my Fathers voice,
Audibly heard from Heav'n, pronounc'd me his,
Mee his beloved Son, in whom alone   285
He was well pleas'd; by which I knew the time
Now full, that I no more should live obscure,
But openly begin, as best becomes
Th'Autority which I deriv'd from Heaven.
And now by som strong motion I am led   290
Into this wilderness, to what intent
I learn not yet, perhaps I need not know;
For what concerns my knowledge God reveals.
    So spake our Morning Star then in his rise,
And looking round on every side beheld   295
A pathless Desert, dusk with horrid shades;
The way he came not having markt, return
Was difficult, by human steps untrod;
And he still on was led, but with such thoughts
Accompanied of things past and to come   300
Lodg'd in his brest, as well might recommend
Such Solitude before choicest Society.
Full forty days he passd, whether on hill
Somtimes, anon in shady vale, each night
Under the covert of som ancient Oak   305
Or Cedar, to defend him from the dew,
Or harbourd in som Cave, is not reveal'd;
Nor tasted human food, nor hunger felt
Till those days ended, hungerd then at last
Among wild Beasts: they at his sight grew mild,   310
Nor sleeping him nor waking harmd, his walk
The fiery Serpent fled, and noxious Worm,
The Lion and fierce Tiger glar'd aloof.
But now an aged man in rural weeds,
Following, as seemd, the quest of some stray Ewe,   315
Or witherd sticks to gather, which might serve
Against a Winters day when winds blow keen
To warm him wet returnd from field at Eve,
He saw approach; who first with curious eye
Perus'd him, then with words thus utterd spake.   320
    Sir what ill chance hath brought thee to this place
So far from path or road of men, who pass
In Troop or Caravan? for single none

277 Mee] Me *1671*   285 Mee] Me *1671*   307 som] one *1671*

Durst ever, who returnd, and dropd not here
His Carcass, pin'd with hunger and with drouth.   325
I ask the rather, and the more admire,
For that to mee thou seemst the man, whom late
Our new baptizing Prophet at the Ford
Of *Jordan* honourd so, and calld thee Son
Of God; I saw and heard, for we somtimes   330
Who dwell this Wild, constraind by want, come forth
To Town or Village nigh (nighest is far)
Where aught we hear, and curious are to hear,
What happens new; Fame also finds us out.
   To whom the Son of God.   Who brought me hither
Will bring me hence, no other Guide I seek.   336
   By Miracle he may, repli'd the Swain,
What other way I see not, for we here
Live on tough roots and stubs, to thirst inur'd
More than the Camel, and to drink go far,   340
Men to much misery and hardship born:
But if thou be the Son of God, Command
That out of these hard stones be made thee bread;
So shalt thou save thy self and us relieve
With Food, whereof we wretched seldom taste.   345
   He ended, and the Son of God repli'd.
Thinkst thou such force in Bread? is it not written
(For I discern thee other than thou seemst)
Man lives not by Bread onely, but each Word
Proceeding from the mouth of God? who fed   350
Our Fathers here with Manna; in the Mount
Moses was forty days, nor eat nor drank,
And forty days *Elijah* without food
Wanderd this barren waste, the same I now:
Why dost thou then suggest to me distrust,   355
Knowing who I am, as I know who thou art?
   Whom thus answerd th' Arch Fiend now undisguis'd.
'Tis true, I am that Spirit unfortunate,
Who leagu'd with millions more in rash revolt
Kept not my happy Station, but was driv'n   360
With them from bliss to the bottomless Deep;
Yet to that hideous place not so confin'd
By rigor unconniving, but that oft
Leaving my dolorous Prison I enjoy
Large liberty to round this Globe of Earth,   365
Or range in th' Air; nor from the Heav'n of Heav'ns
Hath he excluded my resort somtimes.
I came among the Sons of God, when he
Gave up into my hands *Uzzean Job*

327 mee] me *1671*
353 Elijah] Eliah *1671 and at ii. 19, but* Elijah *at ii. 268, 277*

To prove him and illustrate his high worth; 370
And when to all his Angels he propos'd
To draw the proud King *Ahab* into fraud
That he might fall in *Ramoth*, they demurring,
I undertook that office, and the tongues
Of all his flattering Prophets glibbd with lies 375
To his destruction, as I had in charge;
For what he bids I do. Though I have lost
Much lustre of my native brightness, lost
To be belov'd of God, I have not lost
To love, at least contemplate and admire 380
What I see excellent in good or fair
Or vertuous; I should so have lost all sense.
What can be then less in me than desire
To see thee and approach thee, whom I know
Declar'd the Son of God, to hear attent 385
Thy wisdom, and behold thy God-like deeds?
Men generally think me much a foe
To all mankind: why should I? they to mee
Never did wrong or violence, by them
I lost not what I lost, rather by them 390
I gaind what I have gaind, and with them dwell
Copartner in these Regions of the World,
If not disposer; lend them oft my aid,
Oft my advice by presages and signs,
And answers, oracles, portents and dreams, 395
Whereby they may direct their future life.
Envy they say excites me, thus to gain
Companions of my misery and woe.
At first it may be; but long since with woe
Nearer acquainted, now I feel by proof, 400
That fellowship in pain divides not smart,
Nor lightens aught each mans peculiar load.
Small consolation then, were Man adjoind:
This wounds me most (what can it less) that Man,
Man fall'n shall be restor'd, I never more. 405
  To whom our Saviour sternly thus repli'd.
Deservedly thou griev'st, compos'd of lies
From the beginning, and in lies wilt end;
Who boastst release from Hell, and leave to come
Into the Heav'n of Heavens; thou comst indeed, 410
As a poor miserable captive thrall
Comes to the place where he before had sat
Among the Prime in Splendor, now depos'd,
Ejected, emptied, gaz'd, unpittied, shunnd,
A spectacle of ruin or of scorn 415
To all the Host of Heaven; the happy place
Imparts to thee no happiness, no joy,
Rather inflames thy torment, representing

Lost bliss, to thee no more communicable,
So never more in Hell than when in Heaven.   420
But thou art serviceable to Heavens King.
Wilt thou impute to obedience what thy fear
Extorts, or pleasure to do ill excites?
What but thy malice mov'd thee to misdeem
Of righteous *Job*, then cruelly to afflict him   425
With all inflictions? but his patience won.
The other service was thy chosen task,
To be a liar in four hunderd mouths;
For lying is thy sustenance, thy food.
Yet thou pretendst to truth; all Oracles   430
By thee are giv'n, and what confest more true
Among the Nations? that hath been thy craft,
By mixing somewhat true to vent more lies.
But what have been thy answers, what but dark
Ambiguous and with double sense deluding?   435
Which they who askd have seldom understood,
And not well understood as good not known.
Who ever by consulting at thy shrine
Returnd the wiser, or the more instruct
To flie or follow what concernd him most,   440
And run not sooner to his fatal snare?
For God hath justly giv'n the Nations up
To thy Delusions; justly, since they fell
Idolatrous: but when his purpose is
Among them to declare his Providence   445
To thee not known, whence hast thou then thy truth,
But from him or his Angels President
In every Province, who themselves disdaining
To approach thy Temples, give thee in command
What to the smallest tittle thou shalt say   450
To thy Adorers? thou with trembling fear,
Or like a Fawning Parasite obeyst;
Then to thy self ascrib'st the truth foretold.
But this thy glory shall be soon retrencht;
Nor more shalt thou by oracling abuse   455
The Gentiles; henceforth Oracles are ceas't,
And thou no more with Pomp and Sacrifice
Shalt be enquir'd at *Delphos* or elsewhere;
At least in vain, for they shall find thee mute.
God hath now sent his living Oracle   460
Into the World, to teach his final Will,
And sends his Spirit of Truth henceforth to dwell
In pious Hearts, an inward Oracle
To all truth requisite for men to know.
  So spake our Saviour; but the suttle Fiend,   465
Though inly stung with anger and disdain,
Dissembl'd, and this answer smooth returnd.

Sharply thou hast insisted on rebuke,
And urg'd me hard with doings, which not will
But misery hath wrested from me: where   470
Easily canst thou find one miserable,
And not inforc't oft-times to part from truth,
If it may stand him more in stead to lie,
Say and unsay, feign, flatter, or abjure?
But thou art plac't above me, thou art Lord;   475
From thee I can and must submiss endure
Check or reproof, and glad to scape so quit.
Hard are the ways of truth, and rough to walk,
Smooth on the tongue discourst, pleasing to th' ear,
And tuneable as Silvan Pipe or Song;   480
What wonder then if I delight to hear
Her dictates from thy mouth? most men admire
Vertue, who follow not her lore: permit mee
To hear thee when I come (since no man comes)
And talk at least, though I despair to attain.   485
Thy Father, who is holy, wise and pure,
Suffers the Hypocrite or Atheous Priest
To tread his Sacred Courts, and minister
About his Altar, handling holy things,
Praying or vowing, and voutsaf'd his voice   490
To *Balaam* Reprobate, a Prophet yet
Inspir'd; disdain not such access to me.
    To whom our Saviour with unalterd brow.
Thy coming hither, though I know thy scope,
I bid not or forbid; doe as thou find'st   495
Permission from above; thou canst not more.
    He added not; and Satan bowing low
His gray dissimulation, disappear'd
Into thin Air diffus'd: for now began
Night with her sullen wing to double-shade   500
The Desert, Fowls in thir clay nests were coucht;
And now wild Beasts came forth the woods to roam.

The End of the First Book

BOOK II

Mean while the new-baptiz'd, who yet remaind
At *Jordan* with the Baptist, and had seen
Him whom they heard so late expressly calld
Jesus Messiah, Son of God declar'd,
And on that high Autority had believ'd,   5
And with him talkt, and with him lodg'd, I mean
Andrew and *Simon*, famous after known
With others though in Holy Writ not nam'd;
Now missing him thir joy so lately found,
So lately found, and so abruptly gon,   10
Began to doubt, and doubted many days,
And as the days increas'd, increas'd thir doubt:
Somtimes they thought he might be only shewn,
And for a time caught up to God, as once
Moses was in the Mount, and missing long;   15
And the great *Thisbite* who on fiery wheels
Rode up to Heaven, yet once again to come.
Therefore as those young Prophets then with care
Sought lost *Elijah*, so in each place these
Nigh to *Bethabara*; in *Jerico*   20
The City of Palms, *Ænon*, and *Salem* Old,
Machærus and each Town or City walld
On this side the broad lake *Genezaret*,
Or in *Perea*; but returnd in vain.
Then on the bank of *Jordan*, by a Creek   25
Where winds with Reeds and Osiers whisp'ring play,
Plain Fishermen, no greater men them call,
Close in a Cottage low together got,
Thir unexpected loss and plaints outbreath'd.
Alas, from what high hope to what relapse   30
Unlookt for are we fall'n! our eyes beheld
Messiah certainly now come, so long
Expected of our Fathers; we have heard
His words, his wisdom full of grace and truth,
Now, now, for sure, deliverance is at hand,   35
The Kingdom shall to *Israel* be restor'd:
Thus we rejoic'd, but soon our joy is turnd
Into perplexity and new amaze:
For whither is he gon, what accident
Hath rapt him from us? will he now retire   40
After appearance, and again prolong
Our expectation?   God of *Israël*,

Send thy Messiah forth, the time is come;
Behold the Kings of th'Earth how they oppress
Thy chosen, to what highth thir power unjust   45
They have exalted, and behind them cast
All fear of thee; arise and vindicate
Thy Glory, free thy people from thir yoke!
But let us wait; thus far he hath performd,
Sent his Anointed, and to us reveal'd him   50
By his great Prophet, pointed at and shown
In public, and with him we have convers't;
Let us be glad of this, and all our fears
Lay on his Providence; he will not fail
Nor will withdraw him now, nor will recall,   55
Mock us with his blest sight, then snatch him hence,
Soon we shall see our hope, our joy return.
      Thus they out of thir plaints new hope resume
To find whom at the first they found unsought:
But to his Mother *Mary*, when she saw   60
Others returnd from Baptism, not her Son,
Nor left at *Jordan* tidings of him none;
Within her brest though calm, her brest though pure,
Motherly cares and fears got head, and rais'd
Som troubl'd thoughts, which she in sighs thus clad.   65
      O what avails me now that honour high
To have conceiv'd of God, or that salute
Haile highly favour'd, among women blest!
While I to sorrows am no less advanc't,
And fears as eminent, above the lot   70
Of other women, by the birth I bore,
In such a season born when scarce a Shed
Could be obtaind to shelter him or me
From the bleak air; a Stable was our warmth,
A Manger his; yet soon enforc't to flye   75
Thence into *Egypt*, till the Murd'rous King
Were dead, who sought his life, and missing filld
With Infant blood the streets of *Bethlehem*;
From *Egypt* home returnd, in *Nazareth*
Hath been our dwelling many years, his life   80
Privat, unactive, calm, contemplative,
Little suspicious to any King; but now
Full grown to Man, acknowledg'd, as I hear,
By *John* the Baptist, and in public shown,
Son ownd from Heaven by his Fathers voice;   85
I lookd for som great change; to Honour? no,
But trouble, as old *Simeon* plain foretold,
That to the fall and rising he should be
Of many in *Israël*, and to a sign
Spoken against, that through my very Soul   90
A sword shall pierce; this is my favour'd lot,

My Exaltation to Afflictions high;
Afflicted I may be, it seems, and blest;
I will not argue that, nor will repine.
But where delays he now? som great intent   95
Conceals him: when twelve years he scarce had seen,
I lost him, but so found, as well I saw
He could not lose himself; but went about
His Fathers buisness; what he meant I mus'd,
Since understand; much more his absence now   100
Thus long to some great purpose he obscures.
But I to wait with patience am inur'd;
My heart hath been a store-house long of things
And sayings laid up, portending strange events.
    Thus *Mary* pondering oft, and oft to mind   105
Recalling what remarkably had past
Since first her Salutation heard, with thoughts
Meekly compos'd awaited the fulfilling:
The while her Son tracing the Desert wild,
Sole but with holiest Meditations fed,   110
Into himself descended, and at once
All his great work to come before him set;
How to begin, how to accomplish best
His end of being on Earth, and mission high:
For Satan with slye preface to return   115
Had left him vacant, and with speed was gone
Up to the middle Region of thick Air,
Where all his Potentates in Council sate;
There without sign of boast or sign of joy,
Solicitous and blank he thus began.   120
    Princes, Heav'ns ancient Sons, Ethereal Thrones,
Demonian Spirits now, from the Element
Each of his reign allotted, rightlier calld,
Powers of Fire, Air, Water, and Earth beneath,
So may we hold our place and these mild seats   125
Without new trouble; such an Enemy
Is risen to invade us, who no less
Threatens than our expulsion down to Hell;
I, as I undertook, and with the vote
Consenting in full frequence was impowrd,   130
Have found him, viewd him, tasted him, but find
Far other labour to be undergone
Than when I dealt with *Adam* first of Men,
Though *Adam* by his Wives allurement fell;
However to this Man inferior far,   135
If he be Man by Mothers side at least,
With more than human gifts from Heav'n adornd,
Perfections absolute, Graces divine,
And amplitude of mind to greatest Deeds.
Therefore I am returnd, lest confidence   140

Of my success with *Eve* in Paradise
Deceive ye to persuasion over-sure
Of like succeeding here: I summon all
Rather to be in readiness, with hand
Or counsel to assist; lest I who erst   145
Thought none my equal, now be over-matcht.
  So spake th'old Serpent doubting, and from all
With clamor was assur'd thir utmost aid
At his command: when from amidst them rose
Belial the dissolutest Spirit that fell,   150
The sensuallest, and after *Asmodai*
The fleshliest Incubus; and thus advis'd.
  Set women in his eye and in his walk,
Among daughters of men the fairest found;
Many are in each Region passing fair   155
As the noon Skie; more like to Goddesses
Than Mortal Creatures, graceful and discreet,
Expert in amorous Arts, enchanting tongues
Persuasive, Virgin majesty with mild
And sweet allayd, yet terrible to approach,   160
Skilld to retire, and in retiring draw
Hearts after them tangl'd in Amorous Nets.
Such object hath the power to soft'n and tame
Severest temper, smooth the ruggedst brow,
Enerve, and with voluptuous hope dissolve,   165
Draw out with credulous desires, and lead
At will the manliest, resolutest brest,
As the Magnetic hardest Iron draws.
Women, when nothing else, beguil'd the heart
Of wisest *Solomon*, and made him build,   170
And made him bow to the Gods of his Wives.
  To whom quick answer Satan thus returnd.
Belial, in much uneven scale thou weighst
All others by thy self; because of old
Thou thy self doatst on womankind, admiring   175
Thir shape, thir colour, and attractive grace,
None are, thou thinkst, but taken with such toys.
Before the Flood thou with thy lusty Crew,
False titl'd Sons of God, roaming the Earth
Cast wanton eyes on the daughters of men,   180
And coupl'd with them, and begot a race.
Have we not seen, or by relation heard,
In Courts and Regal Chambers how thou lurkst,
In Wood or Grove by mossie Fountain side,
In Valley or Green Meddow, to way-lay   185
Som beauty rare, *Calisto, Clymene,*
Daphne, or *Semele, Antiopa,*
Or *Amymone, Syrinx,* many more
Too long, then layst thy scapes on names ador'd,

Apollo, Neptune, Jupiter or *Pan*,   190
Satyr or *Fawn* or *Silvan*?   But these haunts
Delight not all; among the Sons of Men
How many have with a smile made small account
Of beauty and her lures, easily scornd
All her assaults, on worthier things intent!   195
Remember that *Pellean* Conqueror,
A youth, how all the Beauties of the East
He slightly viewd, and slightly over-passd;
How hee sirnam'd of *Africa* dismissd
In his prime youth the fair *Iberian* maid.   200
For *Solomon* he liv'd at ease, and full
Of honour, wealth, high fare, aimd not beyond
Higher design than to enjoy his State;
Thence to the bait of Women lay expos'd:
But hee whom wee attempt is wiser far   205
Than *Solomon*, of more exalted mind,
Made and set wholly on th' accomplishment
Of greatest things; what woman will you find,
Though of this Age the wonder and the fame,
On whom his leasure will voutsafe an eye   210
Of fond desire? or should she confident,
As sitting Queen ador'd on Beautys Throne,
Descend with all her winning charms begirt
To enamour, as the Zone of *Venus* once
Wrought that effect on *Jove*, so Fables tell;   215
How would one look from his Majestic brow,
Seated as on the top of Vertues hill,
Discount'nance her despis'd, and put to rout
All her array; her femal pride deject,
Or turn to reverent awe! for Beauty stands   220
In th'admiration only of weak minds
Led captive; cease to admire, and all her Plumes
Fall flat and shrink into a trivial toy,
At every sudden slighting quite abasht:
Therefore with manlier objects we must try   225
His constancy, with such as have more shew
Of worth, of honour, glory and popular praise;
Rocks whereon greatest men have oftest wreckt;
Or that which only seems to satisfie
Lawful desires of Nature, not beyond: 230
And now I know he hungers where no food
Is to be found, in the wide Wilderness;
The rest commit to me, I shall let pass
No advantage, and his strength as oft assay.
     He ceas'd, and heard thir grant in loud acclaim;   235

191 haunts] haunts. *1671*
205 hee . . . wee] he . . . we *1671*

Then forthwith to him takes a chosen band
Of Spirits likest to himself in guile
To be at hand, and at his beck appear,
If cause were to unfold som active Scene
Of various persons each to know his part;   240
Then to the Desert takes with these his flight;
Where still from shade to shade the Son of God
After forty days fasting had remaind,
Now hungring first, and to himself thus said.
   Where will this end? four times ten days I have passd
Wandring this woody maze, and human food   246
Nor tasted, nor had appetite: that Fast
To Vertue I impute not, or count part
Of what I suffer here; if Nature need not,
Or God support Nature without repast   250
Though needing, what praise is it to endure?
But now I feel I hunger, which declares
Nature hath need of what she asks; yet God
Can satisfie that need som other way,
Though hunger still remain: so it remain   255
Without this bodys wasting, I content me,
And from the sting of Famin fear no harm,
Nor mind it, fed with better thoughts that feed
Mee hungring more to do my Fathers will.
   It was the hour of night, when thus the Son   260
Commun'd in silent walk, then laid him down
Under the hospitable covert nigh
Of Trees thick interwoven; there he slept,
And dream'd, as appetite is wont to dream,
Of meats and drinks, Natures refreshment sweet;   265
Him thought, he by the Brook of *Cherith* stood
And saw the Ravens with thir horny beaks
Food to *Elijah* bringing Ev'n and Morn,
Though ravenous, taught to abstain from what they brought:
He saw the Prophet also how he fled   270
Into the Desert, and how there he slept
Under a Juniper; then how awak't
He found his Supper on the coals prepar'd,
And by the Angel was bid rise and eat,
And eat the second time after repose,   275
The strength whereof suffic'd him forty days:
Somtimes that with *Elijah* he partook,
Or as a guest with *Daniel* at his pulse.
Thus wore out night; and now the Herald Lark
Left his ground-nest, high touring to descry   280
The morns approach, and greet her with his Song:
As lightly from his grassy Couch up rose
Our Saviour, and found all was but a dream;
Fasting he went to sleep, and fasting wak'd.

Up to a hill anon his steps he rear'd,   285
From whose high top to ken the prospect round,
If Cottage were in view, Sheep-cote or Herd;
But Cottage, Herd or Sheep-cote none he saw,
Onely in a bottom saw a pleasant Grove,
With chaunt of tuneful Birds resounding loud;   290
Thither he bent his way, determind there
To rest at noon, and enterd soon the shade
High rooft and walks beneath, and alleys brown
That opend in the midst a woody Scene,
Natures own work it seemd (Nature taught Art)   295
And to a Superstitious eye the haunt
Of Wood-Gods and Wood-Nymphs; he viewd it round,
When suddenly a man before him stood,
Not rustic as before, but seemlier clad,
As one in City or Court or Palace bred,   300
And with fair speech these words to him addressd.
    With granted leave officious I return,
But much more wonder that the Son of God
In this wild solitude so long should bide
Of all things destitute, and well I know   305
Not without hunger.   Others of som note,
As story tells, have trod this Wilderness;
The Fugitive Bond-woman with her Son
Out-cast *Nebaioth*, yet found hee relief
By a providing Angel; all the race   310
Of *Israel* here had famisht, had not God
Raind from Heav'n Manna; and that Prophet bold,
Native of *Thebez*, wandring here was fed
Twice by a voice inviting him to eat.
Of thee these forty days none hath regard,   315
Forty and more deserted here indeed.
    To whom thus Jesus: What conclud'st thou hence?
They all had need, I as thou seest have none.
    How hast thou hunger then?   Satan repli'd,
Tell me if Food were now before thee set,   320
Wouldst thou not eat?   Thereafter as I like
The giver, answerd Jesus.   Why should that
Cause thy refusal? said the suttle Fiend.
Hast thou not right to all Created things?
Owe not all Creatures by just right to thee   325
Duty and Service, nor to stay till bid,
But tender all thir power? nor mention I
Meats by the Law unclean, or offerd first
To Idols, those young *Daniel* could refuse;
Nor profferd by an Enemy, though who   330
Would scruple that, with want opprest?   Behold

309 hee] he *1671*

Nature asham'd, or better to express,
Troubl'd that thou shouldst hunger, hath purveyd
From all the Elements her choicest store
To treat thee as beseems, and as her Lord   335
With honour: only deign to sit and eat.
    He spake no dream; for as his words had end,
Our Saviour lifting up his eyes beheld
In ample space under the broadest shade
A Table richly spred, in regal mode,   340
With dishes pil'd, and meats of noblest sort
And savour, Beasts of chase or Fowl of game,
In pastry built or from the spit or boild,
Gris-amber-steam'd; all Fish from Sea or Shore,
Freshet or purling Brook, of shell or fin,   345
And exquisitest name, for which was draind
Pontus and *Lucrine* Bay and *Afric* Coast.
Alas how simple, to these Cates compar'd,
Was that crude Apple that diverted *Eve*!
And at a stately side-board by the wine   350
That fragrant smell diffus'd, in order stood
Tall stripling youths rich clad, of fairer hue
Than *Ganymed* or *Hylas*; distant more
Under the Trees now tripd, now solemn stood
Nymphs of *Diana*'s train, and *Naiades*   355
With fruits and flowrs from *Amalthea*'s horn,
And Ladies of th' *Hesperides*, that seemd
Fairer than feignd of old, or fabl'd since
Of Fairy Damsels met in Forest wide
By Knights of *Logres*, or of *Lyones*,   360
Lancelot or *Pelleas* or *Pellenore*;
And all the while Harmonious Airs were heard
Of chiming strings or charming pipes, and winds
Of gentlest gale *Arabian* odours fannd
From thir soft wings, and *Flora*'s earliest smells.   365
Such was the Splendor, and the Tempter now
His invitation earnestly renewd.
    What doubts the Son of God to sit and eat?
These are not Fruits forbidden, no interdict
Defends the touching of these viands pure,   370
Thir taste no knowledge works, at least of evil,
But life preserves, destroys lifes enemy
Hunger, with sweet restorative delight.
All these are Spirits of Air and Woods and Springs,
Thy gentle Ministers, who come to pay   375
Thee homage, and acknowledge thee thir Lord:
What doubtst thou Son of God? sit down and eat.
    To whom thus Jesus temperatly repli'd:
Saidst thou not that to all things I had right?
And who withholds my power that right to use?   380

Shall I receive by gift what of my own,
When and where likes me best, I can command?
I can at will, doubt not, as soon as thou,
Command a Table in this Wilderness,
And call swift flights of Angels ministrant   385
Arrayd in Glory on my cup to attend:
Why shouldst thou then obtrude this diligence,
In vain, where no acceptance it can find?
And with my hunger what hast thou to do?
Thy pompous Delicacies I contemn,   390
And count thy specious gifts no gifts, but guiles.
    To whom thus answerd Satan malecontent.
That I have also power to give thou seest;
If of that power I bring thee voluntary
What I might have bestowd on whom I pleas'd,   395
And rather opportunely in this place
Chose to impart to thy apparent need,
Why shouldst thou not accept it? but I see
What I can do or offer is suspect;
Of these things others quickly will dispose   400
Whose pains have earnd the far-fet spoil.   With that
Both Table and Provision vanishd quite
With sound of Harpies wings and Talons heard;
Onely th'importune Tempter still remaind;
And with these words his temptation persu'd.   405
    By hunger, that each other Creature tames,
Thou art not to be harmd, therefore not mov'd;
Thy temperance invincible besides,
For no allurement yields to appetite;
And all thy heart is set on high designs,   410
High actions: but wherewith to be achiev'd?
Great acts require great means of enterprise;
Thou art unknown, unfriended, low of birth,
A Carpenter thy Father known, thy self
Bred up in poverty and straits at home;   415
Lost in a Desert here and hunger-bit:
Which way or from what hope dost thou aspire
To greatness? whence Autority deriv'st?
What Followers, what Retinue canst thou gain,
Or at thy heels the dizzy Multitude,   420
Longer than thou canst feed them on thy cost?
Money brings Honour, Friends, Conquest and Realms:
What rais'd *Antipater* the *Edomite*,
And his Son *Herod* plac'd on *Judah*'s Throne
(Thy throne) but gold that got him puissant friends? 425
Therefore, if at great things thou wouldst arrive,
Get Riches first, get Wealth, and Treasure heap,
Not difficult, if thou hearken to me,
Riches are mine, Fortune is in my hand;

They whom I favour thrive in wealth amain,   430
While Virtue, Valour, Wisdom sit in want.
    To whom thus Jesus patiently repli'd.
Yet Wealth without these three is impotent
To gain dominion or to keep it gaind.
Witness those ancient Empires of the Earth,   435
In highth of all thir flowing wealth dissolv'd:
But men endu'd with these have oft attaind
In lowest poverty to highest deeds;
Gideon and *Jephtha*, and the Shepherd lad
Whose offspring on the Throne of *Judah* sat   440
So many Ages, and shall yet regain
That seat, and reign in *Israel* without end.
Among the Heathen (for throughout the World
To me is not unknown what hath been done
Worthy of Memorial) canst thou not remember   445
Quintius, Fabricius, Curius, Regulus?
For I esteem those names of men so poor
Who could do mighty things, and could contemn
Riches though offerd from the hand of Kings.
And what in me seems wanting, but that I   450
May also in this poverty as soon
Accomplish what they did, perhaps and more?
Extoll not Riches then, the toil of Fools,
The wise mans cumbrance if not snare, more apt
To slacken Vertue and abate her edge   455
Than prompt her to do aught may merit praise.
What if with like aversion I reject
Riches and Realms? yet not for that a Crown,
Golden in shew, is but a wreath of thorns,
Brings dangers, troubles, cares, and sleepless nights   460
To him who wears the Regal Diadem,
When on his shoulders each mans burden lies;
For therein stands the office of a King,
His Honour, Vertue, Merit and chief Praise,
That for the Public all this weight he bears.   465
Yet he who reigns within himself, and rules
Passions, Desires and Fears, is more a King;
Which every wise and vertuous man attains:
And who attains not, ill aspires to rule
Cities of men, or head-strong Multitudes,   470
Subject himself to Anarchy within
Or lawless passions in him which he serves.
But to guide Nations in the way of truth
By saving Doctrin, and from error lead
To know, and knowing worship God aright,   475
Is yet more Kingly; this attracts the Soul,
Governs the inner man, the nobler part,
That other ore the body only reigns,

And oft by force, which to a generous mind
So reigning can be no sincere delight.   480
Besides to give a Kingdom hath been thought
Greater and nobler don, and to lay down
Far more magnanimous than to assume.
Riches are needless then, both for themselves,
And for thy reason why they should be sought,   485
To gain a Scepter, oftest better misst.

The End of the Second Book

BOOK III

So spake the Son of God, and Satan stood
A while as mute, confounded what to say,
What to reply, confuted and convinc't
Of his weak arguing and fallacious drift;
At length collecting all his Serpent wiles,   5
With soothing words renewd, him thus accosts.
  I see thou knowst what is of use to know,
What best to say canst say, to do canst do;
Thy actions to thy words accord, thy words
To thy large heart give utterance due, thy heart   10
Contains of good, wise, just, the perfet shape.
Should Kings and Nations from thy mouth consult,
Thy Counsel would be as the Oracle
Urim and *Thummim*, those oraculous gems
On *Aarons* brest, or tongue of Seers old   15
Infallible; or wert thou sought to deeds
That might require th' array of war, thy skill
Of conduct would be such, that all the world
Could not sustain thy Prowess, or subsist
In battel, though against thy few in arms.   20
These God-like Vertues wherefore dost thou hide,
Affecting privat life, or more obscure
In savage Wilderness? Wherefore deprive
All Earth her wonder at thy acts, thy self
The fame and glory? glory the reward   25
That sole excites to high attempts the flame
Of most erected Spirits, most temperd pure
Ethereal, who all pleasures else despise,
All treasures and all gain esteem as dross,
And dignities and powers all but the highest.   30
Thy years are ripe, and over-ripe; the Son
Of *Macedonian Philip* had ere these
Won *Asia* and the Throne of *Cyrus* held
At his dispose, young *Scipio* had brought down
The *Carthaginian* pride, young *Pompey* quelld   35
The *Pontic* King and in triumph had rode.
Yet years, and to ripe years judgment mature,
Quench not the thirst of glory, but augment.
Great *Julius*, whom now all the world admires,
The more he grew in years, the more inflam'd   40
With glory, wept that he had liv'd so long
Inglorious: but thou yet art not too late.

To whom our Saviour calmly thus repli'd.
Thou neither dost persuade me to seek wealth
For Empires sake, nor Empire to affect   45
For glorys sake by all thy argument.
For what is glory but the blaze of fame,
The peoples praise, if always praise unmixt?
And what the people but a herd confus'd,
A miscellaneous rabble, who extoll   50
Things vulgar, and well weighd, scarce worth the praise?
They praise and they admire they know not what;
And know not whom, but as one leads the other;
And what delight to be by such extolld,
To live upon thir tongues and be thir talk,   55
Of whom to be disprais'd were no small praise?
His lot who dares be singularly good.
Th' intelligent among them and the wise
Are few, and glory scarce of few is rais'd.
This is true glory and renown, when God   60
Looking on th'Earth, with approbation marks
The just man, and divulges him through Heaven
To all his Angels, who with true applause
Recount his praises; thus he did to *Job*,
When to extend his fame through Heav'n and Earth,   65
As thou to thy reproach mayst well remember,
He askd thee, Hast thou seen my servant *Job*?
Famous he was in Heaven, on Earth less known;
Where glory is false glory, attributed
To things not glorious, men not worthy of fame.   70
They err who count it glorious to subdue
By Conquest far and wide, to over-run
Large Countries, and in field great Battels win,
Great Cities by assault: what do these Worthies
But rob and spoil, burn, slaughter, and enslave   75
Peaceable Nations, neighbouring or remote,
Made Captive yet deserving freedom more
Than those thir Conquerors, who leave behind
Nothing but ruin wheresoe're they rove,
And all the flourishing works of peace destroy?   80
Then swell with pride, and must be titl'd Gods,
Great Benefactors of mankind, Deliverers,
Worshipt with Temple, Priest and Sacrifice;
One is the Son of *Jove*, of *Mars* the other,
Till Conqueror Death discover them scarce men,   85
Rouling in brutish vices, and deformd,
Violent or shameful death thir due reward.
But if there be in glory aught of good,
It may by means far different be attaind
Without ambition, war or violence;   90
By deeds of peace, by wisdom eminent,

By patience, temperance: I mention still
Him whom thy wrongs with Saintly patience borne
Made famous in a Land and times obscure;
Who names not now with honour patient *Job*?   95
Poor *Socrates* (who next more memorable?)
By what he taught, and sufferd for so doing,
For truths sake suffering death unjust, lives now
Equal in fame to proudest Conquerors.
Yet if for fame and glory aught be don,   100
Aught sufferd; if young *African* for fame
His wasted Country freed from *Punic* rage,
The deed becomes unprais'd, the man at least,
And loses, though but verbal, his reward.
Shall I seek glory then, as vain men seek   105
Oft not deserv'd?   I seek not mine, but his
Who sent me, and thereby witness whence I am.
       To whom the Tempter murmuring thus repli'd.
Think not so slight of glory; therein least
Resembling thy great Father: he seeks glory,   110
And for his glory all things made, all things
Orders and governs, nor content in Heaven
By all his Angels glorifi'd, requires
Glory from men, from all men good or bad,
Wise or unwise, no difference, no exemption;   115
Above all Sacrifice or hallowd gift
Glory he requires, and glory he receives
Promiscuous from all Nations, Jew or Greek
Or Barbarous, nor exception hath declar'd:
From us his foes pronounc't glory he exacts.   120
       To whom our Saviour fervently repli'd.
And reason; since his Word all things produc'd,
Though chiefly not for glory as prime end,
But to shew forth his goodness, and impart
His good communicable to every soul   125
Freely; of whom what could he less expect
Than glory and benediction, that is thanks,
The slightest, easiest, readiest recompense
From them who could return him nothing else,
And not returning that would likeliest render   130
Contempt instead, dishonour, obloquy?
Hard recompense, unsutable return
For so much good, so much beneficence.
But why should man seek glory? who of his own
Hath nothing, and to whom nothing belongs   135
But condemnation, ignominy and shame;
Who for so many benefits receiv'd
Turnd recreant to God, ingrate and false,
And so of all true good himself despoild,
Yet sacrilegious, to himself would take   140

That which to God alone of right belongs:
Yet so much bounty is in God, such grace,
That who advance his glory, not thir own,
Them he himself to glory will advance.

    So spake the Son of God; and here again   145
Satan had not to answer, but stood struck
With guilt of his own sin, for he himself
Insatiable of glory had lost all;
Yet of another Plea bethought him soon.

    Of glory as thou wilt, said he, so deem,   150
Worth or not worth the seeking, let it pass:
But to a Kingdom thou art born, ordaind
To sit upon thy Father *Davids* Throne;
By Mothers side thy Father, though thy right
Be now in powerful hands, that will not part   155
Easily from possession won with arms;
Judæa now and all the promis'd land,
Reduc't a Province under *Roman* yoke,
Obeys *Tiberius*; nor is always rul'd
With temperat sway; oft have they violated   160
The Temple, oft the Law with foul affronts,
Abominations rather, as did once
Antiochus: and thinkst thou to regain
Thy right by sitting still or thus retiring?
So did not *Machabeus*: he indeed   165
Retir'd unto the Desert, but with arms;
And ore a mighty King so oft prevaild
That by strong hand his Family obtaind,
Though Priests, the Crown, and *Davids* Throne usurpd,
With *Modin* and her Suburbs once content.   170
If Kingdom move thee not, let move thee Zeal
And Duty; Zeal and Duty are not slow,
But on Occasions forelock watchful wait:
They themselves rather are occasion best;
Zeal of thy Fathers house, Duty to free   175
Thy Country from her Heathen servitude.
So shalt thou best fulfill, best verifie
The Prophets old, who sung thy endless reign,
The happier reign the sooner it begins:
Reign then; what canst thou better do the while?   180

    To whom our Saviour answer thus returnd.
All things are best fulfilld in thir due time,
And time there is for all things, Truth hath said:
If of my reign Prophetic Writ hath told
That it shall never end, so when begin   185
The Father in his purpose hath decreed,
Hee in whose hand all times and seasons roul.

What if he hath decreed that I shall first
Be tri'd in humble state, and things adverse,
By tribulations, injuries, insults,   190
Contempts and scorns and snares and violence,
Suffering, abstaining, quietly expecting
Without distrust or doubt, that he may know
What I can suffer, how obey? who best
Can suffer, best can do; best reign, who first   195
Well hath obeyd; just trial ere I merit
My exaltation without change or end.
But what concerns it thee, when I begin
My everlasting Kingdom, why art thou
Solicitous, what moves thy inquisition?   200
Knowst thou not that my rising is thy fall,
And my promotion will be thy destruction?
    To whom the Tempter inly rackt repli'd.
Let that come when it comes; all hope is lost
Of my reception into grace; what worse?   205
For where no hope is left, is left no fear;
If there be worse, the expectation more
Of worse torments me than the feeling can.
I would be at the worst; worst is my Port,
My harbour and my ultimate repose,   210
The end I would attain, my final good.
My error was my error, and my crime
My crime; whatever for it self condemnd,
And will alike be punisht; whether thou
Reign or reign not; though to that gentle brow   215
Willingly I could fly, and hope thy reign,
From that placid aspect and meek regard,
Rather than aggravate my evil state,
Would stand between me and thy Fathers ire,
(Whose ire I dread more than the fire of Hell)   220
A shelter and a kind of shading cool
Interposition, as a summers cloud.
If I then to the worst that can be haste,
Why move thy feet so slow to what is best,
Happiest both to thy self and all the world,   225
That thou who worthiest art shouldst be thir King?
Perhaps thou lingerst in deep thoughts detaind
Of th'enterprize so hazardous and high;
No wonder, for though in thee be united
What of perfection can in man be found,   230
Or human nature can receive, consider
Thy life hath yet been privat, most part spent
At home, scarce viewd the *Gallilean* Towns,
And once a year *Jerusalem*, few days
Short sojourn; and what thence couldst thou observe? 235
The world thou hast not seen, much less her glory,

Empires, and Monarchs, and thir radiant Courts,
Best school of best experience, quickest insight
In all things that to greatest actions lead.
The wisest, unexperienc't, will be ever   240
Timorous and loath, with novice modesty
(As he who seeking Asses found a Kingdom),
Irresolute, unhardy, unadventrous:
But I will bring thee where thou soon shalt quit
Those rudiments, and see before thine eyes   245
The Monarchies of the Earth, thir pomp and state,
Sufficient introduction to inform
Thee, of thy self so apt, in regal Arts
And regal Mysteries; that thou mayst know
How best thir opposition to withstand.   250
   With that (such power was giv'n him then) he took
The Son of God up to a Mountain high.
It was a Mountain at whose verdant feet
A spacious plain outstretcht in circuit wide
Lay pleasant; from his side two rivers flowd,   255
Th' one winding, th'other straight, and left between
Fair Champain with less rivers interveind,
Then meeting joind thir tribute to the Sea:
Fertil of corn the glebe, of oil and wine,
With herds the pastures throngd, with flocks the hills, 260
Huge Cities and high towrd, that well might seem
The seats of mightiest Monarchs; and so large
The Prospect was, that here and there was room
For barren desert fountainless and dry.
To this high mountain top the Tempter brought   265
Our Saviour, and new train of words began.
   Well have we speeded, and ore hill and dale,
Forrest and field and flood, Temples and Towers,
Cut shorter many a league: Here thou beholdst
Assyria and her Empires ancient bounds,   270
Araxes and the *Caspian* lake, thence on
As far as *Indus* East, *Euphrates* West,
And oft beyond; to South the *Persian* Bay,
And inaccessible th'*Arabian* drouth:
Here *Ninevee*, of length within her wall   275
Several days journey, built by *Ninus* old,
Of that first golden Monarchy the seat,
And seat of *Salmanassar*, whose success
Israel in long captivity still mourns;
There *Babylon* the wonder of all tongues,   280
As ancient, but rebuilt by him who twice
Judah and all thy Father *Davids* house
Led captive, and *Jerusalem* laid waste,
Till *Cyrus* set them free; *Persepolis*
His City there thou seest, and *Bactra* there;   285

Ecbatana her structure vast there shews,
And *Hecatompylos* her hunderd gates,
There *Susa* by *Choaspes*, amber stream,
The drink of none but Kings; of later fame
Built by *Emathian* or by *Parthian* hands,   290
The great *Seleucia*, *Nisibis*, and there
Artaxata, *Teredon*, *Tesiphon*
Turning with easie eye thou mayst behold.
All these the *Parthian*, now som Ages past,
By great *Arsaces* led, who founded first   295
That Empire, under his dominion holds,
From the luxurious Kings of *Antioch* won.
And just in time thou comst to have a view
Of his great power; for now the *Parthian* King
In *Ctesiphon* hath gatherd all his Host   300
Against the *Scythian*, whose incursions wild
Have wasted *Sogdiana*; to her aid
He marches now in haste; see, though from far,
His thousands, in what martial equipage
They issue forth, Steel Bows and Shafts thir arms   305
Of equal dread in flight or in persuit;
All Horsemen, in which fight they most excell;
See how in warlike muster they appear,
In Rhombs and wedges, and half-moons, and wings.

   He lookd and saw what numbers numberless   310
The City gates out pourd, light armed Troops
In coats of Mail and military pride;
In Mail thir horses clad, yet fleet and strong,
Prancing thir riders bore, the flowr and choice
Of many Provinces from bound to bound;   315
From *Arachosia*, from *Candaor* East,
And *Margiana* to th'*Hyrcanian* cliffs
Of *Caucasus* and dark *Iberian* dales,
From *Atropatia* and the neighbouring plains
Of *Adiabene*, *Media*, and the South   320
Of *Susiana* to *Balsara*'s hav'n.
He saw them in thir forms of battel rang'd,
How quick they wheeld, and flying behind them shot
Sharp sleet of arrowie showrs against the face
Of thir persuers, and overcame by flight;   325
The field all iron cast a gleaming brown:
Nor wanted clouds of foot, nor on each horn
Cuirassiers all in steel for standing fight,
Chariots or Elephants endorst with Towrs
Of Archers, nor of labouring Pioners   330
A multitude with Spades and Axes armd
To lay hills plain, fell woods, or valleys fill,
Or where plain was raise hill, or overlay
With bridges rivers proud, as with a yoke;

Mules after these, Camels and Dromedaries,   335
And Waggons fraught with Utensils of war.
Such forces met not, nor so wide a camp,
When *Agrican* with all his Northern powers
Besieg'd *Albracca*, as Romances tell,
The City of *Gallaphrone*, from thence to win   340
The fairest of her Sex *Angelica*
His daughter, sought by many Prowest Knights,
Both *Paynim* and the Peers of *Charlemane*.
Such and so numerous was thir Chivalrie;
At sight whereof the Fiend yet more presum'd,   345
And to our Saviour thus his words renewd.
   That thou mayst know I seek not to engage
Thy Vertue, and not every way secure
On no slight grounds thy safety; hear, and mark
To what end I have brought thee hither and shewn   350
All this fair sight: Thy Kingdom though foretold
By Prophet or by Angel, unless thou
Endevor, as thy Father *David* did,
Thou never shalt obtain; prediction still
In all things, and all men, supposes means;   355
Without means us'd, what it predicts revokes.
But say thou wert possest of *Davids* Throne
By free consent of all, none opposite,
Samaritan or *Jew*; how couldst thou hope
Long to enjoy it quiet and secure,   360
Between two such enclosing enemies
Roman and *Parthian*? therefore one of these
Thou must make sure thy own; the *Parthian* first
By my advice, as nearer and of late
Found able by invasion to annoy   365
Thy country, and captive lead away her Kings
Antigonus and old *Hyrcanus* bound,
Maugre the *Roman*: it shall be my task
To render thee the *Parthian* at dispose;
Choose which thou wilt, by conquest or by league;   370
By him thou shalt regain, without him not,
That which alone can truly reinstall thee
In *Davids* royal Seat, his true Successor,
Deliv'rance of thy brethren, those ten Tribes
Whose offspring in his Territory yet serve   375
In *Habor*, and among the *Medes* disperst;
Ten Sons of *Jacob*, two of *Joseph* lost
Thus long from *Israel*, serving as of old
Thir Fathers in the land of *Egypt* serv'd,
This offer sets before thee to deliver.   380
These if from servitude thou shalt restore
To thir inheritance, then, nor till then,
Thou on the Throne of *David* in full glory,

From *Egypt* to *Euphrates* and beyond
Shalt reign, and *Rome* or *Cæsar* not need fear.   385
   To whom our Saviour answerd thus, unmov'd.
Much ostentation vain of fleshly arm,
And fragile arms, much instrument of war
Long in preparing, soon to nothing brought,
Before mine eyes thou hast set; and in mine ear   390
Vented much pollicy, and projects deep
Of enemies, of aids, battels and leagues,
Plausible to the world, to mee worth naught.
Means I must use thou sayst, prediction else
Will unpredict and fail me of the Throne: 395
My time I told thee (and that time for thee
Were better fardest off) is not yet come;
When that comes think not thou to find me slack
On my part aught endevoring, or to need
Thy politic maxims, or that cumbersome   400
Luggage of war there shewn me, argument
Of human weakness rather than of strength.
My brethren, as thou callst them, those Ten Tribes
I must deliver, if I mean to reign
Davids true heir, and his full Scepter sway   405
To just extent over all *Israels* Sons:
But whence to thee this zeal? where was it then
For *Israel*, or for *David*, or his Throne,
When thou stoodst up his Tempter to the pride
Of numbring *Israël*, which cost the lives   410
Of threescore and ten thousand *Israelites*
By three days Pestilence? such was thy zeal
To *Israel* then, the same that now to me.
As for those captive Tribes, themselves were they
Who wrought thir own captivity, fell off   415
From God to worship Calves, the Deities
Of *Egypt*, *Baäl* next and *Ashtaroth*,
And all th' Idolatries of Heathen round,
Besides thir other worse than heathenish crimes;
Nor in the land of thir captivity   420
Humbl'd themselves, or penitent besought
The God of thir forefathers; but so di'd
Impenitent, and left a race behind
Like to themselves, distinguishable scarce
From Gentiles, but by Circumcision vain,   425
And God with Idols in thir worship joind.
Should I of these the liberty regard,
Who freed, as to thir ancient Patrimony,
Unhumbl'd, unrepentant, unreformd,
Headlong would follow; and to thir Gods perhaps   430

393 mee] me 1671

Of *Bethel* and of *Dan*? no, let them serve
Thir enemies, who serve Idols with God.
Yet he at length, time to himself best known,
Remembring *Abraham* by som wond'rous call
May bring them back repentant and sincere,   435
And at thir passing cleave th'*Assyrian* flood,
While to thir native land with joy they haste,
As the *Red Sea* and *Jordan* once he cleft
When to the *Promis'd Land* thir Fathers passd:
To his due time and providence I leave them.   440
    So spake *Israels* true King, and to the Fiend
Made answer meet, that made void all his wiles.
So fares it when with truth falsehood contends.

The End of the Third Book

BOOK IV

Perplext and troubl'd at his bad success
The Tempter stood, nor had what to reply,
Discoverd in his fraud, thrown from his hope
So oft, and the persuasive Rhetoric
That sleekd his tongue, and won so much on *Eve*,   5
So little here, nay lost; but *Eve* was *Eve*,
This far his over-match, who self deceiv'd
And rash, before hand had no better weighd
The strength he was to cope with, or his own:
But as a man who had been matchless held   10
In cunning, over-reach't where least he thought,
To salve his credit, and for very spite
Still will be tempting him who foils him still,
And never cease, though to his shame the more;
Or as a swarm of flies in vintage time,   15
About the wine-press where sweet moust is pourd,
Beat off, returns as oft with humming sound;
Or surging waves against a solid rock,
Though all to shivers dasht, th'assault renew,
Vain battry, and in froth or bubbles end: 20
So Satan, whom repulse upon repulse
Met ever; and to shameful silence brought,
Yet gives not o'er though desperat of success,
And his vain importunity persues.
He brought our Saviour to the western side   25
Of that high mountain, whence he might behold
Another plain, long but in bredth not wide;
Washt by the Southern Sea, and on the North
To equal length backt with a ridge of hills
That screend the fruits of th'earth and seats of men   30
From cold *Septentrion* blasts; thence in the midst
Divided by a river, of whose banks
On each side an Imperial City stood,
With Towrs and Temples proudly elevate
On sev'n small Hills, with Palaces adornd,   35
Porches and Theatres, Baths, Aqueducts,
Statues and Trophees, and Triumphal Arcs,
Gardens and Groves presented to his eyes,
Above the highth of Mountains interpos'd:
By what strange Parallax or Optic skill   40
Of vision multipli'd through air, or glass
Of Telescope, were curious to enquire.
And now the Tempter thus his silence broke.

The City which thou seest no other deem
Than great and glorious *Rome*, Queen of the Earth   45
So far renownd, and with the spoils enricht
Of Nations; there the Capitol thou seest
Above the rest lifting his stately head
On the *Tarpeian* rock, her Cittadel
Impregnable, and there Mount *Palatine*   50
Th'Imperial Palace, compass huge, and high
The Structure, skill of noblest Architects,
With gilded battlements, conspicuous far,
Turrets and Terraces, and glittering Spires.
Many a fair Edifice besides, more like   55
Houses of gods (so well I have dispos'd
My Aerie Microscope) thou mayst behold
Outside and inside both, pillars and roofs
Carv'd work, the hand of fam'd Artificers
In Cedar, Marble, Ivory or Gold.   60
Thence to the gates cast round thine eye, and see
What conflux issuing forth or entring in,
Pretors, Proconsuls to thir Provinces
Hasting or on return, in robes of State;
Lictors and rods the ensigns of thir power,   65
Legions and Cohorts, turmes of horse and wings:
Or Embassies from Regions far remote
In various habits on the *Appian* road,
Or on th'*Æmilian*; some from fardest South,
Syene, and where the shaddow both way falls,   70
Meroe, Nilotic Ile, and more to West,
The Realm of *Bocchus* to the Black-moor Sea;
From the *Asian* Kings and *Parthian* among these,
From *India* and the golden *Chersoness*,
And utmost *Indian* Isle *Taprobane*,   75
Dusk faces with white silken Turbants wreath'd;
From *Gallia, Gades*, and the *Brittish* West,
Germans and *Scythians*, and *Sarmatians* North
Beyond *Danubius* to the *Tauric* Pool.
All Nations now to *Rome* obedience pay,   80
To *Romes* great Emperor, whose wide domain
In ample Territory, wealth and power,
Civility of Manners, Arts and Arms
And long Renown, thou justly mayst preferr
Before the *Parthian*; these two Thrones except,   85
The rest are barbarous, and scarce worth the sight,
Shar'd among petty Kings too far remov'd;
These having shewn thee, I have shewn thee all
The Kingdoms of the World, and all thir glory.
This Emperor hath no Son, and now is old,   90
Old and lascivious, and from *Rome* retir'd
To *Capreæ* an Iland small but strong

On the *Campanian* shore, with purpose there
His horrid lusts in privat to enjoy,
Committing to a wicked Favourite   95
All public cares, and yet of him suspicious,
Hated of all, and hating; with what ease
Indu'd with Regal Vertues as thou art,
Appearing, and beginning noble deeds,
Mightst thou expell this monster from his Throne   100
Now made a stye, and in his place ascending
A victor people free from servil yoke?
And with my help thou mayst; to me the power
Is giv'n, and by that right I give it thee.
Aim therefore at no less than all the World,   105
Aim at the highest: without th' highest attaind
Will be for thee no sitting, or not long
On *Davids* Throne, be propheci'd what will.
    To whom the Son of God unmov'd repli'd.
Nor doth this grandeur and majestic show   110
Of luxury, though calld magnificence,
More than of arms before, allure mine eye,
Much less my mind; though thou shouldst add to tell
Thir sumptuous gluttonies, and gorgeous feasts
On *Citron* tables or *Atlantic* stone   115
(For I have also heard, perhaps have read),
Thir wines of *Setia*, *Cales* and *Falerne*,
Chios and *Creet*, and how they quaff in Gold,
Crystal and Myrrhine cups imbost with Gems
And studs of Pearl; to mee shouldst tell who thirst   120
And hunger still: then Embassies thou shewst
From Nations far and nigh; what honour that,
But tedious waste of time to sit and hear
So many hollow compliments and lies,
Outlandish flatteries?   Then proceedst to talk   125
Of th'Emperor, how easily subdu'd,
How gloriously; I shall, thou sayst, expell
A brutish monster: what if I withall
Expell a Devil who first made him such?
Let his tormenter Conscience find him out,   130
For him I was not sent; nor yet to free
That people victor once, now vile and base,
Deservedly made vassal, who once just,
Frugal and mild and temperat, conquerd well
But govern ill the Nations under yoke,   135
Peeling thir Provinces, exhausted all
By lust and rapine; first ambitious grown
Of triumph, that insulting vanity;
Then cruel, by thir sports to blood enur'd

120 mee] me *1671*

Of fighting beasts, and men to beasts expos'd;   140
Luxurious by thir wealth, and greedier still,
And from the daily Scene effeminate.
What wise and valiant man would seek to free
These thus degenerat, by themselves enslav'd,
Or could of inward slaves make outward free?   145
Know therefore when my season comes to sit
On *Davids* Throne, it shall be like a tree
Spreading and overshaddowing all the Earth,
Or as a stone that shall to pieces dash
All Monarchies besides throughout the World;   150
And of my Kingdom there shall be no end:
Means there shall be to this, but what the means
Is not for thee to know, nor me to tell.
        To whom the Tempter impudent repli'd.
I see all offers made by me how slight   155
Thou valu'st, because offerd, and rejectst:
Nothing will please the difficult and nice,
Or nothing more than still to contradict:
On th'other side know also thou, that I
On what I offer set as high esteem,   160
Nor what I part with mean to give for naught;
All these which in a moment thou beholdst,
The Kingdoms of the World to thee I give;
For giv'n to me, I give to whom I please,
No trifle; yet with this reserve, not else,   165
On this condition, if thou wilt fall down
And worship me as thy superior Lord,
Easily don, and hold them all of me;
For what can less so great a gift deserve?
        Whom thus our Saviour answerd with disdain.   170
I never lik'd thy talk, thy offers less,
Now both abhorr, since thou hast dar'd to utter
Th'abominable terms, impious condition;
But I endure the time, till which expir'd
Thou hast permission on me.   It is written   175
The first of all Commandments, Thou shalt worship
The Lord thy God, and only him shalt serve;
And dar'st thou to the Son of God propound
To worship thee accurst? now more accurst
For this attempt, bolder than that on *Eve*   180
And more blasphemous; which expect to rue.
The Kingdoms of the World to thee were giv'n,
Permitted rather, and by thee usurpt;
Other donation none thou canst produce:
If giv'n, by whom but by the King of Kings,   185
God over all supream? if giv'n to thee,
By thee how fairly is the Giver now
Repaid?   But gratitude in thee is lost

Long since.   Wert thou so void of fear or shame
As offer them to mee the Son of God,   190
To mee my own, on such abhorred pact,
That I fall down and worship thee as God?
Get thee behind me; plain thou now appear'st
That Evil one, Satan for ever damnd.
    To whom the Fiend with fear abasht repli'd.   195
Be not so sore offended, Son of God;
Though Sons of God both Angels are and Men,
If I to try whether in higher sort
Than these thou bear'st that title, have propos'd
What both from Men and Angels I receive,   200
Tetrarchs of fire, air, flood, and on the earth
Nations besides from all the quarterd winds,
God of this World invok't and World beneath:
Who then thou art, whose coming is foretold
To me so fatal, me it most concerns.   205
The trial hath indamag'd thee no way,
Rather more honour left and more esteem;
Mee naught advantag'd, missing what I aim'd.
Therefore let pass, as they are transitory,
The Kingdoms of this World; I shall no more   210
Advise thee, gain them as thou canst, or not.
And thou thy self seemst otherwise inclin'd
Than to a worldly Crown, addicted more
To contemplation and profound dispute,
As by that early action may by judg'd   215
When slipping from thy Mothers eye thou wentst
Alone into the Temple; there wast found
Among the gravest Rabbies disputant
On points and questions fitting *Moses* Chair,
Teaching not taught; the childhood shews the man,   220
As morning shews the day.   Be famous then
By wisdom; as thy Empire must extend,
So let extend thy mind ore all the World
In knowledge, all things in it comprehend:
All knowledge is not coucht in *Moses* Law,   225
The *Pentateuch* or what the Prophets wrote,
The Gentiles also know, and write, and teach
To admiration, led by Natures light;
And with the Gentiles much thou must converse,
Ruling them by persuasion as thou mean'st;   230
Without thir learning how wilt thou with them
Or they with thee hold conversation meet?
How wilt thou reason with them, how refute
Thir Idolisms, Traditions, Paradoxes?
Error by his own arms is best evinc't.   235

190 mee] me *1671*   191 mee] me *1671*
208 Mee] Me *1671*   217 wast] was *1671*

Look once more ere we leave this specular Mount
Westward, much nearer by Southwest, behold
Where on the Ægean shore a City stands
Built nobly, pure the air, and light the soil,
Athens the eye of Greece, Mother of Arts   240
And Eloquence, native to famous wits
Or hospitable, in her sweet recess,
City or Suburban, studious walks and shades.
See there the Olive Grove of Academe,
Plato's retirement, where the Attic Bird   245
Trills her thick-warbl'd notes the summer long;
There flowrie hill Hymettus with the sound
Of Bees industrious murmur oft invites
To studious musing; there Ilissus rouls
His whispering stream.   Within the walls then view   250
The schools of ancient Sages; his who bred
Great Alexander to subdue the world,
Lyceum there, and painted Stoa next:
There thou shalt hear and learn the secret power
Of harmony in tones and numbers hit   255
By voice or hand, and various-measur'd verse,
Æolian charms and Dorian Lyric Odes,
And his who gave them breath, but higher sung,
Blind Melesigenes thence Homer calld,
Whose Poem Phœbus challeng'd for his own.   260
Thence what the lofty grave Tragœdians taught
In Chorus or Iambic, teachers best
Of moral prudence, with delight receiv'd
In brief sententious precepts, while they treat
Of fate and chance and change in human life;   265
High actions and high passions best describing.
Thence to the famous Orators repair,
Those ancient, whose resistless eloquence
Wielded at will that fierce Democratie,
Shook th'Arsenal and fulmind over Greece   270
To Macedon, and Artaxerxes Throne.
To sage Philosophy next lend thine ear,
From Heav'n descended to the low-rooft house
Of Socrates, see there his Tenement,
Whom well inspir'd the Oracle pronounc'd   275
Wisest of men; from whose mouth issu'd forth
Mellifluous streams that waterd all the schools
Of Academics old and new, with those
Sirnam'd Peripatetics, and the Sect
Epicurean, and the Stoic severe;   280
These here revolve, or, as thou lik'st, at home,
Till time mature thee to a Kingdoms weight;
These rules will render thee a King complete
Within thy self, much more with Empire joind.

To whom our Saviour sagely thus repli'd.   285
Think not but that I know these things, or think
I know them not; not therefore am I short
Of knowing what I ought: hee who receives
Light from above, from the fountain of light,
No other doctrin needs, though granted true;   290
But these are false, or little else but dreams,
Conjectures, fancies, built on nothing firm.
The first and wisest of them all professd
To know this only, that he nothing knew;
The next to fabling fell and smooth conceits;   295
A third sort doubted all things, though plain sense;
Others in vertue plac'd felicity,
But vertue joind with riches and long life;
In corporal pleasure he, and careless ease:
The Stoic last in Philosophic pride,   300
By him calld vertue; and his vertuous man,
Wise, perfet in himself, and all possessing
Equal to God, oft shames not to preferr,
As fearing God nor man, contemning all
Wealth, pleasure, pain or torment, death and life,   305
Which when he lists, he leaves, or boasts he can,
For all his tedious talk is but vain boast
Or suttle shifts conviction to evade.
Alas what can they teach, and not mislead?
Ignorant of themselves, of God much more,   310
And how the World began, and how man fell
Degraded by himself, on Grace depending.
Much of the Soul they talk, but all awrie,
And in themselves seek vertue, and to themselves
All glory arrogate, to God give none,   315
Rather accuse him under usual names,
Fortune and Fate, as one regardless quite
Of Mortal things.   Who therefore seeks in these
True wisdom, finds her not, or by delusion
Far worse, her false resemblance only meets,   320
An empty cloud.   However, many books
Wise men have said are wearisom; who reads
Incessantly, and to his reading brings not
A spirit and judgement equal or superior,
(And what he brings, what needs he elsewhere seek?)   325
Uncertain and unsettl'd still remains,
Deep verst in books and shallow in himself,
Crude or intoxicate, collecting toys
And trifles for choice matters, worth a spunge;
As Childern gathering pibles on the shore.   330
Or if I would delight my privat hours

288 hee] he *1671*

With Music or with Poem, where so soon
As in our native Language can I find
That solace?   All our Law and Story strewd
With Hymns, our Psalms with artful terms inscrib'd,   335
Our Hebrew Songs and Harps in *Babylon*,
That pleas'd so well our Victors ear, declare
That rather *Greece* from us these Arts deriv'd;
Ill imitated, while they loudest sing
The vices of thir Deities, and thir own   340
In Fable, Hymn or Song, so personating
Thir Gods ridiculous, and themselves past shame.
Remove thir swelling Epithetes thick laid
As varnish on a Harlots cheek, the rest,
Thin sown with aught of profit or delight,   345
Will far be found unworthy to compare
With *Sions* songs, to all true tastes excelling,
Where God is prais'd aright, and Godlike men,
The Holiest of Holies, and his Saints;
Such are from God inspir'd, not such from thee;   350
Unless where moral vertue is exprest
By light of Nature not in all quite lost.
Thir Orators thou then extollst, as those
The top of Eloquence, Statists indeed,
And lovers of thir Country, as may seem;   355
But herein to our Prophets far beneath,
As men divinely taught, and better teaching
The solid rules of Civil Government
In thir majestic unaffected style
Than all the Oratory of *Greece* and *Rome*:   360
In them is plainest taught, and easiest learnt,
What makes a Nation happy, and keeps it so,
What ruins Kingdoms, and lays Cities flat;
These only with our Law best form a King.
    So spake the Son of God; but Satan now   365
Quite at a loss, for all his darts were spent,
Thus to our Saviour with stern brow repli'd.
    Since neither wealth nor honour, arms nor arts,
Kingdom nor Empire pleases thee, nor aught
By me propos'd in life contemplative   370
Or active, tended on by glory or fame,
What dost thou in this World? the Wilderness
For thee is fittest place; I found thee there,
And thither will return thee: yet remember
What I foretell thee, soon thou shalt have cause   375
To wish thou never hadst rejected thus
Nicely or cautiously, my offerd aid,
Which would have set thee in short time with ease
On *Davids* Throne; or Throne of all the world,
Now at full age, fulness of time, thy season,   380

When Prophesies of thee are best fullfilld.
Now contrary, if I read aught in Heaven,
Or Heav'n write aught of Fate, by what the Stars
Voluminous, or single characters,
In thir conjunction met, give me to spell,   385
Sorrows and labours, opposition, hate
Attend thee, scorns, reproaches, injuries,
Violence and stripes, and lastly cruel death:
A Kingdom they portend thee, but what Kingdom,
Real or Allegoric I discern not,   390
Nor when, eternal sure, as without end
Without beginning; for no date prefixt
Directs me in the Starry Rubric set.
    So saying he took (for still he knew his power
Not yet expir'd) and to the Wilderness   395
Brought back the Son of God, and left him there,
Feigning to disappear.   Darkness now rose,
As day-light sunk, and brought in louring night
Her shaddowy offspring, unsubstantial both,
Privation mere of light, and absent day.   400
Our Saviour meek and with untroubl'd mind
After his aerie jaunt, though hurried sore,
Hungry and cold betook him to his rest,
Wherever, under some concourse of shades
Whose branching arms thick intertwin'd might shield 405
From dews and damps of night his shelterd head;
But shelterd slept in vain, for at his head
The Tempter watchd, and soon with ugly dreams
Disturbd his sleep.   And either Tropic now
'Gan thunder, and both ends of Heav'n; the Clouds   410
From many a horrid rift abortive pourd
Fierce rain with lightning mixt, water with fire
In ruin reconcil'd; nor slept the winds
Within thir stony caves, but rushd abroad
From the four hinges of the World, and fell   415
On the vext Wilderness, whose tallest Pines,
Though rooted deep as high, and sturdiest Oaks
Bowd thir Stiff necks, loaden with stormy blasts,
Or torn up sheer: ill wast thou shrouded then,
O patient Son of God, yet onely stoodst   420
Unshaken: nor yet stayd the terror there;
Infernal Ghosts, and Hellish Furies, round
Environd thee; som howld, som yelld, som shriekd,
Som bent at thee thir fiery darts, while thou
Satst unappalld in calm and sinless peace.   425
Thus passd the night so foul till morning fair
Came forth with Pilgrim steps in amice gray;

387 Attend] Attends *1671*

Who with her radiant finger stilld the roar
Of thunder, chas'd the clouds, and laid the winds
And grisly Spectres, which the Fiend had rais'd   430
To tempt the Son of God with terrors dire.
And now the Sun with more effectual beams
Had cheerd the face of Earth, and dri'd the wet
From drooping plant or dropping tree; the birds
Who all things now behold more fresh and green,   435
After a night of storm so ruinous,
Clear'd up thir choicest notes in bush and spray
To gratulate the sweet return of morn:
Nor yet amidst this joy and brightest morn
Was absent, after all his mischief don,   440
The Prince of Darkness, glad would also seem
Of this fair change, and to our Saviour came,
Yet with no new device, they all were spent,
Rather by this his last affront resolv'd,
Desperat of better course, to vent his rage,   445
And mad despite to be so oft repelld.
Him walking on a Sunny hill he found,
Backt on the North and West by a thick wood;
Out of the wood he starts in wonted shape,
And in a careless mood thus to him said.   450
    Fair morning yet betides thee Son of God,
After a dismal night; I heard the rack
As Earth and Skie would mingle; but my self
Was distant; and these flaws, though mortals fear them
As dangerous to the pillard frame of Heaven,   455
Or to the Earths dark basis underneath,
Are to the main as inconsiderable
And harmless, if not wholsom, as a sneeze
To mans less universe, and soon are gon;
Yet as being oft times noxious where they light   460
On man, beast, plant, wasteful and turbulent,
Like turbulencies in th' affairs of men,
Over whose heads they roar, and seem to point,
They oft fore-signifie and threaten ill:
This Tempest at this Desert most was bent;   465
Of men at thee, for only thou here dwellst.
Did I not tell thee, if thou didst reject
The perfet season offerd with my aid
To win thy destind seat, but wilt prolong
All to the push of Fate, persue thy way   470
Of gaining *Davids* Throne no man knows when,
For both the when and how is no where told,
Thou shalt be what thou art ordaind, no doubt;
For Angels have proclaimd it, but concealing
The time and means: each act is rightliest don,   475
Not when it must, but when it may be best.

If thou observe not this, be sure to find,
What I foretold thee, many a hard assay
Of dangers, and adversities and pains,
Ere thou of *Israels* Scepter get fast hold;   480
Whereof this ominous night that clos'd thee round,
So many terrors, voices, prodigies
May warn thee, as a sure foregoing sign.

    So talkd he, while the Son of God went on
And stayd not, but in brief him answerd thus.   485

    Mee worse than wet thou find'st not; other harm
Those terrors which thou speak'st of, did me none;
I never fear'd they could, though noising loud
And threatning nigh; what they can do as signs
Betok'ning, or ill boding, I contemn   490
As false portents, not sent from God, but thee;
Who knowing I shall reign past thy preventing,
Obtrud'st thy offerd aid, that I accepting
At least might seem to hold all power of thee,
Ambitious spirit, and wouldst be thought my God;   495
And stormst refus'd, thinking to terrifie
Mee to thy will: desist, thou art discernd
And toilst in vain; nor me in vain molest.

    To whom the Fiend now swoln with rage repli'd:
Then hear O Son of *David*, Virgin-born;   500
For Son of God to me is yet in doubt:
Of the Messiah I have heard foretold
By all the Prophets; of thy birth at length
Announc't by *Gabriel* with the first I knew,
And of th'Angelic Song in *Bethlehem* field   505
On thy birth-night, that sung thee Saviour born.
From that time seldom have I ceas't to eye
Thy infancy, thy childhood, and thy youth,
Thy manhood last, though yet in privat bred;
Till at the Ford of *Jordan* whither all   510
Flockd to the Baptist, I among the rest,
Though not to be Baptiz'd, by voice from Heav'n
Heard thee pronounc't the Son of God belov'd.
Thenceforth I thought thee worth my nearer view
And narrower Scrutiny, that I might learn   515
In what degree or meaning thou art calld
The Son of God, which bears no single sense;
The Son of God I also am, or was,
And if I was, I am; relation stands;
All men are Sons of God: yet thee I thought   520
In some respect far higher so declar'd.
Therefore I watchd thy footsteps from that hour,
And followd thee still on to this waste wild;
Where by all best conjectures I collect
Thou art to be my fatal enemy.   525

Good reason then, if I beforehand seek
To understand my Adversary, who
And what he is, his wisdom, power, intent;
By parl or composition, truce or league
To win him, or win from him what I can.   530
And opportunity I here have had
To try thee, sift thee, and confess have found thee
Proof against all temptation as a rock
Of Adamant, and as a Center, firm;
To th'utmost of mere man both wise and good,   535
Not more: for Honours, Riches, Kingdoms, Glory
Have been before contemnd, and may again.
Therefore to know what more thou art than man,
Worth naming Son of God by voice from Heav'n,
Another method I must now begin.   540
    So saying he caught him up, and without wing
Of *Hippogrif* bore through the Air sublime
Over the Wilderness and ore the Plain;
Till underneath them fair *Jerusalem*
The holy City lifted high her Towers,   545
And higher yet the glorious Temple rear'd
Her pile, far off appearing like a Mount
Of Alablaster, topt with golden Spires:
There on the highest Pinnacle he set
The Son of God; and added thus in scorn: 550
    There stand, if thou wilt stand; to stand upright
Will ask thee skill; I to thy Fathers house
Have brought thee, and highest plac't, highest is best;
Now shew thy Progeny; if not to stand,
Cast thy self down; safely if Son of God: 555
For it is written, He will give command
Concerning thee to his Angels, in thir hands
They shall up lift thee, lest at any time
Thou chance to dash thy foot against a stone.
    To whom thus *Jesus*: Also it is written,   560
Tempt not the Lord thy God; he said, and stood.
But *Satan* smitten with amazement fell.
As when Earths Son *Antæus* (to compare
Small things with greatest) in *Irassa* strove
With *Joves Alcides*, and oft foild still rose,   565
Receiving from his mother Earth new strength,
Fresh from his fall, and fiercer grapple joind,
Throttl'd at length in th'Air, expir'd and fell;
So after many a foil the Tempter proud,
Renewing fresh assaults, amidst his pride   570
Fell whence he stood to see his Victor fall.
And as that *Theban* Monster that propos'd
Her riddle, and him, who solv'd it not, devourd;
That once found out and solv'd, for grief and spite

Cast her self headlong from th' *Ismenian* steep;   575
So strook with dread and anguish fell the Fiend,
And to his crew, that sat consulting, brought
Joyless triumphals of his hop't success,
Ruin and desperation and dismay,
Who durst so proudly tempt the Son of God.   580
So Satan fell: And straight a fiery Globe
Of Angels on full sail of wing flew nigh,
Who on thir plumy Vans receiv'd him soft
From his uneasie station, and upbore
As on a floating couch through the blithe Air,   585
Then in a flowry valley set him down
On a green bank, and set before him spred
A table of Celestial Food, Divine,
Ambrosial, Fruits fetcht from the Tree of Life,
And from the Fount of Life Ambrosial drink,   590
That soon refreshd him wearied, and repaird
What hunger, if aught hunger had impaird
Or thirst; and as he fed, Angelic Quires
Sung Heavenly Anthems of his victory
Over temptation and the Tempter proud.   595
     True Image of the Father, whether thron'd
In the bosom of bliss, and light of light
Conceiving, or remote from Heaven, enshrin'd
In fleshly Tabernacle and human form,
Wandring the Wilderness; whatever place,   600
Habit or state or motion, still expressing
The Son of God, with Godlike force indu'd
Against th' Attempter of thy Fathers Throne,
And Thief of Paradise; him long of old
Thou didst debell, and down from Heav'n cast   605
With all his Army, now thou hast aveng'd
Supplanted *Adam*, and by vanquishing
Temptation hast regaind lost Paradise,
And frustrated the conquest fraudulent:
He never more henceforth will dare set foot   610
In Paradise to tempt; his snares are broke:
For though that seat of earthly bliss be faild,
A fairer Paradise is founded now
For *Adam* and his chosen Sons, whom thou
A Saviour art come down to re-install,   615
Where they shall dwell secure, when time shall be
Of Tempter and Temptation without fear.
But thou, Infernal Serpent, shalt not long
Rule in the Clouds; like an Autumnal Star
Or Lightning thou shalt fall from Heav'n trod down   620
Under his feet: for proof, ere this thou feelst
Thy wound, yet not thy last and deadliest wound
By this repulse receiv'd, and holdst in Hell

No triumph; in all her gates *Abaddon* rues
Thy bold attempt; hereafter learn with awe   625
To dread the Son of God: hee all unarmd
Shall chase thee with the terror of his voice
From thy Demoniac holds, possession foul,
Thee and thy Legions; yelling they shall fly,
And beg to hide them in a herd of Swine,   630
Lest he command them down into the Deep
Bound, and to torment sent before thir time.
Haile Son of the most High, heir of both Worlds,
Queller of Satan, on thy glorious work
Now enter, and begin to save mankind.   635
    Thus they the Son of God our Saviour meek
Sung Victor, and from Heav'nly Feast refresht
Brought on his way with joy; hee unobserv'd
Home to his Mothers house privat returnd.

626 hee] he *1671*

The End

[Many corrections of emphatic and unemphatic forms of the pronouns
have been silently made in the present texts of *Paradise Regain'd* and *Samson
Agonistes,* especially of *their* to *thir.*]

SAMSON AGONISTES

SAMSON
AGONISTES,
A
DRAMATIC POEM.

The Author
JOHN MILTON.

Aristot. Poet. Cap. 6.

Τεαγωδία μίμησις πεαξεως σπυδαίας, &c.

Tragœdia est imitatio actionis seriæ, &c. Per misericordiam &
metum perficiens talium affectuum lustrationem.

LONDON,

Printed by *J. M.* for *John Starkey* at the
Mitre in *Fleetstreet*, near *Temple-Bar.*
MDCLXXI.

I

Of that sort of Dramatic Poem
which is called Tragedy

Tragedy, as it was antiently compos'd, hath been ever
held the gravest, moralest, and most profitable of all other
Poems: therefore said by *Aristotle* to be of power by raising
pity and fear, or terror, to purge the mind of those and such
like passions, that is to temper and reduce them to just   5
measure with a kind of delight, stirr'd up by reading or
seeing those passions well imitated.   Nor is Nature wanting
in her own effects to make good his assertion: for so
in Physic things of melancholic hue and quality are us'd
against melancholy, sour against sour, salt to remove salt   10
humours.   Hence Philosophers and other gravest Writers,
as *Cicero*, *Plutarch*, and others, frequently cite out of Tragic
Poets, both to adorn and illustrate thir discourse.   The
Apostle *Paul* himself thought it not unworthy to insert a
verse of *Euripides* into the Text of Holy Scripture, 1 *Cor.*   15
15. 33; and *Paræus* commenting on the *Revelation*, divides
the whole Book as a Tragedy, into Acts distinguisht each by
a Chorus of Heavenly Harpings and Song between.   Here-
tofore Men in highest dignity have labour'd not a little to
be thought able to compose a Tragedy.   Of that honour   20
Dionysius the elder was no less ambitious, then before of his
attaining to the Tyranny.   *Augustus Cæsar* also had begun
his *Ajax*, but unable to please his own judgment with what
he had begun, left it unfinisht.   *Seneca* the Philosopher is
by some thought the Author of those Tragedies (at least the   25
best of them) that go under that name.   *Gregory Nazianzen*
a Father of the Church, thought it not unbeseeming the
sanctity of his person to write a Tragedy, which he entitl'd,
Christ suffering.   This is mention'd to vindicate Tragedy
from the small esteem, or rather infamy, which in the ac-   30
count of many it undergoes at this day with other common
Interludes; hap'ning through the Poets error of intermixing
Comic stuff with Tragic sadness and gravity; or introducing trivial and vulgar persons, which by all judicious hath
bin counted absurd; and brought in without discretion, cor-   35
ruptly to gratifie the people.   And though antient Tragedy
use no Prologue, yet using sometimes, in case of self defence,
or explanation, that which *Martial* calls an Epistle; in behalf
of this Tragedy coming forth after the antient manner, much
different from what among us passes for best, thus much   40
before-hand may be Epistl'd; that *Chorus* is here introduc'd

after the Greek manner, not antient only but modern, and
still in use among the *Italians*.   In the modelling therefore
of this Poem, with good reason, the Antients and *Italians*
are rather follow'd, as of much more authority and fame.   45
The measure of Verse us'd in the Chorus is of all sorts, call'd
by the Greeks *Monostrophic*, or rather *Apolelymenon*, without regard had to *Strophe*, *Antistrophe* or *Epod*, which were
a kind of Stanza's fram'd only for the Music, then us'd with
the Chorus that sung; not essential to the Poem, and there-   50
fore not material; or being divided into Stanza's or Pauses,
they may be call'd *Allæostropha*.   Division into Act and
Scene referring chiefly to the Stage (to which this work never
was intended) is here omitted.   It suffices if the whole
Drama be found not produc't beyond the fift Act.   55

   Of the style and uniformitie, and that commonly call'd
the Plot, whether intricate or explicit, which is nothing
indeed but such œconomy or disposition of the fable as may
stand best with verisimilitude and decorum; they only will
best judge who are not unacquainted with *Æschulus*, *So-*   60
phocles, and *Euripides*, the three Tragic Poets unequall'd yet
by any, and the best rule to all who endeavour to write
Tragedy.   The circumscription of time wherein the whole
Drama begins and ends, is according to antient rule, and
best example, within the space of 24 hours.   65

   54 omitted.] *1671 ends the paragraph here, whereas it should obviously end
at* 'fift Act.'
   55 Act.] Act, *1671*
   56 Of the style] of the style *1671*

The ARGUMENT

Samson *made Captive, Blind, and now in the Prison at* Gaza, *there to labour as in a common work-house, on a Festival day, in the general cessation from labour, comes forth into the open Air, to a place nigh, somewhat retir'd, there to sit a while and bemoan his condition. Where he happens at length to be visited by certain friends and equals of his tribe, which make the Chorus, who seek to comfort him what they can ; then by his old Father* Manoah, *who endeavours the like, and withall tells him his purpose to procure his liberty by ransom ; lastly, that this Feast was proclaim'd by the* Philistins *as a day of Thanksgiving for thir deliverance from the hands of* Samson, *which yet more troubles him.* Manoah *then departs to prosecute his endeavour with the* Philistian *Lords for* Samson's *redemption ; who in the mean while is visited by other persons; and lastly by a public Officer to require his coming to the Feast before the Lords and People, to play or shew his strength in thir presence ; he at first refuses, dismissing the public Officer with absolute denial to come ; at length persuaded inwardly that this was from God, he yields to go along with him, who came now the second time with great threatnings to fetch him ; the Chorus yet remaining on the place,* Manoah *returns full of joyful hope, to procure ere long his Sons deliverance : in the midst of which discourse an Ebrew comes in haste confusedly at first ; and afterward more distinctly relating the Catastrophe, what* Samson *had done to the* Philistins, *and by accident to himself; wherewith the Tragedy ends.*

The Persons

Samson
Manoah *the Father of* Samson
Dalila *his Wife*
Harapha *of* Gath
Public Officer
Messenger
Chorus *of* Danites

The Scene before the Prison in Gaza

SAMSON
AGONISTES

Samson. A little onward lend thy guiding hand
To these dark steps, a little furder on;
For yonder bank hath choice of Sun or shade;
There I am wont to sit, when any chance
Relieves me from my task of servil toil,   5
Daily in the common Prison else enjoind me,
Where I a Pris'ner chaind, scarce freely draw
The air imprisond also, close and damp,
Unwholsom draught: but here I feel amends,
The breath of Heav'n fresh-blowing, pure and sweet,   10
With day-spring born; here leave me to respire.
This day a solemn Feast the people hold
To *Dagon* thir Sea-Idol, and forbid
Laborious works; unwillingly this rest
Thir Superstition yields me: hence with leave   15
Retiring from the popular noise, I seek
This unfrequented place to find som ease;
Ease to the body som, none to the mind
From restless thoughts, that like a deadly swarm
Of Hornets armd, no sooner found alone,   20
But rush upon me thronging, and present
Times past, what once I was, and what am now.
O wherefore was my birth from Heav'n foretold
Twice by an Angel, who at last in sight
Of both my Parents all in flames ascended   25
From off the Altar, where an Off'ring burnd,
As in a fiery column charioting
His Godlike presence, and from some great act
Or benefit reveal'd to *Abrahams* race?
Why was my breeding orderd and prescrib'd   30
As of a person separate to God,
Design'd for great exploits, if I must die
Betrayd, Captiv'd, and both my Eyes put out,
Made of my Enemies the scorn and gaze,
To grind in Brazen Fetters under task   35
With this Heav'n-gifted strength? O glorious strength
Put to the labour of a Beast, debas't
Lower than bondslave!   Promise was that I
Should *Israel* from *Philistian* yoke deliver;

Ask for this great Deliverer now, and find him   40
Eyeless in *Gaza* at the Mill with slaves,
Himself in bonds under *Philistian* yoke:
Yet stay, let me not rashly call in doubt
Divine Prediction; what if all foretold
Had been fulfilld but through mine own default,   45
Whom have I to complain of but my self?
Who this high gift of strength committed to me,
In what part lodg'd, how easily bereft me,
Under the Seal of silence could not keep,
But weakly to a woman must reveal it   50
O'ercome with importunity and tears.
O impotence of mind, in body strong!
But what is strength without a double share
Of wisdom? vast, unwieldy, burdensom,
Proudly secure, yet liable to fall   55
By weakest suttleties, not made to rule,
But to subserve where wisdom bears command.
God, when he gave me strength, to shew withall
How slight the gift was, hung it in my Hair.
But peace, I must not quarrel with the will   60
Of highest dispensation, which herein
Haply had ends above my reach to know:
Suffices that to mee strength is my bane,
And proves the source of all my miseries;
So many, and so huge, that each apart   65
Would ask a life to wail, but chief of all,
O loss of sight, of thee I most complain!
Blind among enemies, O worse than chains,
Dungeon or beggery or decrepit age!
Light the prime work of God to me is extinct,   70
And all her various objects of delight
Annulld, which might in part my grief have eas'd,
Inferior to the vilest now become
Of man or worm; the vilest here excell me,
They creep, yet see, I dark in light expos'd   75
To daily fraud, contempt, abuse and wrong,
Within doors or without, still as a fool,
In power of others, never in my own;
Scarce half I seem to live, dead more than half.
O dark, dark, dark, amid the blaze of noon,   80
Irrecoverably dark, total Eclipse
Without all hope of day!
O first created Beam, and thou great Word,
Let ther be light, and light was over all;
Why am I thus bereav'd thy prime decree?   85
The Sun to me is dark

62 Haply] Happ'ly *Ed. 1*   63 mee] me *Ed. 1*

And silent as the Moon,
When she deserts the night
Hid in her vacant interlunar cave.
Since light so necessary is to life,   90
And almost life itself, if it be true
That light is in the Soul,
Shee all in every part; why was the sight
To such a tender ball as th' eye confin'd,
So obvious and so easie to be quencht,   95
And not as feeling through all parts diffus'd,
That she might look at will through every pore?
Then had I not bin thus exil'd from light;
As in the land of darkness yet in light,
To live a life half dead, a living death,   100
And buried; but O yet more miserable!
My self, my Sepulcher, a moving Grave,
Buried, yet not exempt
By priviledge of death and burial
From worst of other evils, pains and wrongs,   105
But made hereby obnoxious more
To all the miseries of life,
Life in captivity
Among inhuman foes.
But who are these? for with joint pace I hear   110
The tread of many feet steering this way;
Perhaps my enemies who come to stare
At my affliction, and perhaps to insult,
Thir daily practice to afflict me more.
    Chorus. This, this is he; softly a while,   115
Let us not break in upon him:
O change beyond report, thought or belief!
See how he lies at random, carelessly diffus'd,
With languisht head unpropt,
As one past hope, abandond   120
And by himself giv'n over;
In slavish habit, ill-fitted weeds
Oreworn and soild;
Or do my eyes misrepresent?   Can this be hee,
That Heroic, that Renownd,   125
Irresistible *Samson*? whom unarmd
No strength of man or fiercest wild beast could withstand;
Who tore the Lion, as the Lion tears the Kid,
Ran on embatteld Armies clad in Iron,
And weaponless himself   130
Made Arms ridiculous, useless the forgery
Of brazen shield and spear, the hammerd Cuirass,
Chalybean temperd steel, and frock of mail
Adamantean Proof;
But safest he who stood aloof,   135

When insupportably his foot advanc't,
In scorn of thir proud arms and warlike tools,
Spurnd them to death by Troops.   The bold *Ascalonite*
Fled from his Lion ramp, old Warriors turnd
Thir plated backs under his heel;   140
Or grovling soild thir crested helmets in the dust.
Then with what trivial weapon came to hand,
The Jaw of a dead Ass, his sword of bone,
A thousand foreskins fell, the flowr of *Palestine*
In *Ramath-lechi* famous to this day: 145
Then by main force pulld up, and on his shoulders bore
The Gates of *Azza*, Post and massie Bar
Up to the Hill by *Hebron*, seat of Giants old,
No journey of a Sabbath day, and loaded so;
Like whom the Gentiles feign to bear up Heav'n.   150
Which shall I first bewail,
Thy Bondage or lost Sight,
Prison within Prison
Inseparably dark?
Thou art become (O worst imprisonment!)   155
The Dungeon of thy self; thy Soul
(Which Men enjoying sight oft without cause complain)
Imprisond now indeed,
In real darkness of the body dwells,
Shut up from outward light   160
To incorporate with gloomy night;
For inward light alas
Puts forth no visual beam.
O mirror of our fickle state,
Since man on earth unparaleld!   165
The rarer thy example stands,
By how much from the top of wondrous glory,
Strongest of mortal men,
To lowest pitch of abject fortune thou art fall'n.
For him I reckon not in high estate   170
Whom long descent of birth
Or the sphear of fortune raises;
But thee whose strength, while vertue was her mate
Might have subdu'd the Earth,
Universally crownd with highest praises.   175
    Sam. I hear the sound of words, thir sense the air
Dissolves unjointed ere it reach my ear.
    Chor. He speaks, let us draw nigh.   Matchless in might,
The glory late of *Israel*, now the grief;
We come thy friends and neighbours not unknown   180
From *Eshtaol* and *Zora*'s fruitful Vale
To visit or bewail thee, or if better,
Counsel or Consolation we may bring,
Salve to thy Sores; apt words have power to swage

The tumors of a troubl'd mind, 185
And are as Baum to festerd wounds.
   Sam. Your coming, Friends, revives me, for I learn
Now of my own experience, not by talk,
How counterfeit a coin they are who friends
Bear in thir Superscription (of the most 190
I would be understood): in prosperous days
They swarm, but in adverse withdraw thir head
Not to be found, though sought. Yee see, O friends,
How many evils have enclos'd me round;
Yet that which was the worst now least afflicts me, 195
Blindness: for had I sight, confus'd with shame
How could I once look up or heave the head,
Who like a foolish Pilot have shipwrackt
My Vessel trusted to me from above,
Gloriously riggd; and for a word, a tear, 200
Fool, have divulg'd the secret gift of God
To a deceitful Woman: tell me Friends,
Am I not sung and proverbd for a Fool
In every street, do they not say, how well
Are come upon him his deserts? yet why? 205
Immeasurable strength they might behold
In me, of wisdom nothing more than mean;
This with the other should, at least, have paird,
These two proportiond ill drove me transverse.
   Chor. Tax not divine disposal; wisest Men 210
Have errd, and by bad Women been deceiv'd;
And shall again, pretend they ne're so wise.
Deject not then so overmuch thy self,
Who hast of sorrow thy full load besides;
Yet truth to say, I oft have heard men wonder 215
Why thou shouldst wed *Philistian* women rather
Than of thine own Tribe fairer, or as fair,
At least of thy own Nation, and as noble.
   Sam. The first I saw at *Timna*, and she pleas'd
Mee, not my Parents, that I sought to wed 220
The daughter of an Infidel: they knew not
That what I motiond was of God; I knew
From intimate impulse, and therefore urg'd
The Marriage on; that by occasion hence
I might begin *Israels* Deliverance, 225
The work to which I was divinely calld;
She proving false, the next I took to Wife
(O that I never had! fond wish too late)
Was in the Vale of *Sorec*, *Dalila*,
That specious Monster, my accomplisht snare. 230
I thought it lawful from my former act,
And the same end; still watching to oppress
Israels oppressors: of what now I suffer

She was not the prime cause, but I my self,
Who vanquisht with a peal of words (O weakness!)   235
Gave up my fort of silence to a Woman.
   Chor. In seeking just occasion to provoke
The *Philistine*, thy Countrys Enemy,
Thou never wast remiss, I bear thee witness:
Yet *Israël* still serves with all his Sons.   240
   Sam. That fault I take not on me, but transferr
On *Israels* Governors, and Heads of Tribes,
Who seeing those great acts which God had done
Singly by mee against thir Conquerors
Acknowledg'd not or not at all considerd   245
Deliverance offerd: I on th' other side
Us'd no ambition to commend my deeds,
The deeds themselves, though mute, spoke loud the dooer;
But they persisted deaf, and would not seem
To count them things worth notice, till at length   250
Thir Lords the *Philistines* with gatherd powers
Enterd *Judea* seeking me, who then
Safe to the rock of *Etham* was retir'd,
Not flying, but forecasting in what place
To set upon them, what advantag'd best;   255
Mean while the men of *Judah*, to prevent
The harrass of thir Land, beset me round;
I willingly on some conditions came
Into thir hands, and they as gladly yield me
To the uncircumcis'd a welcom prey,   260
Bound with two cords; but cords to me were threds
Toucht with the flame: on thir whole Host I flew
Unarmd, and with a trivial weapon felld
Thir choicest youth; they only liv'd who fled.
Had *Judah* that day joind, or one whole Tribe,   265
They had by this possesst the Towrs of *Gath*,
And lorded over them whom now they serve;
But what more oft in Nations grown corrupt,
And by thir vices brought to servitude,
Than to love Bondage more than Liberty,   270
Bondage with ease than strenuous Liberty;
And to despise or envy or suspect
Whom God hath of his special favour rais'd
As thir Deliverer; if he aught begin,
How frequent to desert him, and at last   275
To heap ingratitude on worthiest deeds!
   Chor. Thy words to my remembrance bring
How *Succoth* and the Fort of *Penuel*
Thir great Deliverer contemnd,
The matchless *Gideon* in persuit   280

    244 mee] me *Ed. 1*   252 me] mee *Ed. 1*

Of *Madian* and her vanquisht Kings:
And how ingrateful *Ephraim*
Had dealt with *Jephtha*, who by argument
Not worse than by his shield and spear
Defended *Israel* from the *Ammonite*,   285
Had not his prowess quelld thir pride
In that sore battel when so many di'd
Without Reprieve adjudg'd to death,
For want of well pronouncing *Shibboleth*.
   Sam. Of such examples adde mee to the roul;   290
Mee easily indeed mine may neglect,
But Gods propos'd deliverance not so.
   Chor. Just are the ways of God,
And justifiable to Men;
Unless there be who think not God at all,   295
If any be, they walk obscure;
For of such Doctrin never was there School
But the heart of the Fool,
And no man therein Doctor but himself.
   Yet more there be who doubt his ways not just,   300
As to his own edicts found contradicting,
Then give the reins to wandring thought,
Regardless of his glorys diminution;
Till by thir own perplexities involv'd
They ravel more, still less resolv'd,   305
But never find self-satisfying solution.
   As if they would confine th' interminable,
And tie him to his own prescript,
Who made our Laws to bind us, not himself.
And hath full right to exempt   310
Whom so it pleases him by choice
From National obstriction, without taint
Of sin or legal debt;
For with his own Laws he can best dispense.
   He would not else, who never wanted means,   315
Nor in respect of th'enemy just cause
To set his people free,
Have prompted this Heroic *Nazarite*,
Against his vow of strictest purity,
To seek in marriage that fallacious Bride,   320
Unclean, unchaste.
   Down Reason then, at least vain reasonings down,
Though Reason here averr
That moral verdit quits her of unclean:
Unchaste was subsequent, her stain not his.   325
   But see here comes thy reverend Sire
With careful step, Locks white as down,
Old *Manoah*: advise
Forthwith how thou oughtst to receive him.

Sam. Ay me, another inward grief awak't   330
With mention of that name renews th' assault.
  Manoah. Brethren and men of *Dan*, for such ye seem,
Though in this uncouth place; if old respect,
As I suppose, towards your once gloried friend,
My Son now Captive, hither hath informd   335
Your younger feet, while mine cast back with age
Came lagging after; say if he be here.
  Chor. As signal now in low dejected state,
As erst in highest, behold him where he lies.
  Man. O miserable change! is this the man,   340
That invincible *Samson*, far renownd,
The dread of *Israels* foes who with a strength
Equivalent to Angels walkd thir streets,
None offering fight; who single combatant
Duelld thir Armies rankt in proud array,   345
Himself an Army, now unequal match
To save himself against a coward armd
At one spears length.   O ever failing trust
In mortal strength! and oh what not in man
Deceivable and vain! Nay what thing good   350
Prayd for, but often proves our woe, our bane?
I prayd for Childern, and thought barrenness
In wedlock a reproach; I gaind a Son,
And such a Son as all Men haild me happy;
Who would be now a Father in my stead?   355
O wherefore did God grant me my request,
And as a blessing with such pomp adornd?
Why are his gifts desirable, to tempt
Our earnest Prayers, then giv'n with solemn hand
As Graces, draw a Scorpions tail behind?   360
For this did th'Angel twice descend? for this
Ordaind thy nurture holy, as of a Plant?
Select and Sacred, Glorious for a while,
The miracle of men: then in an hour
Ensnar'd, assaulted, overcome, led bound,   365
Thy Foes derision, Captive, Poor, and Blind
Into a Dungeon thrust, to work with Slaves.
Alas methinks whom God hath chosen once
To worthiest deeds, if he through frailty err,
He should not so orewhelm, and as a thrall   370
Subject him to so foul indignities,
Be it but for honours sake of former deeds.
  Sam. Appoint not heav'nly disposition, Father,
Nothing of all these evils hath befall'n me
But justly; I my self have brought them on,   375
Sole Author I, sole cause: if aught seem vile,
As vile hath been my folly, who have profan'd
The mystery of God giv'n me under pledge

Of vow, and have betrayd it to a woman,
A *Canaanite*, my faithless enemy.   380
This well I knew, nor was at all surpris'd,
But warnd by oft experience: did not she
Of *Timna* first betray me, and reveal
The secret wrested from me in her highth
Of Nuptial Love profest, carrying it straight   385
To them who had corrupted her, my Spies
And Rivals?   In this other was there found
More Faith? who also in her prime of love,
Spousal embraces, vitiated with Gold,
Though offerd only, by the scent conceiv'd   390
Her spurious first-born; Treason against me!
Thrice she assayd with flattering prayers and sighs
And amorous reproaches to win from me
My capital secret, in what part my strength
Lay stor'd, in what part summd, that she might know:
Thrice I deluded her, and turnd to sport   396
Her importunity, each time perceiving
How openly, and with what impudence
She purpos'd to betray me, and (which was worse
Than undissembl'd hate) with what contempt   400
She sought to make me Traitor to my self;
Yet the fourth time, when mustring all her wiles,
With blandisht parlies, feminine assaults,
Tongue-batteries, she surceas'd not day nor night
To storm me over-watcht and wearied out,   405
At times when men seek most repose and rest
I yielded, and unlockd her all my heart,
Who with a grain of manhood well resolv'd
Might easily have shook off all her snares:
But foul effeminacy held me yok't   410
Her Bond-slave; O indignity, O blot
To Honour and Religion! servil mind
Rewarded well with servil punishment!
The base degree to which I now am fall'n,
These rags, this grinding, is not yet so base   415
As was my former servitude, ignoble,
Unmanly, ignominious, infamous,
True slavery, and that blindness worse than this,
That saw not how degeneratly I serv'd.
  Man. I cannot praise thy Marriage choices, Son,   420
Rather approv'd them not; but thou didst plead
Divine impulsion prompting how thou mightst
Find some occasion to infest our Foes.
I state not that; this I am sure, our Foes
Found soon occasion thereby to make thee   425
Thir Captive, and thir triumph; thou the sooner
Temptation foundst, or over-potent charms

To violate the sacred trust of silence
Deposited within thee; which to have kept
Tacit, was in thy power; true; and thou bear'st   430
Anough and more the burden of that fault;
Bitterly hast thou paid, and still art paying
That rigid score.   A worse thing yet remains,
This day the *Philistines* a popular Feast
Here celebrate in *Gaza*; and proclaim   435
Great Pomp and Sacrifice and Praises loud
To *Dagon*, as their God who hath deliverd
Thee *Samson* bound and blind into thir hands,
Them out of thine, who slewst them many a slain.
So *Dagon* shall be magnifi'd, and God,   440
Besides whom is no God, compar'd with Idols,
Disglorifi'd, blasphem'd, and had in scorn
By th' Idolatrous rout amidst thir wine;
Which to have come to pass by means of thee
Samson, of all thy sufferings think the heaviest,   445
Of all reproach the most with shame that ever
Could have befall'n thee, and thy Fathers house.
   Sam. Father, I do acknowledge and confess
That I this honour, I this pomp have brought
To *Dagon*, and advanc't his praises high   450
Among the Heathen round; to God have brought
Dishonour, obloquie, and op't the mouths
Of Idolists and Atheists; have brought scandal
To *Israel*, diffidence of God, and doubt
In feeble hearts, propense anough before   455
To waver, or fall off and join with Idols;
Which is my chief affliction, shame and sorrow,
The anguish of my Soul, that suffers not
Mine eye to harbour sleep, or thoughts to rest.
This only hope relieves me, that the strife   460
With mee hath end: all the contest is now
'Twixt God and *Dagon*; *Dagon* hath presum'd,
Mee overthrown, to enter lists with God,
His Deity comparing and preferring
Before the God of *Abraham*.   He, be sure,   465
Will not connive or linger, thus provok't,
But will arise and his great name assert:
Dagon must stoop, and shall ere long receive
Such a discomfit, as shall quite despoil him
Of all these boasted Trophies won on me,   470
And with confusion blank his Worshippers.
   Man. With cause this hope relieves thee, and these words
I as a Prophecy receive: for God,
Nothing more certain, will not long deferr

To vindicate the glory of his name 475
Against all competition, nor will long
Endure it, doubtful whether God be Lord
Or *Dagon*.   But for thee what shall be don?
Thou must not in the mean while here forgot
Lie in this miserable loathsom plight 480
Neglected.   I already have made way
To some *Philistian* Lords, with whom to treat
About thy ransom: well they may by this
Have satisfi'd thir utmost of revenge
By pains and slaveries, worse than death inflicted 485
On thee, who now no more canst do them harm.

    Sam. Spare that proposal, Father, spare the trouble
Of that solicitation; let me here,
As I deserve, pay on my punishment;
And expiate, if possible, my crime, 490
Shameful garrulity.   To have reveal'd
Secrets of men, the secrets of a friend,
How heinous had the fact been, how deserving
Contempt, and scorn of all, to be excluded
All friendship, and avoided as a blab, 495
The mark of fool set on his front!   But I
Gods counsel have not kept, his holy secret
Presumptously have publisht, impiously,
Weakly at least, and shamefully: A sin
That Gentiles in thir Parables condemn 500
To thir abyss and horrid pains confin'd.

    Man. Be penitent and for thy fault contrite,
But act not in thy own affliction, Son,
Repent the sin, but if the punishment
Thou canst avoid, self-preservation bids; 505
Or th' execution leave to high disposal,
And let another hand, not thine, exact
Thy penal forfeit from thy self: perhaps
God will relent, and quit thee all his debt;
Who evermore approves and more accepts 510
(Best pleas'd with humble and filial submission)
Him who imploring mercy sues for life,
Than who self-rigorous chooses death as due;
Which argues over-just, and self-displeas'd
For self-offence, more than for God offended. 515
Reject not then what offerd means, who knows
But God hath set before us, to return thee
Home to thy country and his sacred house,
Where thou mayst bring thy off'rings, to avert
His further ire, with prayers and vows renewd. 520

    Sam. His pardon I implore; but as for life,

496 But I] *Misplaced to next line in Ed. 1*

To what end should I seek it? When in strength
All mortals I excelld, and great in hopes
With youthful courage and magnanimous thoughts
Of birth from Heav'n foretold and high exploits,   525
Full of divine instinct, after som proof
Of acts indeed heroic, far beyond
The Sons of *Anac*, famous now and blaz'd,
Fearless of danger, like a petty God
I walkd about admir'd of all and dreaded   530
On hostile ground, none daring my affront;
Then swoll'n with pride into the snare I fell
Of fair fallacious looks, venereal trains,
Softend with pleasure and voluptuous life;
At length to lay my head and hallowd pledge   535
Of all my strength in the lascivious lap
Of a deceitful Concubine who shore me
Like a tame Wether, all my precious fleece,
Then turnd me out ridiculous, despoild,
Shav'n, and disarmd among my enemies.   540
   Chor. Desire of wine and all delicious drinks,
Which many a famous Warrior overturns,
Thou couldst repress, nor did the dancing Rubie
Sparkling out-pour'd, the flavor or the smell
Or taste that cheers the heart of Gods and men,   545
Allure thee from the cool Crystallin stream.
   Sam. Wherever fountain or fresh current flowd
Against the Eastern ray, translucent, pure
With touch ethereal of Heav'ns fiery rod,
I drank, from the clear milkie juice allaying   550
Thirst, and refresht; nor envied them the grape
Whose heads that turbulent liquor fills with fumes.
   Chor. O madness, to think use of strongest wines
And strongest drinks our chief support of health,
When God with these forbidd'n made choice to rear   555
His mighty Champion, strong above compare,
Whose drink was onely from the liquid brook.
   Sam. But what availd this temperance, not complete
Against another object more enticing?
What boots it at one gate to make defence,   560
And at another to let in the foe
Effeminatly vanquisht? by which means,
Now blind, disheartend, sham'd, dishonourd, quelld,
To what can I be useful, wherein serve
My Nation, and the work from Heav'n impos'd,   565
But to sit idle on the household hearth,
A burd'nous drone? to visitants a gaze
Or pittied object, these redundant locks
Robustious to no purpose clustring down,
Vain monument of strength; till length of years   570

And sedentary numness craze my limbs
To a contemptible old age obscure.
Here rather let me drudge and earn my bread,
Till vermin or the draff of servil food
Consume me, and oft-invocated death   575
Hasten the welcom end of all my pains.
   Man. Wilt thou then serve the *Philistines* with that gift
Which was expressly giv'n thee to annoy them?
Better at home lie bed-rid, not only idle,
Inglorious, unimployd, with age out-worn.   580
But God who caus'd a fountain at thy prayer
From the dry ground to spring, thy thirst to allay
After the brunt of battel, can as easie
Cause light again within thy eyes to spring,
Wherewith to serve him better than thou hast;   585
And I persuade me so; why else this strength
Miraculous yet remaining in those locks?
His might continues in thee not for naught,
Nor shall his wondrous gifts be frustrate thus.
   Sam. All otherwise to me my thoughts portend,   590
That these dark orbs no more shall treat with light,
Nor th' other light of life continue long,
But yield to double darkness nigh at hand:
So much I feel my genial spirits droop,
My hopes all flat, nature within me seems   595
In all her functions weary of herself;
My race of glory run, and race of shame,
And I shall shortly be with them that rest.
   Man. Believe not these suggestions which proceed
From anguish of the mind and humours black,   600
That mingle with thy fancy.   I however
Must not omit a Fathers timely care
To prosecute the means of thy deliverance
By ransom or how else: mean while be calm,
And healing words from these thy friends admit.   605
   Sam. O that torment should not be confin'd
To the bodys wounds and sores
With maladies innumerable
In heart, head, brest and reins;
But must secret passage find   610
To th' inmost mind,
There exercise all his fierce accidents,
And on her purest spirits prey,
As on entrails, joints and limbs,
With answerable pains, but more intense,   615
Though void of corporal sense.
   My griefs not only pain me
As a lingring disease,
But finding no redress, ferment and rage,

Nor less than wounds immedicable   620
Rankle and fester and gangrene
To black mortification.
Thoughts my Tormenters armd with deadly stings
Mangle my apprehensive tenderest parts,
Exasperate, exulcerate, and raise   625
Dire inflammation which no cooling herb
Or medcinal liquor can assuage,
Nor breath of Vernal Air from snowy *Alp*.
Sleep hath forsook and giv'n me ore
To deaths benumming Opium as my onely cure.   630
Thence faintings, swoonings of despair,
And sense of Heav'ns desertion.
     I was his nursling once and choice delight,
His destind from the womb,
Promis'd by Heavenly message twice descending.   635
Under his special eye
Abstemious I grew up and thriv'd amain;
He led me on to mightiest deeds
Above the nerve of mortal arm
Against th'uncircumcis'd, our enemies.   640
But now hath cast me off as never known,
And to those cruel enemies,
Whom I by his appointment had provok't,
Left me all helpless with th' irreparable loss
Of sight, reserv'd alive to be repeated   645
The subject of thir cruelty or scorn.
Nor am I in the list of them that hope;
Hopeless are all my evils, all remediless;
This one prayer yet remains, might I be heard,
No long petition, speedy death,   650
The close of all my miseries, and the baum.
     Chor. Many are the sayings of the wise
In ancient and in modern books enrould,
Extolling Patience as the truest fortitude;
And to the bearing well of all calamities,   655
All chances incident to mans frail life
Consolatories writ
With studied argument, and much persuasion sought
Lenient of grief and anxious thought:
But with th' afflicted in his pangs thir sound   660
Little prevails, or rather seems a tune
Harsh and of dissonant mood from his complaint,
Unless he feel within
Som source of consolation from above;
Secret refreshings, that repair his strength   665
And fainting spirits uphold.
     God of our Fathers, what is man!
That thou towards him with hand so various,

Or might I say contrarious,
Temperst thy providence through his short course, 670
Not evenly, as thou rul'st
Th'Angelic orders and inferior creatures mute,
Irrational and brute.
Nor do I name of men the common rout,
That wandring loose about 675
Grow up and perish, as the summer flie,
Heads without name no more rememberd,
But such as thou hast solemnly elected,
With gifts and graces eminently adornd,
To some great work, thy glory, 680
And peoples safety, which in part they effect:
Yet toward these thus dignifi'd, thou oft
Amidst thir highth of noon
Changest thy count'nance, and thy hand with no regard
Of highest favours past 685
From thee on them, or them to thee of service.
    Nor only dost degrade them, or remit
To life obscur'd, which were a fair dismission,
But throwst them lower than thou didst exalt them high,
Unseemly falls in human eye, 690
Too grievous for the trespass or omission;
Oft leav'st them to the hostile sword
Of Heathen and profane, thir carcasses
To dogs and fowls a prey, or else captiv'd;
Or to th'unjust tribunals, under change of times, 695
And condemnation of th'ingrateful multitude.
If these they scape, perhaps in poverty
With sickness and disease thou bowst them down,
Painful diseases and deformd,
In crude old age; 700
Though not disordinate, yet causeless suffring
The punishment of dissolute days; in fine,
Just or unjust, alike seem miserable,
For oft alike, both come to evil end.
    So deal not with this once thy glorious Champion, 705
The Image of thy strength, and mighty minister.
What do I beg? how hast thou dealt already?
Behold him in this state calamitous, and turn
His labours, for thou canst, to peaceful end.
    But who is this, what thing of Sea or Land? 710
Femal of sex it seems,
That so bedeckt, ornate and gay,
Comes this way sailing
Like a stately Ship
Of *Tarsus*, bound for th' Iles 715
Of *Javan* or *Gadier*
With all her bravery on, and tackle trim,

Sails filld, and streamers waving,
Courted by all the winds that hold them play,
An Amber scent of odorous perfume   720
Her harbinger, a damsel train behind;
Som rich *Philistian* Matron she may seem,
And now at nearer view, no other certain
Than *Dalila* thy wife.
    Sam. My Wife, my Traitress, let her not come near me.
    Chor. Yet on she moves, now stands and eyes thee
       fixt,   726
About t' have spoke, but now, with head declin'd
Like a fair flowr surcharg'd with dew, she weeps,
And words addrest seem into tears dissolv'd,
Wetting the borders of her silken veil: 730
But now again she makes address to speak.
    Dalila. With doubtful feet and wavering resolution
I came, still dreading thy displeasure, *Samson*,
Which to have merited, without excuse
I cannot but acknowledge; yet if tears   735
May expiate (though the fact more evil drew
In the perverse event than I foresaw)
My penance hath not slackend, though my pardon
No way assur'd.   But conjugal affection
Prevailing over fear and timorous doubt   740
Hath led me on desirous to behold
Once more thy face, and know of thy estate,
If aught in my ability may serve
To lighten what thou sufferst, and appease
Thy mind with what amends is in my power,   745
Though late, yet in som part to recompense
My rash but more unfortunate misdeed.
    Sam. Out, out *Hyæna*; these are thy wonted arts,
And arts of every woman false like thee,
To break all faith, all vows, deceive, betray,   750
Then as repentant to submit, beseech,
And reconcilement move with feignd remorse,
Confess, and promise wonders in her change,
Not truly penitent, but chief to try
Her husband, how far urg'd his patience bears,   755
His vertue or weakness which way to assail:
Then with more cautious and instructed skill
Again transgresses, and again submits;
That wisest and best men full oft beguil'd
With goodness principl'd not to reject   760
The penitent, but ever to forgive,
Are drawn to wear out miserable days,
Entangl'd with a pois'nous bosom snake,
If not by quick destruction soon cut off
As I by thee; to Ages an example.   765

Dal. Yet hear me *Samson*; not that I endevor
To lessen or extenuate my offence,
But that on th' other side if it be weighd
By it self, with aggravations not surcharg'd,
Or else with just allowance counterpois'd,   770
I may, if possible, thy pardon find
The easier towards me, or thy hatred less.
First granting, as I do, it was a weakness
In me, but incident to all our sex,
Curiosity, inquisitive, importune   775
Of secrets, then with like infirmity
To publish them, both common femal faults:
Was it not weakness also to make known
For importunity, that is for naught,
Wherein consisted all thy strength and safety?   780
To what I did thou shewdst me first the way.
But I to enemies reveal'd, and should not:
Nor shouldst thou have trusted that to womans frailty;
Ere I to thee, thou to thy self wast cruel.
Let weakness then with weakness come to parl,   785
So near related, or the same of kind,
Thine forgive mine; that men may censure thine
The gentler, if severely thou exact not
More strength from me, than in thy self was found.
And what if Love, which thou interpretst hate,   790
The jealousie of Love, powerful of sway
In human hearts, nor less in mine towards thee,
Caus'd what I did? I saw thee mutable
Of fancy, fear'd lest one day thou wouldst leave me
As her at *Timna,* sought by all means therefore   795
How to endear, and hold thee to me firmest:
No better way I saw than by importuning
To learn thy secrets, get into my power
Thy key of strength and safety: thou wilt say,
Why then reveal'd?   I was assur'd by those   800
Who tempted me, that nothing was design'd
Against thee but safe custody and hold:
That made for me, I knew that liberty
Would draw thee forth to perilous enterprises,
While I at home sate full of cares and fears   805
Wailing thy absence in my widowd bed;
Here I should still enjoy thee day and night
Mine and Loves pris'ner, not the *Philistines,*
Whole to my self, unhazarded abroad,
Fearless at home of partners in my love.   810
These reasons in Loves law have past for good,
Though fond and reasonless to some perhaps:
And Love hath oft, well meaning, wrought much woe,
Yet always pitty or pardon hath obtaind.

Be not unlike all others, not austere   815
As thou art strong, inflexible as steel.
If thou in strength all mortals dost exceed,
In uncompassionate anger do not so.
   Sam. How cunningly the sorceress displays
Her own transgressions, to upbraid me mine!   820
That malice not repentance brought thee hither,
By this appears: I gave, thou sayst, th' example,
I led the way; bitter reproach, but true,
I to my self was false ere thou to me,
Such pardon therefore as I give my folly,   825
Take to thy wicked deed: which when thou seest
Impartial, self-severe, inexorable,
Thou wilt renounce thy seeking, and much rather
Confess it feignd.   Weakness is thy excuse,
And I believe it, weakness to resist   830
Philistian gold: if weakness may excuse,
What Murtherer, what Traitor, Parricide,
Incestuous, Sacrilegious, but may plead it?
All wickedness is weakness: that plea therefore
With God or Man will gain thee no remission.   835
But Love constraind thee; call it furious rage
To satisfie thy lust: Love seeks t'have Love;
My love how couldst thou hope, who tookst the way
To raise in me inexpiable hate,
Knowing, as needs I must, by thee betrayd?   840
In vain thou striv'st to cover shame with shame,
Or by evasions thy crime uncoverst more.
   Dal. Since thou determinst weakness for no plea
In man or woman, though to thy own condemning,
Hear what assaults I had, what snares besides,   845
What sieges girt me round, ere I consented;
Which might have awd the best resolv'd of men,
The constantest, t'have yielded without blame.
It was not gold, as to my charge thou layst,
That wrought with me: thou knowst the Magistrates   850
And Princes of my country came in person,
Solicited, commanded, threatend, urg'd,
Adjur'd by all the bonds of civil Duty
And of Religion, pressd how just it was,
How honourable, how glorious to entrap   855
A common enemy, who had destroyd
Such numbers of our Nation: and the Priest
Was not behind, but ever at my ear,
Preaching how meritorious with the gods
It would be to ensnare an irreligious   860
Dishonourer of *Dagon*: what had I

829 feignd.   Weakness] feign'd, weakness *Ed. 1*   842 Or] For *1705*

To oppose against such powerful arguments?
Onely my love of thee held long debate;
And combated in silence all these reasons
With hard contest: at length that grounded maxim   865
So rife and celebrated in the mouths
Of wisest men; that to the public good
Privat respects must yield; with grave autority
Took full possession of me and prevaild;
Vertue, as I thought, truth, duty so enjoining.   870
   Sam. I thought where all thy circling wiles would end;
In feignd Religion, smooth hypocrisie.
But had thy love, still odiously pretended,
Bin, as it ought, sincere, it would have taught thee
Far other reasonings, brought forth other deeds.   875
I before all the daughters of my Tribe
And of my Nation chose thee from among
My enemies, lov'd thee, as too well thou knewst,
Too well, unbosomd all my secrets to thee,
Not out of levity, but overpow'rd   880
By thy request, who could deny thee nothing;
Yet now am judg'd an enemy. Why then
Didst thou at first receive me for thy husband?
Then, as since then, thy countrys foe profest:
Being once a wife, for me thou wast to leave   885
Parents and country; nor was I their subject,
Nor under their protection but my own,
Thou mine, not theirs; if aught against my life
Thy country sought of thee, it sought unjustly,
Against the law of nature, law of nations,   890
No more thy country, but an impious crew
Of men conspiring to uphold thir state
By worse than hostile deeds, violating th' ends
For which our country is a name so dear;
Not therefore to be obeyd. But zeal mov'd thee;   895
To please thy gods thou didst it; gods unable
To acquit themselves and prosecute thir foes
But by ungodly deeds, the contradiction
Of thir own deity, Gods cannot be;
Less therefore to be pleas'd, obeyd, or fear'd: 900
These false pretexts and varnisht colours failing,
Bare in thy guilt how foul must thou appear!
   Dal. In argument with men a woman ever
Goes by the worse, whatever be her cause.
   Sam. For want of words no doubt, or lack of breath;
Witness when I was worried with thy peals.   906
   Dal. I was a fool, too rash, and quite mistaken
In what I thought would have succeeded best.
Let me obtain forgiveness of thee *Samson*,
Afford me place to shew what recompense   910

Towards thee I intend for what I have misdon,
Misguided: only what remains past cure
Bear not too sensibly, nor still insist
To afflict thy self in vain: though sight be lost,
Life yet hath many solaces, enjoyd   915
Where other senses want not thir delights
At home in leasure and domestic ease,
Exempt from many a care and chance to which
Eyesight exposes daily men abroad.
I to the Lords will intercede, not doubting   920
Thir favourable ear, that I may fetch thee
From forth this loathsom prison-house, to abide
With me, where my redoubl'd love and care
With nursing diligence, to me glad office,
May ever tend about thee to old age   925
With all things grateful cheerd, and so suppli'd
That what by me thou hast lost thou least shalt miss.
    Sam. No, no, of my condition take no care;
It fits not; thou and I long since are twain:
Nor think me so unwary or accurst   930
To bring my feet again into the snare
Where once I have been caught; I know thy trains,
Though dearly to my cost, thy ginns and toils;
Thy fair enchanted cup and warbling charms
No more on me have power, thir force is nulld: 935
So much of Adders wisdom I have learnt
To fence my ear against thy sorceries.
If in my flowr of youth and strength, when all men
Lov'd, honourd, fear'd me, thou alone could hate me
Thy Husband, slight me, sell me, and forgo me;   940
How wouldst thou use me now, blind, and thereby
Deceivable, in most things as a child
Helpless, thence easily contemnd and scornd,
And last neglected? How wouldst thou insult
When I must live uxorious to thy will   945
In perfet thraldom, how again betray me,
Bearing my words and doings to the Lords
To gloss upon, and censuring, frown or smile?
This Jail I count the house of Liberty
To thine whose doors my feet shall never enter.   950
    Dal. Let me approach at least, and touch thy hand.
    Sam. Not for thy life, lest fierce remembrance wake
My sudden rage to tear thee joint by joint.
At distance I forgive thee, go with that;
Bewail thy falsehood, and the pious works   955
It hath brought forth to make thee memorable
Among illustrious women, faithful wives:
Cherish thy hastend widowhood with the gold
Of Matrimonial treason: so farewell.

Dal. I see thou art implacable, more deaf   960
To prayers, than winds and seas; yet winds to seas
Are reconcil'd at length, and Sea to Shore:
They anger, unappeasable, still rages,
Eternal tempest never to be calmd.
Why do I humble thus my self, and suing   965
For peace, reap nothing but repulse and hate?
Bid go with evil omen and the brand
Of infamy upon my name denounc't?
To mix with thy concernments I desist
Henceforth, nor too much disapprove my own.   970
Fame if not double-fac't is double-mouth'd,
And with contrary blast proclaims most deeds;
On both his wings, one black the other white,
Bears greatest names in his wild aerie flight.
My name perhaps among the Circumcis'd   975
In *Dan*, in *Judah*, and the bordering Tribes,
To all posterity may stand defam'd,
With malediction mentiond, and the blot
Of falsehood most unconjugal traduc't.
But in my country where I most desire,   980
In *Ecron*, *Gaza*, *Asdod*, and in *Gath*
I shall be nam'd among the famousest
Of Women, sung at solemn festivals,
Living and dead recorded, who to save
Her country from a fierce destroyer, chose   985
Above the faith of wedlock-bands; my tomb
With odours visited and annual flowers:
Not less renownd than in Mount *Ephraim*
Jaël, who with inhospitable guile
Smote *Sisera* sleeping, through the Temples naild.   990
Nor shall I count it heinous to enjoy
The public marks of honour and reward
Conferrd upon me, for the piety
Which to my country I was judg'd t'have shewn.
At this who ever envies or repines   995
I leave him to his lot, and like my own.
   Chor. She's gon, a manifest Serpent by her sting
Discoverd in the end, till now conceal'd.
   Sam. So let her go, God sent her to debase me,
And aggravate my folly who committed .   1000
To such a viper his most sacred trust
Of secresie, my safety, and my life.
   Chor. Yet beauty, though injurious, hath strange
     power,
After offence returning, to regain
Love once possest, nor can be easily   1005
Repuls't, without much inward passion felt
And secret sting of amorous remorse.

Sam. Love-quarrels oft in pleasing concord end,
Not wedlock-trechery endangering life.
    Chor. It is not vertue, wisdom, valour, wit,   1010
Strength, comliness of shape, or amplest merit
That womans love can win or long inherit;
But what it is, hard is to say,
Harder to hit
(Which way soever men refer it),   1015
Much like thy riddle, *Samson*, in one day
Or sev'n, though one should musing sit;
    If any of these or all, the *Timnian* bride
Had not so soon preferrd
Thy Paranymph, worthless to thee compar'd,   1020
Successor in thy bed,
Nor both so loosely disalli'd
Thir nuptials, nor this last so trecherously
Had shorn the fatal harvest of thy head.
Is it for that such outward ornament   1025
Was lavish't on thir Sex, that inward gifts
Were left for haste unfinisht, judgment scant,
Capacity not rais'd to apprehend
Or value what is best
In choice, but oftest to affect the wrong?   1030
Or was too much of self-love mixt,
Of constancy no root infixt,
That either they love nothing, or not long?
    What e're it be, to wisest men and best
Seeming at first all heav'nly under virgin veil,   1035
Soft, modest, meek, demure,
Once joind, the contrary she proves, a thorn
Intestin, far within defensive arms
A cleaving mischief, in his way to vertue
Adverse and turbulent, or by her charms   1040
Draws him awry enslav'd
With dotage, and his sense deprav'd
To folly and shameful deeds which ruin ends.
What Pilot so expert but needs must wreck
Embarkt with such a Steers-mate at the Helm?   1045
    Favourd of Heav'n who finds
One vertuous, rarely found,
That in domestic good combines:
Happy that house! his way to peace is smooth:
But vertue which breaks through all opposition,   1050
And all temptation can remove,
Most shines and most is acceptable above.
    Therefore Gods universal Law
Gave to the man despotic power
Over his femal in due awe,   1055
Nor from that right to part an hour,

Smile she or lour:
So shall he least confusion draw
On his whole life, not swayd
By femal usurpation, nor dismayd.   1060
     But had we best retire?   I see a storm.
     Sam. Fair days have oft contracted wind and rain.
     Chor. But this another kind of tempest brings.
     Sam. Be less abstruse, my riddling days are past.
     Chor. Look now for no inchanting voice, nor fear   1065
The bait of honied words; a rougher tongue
Draws hitherwards; I know him by his stride,
The Giant *Harapha* of *Gath*, his look
Haughty as is his pile high-built and proud.
Comes he in peace? what wind hath blown him thither
I less conjecture than when first I saw   1071
The sumptuous *Dalila* floating this way:
His habit carries peace, his brow defiance.
     Sam. Or peace or not, alike to me he comes.   1074
     Chor. His fraught we soon shall know, he now arrives.
     Harapha. I come not *Samson*, to condole thy chance,
As these perhaps, yet wish it had not been,
Though for no friendly intent.   I am of *Gath*,
Men call me *Harapha*; of stock renownd
As *Og* or *Anak* and the *Emims* old   1080
That *Kiriathaim* held, thou knowst me now
If thou at all art known.   Much I have heard
Of thy prodigious might and feats performd
Incredible to me; in this displeas'd,
That I was never present on the place   1085
Of those encounters, where we might have tri'd
Each others force in camp or listed field:
And now am come to see of whom such noise
Hath walkt about, and each limb to survey,
If thy appearance answer loud report.   1090
     Sam. The way to know were not to see but taste.
     Har. Dost thou already single me?   I thought
Gives and the Mill had tam'd thee.   O that fortune
Had brought me to the field where thou art fam'd
T'have wrought such wonders with an Asses Jaw;   1095
I should have forc't thee soon wish other arms,
Or left thy carcass where the Ass lay thrown:
So had the glory of Prowess been recoverd
To *Palestine*, won by a *Philistine*
From the unforeskinnd race, of whom thou bear'st   1100
The highest name for valiant Acts; that honour
Certain to have won by mortal duel from thee,
I lose, prevented by thy eyes put out.
     Sam. Boast not of what thou wouldst have don, but do
What then thou wouldst; thou seest it in thy hand.   1105

Har. To combat with a blind man I disdain,
And thou hast need much washing to be toucht.
  Sam. Such usage as your honourable Lords
Afford me assassinated and betrayd,
Who durst not with thir whole united powers   1110
In fight withstand me, single and unarmd,
Nor in the house with chamber Ambushes
Close-banded durst attack me, no not sleeping,
Till they had hir'd a woman with thir gold,
Breaking her Marriage Faith to circumvent me.   1115
Therefore without feignd shifts let be assign'd
Som narrow place enclos'd, where sight may give thee,
Or rather flight, no great advantage on me;
Then put on all thy gorgeous arms, thy Helmet
And Brigandine of brass, thy broad Habergeon,   1120
Vant-brass and Greves, and Gauntlet, add thy Spear
A Weavers beam, and sev'n-times-folded shield;
I only with an Oaken staff will meet thee,
And raise such outcries on thy clatterd Iron,
Which long shall not withhold mee from thy head,   1125
That in a little time, while breath remains thee,
Thou oft shalt wish thy self at *Gath* to boast
Again in safety what thou wouldst have done
To *Samson*; but shalt never see *Gath* more.
  Har. Thou durst not thus disparage glorious arms   1130
Which greatest Heroes have in battel worn,
Thir ornament and safety, had not spells
And black enchantments, some Magicians Art
Armd thee or charmd thee strong, which thou from Heaven
Feigndst at thy birth was giv'n thee in thy hair,   1135
Where strength can least abide, though all thy hairs
Were bristles rang'd like those that ridge the back
Of chaf't wild Boars or ruffl'd Porcupines.
  Sam. I know no Spells, use no forbidden Arts;
My trust is in the living God who gave me   1140
At my Nativity this strength, diffus'd
No less through all my sinews, joints and bones
Than thine, while I preserv'd these locks unshorn,
The pledge of my unviolated vow.
For proof hereof, if *Dagon* be thy god,   1145
Goe to his Temple, invocate his aid
With solemnest devotion, spread before him
How highly it concerns his glory now
To frustrate and dissolve these Magic spells,
Which I to be the power of *Israels* God   1150
Avow, and challenge *Dagon* to the test,
Off'ring to combat thee his Champion bold,
With th' utmost of his Godhead seconded:

Then thou shalt see, or rather to thy sorrow
Soon feel, whose God is strongest, thine or mine.   1155
   Har. Presume not on thy God, what e're he be,
Thee he regards not, owns not, hath cut off
Quite from his people, and deliverd up
Into thy Enemies hand, permitted them
To put out both thine eyes, and fetterd send thee   1160
Into the common Prison, there to grind
Among the Slaves and Asses thy comrades,
As good for nothing else, no better service
With those thy boistrous locks, no worthy match
For valour to assail, nor by the sword   1165
Of noble Warrior, so to stain his honour,
But by the Barbars razor best subdu'd.
   Sam. All these indignities, for such they are
From thine, these evils I deserve and more,
Acknowledge them from God inflicted on me   1170
Justly, yet despair not of his final pardon
Whose ear is ever open; and his eye
Gracious to re-admit the suppliant:
In confidence whereof I once again
Defie thee to the trial of mortal fight,   1175
By combat to decide whose god is God,
Thine or whom I with *Israels* Sons adore.
   Har. Fair honour that thou dost thy God, in trusting
He will accept thee to defend his cause,
A Murtherer, a Revolter, and a Robber.   1180
   Sam. Tongue-doughtie Giant, how dost thou prove me
    these?
   Har. Is not thy Nation subject to our Lords?
Thir Magistrates confessd it, when they took thee
As a League-breaker and deliverd bound
Into our hands: for hadst thou not committed   1185
Notorious murder on those thirty men
At *Askalon*, who never did thee harm,
Then like a Robber stripdst them of thir robes?
The *Philistines*, when thou hadst broke the league,
Went up with armed powers, thee only seeking,   1190
To others did no violence nor spoil.
   Sam. Among the Daughters of the *Philistines*
I chose a Wife, which argu'd me no foe;
And in your City held my Nuptial Feast:
But your ill-meaning Politician Lords,   1195
Under pretence of Bridal friends and guests,
Appointed to await me thirty spies,
Who threatning cruel death constraind the bride
To wring from me and tell to them my secret,

    1158 deliverd] delivered *Ed. 1*
    1181 Tongue-doughtie] Tongue-doubtie *Ed. 1*

That solv'd the riddle which I had propos'd.   1200
When I perceiv'd all set on enmity,
As on my enemies, wherever chanc'd,
I us'd hostility, and took thir spoil
To pay my underminers in thir coin.
My Nation was subjected to your Lords!   1205
It was the force of Conquest: force with force
Is well ejected when the Conquerd can.
But I a privat person, whom my Country
As a league-breaker gave up bound, presum'd
Single Rebellion and did Hostile Acts!   1210
I was no privat but a person rais'd
With strength sufficient and command from Heav'n
To free my Country; if their servil minds
Mee thir Deliverer sent, would not receive,
But to thir Masters gave me up for naught,   1215
Th' unworthier they; whence to this day they serve.
I was to do my part from Heav'n assign'd,
And had performd it if my known offence
Had not disabl'd me, not all your force:
These shifts refuted, answer thy appellant   1220
Though by his blindness maimd for high attempts,
Who now defies thee thrice to single fight,
As a petty enterprise of small enforce.
    Har. With thee, a Man condemnd, a Slave enrould,
Due by the Law to capital punishment?   1225
To fight with thee no man of arms will deign.
    Sam. Cam'st thou for this, vain boaster, to survey me,
To descant on my strength, and give thy verdit?
Come nearer, part not hence so slight informd;
But take good heed my hand survey not thee.   1230
    Har. O *Baäl-zebub*! can my ears unus'd
Hear these dishonours, and not render death?
    Sam. No man withholds thee, nothing from thy
        hand
Fear I incurable; bring up thy van,
My heels are fetterd, but my fist is free.   1235
    Har. This insolence other kind of answer fits.
    Sam. Goe baffl'd coward, lest I run upon thee
Though in these chains, bulk without spirit vast,
And with one buffet lay thy structure low
Or swing thee in the Air, then dash thee down   1240
To th' hazard of thy brains and shatterd sides.
    Har. By *Astaroth* ere long thou shalt lament
These braveries in Irons loaden on thee.
    Chor. His Giantship is gone somewhat crestfall'n,
Stalking with less unconsci'nable strides,   1245
And lower looks, but in a sultrie chafe.

1214 Mee] Me *Ed. 1.* thir] their *Ed. 1*

Sam. I dread him not, nor all his Giant-brood,
Though Fame divulge him Father of five Sons
All of Gigantic size, *Goliah* chief.
   Chor. He will directly to the Lords, I fear,   1250
And with malicious counsel stir them up
Some way or other yet further to afflict thee.
   Sam. He must allege som cause, and offerd fight
Will not dare mention, lest a question rise
Whether he durst accept the offer or not,   1255
And that he durst not plain anough appear'd.
Much.more affliction than already felt
They cannot well impose, nor I sustain,
If they intend advantage of my labours
The work of many hands, which earns my keeping   1260
With no small profit daily to my owners.
But come what will, my deadliest foe will prove
My speediest friend, by death to rid me hence;
The worst that he can give, to me the best.
Yet so it may fall out, because thir end   1265
Is hate, not help to me, it may with mine
Draw thir own ruin who attempt the deed.
   Chor. Oh how comely it is and how reviving
To the Spirits of just men long opprest!
When God into the hands of thir deliverer   1270
Puts invincible might
To quell the mighty of the Earth, th' oppressor,
The brute and boistrous force of violent men
Hardy and industrious to support
Tyrannic power, but raging to persue   1275
The righteous and all such as honour Truth;
Hee all thir Ammunition
And feats of War defeats
With plain Heroic magnitude of mind
And celestial vigor armd,   1280
Thir Armories and Magazins contemns,
Renders them useless, while
With winged expedition
Swift as the lightning glance he executes
His errand on the wicked, who surpris'd   1285
Lose thir defence distracted and amaz'd.
   But patience is more oft the exercise
Of Saints, the trial of thir fortitude,
Making them each his own Deliverer,
And Victor over all   1290
That tyrannie or fortune can inflict;
Either of these is in thy lot
Samson, with might endu'd

1277 Hee] He *Ed. 1*

Above the Sons of men; but sight bereav'd
May chance to number thee with those   1295
Whom Patience finally must crown.
This Idols day hath bin to thee no day of rest,
  Labouring thy mind
More than the working day thy hands:
And yet perhaps more trouble is behind.   1300
For I descry this way
Som other tending, in his hand
A Scepter or quaint staff he bears,
Comes on amain, speed in his look.
By his habit I discern him now   1305
A Public Officer; and now at hand.
His message will be short and voluble.
  Officer. *Ebrews*, the Pris'ner *Samson* here I seek.
  Chor. His manacles remark him, there he sits.
  Off. *Samson*, to thee our Lords thus bid me say: 1310
This day to *Dagon* is a solemn Feast,
With Sacrifices, Triumph, Pomp and Games;
Thy strength they know surpassing human rate,
And now som public proof thereof require
To honour this great Feast, and great Assembly: 1315
Rise therefore with all speed and come along,
Where I will see thee heartend and fresh clad
To appear as fits before th' illustrious Lords.
  Sam. Thou knowst I am an *Ebrew*, therefore tell them,
Our Law forbids at thir Religious Rites   1320
My presence; for that cause I cannot come.
  Off. This answer, be assur'd, will not content them.
  Sam. Have they not Sword-players, and ev'ry sort
Of Gymnic Artists, Wrestlers, Riders, Runners,
Juglers and Dancers, Antics, Mummers, Mimics,   1325
But they must pick mee out with shackles tir'd,
And over-labourd at thir public Mill,
To make them sport with blind activity?
Do they not seek occasion of new quarrels
On my refusal to distress me more,   1330
Or make a game of my calamities?
Return the way thou cam'st, I will not come.
  Off. Regard thy self, this will offend them highly.
  Sam. My self? my conscience and internal peace.
Can they think me so broken, so debas'd   1335
With corporal servitude, that my mind ever
Will condescend to such absurd commands?
Although thir drudge, to be thir fool or jester,
And in my midst of sorrow and heart-grief
To shew them feats, and play before thir god,   1340.

1326 mee] me *Ed. 1*

The worst of all indignities, yet on me
Joind with extream contempt?   I will not come.
   Off. My message was impos'd on me with speed,
Brooks no delay: is this thy resolution?
    Sam. So take it with what speed thy message needs.
    Off. I am sorry what this stoutness will produce.   1346
    Sam. Perhaps thou shalt have cause to sorrow indeed.
    Chor. Consider, *Samson*; matters now are straind
Up to the highth, whether to hold or break;
He's gon, and who knows how he may report   1350
Thy words by adding fuel to the flame?
Expect another message more imperious,
More Lordly thundring than thou well wilt bear.
    Sam. Shall I abuse this Consecrated gift
Of strength, again returning with my hair   1355
After my great transgression, so requite
Favour renewd, and add a greater sin
By prostituting holy things to Idols;
A *Nazarite* in place abominable
Vaunting my strength in honour to thir *Dagon*?   1360
Besides, how vile, contemptible, ridiculous!
What act more execrably unclean, profane?
    Chor. Yet with this strength thou serv'st the *Philistines*,
Idolatrous, uncircumcis'd, unclean.
    Sam. Not in thir Idol-worship, but by labour   1365
Honest and lawful, to deserve my food
Of those who have me in thir civil power.
    Chor. Where the heart joins not, outward acts defile
   not.
    Sam. Where outward force constrains, the sentence
   holds;
But who constrains me to the Temple of *Dagon*,   1370
Not dragging? the *Philistian* Lords command:
Commands are no constraints.   If I obey them,
I do it freely; venturing to displease
God for the fear of Man, and Man preferr,
Set God behind: which in his jealousie   1375
Shall never, unrepented, find forgiveness.
Yet that he may dispense with me or thee
Present in Temples at Idolatrous Rites
For some important cause, thou needst not doubt.
    Chor. How thou wilt here come off surmounts my
   reach.   1380
    Sam. Be of good courage, I begin to feel
Som rouzing motions in me which dispose
To something extraordinary my thoughts.
I with this Messenger will go along,
Nothing to do, be sure, that may dishonour   1385
Our Law, or stain my vow of *Nazarite*.

If there be aught of presage in the mind,
This day will be remarkable in my life
By some great act, or of my days the last.
   Chor. In time thou hast resolv'd, the man returns.   1390
   Off. Samson, this second message from our Lords
To thee I am bid say. Art thou our Slave,
Our Captive, at the public Mill our drudge,
And dar'st thou at our sending and command
Dispute thy coming? come without delay;   1395
Or we shall find such Engins to assail
And hamper thee, as thou shalt come of force,
Though thou wert firmlier fastend than a rock.
   Sam. I could be well content to try thir Art,
Which to no few of them would prove pernicious.   1400
Yet knowing thir advantages too many,
Because they shall not trail me through thir streets
Like a wild Beast, I am content to go.
Masters commands come with a power resistless
To such as owe them absolute subjection;   1405
And for a life who will not change his purpose?
(So mutable are all the ways of men)
Yet this be sure, in nothing to comply
Scandalous or forbidden in our Law.
   Off. I praise thy resolution, doff these links: 1410
By this compliance thou wilt win the Lords
To favour, and perhaps to set thee free.
   Sam. Brethren farewell, your company along
I will not wish, lest it perhaps offend them
To see me girt with Friends; and how the sight   1415
Of mee as of a common Enemy,
So dreaded once, may now exasperate them
I know not. Lords are Lordliest in thir wine;
And the well-feasted Priest then soonest fir'd
With zeal, if aught Religion seem concernd: 1420
No less the people on thir Holy-days
Impetuous, insolent, unquenchable;
Happen what may, of me expect to hear
Nothing dishonourable, impure, unworthy
Our God, our Law, my Nation, or my self,   1425
The last of me or no I cannot warrant.
   Chor. Go, and the Holy One
Of *Israel* be thy guide
To what may serve his glory best, and spread his name
Great among the Heathen round: 1430
Send thee the Angel of thy Birth, to stand
Fast by thy side, who from thy Fathers field
Rode up in flames after his message told
Of thy conception, and be now a shield
Of fire; that Spirit that first rushd on thee   1435

In the camp of *Dan*
Be efficacious in thee now at need.
For never was from Heav'n imparted
Measure of strength so great to mortal seed,
As in thy wondrous actions hath bin seen.   1440
But wherefore comes old *Manoah* in such haste
With youthful steps? much livelier than erewhile
He seems: supposing here to find his Son,
Or of him bringing to us som glad news?
   Man. Peace with you brethren; my inducement hither
Was not at present here to find my Son,   1446
By order of the Lords new parted hence
To come and play before them at thir Feast.
I heard all as I came, the City rings
And numbers thither flock, I had no will,   1450
Lest I should see him forc't to things unseemly.
But that which mov'd my coming now, was chiefly
To give ye part with me what hope I have
With good success to work his liberty.
   Chor. That hope would much rejoice us to partake 1455
With thee; say reverend Sire, we thirst to hear.
   Man. I have attempted one by one the Lords
Either at home, or through the high street passing,
With supplication prone and Fathers tears
T'accept of ransom for my Son thir pris'ner.   1460
Some much averse I found and wondrous harsh,
Contemptuous, proud, set on revenge and spite;
That part most reverenc'd *Dagon* and his Priests:
Others more moderat seeming, but thir aim
Privat reward, for which both God and State   1465
They easily would set to sale: a third
More generous far and civil, who confessd
They had anough reveng'd, having reduc't
Thir foe to misery beneath thir fears,
The rest was magnanimity to remit,   1470
If some convenient ransom were propos'd.
What noise or shout was that? it tore the Skie.
   Chor. Doubtless the people shouting to behold
Thir once great dread, captive and blind before them,
Or at som proof of strength before them shown.   1475
   Man. His ransom, if my whole inheritance
May compass it, shall willingly be paid
And numberd down: much rather I shall choose
To live the poorest in my Tribe than richest,
And he in that calamitous prison left.   1480
No, I am fixt not to part hence without him.
For his redemption all my Patrimony,
If need be, I am ready to forgo
And quit: not wanting him, I shall want nothing.

Chor. Fathers are wont to lay up for thir Sons,   1485
Thou for thy Son art bent to lay out all;
Sons wont to nurse thir Parents in old age,
Thou in old age car'st how to nurse thy Son,
Made older than thy age through eyesight lost.
    Man. It shall be my delight to tend his eyes,   1490
And view him sitting in the house, enobl'd
With all those high exploits by him achiev'd,
And on his shoulders waving down those locks
That of a Nation armd the strength containd:
And I persuade me God had not permitted   1495
His strength again to grow up with his hair
Garrisond round about him like a Camp
Of faithful Souldiery, were not his purpose
To use him furder yet in some great service,
Not to sit idle with so great a gift   1500
Useless, and thence ridiculous about him.
And since his strength with eyesight was not lost,
God will restore him eyesight to his strength.
    Chor. Thy hopes are not ill founded nor seem vain
Of his delivery, and thy joy thereon   1505
Conceiv'd, agreeable to a Fathers love;
In both which wee as next participate.
    Man. I know your friendly minds and—O what noise!
Mercy of Heav'n what hideous noise was that!
Horribly loud, unlike the former shout.   1510
    Chor. Noise call you it or universal groan
As if the whole inhabitation perishd?
Blood, death, and deathful deeds are in that noise,
Ruin, destruction at the utmost point.
    Man. Of ruin indeed methought I heard the noise,
Oh it continues, they have slain my Son.   1516
    Chor. Thy Son is rather slaying them, that outcry
From slaughter of one foe could not ascend.
    Man. Som dismal accident it needs must be;
What shall we do, stay here or run and see?   1520
    Chor. Best keep together here, lest running thither
We unawares run into dangers mouth.
This evil on the *Philistines* is fall'n,
From whom could else a general cry be heard?
The sufferers then will scarce molest us here;   1525
From other hands we need not much to fear.
What if his eyesight (for to *Israels* God
Nothing is hard) by miracle restor'd,
He now be dealing dole among his foes,
And over heaps of slaughterd walk his way?   1530
    Man. That were a joy presumptuous to be thought.

1507 wee] we, *Ed. 1*

Chor. Yet God hath wrought things as incredible
For his people of old; what hinders now?
    Man. He can I know, but doubt to think he will;
Yet Hope would fain subscribe, and tempts Belief.   1535
A little stay will bring som notice hither.
    Chor. Of good or bad so great, of bad the sooner;
For evil news rides post, while good news baits.
And to our wish I see one hither speeding,
An *Ebrew*, as I guess, and of our Tribe.   1540
    Messenger. O whither shall I run, or which way flie
The sight of this so horrid spectacle
Which erst my eyes beheld and yet behold;
For dire imagination still persues me.
But providence or instinct of nature seems,   1545
Or reason though disturbd and scarce consulted,
To have guided me aright, I know not how,
To thee first reverend *Manoah*, and to these
My Countrymen, whom here I knew remaining,
As at som distance from the place of horror,   1550
So in the sad event too much concernd.
    Man. The accident was loud, and here before thee
With rueful cry, yet what it was we hear not;
No Preface needs, thou seest we long to know.
    Mess. It would burst forth, but I recover breath   1555
And sense distract, to know well what I utter.
    Man. Tell us the sum, the circumstance deferr.
    Mess. Gaza yet stands, but all her Sons are fall'n,
All in a moment overwhelmd and fa!l'n.
    Man. Sad, but thou knowst to *Israelites* not saddest   1560
The desolation of a Hostile City.
    Mess. Feed on that first, there may in grief be surfet.
    Man. Relate by whom.   *Mess.* By *Samson.*
      Man. That still lessens
The sorrow, and converts it nigh to joy.
    Mess. Ah *Manoah* I refrain, too suddenly   1565
To utter what will come at last too soon;
Lest evil tidings with too rude irruption
Hitting thy aged ear should pierce too deep.
    Man. Suspense in news is torture, speak them out.
    Mess. Then take the worst in brief, *Samson* is dead.   1570
    Man. The worst indeed, O all my hopes defeated
To free him hence! but death who sets all free
Hath paid his ransom now and full discharge.
What windy joy this day had I conceiv'd
Hopeful of his Delivery, which now proves   1575
Abortive as the first-born bloom of spring
Nipt with the lagging rear of winters frost.

1571 hopes *1720*] hope's *Ed. 1*

Yet ere I give the reins to grief, say first,
How di'd he? death to life is crown or shame.
All by him fell thou sayst: by whom fell he,   1580
What glorious hand gave *Samson* his deaths wound?
  Mess. Unwounded of his enemies he fell.
  Man. Wearied with slaughter then or how? explain.
  Mess. By his own hands. *Man.* Self-violence? what cause
Brought him so soon at variance with himself   1585
Among his foes? *Mess.* Inevitable cause
At once both to destroy and be destroyd;
The Edifice where all were met to see him
Upon thir heads and on his own he pulld.
  Man. O lastly over-strong against thy self!   1590
A dreadful way thou tookst to thy revenge.
More than anough we know; but while things yet
Are in confusion, give us if thou canst,
Eye-witness of what first or last was don,
Relation more particular and distinct.   1595
  Mess. Occasions drew me early to this City,
And as the gates I enterd with Sun-rise,
The morning Trumpets Festival proclaimd
Through each high street: little I had dispatcht
When all abroad was rumord that this day   1600
Samson should be brought forth to shew the people
Proof of his mighty strength, in feats and games;
I sorrowd at his captive state, but minded
Not to be absent at that spectacle.
The building was a spacious Theatre   1605
Half round on two main Pillars vaulted high,
With seats where all the Lords and each degree
Of sort, might sit in order to behold;
The other side was open, where the throng
On banks and scaffolds under Skie might stand;   1610
I among these aloof obscurely stood.
The Feast and noon grew high, and Sacrifice
Had filld thir hearts with mirth, high cheer, and wine,
When to thir sports they turnd.   Immediatly
Was *Samson* as a public servant brought,   1615
In thir state Livery clad; before him Pipes
And Timbrels, on each side went armed guards,
Both horse and foot before him and behind,
Archers and Slingers, Cataphracts and Spears.
At sight of him the people with a shout   1620
Rifted the Air, clamoring thir god with praise,
Who had made thir dreadful enemy thir thrall.
He, patient but undaunted where they led him,
Came to the place, and what was set before him
Which without help of eye, might be assayd,   1625

To heave, pull, draw or break, he still performd
All with incredible, stupendious force,
None daring to appear Antagonist.
At length for intermission sake they led him
Between the pillars; he his guide requested   1630
(For so from such as nearer stood we heard)
As over-tir'd to let him lean a while
With both his arms on those two massie Pillars
That to the arched roof gave main support.
Hee unsuspicious led him; which when *Samson*   1635
Felt in his arms, with head a while enclin'd
And eyes fast fixt he stood, as one who prayd,
Or some great matter in his mind revolv'd.
At last with head erect thus cri'd aloud,
Hitherto, Lords, what your commands impos'd   1640
I have performd, as reason was, obeying,
Not without wonder or delight beheld.
Now of my own accord such other trial
I mean to shew you of my strength, yet greater;
As with amaze shall strike all who behold.   1645
This utterd, straining all his nerves he bowd,
As with the force of winds and waters pent
When Mountains tremble; those two massie Pillars
With horrible convulsion to and fro,
He tuggd, he shook, till down they came and drew   1650
The whole roof after them, with burst of thunder
Upon the heads of all who sate beneath,
Lords, Ladies, Captains, Councellors or Priests,
Thir choice nobility and flowr, not onely
Of this but each *Philistine* City round   1655
Met from all parts to solemnize this Feast.
Samson with these immixt, inevitably
Pulld down the same destruction on himself;
The vulgar onely scap'd who stood without.
    Chor. O dearly-bought revenge, yet glorious!   1660
Living or dying thou hast fulfilld
The work for which thou wast foretold
To *Israel*, and now li'st victorious
Among thy slain self-killd
Not willingly, but tangl'd in the fold   1665
Of dire necessity, whose law in death conjoind
Thee with thy slaughterd foes in number more
Than all thy life had slain before.
    Semichorus. While thir hearts were jocond and sublime,
Drunk with Idolatry, drunk with Wine,   1670
And fat regorg'd of Bulls and Goats,
Chaunting thir Idol, and preferring

1635 Hee] He *1671*

Before our living Dread who dwells
In *Silo* his bright Sanctuary:
Among them hee a spirit of phrenzie sent,   1675
Who hurt thir minds,
And urg'd them on with mad desire
To call in haste for thir destroyer;
They only set on sport and play
Unweetingly importun'd   1680
Thir own destruction to come speedy upon them.
So fond are mortal men
Fall'n into wrath divine,
As thir own ruin on themselves to invite,
Insensate left, or to sense reprobate,   1685
And with blindness internal struck.
   Semichor. But he, though blind of sight,
Despis'd and thought extinguisht quite,
With inward eyes illuminated
His fierie vertue rous'd   1690
From under ashes into sudden flame,
And as an ev'ning Dragon came,
Assailant on the perched roosts
And nests in order rang'd
Of tame villatic Fowl; but as an Eagle   1695
His cloudless thunder bolted on thir heads.
So vertue giv'n for lost,
Deprest and overthrown, as seemd,
Like that self-begotten bird
In the *Arabian* woods embost,   1700
That no second knows nor third,
And lay erewhile a Holocaust,
From out her ashie womb now teemd
Revives, reflourishes, then vigorous most
When most unactive deemd,   1705
And though her body die, her fame survives,
A secular bird ages of lives.
   Man. Come, come, no time for lamentation now,
Nor much more cause; *Samson* hath quit himself
Like *Samson*, and heroicly hath finisht   1710
A life Heroic; on his Enemies
Fully reveng'd, hath left them years of mourning,
And lamentation to the Sons of *Caphtor*
Through all *Philistian* bounds. To *Israël*
Honour hath left and freedom, let but them   1715
Find courage to lay hold on this occasion,
To himself and Fathers house eternal fame;
And which is best and happiest yet, all this
With God not parted from him, as was fear'd,

1675 hee] he *Ed. 1*

But favouring and assisting to the end.   1720
Nothing is here for tears, nothing to wail
Or knock the brest, no weakness, no contempt,
Dispraise or blame, nothing but well and fair,
And what may quiet us in a death so noble.
Let us go find the body where it lies   1725
Soakt in his enemies blood, and from the stream
With lavers pure and cleansing herbs wash off
The clotted gore.   I with what speed the while
(*Gaza* is not in plight to say us nay)
Will send for all my kindred, all my friends   1730
To fetch him hence and solemnly attend
With silent obsequie and funeral train
Home to his Fathers house: there will I build him
A Monument, and plant it round with shade
Of Laurel ever green and branching Palm,   1735
With all his Trophies hung, and Acts enrould
In copious Legend or sweet Lyric Song.
Thither shall all the valiant youth resort,
And from his memory inflame thir brests
To matchless valour and adventures high: 1740
The Virgins also shall on feastful days
Visit his Tomb with flowrs, onely bewailing
His lot unfortunate in nuptial choice,
From whence captivity and loss of eyes.
    Chor. All is best, though we oft doubt,   1745
What th' unsearchable dispose
Of highest wisdom brings about,
And ever best found in the close.
Oft he seems to hide his face,
But unexpectedly returns   1750
And to his faithful Champion hath in place
Bore witness gloriously; whence *Gaza* mourns
And all that band them to resist
His uncontroulable intent.
His servants he with new acquist   1755
Of true experience from this great event
With peace and consolation hath dismist,
And calm of mind all passion spent.

The End

NOTES

[pp. 5–9]

The Authorized Version of the Bible, otherwise known as the King James Version, is abbreviated as A.V., and the Revised Version as R.V. O.T. and N.T. refer to the Old and New Testaments, LXX refers to the Greek version of the O.T., the Septuagint.

MISCELLANEOUS POEMS

The quotation from Virgil on the 1645 title-page means 'Wreathe my forehead with bacchar, and let not an evil tongue injure the destined poet.'

On the Morning of Christ's Nativity

Milton describes the 'Nativity Ode' in *Elegia* VI 79–88, noting that it was composed early on Christmas day (1629).

5 holy Sages] Hebrew prophets.

15 Heav'nly Muse] Urania; see *PL* VII 1n.

24 prevent] anticipate.

28] Isa. vi. 6–7; 'secret' means 'set apart'.

48 sphear] the firmament of the Mosaic cosmology (*PL* VII 261–75, Gen. i. 6–8) and the spheres of the Ptolemaic cosmology.

50 Turtle] turtle dove.
   amorous] fond of peace.

56 hooked] equipped with scythes.

64 whist] hushed.

68 Birds of Calm] halcyons. The line recalls the classical belief that the sea remained calm during the days preceding and following the winter solstice to enable the birds to brood on their floating nests, and also echoes the image of Gen. i. 2 and *PL* VII 234–5.

71 one way] i.e. towards Bethlehem.

74 *Lucifer*] the morning star, Venus.

75 Orbs] in the Ptolemaic cosmology, orbs are the concentric hollow spheres which carry the planets and fixed stars around the earth.

81 as] as if.

88 than] then.

89 *Pan*] The Greek god was a guardian of sheep, and in the Renaissance he was commonly compared to Christ as the good shepherd. The name Pan was associated with *pan* (all) in antiquity (though the words are etymologically distinct), and he became a universal god in late Greek theology. Cf. *PL* IV 266.

92 silly] simple and innocent.

98 took] bewitched.

100 close] the end of a musical phrase.

102–3 hollow . . . seat] the sphere of the moon; see *Elegia* V 46n.

115 quire] refers to musical choirs and to each of the nine orders of angels.

116 unexpressive] inexpressible.

122 hinges] the earth's axis.

125–32] According to a tradition deriving from Pythagoras each of the spheres surrounding the earth was said to produce a note as it revolved. Cf. *Arcades* 62–73, *Solemn Music* 19–24, *Comus* 1019–20, *PL* V 178.

140 peering] may mean 'appearing' or 'prying'.

141 Justice] Astrea, who lived on earth during the golden age, and was later stellified as the constellation Virgo (cf. *Elegia* IV 81–2, *Fair Infant* 50–2, *PL* IV 998). Milton conflates her return with that of Truth and Mercy as recorded in Psalm lxxxv. 10–11, where the 'righteousness' of the A.V. is *justitia* in the Vulgate. Peace (introduced in stanza III), Truth, Justice, and Mercy were the four daughters of God in a prominent medieval allegorical tradition which survived into the Renaissance.

149 wisest Fate] the will of God (see *PL* VII 173).

151 Infancy] may retain the Latin sense of 'inability to speak'.

155 ychaind] The 'y' is an archaism which derives from the Anglo-Saxon 'ge', the prefix for past participles. As 'chain' derives from Old French rather than Anglo-Saxon, the archaism is a false one. The prosthesis is occasioned by the demands of metre. Cf. 'ypointing' in *Shakespeare* 4 and 'ycleapt' in *Allegro* 12.

158–9] Exod. xix. 16–18; cf. *PL* VI 56–60.

159 smouldring] stifling (not, as now, 'burning slowly').

160–2] Psalm cxiv. 7 (l. 15 of Milton's English version, l. 19 of his Greek version).

164 middle Air] the 'clouds of heaven' of Matt. xxiv. 30; see I Thess. iv. 17.

168 Dragon] Rev. xii, xx; cf. *PL* IV 3.

172 Swindges] lashes.

173] Milton is drawing on the ancient tradition that the pagan oracles ceased at the advent of Christ. Cf. *PR* I 456.

179 nightly] nocturnal.

186 Genius] local god, the Roman *genius loci*. Cf. *Arcades* 25–6, *Lycidas* 183–5, *Penseroso* 154.

191 *Lars, Lemures*] *Lemures*: spirits of the dead – may be good (Lares) or evil (Larvæ), but Milton's identification of Lemures with Larvæ is not uncommon.

194 Flamins] an order of Roman priests.

197 *Peor* and *Baälim*] *Peor* is the name of a mountain, the god of which was Baal-Peor (see Psalm cvi. 28). Cf. *PL* I 412. *Baälim* is the plural of Baal (see Judges ii. 11), and alludes to other forms of the god, such as Baäl-zebub (*SA* 1231).

199 twice-batterd god] Dagon. See I Sam. v. 2–4, and cf. *PL* I 457–66 and *SA* 13.

200 *Ashtaroth*] the collective name for the manifestations of Ashtoreth, the Syrian goddess. Cf. *PL* I 438–9, *PR* III 417, and *SA* 1242. *Baälim* and *Ashtaroth* are contrasted in *PL* I 421–3. Ashtoreth entered Greek mythology (through Cyprus) as Aphrodite.

203 *Hammon*] An Egyptian god whose oracle in Lybia was well known to the Greeks. Cf. *PL* IV 277.

204 *Tyrian . . . Thamuz*] Thammuz, who was identified by Jerome with Adonis, was worshipped in Phoenicia, of which Tyre was an important city. Cf. Ezek. viii. 14 and *PL* I 446–57.

205 *Moloch*] Ammonite fire-god, associated in the O.T. with the sacrifice of children. See Lev. xviii. 21, II Kings xxiii. 10, Psalm cvi. 37–8. In *PL* he is a fallen angel (I 392 ff.).

212–13] *Isis*, the Egyptian goddess of the moon, is the wife and sister of *Osiris*, the sun-god, and the mother of *Orus* (usually Horus). All three appear as rebel angels in *PL* I 478. *Anubis* is a son of Osiris and Nephthys, reared by *Isis*.

223 eyn] archaic plural of 'eye'.

226 *Typhon*] A conflation of the Egyptian Typhon, who killed Osiris, and the Greek monster, half serpent, who was killed by Zeus.

227–8] Milton is comparing Christ to the infant Hercules, who strangled serpents in his cradle. Cf. *Passion* 13–14.

Psalm 114

fifteen years old] i.e. 1624. This and the following psalm may have been school
   exercises based primarily on Latin and Greek versions of the Bible. Milton may
   also have consulted the Hebrew version, for he began his study of Hebrew in
   1624. He later composed a Greek version of the same psalm (printed on p.
   137).
1 *Terah's* faithful Son] Abraham.
3 *Pharian* Fields] Pharos, a small island near Alexandria, here represents Egypt.

Psalm 136

46 *Erythræan* main] The Red Sea.
65 *Seon*] Sihon, king of the Amonites (Num. xxi. 21–32).
69 *Og*] king of Bashan (Num. xxi. 33–35, Deut. iii. 1–5). On his huge limbs see
   Deut. iii. 11. Cf. *SA* 1080.
73 Servant *Israël*] Jacob.

On the Death of a Fair Infant

The date of composition is debatable. Edward Phillips, Milton's nephew, wrote in
1694 that the poem was occasioned by 'the Death of one of his Sister's Children (a
daughter), who died in her infancy.' Should this be true, then Milton's 'Anno ætatis
17' (i.e. 9 December 1625–8 December 1626) may be an error, for Milton's eldest
niece, Anne Phillips, died on 22 January 1628. On the other hand, the plague to
which Milton refers in stanza X is almost certainly the great plague of 1625.
2 timelesslie] unseasonably.
8 Aquilo] Boreas, the north wind, who abducted Orithyia, the 'Athenian damsel'.
   Cf. *Naturam* 55 and the *pessimus ventorum* of *Salsillum* 11.
13 eld] old age.
16 middle . . . aire] the middle of the three layers of air above the earth, and the
   one in which inclement weather was generated.
23–6] *Hyacinth* was accidentally killed by the discus of his lover *Apollo*, who
   transformed the blood of *Hyacinth* into a flower (*Metamorphoses* x 162–219;
   cf. *Naturam* 62, *Lycidas* 106, *Procan* 44, *PL* IV 301. *Eurotas* is a river in
   Laconia, and flows by Sparta.
39 first-moving Sphear] the *primum mobile* of Ptolemaic cosmology was the
   outermost sphere, where motion originated. Cf. *Naturam* 37 (*rota prima*), *PL*
   III 482–3, VIII 133–6.
40 Elisian fields] Not the paradise of Homer, which was at the extremity of the
   earth, but that of Plato, which was in the highest heaven. Cf. *PL* III 472.
50–52] See *Nativity* 141n.
53 Mercy] A traditional editorial conjecture. Two syllables are clearly missing in
   the original version (which is printed at the bottom of the page). Other
   suggestions for the missing disyllable are 'Virtue', 'Peace, in', 'Honour', and
   'Temperance' (pronounced as a disyllable).
77] Isa. lvi. 5.

At a Vacation Exercise

The poem was written in 1628. The Latin speeches to which Milton alludes consist
of an oration and a prolusion which Milton delivered at Christ's College in July
1628. The prolusion ends with the announcement that Milton is adding a section in
English to the Latin discourse.
34 wheeling poles] The poles are the extremities of the axis around which the
   spheres revolve.
36 thunderous throne] of Jove, the thunderer.

37 unshorn] a common classical epithet for Apollo.

38 *Hebe*] daughter of Zeus and Hera; she frequently personifies youth. Cf. *Allegro* 29, *Comus* 289, *Salsillum* 23.

40 Sphears of watchful fire] The exact reference of the phrase is difficult to determine. Milton may be referring to the spheres of the Ptolemaic system, the heavenly bodies of which were located in the region of fire, and were according to Plato created to watch over the numbers of time. Alternatively, he may be referring to a layer of fire directly under the sphere of the moon; this layer could be said to be 'watchful' in that it protects the supralunar vault from contamination.

41–2] See *Fair Infant* 16n.

46 Beldam] may mean grandmother, or nurse.

48–52] In *Odyssey* viii 487–543 the minstrel *Demodocus* sings of the fall of Troy while Odysseus is being entertained by *Alcinous*, king of the Phæacians; the song moves Odysseus to tears.

56 Predicament] Milton plays on the common meaning of the word and the technical meaning (an Aristotelian category).

Stage Direction] In the satirical entertainment which Milton is introducing, he acts the part of Ens, or 'Being', himself, and ten of his fellow undergraduates act the parts of the 'Sons', Aristotle's ten categories, of which four – Substance, Quantity, Quality, and Relation – are represented in the portion of the play which Milton has preserved.

69 *Sybil*] a prophetic hag.

91 Rivers arise] The part of Relation was evidently played by one of the two Rivers brothers who had been admitted to Christ's College on 28 May 1628. The catalogue of rivers that follows is a parody of the catalogues of rivers composed by Spenser and Drayton.

92 utmost] i.e. outermost, as the Tweed formed the border between England and Scotland.

gulphie] i.e. full of eddies; the river is the Don, in Yorkshire.

96 Maidens death] The maiden is Sabrina; see *Comus* 823ff.

98 hallowd] The changes in the course of the Dee were said to be prophetic. Cf. *Lycidas* 55.

The Passion

As the first four lines of the poem clearly allude to the 'Nativity Ode' it seems likely that this poem was written the following Easter; in 1630 Good Friday fell on 26 March.

4 divide] Milton conflates the primary meaning ('to join') with the technical meaning in music ('to execute a florid melodic variation').

13–14] The *Hero* is Christ, whose trials Milton compares to the labours of Hercules. Cf. *Nativity* 227–8.

17 fleshly Tabernacle] See Heb. ix. 11–12, and cf. *PR* IV 599.

21] See Heb. ii. 17.

23 *Phoebus*] Apollo, god of the sun, was often identified with poetic inspiration.

26 ore] over.

Cremona's Trump] The *Christiad*, a Latin poem by Vida, published in Cremona in 1535.

28 still] quiet.

30 Pole] the sky. Cf. *Vacation Exercise* 34n.

36–40] Milton's account of Ezekiel's vision is based on Ezek. i and x. The vision occurred by the river of *Chebar*; *Salem* was the ancient name for Jerusalem. Cf. *Penseroso* 53 and *PL* VI 750–53.

50 viewless] invisible.
51 Jer. ix. 10.
56] Probably an allusion to the story of Ixion, who begot Centaurus on a cloud shaped like Hera. Cf. *PR* IV 318–21.

On Time

The date of the poem is not known. In the manuscript Milton wrote (and afterwards deleted) the phrase 'to be set on a clock case' under the title. This phrase explains the appropriateness of the metaphor of the lead plummet in ll. 1–3.

3 Plummet] the weight (not the pendulum) of a clock.
4] Cf. *Naturam* 14–15n.
9 when as] when.
12 individual] probably means inseparable (cf. *PL* V 610), but may also encompass the modern meaning, which existed in Milton's time, in which case the word affirms personal immortality.
14 sincerely] purely, wholly.
18 happy-making sight] an Anglicized form of the term 'beatific vision'. See *PL* I 684n.

Upon the Circumcision

The poem was probably written as the Feast of the Circumcision, which falls on 1 January. The year of composition is not known, though 1633 is not improbable. In the poem Milton regards the circumcision as the first act of the passion, and a foreshadowing of the crucifixion.

1 Powers] one of the nine orders of angels.
10 heraldry] heraldic pomp.
14 sease] seize.
20 Emptied his glory]. In the Greek of Phil. ii. 7 Christ is said to have emptied (ἐκένωσε) himself.
21 that great Cov'nant] of works.
24 excess] extravagant violation of law and morality. Cf. *PL* XI 111.

At a Solemn Music

The date is uncertain, but the poem was probably written sometime between 1631 and 1637. The 'solemn music' of the title would nowadays be called a 'sacred concert'.

1–2 Sirens . . . Sphear-born] In the manuscript versions of the poem Milton uses 'borne', but in the two printed versions 'born'. He may have distinguished the two words. If 'borne' is intended, then these are the sirens of *Arcades* 63–4, for the sirens 'sit upon the . . . Sphears'; if 'born' is intended then the sirens should be compared with Echo in *Comus* 240, for she is '*Daughter of the Sphear*'.
4] alludes to the myth of Orpheus. See *Allegro* 145–50n.
6 concent] harmony.
7 saphire-colour'd throne] the throne of God in Ezekiel's vision. See Ezek. i. 26, x. 1.
10 Seraphim] one of the nine orders of angels. Cherubim, in l. 12, are another order.
23 Diapason] harmony.

An Epitaph on the Marchioness of Winchester

Jane Savage, Marchioness of Winchester, died on 15 April 1631. She was a Catholic (though one seventeenth-century source says that 'she was inclining to become a protestant') and a Royalist. No connection between Milton and the family of the Marchioness is known, so the poem may have been composed as a contribution to a collection of memorial verses by Cambridge poets.

18 The God] Hymen.

20 scarce-wel-lighted flame] At the marriage of Orpheus and Eurydice the torch of Hymen is smoky. Contrast *Allegro* 125–6, where Hymen's taper is 'clear'.

24 son] Charles, born 1629, later the sixth Marquis.

26 *Lucina*] Roman goddess of childbirth.

28 *Atropos*] One of the three Parcæ, Roman goddesses of birth and fate. *Atropos* cut the thread of life (cf. *Lycidas* 75) which Clotho spun and Lachesis measured.

43–6] Cf. *Novembris* 133–5n.

52 lives] life's.

56 *Helicon*] A mountain in Boeotia, sacred to Apollo and muses.

59 *Came*] The river Cam, in Cambridge.

63 *Syrian* Shepherdess] Rachel. See Gen. xxix and xxx.

66 him] Jacob.

67 her next birth] Benjamin. For the significance of the analogy see Gen. xxxv. 18.

Song on May Morning

The many similarities to *Elegia* V suggest that the poem may have been written on 1 May 1629, or possibly the same date in 1630 or 1631.

On Shakespear. 1630

The poem was first published in the Second Folio of Shakespeare (1632).

4 Star-ypointing] a present participle. See *Nativity* 155n.

11 unvalu'd] invaluable.

12 Delphic lines] Apollo, the patron of poetry, had his oracle at Delphi.

On the University Carrier

Thomas Hobson died, aged 86, on 1 January 1631. He had been well known in Cambridge for over 60 years. He drove a weekly coach to London, and also hired out horses. His insistence that each customer take the horse nearest the door is the origin of the proverbial phrase 'Hobson's choice'. His death prompted the composition of many light-hearted commemorative poems by Cambridge students.

1 girt] saddle girth.

5 shifter] trickster, evader.

8 Bull] the Bull Inn, Bishopsgate, London.

13 tane] taken.

14 Chamberlin] an attendant in charge of the bed-chambers in an inn.

Another on the Same

See previous headnote.

5 sphear-metal] Aristotle argued that the material of which the celestial spheres were composed was indestructible.

7 Time numbers motion] Aristotle described time as the measure of motion. Cf. *PL* V 580–82.

9 Engin] a machine, here a clock.

10 principles] source of motion.

12 breathing] time for rest.

14–34] The lines contain a series of puns. 'Vacation' and 'term' (14) have a special university sense, but also mean 'freedom from business' and 'end' respectively. 'Drive . . . away' (15) contains an obvious pun. In l. 18 Milton plays on the phrase 'fetch and carry', and 'fetcht' also means 'restored to consciousness'.

'Put down' (20) means 'dismissed from office' or 'killed'. 'Bearers' (20) refers to porters and pall bearers. 'Heaviness' (22) refers to sadness and weight. 'Waight' (26) plays on 'wait'. 'Wain' (32) means both 'waggon' and 'decrease'. 'Superscription' (34) refers to the addresses on the letters which Hobson carried, and to the epitaph on his gravestone.

30 In course reciprocal] i.e. like the tides.

L'Allegro

L'Allegro and *Il Penseroso* cannot be dated precisely, but they may have been written while Milton was in Hammersmith (1632–5) or Horton (1635–8).

title] The phrase is Italian, and means 'the cheerful man'.

1–2] Melancholy was not a personage in classical myth; Milton has invented her parentage. In classical myth Erebus was the brother and husband of Night (*Novembris* 69, *Eliensis* 32–3), but Milton has substituted *Cerberus*, the hound of Hades, for Erebus, possibly in view of the usual derivation of *Cerebus* from Κὴρ Βορός, heart-devouring.

3 *Stygian* cave] Cerberus had a cave on the bank of the Styx.

5 uncouth cell] desolate cave.

8 shades] trees.

10 *Cimmerian*] The land of the Cimmerians, which Odysseus visited (*Odyssey* xi 13–22) was proverbially dark. Cf. *Novembris* 60.

12 ycleapt] called. See *Nativity* 155n.

12–16] The three Graces were Euphrosyne (Mirth), Aglaia (Brilliance), and Thalia (Bloom). According to one tradition they were the daughters of Venus and Bacchus.

19] *Zephir* is the west wind, *Aurora* the dawn.

24 buxom] yielding.

27 Cranks] jokes dependent on verbal twists.

28 Becks] upward nods corresponding to a beckoning by hand.

29 *Hebe*] see *Vacation Exercise* 38n.

33 trip] move lightly.

55 Hoar] i.e. grey with mist.

60 state] the stately progress of the sun, as described in *PL* VI 12–15.

62 dight] clothed.

67 tells his tale] either 'counts his sheep' or 'tells his story'.

70 Lantskip] landscape.

74 labouring clouds] echoes the story of Ixion. Cf. *Passion* 56n.

75 pide] variegated.

80 Cynosure] See *Comus* 341n.

83–88] The names of Milton's rustics occur commonly in classical and Renaissance pastoral poetry.

91 secure] here used in the Latin sense of 'carefree'.

94 rebecks] early bowed instruments.

102 *Mab*] queen of the fairies.

104 Friars Lanthorn] the will-o'-the-wisp.

110 Lubbar Fend] drudging fiend.

111 Chimney] fireplace.

120 weeds] clothes.

triumphs] pageants or spectacles.

121–2] The bright eyes are compared to stars, the ethereal fluid of which rains on mankind, thus controlling character and destiny.

125–6] See *Winchester* 20n.

132 Sock] low-heeled slipper worn by Greek comic actors.

136 *Lydian*] a musical mode usually thought to be morally enervating. In a minority tradition which can be traced to Cassiodorus the Lydian mode was deemed to be relaxing and delightful.

145 *Orpheus*] a possessive.

145-50] *Orpheus* sang so beautifully that human beings, beasts, and even inanimate nature responded. He went to Hades in order to recover his dead wife *Eurydice*, and so moved *Pluto* and Proserpina with his music that they consented to *Eurydice*'s return, on condition that *Orpheus* should not look back upon her until he emerged into the upper air. Near the end of the journey he looked back, and *Eurydice*, 'half regaind', vanished.

Il Penseroso

title] The phrase is Italian, and means 'the contemplative man'.

3 bested] help.

10 Pensioners] attendants.

Morpheus] the god of dreams, one of the sons of Somnus (sleep).

18 Prince *Memnons* sister] In late antiquity the mythical Ethiopian Prince Memnon was given a beautiful sister called Hemera.

19-21] Cassiopeia, wife of Ethiopean king Cephalus, boasted that she was more beautiful than the Nereids ('Sea Nymphs'), and after her death was translated into a constellation ('starrd').

23-30] 'Melancholy's parentage is Milton's invention. *Vesta* was the virgin goddess of the hearth, born to *Saturn* before *Saturn* was overthrown by *Jove* (hence l. 30). *Ida* is the name of a mountain near Troy, and of another mountain on Crete.

31 Nun] The primary meaning is that of a pagan priestess, but a suggestion of the modern meaning is evident in Milton's association of the nun with contemplation.

33 grain] colour.

35 *Cypress* Lawn] fine black linen.

43 sad] serious.

53] see *Passion* 36-40n.

55 hist] to call with the exclamation 'hist'.

73 Plat] plot.

77 Air] weather.

83 Belmans drowsie charm] night-watchman's drowsy chant.

87 outwatch the *Bear*] stay up all night. The Bear (Ursa Major) never sets.

88 *Hermes*] Hermes Trismegistus ('thrice-great'), the Greek name for Thoth, the Egyptian god of letters, to whom were attributed many occult works written by Alexandrian Greeks in the second and third centuries AD. Cf. *Idea* 32-3.

unsphear] call back.

99 *Thebs*] the scene of tragedies about Oedipus and his family.

Pelops line] plays about Agamemnon, Orestes, Electra, and Iphigenia. Cf. *Elegia* I 45-6.

100 *Troy*] the setting of such plays as Euripides' *Trojan Women* and Sophocles' *Ajax*.

102 *Buskind*] the buskin was a high boot worn by Greek tragic actors.

104 *Musaeus*] a mythical Greek singer.

105-8] See *Allegro* 145-50n.

109-15] refers to Chaucer's unfinished *Squire's Tale*.

116–20] refers principally to Spenser, but also to Tasso and Ariosto, whose epics had been allegorized.

122–4] The 'Attic Boy' is Cephalus, who replaced the aged Tithonus as the lover of Aurora the dawn. 'Civil-suited' means soberly dressed; 'trickt and frounc't' means adorned and curly-haired. Cf. *Elegia* III 67, *Elegia* V 49–52.

127 still] quiet.

130 minute] falling at intervals of one minute.

134 *Sylvan*] Roman god of fields and forests.

145 consort] musical harmony.

154 Genius of the Wood] See *Nativity* 186n.

156 pale] enclosure.

157 embowed] vaulted.

158 antic] may mean 'old' or 'fantastic, grotesque'.

massy proof] massive, and proof against the weight of the roof.

159 storied] depicting biblical stories.

163 Service, Anthems] The terms are both Protestant. A service is a setting of the canticles, and an anthem is the vernacular Protestant equivalent of the Latin motet, from which it derives.

170/71 spell/Of] interpret.

The Fifth Ode of Horace

The date of the translation is unknown but its absence from the Trinity MS may suggest a date before 1632. The text of 'Ad Pyrrham' which Milton used is printed below his translation.

Arcades

This short pastoral was performed at an unknown date early in the 1630s for Alice, Dowager Countess of Derby. The performance was held in the garden of Harefield, her estate near Uxbridge. The elderly Countess (b. 1559) had long been a notable patroness of literature; in her youth her virtues had been celebrated by Spenser. One of her daughters (Lady Frances) by her first husband (Lord Derby) married John Egerton, the son by a previous marriage of Lady Alice's second husband, Sir Thomas Egerton. The children of Frances and John Egerton (to whom Lady Alice was both maternal grandmother and stepmother of their father) were later to act in Milton's *Comus*, and one or more of them was probably included in the 'Noble Persons of her Family' who acted in *Arcades*.

title] refers to the inhabitants of ancient Arcadia, a mountainous area in central Peloponnesus which was often used as the setting of Renaissance pastoral fictions.

12 less than half] I Kings x. 7.

20 *Latona*] See *Sonnet* XII 5–7n.

21 *Cybele*] mother of the gods, often portrayed with a crown of towers.

23 *Juno*] wife of Jove, queen of the gods.

25/6 genius of the Wood] See *Nativity* 186n.

30–31] *Alpheus* is a river in Arcadia. The youth *Alpheus* loved the nymph Arethusa. She fled to Sicily, and became a fountain, and he, changed to a river, flowed to her by a hidden channel under the sea. Cf. *Lycidas* 85n and 132.

48 nightly] nocturnal.

52 Planet] Saturn, the malign planet.

63–73] Not Homer's Sirens, but Plato's (*Republic* x 616–17). In Plato's account a spindle of adamant rests on the knees of Necessity, whose three daughters, the Fates (see *Winchester* 28n.) turn the spindle upon which are threaded the eight concentric whorls of the universe; a Siren stood on the rim of each circle. In accordance with Renaissance Ptolemaic thought Milton has nine spheres rather than Plato's eight. Cf. *Solemn Music* 1–2.

82 stemm] descent.

84 enameld] beautified with various colours.

97] The Ladon was a river in Arcadia.

98–102] names of Arcadian mountains associated with Pan.

105 *Syrinx*] a nymph beloved of Pan.

Lycidas

On 10 August 1637 Edward King, a Fellow of Christ's College Cambridge, was drowned. Milton dated his pastoral elegy 'November, 1637' in the Trinity MS, and published it the following year in a commemorative volume entitled *Justa Eduardo King*, a collection of poems in Latin, Greek, and English written by King's Cambridge contemporaries.

title] Lycidas is a common name in pastoral verse.

epigraph] The first line appears in the MS, but the second does not. Neither is printed in the 1638 version, but the complete epigraph is printed in Milton's 1645 *Poems*.

1 Yet once more] see Heb. xii. 26–27.

2 sear] dry, withered.

3 crude] used in the Latin sense of 'unripe'.

4 rude] used in the Latin sense of 'unskilled'.

8 ere his prime] King was twenty-five.

12 bear] bier.

13 welter] writhe. Cf. *PL* I 78.

14 meed] reward.

tear] Collections of elegies issued by the universities were often entitled *Lacrymæ*, so 'tear' means 'elegy'.

15–16] The Sisters are the muses, the sacred well is Aganippe, on Mount Helicon, and the seat of Jove is the altar to Zeus on the same mountain.

22 sable] black.

36 *Damaetus*] a pastoral name, here probably used as an allusion to a tutor at Christ's.

54 *Mona*] Anglesey.

55 *Deva*] The Dee. See *Vacation Exercise* 98n.

58–63] The muse is Calliope; in the course of the orgies of Bacchus her son *Orpheus* was dismembered by the Mænads, who threw his head (and his lyre) into the *Hebrus* River, from which both floated to the island of Lesbos. Cf. *PL* VII 32–8.

64 boots] avails, profits.

68–9] Both names are common in pastoral verse. *Neaera's* tangled hair often appears in Renaissance verse.

75 *Fury*] Atropos is of course a Fate (see *Winchester* 28n.), but Milton endows her with the menacing and repulsive character of a Fury.

77 *Phoebus*] See *Passion* 23n.

79 foil] the setting of a jewel.

85 *Arethuse*] represents the Greek pastoral poetry of Sicily; see *Arcades* 30–31n.

86 *Mincius*] represents Roman pastoral poetry, especially that of Virgil, who was born near Mantua, which is situated on two islands in the Mincio.

87 mood] musical mode.

89 Herald] Triton. See *Comus* 872n.

91 Fellon] means 'savage, wild' (the primary meaning), and 'felonious'.

96 *Hippotades*] means son of Hippotes, and refers to Aeolus, god of the winds.
97 dungeon] the cave of Aeolus, in which Jove imprisoned the winds.
99 *Panope*] one of the fifty sea nymphs (Nereids).
103 *Camus*] the river Cam represents the University of Cambridge.
106 flowr] the hyacinth; see *Fair Infant* 23–6n.
107 pledge] child.
109 The Pilot] St Peter, who was a Galilean fisherman when Jesus called him. (Luke v. 3–11).
110] Matt. xvi. 19.
111 amain] with full force.
112 Miterd] St Peter was the first bishop of the church, and so wears a mitre.
113–21] See the parable in John x. 1–28.
114 Anow] plural of 'enough'.
122 sped] satisfied.
123 list] choose, desire.
flashy] trifling, destitute of solidity or purpose.
124 scrannel] thin, weakly.
130 two-handed engin] the most famous crux in Milton's poetry; scores of interpretations have been advanced. The engine is evidently an instrument of retribution or reform. The second line of Milton's headnote seems to refer to ll. 130–31.
132 *Alpheus*] see *Arcades* 30–31n.
136 use] go habitually.
138 swart Star] probably refers to Sirius, the Dog Star, the heliacal rising of which occurs in mid-summer. 'Swart' (blackened by heat) has been transferred from effect to cause.
142 rathe] early.
149 *Amarantus*] see *PL* III 352–61n.
158 monstrous world] the world of sea-monsters.
160 *Bellerus*] Milton's invention, by analogy to Bellerium, the Latin name for Land's End.
161] According to a Cornish legend in the year 495 St Michael appeared to some fishermen who saw him standing on the Mount that now bears his name.
162] *Namancos* and *Bayona* represent Spain, the Catholicism of which St Michael guards against.
163 ruth] pity.
164] may refer to the myth of Arion, the singer and lyric poet who was saved from drowning by a dolphin.
168 day-star] the sun.
170 tricks] adorns.
173 him] Jesus. See Math. xiv. 25–31.
174] See Rev. xxii. 1–2, vii. 17.
176 unexpressive] inexpressible.
nuptial Song] Rev. xix. 6–9.
181] See Isa. xxv. 8, Rev. vii. 17, xxi. 4.
183] See *Nativity* 186n.
186 uncouth] may mean 'unknown' or 'rustic'.
189 *Doric* lay] pastoral song. Theocritus, Moschus, and Bion wrote in the *Doric* dialect.

A Mask

A Mask Presented at Ludlow Castle, which has been popularly known as *Comus* since the late seventeenth century, was first performed on 29 September 1634 at the Shropshire home of the Earl of Bridgewater as part of the festivities celebrating his appointment as Lord President of Wales. The parts of the Lady and the two Brothers were acted by the Earl's children, and the part of the Attendant Spirit was acted by Henry Lawes, the children's music tutor. Lawes wrote the music for the songs, and was probably responsible for the commission to Milton to compose the text. In 1637 Lawes published the text.

Title page] The Latin epigraph is taken from Virgil's Second Eclogue (ll. 58–9), and means 'Alas, what have I wished on my miserable self! Destroyed, I have let the south wind blow on my flowers'.

The Copy of a Letter, pp. 49–51] Sir Henry Wotton (1568–1639) had served as an ambassador to various countries in Europe for 20 years, and in 1624 had returned to England to become Provost of Eton. On 6 April 1638 Milton wrote to Wotton, enclosing a copy of *Comus* and mentioning his plans to travel to Italy in the next few weeks. This letter is Wotton's reply.

p. 49 Mr. *H.*] traditionally identified as the 'ever-memorable' John Hales, a Fellow of Eton.

p. 50 *Ipsa mollities*] delicacy itself.

Mr. *R.*] has not been identified with certainty.

late *R's* Poems] refers to Thomas Randolph's *Poems* (Oxford, 1638).

Con la bocca dolce] i.e. with a sweet taste in his mouth.

blanch] avoid.

Mr. *M.B.*] Michael Branthwaite, who had served with Wotton in Venice.

Lord *S.*] James Scudamore, son of Viscount Scudamore, the ambassador in Paris.

Signor . . . sciolto] translated by Wotton as 'My Signor Harry, your thoughts close and your countenance loose'.

p. 51 Home-Novelties] newsletters.

p. 52 *Lord Bracly*] In September 1634 John Egerton, Viscount Bracly, was 11 years old; he acted the part of the elder brother. In 1638 Lawes dedicated his edition of *Comus* to Lord Bracly (see p. 49).

Thomas Egerton] 9 years old in September 1634; he acted the part of the second brother.

Lady Alice Egerton] 15 years old in September 1634; she played the part of the Lady.

4 serene] used in the Latin sense of 'clear, bright'.

7 pesterd] crowded.

pin-fold] animal pound.

11] See Rev. iv. 4.

13 Golden Key] cf. *Lycidas* 111.

16 Ambrosial weeds] immortal clothes.

18–20] Jove ruled the heavens, *Neptune* the sea, and Pluto ('nether *Jove*') the underworld.

24 grace] honour.

31 Peer] The Earl of Bridgewater.

37 perplext] used in the Latin sense of 'entangled'.

48 transformd] i.e. were transformed (a Latinism). Bacchus transformed the sailors who had kidnapped him into dolphins.

50 *Circes* Iland] Aeaea, in the Tyrrhenian Sea. Circe, the daughter of the sun (Helios), was visited by Odysseus, and according to one tradition bore him a

son, Telegonus (see *Procan* 18). She turned his sailors into swine by means of a magic potion (*Odyssey* x 135 ff.).

58 *Comus*] The name means 'revelry' in Greek. His parentage is Milton's invention.

60 *Celtic* and *Iberian*] French and Spanish.

65 orient] bright, like pearls from the east.

66 drouth of *Phoebus*] thirst caused by the sun.

71 Ounce] name used of various small feline beasts, vaguely identified.

83 *Iris* Wooff] the woven fabric of the rainbow, of which *Iris* was the goddess.

92 viewless] invisible.

93 Star] Hesperus, the evening star.

95 Car of Day] the chariot of the sun.

97 stream] the ancients believed that the earth was encircled by a river, Oceanus.

110 Saws] sententious sayings.

113 watchful Sphears] see *Vacation Exercise* 40n.

116 Morrice] Morris dance.

117 Shelves] sandbanks or shallows.

126ff.] John iii. 19–20.

129 *Cotytto*] Thracian goddess celebrated in nocturnal orgies.

135 *Hecat'*] goddess of witchcraft.

151 trains] deceits.

154 spungy] absorbent.

161 glozing] flattering.

165 vertue] power, efficacy.

168 fairly] quietly.

173 loose unletterd Hinds] dissolute and illiterate rustics.

175 *Pan*] Greek god of woods, fields, and shepherds.

178 Wassailers] revellers.

188] 'Sad' means both 'serious' and 'darkly dressed'. A 'Votarist' is one bound by a vow. 'Palmer' is not used in the strict sense of 'one who has been to the Holy Land', but simply means 'pilgrim'.

196 dark Lantern] a lantern, the light from which can be darkened with a shutter.

211 siding] supporting.

227 venter] venture.

229 *Echo*] a Greek nymph who loved Narcissus, a beautiful youth. Narcissus spurned her love, and was punished by Aphrodite, who made him fall in love with his own reflection in the water; he pined away, and was transformed into a flower (*Metamorphoses* iii 402–510).

231 Meander] a winding river in Asia Minor.

240 *Parly*] speech.

Daughter of the Sphear] See *Solemn Music* 1–2n.

250 fall] cadence.

252 Sirens] In Homer two Sirens (named by Milton in ll. 876 and 878) lure sailors to their deaths (*Odyssey* xii 166–200); later authors speak of three or four Sirens.

253 *Naiades*] river and fountain nymphs.

256–8] Monsters associated with the rocks of *Scylla* and the whirlpool of *Charybdis* were the twin hazards of the Straits of Messina (*Odyssey* xii 73–100; cf. *PL* II 1019–20).

261 home-felt] intimately felt.

266 Unless the Goddess] Unless you are the goddess.

267 *Silvan*] Silvanus, the Roman forest god.

276–89] This dialogue in alternative single lines imitates the stichomythia of Greek drama.

289 *Hebe*] see *Vacation Exercise* 38n.

292 swinkt] tired.

296 port] deportment, bearing.

300 plighted] plaited, interwoven.

311 Dingle] wooded hollow.

312 bosky bourn] small stream overhung with bushes.

314 attendance] attendants.

317 thatcht pallat] straw bed.

331 benizon] blessing.

340 star of *Arcady*] Arcturus, in the constellation Boötes, was the pole star of the ancient Greeks. Arcturus was thought by the Greeks to be a stellification of Arcus, the son of Callisto, an Arcadian princess (hence 'of *Arcady*') who was stellified as Ursa Major.

341 *Tyrian* Cynosure] The Phoenician (or Tyrian) pole star, which is also the modern pole star, is in Ursa Minor, which the Greeks called *Cynosura* (dog's tail).

358 over-exquisite] too precise.

359 cast] forecast.

365 to seek] deficient.

379 to] an archaic intensive prefix.

381 center] of the earth.

385 affects] loves.

392–4] In the garden of the Hesperides a tree bearing golden apples was guarded by the beautiful daughters of Hesperus (the Hesperides) and by a sleepless dragon. Cf. ll. 980–82.

403 it recks me not] I am not concerned.

406 unowned] lost.

410 arbitrate th'event] decide the outcome.

422 unharbourd] offering no shelter.

432 fire] will-o'-the-wisp.

440–41] Diana, the virgin goddess and huntress, was also a moon-goddess, and the shafts may be moonbeams (hence 'silver') as well as arrows.

443 pard] panther or leopard.

446–51] *Minerva*, the virgin goddess of the arts, of war, and of healing, wore on her shield the head of Medusa (one of the three Gorgons), whose hair Minerva had transformed into snakes. The gaze of a Gorgon turned the beholder into stone.

462–74] An adaptation of Plato, *Phædo* 81.

464 lavish] licentious.

467 Imbodies and imbrutes] becomes corporeal and bestial.

479 crude] indigestible.

482 night-founderd] engulfed in night.

490 stakes] swords.

493 *Thyrsis*] common name in pastoral poetry, sometimes used for shepherd singers.

508 sadly] seriously.

516 *Chimera*] a fire-breathing monster with the head of a lion, the body of a female goat, and the tail of a dragon.

532 monstrous rout] rout of monsters.

541 dew-besprent] sprinkled with dew.

546 meditate] practise.

584 period] sentence.

585 for me] for my part.

597 pillard firmament] the dome of the sky supported by pillars. Cf. *PR* IV 455 and Job xxvi. 11.

603 *Acheron*] one of the rivers of the underworld; see *PL* II 578.

604 *Harpies*] long-clawed birds with the faces of hags who lived at the entrance to the underworld.

Hydras] here refers to a fifty-headed monster, a guardian in the underworld.

609 Emprise] chivalric prowess.

619 to see to] to look at.

620 vertuous] efficacious.

625 scrip] bag.

626 simples] medicinal herbs.

627 faculties] properties.

634 clouted shoon] shoes protected with iron plates, or studded with large-headed nails.

635 *Moly*] Plant given to *Ulysses* to protect him from Circe (*Odyssey* x 305).

636 *Hermes*] Hermes (Mercury), the messenger of Zeus and god of good fortune.

637 *Haemony*] Milton probably derived the name from Hæmonia (Thessaly), the land of magic (cf. *Elegia* II 7), but other etymologies are possible.

645 lime-twigs] twigs smeared with bird-lime for trapping birds.

654 *Vulcan*] god of fire and volcanoes; one of his sons, Cacus, belched out smoke in an unsuccessful attempt to protect himself from Hercules.

660–61] See *PL* IV 272–4n.

671 Julep] literally a sweet drink, but the word carries a secondary sense of a drink to cool the heat of passion.

674–5] *Nepenthes* means in Greek 'banishing pain and sorrow'. *Pharmakon Nepenthes* was a drug, possibly opium, given to Helen on her way home from Troy by Polydamna, the wife of the Egyptian Thon.

699 lickerish] 'pleasant to the palate', but the word carries a secondary sense of 'lecherous, lustful'.

706–7] Stoics and Cynics were ancient groups of philosophers who abjured all luxury. The Stoic school was founded by Zeno, and by the 'Doctors' of the school Milton might mean ancients such as Seneca, Epictetus, and Marcus Aurelius. The Cynic school was founded by Antisthenes, and one of its leaders, Diogenes, lived in a tub. 'Budge' means 'solemn' or 'pompous', but the word 'Furr' at the end of the line brings out the secondary meaning of 'budge', 'the fur used to trim academic robes'.

720–21] See Dan. i. 8–16. Frieze is a coarse woollen cloth.

732 Deep] centre of the earth, the 'forhead' of which is the roof of the inside of the earth.

733 they below] the spirits of the underworld.

749 grain] hue.

756 Jugler] 'sorcerer', with a secondary suggestion of 'trickster'.

758 prankt] showily dressed.

759 bolt] may mean 'refine', or 'utter hastily'.

777 besotted] intellectually or morally stupefied or blinded.

781 Sun-clad] see Rev. xii. 1.

790 fence] the art of fencing.

792 uncontroled] indisputable.

796 nerves] sinews.

802–4] *Jove* used thunderbolts to depose his father *Saturn*, and then chained *Saturn* and his supporters ('crew'), the Titans, in *Erebus*, the underworld.

808 lees] sediment.

821 *Melibaeus*] commonly identified with Spenser, who told the story of Sabrina in *Faerie Queene* II. x. 14–19.

822 soothest] most truthful.

825ff.] Milton's version of the legend of *Sabrina*, goddess of the Severn, differs from the multitude of earlier versions in emphasizing her virginity and in obscuring the fact that she was born of the adulterous union of *Locrine* and Estrildis.

827 *Brute*] great-grandson of Aeneas, legendary founder of Britain.

834 *Nereus*] father of the fifty Nereids (sea-nymphs).

835 lank] drooping.

837 lavers] basins.

Asphodil] the immortal flower of the Elysian fields.

844 urchin blasts] infections breathed by mischievous fairies.

851 Swain] Melibaeus.

867 *Oceanus*] see l. 97n.

868 earth-shaking] the Homeric epithet for Poseidon (Neptune), who carries a trident ('mace').

869 *Tethys*] wife of Oceanus.

871 *Carpathian* wizard] Proteus, who according to one tradition lived in the sea near the island of Carpathos (between Rhodes and Crete), was a seer ('wizard'), and was the shepherd (hence 'hook') of Poseidon's seals.

872 *Triton*] Son of Poseidon (Neptune) who blew on his conch-shell to calm the seas. Cf. *Lycidas* 89 and *Naturam* 58.

873 *Glaucus*] a Greek fisherman who ate a magic herb and was changed into a sea-god with prophetic powers.

874 *Leucothea*] a sea-goddess, whose name in Greek means 'white goddess'.

875 her son] Melicertes, god of harbours.

876 *Thetis*] One of the Nereids (sea-nymphs); her Homeric epithet was 'silver footed'.

878 *Parthenope*] one of the Sirens; her tomb was near Naples, the ancient name of which was *Parthenope*.

879 *Ligea*] the other Homeric Siren (according to a late tradition).

920 *Amphitrite*] Neptune's wife.

922 *Anchises*] father of Aeneas. See 827n.

963 *Dryades*] woodland nymphs.

969 *timely*] early.

971 *assays*] tests and tribulations.

979 liquid] clear, bright.

980–82] see 392–4n.

983 crisped] the precise meaning is not clear, but the word may mean 'curled' or 'ruffled'.

985 Graces] See *Allegro* 12–16n.

Hours] Greek goddesses who presided over the changing seasons and protected the rural order.

988 West winds] the Zephyrs, harbingers of spring.

989 cedar'n] composed of cedars.

990 *Nard* and *Cassia*] aromatic plants.

991 *Iris*] goddess of the rainbow.

994 purfl'd] variegated.

995–1110] Milton intended his readers to recall Spenser's Garden of Adonis, *Faerie Queene* III. vi. 43–50.

998–1001] *Adonis*, a youthful hunter beloved of Venus (the '*Assyrian* Queen'), was slain by a boar.

1102–10] In the fable of Apuleius *Cupid* fell in love with *Psyche* (whose name means 'breath' or 'soul'), and visited her in darkness. When she discovered her lover's identity, he fled. She roamed the world in search of him ('wandring labours') and after they were reconciled bore him a son, *Voluptas*. In Spenser's version the child is called Pleasure. Milton gives them twins.

1003 advanc't] elevated.

1014 bowd welkin] the curved vault of the sky.

1016 corners] may be a Latinism meaning 'horns' (from *cornu*).

1020 Spheary chime] the music of the sphears.

SONNETS

Sonnet I

The date of composition is not known. It is a poem of spring, like *Elegia* V and 'May Morning', and may have been composed at the same time as a Petrarchan variation on the theme.

1–2] virtually translates *Elegia* V 25–6.

4 hours] See *Comus* 985n.

9 Bird of Hate] the cuckoo.

10 ny] the unusual spelling may reflect the conscious creation of an eye-rhyme.

The Italian Sonnets

Milton's six Italian sonnets are love poems written for a lady called Emilia, who may have been real or imaginary. They were written in 1629 or 1630, long before Milton went to Italy in 1638.

Sonnet II

Lovely lady, whose beautiful name honours[1] the grassy valley of Reno and the famous ford,[2] truly is he destitute of all value who is not charmed by your gentle spirit, which sweetly shows itself, never sparing its gracious gestures, and by the gifts which are the bows and arrows of Love there[8] where your lofty virtue flowers.

When you speak beautifully, or sing joyfully, which can move hard mountainous trees,[10] let whoever is unworthy of you[12] guard the entrance of his eyes and ears.[11] Only grace from above can help him, before amorous desire becomes inveterate in his heart.

1–2] The Reno is a river in the province of Emilia, and the famous ford is the Rubicon, which is also in Emilia. Milton is explaining the name of the lady in a form that had precedent in Italian sonnets.

8 Là] i.e. in her eyes.

10] a comparison to Orpheus.

11–12] a comparison of the Lady to Homer's Sirens, the sweetness of whose song Milton affirmed in *Comus* 877. Cf. *Sonnet IV* 14.

Sonnet III

As on a rugged hill, at the twilight of evening, a youthful shepherdess, at home there, waters a strange and beautiful plant which scarcely spreads its leaves in the unfamiliar air, parted from its life-giving native springtime, so Love in me upon my nimble tongue awakens the strange flower of a foreign speech, as I sing to you, charmingly proud lady, not understood by my own good countrymen, and I exchange the beautiful Thames for the beautiful Arno.[10] Love willed it, and I have learned from the distress of others that Love never willed anything in vain. Ah, would that my slow heart and hard breast were as good a soil to Him who plants from heaven.

10] The Thames represents the English language, and the Arno, which flows through Tuscany, represents the Tuscan dialect of Italian, i.e. the classic literary form.

Canzone

A *canzone* is an Italian (or Provençal) lyric consisting of several long stanzas with lines of irregular length and concluding with a short stanza called the *commiato* (dismissal). Milton's *canzone* would more commonly be termed a *stanza di canzone*, since it consists of only one stanza and an envoy.

Amorous young men and women laugh, and gathering about me, ask 'Why do you write, why do you write in a strange and unknown language, versifying about love? How dare you? Tell us, so that your hope may never be vain, and your best wishes may be fulfilled.' Thus they make fun of me: 'Other streams, other shores await you, and other waters on whose green margins appear for you from time to time the immortal guerdon of undying fronds for your hair: why add an excessive burden to your shoulders?'

Canzone, I shall tell you, and you will answer for me: my lady says, and her word is my heart, 'This is the language in which Love prides himself.'

Sonnet IV

Diodati,[1] I shall say it to you with astonishment, I, that reluctant one who used to despise Love, and frequently laughed at his snares, have now fallen where a good man sometimes entangles himself. Neither tresses of gold nor rosy cheeks have dazzled me so, but a foreign beauty modelled on a rare idea delights my heart, a bearing proud and modest, a clear blaze of lovely darkness in her eyes, speech adorned by more than one language, and singing which might well lead the labouring moon[12] astray in the middle of the sky. And from her eyes there shoots such fierce flame that to stop my ears with wax would be of little use.[14]

1 *Diodati*] Charles Diodati was the most intimate friend of Milton's early life. His family home was near Milton's, and he was a fellow pupil with Milton at St Paul's School before going up to Oxford. Milton's *Elegia* I and *Elegia* VI are both addressed to Diodati, as are two of Milton's *Familiar Letters*. Milton commemorated Diodati's death in *Epitaphium Damonis*.

12 *faticosa Luna*] Cf. *PL* II 665.

14] Odysseus put wax in the ears of his crew so that they would not be able to hear the song of the sirens. Cf. *Sonnet* II 11–12.

Sonnet V

In truth, my lady, your beautiful eyes can be for me nothing other than the sun. They strike me as powerfully as does the sun on one who makes his way across the sands of Libya; meanwhile a hot vapour (which I have not felt before) presses up from the side where I am aching. Perhaps lovers in their language call it a sigh; I do not know what it may be. Part of it, confined and agitated, hides itself, and having shaken my breast, a little escapes, and all around here it is either chilled or frozen. But that part of it which finds a place in my eyes makes every night a rainy one for me, until my Dawn returns, brimming with roses.

Sonnet VI

Youthful, gentle, and artless lover that I am, since I am in doubt about how to escape from myself, I shall devoutly make a humble gift of my heart to you, my lady. I have tested it many times, and found it loyal, fearless, constant, and in its thoughts gracious, circumspect, and kind. When the great world roars and the thunder claps, my heart arms itself with itself and with complete adamant, as safe from chance and envy, from the fears and hopes of common people, as it is eager for distinction of mind and high worth, for the resounding lyre and the Muses. You will find it less hard only in the place where Love has put his incurable sting.

Sonnet VII

Line 2 suggests a date of composition on or near 9 December 1631, Milton's twenty-third birthday.

4 semblance] appearance.

7 timely] 'seasonable', with a secondary sense of 'early'.

indu'th] is inherent in.

10 still] forever.

10–11] ev'n/To] appropriate to, equal to.

Sonnet VIII

The poem is dated 1642 in the Trinity MS. After the battle of Edgehill on 23 October 1642 the Parliamentary army retreated to Warwick, thus leaving the road to London open to the army of Charles, who advanced as far as Turnham Green, which was only a few miles from Milton's house on Aldersgate Street. The prospect of the fall of London may have occasioned the poem.

10–12] When the army of Alexander (who is here called *Emathian*, Emathia being a district of Macedon) was destroying Thebes, Alexander spared the house in which Pindar had lived, and also spared the descendants of the poet.

12–14] The Spartans defeated Athens in 404 BC, and were allegedly restrained from destroying the city by a Phocian who sang the first chorus of Euripides' *Electra*, and thus persuaded the conquerors to spare the city that had produced such a great poet.

Sonnet IX

As the identity of the Lady is not known, the date of composition is uncertain. In the Trinity MS it follows *Sonnet* VIII, which suggests that it was written after 1642.

2 broad way] Matt. vii. 13–14.

5 *Mary*] Luke x. 38–42.

Ruth] Ruth i. 14ff.

9–14] based on the parable of the virgins, Matt. xxv. 1–13.

11 Hope . . . shame] cf. Rom. v. 5.

Sonnet X

The daughter is identified by the title of the poem in the Trinity MS as Lady Margaret Ley, who, according to Edward Phillips, Milton's nephew, 'took much delight in [Milton's] company, as likewise her husband Captain Hobson'. Captain Hobson (who fought on the side of Parliament) and his wife lived in Aldersgate Street, and were therefore Milton's neighbours. The poem cannot be dated exactly, but was probably written between 1642 and 1645.

1–2] The 'good Earl' was James Ley, who in 1624 became Lord High Treasurer, in 1628 was created Earl of Marlborough, and in 1628 became for a short time Lord President of the Council.

4] Ley retired as Lord President of the Council on 28 December 1628. According to Clarendon he 'was removed under pretence of his age and disability for the work'.

5] On 2 March 1629 Charles ordered the dissolution of Parliament. The Parliamentarians rebelled, and forcibly held the Speaker in his chair while passing Sir John Eliot's three resolutions condemning the King's administration. Parliament was finally dissolved on 10 March 1629.

6 broke him] Ley died on 14 March 1629.

6–8] The 'Old man' is the Athenian orator Isocrates, who was so distressed by Philip of Macedon's victory over the Athenian and Theban forces at *Chaeronea* in 338 BC that he starved himself to death. 'Dishonest' means 'shameful'.

Sonnet XI

The 'certain treatises' of the MS title are Milton's four divorce tracts: *Doctrine and Discipline of Divorce*, *The Judgement of Martin Bucer*, *Tetrachordon*, and *Colasterion*. Milton's *Tetrachordon* was published on 4 March 1645. The phrases 'it walkd the Town a while' (line 3) and 'now seldom por'd on' (line 4) suggest that the sonnet was written after an interval of several months.

1 *Tetrachordon*] The Greek word *tetrachordon* means 'four-stringed', and refers to a scale of four notes. Milton applied the word to the four texts of Scripture which he wished to compare and explain.

6–7 Mile-/End Green] a common at the eastern limit of London.

7–8] The Scottish names were doubtless chosen for their harsh sounds, but they may refer to individuals, presumably followers of Montrose.

11 *Quintilian*] In his *Institutes* Quintilian, the Roman rhetorician, censures foreign words as a threat to the purity of Latin.

12–14] Sir *John Cheke* (1514–57), tutor to Edward VI, was Professor of Greek at Cambridge.

Sonnet XII

The title 'On the Same' refers to Milton's four divorce tracts rather than to *Tetrachordon* in particular. The poem was probably written in the second half of 1645.

1 quit their cloggs] throw off their shackles.

5–7] *Latona* was the mother of Apollo and Diana, who were later to possess (hold 'in fee') the sun and moon. *Latona* stopped at a pool to drink, and when prevented from doing so by some peasants ('hinds') who stirred up the water to make it muddy, turned them into frogs (*Metamorphoses* vi 317–81; cf. *Arcades* 20).

8] Matt. vii. 6.

10] John viii. 32.

Sonnet XIII. On the New Forcers of Conscience under the Long Parlament

The latest event to which Milton alludes in the poem is the decree of 28 August 1646, when Parliament established the ordination of ministers by 'the Classical Presbyteries'. The phrase 'just Fears' in line 18 may mean that the poem was written in horrified anticipation of this decree shortly before it was passed.

The sonnet is unique among Milton's sonnets in that it is a *sonetto caudato*, a sonnet with *coda* (tail). Milton's sonnet has two *code*, each consisting of a half-line and a couplet.

title] The new forcers of conscience are the Presbyterians, who had led the Puritan attack on Laudian episcopacy and since 1643 had gradually established a presbyterian system. The phrase 'under the Long Parlament' does not appear in the Trinity MS, but was added in 1673, by which time the phrase 'Long

Parliament' was understood to refer to the parliament which extended (with interruptions) from 1640 to 1660.

1] Although the act abolishing archbishops and bishops was not passed until 9 October 1646, episcopacy had been effectively abolished since January 1643.

2] refers to the abolition of the *Book of Common Prayer* and the adoption of the *Directory for Public Worship* on 4 January 1645.

3 widowd whore Pluralitie] Milton's personification of the practice of securing the income from more than one benefice at a time. She is 'widowd' because the Anglican clergyman who had indulged in the practice had been replaced by Presbyterians.

4 abhorrd] plays on 'whore' (line 3).

5 Civil Sword] the authority of the state. See *Sonnet* XVIII 12n.

7 classic] refers to the *classis*, or presbytery, a body of elders acting as an ecclesiastical court.

Hierarchy] refers to the hierarchy of four courts under the Presbytery system: consistory, *classis*, synod, and national assembly. Milton intended the word to recall the Anglican hierarchy.

8 *A.S.*] Adam Stewart, a Scottish Presbyterian living in London in the 1640s. Pamphlets, including Stewart's anti-Independent pamphlets, were often signed by initials rather than names, and Milton's use of initials alludes to Stewart's pamphleteering activities.

Rotherford] Samuel Rutherford, one of the four Commissioners sent by the Church of Scotland to the Westminster Assembly.

12 *Edwards*] Thomas Edwards, English Presbyterian apologist, and the author of *Gangrena* (1646), which included an attack on Milton's divorce tracts.

Scotch what-d'ye-call] Usually identified (without proof) as Robert Baillie, one of the Scottish Commissioners, and the author of *Dissuasive from the Errors of the Time* (1645), which included an attack on Milton's divorce tracts.

14] A comparison of the Westminster Assembly to the Council of *Trent* (1545–63), at which the Protestant delegates were a minority in a council 'packed' in the Catholic interest.

17 Phylacteries] here used metaphorically to mean an ostentatious display of piety. See Matt. xxiii. 5.

bauk your Ears] 'bauk' means 'ignore'. The phrase glances at the fate of William Prynne, whose ears had been clipped in 1634 as a punishment for alleged defamation of the King and Queen in his *Histriomastix*; in 1637 his ears were removed completely for another offence. The MS version of the line makes the allusion clearer: 'Cropp yee as close as marginall P–s eares'.

20] Etymologically 'priest' is an abbreviated form of 'presbyter'.

Sonnet XIV. To Mr. H. Lawes, on his Aires

The sonnet is dated in MS 9 February 1645 (i.e. 1646), and was first published by Henry Lawes (the court musician with whom Milton had collaborated in *Comus*) in *Choice Psalmes* (1648), which was dedicated to Charles I, who was then a prisoner.

4 *Midas*] King of Phrygia who preferred the music of Pan to that of Apollo, whereupon Apollo changed his ears to those of an ass.

10 *Phoebus*] see *Passion* 23n.

12–14] In *Purgatorio* ii Dante meets his friend *Casella* the musician, and asks him to sing. Casella sings Dante's own *canzone* 'Amor che ne la mente mi ragiona'.

Sonnet XV

The MS title indicates that the sonnet was written in memory of Mrs Catherine

Thomason, who died in December 1646. Mrs Thomason was the wife of Milton's friend, George Thomason, the bookseller and collector of civil war pamphlets.

Sonnet XVI. On the Lord Gen. Fairfax at the siege of Colchester

Sir Thomas Fairfax was commander-in-chief of the New Model Army. He was a military genius of immense personal courage, and led the parliamentary army to a series of victories. He besieged Colchester on 13 June 1647, and the city fell on 27 August. Milton's hopes for Fairfax, as expressed in the sestet, never came to fruition, for Fairfax withdrew from public life after the execution of Charles, to which he objected.

5 vertue] means both 'valour' and 'moral worth'.

6 new rebellions] the Royalist rebellions of 1648, i.e. the Second Civil War.

7 Hydra] mythical water serpent with seven or more heads, killed by Hercules.

7–8 false . . . league] The 'false North' is Scotland, and the 'broken league' is the Solemn League and Covenant (on which see *Sonnet* XVII 4n), which the Scots violated by invading England on 8 July 1648.

8 imp . . . wings] to strengthen or improve the flight of a bird by engrafting new feathers in the wing.

12–14] Milton often denounced the well-attested corruption of the Long Parliament.

Sonnet XVII. To the Lord General Cromwell May 1652

In February 1652 Parliament appointed a Committee for the Propagation of the Gospel to consider the proposals of fifteen ministers, whose number included John Owen, formerly Cromwell's chaplain, and Philip Nye, one of the original Dissenting Brethren. The ministers proposed, *inter alia*, limited toleration and a stipendiary clergy. In this sonnet Milton addresses Cromwell as a member of the committee.

4 peace and truth] a popular catch-phrase, Biblical in origin (Isa. xxxix. 8), here quite possibly used as an allusion to the Solemn League and Covenant (the league between England and Scotland on the basis of the establishment of Presbyterianism in both countries, signed in 1643), of which these were the closing words.

5 crowned Fortune] Fortuna, the pagan goddess, here represents Charles I, who had been executed on 30 January 1649. See l. 9n.

7 *Darwen* stream] refers to the Battle of Preston, which was fought near the river Darwen in Lancashire from 17–19 August 1648, and at which Cromwell defeated the Covenanters under the Duke of Hamilton, half of whose army was destroyed in the engagement.

8 *Dunbarr field*] refers to the Battle of Dunbar on 3 September 1650 at which Cromwell defeated the Covenanters under Leslie and went on to occupy Scotland.

9 *Worsters* laureat wreath] On 3 September 1651, the anniversary of Dunbar, Cromwell crushed the Covenanters under Charles II (who had been crowned king in Scotland on 1 January 1651, and may therefore be included in the phrase 'crowned Fortune' in l. 5).

12 secular chaines] alludes to the proposal that the state should enforce the limits of toleration.

14 hireling wolves] stipendiary clergy.

Sonnet XVIII. To Sir Henry Vane the younger

Sir Henry Vane the Younger (so called to distinguish him from his eminent father), 1613–62, was an important figure in the Puritan cause. Unlike Milton, he advocated toleration for all religious opinions. Though not a regicide, he was executed after the Restoration. Milton sent the sonnet to Vane on 3 July 1652.

3 gowns] civil power. The phrase 'gowns not arms' alludes to the ancient dictum *Cedant arma togæ* (let arms yield to the gown).

3–4] alludes to accounts of the firmness of the Roman senate in the face of invasions by Pyrrhus, king of Epirus, and the African Hannibal.

6 hollow states] 'hollow' puns on Holland, and retains the secondary meanings of 'insincere' and 'low-lying', while 'states' puns on States-General, the Dutch legislative assembly. Vane had attempted to negotiate a union between the Commonwealth and the Dutch Republic. The attempt failed, and shortly before Milton wrote his sonnet the First Anglo-Dutch War began.

spelld] comprehended.

12 either sword] the spiritual sword and the civil sword. See *Sonnet* XIII 5.

Sonnet XIX. On the late Massacre in Piemont

The sect known as the Vaudois or Waldenses were believed by seventeenth-century Protestants to represent the continuity of Protestantism from earliest times to the Reformation. The Vaudois sect had been persecuted since its foundation in the twelfth century, and the frequency and intensity of the persecution increased as the sect became absorbed into the Protestant movement. The massacre to which Milton's sonnet seems to be an immediate response was perpetuated by French and Irish troops sent to the Vaudois valleys by the Duke of Savoy. On 24 April 1655 this army began the mutilation, torture and slaughter of the members of the sect, and a few days later over 1700 Vaudois were dead. Protestant Europe was outraged and Cromwell protested to the Duke of Savoy with a letter written by Milton.

1] See Luke xviii. 7, Rev. vi. 9–10.

2] See Psalm cxli. 7.

4 Stocks and Stones] See Jer. ii. 27.

5 book] Rev. xx. 12.

10 martyrd ... sow] Alludes to Tertullian's famous maxim 'The blood of the martyrs is the seed of the church' (*Plures efficimur, quoties metimur a vobis: semen est sanguis Christianorum*). The phrase also introduces an extended allusion to the parable of the sower (Matt. xiii. 3–9).

12 triple Tyrant] the pope, whose crown has three tiers. Cf. *Novembris* 55 and 94, and *Bombardicam* III 3.

14 *Babylonian*] The Protestants commonly identified the Babylon of Revelation with papal Rome.

Sonnet XX

The date of composition is not known, but it may have been written shortly after Milton went blind early in 1652. The fact that the poem follows the Piedmont massacre sonnet in Milton's 1673 *Poems* may, on the other hand, indicate a date of 1655.

3–6] The lines are based on the parable of the talents, Matt. xxv. 14–30.

11 milde yoke] Matt. xi. 29–30.

Sonnet XXI

According to Edward Phillips, Milton's nephew, Milton was often visited by 'young Laurence (the Son of him that was President of *Oliver's* Council)'. 'Young Laurence' is probably Edward Lawrence (1633–57), who may have been a pupil of Milton. Lawrence became an MP in 1656 and died, aged 24, in the second half of 1657.

The poem could have been written at any time from the winter of 1651–2, when Milton moved to Westminster and began to be visited by Lawrence, to the winter of 1656–7.

1 Father] Edward Lawrence was the eldest son of Henry Lawrence, a prominent figure in Cromwell's Council of State and the author of several theological treatises.

6 *Favonius*] Roman personification of the west wind, and the messenger of spring.

8] Matt. vi. 28.

10 Attic taste] taste characterized by the simple and refined elegance of Athens.

13–14 spare/To interpose] The phrase is ambiguous, and may mean 'refrain from interposing', or may signify the opposite, 'spare time for interposing'.

Sonnet XXII

Cyriack Skinner (1627–1700) was a pupil of Milton in the 1640s, and a regular visitor at his house in the 1650s. The sonnet was probably written in 1655.

1 Grandsire] Skinner's maternal grandfather was Sir Edward Coke, the most distinguished lawyer of his generation, famed as the defender of law and Parliament against archbishops and kings.

Royal Bench] Coke became Chief Justice of the King's Bench in 1613.

2 *Themis*] Greek goddess of law, called Justitia by the Romans.

3 volumes] Coke was the author of *Reports*, *Booke of Entries*, and *Institutes of the Laws of England*.

7] *Euclid* and *Archimedes* represent Skinner's interest in mathematics and physics.

8] The *Swede* is probably Charles X, who in 1655 was commanding his army in Poland. The *French* alludes to the war between France and Spain, and to Cardinal Mazarin (the chief minister of France) in particular. Together the allusions constitute a reference to Skinner's interest in politics.

Sonnet XXIII. To Mr Cyriack Skinner upon his Blindness

On Skinner see headnote to previous poem. The phrase 'three years day' suggests a date of composition in 1655.

10 conscience] inward knowledge.

Sonnet XXIV

The date of composition is not known, as it is not clear whether the subject of the poem is Milton's first wife, Mary Powell, who died in May 1652, three days after the birth of their daughter Deborah, or his second wife, Katherine Woodcock, who died in February 1658 after giving birth in October 1657 to their daughter Katherine, who died six weeks after her mother.

2–3] In Euripides' *Alcestis* Hercules ('*Joves* great Son') rescues *Alcestis* from Death and returns her, veiled, to Admetus, her husband. In antiquity *Alcestis* represented conjugal fidelity and devotion.

6] See Lev. xii. 4–8.

9 vested all in white] See Rev. vii. 13–14.

PSALMS

Psalms i–viii were translated from the original Hebrew in 1653, when Milton had been blind for a year and a half.

Ps. ii. *Terzetti*] the translation is written in the *terza rima* of Dante, i.e. as a series of interlocking tercets in which the second line of each tercet rhymes with the first and third lines of the succeeding tercet.

Psalms lxxx–lxxxviii were translated in April 1647, at a time when there was considerable controversy over the metrical psalter. This controversy may have occasioned Milton's translations.

Psalm LXXX

11 Awake thy strength] *Gnorera* means 'rouse'.

18–19 declare/Thy smoking wrauth] *Gnashanta* means 'you are smoking'.

23 largely] *Shalish* is probably the name of a measure, one third of a unit; cf. Isa. xl. 12 (and A.V. marginal note), its only other occurrence.

27–8 laugh . . . throw] The verb *Jilgnagu* means 'scorn'.

Psalm LXXXI

29 in thunder deep] *Besether ragnam* means 'in the secret place of thunder'.

Psalm LXXXII

1 great assembly] *Bagnadath-el* may mean 'assembly of the mighty one' or 'assembly of God'.

3 Among, on both his hands] *Bekerev* means 'in the midst of'.

5–6 pervert . . . wrong] *Tishphetu gnavel* means 'judge perversely'.

9–10 Regard . . . cause] *Shiphtu-dal* means 'judge the poor' or 'judge the weak'.

11–12 raise . . . Laws] *Hatzdiku* means 'declare right or just'.

19–20 are mov'd . . . gon] *Jimmotu* means 'moved'.

25–6 judge . . . redress] The verb *Shophta* (not *Shiphta*) means 'judge'.

Psalm LXXXIII

5–6 swell . . . outrageously] *Jehemajun* means 'are in turmoil'.

9–10 contrive . . . deep] *Jagnarimu Sod* means 'deliberate cunningly'.

11 to ensnare . . . strive] *Jithjagnatsu gnal* means 'conspire against'.

11–12 Them, Whom . . . keep] *Tsephuneca* means 'your hidden things'.

17 with all thir might] *Lev jachdau* means 'together with one heart'.

47–8 Gods houses . . . Thir stately Palaces] In the phrase *Neoth Elohim bears both* Milton asserts (correctly) that the Hebrew phrase is ambiguous, and can be translated by either English phrase. *Elohim* means 'God', but can also be used as a superlative; *Neoth* is really 'pastures' (as in Psalm xxiii. 2), thence 'dwelling places', but hardly 'palaces'.

Psalm LXXXVIII

31–2] In the phrase '*The* Heb. *bears both*' Milton asserts (incorrectly) that the Hebrew phrase is ambiguous, and can be translated by either English phrase. In fact only line 31 is a correct translation.

60 shake] The phrase *Prae Concussione* is not a clarification of the Hebrew (it merely translates Milton's English phrase), but rather an assertion of Milton's preference for the meaning 'shaking'. The Hebrew word means 'youth' (cf. A.V. 'from my youth up'), but Milton has enlisted an homonymous root that means 'to shake' to help him understand a difficult line.

LATIN POEMS

Tributes

The author knows that the tributes concerning himself which follow, are not so much words of praise as overpraise, because men of remarkable talent who are also friends are wont, for the most part, to eulogize and fashion all things with excessive warmth according to their own excellence rather than be consistent with the truth. However, the author was not willing that their good wishes for him not be known, especially since others have earnestly urged that he make them known. For while he seeks with all his strength to ward off the odium of excessive praise, and prefers that he should not have attributed to him more than is fair, nevertheless, he cannot deny that he considers these judgements of wise and distinguished men a supreme honour.

Ut mens

Giovanni Battista Manso, Marquis of Villa, of Naples, to John Milton, Englishman

If your piety were as your mind, your form, your elegance, appearance and manner, then you would not be an Angle, but, by Hercules, a true angel.

Cf. the poem which Milton wrote to Mansus, p. 139.

Cede Meles

An Epigram by Giovanni Salsilli, of Rome, to John Milton, Englishman, who deserves to be crowned with the triple laurel of poesy, Greek certainly, Latin and Etruscan.

Yield Meles; let Mincius yield with lowered urn; let Sebetus cease to speak all the time of Tasso. But let the victorious Thames flow more deeply than all other streams, for through you, Milton, he alone will be equal to all three.

Cf. the poem which Milton wrote to Salsilli, p. 138.

Meles] Homer; see *PR* IV 259n.
Mincius] Virgil; see *Lycidas* 86n.
Sebetus] a river near Sorrento (in Campania), where Tasso was born.

Græcia Mæonidem
To John Milton

Let Greece boast of Mæonides and Rome of Maro, England boasts of Milton, the equal of them both. Selvaggi.

The identity of Selvaggi has not been established.
Mæonidem] Homer.
Moronem] Virgil.

Ergimi all' Etra
To Mr John Milton, English Nobleman
Ode

Raise me to the sky, O Clio,[1] for of stars shall I plait the wreath, not of the eternal foliage of Pindus[4] and Helicon on the fair-haired god,[3] for greater ornaments are appropriate to greater merit, divine virtue to divine praise.

Exalted eternal worth cannot be left a prey to devouring time, rapacious oblivion cannot steal lofty honour from memory. May virtue fit a strong arrow to the bow of my harp, and I shall wound death.

Surrounded by the wide expanses of the deep ocean, England resides severed from the world, so her worth exceeds that of other people. This fecundity produces heroes whom we rightly deem superhuman.

In their breasts a refuge is found for banished virtue, which is alone welcome to them, because in it they can find joy and delight; you repeat it, John, and show by your true virtue the truth of my song.

Industrious Zeuxis[26] was driven far from the shores of his native land by ardent desire, for he had heard the cry of the golden horn of fame roaring Helen's fame, and to make her effigy adequately he drew the rarest of most beautiful ideas.

So the industrious bee laboriously extracts its precious liquid from the lily and the rose and from all the lovely flowers that adorn the meadow; various strings make one sweet sound, various voices make an harmonious melody.

Loving beautiful glory, Milton, you quit your native clime and turned your wandering foot to other countries, seeking sciences and arts; you saw the kingdoms of the prevailing Gaul, and the worthiest heroes of Italy.

Artisan almost divine, your thought, seeking only virtue, saw in every land those who walk the path of noble worth; it selected the best from the good to forge the Idea of all virtues.

All those born in Florence, or who there learned the art of speaking the Tuscan tongue, those whose memory is perpetuated in scholarly books, you sought for your treasuring, and spoke with them in their works.

In vain for you did Jove confuse the tongues in lofty Babel when the tower, a monument of various languages, fell to the plain. For not only England hears you speak her worthy language, but also Spain, France, Tuscany, Greece and Rome.

The deepest mysteries which Nature hides in heaven or on earth, too often avariciously hiding them from superhuman minds, you have penetrated, reaching at last the great limit of moral virtue.

Let time cease to thrash its wings, let it be motionless, and let the years which elapse and are insulting to immortal virtue stop; for if ever there were deeds worthy of poem or history, you have them present in your memory.

Give me your sweet harp if I am to speak of your sweet song, which exalts you to the sky and in making you a heavenly man attains honour. The Thames will proclaim, through you its swan, equality with Permessus.[78]

I who on the bank of the Arno attempt to proclaim your high and prominent merit do so in vain, for I learn how to admire it but not how to praise it; consequently I restrain my tongue and listen to my heart which with amazement undertakes to praise you.

Antonio Francini is mentioned in *Damonis* 137.

1 *Clio*] the muse of history.
3 *Biondo Dio*] Apollo.
4] Pindus is the ancient name for the mountain range which separates Thessaly from Epirus; on Helicon see *Winchester* 56n.
26 *Zeusi*] Zeuxis, an ancient Greek painter, painted a Helen that was an ideal picture compiled from several models.
78 *Permesso*] a river on Mount Helicon.

Juveni Patria

To John Milton of London

To a young man distinguished for his birthplace and his excellence.

To a man who in his travels has explored many places on earth and in his studies examined them all, so that like a modern Ulysses he might everywhere grasp the knowledge of everything offered by all people.

To a polyglot on whose lips languages already dead come to life again, so that all forms of expression in his praise are ineloquent. He knows these forms so well that he understands the expressions of popular admiration and applause excited by his special wisdom.

To him whose endowments of body and soul drive the senses to admiration, yet on account of this admiration deprive the senses of their impulses. His works inspire applause but by their charm deprive his eulogizers of their speech.

To one who has a memory of the whole world; in whose intellect is wisdom; in whose desires a passion for fame; in whose mouth eloquence; who with Astronomy as guide hears the harmonious sounds of the heavenly spheres; who with Philosophy as teacher selects the marks of nature's wondrous deeds through which the greatness of God is portrayed; who with the constant reading of writers as his companion he investigates, restores, traverses, in the hiding-places of antiquity's history, in the ruins of former times, and in the digressions of erudition (but why do I struggle up the steeps?).

To him in the publishing of whose virtues the tongues of Rumour would not suffice, nor is the amazement of men in their praises enough, with respect and love this tribute of admiration, the just desert of his merits, is offered by Charles Dati, Patrician of Florence, humble servant of so great a man and lover of such excellence.

Carlo Dati is mentioned in *Damonis* 137. One of Milton's letters to Dati survives, as do two of Dati's to Milton.

A Book of Elegies
Elegia Prima
Elegy One to Charles Diodati

At last, beloved friend, your letter has reached me. This messenger of yours has brought your words, brought them from the western bank of the River Dee at Chester where in a downward torrent the water seeks the Vergivian Sea.[4] Believe me, it is a great joy that distant lands have nourished a heart which loves me, and a mind so true, that an agreeable companion is owed to me by a remote country, which, when asked, is willing to restore him to me presently. I remain in the city washed by the tides of the Thames, and am not unwilling to stay here in the delightful place of my birth. At this time I am not troubled by an urge to revisit the reedy Cam, nor by a desire for the home which is now forbidden to me. Bare fields without gentle shade do not give satisfaction. How badly suited is that place to the votaries of Phoebus.[14] I do not care to endure continually the threats of a harsh teacher, nor the other things inappropriate to my disposition. If this be exile – to return to one's home and enjoy an agreeable ease, free from cares – then I do not reject the name or lot of a fugitive, but cheerfully enjoy my banishment. If only the poet,[21] the lamentable exile in the land of Tomis[22] had endured nothing more burdensome, then he would have yielded nothing to Ionian Homer, and you, Virgil, he would have vanquished and deprived of highest praise. For here I can freely give my time to the gentle muses, and be possessed completely by the books which make up the whole of my life. When I am weary, I am drawn out by the display of the curved theatre, and the flowing words of the stage call for applause. Sometimes I hear a wise old man, sometimes a prodigal heir; now a suitor appears, now a soldier without his helmet, or a lawyer, grown rich from a ten-year dispute, thunders out his barbarous phrases to a disorderly courtroom. Often a cunning slave assists a son in his love affair to deceive his stern father right under his nose. Often too, a young girl, wondering at new warmth within, falls in love, even though she does not know what love is. Raging tragedy, with dishevelled hair and rolling eyes shakes her blood-stained sceptre. It pains me to watch and yet there is a pleasure in the pain of watching. Occasionally there is a sweet bitterness in the tears, when an unfortunate young man leaves behind untroubled pleasures, and sinks weeping for a lost love, or when a cruel avenger of wrong returns from the darkness across the Styx troubling the guilty hearts with his destructive torch, or the house of Pelops or that of noble Ilus[45] mourns, or the court of Creon atones for incestuous ancestors.[46] But I am not always hidden away under a roof, nor in the city, and springtime is not without its significance for me. I too enjoy the densely planted elm grove and a spot near the city well known for its shade. Here, one can often see clusters of maidens pass by, stars inspiring pleasant passions. Ah, how often did I marvel at a beauteous form which could rejuvenate even old Jove and how many times have I seen eyes brighter than precious stones or all the stars that revolve about both poles, and necks which would surpass the arms of twice-alive Pelops[57] and the way[58] that overflows with pure nectar, a forehead of extraordinary grace, waving hair that is a snare of gold extended by deceitful Love, enticing cheeks beside which the crimson of the hyacinth and even the redness of your flower,[62] Adonis, are to be despised. Yield Heroides,[63] often praised in the past, and every woman that has charmed inconstant Jove. Yield Achaemenian girls with towering hats, and everyone that lives in Susa and in Memmonian Ninevah.[66] Admit defeat nymphs of Danaus,[67] and women of Troy and of Rome. Let not the Tarpeian Muse vaunt Pompey's colonnade[69] or a theatre full of Ausonian robes.[70] The most distinguished praise must be reserved for the maidens of Britain, and your foreign women must be content to follow. And you, London, a city built by Trojan colonists, and celebrated far and wide for your turreted head,[74] are exceedingly favoured to contain within your walls whatever beauty this pendant orb contains. The stars that glitter in the clear sky – the multitude of handmaidens serving the goddess of Endymion[78] – do not equal in number the host of fair maidens, conspicuous for their beauty, which can be seen gracing your streets. It is believed that kindly Venus, drawn by her twin doves and escorted by her quiver-bearing soldier, came to this place and preferred it to Cnidos, to the valleys watered by the Simois,[83] to Paphos[83] and to rosy Cyprus.

But I am preparing to leave this favoured city with all speed, while the indulgence of the blind boy permits, and, with the help of the divine moly,[88] to shun the infamous halls of faithless Circe.[87] I am to return to the reedy fens of the Cam and hear once more the hoarse hum of the university.

Meanwhile, accept the small tribute of a faithful friend, these few words rendered in elegiac measures.[92]

The poem was written in the spring of 1626. On Diodati see *Sonnet* IV 1n.

4 Vergivium . . . salum] The Irish Sea.

14 Phœbicolis] i.e. poets and students of poetry. See *Passion* 23n.

21–2 In AD 8 Ovid was banished by Augustus to Tomis (modern Constanta, on the Black Sea coast of Romania).

45–6] Cf. *Il Penseroso* 99–100 notes. Ilus was the legendary founder of Troy, and Creon was the brother of Jocasta, the mother and wife of Oedipus.

57] Pelops was murdered by his father Tantalus, who served him as a feast to the gods; the crime was discovered, Pelops was restored to life, and Tantalus punished (see *PL* II 607–14). The portion of Pelops' shoulder (not arm) which had been eaten was replaced with ivory.

58 via] The Milky Way.

62 floris] the anemone, which Venus caused to grow from the blood of Adonis, who had been slain by a boar. (*Metamorphoses* x 731–9).

63 Heroides] the heroines of Ovid's *Heroides*.

66] See *PL* X 306–11n, *PR* III 275–9n.

67 Danaæ] an ancient epithet which means 'Greek'; it refers to the mythical Lybian king Danaus, who founded Argos.

69 Tarpëia Musa] Ovid, whose house was near the Tarpeian rock (see *PR* IV 49n.).

Pompeianas . . . columnas] refers to the portico of the Theatre of Pompey, on the Campus Martius, in Rome.

70 Ausoniis] In Augustan poetry (e.g. *Aeneid* x 54) Ausonia is a synonym for Italy. The *stola* was the robe worn by Roman matrons.

74] Cf. *Arcades* 21n.

78] i.e. the stars that serve the moon, who was the lover of Endymion.

83] Cnidos, a Greek city in Asia Minor, was famed in antiquity for the Venus which Praxiteles had sculpted for the temple. The river Simois rose on Mount Ida, the scene of the judgement of Paris (see *PL* V 381–2n.).

84] Paphos, an ancient city of Cyprus, possessed a famous temple of Venus, and was regarded by Homer as her chief resort.

87–8] See *Comus* 50n. (on Circe) and 635n. (on moly).

92] refers to the alternating hexameters and pentameters that comprise the elegiac distich.

Elegia Secunda

Elegy 2 At the age of seventeen. On the death of the Beadle of the University of Cambridge.

Cruel death, the last of all beadles, shows her own office no favour, and takes you, a fellow beadle. How distinguished you were on the many occasions that you carried the glittering mace, and called together the Palladian flock.[2] Though your temples were whiter than the plumes[5] beneath which, we are told, Love hid,[6] yet you deserved to grow young again by an Haemonian potion.[7] You deserved to live on to the age of Aeson,[8] and to be recalled from the Stygian waters by Coronides' healing art through the persistent begging of a goddess.[10] If you were ordered by your Apollo[12] to be his swift messenger and summon the gowned ranks, you were like wing-footed Cyllenius[13] when he was sent from his father's celestial citadel,[14] and stood in the Trojan court. You were like Eurybates as he faced the harsh demands of his leader Atrides.[16] Great queen of sepulchres, attendant of Avernus,[17] too cruel to the Muses, too cruel to Pallas, why not carry off those who are a useless burden to the earth? That is the crowd for you to attack with your darts.

Mourn for this man, University, and wear your dark robes. May his black bier be wet with your tears. Let plaintive Elegy herself pour forth sad measures and let melancholy dirges resound in all the schools.

Richard Ridding, who had held the ceremonial office of university beadle for thirty years, died in the autumn of 1626. Milton wrote the poem before his eighteenth birthday on 9 December.

2 Palladium . . . gregem] i.e. those who follow Pallas Athena, the Greek goddess who ultimately became allegorized into a personification of wisdom.

5–6] When Jove visited Leda he assumed the form of a very white swan.

7–8] Medea rejuvenated Aeson by filling his veins with a brew that included roots cut in a valley in Haemonia (i.e. Thessaly. *Metamorphoses* vii 264; cf. *Comus* 637n.).

10] Aesculapius, the god of medicine (here called Coronides after his mother Coronis) restored Hippolytus to life in response to the prayer of Diana.

12 Phœbo . . . tuo] i.e. the Vice-Chancellor.

13–14] Mercury (here called Cyllenius after his birthplace, Mount Cyllene in Arcadia) was sent by Jove to guide Priam; in Homer's account they do not meet in the court (*Iliad* xxiv 334 ff.).

15–16] Eurybates, one of the heralds of Agamemnon (here called Atrides after his father Atreus), was sent with another herald to Achilles to secure Briseis; in Homer's account they do not set out the demands of Agamemnon, but stand in silence (*Iliad* i 320–44).

17] Avernus, a deep lake near Naples, was anciently believed to lead to the underworld.

Elegia Tertia

Elegy 3 At the age of seventeen. On the death of the Bishop of Winchester.

I was sad, and sat silent and alone. Many sorrows perplexed my soul, when suddenly there came a vision of the dismal massacre wrought by Libitina[4] on England's soil. Grim death, fearful with her sepulchral torch, entered the brilliant marble palaces of princes, struck the walls laden with gold and jasper, and did not hesitate to cut down troops of rulers with her scythe. Then I recalled the glorious leader and his venerable brother[9] whose bones were burned on untimely funeral pyres, and the heroes Belgia[12] saw snatched up to the heavens, lost princes for whom the whole country mourned. But it was especially for you I mourned, most worthy bishop, at one time the great glory of your Winchester. I melted into tears and lamented with these mournful words: 'Cruel Death, goddess second to Tartarean Jove,[16] is it not enough that the woods feel your rage, that you are given power over the grassy fields and that the lilies, crocus, and sacred rose of beautiful Cypris[20] wither when touched by your putrid breath? Is it not enough that you forbid the oak tree on the river bank to gaze for ever at the water passing by? The unnumbered birds which spread out on wings across the clear sky succumb to you, despite their prophetic powers, as do the thousand beasts wandering in the dark forests and the silent herd which the caves of Proteus[26] sustain. Envious one, when such great power has been conceded to you, what delight is there in staining your hands with human blood, in sharpening your certain darts against a noble breast or in driving out a half-divine spirit from its dwelling place?'

While I wept and brooded upon these matters in my heart, dewy Hesperus rose out of the western waters, and Phoebus, after measuring his passage from the eastern shore, submerged his chariot in the Tartessian[33] sea. Without delay I stretched out on the hollow bed in order to refresh my limbs. Night and sleep had closed my eyes, when it seemed to me that I was walking about a wide plain. Alas, my talents are insufficient to describe what I saw. There everything shone with a rosy light, like mountain tops coloured by the early morning sun. The earth was bright with a many-coloured garment as when the daughter of Thaumas[41] spreads out her riches for display. Chloris, the goddess loved by delicate Zephyrus did not adorn the garden of Alcinous[44] with such varied blossoms. Silver streams washed verdant plains, their sands more richly golden than the Hesperian Tagus.[46] Through the perfumed riches gradually spreads the soft breath of Favonius[47] – a dewy breath born under countless roses. Such a place, on the most distant shore of the land of the Ganges, is imagined to be the home of royal Lucifer.[50] While I marvel at the thick shadows under clustering vines and the shining places around me, suddenly, the Bishop of Winchester stands near by. A heavenly radiance shone on his bright face, shining white garments flowed down to his golden sandals, and a white fillet wreathed his divine head. And while the venerable man advanced thus clad, the shining earth trembled with a joyful noise. The heavenly hosts clap their jewelled wings and the undefiled sky resounds with a triumphal trumpet. Each one greets his new companion with an embrace and a song, and one of them uttered these words from his quiet lips: 'Come my son, and receive joyously the delights of your father's kingdom, and be free forever from your troublesome labour.' He spoke, and the winged throng touched their harps. But my golden rest was banished with the night and I wept for the sleep that was disturbed by Cephalus' mistress.[67]

May such dreams often befall me.[68]

Lancelot Andrewes, the distinguished scholar and divine, died on 25 September 1626. Milton wrote the poem before his eighteenth birthday on 9 December.

4 Libitina] goddess of corpses and burial; more than 35000 people died when the plague struck London in 1625.

9–12] the *clarus dux*, his *frater verendus*, and the heroes of Belgia have not been identified with certainty.

16 Tartareo . . . Jovi] Pluto.

20 Cypridi] Venus. See *Elegia* I 84n.

26] Proteus (on whom see *PL* III 604n.) tended the seals of Poseidon (see *Comus* 871n.).

33 Tartessiaco . . . æquore] the Atlantic, here called after Tartessus, an ancient city in southern Spain.

41 Thaumantia proles] Iris, goddess of the rainbow, was the daughter of the sea god Thaumas.

44] See *PL* V 16n., 339–41n.

46 Hesperio . . . Tago] the river Tagus (now Tejo), which rises in eastern Spain and flows through Portugal to Lisbon, had been famed since antiquity for its golden sand. 'Hesperian' here means 'Spanish'.

47 Favoni] the west wind.

50 Luciferi] the 'light-bearer', i.e. the sun.

67 Cephaleiâ pellice] Aurora; see *Penseroso* 122–4n.

68] a rather startling adaptation of the last line of Ovid's *Amores* I v, in which the poet is referring to making love to Corinna.

Elegia Quarta

Elegy 4 At the age of eighteen. To Thomas Young, his tutor, now performing the duties of pastor to the English merchants in Hamburg.

Fly, my letter, quickly across the boundless sea. Go! Seek Teutonic lands across the smooth waters. Shake off lingering delays, and let nothing, I pray, oppose your going or hinder the hastening of your journey. I myself will urge Aeolus,[6] who restrains the winds in his Sicanian[5] cave, the green gods, and azure Doris[7] with her company of nymphs, to give you a quiet journey through their kingdoms. But you, if you are able, lay hold of the swift team that carried the Colchian[10] when she fled from the face of her husband, or that by which Triptolemus reached the Scythian borders,[11] a welcome messenger from the city of Eleusis.[12] And when you see the yellow sands of Germany, turn your steps to the walls of wealthy Hamburg, which is said to take its name from Hama,[15] who, they say, was slain by a Cimbric[16] club. In that city lives a pastor, well-known for his allegiance to the primitive faith, instructed to tend the Christian flock. He is, indeed, more than half my soul. I am constrained to live a half-life. Alas, how many seas, how many mountains intervene to cut me off from that other part of myself? Dearer is he to me than you, most learned of the Greeks,[23] were to Cliniades, who was a descendant of Telamon;[24] dearer than the great Stagirite to his noble pupil[25] whom the gentle woman of Chaonia bore to Libyan Jove.[26] What the son of Amyntor, and what the heroic son of Philyra[27] were to the king of the Myrmidons, such is this man to me.[28] With him leading the way I first visited the Aonian retreats[29] and the sacred groves of the twin-peaked summit,[30] drained the Pierian springs and by Clio's favour[31] thrice moistened my grateful lips with the wine of Castilia.[32] Three times flaming Aethon saw the sign of the Ram[33] and overlaid its woolly back with new gold; twice Chloris[35] have you scattered new grass over the old earth and twice Auster[36] took away your riches; but not yet was I allowed to nourish my eyes on his face or my ears to drink in the sweet sounds of his voice.

Go, therefore, and outstrip sonorous Eurus[39] in your journey. What need there be for my warning, circumstances teach, and you yourself see. Perhaps you will come upon him sitting with his sweet wife, caressing on his lap the precious pledges of their love. Perchance he may be studying the large volumes of the ancient Fathers or the holy scriptures of the true God, or nourishing tender spirits with heavenly dew, the great healing task of religion. Let it be your concern to give a warm greeting, as the custom is, to say what would befit your master, were he present. Remember also to fix your eyes modestly on the ground for a short time and to speak these words with reverence: if there be time for the gentle Muses amidst the fighting,[51] a faithful hand sends these lines from England's shores. Accept his sincere, though late, salutation; let it be for that reason even more welcome to you. Late, indeed, but genuine was the greeting that chaste Penelope daughter of Icarus received from her lingering husband.[56] But why should I want to deny the existence of an obvious fault, which cannot in any way be lessened. He is justly accused of delay, he acknowledges his offence, and he is ashamed to have failed in his duty. Only grant forgiveness, for I have confessed the fault and beg your pardon. Faults which are acknowledged are wont to be lessened. No wild beast opens its gaping jaw against those who tremble, nor does the lion tear at those who are prostrate with his wounding claw. Often the cruel hearts of lance-bearing Thracians were softened by the sorrowful entreaties of humble petitioners. Uplifted hands turn aside the stroke of the thunderbolt and a small sacrifice placates angry gods.

For a long time he has felt the urge to write to you, and now love suffers no further delay, for wandering Rumour (alas, true messenger of misfortune) reports that wars are ready to burst out in areas bordering yours and that fierce soldiers surround you and your city and that the Saxon leaders are now furnished with arms. Everywhere around you Enyo[75] is despoiling the land, and blood now waters the fields sown with the flesh of men. Thrace has consigned her Mars to Germany; thither Father Mars has driven his Odrysian horses.[78] The ever-luxuriant olive now withers and the Goddess[80] who hates the sound of the brazen trumpet has fled (look!) fled from the earth, and indeed, it is thought the just Virgin[81] was not the last to take flight to the mansions above. Meanwhile the horror of war resounds on every side and you live alone and helpless in a strange land. Needy, you seek in a foreign country the sustenance which your fatherland did not supply. Native land, unfeeling parent, and more cruel than the white rocks that are struck by the foaming waves of your coast, does it become you thus to expose your innocent offspring,[89] do you thus consign to foreign soil and allow to seek nourishment in distant lands those whom God in his providence has sent to you, who bear glad tidings from heaven and who teach the way which after death leads to the stars? You deserve to live imprisoned by Stygian darkness and to perish from eternal hunger of the soul. Even thus did the prophet of the land of the Tishbites[97] once tread with unaccustomed foot the inaccessible wastes and the rough deserts of Arabia when he fled from the hands of King Ahab and from yours also, dreadful woman of Sidon.[100] And in this way Cilician Paul was driven from the Emathian city,[102] his flesh mutilated by the horrisonant scourge,[101] and Jesus himself was ordered by the ungrateful citizens of Gergessa to leave their territories.[104]

But take courage and let not uneasy hope succumb to cares nor pallid fear trouble your frame. Though you are beset by blazing arms and a thousand darts threaten death, yet no weapon shall injure your defenceless side, no spear shall drink your blood. For truly, you will be out of danger under the radiant shield of God. He will be your defender and your champion. He in the stillness of night vanquished the Assyrian host[114] beneath the ramparts of the citadel of Zion[113] and put to flight those whom old Damascus had sent from her ancient plains[116] into the Samaritan borders.[115] He terrified the thickset cohort with their trembling king[117] when in the clear air the brilliant trumpet sounded,[118] the horny hoofs beat the dusty plain,[119] and the hard-driven chariot beat the sandy ground.[120] There was heard the neighing of horses rushing to battle,[121] the clash of arms and the deep cries of men.[122] Remember to hope, for this is what remains to the wretched, and overcome your misfortunes with a magnanimous[124] spirit. Do not doubt that you will someday enjoy better seasons, and once again will be able to see your native home.'

Thomas Young (*c.* 1587–1665) was Milton's tutor for an unknown period sometime before 1620, when Young moved to Hamburg. The poem was written in 1627.

5–6] Aeolus, ruler of the winds, was thought to keep the winds in a cave on Aeolia, a floating island often located near Sicily, which is here called Sicania (after the ancient inhabitants of west-central Sicily).

7 Dorida] Doris was the wife of Nereus and the mother of the fifty Nereids.

10 Colchis] Medea, who fled from her husband Jason in a cart drawn by dragons after killing their children and Jason's new bride.

11–12] Ceres sent Triptolemus from Eleusis (a city in Attica) to Scythia (in southern Russia) in a chariot drawn by dragons (Ovid, *Metamorphoses* v 642–61).

15–16] Hama, a Saxon, was slain by Starchater, a Dane (here called Cimbric after the tribe from north Jutland).

23 doctissime Graiûm] Socrates.

24] Alcibiades, here called Cliniades after his father Clinias, claimed descent from the mythical hero Telemon. Plato represented Socrates and Alcibiades as intimate friends.

25–6] Aristotle, here called the Stagirite after his birthplace Stagirus (later Stagira) in Chalcidice, was the tutor of Alexander the Great, whose mother Olympias is here called the gentle woman of Chaonis (Epirus). See *PL* IX 507–9n.

27–8] Phoenix, here called Amyntorides after his father Amyntor, and Chiron, son of the nymph Philyra, were both tutors of Achilles, the king of the Myrmidons.

29] The Aonian retreats are Mount Helicon and its fountains Aganippe and Hippocrene; the mountain and its fountains were sacred to poets. The precise reference of *primus* is not clear.

30 bifidi . . . jugi] Parnassus, which was sacred to the muses.

31–2] The muses were born at Pieria, near Mount Olympus; the Castilian spring, at the foot of Mount Parnassus, was sacred to Clio, the muse of history.

33] Aethon is one of the four horses of the sun, which enters Aries, the sign of the Ram, at the vernal equinox.

35 Chlori] The Greek name for Flora, goddess of flowers, whose festival, the Floralis, began on 28 April.

36 Auster] the south wind.

39 Eurum] Eurus, the south-east wind.

51 inter prælia] refers to the battles of the Thirty Years' War.

56 viro] Odysseus.

75 Enyo] Greek goddess of war.

77] Mars (Ares) was traditionally associated with Thrace.

78 Odrysios] Thracian.

80 Diva] Eirene (Pax), goddess of peace, one of the Horae (Hours); see *Comus* 985n.

81 Virgo] Astrea; see *Nativity* 141n.

89] refers to the ancient practice of killing unwanted infants by exposure.

97–100] On Elijah as a Tishbite see *PR* II 16–17n., 312–14n. *Sidoni dira* is
    Jezebel, daughter of Ethbaal, king of Sidon, and wife of Ahab, king of Israel.
    See I Kings xix.

101–2] Paul was 'a Jew of Tarsus, a city in Cilicia' (Acts xxi. 39); on his scourging
    see Acts xvi. 19–40. The Emathian (Macedonian) city is Philippi.

103–4] Matt. viii. 34.

113–14] refers to Sennacherib's attack on Jerusalem; see II Kings xix. 35–6.

115–22] See II Kings vii. 6–7. The king is Ben-hadad II.

124 magnanimo] See *PL* VII 511n.

Elegia Quinta

Elegy 5 At the age of Twenty On the coming of spring.

Time, revolving in its perpetual circuit, now, in the warmth of spring, calls back
new zephyrs. Earth restored displays her brief youth and the ground now free of
frost takes on a soft greenness. Am I deceived? Or do my powers of verse return?
Does spring bear the gift of inspiration? It is here by the favour of spring and
flourishes once again, and (who would believe it?) now begs some employment for
itself. The Castalian spring and the twin peaks hover before my eyes[9] and dreams
bring Pirene to me at night.[10] Aroused, my soul burns with its secret passion. I am
stirred up by the madness and divine sounds within. The Delian god himself comes,
I see the hair entwined with Penean laurel;[13] the Delian himself comes.[14] Now my
mind is transported to the clear sky on high, and free from the body, I pass through
the wandering clouds. Through shades and caverns, the sanctuaries of poets, am I
led, and the hidden temples of the gods are open to me. My spirit wonders at all that
is done on Olympus and dark Tartarus does not escape my notice. What grand song
will my spirit pour forth from open lips? What will this fury, this divine madness,
bring forth? Spring, which gave the inspiration to me, will be the subject of my
song. In this way, the gifts will be returned to repay spring.

Now, Philomel, hidden by new leaves,[25] begin your melodies while all the woods
keep silent.[26] Let us begin together, I in the city and you in the woodlands, and
together celebrate the coming of spring. What joy! The changing spring has
returned. Let us praise the glories of spring and let the Muse take on her
perennial[30] task. The sun, now fleeing from Ethiopia and the fields of Tithonus,[31]
turns his golden reins to northern lands.[32] Night's journey is brief, brief the stay of
shady night. She is exiled with her horrid darkness. And now Lycaonian Boötes
does not follow wearily the heavenly wain[35] in its long path, as he did before. Now,
in all the heavens, only a few stars keep their accustomed watch around the courts
of Jove. For fraud, killing and violence have vanished with night, and the Gods do
not fear the wickedness of the Giants.[40] Perhaps some shepherd reclining on a
rocky peak while the dewy earth reddens with the first sun declares 'This night, O
Phoebus, certainly this night have you been deprived of your beloved who restrains
your swift horses!' Joyfully Cynthia[46] returns to her woods and takes up her quiver
when from on high she sees the light-bringing chariot. Setting aside her weak
moonbeams she seems to rejoice that her own task is made so brief by her
brother's[48] aid. 'Aurora' cries Phoebus, 'Forsake the marriage-bed of an old man.[49]
What pleasure is there to lie beside a worn-out spouse?[50] The hunter Aeolides
awaits you in the green fields.[51] Arise! Your flame is on the heights of Hymettus![52]
The blushing goddess acknowledges her guilt and urges the horses of the morning
to be swifter.

Earth, renewed, casts off detested old age and longs to have your embraces,
Phoebus. She desires them, and is worthy of them. What, truly, is more beautiful

than earth as she exuberantly bares her fertile bosom, breathes out Arabian harvests, and from her charming lips pours forth mellow spices and Paphian[60] roses. Behold, her lofty brow is wreathed by a sacred grove, as Idean Ops is encompassed by a turret of pines.[62] She plaits her dewy hair with many-hued flowers, flowers which seem to give her the power to charm, just as the Sicanian goddess when she wreathed her flowing tresses with flowers charmed the Taenarian God.[66] 'Look, Phoebus, willing lovers are urging you on, and the spring breezes carry honey-sweet entreaties. Fragrant Zephyr gently waves his cinnamon-scented wings, and the birds seem to carry blandishments to you. Not without a dowry does Earth thoughtlessly seek your love, nor because of poverty does she beg for the marriage she desires. She kindly proffers health-bringing herbs for medicines,[73] and thus she enhances your fame.[74] If a reward or sparkling gifts move you (for love is often bought with such gifts) then she holds out to you whatever riches she conceals in the vast sea or under the soaring mountains. Ah, how often has she cried, when wearied by the heights of Olympus you have thrown yourself into the western sea.

'Why Phoebus, when you are faint from your day's journey, does the cerulean mother receive you into the Hesperian sea?[82] What have you to do with Tethys? What with the Tartessian waters?[83] Why bathe your divine face in the foul sea? It is better, Phoebus, to look for coolness in my shades. Come hither, and dip your fiery tresses in my dew. Sweeter sleep will come to you on the cool grass. Come hither, and lay your splendours in my lap. Where you lie, the gently murmuring breeze will caress our bodies on their bed of dewy roses. Believe me, neither the fate of Semele,[91] nor the smoking wheel of Phaeton's chariot terrifies me.[92] When you Phoebus use your flame more prudently, come hither and place your splendours in my lap.'

Thus wanton earth breathes forth her desires and her thronging children hasten to follow her example. Now roving Cupid runs throughout the whole world and kindles his feeble torch with the fire of the sun. His deadly bow resounds with new strings, and his flashing arrows gleam harshly with new tips. Now he tries to conquer even the unconquerable Diana[101] and chaste Vesta[102] who sits by the sacred hearth. Venus herself each year renews her aging beauty, and seems to have soared again from the warm sea. Through the marble cities the young men call out 'Hymenaeus'[105] and the shore and hollow rocks resound with 'Io Hymen'.[106] Hymen himself appears in festal attire, becomingly robed in a suitable tunic, his fragrant clothes perfumed with purple crocuses. Crowds of girls, their youthful breasts encircled with gold, go forth to enjoy the delightful spring. Each one has her own desire, yet the desire of all is the same: that Cytherea[112] would give her the man she longs for. Now too, the shepherd plays his seven-reeded pipe, and Phyllis[114] has her songs to add to his. At night the sailor satisfies his stars with song, and calls the playful dolphins to the surface of the waves. High on Olympus, Jupiter himself frolics with his consort and assembles even the servile gods at his feast. Now the Satyrs also, rising at the late twilight hour, flit about the blossoming countryside in swift bands, and with them Silvanus, the half-goat God, half-God goat,[122] crowned with his garland of cypress.[121] The dryads[123] that have been hiding under the ancient trees now wander around the mountains and across the deserted fields. Maenalian[125] Pan sports in the sown fields and thickets; hardly is Mother Cybele safe from him, hardly is Ceres.[126] Lustful Faunus seeks to ravish some oread[127] while the nymph takes to her restless feet. Now she hides, but hiding ill-concealed she wishes to be seen; she flees, but while fleeing greatly desires to be captured. The gods do not hesitate to prefer the woods to heaven, and every grove has its own deities.

And long may each grove have its own deities. I beseech you gods, do not leave your forest homes. May the ages of gold restore you, Jupiter, to the miserable earth! Why return to the clouds with their harsh weapons? At least, Phoebus, drive your impetuous team as slowly as you can, and let the springtime pass gently. Let foul winter be tardy in bringing back the long nights, and let the shadows fall later upon our sky.

The poem was composed in the spring of 1629.

9] See *Elegia* IV 30n., 31–2n.

10 Pyrenen] Pirene, a fountain on the acropolis of Corinth, was sacred to the muses.

13–14] On Daphne (here named after her father Peneus) and Apollo (here named after his birthplace Delos) see *PL* IV 272–4n.

25–6] See *Sonnet* I 1–2n.

30] See textual note. Salmasius noted the false quantity in *quotannis* (annual), in which the last syllable is long; in 1673 Milton substituted *perennis* (perennial), in which the last syllable is short.

31–2] Ethiopia here represents the equator (cf. *PL* IV 282), and the fields of Tithonus (the husband of Aurora, the dawn) represent the east. After the vernal equinox the sun moves towards the north.

35–6] Lycaon, king of Arcadia, was the father of Callisto (see *Comus* 340n.); here Lycaonian means 'northern'. The *plaustrum* (wain), another name for Ursa Major, was driven by Bootes, the ploughman.

40] See *PL* I 197–200n. and *Novembris* 174n.

46 Cynthia] Diana, the moon-goddess, here named after her birthplace, Mount Cynthus, on Delos. Cf. *Nativity* 103, *Penseroso* 59, *Mansus* 55n.

48 fratris] Phoebus Apollo, the sun.

49–52] See *Penseroso* 122–4n. Cephalus, here named Aeolides after his father Aeolus, was hunting on Mount Hymettus (in Attica) when first seen by Aurora.

60 Paphiis] See *Elegia* I 84n.

62] Cybele (Ops) was associated with Mount Ida (see *PL* V 381–2n.); on her turret, see *Arcades* 21n.

66 Tenario ... Deo] Pluto, here named after an entrance to the underworld through a cave in the promontory of Taeranus in Laconia. The *diva Siciana* is Proserpina. See *PL* IV 268–72n.

73–4] Phoebus was the god of healing and the father of Aesculapius.

82] *Hesperiis* here means 'western'; *cærula mater* is Tethys, wife of Oceanus.

83 Tartesside lympha] See *Elegia* III 33n.

91] Semele was consumed by the fire of her lover, Jove (Ovid, *Metamorphoses* iii 253–315). Her posthumous child by Jove was Bacchus.

92] Phaeton attempted to drive the chariot of his father Phoebus Apollo; he lost control of the horses, and Jove destroyed him with a thunderbolt lest he destroy the earth. Cf. *Naturam* 25, *Patrem* 97–100.

101] Diana was pledged to chastity. See *Comus* 440–41n.

102 Vesta] See *Penseroso* 23–30n.

105–6] See *PL* IV 711n. 'Io' is a joyous interjection in Greek (ἰώ) and Latin.

112 Cytherea] Venus, here named after the island of Cythera, near which she rose from the sea.

114 Phyllis] a common name for shepherdesses in pastoral poetry.

121] Silvanus, the Roman forest god, wore cyprus as a memorial of the boy whom he loved, Cyparissus, who was transformed into a cyprus after dying of grief at the death of a deer.

122] a witty imitation of Ovid, *Ars Amatoria* ii. 24.

123 Dryades] nymphs of forests and groves.
125] Pan was associated with the Arcadian mountain range Maenalus.
126] Cybele (see 62n.) was the mother of Ceres, the Roman goddess of agricul-
      ture.
127] An oread was a mountain nymph; Faunus was a Roman god of fields and
      woods.

Elegia Sexta
Elegy 6 To Charles Diodati, now staying in the country.

Who, having written on the 13th of December and asked that his verses be
excused if they were not as good as usual, declared that in the midst of the
splendour with which he had been received by his friends, he was not able to
serve the muses productively. He received this reply.

I, with an empty stomach, send you a wish for good health, which you, with your
full one, may perhaps lack. But why does your muse provoke mine,[3] and not permit
it to pursue the obscurity it longs for? Would you like to hear in verse that I return
your love and cherish you? Believe me, you could hardly learn that from this poem,
for my love cannot be restrained by strict metres, nor its perfection expressed in
lame feet.[8]

How well you describe the festive banquets and December merriment, the feasts
which honour the heaven-sent God, the delights and joys of the country in winter
and the Gallic must drunk beside a pleasant fireside.

Why do you complain that poetry is a fugitive from wine and feasting? Song
loves Bacchus and Bacchus loves song. Phoebus was not ashamed to wear the
green ivy clusters[15] or to prefer the ivy to his own laurel.[16] Many times on the
Aonian hills[17] has the chorus of nine intermingled with the Thyonean[18] throng and
cried out 'Euoe'.[17] Naso sent bad poetry from the Corallian fields[19] because there
were no feasts, nor vines planted. Of what other than wine, roses, and the
cluster-crowned Lyaeus[21] did the Teian Muse[22] sing in his brief measures?
Teumesian Euan[23] inspires Pindar's verses and every page smells of the wine he
enjoyed;[24] with a crash the heavy chariot is thrown backwards by its broken axle[25]
and the horseman, dark with Elean dust, flies by.[26] When the Roman lyrist's lips
are moistened with four-year old wine,[27] he sings sweetly of Glycera and golden-
haired Chloe.[28] Your splendid table furnished with excellent provisions nourishes
your mind and encourages your talents. The Massic cups[31] foam with a fruitful
pulse and from that wine jar you pour out verses from the treasure within. To these
we add artistry and the penetration of Phoebus to your innermost heart. Bacchus,
Apollo and Ceres all befriend you. It is no wonder that such beautiful verses have
been composed by you when these three gods have combined their powers.

Now, too, for you sounds the gold-engraved Thracian[37] lyre, gently plucked by a
skilled hand. In tapestried rooms is heard the lyre, whose spirited music directs the
maidens' feet.

Let these sights at least, take possession of your muses and let them recall the
inspiration that idle intoxication drives away. Believe me, when the ivory plays and
festive dancers, moving with the beat of a plectrum, fill up the fragrant rooms, you
will feel Phoebus silently steal into your heart, like a sudden warmth that
penetrates your bones. Through a maiden's eyes and a musician's fingers Thalia[48]
slides into your soul and assumes complete control. For light Elegy is the concern
of many gods, and calls whom it will to its measures. Liber assists elegies and so do
Erato, Ceres, Venus,[51] and tender Love with his beautiful mother. Such poets are
allowed to have sumptuous feasts and frequent mellowing of old wine. But he who
sets forth wars, and the heaven of mature Jove, dutiful heroes and leaders

half-divine, and at one time sings of the decrees of the gods above and at another of the deep kingdoms where the wild dog[58] barks, he must live frugally indeed, adopting the habits of the teacher of Samos,[59] and let green herbs supply him with harmless nourishment. Let a beechwood bowl of clear water stand near him, and let him drink sober draughts from the pure spring. In addition to this, let him have a youth chaste and free from crime, strict morals, and his hand unstained, like a priest when, gleaming in sacred vestment, from the waters of purification you rise to face the angry gods. In this manner lived wise Tiresias after he lost his eyesight, Theban Linus,[68] Calchas, a fugitive from his doomed home,[69] and aged Orpheus when he tamed wild beasts among lonely caves.[70] Thus Homer, eating meagre meals and drinking only water, transported the man of Dulichium[72] across the vast seas, through the monster-making palace of the daughter of Perseis and Phoebus[73] and the shallows made dangerous by the songs of women, and through your house, infernal king, where it is said, black blood[75] held back the bands of ghosts.[76] Truly, the poet is sacred to the gods, he is a priest of the gods. His secret heart and lips are full of Jove.

But if you want to know what I am doing (if indeed you consider it to be of consequence to know whether I am doing anything) I am singing of the peace-bringing king of heavenly seed and the blessed ages promised by the sacred books, the infant cries of God, and the stabling beneath a poor roof of him, who with his father, dwells in the realms above; of the starry sky and the hosts that sang in the heavens, and of the sudden shattering of gods in their own shrines. These are the gifts I have given for the birthday of Christ; the first light of dawn brought them to me. For you also these simple strains composed on my native pipes are waiting.[89] When I recite them to you, you will be my judge.

The poem was written in December 1629. On Diodati see *Sonnet* IV 1n. Diodati's letter of 13 December has not survived.

3] The Camenæ were Roman water-goddesses; the tradition which identifies them with the muses originates in the *Odyssia* of Livius Andronicus.

8] The elegaic distich is lame because its first line (a hexameter) is a foot longer than its second (a pentameter). Cf. *Salsillum* 1.

15–16] Ivy was traditionally associated with Bacchus (cf. *Allegro* 16, *Comus* 54–5).

17] On the Aonian hills see *Elegia* IV 29n. *Euoe* was the shout of joy at the festivals of Bacchus.

18 Thyoneo] Bacchic. Semele (see *Elegia* V 91) was also known as Thyone.

19 Naso] Ovid, on whose banishment see *Elegia* I 21–2n. The Coralli were a barbarian tribe from the Danube.

21 Lyæum] means 'the relaxer, the deliverer from care', and refers to Bacchus.

22 Tëia Musa] The lyric poet Anacreon, here named after his birthplace, Teos, in Asia Minor.

23 Teumesius Euan] Boeotian Bacchus, so named from the mountain range Teumessus and the shout of his followers (17n.).

23-6] Pindar, who was a Boeotian, wrote odes to honour the victors of the chariot races in the Olympic games held in Elis.

27–8 Lyricen Romanus] Horace; on the wine see *Odes* I. ix. 7–8, on Glycera I. xix, xxx. 3, xxxiii, on Chloe I. xxiii, III. vii. 10, ix. 9, 19 (where she is *flava*), xxvi. 12.

31] The wine from Mount Massicus, on the border of Latium and Campania, was famous in antiquity.

37 Thressa] the lyre is so called because Orpheus was 'the *Thracian* Bard' (*PL* VII 34).

48 Thalia] the muse of comedy; she was also associated with pastoral verse.

51] Liber was an Italian god later identified with Bacchus; Erato was the muse of lyric poetry and love songs.

58 cane] Cerberus, on whom see *Allegro* 1–2n.

59 Samii . . . magistri] Pythagoras, who was born at Samos and founded in Croton a religious society membership of which entailed a strict discipline of purity, one element of which was abstention from flesh and wine.

68] On Tiresias see *PL* III 36n. Linus was a mythical musician of Thebes (which is here named after its founder, Ogyges); he taught Orpheus and Hercules.

69] Calchas was a soothsayer who accompanied the Greek army to Troy. A medieval tradition embodied in Chaucer's *Troilus and Criseyde* made him a Trojan.

70] See *Allegro* 145–50n.

72 Dulichium . . . virum] Odysseus, whose kingdom included the island of Dulichium.

73 Perseiæ Phœbados] Circe, on whom see *Comus* 50n.

75–6] *Odyssey* xi. The infernal king is Pluto.

79–88] refer to Milton's *Nativity Ode*.

89 patriis . . . cicutis] The phrase is ambiguous, for it may refer to Diodati's native language, in the which case the poems which await Diodati are Milton's Italian sonnets; alternatively, the phrase may refer to Milton's native language, in which case the line may continue the reference to the *Nativity Ode* or refer to another English poem.

Elegia Septima

Elegy 7 In my nineteenth year.

I was not yet acquainted with your laws, seductive Amathusia,[1] and my heart was free from Paphian[2] fire. Often I rejected Cupid's arrows as childish weapons and scorned especially your divine power, Love. 'Boy', I said, 'shoot the timid doves, for gentle battles are appropriate to a tender leader. Pursue your excited triumphs over sparrows, little one. These are the trophies worthy of your warfare. Why aim your petty weapons at human beings? Your quiver has no power against strong men.' This the Cyprian[11] could not bear (for no God is quicker to anger) and the fierce boy was now inflamed with double fire.

It was spring, and the sun, shining over the roof-tops of the village, brought to you, May, your first day. But my eyes still sought the receding night and could not endure the splendour of the dawn. By my bed stood Love, unwearied Love with his coloured wings. The movement of his quiver betrayed the presence of the god. His face too, and his sweetly threatening eyes, betrayed him, as did whatever else becomes a boy and Love. Thus young Sigean appears on eternal Olympus[21] as he prepares copious goblets for the amorous Jove;[22] or Hylas, son of Theiodamas,[24] who enticed the beautiful nymphs to his kisses[23] and was carried off by a naide.[24] He was full of rage, but you would have considered this becoming to him, and he uttered harsh threats, full of bitterness.

'Wretch,' he said, 'you would have learned more safely from the example of others; now you yourself shall witness what my right hand can do. You will be numbered amongst those who have experienced my power, and through your suffering I shall assuredly establish men's faith in me. You may not know that it was I who subdued Phoebus, arrogant[31] after his victory over the Python; even he yielded to me.[32] As often as he thinks of Peneus' daughter, he acknowledges[33] that my darts inflict a more certain and more painful injury.[34] The Parthian horseman who conquers as he flees[36] cannot draw the stretched bow more skilfully than I. To me yields the Cydonian hunter[37] and also he who was the unwitting author of his own wife's death.[38] I also conquered huge Orion,[39] mighty Hercules, and the companion of Hercules.[40] Jupiter himself may hurl his thunderbolts at me, but my darts will pierce the side of Jove.[42] Whatever your doubts, you will be better instructed by my arrows, and by your heart, which I shall not lightly seek out. Fool! Your muses will not be able to protect you, nor will Phoebus' serpent extend aid to you.[46] He spoke, and brandishing an arrow with a golden point,[47] flew away to the warm breast of Cypris.[48] But I was ready to laugh as he wildly thundered his threats, and I had no fear at all of the boy.

At times the city where the citizens walk about afforded me pleasure, at other times the fields close to villages. A great crowd, most like a glittering crowd of goddesses, came and went along the walks. With this added brilliance, the day gleams with double splendour. Am I deceived, or is it from them that Phoebus too draws his rays? I did not shun austerely these pleasing sights, but followed where youthful impulse led. Giving no thought to prudence, I let my glance meet theirs, and then was not able to control my eyes. By chance, I noticed one who surpassed the others; that sight was the beginning of my misfortune. Thus Venus herself might wish to appear to mortals; thus the queen of the gods[64] should have been admired. That mischievous Cupid, not forgetting his threats, threw her into my sight: he alone had already laid this snare for me. This crafty one lurked nearby with many arrows, the weighty burden of his torch hung from his back. Without delay he clung now to her eyelids, now to the maiden's face. From there he leapt to her lips and then settled on her cheeks. Wherever the nimble archer hovered, woe to me! From a thousand points he struck my defenceless heart. Immediately strange passions assaulted my heart. I was consumed within with love, and was all ablaze. Meanwhile, she who alone now gave me pleasure in my misery was carried off, never to return to my sight.

And now I went on, complaining to myself and discouraged, and in doubt I often wished to retrace my steps. I am split in two; one part stays here, the other part follows my desire. It is a pleasure to weep for joys so suddenly snatched away. Thus grieved Juno's son for his lost heaven[81] when he was thrown down among the Lemnian hearths.[82] Such was the grief of Amphiaraus looking upon the disappearing sun[83] as he was carried off to Orcus by his terrified horses.[84] What shall I do, unhappy as I am and overcome with grief? This incipient love I can neither lay aside nor follow. If only it were given to me to gaze once more on those beloved features and to speak of my sadness face to face. Perhaps she is not made of hard adamant, perhaps she would not be deaf to my prayers. Believe me, no one was ever thus unhappily consumed with love. I may be considered the first and only example. Have mercy, I pray, since you are the winged god of tender love. Do not let your deeds contradict your duty. Now, surely, your bow fills me with terror. Child of a goddess, you are powerful because of your darts, no less than for your fire. Your altars will smoke with my sacrifices. For me, you alone will be supreme among the gods. Take away my madness then – and yet – do not take it away. I do not understand why every lover is sweetly miserable. Only be gracious and grant that if ever any maiden is to be mine an arrow will transfix as one the destined lovers.

The poem was probably written in 1628.

1 Amathusia] Venus, here named after her temple at Amathus, in Cyprus.

2 Paphio] See *Elegia* I 84n.

11 Cyprius] Cupid. The name was not used of Cupid in antiquity.

21–4] *Sigeus* means Trojan (so called from a promontory near Troy), and here refers to Ganymede, the beautiful youth who was taken to Olympus to become the cupbearer of Jove. Hylas, the son of Theiodamas and the page of Hercules, was dragged into a spring by a naide (fountain nymph) enamoured of his beauty. Cf. *PR* II 353, *Damonis* 1.

31–2] See *PL* X 529–31n.

33–4] See *PL* IV 272–4n.

36] Cf. *PR* III 306, 322–5.

37 Cydoniusque . . . venator] Cydonia was a port in Crete, which was famous for its archers.

38] Cephalus (on whom see *Penseroso* 122–4n) accidentally slew his wife Procris when he mistook her for an animal.

39] The amatory adventures of Orion include the pursuit of the Pleiades, capture by Aurora, and a fatal attempt on the chastity of Diana.

40] Hercules had a demeaning affair with Omphale, Queen of Lydia. The identity of the companion of Hercules is uncertain, as at least eight men were so described in antiquity; the reference may be to Jason, or Hylas, or Theseus, all of whom were Cupid's victims.

42] Jove had many love affairs (see e.g. *PL* IX 396, *PR* II 186–8n.).

46] On Aesculapius (the son of Apollo) as a serpent see *PL* IX 506–7n.

47 aurato . . . mucrone] see *PL* IV 763n.

48 Cypridos] Venus. See *Elegia* I 84n.

64 regina Deum] Juno, wife and sister of Jove.

81–2] Juno's son is Vulcan; see *PL* I 738–46.

83–4] Amphiaraus was one of the seven against Thebes; as he fled from the Homoloian Gate which he had attacked, he and his chariot and horses fell into a cleft (made by Zeus' thunderbolt) to Hades, which is here called Orcus.

Hæc ego mente

Some time ago, with foolish mind and idle zeal I fashioned these verses, vain trophies of my wantonness. It is clear that destructive error thus carried me off, and untaught youth was my faithless teacher, until the shady Academy offered its Socratic streams[5] and taught me to reject the yoke I had accepted. Immediately the flames were quenched, and from that time my breast has been numbed by a thick cover of ice, thus the boy himself is afraid of the cold for his arrows and even Venus fears my Diomedean strength.[10]

This retraction may refer to *Elegia* VII alone, or to the erotic portions of I, V, and VII. The printer's line which separates the poem from *Elegia* VII suggests a third possibility, namely that the retraction is a separate epigram, like the pieces which follow it; the *Poemata* begin with the phrase *Elegiarum Liber Primus*, and this line may mark the beginning of the otherwise unmarked *Liber Secundus*. The date of composition is unknown.

5] See *PR* IV 276–7n.

10] In *Iliad* v 334–417 Venus is wounded by Diomedes while trying to protect her son Aeneas.

In Proditionem Bombardicum
On the Gunpowder Plot

When lately, treacherous Fawkes, you attempted your unspeakable crime against the king and the British lords, am I mistaken, or did you wish to appear in some degree kind, and to compensate for your crime with a wicked piety? Evidently you were going to send them to the courts of high heaven in a sulphurous chariot with wheels of flame, just as he, whom the cruel Fates[7] found inviolable, was taken up from the fields of the Jordan in a whirlwind.[8]

The dates of composition of the four epigrams on the Gunpowder Plot and the related poem on the inventor of gunpowder are not known, though line 5 of the second poem suggests that it was written after the death of James on 27 March 1625.

7 Parcis] See *Winchester* 28n.

8] See *PL* III 522n.

On the Same

Was it thus, Beast that lurks on the seven hills,[2] that you tried to send James to heaven? Unless your divinity is able to bestow better presents, be sparing, I pray deceitful one, of your gifts. He, indeed, went to the fellowship of heaven at a ripe old age,[5] without your aid, or that of your hellish gunpowder. Rather hurl to heaven in this way your detestable cowls, and all the dumb gods that profane Rome contains; for unless you help each one by this or some other means, they will only ascend the way to heaven with difficulty.

2] Protestants identified the Beast of the Apocalypse with the Papacy.

5] See note, above.

On the Same

James scoffed at purgatorial fire, without which the soul cannot approach its home above. At this the triple-crowned monster of Latium[3] gnashed its teeth and shook its ten horns[4] with dreadful threats. 'Not unavenged, Briton, will you scorn my sacred mysteries,' it said. 'You shall pay the penalty for spurning my religion, and if ever you enter the starry citadels, only a disagreeable way through flames will be open to you.'

Oh, how close to the dismal truth did you prophesy. Your words scarcely lacked complete fulfilment, for he nearly went to the celestial shores a burnt ghost, whirled aloft by Tartarean fire.

3] See *Sonnet* XIX 12n.

4] Rev. xiii. 1.

On the Same

Him, whom impious Rome had lately cursed with execrations and condemned to the Styx and Tænarian Cave,[2] him now, by a complete change she longs instead to elevate to the stars and desires to bear him aloft even to the gods above.

2 Tænarioque sinu] See *Elegia* V 66n.

On the Inventor of Gunpowder

The ancients blindly praised the son of Iapetus,[1] who brought celestial fire from the axle of the sun. But greater, I think, will be the man who is believed to have stolen the ghastly weapons and three-forked thunderbolt from Jove.

1 Iapetionidem] Prometheus.

Ad Leonoram Romæ canentem
To Leonora singing in Rome.

Believe me, you nations, a winged angel from the celestial ranks protects each individual. Is it a wonder, Leonora, if a greater honour is yours? For your voice itself utters the presence of God – either God, or certainly a third mind[5] freed from heaven that creeps forcefully through your throat. Forcefully it creeps and easily teaches mortal hearts gradually how to become accustomed to immortal sound. If God is all things, and through all things diffused, in you alone He speaks, the rest He holds in silence.

Milton heard Leonora Baroni sing late in 1638 or early in 1639.

5 mens tertia] an obscure reference, possibly to the Holy Spirit.

To the Same

Another Leonora possessed the poet Torquato,[1] who for frantic love of her became mad.[2] Ah, poor wretch! How much more happily would he have been ruined in your lifetime, and because of you, Leonora. He would have heard you singing with your Pierian voice[5] and the golden strings of your mother's lyre vibrating.[6] Although he rolled his eyes more fiercely than Dircaean Pentheus,[7] or was foolish and not understanding, you could have composed by your voice his senses wandering in their blind whirl; and, breathing peace into his troubled heart, you could have restored him to himself by your soul-moving song.

1–2] Tasso's insanity was sometimes ascribed to an infatuation with Leonora d'Este, and Milton's friend Manso mentioned in his *Vita del Tasso* two other Leonoras whom Tasso loved.

5] Pieriâ . . . voce] See *Elegia* IV 31–2n.

6] Adriana Baroni, Leonora's mother, was a celebrated musician.

7] Dircaean refers to a fountain near Thebes, and means 'Theban'. Pentheus, King of Thebes, opposed the Bacchic orgies and was consequently dismembered by the Bacchantes.

To the Same

Why, credulous Naples, do you boast of your clear-voiced Siren,[1] and of the famous shrine of Achelous' daughter Parthenope,[2] the shore naiad, and that, when she died on your coasts you gave her sacred body to a Chalcidian[4] pile? In fact, she still lives, and has exchanged the grating murmurs of Posillipo[6] for the pleasant waves of the Tiber. There, applauded with enthusiasm by the sons of Romulus she entrances both men and gods with song.

1–2] As Leonora was a Neapolitan, Milton associates her with Parthenope (see *Comus* 878n.), the daughter of the river-god Achelous.

4 Chalcidico] Neapolitan, so called because Greek colonists from Chalcis (in Euboea) had settled in Naples in the eighth century BC.

6 Pausilipi] Naples. The precise reference is to Mount Posillipo near Naples. The murmurs may be the noise of traffic that went through the tunnel under the mountain, or the sound of waves beating against the foot of the mountain.

Apologus de Rustico et Hero

The Fable of a Peasant and his Master

A peasant gathered every year the best tasting fruits from his apple tree and carried them to his master who lived in the city. The latter, fascinated by the incredible sweetness of the fruit, transplanted the apple tree itself in his own gardens. Up to this time the tree had been fertile, but it was weak with old age, and when moved from its accustomed soil it immediately withered and bore nothing. When at length, it was evident to his master that he had been deceived by a vain hope, he condemned the hands that had been so swift to cause their own injury.

'Alas,' he said, 'How much better it was to receive with gratitude those gifts of my tenant, small though they were. Would that I could have restrained my avarice and devouring appetite, for now, I have lost both fruit and the tree.'

The date of composition is unknown, but it may have been a grammar school exercise in imitative versifying, as it imitates a fable by Mantuan.

The End of the Elegies

A Book of Sylvæ

In Obitum Procancellarii Medici

At the age of 16. On the death of the Vice-Chancellor, a Physician

Learn to submit to the laws of fate, and offer now entreating hands to the goddess of destiny,[2] you descendants of Iapetus[4] who inhabit the pendulous orb of the earth. If, leaving Taenarus,[5] the doleful wanderer Death has once called you, alas, delays and deceits are attempted in vain, for the way through Stygian darkness is fixed. If the right hand were strong enough to drive back destined Death, fierce Hercules[10] would not have lain dead on Emathian Oeta,[12] poisoned by the blood of Nessus;[11] nor would Ilium have seen Hector killed[14] through the base deceit of envious Pallas,[13] or him whom the spectre of Peleus' son[15] cut off with Locrian sword, while Jove wept.[16] If the spells of Hecate[17] could chase away gloomy Fate the disreputable mother of Telegonus[18] would have survived, as would the sister of Aegialeus,[20] by the use of her powerful wand. If the arts of physicians or unknown herbs could deceive the triple divinity,[21] then Machaon, with his knowledge of herbs[23], would not have fallen to the spear of Eurypylus;[24] nor would the arrow smeared with the blood of the Lernaean hydra[26] have wounded you, son of Philyra;[25] nor would the weapons and thunderbolts of your grandfather have injured you,[27] boy, cut from your mother's womb.[28] And you, greater than your pupil Apollo, to whom was given the government of the gowned tribe and for whom now laments leafy Cirrha,[31] and Helicon[32] amid its streams, you would be alive still, happy and honoured to protect Palleas' flock.[33] You would not have traversed the dreadful recesses of the abyss in Charon's boat.[35] But Persephone broke the thread of your life,[37] furious when she saw that by your arts and powerful potions you snatched so many from the black jaws of death. Reverend Master, I pray that your limbs may rest in the soft turf and from your grave may spring roses and marigolds and the purple-bloomed hyacinth.[44] May the judgement Aeacus passes upon you be mild and may Aetnaean[46] Proserpina smile. May you walk forever among the blessed in the Elysian fields.

John Gostlin, Master of Caius College (1619–26), Regius Professor of Physic (1623–5) and Vice-Chancellor (1625–6), died on 21 October 1626, when Milton was 17. Milton's date, which he added to the poem in 1645, is therefore an error.

2 Parcæ] see *Winchester* 28n.

4 Iäpeti . . . nepotes] All mankind was said to descend from Iapetus, on whom see *PL* IV 714–19n.

5 Tænaro] See *Elegia* V 66n.

10–12] See *PL* II 542–6n; Emathian means Macedonian.

13–14] Pallas Athene precipitated the death of Hector by appearing to him in the guise of his brother Deiphobus and persuading him to fight Achilles. (*Iliad* xxii 224–404).

15–16] Jove wept because his son Sarpedon was killed by the Ionian Patroclus, who was wearing the armour of Achilles, son of Peleus.

17] Hecate was the goddess of witchcraft.

18 Telegoni parens] Circe; see *Comus* 50n.

20 Ægiali soror] Medea, who killed her brother Aegialeus, who is usually called Absyrtus.

21 Numenque trinum] the Parcæ; see *Winchester* 28n.

23–4] Machaon, the son of Aesculapius, was a physician with the Greek army at Troy. His death at the hand of Eurypylus is a post-Homeric tradition.

25–6] Chiron, son of the nymph Philyra, was famous for his knowledge of medicine; he was accidentally killed by one of Hercules' arrows, which had been poisoned with the blood of the Lernæan hydra.

27–8] Aesculapius, the son of Apollo and the grandson of Zeus, was cut from the womb of his mother Coronis by Apollo, instructed in medicine by Chiron, and slain by Zeus because he learned to bring the dead back to life.

31 Cirrha] a port near Delphi, which was sacred to Apollo.

32 Helicon] see *Winchester* 56n.

33 Palladio gregi] See *Elegia* II 2n.

35] Charon was the ferryman who rowed the shades of the dead across the Styx.

37] Persephone, or Proserpina (line 46), on whom see *PL* IV 268–72n., is here given the function of Atropos, on whom see *Winchester* 28n.

44] See *Fair Infant* 23–6n.

45 Æaci] a judge in Hades.

46 Ætnæa] here means 'Sicilian'.

In quintum Novembris
On the Fifth of November. At the age of 17

By this time[1] pious James, coming from the far north, was master of the Troy-sprung people and the far-reaching realms of Albion, and already an inviolable treaty had united the sceptres of the English and the Caledonian Scots. Peace-loving, happy and rich, he sat on his new throne, untroubled by secret plot or enemy, when the fierce tyrant ruling Acheron's river of fire,[7] the father of the Eumenides[8] and a wandering exile from ethereal Olympus, had by chance wandered over the boundless orb of the earth counting his companions in crime and the faithful slaves who were to be partners in his kingdom after their unhappy deaths. Here he stirs up dreadful tempests in the middle air,[12] there spreads hatred amongst inseparable friends. He arms invincible nations for deadly war against one another, and overturns kingdoms where the olive of peace blossoms. Any lover of undefiled virtue whom he sees, he longs to have under his dominion, and the master of fraud strives to corrupt the heart that is not open to wickedness. He sets secret snares and stretches concealed nets to catch the unwary, just as the Caspian Tigress follows her alarmed prey over abandoned wastes at night with no moonlight and the stars blinking with sleep. With such attacks does Summanus,[23] girdled in a smoking whirlwind of blue flames, destroy peoples and cities.

And now the white coast where the breakers dash against the cliffs comes in sight, and the land loved by the god of the sea to which, long ago, Neptune's son had given his name,[27] he who, having crossed the sea[28] did not hesitate to challenge Amphitryon's fierce son[29] in dreadful combat, before the cruel times of the fall of Troy.[30] But as soon as he looked upon this land blessed with riches and festal peace, its fields rich with Ceres' gifts, and, what grieved him more, a nation worshipping the sacred will of the true God, he finally burst into sighs that smelled of Tartarean fires and ghastly sulphur, such sighs as issued from the diseased mouth of the savage monster Typhoeus[37] imprisoned by Jove on Trinacrian Etna.[36] His eyes burned and his adamantine teeth gnashed with the noise of weapons crashing, spear striking spear.

'I have wandered through the whole world,' he said, 'and I have found that only this sight brings tears to my eyes. This nation alone rebels against me, disdaining my yoke, more powerful than my art. Yet, if my efforts can accomplish anything it will not long do this with impunity, nor will it go unpunished.' Thus he spoke, and with pitch-black wings swims through the liquid air. Wherever he flies bands of contrary winds hasten on before him, clouds thicken, thunder and lightning flash repeatedly. Now in swift flight, he rose above the frosty Alps and reached the borders of Ausonia[49]; on his left were the storm-bringing Appenines, and the ancient Sabine country; on his right was Etruria, notorious for its sorceries. And he saw you, Tiber, stealing kisses from Thetis.[52] Soon he alights on the citadel of Quirinus, the son of Mars.[53] Late evening rendered the light uncertain when he who wears the triple crown[55] travels about the whole city conveyed on the shoulders of men, and carrying the gods made of bread. Kings come before him on bended knee, and a long line of mendicant friars bearing wax tapers in their hands, blind men, for they are born and drag out their lives in Cimmerian darkness.[60] Then they enter the temples bright with many torches, for it was St Peter's Eve,[62] and the sound of singing fills the empty domes and hollow spaces, like the howls of Bromius[64] and the Bromian troop celebrating their orgies on Echionian Aracynthus[65] while stunned Asopus[66] trembles in his glassy waves, and from afar even Cithaeron[67] in his hollow cliff sends a reply. When at length these solemn rites were completed according to custom, Night silently left the embrace of aged Erebus[69] and with a goading whip drove her galloping horses, sightless Typhlon,[71] fierce Melanchaetes,[71] numb Siope born of an Acherontean sire,[72] and Phrix rough with bristly hair.[73]

Meanwhile the king-tamer, heir of Phlegethon,[74] enters his bridal-chamber (for the secret adulterer passes no barren nights without a pliant concubine) but scarcely had sleep closed his calm eyes when the black lord of the shades, master of the silent dead and plunderer of men, stood near him under a false disguise. His temples gleamed with the white hair he had put on; a long beard covered his chest; his ash-coloured robe swept the ground with its long skirt; a cowl hung down from his shaven head; and, that his device be lacking in nothing, he had bound his lustful loins with a hemp rope, and with slow steps moved his feet clad with latticed sandals. In this disguise, according to tradition, Francis used to wander through the vast wilderness, alone in the hideous haunts of wild beasts, and although wicked himself, brought the blessed words of salvation to the people of the forest and tamed wolves and Libyan lions.

Thus attired the cunning, deceitful Serpent uttered these words from his detestable lips: 'Are you asleep, my son? Does sleep even overwhelm your limbs?[92] O neglector of the faith and forgetter of your flock while a barbarous nation born under the northern sky laughs at your throne, venerable father, and your triple diadem, while quiver-bearing Britons scorn your authority. Arise! come on, you sluggard, whom the Roman Caesar[97] worships; you, to whom the unlocked gate of the vaulted heaven lies open. Crush haughty spirits and wanton arrogance, let the wicked know the power of your curse, and the power of the keeper of the Apostolic key.[101] Remember to avenge Hesperia's scattered fleet[102] and the Iberian banners sunk in the wide deep,[103] and the bodies of so many saints fixed on the shameful cross[104] during the recent reign of the Thermodontean Maiden.[105] But, if you prefer to grow stiff on a soft bed and refuse to crush the growing strength of the enemy, he will fill the Tyrrhenian Sea with his soldiery and plant his glittering standards on the Aventine hill.[109] He will break and consume in flames the relics of the ancients, and tread with wicked feet upon your holy neck, on you whose shoes kings rejoiced to kiss. But do not challenge him to war or open battle; that would be wasted effort. You must be cunning and use fraud; any kind of snare may be used against heretics. Even now the great king summons to council from the uttermost ends of the kingdom, the gentry and nobles of high birth,[117] and the venerable old fathers with their robes and grey hair.[118] These you will be able to scatter limb from limb into the air and burn to ashes by igniting nitrous powder in the depths of the building where they assemble. Immediately, therefore, warn whatever faithful remain in England of our intention and deed. Will any of your followers dare to disobey the commands of the supreme Pope? When the people are overcome with fear and stunned by the catastrophe let either the dreadful Gaul or fierce Iberian invade. Thus, the Marian age[127] will finally return to that land and you will again have dominion over the warlike English. You need not fear anything. Understand that you have the favour of gods and goddesses, all those divinities who are celebrated in your feasts.' Thus spoke the Deceiver and, laying aside his disguise, fled to the gloomy kingdom, abominable Lethe.[132] Now rosy Tithonia is opening the gates of the East[133] and attires the gilded earth with returning light.[134] Still mourning the sorrowful death of her dark son,[135] she moistens the mountain peaks with ambrosial drops,[135] while the doorkeeper of the starry court banished sleep and reflected upon nocturnal visions and pleasant dreams.

There is a place surrounded by the eternal darkness of night, at one time the foundations of a ruined building and now the den of fierce Murder and double-tongued Treachery whom savage Discord bore at one birth. Here among broken[143] stones and rocks lie unburied the bones of men and corpses pierced with iron. Here ever sits dark Guile with twisted eyes, Strife, and Calumny, her jaws armed with fangs, and Fury, and a thousand ways of dying are seen, and Fear, and bloodless Horror flies around the place, and ghosts are perpetually flitting in the deep silence. The knowing Earth howls and stagnates with blood. In the inner cave hide Murder and Treachery. They too are terrified, and though no one follows them through the cave – this dreadful craggy cave, dark with deathly shades – the guilty pair flee with backward glances. These champions of Rome, faithful through long ages, the Babylonian[156] priest calls forth and addresses in this manner:

'On the western borders, surrounded by the sea, dwells a nation that I hate. Prudent Nature refused to unite this wholly unworthy people with our world. Hasten to that place, I command, with all speed. Let king and nobles alike, a polluted race, be blown into thin air by Tartarean powder. As many as are inflamed with love for the true faith receive as fellows in your deliberations and assistants in the work.' He finished, and the ruthless twins eagerly obeyed.

Meanwhile, the Lord who sends the lightning from his ethereal citadel and turns the heavens in their vast arc, looks down and laughs at the vain attempt of the evil throng,[168] and himself resolves to defend the cause of his people.

There is a place, it is said, which separates fertile Europe from Asia and faces the waters of Mareotis.[171] Here the high tower of Titanean Fame is built – bronze, broad, reverberating, and nearer the glittering stars than Athos, or Pelion piled on Ossa.[174] A thousand doors and entrances stand open, and just as many windows and spacious halls shine through the thin walls. Here a dense crowd of people raises an agitated mutter, like swarms of humming flies[179] buzzing around milk pails[178] or in wattled sheepfolds when the Dog Star seeks its summer summit in the heights of heaven. Fame herself, the avenger of her mother[181] sits at the top of her citadel and lifts her head wreathed with innumerable ears with which she takes in the slightest sound and snatches the faintest murmurs from the farthest limits of the wide world. Son of Arestor and unkind guardian of the heifer[185] Isis, you did not roll so many eyes in your rough face,[186] eyes that never nodded in silent sleep, eyes observing far and wide the lands below. With her eyes she is wont to survey the places devoid of light and impervious to the beaming sun. Chattering with a thousand tongues she pours out imprudently to anyone all she has seen and heard. This deceiver at one time diminishes the truth, at another augments it with invented tales.

Nevertheless, Fame, you deserve praise in my song,[194] for one good report, truer than any other.[195] You are worthy of my song, and I do not regret having celebrated you in verse of such length, for it is plain that the English were preserved by your good offices, wandering goddess, and we give our just thanks to you. God, who regulates the movement of eternal fires, hurled his thunderbolt and, while the earth trembled, spoke:

'Fame, are you silent? Can you not see the wicked band of Papists plotting against me and my Britons, and the strange murder planned for the sceptre-bearing James?' He said no more. She understood at once the command of the Thunderer, and though swift enough before, she put on hissing wings and covered her thin body with many-coloured plumage and in her right hand carried a resounding trumpet of Temesan[207] brass. Without delay her wings cut through the yielding air, and, not content to outstrip the swift clouds in her journey, she leaves behind now the winds, and now even the horses of the sun. At first, according to her usual habit, she spreads abroad through English cities ambiguous words and uncertain murmurings. Soon she divulges in a clear voice the plots and execrable work of treason, and not only describes the horrid deeds, but also names the instigators of the crime; and in her prattling she does not conceal the place chosen for the secret plot. Stunned by these reports, young men, girls, and feeble old men all tremble as the significance of such a great catastrophe suddenly struck at the hearts of all ages.

But meanwhile the Heavenly Father from on high has compassion for his people and thwarts the cruel undertaking of the Papists. They are captured and carried off to severe punishments. Pious incense is burned and grateful honours are offered to God. At all the rejoicing crossroads smoke rises from the festive bonfires, and crowds of young people dance. In the whole year there is no day more celebrated than the fifth of November.

The poem was written in 1626.

1 Jam] The conspirators planned to blow up King James and the parliament on 5 November 1605.

7] Milton attributes to Acheron the fire of Phlegethon; see *PL* II 578–81.

8 Eumenidum pater] Pluto.

12 medio . . . aëre] See *Fair Infant* 16n.

23 Summanus] god of nocturnal thunderbolts.

27–30] According to Milton's *History of Britain*, Albion, a son of Neptune, ruled for forty-four years, and then crossed to the continent to aid his brother and was slain by Hercules, who is here named after the husband of his mother.

36–7] Jove imprisoned the rebel Typhoeus under Sicily (Trinacria), placing on his head Mount Etna, through which he belched fire.

49 Ausoniæ] See *Elegia* I 70n.

52] Thetis, on whom see *Comus* 876n., here represents the Tyrrhenian Sea.

53] Quirinus was the name given to Romulus, son of Mars, after his deification.

55 Tricoronifer] See *Sonnet* XIX 12n.

60 Cimmeriis . . . tenebris] See *Allegro* 10n.

62] i.e. 28 June; St Peter's feast day is 29 June.

64] Bromius means 'the noisy one' and refers to Bacchus.

65] Echion, one of the Sparti, helped to found Thebes; hence *Echionius* means Theban, or Boeotian. Aracynthus here refers to a mountain on the border of Boeotia and Attica.

66 Asopus] a river and river-god in Boeotia.

67 Cithæron] a mountain range dividing Megaris and Boeotia from Attica, associated with the cult of Dionysus.

69] Erebus is here the god of darkness, brother and husband of Night (Nyx); cf. *Eliensis* 33 and S.B.'s *In Paradisum Amissam* 8.

71–4 The Greek names of the horses are Milton's invention. Typhlon means 'blinding', Melanchætes 'black-haired', Siope 'silence', and Phrix 'shuddering'. On *Acherontæo* and *Phlegetontius* see 7n.

92] See *PL* V 673n.

97 Latius . . . Cæsar] i.e. the Holy Roman Emperors.

101] Matt. xvi. 19.

102–3] Refers to the defeat of the Spanish Armada in 1588. *Hesperiæ* here means Spain.

104–5] The Amazons were said to live on the river Thermodon, so Thermodontean means Amazonian. The lines refer to the executions of Catholics during Elizabeth's reign.

109 Aventino . . . colle] one of the seven hills of Rome.

117 The *patricii* are the members of the House of Commons, the *proceres* of the Lords.

118] refers to the bishops in the House of Lords and the Privy Counsellors.

127 Sæcula . . . Mariana] refers to the reign of Mary (1553–8), a champion of Catholicism, and plays on the ancient sense of the phrase, i.e. the bloody and vindictive rule of Marius.

132] Lethe is 'the River of Oblivion' in Hades (*PL* II 583).

133–5] Aurora, the dawn, here named Tithonia after her husband Tithonus, weeps tears of dew because their son Memnon has been killed by Achilles.

143] See textual note; as in *Elegia* V 30, Salmasius had seized on the false quantity in the 1645 reading.

156 Babylonius] See *Sonnet* XIX 14n.

168] Cf. Milton's translation of Psalm ii. 4 (ll. 8–9).

171] Lake Mareotis is near Alexandria, in Egypt; *Mareotidas* may be a printer's error for *Maeotidas* (see *PL* IX 76–8n.), which was thought to separate Europe and Asia.

174] In some versions of the war of the giants against the gods (see *PL* I 197–200n., cf. *Elegia* V 40), Pelion was piled on Ossa (both are mountains in Thessaly). Mount Athos is on the easternmost of the Chalcidian promontories.

178–9] See *PR* IV 15–17n.

181 matris] Terra (Earth).

185–6] See *PL* XI 131–3n. Io was identified with *Isis*, on whom see *Nativity* 212–13n.

194–5] The Gunpowder Plot was discovered because Lord Monteagle received on 26 October an anonymous letter, apparently from his brother-in-law, the conspirator Francis Tresham, warning him not to attend the opening of Parliament; he immediately informed the government, and the cellar under the House of Lords was found to contain the gunpowder and its custodian Guy Fawkes.

207] Temesa, an ancient city in Calabria, was famed for its copper mines in antiquity.

In Obitum Præsulis Eliensis
At the age of 17. On the Death of the Bishop of Ely

My cheeks were still wet and stained with tears, and my eyes, not yet dry, were still swollen with the flood of salty water that I lately shed in respect as I paid my sorrowful tribute at the precious grave of the bishop of Winchester,[6] when hundred-tongued Fame (alas! ever a true messenger of misfortune and destruction) rumoured through the cities of rich Britain and among the people sprung from Neptune,[10] that you, a jewel of mankind and head of the church[13] in that island that bears the name of Eel,[14] had yielded to death and the cruel sisters.[11] Immediately my restless heart boiled up with burning rage, cursing again and again the powerful goddess of the grave. Naso, in the depths of his heart, did not compose more dreadful execrations against Ibis,[18] and the Greek poet was more sparing[20] when he cursed the foul deceit of Lycambes[21] and Neobule, his betrothed.[22] But behold, while I poured out the grievous curses and called down death upon death, astonished, I seemed to hear these sounds in the gently blowing breeze:

'Calm your blind rage; calm the gleaming bile and vain threats. Why do you dishonour deities who cannot be harmed and are quickly moved to anger? Death is not, as you believe, deluded wretch, the dark daughter of Night, not descended from Erebus or Erinys,[33] nor was she born in vast Chaos. On the contrary, she is sent from the starry heaven, and everywhere gathers the harvest of God. She calls forth to light and air the souls hidden in a mass of flesh just as the fleeting Hours,[39] the daughters of Themis[40] and Jove, rouse the day, and leads them into the presence of the eternal Father. She justly carries away the wicked to the doleful realm of gloomy Tartarus, to infernal dwelling places. I rejoiced when I heard her calling and quickly left my foul prison, and happy amid winged soldiers I was borne aloft to the stars, just as the old prophet was once carried to heaven[49] driving a chariot of fire.[50] I was not alarmed by the wain[52] of shining Boötes,[51] sluggish with the cold, nor by the claws of the dreadful Scorpion, nor by your sword, Orion. We flew past the globe of the glittering sun, and far beneath my feet I saw the triform[57] goddess[56] restraining her dragons[58] with golden reins. I sailed through the ranks of the wandering stars and the Milky Way,[60] often wondering at my unaccustomed speed,[61] until at length I came to the shining gates[62] of Olympus and the crystalline palace[63] and the court paved with emeralds.[64] But here I shall be silent, for who that has a mortal father can describe the loveliness of that place? For me, it is enough to enjoy it forever.'

Nicholas Felton, Bishop of Ely from 1619–26, died on 5 October 1626.

1–6] refers to *Elegia* III.

10] See *Novembris* 27–30.

11 ferreis Sororibus] the Parcæ; see *Winchester* 28n.

13 rex sacrorum] In Republican Rome this phrase was a priestly title.

14 Anguillæ] Etymologically 'Ely' means 'eel-island'.

18 Naso in Ibida] Ovid's *Ibis* is a curse directed at an unnamed enemy.

20–22] Archilochus, the early Greek iambic and elegiac poet, responded to Lycambes' withdrawal of consent to marry his daughter Neobule with satire so powerful that Lycambes and his daughters are said to have hanged themselves.

33] On Erebus see *Novembris* 69n. Erinys is one of the Furies; see *PL* II 596n.

39 Horæ] See *Comus* 985n.

40] On Themis see *Sonnet* XXII 2n.

49–50] See *PL* III 522n.

51–2 Boötis . . . Sarraca] See *Elegia* V 35–6n.

56–8] On the triform goddess see *PL* III 730n.; on the dragons see *Elegia* IV 10n. and *Penseroso* 59n.

60–64] See *PL* VII 577–9n.

Naturam non pati senium

That Nature Does not Suffer from Old Age

Alas, how perpetual are the errors driving man's wandering mind to exhaustion; plunged into vast darkness he ponders in his heart that night[3] of Oedipus. Insanely, he dares to measure the deeds of gods by his own, and to compare laws engraved in everlasting adamant to his, and binds the resolution of fate, which no age will change, to the passing hours. Will the face of Nature wither and be furrowed all over with wrinkles? Will the common mother[9] contract her all-producing womb and grow barren from old age?[10] Will she admit her old age and walk with unsteady feet and starry head trembling? Will loathsome old age and the endless hunger of years and squalor and rust distress the stars? Will insatiable Time[14] hunger for heaven and devour his father?[15] Alas, could not imprudent Jove have fortified his citadels against this horror and delivered them from the evil deeds of Time and given them unceasing revolutions? At some time, therefore, the decayed[19] floors of the vaulted heaven will tumble down[20] with a frightful noise[19] and the poles will crack in collision. The Olympian will fall from his celestial palace, and dreadful Pallas will fall with her Gorgon shield uncovered,[22] even as the son of Juno[23] fell from the sacred threshold of heaven[24] upon Aegean Lemnos.[23] You too, Phoebus, as you fall from your rushing chariot will imitate the fate of your son[25] and be borne down in sudden ruin.[26] Nereus [27] will smoke as your lamp is quenched and the astonished sea will utter fearful hisses. Then, with its foundations torn asunder, the summit of lofty Hæmus[29] will fly in pieces, and the Ceraunian mountains, which were used in fratricidal wars[32] against the gods, will be dashed to the lowest abyss[30] and will terrify Stygian Dis.[31] But the omnipotent father, reflecting upon the sum of things, fixed the stars more firmly, adjusted the scales of the fates with a sure weight, and commanded that each thing in the great order keep to its course forever. Hence, the prime wheel[37] of the world rotates daily and in its revolution also drags along the encircling heavens. Saturn is by no means slower than usual, and Mars, as fierce as ever, glows red with the flashing from his crested helmet.[40] Beautiful Phoebus shines with eternal youth; nor does the god drive his chariot down to warm the exhausted soil in the valleys, but powerfully and with his ever friendly light he hastens on the same way, in the tracks of his wheels. Equally beautiful, a star rises from fragrant India,[45] calling at dawn and in the evening driving to the pasture of the sky[47] the celestial herd that gathers on whitening Olympus,[46] dividing the kingdoms of Time with two colours.[48] By turns Delia[49] waxes and wanes with alternating horns, and grasps the blue fire with unchanged arms. Nor do the elements break faith; with accustomed crashing the lurid lightning bolts are cast and strike the cliffs. Corus[53] rages through the void with no gentler murmur, and wild Aquilo,[55] ever dreaded, holds in check the warlike Geloni,[54] breathes forth the winter and rolls the dark clouds. The king of the sea still strikes at the foot of Sicilian Pelorus[56] and the hollow-sounding shell of the Ocean's trumpeter[58] resounds over the sea. The Balearic whales bear on their backs an Aegaeon[59] no less vast in bulk. Nor, Earth, do you lack the strength of ages long past. Narcissus[61] keeps his perfume; that boy[62] of yours, Phoebus, remains beautiful, and that boy of yours too, Cypris.[63] The earth was not richer in times past when she guiltily concealed the cause of crime, gold in the mountains and gems beneath the sea. Thus, the perfect course of all things will go on forever until the last flames destroy the universe[67] embracing far and wide the poles and the heights of the vast heaven,[68] and the fabric of the world will blaze on an enormous funeral pyre.[69]

The date and circumstances of composition are not known, but the poem may have been an academic exercise written while Milton was at Cambridge.

3 noctem] i.e. blindness.

9–10] See *PL* V 338n.

14–15] Glancing at the traditional identification of Chronos (Time) with Cronos (Saturn), Milton reverses the myth whereby Cronos devours his children and instead makes him devour his father. Cf. *On Time* 4.

19–20] II Pet. iii. 10.

22] On the shield of Pallas Athena (Minerva) see *Comus* 446–51n.

23–4] Juno's son is Vulcan; see *PL* I 738–46n.

25–6] See *Elegia* V 92n.

27 Nereus] The Greek sea-god here represents the sea.

29 Hæmi] a mountain in Thrace.

30–32] The Ceraunian mountains are in Epirus. Dis is the Roman name for Pluto, god of the underworld. On the wars of the gods see *PL* I 197–200n.

37 rota prima] the *primum mobile* (see *Fair Infant* 39n.).

40] Mars is described as the god of war.

45–8] Venus appears as Lucifer, the morning star, and Hesperus, the evening star.

49 Delia] See *PL* IX 387n.

53 Corus] the north-west wind.

54] The Geloni were a Scythian tribe living in what is now the Ukraine.

55 Aquilo] See *Fair Infant* 8n.

56 Pelori] See *PL* I 230–7n.

58 Oceani Tubicen] See *Comus* 872n.

59] Aegaeon (Briareus), one of the Centimani (giants with 100 hands) is here represented as a sea-god.

61 Narcissus] See *Comus* 229n.

62 puer] See *Fair Infant* 23–6n.

63] Cyprus is Venus (see *Elegia* I 84n.) whose boy is Adonis (see *Elegia* I 62n.).

67–9] II Pet. iii. 10.

De Idea Platonica

On the Platonic Ideal Form as Understood by Aristotle.

Declare, O goddesses[1] guarding the sacred groves, and you Memory,[3] blessed mother of the ninefold deity, and you Eternity, who lie idle in a vast cave far away, presenting the chronicles and unalterable laws of Jove, the calendar of heaven and the diaries of the gods, declare who was that first being – eternal, uncorrupted, coeval with the heavens, one and universal, an image of God – after whose likeness skilled Nature has shaped the human race? Surely he is not a twin to the virgin Athene,[11] not an unborn child dwelling in Jove's mind.[12] But however universal his nature is, nevertheless he exists separately, in the manner of an individual, and, strangely enough, is confined within definite spatial limits. Perhaps that perpetual companion of the stars wanders through the ten spheres of heaven[17] or inhabits the globe of the moon, which is nearest earth, or perhaps sitting among the spirits waiting to enter bodies, he lazes beside Lethe's waters of forgetfulness,[20] or perhaps in some far-off region of the earth this huge giant advances, the archetype of man. He raises his head high, frightening the gods, a being taller than Atlas,[24] bearer of the stars. The Dircean augur,[26] whose blindness gave him profound light, did not see this being in the depths of his heart. Nor, in the silence of night, did the wing-footed grandson of Pleione[27] show this one to the band of wise seers. The Assyrian priest did not know him, although he could relate the long ancestry of Ninus,[30] primitive Belus and renowned Osiris.[31] He that is famous with his triple name,[32] the thrice-great Hermes,[33] though skilled in mysteries, did not leave such a being to the worshippers of Isis.[34] But you, everlasting glory of the rural Academy,[35] if you first introduced these monstrosities into the Schools, you must now recall the poets exiled from your city[37] – for you yourself are the greatest fabler[38] – or else you the founder must banish yourself.

The date and circumstances of composition are not known, but the poem may have been written for an academic occasion while Milton was at Cambridge.

1 deæ] may refer to the muses or to Diana and her retinue.

3 Memoria] Mnemosyne, mother of the nine muses.

11–12] See *PL* II 752–9.

17] See *PL* III 481–3n.

20 Lethes] See *Novembris* 132n.

24] On Atlas see *PL* II 306n.

26] The Dircean (see *Leonoram* II 7n.) augur is Tiresias, on whom see *PL* III 36n.

27 Plëiones nepos] Mercury, son of Maia, who was the daughter of Pleione and Atlas. Cf. *Mansus* 72.

30 Nini] See *PR* III 275–9n.

31 Belon] Babylonian Baal; on Osiris see *Nativity* 212–13n.

32–3] See *Penseroso* 88n.

34] On Isis see *Nativity* 212–13n.

35] See *PR* IV 244–6n.

37] Plato banished poets from his ideal state (*Republic* x 595–608).

38 fabulator maximus] Cf *PR* IV 295.

Ad Patrem
To my Father

Now I wish the Pierian[1] fountains would turn their refreshing waters through my heart, and pour through my lips the whole stream that flows from the twin summit,[3] so that my Muse, forgetting her trifling strains, might rise on spirited wings to serve my revered father. This poem, a small work, however acceptable it may be, she meditates for you, excellent father. And yet I do not myself know what I can give more fittingly in return for your gifts to me, though even my greatest gift could not repay you, much less could the meagre gratitude offered in vain words ever equal your gifts. Nevertheless, this page displays my possessions, and what treasures I have are numbered on this paper, for I have nothing except what golden Clio[14] has given to me, what dreams in distant caves, the laurel of sacred groves and the shades of Parnassus have brought to me.

Do not despise the poet's work, divine poetry, for nothing proclaims more completely our celestial beginnings and heavenly seeds, or so extols the human mind for its origin, and retains sacred traces of Promethean fire.[20] The gods above love poetry. Poetry is able to move the trembling depths of Tartarus[21] and to bend the gods below;[22] it restrains the troublesome shades with triple adamant.[23] In poetry Apollo's priestesses and trembling pale-faced sibyls reveal the secrets of the distant future.[25] The sacrificing priest composes poetry at the solemn altars, whether he is casting down the bull shaking its golden horn, or is wisely considering the predictions hidden in the reeking entrails or is seeking for Fate[29] in its warm innards. We too, when we return to our native Olympus and the endless ages of changeless eternity are fixed, shall go through the spaces of heaven with golden crowns,[32] joining our sweet songs with the soft-sounding lyre[33] with which the starry vaults of both hemispheres will resound. The fiery spirit who circles the swift spheres is already singing with the celestial choirs his immortal melody, an indescribable song; while the shining Serpent curbs his parched hissing, wild Orion grows gentle and lowers his sword, and Mauretanian Atlas[40] no longer feels the burden of the stars.

Poems used to ornament the feasts of kings, when luxury and the boundless chasm of insatiable gluttony were not yet known, and the table foamed with a modest wine. Then, according to custom, the poet, sitting at the joyful banquet, his unshorn[45] locks wreathed with oak leaves, sang of the feats of heroes and the deeds to be copied, of Chaos and the broadly-laid foundations of the world, of the creeping gods and the acorns that nourished divinities, and of the thunderbolt not yet brought out of the cave of Etna.[49] Indeed, what help is an empty modulation of the voice, without words, meaning and the rhythms of speech? That song may suit the woodland choir, but not Orpheus,[52] who held back rivers and placed ears on the oak trees[53] with song, not with a lute, and who with singing moved lifeless shades[54] to tears. This fame he owes to song.[55]

Do not, I beg you, continue to despise the sacred Muses, nor reckon vain and poor those by whose gift you are skilled[57] to join a thousand notes to suitable rhythms,[58] and who have taught you to vary your melodious voice in a thousand tunes,[59] so that you deserve to be heir to the name of Arion.[60] Now, why do you marvel that you have happened to bear a poet, and that as we are so closely joined by ties of blood and affection, we pursue kindred arts and related studies? Phoebus, wishing to divide himself between the two of us, gave some gifts to me, the other gifts to my father, and we, father and son, possess the divided god.

You, however, pretend to hate the delicate Muses,[67] though I do not believe you truly hate them. For, father, you did not command me to go where the broad way lies open, where the course of gain is easier, and the golden hope of laying up money shines true. You do not force me to law, and the badly-guarded justice of the nation; nor do you condemn my ears to absurd clamourings. But, desiring that my carefully-tended mind be enriched more completely, you have taken me from the din of the city to the deep retreats of delightful leisure by the Aonian banks,[75] and allowed me to go, a fortunate companion, by Phoebus' side.

I say nothing of the usual kindness of a dear parent, for greater matters summon me. When at your expense, excellent father, I had become fluent in the language of Romulus, the charms of Latin, and the lofty words of the eloquent Greeks, fit for the mighty lips of Jove himself, you urged me to add the flowers that France boasts and the language the modern Italian pours from his degenerate mouth – testifying in his speech to the barbarian invasions – and the mysteries uttered by the Palestinian prophet. Finally, whatever is in the sky, on mother earth beneath the sky, in the air flowing between earth and sky, and all that is hidden by the waves and the restless surface of the sea, all this through you I have been enabled to know, through you, if I choose to know. As the clouds scatter, science comes into view, and naked, inclines her remarkable face to my kisses, unless I wish to flee, and unless I do not find the taste annoying.

Go now and collect riches, all who foolishly prefer the ancestral treasures of Austria and the Peruvian kingdoms. What greater gift could a father, or even Jove himself, have bestowed, had he given all except heaven? No better were the gifts (however safe they were) of him who entrusted to his own son the universal light, the chariot of Hyperion,[99] the reins of day and a tiara abounding with radiant light. Therefore, I am now one, although the humblest, of the learned company, and shall sit among the victors' ivy and laurels. I shall no longer mingle unrecognised in the indolent crowd; my footsteps will shun the gaze of profane eyes. Begone, sleepless cares; begone, complaints, and the twisted glance of Envy's goatish eye. Fierce Calumny, do not open your serpent-bearing jaws. Foul crowd, you can do me no harm. I am not under your law. With untroubled heart I shall walk safely above your viper stroke.

But for you, dear father, since I am not able to give what you rightly deserve, nor to pay back gifts with deeds, let it suffice that I have remembered and recounted your repeated gifts with a grateful heart, and stored them up in a faithful mind.

And you, my youthful verses, my pastimes, if only you dare hope for endless years, and outlive your master's funeral pyre, and look upon the light, and if dark oblivion does not drag you down to crowded Orcus,[118] perhaps these praises, and the name of my father chanted here, you will preserve as an example to a distant age.

The date of composition is not known.

1 Pierios] See *Elegia* IV 31–2n.

3 gemino . . . vertice] See *Elegia* IV 30n.

14 Clio] the muse of history.

20] See *PL* IV 714–19n.

21–3] See *Allegro* 145–50n.

25] The priestesses of Apollo ministered at the temple at Delphi, which contained the famous oracle. The Sibyl of Cumæ revealed the future to Aeneas, and guided him to Hades.

29 Parcam] See *Winchester* 28n.

32–3] Rev. iv. 4, v. 8, xiv. 2.

40] On Mauretania see *PR* IV 69–79n., and on Atlas *PL* XI 402n.

43 Lyæo] See *Elegia* VI 21n.

45 intonsos] See *Vacation Exercise* 37n.

49] Vulcan and the Cyclops forged the thunderbolts of Jove in a cave under Mount Etna.

52–5] See *Allegro* 145–50n.

57–60] Milton's father was a gifted minor composer. On Arion see *Lycidas* 164n.

67 Camœnas] See *Elegia* VI 3n.

75 Aoniæ . . . ripæ] See *Elegia* IV 29n.

99] Hyperion was the father of the sun.

118 Orco] Hades.

Psalm 114

When the children of Israel, when the glorious tribes of Jacob left the land of Egypt, a hateful place of barbarous speech, then indeed were the sons of Judah the only holy race, and among these peoples the mighty God was king. The sea saw this, and rushed in headlong flight, coiled in roaring waves. Sacred Jordan was thrust back towards its silvery source. The immense mountains rushed wildly about, leaping like lusty rams in a rich meadow. All the smaller crags skipped like lambs about their dear mother to the sound of the syrinx. Why, grim and monstrous sea, did you, coiled in roaring waves, rush in headlong flight? Why, sacred Jordan, were you thrust back towards your silvery source? Why, immense mountains, did you rush wildly about, leaping like lusty rams in a rich meadow? Why, smaller crags, did you skip like lambs about their dear mother to the sound of the syrinx? Shake, earth, in fear of God who thunders loudly. Earth, fear God, the highest majesty of the seed of Isaac, who pours roaring rivers out of the crags, and an eternal spring from a weeping rock.

Milton enclosed this translation with a letter to Alexander Gill dated 4 December 1634, explaining that he had written it the previous week. Cf. Milton's English version of the same psalm, p. 12.

Philosophus ad regem

A philosopher on his way to execution suddenly sent these verses to a certain king who had unknowingly condemned him, unrecognized and innocent, when he was captured by chance along with some criminals.

O King, if you destroy me, a man who obeys the law and has done no harm to any man, know that you may easily take away a very wise head, but later you will perceive this, and you will then mourn to your own soul [Ed. 1, 1645: in time then you will mourn very much, fruitlessly] that you have destroyed such a far-famed safeguard of your city.

The date of composition is not known.

In Effigiei ejus Sculptorem
On the Engraver of his Portrait

Looking at its original, you would perhaps say that an ignorant hand had drawn this image. Since you do not recognize the person, my friends, laugh at this bad imitation by a worthless artist.[4]

These verses were printed below the portrait of Milton which had been engraved by William Marshall for Milton's 1645 *Poems*.

4 φαύλον ... ζωγράφου] plays on the senses 'of a worthless artist' and 'by a worthless artist'.

Ad Salsillum

To Salzilli, the Roman Poet, in his Illness.

Scazons.

O Muse, who willingly drags a halting[1] foot, and delights in Vulcan's slow gait,[2] and does not think that in its place it is less agreeable than fair Deiopea, with her noble ankles,[4] as she dances before Juno's golden couch,[5] come hither, and carry, if you will, these few words to Salzilli, to whom our poetry is so agreeable, that he prefers it quite undeservedly to that of the great divines. These lines, therefore, are sent by a native of London, Milton, who lately, leaving his own nest and region of the heavens (where the worst of the winds, powerless to control the raging of its lungs, swiftly drives its panting blasts beneath the sky) came to the fruitful soil of Italy to see the proudly reported cities, the men and the genius of the learned young. That Milton wishes you, Salzilli, much prosperity and good health for your infirm body, where now excessive bile attacks your kidneys and fixed in your stomach spreads its destruction. You were not spared this curse even though you are a cultured man whose Roman lips fashion the song of Lesbos.[22]

O sweet gift of the gods, health, the sister of Hebe,[23] and you, Phœbus – or do you prefer the name Pæan[25] – the terror of diseases since you killed Python, this man is your priest. Oak-groves of Faunus,[27] and hills abounding with the dew of grapes, the seat of gentle Evander,[28] if you put forth health-giving leaves in your valleys, carry them eagerly to help the sick poet. Then, restored anew to his dear Muses, he will delight the neighbouring meadows with sweet song. Numa himself will wonder, when among the dark groves[33] he spends his happy eternity of leisure[34] reclining with his gaze fixed always on his Egeria.[35] Even swollen Tiber, charmed by the song, will favour the yearly hope of the husbandmen, and will not overwhelm the kings in their tombs[38] by rushing along with the left rein too slack,[39] but he will govern closely the reins of his waters all the way to the salty realm of curved Portumnus.[41]

The poem was written late in 1638 or early in 1639, and is addressed to Giovanni Salzilli, apparently in response to Salzilli's quatrain (printed on p. 104).

Title. *Scazontes*] a modification of iambic trimeter in which a spondee or trochee replaces the final iamb.

1 claudum] Scazon means 'limping' in Greek. Cf. *Elegia* VI 8n.

2] Vulcan's fall to Lemnos (see *PL* I 740–6) left him lame.

4–5] Juno thought that Deiopea was the fairest of her fourteen nymphs (*Aeneid* i 71–5).

11 pessimus ... ventorum] Aquilo; see *Fair Infant* 8n.

22 Lesbium ... melos] refers to the poetry of Sappho and Alcaeus, both of whom were natives of Lesbos.

23 Hebes] See *Vacation Exercise* 38n.

25 Pæan] an appellation of Apollo, as the healing deity. On the Python see *PL* X 529–31n.

27 Fauni] the Roman god of fields and woods was also father of Latinus, king of the Latins.

28] Evander was the Arcadian king who founded a colony on the Palatine Hill.

33–5] Numa Pompilius, the second king of Rome, received nocturnal counsel from his consort, the nymph Egeria.
38] probably refers to the mausoleum of Augustus, in the Campus Martius.
39] The left bank of the Tiber was particularly subject to flooding.
41] Portumnus was the god of harbours; *curvus* may refer to the shore which he protects.

Mansus

Manso

Giovanni Battista Manso, the Marquis of Villa, is one of the most celebrated men in Italy, for the fame of his genius and literary studies, and also for his courage in war. There is extant a dialogue on friendship addressed to him by Torquato Tasso. He was a close friend of Tasso and was celebrated by him among the princes of Campania in the poem entitled *Jerusalem Conquered*, Book 20:

> Among magnanimous and courteous knights
> Shines Manso –

When the present author was staying in Naples, Manso honoured him with the greatest kindness, and bestowed on him many gentle favours. Therefore his guest sent him this poem before he left that city in order that he might not appear ungrateful.

These verses too,[1] Manso, the Pierides[2] intend for your praise, for you, Manso, are well known to the choir of Phoebus, for he has not deemed another worthy of equal honour since the death of Gallus and Etruscan Maecenas.[4] You also, if the breath of my muse[5] has power, will sit among the victors' ivy and laurels.

Long ago a happy friendship joined you with the great Tasso, and wrote your names on everlasting records. Soon afterwards the knowing muse entrusted to you the sweet-tongued Marino who was delighted to be called your foster-son when he sang at length the Assyrian loves of the gods[11] and charmed the Ausonian[12] nymphs with his gentler verse. When he died, the poet, conscious of his debt to you alone, to you alone left his body and his last wishes. Your loving affection has not disappointed the departed spirit of your friend, for we have seen the poet smiling from the sculptured bronze. But this did not seem enough for either poet, and your pious offices did not cease at the tomb, for you wished to snatch them from Orcus[18] unharmed and, as far as you could, to frustrate the greedy laws of the Fates.[19] So you set down the ancestry of both,[20] the changing fortunes of their lives, their characters and their gifts from Minerva.[21] You rival the eloquent one born near high Mycale[22] who recounted the life of Aeolian Homer.[23] Therefore, father Manso, in the name of Clio[24] and the great Phoebus, I, a youthful wanderer sent from the Hyperborean heavens, wish you good health and long life. You in your goodwill will not despise a distant muse, who though poorly nourished beneath the icy Bear, of late has rashly dared to fly through the Italian cities.

I believe that in the dusky shadows of night I, too, have heard the swans singing on my river where the silver Thames with pure urns drenches her gray hair in the wide waters of the ocean. Indeed, Tityrus[34] once came to these shores.

But we are not an uncultivated race, nor useless to Phoebus, we that endure the long nights under wintry Boötes in a region of the world furrowed by the sevenfold Triones.[36] We too are devoted to Phoebus; we have sent him gifts – golden ears of grain, baskets of rosy apples, fragrant crocuses (unless antiquity's assertions are groundless) and choirs chosen from the Druids. The Druids, an ancient race skilled in the rites of the gods, used to sing the praises of heroes, and of deeds to be imitated. Hence, as often as the Greek maidens circled the altars in grassy Delos with festal song according to custom, they commemorate in joyful verses

Corineidan Loxo,[46] prophetic Upis, and golden-haired Hecaerge,[47] their bare breasts coloured with Caledonian paint.

Therefore, fortunate old man, wherever in the world the glory and great name of Torquato is celebrated, and wherever the brilliant fame of the immortal Marino shall spread, your name and praise will also frequently be on the lips of men, and in equal flight you will sail along the path to immortality. Then it will be said that Cynthius[55] willingly dwelt in your home and the muses came as servant to your house. Yet it was not willingly, however,[56] that Apollo, a fugitive from heaven, came to the farm of King Pheretiades,[57] although, as host, that king received the great Alcides.[58] But when he wished to avoid the noisy ploughmen, Apollo withdrew to the famous cave of gentle Chiron[60] among the well-watered pastures and leafy shelters beside the river Peneus.[62] There, under the dark oak, overwhelmed by the flattering request of his friend, he would often lighten the hard labours of his exile with a song accompanied by a cithara. Then neither the bank nor the rocks fixed in the lowest abyss stood in their places; the Trachinian cliff[66] swayed and no longer felt the enormous weight of its accustomed forests; uprooted mountain ashes hastened from the hills, and the spotted lynxes were soothed by the unfamiliar song.

Old man loved by the gods, Jupiter must have been friendly to you at your birth, and Phœbus and the grandson of Atlas[72] must have illumined you with their kindly light, for no one, unless dear to the gods from his birth, could have befriended a great poet. Hence, your old age flourishes with lingering blossom and, still full of life, acquires for itself the Aesonian spindles,[75] keeping the honours of your brow unfallen, your genius flourishing and a matured subtlety of mind. O that my fate would grant to me such a friend, who knows so well how to honour the followers of Phœbus, if ever I call back into verse our native kings, and Arthur who waged wars even under the earth, or were I to speak of the magnanimous heroes of the table made invincible by a bond of companionship, and (if only the spirit be present) to break the Saxon phalanxes with a British War. When at last I have measured the span of a not silent life and, full of years, I bequeath to death its due, if that friend, with eyes moist, might stand near my bed, I should be content if I could say to him as he stood there, 'Take me into your care.' He would see to it that my limbs, relaxed by livid death, were gently laid in a little urn. Perhaps he would shape my features in marble, binding the locks on my brow with Paphian[92] myrtle or Parnassian laurel and I might rest in secure peace. Then, too, if there be such a thing as faith, if rewards for the good are certain, I myself, removed to the ethereal homes of the heaven-dwelling gods to which labour, a pure mind, and burning courage convey us, shall see these things from some other part of that secret world – as much as the fates allow – and with my mind completely serene and my smiling face suffused with a rosy light, I shall with joy applaud myself on high Olympus.

When Milton visited Naples late in 1638 he was befriended by Manso, whose couplet addressed to Milton is printed on p. 104.

1 quoque] Many poems had been written in praise of Manso.

2 Pierides] See *Elegia* IV 31–2n.

4] Cornelius Gallus (*c.* 69–26 BC), poet and general, was a friend of Virgil (see *Eclogue* x). Gaius Mæcenas (d. 8 BC) was a famous patron of poets, including Virgil, Horace, and Propertius.

5 Camænæ] See *Elegia* VI 3n.

11] Marino's *L'Adone* (1623), which extends to more than 5000 octaves, tells the story of Venus and Adonis. Venus is Assyrian in *Comus* 1001; see also *Nativity* 200n., 204n., and *PL* I 446–57n.

12 Ausonias] See *Elegia* I 70n.

18 Orco] Hades.

19 Parcarum] See *Winchester* 28n.

20] Manso's life of Tasso was published (in part) in 1621, but his MS life of Marino has not survived.

21 Minervæ] i.e. Pallas Athena (see *Elegia* II 2n.).

22–3] Herodotus, who was born in Halicarnassus, which is south of the promontory of Mycale, was thought to have written a *Life of Homer* (it is no longer attributed to him). The western coast of Asia Minor north of the Hermus (modern Gediz) River constituted Aeolis.

24] Clio was the muse of history.

34 Tityrus] the Virgilian name given by Spenser to Chaucer in *Shepherd's Calendar* (February 92, June 81, December 4). Chaucer visited Italy in 1372–3 and 1378.

36 septeno . . . Trione] The wain, Ursa Major (see *Elegia* V 35–6n.) has seven bright stars, the Septentriones.

46–7] Loxo (whom Milton makes the daughter of Corineus, who came to Britain with Brutus, and after whom Cornwall was thought to be named), Upis, and Hacaerge were the British Druidesses who were thought to have travelled to Delos with offerings to Apollo.

55 Cynthius] Apollo, who was born on Mount Cynthos, in Delos; cf. *Elegia* V 46n.

56–8] Apollo, who was banished from Olympus for killing the Cyclopes, served the king of Pheræ (in Thessaly), Admetus, son of Pheres (hence *Pheretiades*) as a shepherd. On Hercules (Alcides) and Admetus, see *Sonnet* XXIV 2–3n.

60 Chironis] See *Elegia* IV 27–8n., *In Obitum Procancellarii* 27–8n.

62 Peneium] a river (and a river-god; see *PL* IV 272–4n.) in Thessaly.

66 Trachinia rupes] Mount Oeta (the site of the town of Trachis), on which see *PL* II 542–6n.

72 Atlantisque nepos] Mercury; see *Idea* 27n.

75] On Aeson see *Elegia* II 7–8n. The spindles are those of the Parcæ (see *Winchester* 28n.).

92 Paphiâ] See *Elegia* I 84n.

Epitaphium Damonis

Damon's Epitaph

Argument

Thyrsis and Damon, shepherds of the same neighbourhood, had pursued the same interests from childhood, and had been very close friends. Thyrsis, abroad for the improvement of his mind, received the news of Damon's death. After he had returned home and ascertained that it was true, he bewailed himself and his loneliness in this poem. 'Damon' here represents Charles Diodati, whose origin through his father's family was in the Tuscan city of Lucca, but who was in every other respect English. While he lived he was a youth distinguished as a man of genius, learning, and other honourable virtues.

Nymphs of Himera – for you remember Daphnis and Hylas[1] and the long-lamented fate of Bion[2] – sing your Sicilian song through the cities of the Thames; the words and murmurs that wretched Thyrsis[4] poured out and the incessant complaints with which he harassed the caves, the rivers, the wandering streams and the recesses of the woods while he mourned to himself the untimely loss of Damon and wandered through the lonely places filling the depths of night with his lamentations. Twice already had the stalk with its green ear grown up, and twice had the barns contained the golden harvests since Damon's last day had borne him to the shades, and Thyrsis was not yet present, for love of the sweet Muse held that shepherd in a Tuscan city.[13] But when his mind was full and concern for the flock left behind had called him home, as soon as he sat down under his accustomed elm, truly then, then at last he felt the loss of his friend, and thus began to relieve his boundless sorrow.

Go home unfed, my lambs, your master has not time for you now.[18] Ah me, what deities shall I call upon in earth or heaven, since they have snatched you away to cruel death, Damon! Do you leave me thus? Will your virtue go without a name and too soon be united to the company of unknown spirits? But he[23] who divides the souls with his golden wand would not wish that. May he lead you to a company worthy of you, and keep at a distance the whole idle herd of the silent dead.

Go home unfed, my lambs, your master has not time for you now. Whatever happens, unless a wolf sees me first,[27] you will certainly not crumble in the grave unwept. Your fame will endure, and will flourish for a long time among shepherds. They will rejoice to pay their vows to you, next after Daphnis, and, next after Daphnis, to sing your praises, as long as Pales and Faunus[32] love the fields – if it means anything to have honoured the ancient faith and piety and the Palladian arts,[34] and to have had a poetic companion.

Go home unfed, my lambs, your master has not time for you now. For you, Damon, these rewards remain certain; they will be yours. But what is to become of me? What faithful comrade will stay at my side, as you used to, in the severe cold of winter when the fields were covered with frost, or in the fierce sun when the crops were dying of thirst, whether our task was to approach great lions or to frighten hungry wolves from the high sheepfolds? Who will now lull the day to sleep with conversation and song?

Go home unfed, my lambs, your master has not time for you now. To whom shall I entrust my heart? Who will teach me how to soothe devouring cares, or how to lighten the long night with agreeable conversation while the soft pear hisses by a pleasant fire and the nuts sizzle on the hearth, while yet wicked Auster[48] throws everything outside into confusion and thunders through the tops of the elms.

Go home unfed, my lambs, your master has not time for you now. Or in summer, at midday, when Pan takes his sleep hidden in the shade of the oak tree, and the nymphs revisit their familiar haunts under the waters, the shepherds recline in secret, and the ploughman snores under the hedge, who then will bring to me your flatteries, your smile, your Cecropian[56] wit, and your elegant charm?

Go home unfed, my lambs, your master has not time for you now. But now I wander alone through fields, now alone through pastures. Whenever the shadows are deepened by the boughs, there I await the evening. Above my head rain and Eurus[60] cry out sorrowfully in the restless twilight of the trembling forest.

Go home unfed, my lambs, your master has not time for you now. Alas, my once tilled lands are now enveloped with shameless weeds and even the tall corn grows weak with mould. The cluster of grapes withers unwedded[65] to its neglected stalk, and the myrtle groves do not please me. I am weary even of my sheep, but they are sad and turn their faces to their master.

Go home unfed, my lambs, your master has not time for you now. Tityrus calls me to the hazels, Alphesibœus to the mountain-ashes,[69] Aegon to the willows, fair Amyntas to the rivers:[70] 'Here are cool springs. Here is turf covered with moss. Here are the zephyrs. Here the arbutus whispers amid peaceful streams.' But I am deaf to their songs. I reach the thickets and withdraw.

Go home unfed, my lambs, your master has not time for you now. Then came Mopsus – for by chance he had observed me returning – Mopsus, who was skilled in the language of birds and in the stars. 'What is this, Thyrsis?' he said. 'What fierce bile is tormenting you? Either you are dying of love, or an evil star has bewitched you. Saturn's star has often been troublesome to shepherds,[79] and his slanting leaden shaft pierces to the innermost heart.[80]

Go home unfed, my lambs, your master has not time for you now. The nymphs are astonished. 'What is to become of you, Thyrsis? What do you wish?' they say. 'The brow of youth is not usually cloudy, its eyes stern, or its features serious. By right youth seeks dances and pleasant sports, and always love; twice wretched is he who loves too late.'

Go home unfed, my lambs, your master has not time for you now. Hylas came, and Dryope, and Baucis' daughter Aegle,[88] who was skilled in the techniques of the harp but ruined by excessive pride; and Chloris came, a neighbour of the Idumanian river.[90] Their flatteries and soothing words are nothing to me. Nothing in the present moves me, nor is there any hope for the future.

Go home unfed, my lambs, your master has not time for you now. Ah me, how alike one to one another are the young bullocks sporting in the meadows, all comrades under one law; no one singles out a special friend in the herd. In the same way wolves come in packs to their food, and the shaggy wild asses mate in pairs by turns. The law of the sea is the same. On the deserted shore Proteus[99] numbers the troops of seals. Even that worthless bird, the sparrow, always has a mate with whom it cheerfully flies around to every heap of grain, and comes again late to its own nest. If by chance strike its mate dead, whether this fate was brought by the kite with its hooked bill, or it was cast down by a peasant's arrow, forthwith he seeks another to be henceforth his companion in flight. But we men are a harsh race, a tribe harassed by cruel fates, with alienated minds and discordant hearts. A man can hardly find one single friend for himself among thousands; or if Destiny, not unreceptive to your prayers finally gives that one, on an unexpected day, at an hour when you least expect it, he is snatched away, leaving forever a constant loss.

Go home unfed, my lambs, your master has not time for you now. Alas, what wandering delusion drew me to travel to unknown coasts, across lofty cliffs and the snowy Alps. Was it so important to have seen buried Rome – even had it been what it was when long ago Tityrus[117] himself left his sheep and pastures – that I could be without so sweet a companion, that I could place between us so many deep seas, so many mountains, woods, rocks, and roaring rivers? Surely I might have touched his right hand at the end, and closed his eyes as he calmly died, and said, 'Farewell, remember me as you go to the stars.'

Go home unfed, my lambs, your master has not time for you now. Although I shall never weary of your memory, Tuscan shepherds, youths devoted to the Muses, here were Grace and Charm; you too were Tuscan, Damon, and traced your lineage from the ancient city of Lucca. Ah, how great I felt when, stretched by the cool murmuring Arno, in the poplar grove with its soft grass, I could gather, now violets, now sprays of myrtle, and listen to Menalcas contending with Lycidas.[132] I, too, dared to try, and I do not think you were greatly displeased, for with me here are your gifts – woven baskets, bowls, and pipes with wax fastenings; and indeed, Dati and Francini,[137] both renowned for their eloquence and learning, and both of Lydian blood,[138] have taught my name to their beech trees.

Go home unfed, my lambs, your master has not time for you now. These things the dewy moon used to say to me when I was happy and while alone I shut up the young kids in their wattled folds. Ah, how often, when you were already dark ashes I said, 'Now Damon is singing, or now he is stretching nets for the hare, now he is weaving switches for his various uses.' What I then with an easy mind hoped for the future I lightly changed from a wish to an imagined present: 'Ho, good man, have you anything to do? If there is nothing to stop you, let us go and lie down for a little

while in the rustling shade by the waters of Colne or in the fields of Cassivellaunus.[149] You will run through for me your herbs and healing potions – your
hellebore, humble crocus, hyacinth leaf, and all the plants that the marshes yield –
and all the arts of the physicians.' Ah, let the herbs and plants perish, and let the
arts of the physicians perish, since they have profited their master nothing. And
myself, for I know not what grand song my pipe was sounding – it is now eleven
nights and a day since then – perhaps I set my lips to new pipes, but they fell apart,
broken at the fastenings, and were not able to carry the deep sounds; I hesitate to
appear puffed up, yet I shall tell the tale. Give place, forests.

Go home unfed, my lambs, your master has not time for you now. I am going to
tell of the Trojan ships in the Rutupian Sea,[162] of the ancient realm of Imogen, the
daughter of Pandrasus,[163] and of the leaders Brennus and Arviragus, and of old
Belinus,[164] and the Armorican settlers, finally under British law;[165] then of Igerne
pregnant with Arthur by a fatal deceit,[166] when the likeness and arms of Gorlois
were assumed[167] through the deception of Merlin.[168] And then, if life remains to
me, you, my pipe, will hang forgotten on a far-off pine tree unless, changed, you
will utter a British theme in native songs. For indeed, one man cannot do
everything, nor even hope to do all. I shall have ample reward and great glory –
though I may be for ever unknown and completely without fame in foreign parts –
if yellow-haired Ouse reads me, and he who drinks from the Aln[175] and the Abra[176]
with its many whirlpools, and every wood by the Trent, and above all my Thames
and the Tamar[178] darkened with metals, and if the Orkneys in their remote waters
will learn my song.

Go home unfed, my lambs, your master has not time for you now. These things I
was keeping for you under the tough bark of the laurel; these, and more besides,
for I was keeping the two cups[181] that Manso, not the least glory of the Chalcidian[182]
shore, gave me. They are a wonderful work of art, and he too, is wonderful.
Around the cups is a carving with a double theme: in the middle are the waters of
the Red Sea, fragrant spring,[185] the distant shores of Arabia, and trees dripping
balsam.[186] Among the trees the phoenix, the divine bird unparalleled on earth,[187]
shining blue and with many-coloured wings,[188] watches Aurora rise over the glassy
waters.[189] Another part is the boundless sky and great Olympus. Here too (who
would believe it?) is Love, with his quiver painted against a cloud, flashing arms,
torches, and bronze-coloured darts. From there he does not hit trifling spirits and
the ignoble hearts of the rabble, but rolling around his blazing eyes, unwearied, he
always sends his darts upwards through the spheres and never aims his shots
downwards. Hence he inflames holy minds and the divine forms.

You are also among these Damon – for no uncertain hope deceives me – you also
are surely among these, for where else would your sweet and holy simplicity go,
where your shining virtues? It is not right to seek for you in Lethean Orcus,[201] nor
are tears for you appropriate. I shall weep no more. Away tears! Damon dwells in
the pure ether, and pure himself, possesses the ether and thrusts back the rainbow
with his foot. Among the souls of heroes and the immortal gods, he draws from the
heavenly springs, and drinks their delights with his sacred lips. And now, since you
have received the rights of heaven, stand by my side and gently favour me,
whatever your name is to be. Whether you will be our Damon or if you prefer to be
called Diodati, the divine name[210] by which the inhabitants of heaven will know
you, in the forests you will be called Damon. Because you loved a rosy blush and,
stainless youth, because you never tasted the delights of marriage,[213] lo, for you are
reserved the honours of a virgin.[214] Your shining head will be wreathed with a
glowing crown,[215] and bearing the cheerful branches of the leafy palm[216] you will
enact for ever the immortal marriage,[217] where song and the sound of the ecstatic

lyre mingle with the dances of the blessed, and the festal revels rage under the thyrsus[219] of Zion.

Diodati (on whom see *Sonnet* IV 1n.) died in August 1638. Milton wrote the poem after he returned to England from Italy late in the summer of 1639.

1] The Himera is a Sicilian river mentioned by Theocritus (v 124, vii 75), and its nymphs represent the 'Sicilian Muse' (*Lycidas* 133) of Greek pastoral poetry. Daphnis is mourned in Theocritus i; on Hylas see *Elegia* VII 21–4n.

2] Bion, a pastoral poet, was commemorated in *Lament for Bion*, which was traditionally attributed to Moschus.

4] Thyrsis] Milton represents himself with the name of the shepherd who mourns Daphnis in Theocritus i (cf. Virgil, *Eclogue* vii).

7 Damona] Milton represents Diodati with a pastoral name that may recall the intimate friends Damon and Pythias, who were votaries of the Pythagorean discipline extolled in *Elegia* VI, which is addressed to Diodati.

13 Thuscâ ... urbe] Florence, which Milton visited from August–September 1638 and March–April 1639.

18] Virgil, *Eclogue* vii. 44.

23 ille] Mercury; see *Aeneid* iv 242–4.

27] alludes to the ancient belief that a man was struck dumb if seen by a wolf before seeing it.

32] Pales was the Roman goddess of flocks and shepherds, and Faunus the god of fields and woods.

34 Palladiasque artes] See *Elegia* II 2n.

48 Auster] the south wind.

56] Cecrops was the first king of Attica, so *Cecropius* means Attic.

60 Eurus] the south-east wind.

65 Innuba] See *PL* V 215–19n.

69–90] The names are common in pastoral poetry.

79–80] The planet Saturn was associated with bad weather and melancholy temperaments.

90 Idumanii ... fluenti] the Chelmer River, in Essex.

99 Proteus] See *Elegia* III 26n.

117 Tityrus] refers to Virgil's Tityrus (*Eclogue* i)

132] Milton uses the pastoral convention of the singing contest to refer to the literary readings at the Florentine academies.

137] Cf. Dati's prose tribute (p. 107) and Francini's poem (pp. 105–7).

138 Lydorum] The Lydians who migrated to northern Italy were thought to be the ancestors of the Etruscans and Tuscans.

149] The Colne flows near Horton. Cassivellaunus was a British chieftain whose territory was north of the Thames, and would therefore include Horton.

162] Ptolemy's *Rutupiæ* was identified by Camden with Richborough, in Kent.

163] Pandrasus, a Greek king, gave his daughter Imogen to the Trojan Brutus.

164] Brennus and Belinus, the sons of Dunwallo Molmutius, king of Britain, were thought to have overrun Gaul and (in 390 BC) captured Rome. Arviragus, the son of Cymbeline, submitted to Rome but later rebelled.

165] Constantine was thought to have founded a colony of veteran British soldiers in Armorica (Brittany).

166–8] King Uther Pendragon was enabled through Merlin's magic to visit Igerne in the form of her late husband, Gorlois Duke of Cornwall, and to beget a son, Arthur.

175] The Ouse is probably the river that flows from Northamptonshire to the Wash, rather than the rivers in Yorkshire or Sussex. The *Alaunus* may be the

Aln, in Northumbria, or the united Stour and Avon, in Hampshire.
176 Abra] probably the Humber.
178] The Tamar, between Devon and Cornwall, passes close to ancient mines.
181 pocula] may refer to actual cups or to books.
182 Chalcidicæ] See *Ad Leonoram* III 4n.
185–9] See *PL* V 272–4n. Aurora is the dawn.
201] On Lethe see *Novembris* 132n.; Orcus is Pluto.
210 divino nomine] *Diodotus* means 'God-given.'
213–14] Rev. xiv. 1–4.
215] I Pet. v.4, Rev. ii. 10.
216] Rev. vii. 9–10.
217] Rev. xix. 6–8.
219] The thyrsus was a staff or spear tipped with an ornament like a pine-cone and
wreathed with ivy or vines; it was carried by Bacchus and his votaries.

Ad Joannem Rousium
Jan. 23. 1646
To John Rouse. Librarian of Oxford University

An ode on a lost volume of my Poems, which he asked to be sent to him a second
time that he might place it in the public library with my other books.

Strophe I

Two-part book, cheerful in your single covers,[1] but with a double leaf,[2] shining with
the unlaboured elegance once given you by a youthful hand – industrious, but
hardly that of a poet – wandering, he sported now in the Ausonian[7] shades, now in
the green fields of England unconcerned with the public. Withdrawn, he gave
himself up to his native lute, and then presently with Daunian[10] quill sounded a
foreign strain to his neighbours, and scarcely touched the ground with his foot.

Antistrophe

Little book, who deceitfully carried you away from your brothers, when sent from
the city at the persistent requests of my learned friend you were proceeding upon
your famous journey to the cradle of blue Father Thames, where the clear
fountains of the Aonides[21] are, and the sacred Bacchic dance known to the world as
the Heavens turns through the flight of time, and will be famous for ever?

Strophe 2

But what God or demi-god has compassion for the original native qualities of our
race (if we have atoned sufficiently for our earlier faults, effeminate luxury and
degenerate idleness) and will take away the abomination of civil war,[29] and what
divinity will recall nourishing studies[30] and the banished muses now without a
home[31] in almost the entire land of England?[32] Who, using Apollo's quiver will
pierce the foul birds[33] threatening us with their talons,[34] and drive away the plague
of Phineus far from the river of Pegasus?

Antistrophe

But, little book, although by the bad faith or negligence of my messenger you have
at some time strayed from the company of your brothers, though some cave or
hiding place now possesses you, where perhaps you will be rubbed by the base
callous hand of a stupid peddlar, rejoice in your good fortune. Behold, new hope
shines that you may be able to run away from the depths of Lethe[45] and be borne on
soaring wings to the courts of Jove above.

Strophe 3

For Rouse wishes you to be part of his property, complains that you are missing
from the full number promised him and asks that you come to him, to whose care

are entrusted the famous monuments of men. He wants you to be placed in the sacred inner chambers over which he presides, the faithful keeper of immortal works and the treasurer of riches more excellent than the golden tripods and Delphic offerings[59] entrusted to Ion[56] in the splendid temple of his divine father[58] – Ion, the famous grandson of Erechtheus[57] born of Actæan Creusa.[60]

Antistrophe

Therefore you will go to view the delightful groves of the muses, and you will go again to the divine home of Phœbus where he dwells in the Vale of Oxford, preferring that to Delos[65] and the cleft summit of Parnassus. You will go in honour, since you go away with a distinguished fate, urged by the entreaty of a favouring friend. There you will be read among the great names of authors who were the ancient lights and true glory of the Greek and Latin peoples.

Epode

You then, my labours, whatever this barren genius has brought forth, were not in vain. Now at last, I bid you hope for peaceful rest and, having endured envy, the blessed dwellings which good Hermes and the expert care of Rouse shall give you, where the impudent tongue of the vulgar shall not penetrate, and the faithless crowd of readers will remain far off. But our distant descendants and a wiser age will perhaps, with honest mind, bring fairer judgement to all things. Then, with malice buried, a sane posterity will know, thanks to Rouse, the worth of these poems.

The ode has three strophes, the same number of antistrophes, and ends with an epode. Although all parts do not correspond exactly in the number of lines, nor are the metrical sections fixed, I have divided it thus, however, to facilitate reading and not because of respect for an ancient method of versification.

In other respects this sort of poem should perhaps have been more correctly called monostrophic. The metres are in part related and in part free. The Phaleucian lines twice admit a spondee in the third foot; Catullus readily did thus in the second foot.

The ode was written on 23 January 1647 (1646 Old Style). John Rouse, who was Bodley's Librarian from 1620 until his death in 1652, requested from Milton a copy of his 1645 *Poems* to replace a copy that had gone astray on the journey from London to Oxford.

1–2] Milton's 1645 *Poems* was in two parts, English and Latin, each with a separate pagination and a separate title-page (*Fronde . . . geminâ*).

7 Ausonias] See *Elegia* I 70n.

10] Daunia, a part of Apulia, here represents Italy.

21 Aonidum] See *Elegia* IV 29n.

29–32] Oxford was the headquarters of the Royalists from October 1642 until it fell to Fairfax in June 1646.

33–6] The prophet-king Phineus (see *PL* III 36) was punished for blinding his sons by Zeus, who sent Harpies (see *Comus* 604n.) to steal or foul his food. In ancient versions of the story the Harpies are chased away by two of the Argonauts, but Milton substitutes Apollo, who slew the Python (see *PL* X 529–31n.). The river of Pegasus is the Thames, so called because Pegasus had created Hippocrene (see *PL* VII 4n.) and Aganippe (see *Elegia* IV 29n.).

45 Lethen] See *Novembris* 132n.

56–60] Ion, the progenitor of the Ionians, was the son by Apollo of Creusa, who was the daughter of Erechtheus, king of Athens. Ion guarded the treasures in the temple of Apollo at Delphi; the treasures included the Platæan tripod, which consisted of a golden basin supported by a bronze serpent with three

heads. *Actæâ* here means Attic, so called from Acte, an early name for Attica.
65] Delos (see *PL* V 264–5n.) was the birthplace of Apollo.
Postscript] On the technical terms see the preface to *SA* 47–52n. (where ἀπολελυμένα is *Apolelymenon*). Phaleucian metre consisted of a spondee, a dactyl, and three trochees.

PARADISE LOST

Milton originally conceived of *Paradise Lost* as a tragedy, and four drafts written about 1640 survive in the Trinity MS. Edward Phillips, Milton's nephew, explains in his biography of his uncle that Milton showed him the opening lines of the tragedy many years before he began to compose the epic. The passage which Phillips was shown survives in the epic as *PL* IV 32–41. The composition of the poem was probably begun in 1658, and although it was not published until 1667 it was certainly completed by 1665, possibly two years earlier. The notes that follow do not attempt to list allusions to *Gen*. i–iii, unless Milton alludes to versions other than the A.V.

In Paradisum Amissam

On Paradise Lost, by John Milton, The Greatest Poet.

You who read *Paradise Lost*, the sublime poem of the great Milton, what do you read except the whole poem? That book contains all things, the first beginnings of all things, their destinies and their final ends. The innermost chambers of the great world are thrown open and whatever in the world lies hidden is described: the lands and the stretches of sea, the depths of the heavens, and the sulphurous, flame-vomiting den of Erebus;[8] all that dwell on earth, in the sea, and in dark Tartarus[9] and in the bright kingdom of highest heaven; whatever is confined anywhere by any bounds, and also boundless chaos and boundless God, and more that is boundless, if anything be more without limits, love among men united in Christ. Who that had hoped for this would believe that it would ever be written? And yet the land of Britain reads these things today. O, what leaders in war, what arms, appear! What fearful battles he sings on the war-trumpet! Celestial armies and heaven in conflict! What a battle, fit for the celestial fields! What a Lucifer, bearing ethereal armour, and as he walks, hardly inferior to Michael himself! With what great and deadly anger do they join battle. While the latter fiercely defends the stars the former assaults. While they fling uprooted mountains at each other as darts, rain falls from above with immortal fire. Olympus stands doubtful to which side it will submit, and fears that it may not survive its own battle. But as soon as the standards of the Messiah glisten in the heavens with living chariots and armour worthy of God, the wheels creak horribly and fierce flashes burst forth from savage eyes, the flames threaten and real thunder mixed with flames resounds hoarsely in the heavens. All the boldness and fury of the amazed foe fails, and useless weapons fall from hands that have lost all strength. They flee to their punishments as if Orcus[37] were a refuge and they struggle to hide themselves in the infernal darkness. Yield writers of Rome, yield writers of Greece and those whom fame, recent or ancient, has celebrated. Who reads this poem will think Mæonides[42] sang of frogs, Virgil of gnats.

8 *Erebi*] See *Novembris* 69n.
9 *Tartara*] See *PL* II 69n.
37 *Orcus*] See *PL* II 964n.
42 Mæonidem] Homer. Cf. *PL* III 35.

On Paradise Lost (Marvell)

9] Milton had published *SA* in 1671.

18–22] The lines allude to Dryden, to whom (according to John Aubrey) Milton had granted permission to 'putt his Paradise Lost into a drama in rhymne'.

39–40] Birds of Paradise were popularly believed to have no feet, and therefore to be perpetually in flight.

42 *Tiresias*] See *PL* III 36n.

47 *Bayes*] a popular nickname for Dryden, originating in the satire on Dryden in Buckingham's *The Rehearsal* (1672).

45–54] Rhyme was a much-debated subject at the time. Marvell alludes specifically to Milton's remarks on the subject in his note on 'The Verse' (p. 156).

49 Bushy-points] tassled hose-fasteners.

Book I

1 Fruit] means 'fruit' and 'result'.

4 greater Man] Jesus. See Rom. v. 12, 19.

6 Heav'nly Muse] Urania. See *PL* VII 1n.

7–8] Moses saw the burning bush on Mount Horeb (Exod. iii). There is some confusion in the Pentateuch about the mountain on which Moses received the tablets of the law, for the names Sinai and Horeb seem to be interchangeable. See Exod. xix. 16–25 and Deut. iv. 10–13. The 'chosen Seed' is Israel, whom Moses taught about the creation in Genesis.

10 *Sion* Hill] one of the hills of Jerusalem, and the site of the temple.

11 *Siloa*] a pool near the temple in Jerusalem. See Isa. viii. 6, John ix. 7, 11.

15 *Aonian* Mount] Helicon, home of the muses.

16] An ironic translation of the second line of Ariosto's *Orlando Furioso*: *Cosa non detta in prosa mai, né in rima*'.

21] Gen. i. 2; Luke iii. 22.

34 infernal Serpent] Satan. See Rev. xii. 9.

38–48] a tissue of Biblical phrases (e.g. Isa. xiv. 13–15, Luke x. 18, Rev. xvii. 8, II Pet. ii. 4, Jude 6).

50] Recalls the fall of the Titans, who according to Hesiod fell nine days and nights into Tartarus (*Theogony* 664–735).

57 witnessd] bore witness to.

59 Angels] May be a possessive, in the which case 'kenn' is a noun.

66] Alludes to the inscription over the gate of Hell in Dante's *Inferno* iii. 9, *Lasciate ogni speranza voi ch'entrate* ('Abandon all hope, you who enter here).

72 utter] outer.

81 *Beëlzebub*] 'prince of devils' (Matt. xii. 24), and in the O.T. a Philistine God (See *SA* 1231 and 2 Kings i. 2) whose name means 'Lord of the Flies' in Hebrew.

82 *Satan*] the name means 'adversary', or 'one who plots against another' in Hebrew. See the A.V. marginal note to Job i. 6.

84–5] Isa. xiv. 12, *Æneid* ii. 274–5.

114 Doubted] feared for.

128 Powers] one of the orders of angels; seraphim (l. 129) and cherubim (l. 157) are other orders.

167 fail] err.

187 offend] injure.

197–200] *Briarios* was a Titan, *Typhon*, a Giant; both were sons of Gæa (Mother Earth). The Titans and the Giants (the two races were sometimes confused in antiquity) rebelled against Zeus. A later Christian tradition established the parallel between these rebellions and the rebellion of Satan.

200–208] *Leviathan*, the sea-monster of Job xli, was often thought to be a whale.

The story of the illusory island occurs in *Physiologus* ('The Naturalist'), the moralizing anecdotes of which were translated into the main languages of Europe and the Near East. Many versions of the story exist in mediæval and Renaissance art and literature.

202 Ocean stream] See *Comus* 97n.

208 Invests] covers, envelops.

224 horrid] The primary sense is 'bristling' (with 'pointing spires'), but the word probably carries the secondary sense of 'abominable'. The image ironically echoes Exod. xiv. 21–2.

230–37] The lines conflate Virgil's and Ovid's descriptions of Etna (*Æneid* iii. 570–77, *Metamorphoses* xv. 298–306). In antiquity and in the Renaissance volcanoes and earthquakes were attributed to the periodic escape of winds trapped in the earth. *Pelorus* is the promontory at the north-eastern corner of Sicily, near Etna. 'Sublim'd' is an alchemical term meaning 'vaporized'.

239 *Stygian*] here means 'dark'. Cf. *Comus* l. 132 and *Elegia* IV 95.

254–5] The heresy that heaven and hell are merely states of mind was devised by Amalric of Bena (near Chartres), a scholastic philosopher whose doctrines were condemned in 1204, and probably has its ultimate origins in Stoic doctrine.

263] Cf. Milton's translation of Psalm lxxxiv. 10. The sentiment is virtually proverbial in antiquity and the Renaissance.

266 oblivious Pool] Milton's 'forgetful Lake' (II 74) is an adaptation of the river Lethe of the classical underworld, for the devil's loss of memory is temporary. Cf. the classic version of Lethe in *PL* II 582–6, 604–14.

276 edge] carries the Latin sense of 'front line'.

285 Ethereal temper] tempered by celestial fire.

288–91] The '*Tuscan* artist' (i.e. scientist) is Galileo, whom Milton visited in Fiesole, which overlooks the valley of Arno (*Valdarno*). Cf. III 588–90, V 261–3.

294 Ammiral] flagship.

296 Marle] a kind of soil.

299 Nathless] nevertheless.

303] *Vallombrosa* is a wooded valley in Tuscany (ancient Etruria); Milton probably visited the convent there.

305] The late rising of *Orion* was anciently thought to portend stormy weather.

306–11] The Pharaoh of Exod. xiv was sometimes identified with the mythical king *Busiris*. *Memphis* was the ancient capital of Egypt; *Goshen* was the area east of the Nile where the Israelites lived. The connection between the destruction of Pharaoh's cavalry and Orion may have been suggested by Amos v. 8.

338–43] Moses was the son of *Amram*. See Exod. x. 12–15, and cf. *PL* XII 184–8.

351–5] refers to the barbarian invasions of late antiquity. *Rhene* is the Rhine, *Danaw* the Danube.

363 Books of Life] Rev. iii. 5, xx. 15, xxi. 27; Exod. xxxii. 32–3.

365 new Names] an ironic contrast to Rev. iii. 12, for the new names of the fallen angels are those of the idols of l. 375.

368–71] Rom. i. 23.

372 Religions] religious rites.

376] The Homeric and Virgilian catalogues which Milton is about to imitate begin with appeals to the muse (*Iliad* ii 484, *Æneid*, vii 641).

387 Between the Cherubim] Cf. Milton's translation of Psalm lxxx. 1.

392] *Moloch* means 'king' in Hebrew. See *Nativity* 205–12 and 205n.

396–7] *Rabba*, the royal city of the *Ammonites*, was conquered by David (II Sam. xii. 26–31).

398–9] The Israelites conquered the Ammonites of *Argob* and *Basan*, parts of the kingdom of Og, as far as the border with the Moabites, the stream of *Arnon* (Deut. iii. 1–13).

400–403] I Kings xi. 7. The 'opprobrious Hill' is the Mount of Olives, the 'Hill of scandal' of l. 416, the 'offensive Mountain' of l. 443, and the 'mount of corruption' of II Kings xxiii. 13.

404–5] II Kings xxiii. 10. The Greek word *Gehenna* (Matt. v. 29) derives from the Hebrew phrase which means 'valley of *Hinnom*'.

406] I Kings xi. 7.

407–8] I Chron. v. 8. On *Aroer* see Deut. ii. 36 and Jer. xlviii. 19. Milton's *Nebo* may be the town in Moab, or the mountain from which Moses viewed the promised land; the city was near the *Abarim* mountains, and the mountain was part of the range.

408–11] Isa. xv. 4–5, xvi. 8–9. *Seon* was an Amorite king: see Numbers xxi. 21–30. The '*Asphaltic* Pool' is the Dead Sea, called *Asphaltites* by Josephus because of its deposits of bitumen.

412 *Peor*] See *Nativity* 197n.

412–14] Numbers xxv. 1–9. On the 'woe' see also I Cor. x. 8.

418] On *Josiah* see II Kings xxii–xxiii.

420 Brook] Besor. I Sam. xxx. 9, 10, 21.

422–3] See *Nativity* 197n., 200n.; 'im' is normally a masculine plural inflection, 'oth' a feminine plural inflection.

432–3] I Sam. xv. 29.

438–9] See *Nativity* 200n.

441 *Sidonian*] of Sidon, the Phoenician city.

444 King] Solomon, whose wives 'turned away his heart after other gods' (I Kings xi 1–8).

446–57] See *Nativity* 204n. and Ezek. viii. 14. It is appropriate for *Thammuz* to follow *Ashtoreth* because Adonis (*Thammuz*) was the lover of Astarte-Aphrodite.

457–66] See *Nativity* 199n. 'Grunsel' (460) means 'threshold'.

464–6] The five chief cities of Philistia were *Azotus* (or Asdod), *Gath*, *Ascalon*, *Accaron* (or Ecron) and *Gaza* (or Azza). The forms in parentheses appear in *SA*.

467 *Rimmon*] a Syrian god.

468–71] In II Kings v Elisha tells the Syrian leper Naaman to wash in the Jordan, and Namaan replies (v. 12) 'Are not Abana and Pharpar, rivers of Damascus, better than all the waters of Israel?'

471–6] The king is Ahaz; see II Kings xvi.

478] See *Nativity* 212–13n.

482–4] Exod. xxxii; Psalm cvi. 19. The connection with Egypt is the traditional identification of the golden calf with the Egyptian Apis. On the gold having been 'borrow'd' see Exod. xii. 35.

484–5] The 'Rebel King' is Jereboam, who 'doubl'd that sin' by making two calves of gold, one for *Bethel* and one for *Dan* (I Kings xii. 28–9).

486] Psalm cvi. 19–20.

487–9] Exod. xii. 12–30.

490 *Belial*] The word *Belial* in Hebrew is not a proper name, but an abstraction, and can mean either 'worthlessness' or 'destruction'; it is usually rendered in the Vulgate as a proper name. In II Cor. vi. 15 the word appears as a proper name.

494–6] I Sam. ii. 12–25.

502 flown] This archaic past-participle of 'flow' (not 'fly') literally means 'swollen' or 'in flood'.

503–5] Gen. xix. 4–11; Judges xix. 12–30.

508] *Javan*, the grandson of Noah (Gen. x. 1–5) was thought to be the progenitor of the Ionians.

509–21] Uranus and Gæa ('Heav'n and Earth') were the parents of the twelve *Titans*, two of whom were *Saturn* and *Rhea*, who became the parents of *Jove*. *Jove*, who was born in a cave on Mount *Ida* (in *Crete*), overthrew his father. Jove lived on Mt *Olympus* (on 'middle Air' see *Fair Infant* 16n.), and was venerated at *Dodona* (in northern Greece), and throughout Greece ('Doric land'); his son Apollo revealed the will of the gods at *Delphi*. *Saturn* was eventually banished by Jove, and fled across the Adriatic (*Adria*) to Italy ('*Hesperian* Fields'). Later he fled to France ('*Celtic*' fields) and finally to the 'utmost Iles', the *ultima Thule* of classical antiquity. The story of Titan to which Milton alludes (l. 510) exists only in a late tradition transmitted by Lactantius.

533–4] The word translated as 'scapegoat' in Lev. xvi refers in Hebrew to the goat 'for *Azazel*', *Azazel* being the name of the spirit living in the wilderness to whom the goat was sent. In a cabbalistic tradition with which Milton was familiar the spirit Azazel is represented as an angel who serves in Satan's army as a standard-bearer.

543 Reign] realm.

550 *Dorian* mood] one of the musical modes of ancient Greece, characterized by simplicity and solemnity.

551] The Spartan army went into battle to the music of the flute (whereas the Romans used trumpets).

563 horrid] means both 'bristling' (with spears) and 'abominable'.

571–3] Dan. v. 20.

575 small infantry] Pygmies. On the attack of the pygmies by cranes see *Iliad* iii 3–6. *Infantry* may be a pun.

577 *Phlegra*] the warfare of the Giants and the gods took place on the Phlegræan plains in Macedonia, and on the Phlegræan Fields near Naples.

578] The fates of the Theban princes and the tale of Troy (*Ilium*) were the central material of Greek tragedy and epic.

580–81] *Uther*'s son is King Arthur, some of whose knights were Breton ('*Armoric*').

583–4] *Aspramont*, a mountain in Calabria, was celebrated in romances as the site of one of Charlemagne's victories over the Saracens. *Montalban*, in Languedoc, was the home of Rinaldo, whose story was a popular romance subject; Damascus (*Damasco*) is the scene of a tournament in one of these romances, *Orlando Furioso* (xvii); *Trebisond*, the Byzantine city on the Black Sea, was associated with the romance tradition.

585 *Biserta*] a Tunisian port.

586–7] No extant version of the Charlemagne legend records Charlemagne's death at *Fontarabbia* (Fuenterrabia, in the Pyrenees), though several late versions record the massacre of Roland (Orlando) and his rearguard at Roncesvalles, about forty miles from Fuenterrabia, and the Spanish historian Juan de Mariana placed the massacre at Fuenterrabia.

597 disastrous] foreboding disaster.

603 considerat] considered, deliberate.

609 amerc'd] deprived.

636 different] may mean 'differing' or 'procrastinating'.

678] *Mammon*, the Aramaic word for 'riches', is personified in Matt. vi. 24 and Luke xvi. 13. In later traditions this personification became identified with Plutus, the Greek god of wealth, and with Pluto, the god of the underworld. Burton made him prince of the ninth order of devils (*Anatomy of Melancholy* I ii I 2).

679 erected] exalted.

682] Rev. xxi. 21.

684 vision beatific] the Scholastic term for the 'sight of God' promised in Matt. v. 8. Cf. 'On Time' 18, and *PL* V 613.

684–92] See *Metamorphoses* i 137–42 and cf. *Naturam* 63–5.

694] Alludes to the tower of Babel (cf. *PL* XII 38–62) and the pyramids of Egypt.

718 *Alcairo*] Memphis, the ancient city near modern Cairo.

720 *Belus*] Babylonian Baal.

Serapis] The state god of Ptolemaic Egypt, a combination of Apis and Osiris.

738–46] *Mulciber* (Vulcan), the god of fire and of arts for which fire is needed, was known in Greece as Hephæstus. On *Ausonian* see *Elegia*. I 70n. See *Iliad* i 588–95, and cf. *Elegia* VII 81–2 and *Naturam* 23–4.

756 *Pandæmonium*] Milton's coinage, probably formed from πάν (all) + δαίμον ('demon, evil spirit', especially in New Testament Greek) + ιον, a suffix which here suggests 'place'.

765 *Panim*] pagan.

766 career] a charge or encounter at a tournament.

768–75] A common metaphor in antiquity. See *Iliad* ii 87–90, *Æneid* i 430–36, and especially Virgil's *Georgics* iv 149–227.

769] The sun enters the zodiacal sign of *Taurus* in April.

774 expatiate] to walk about at large.

780–81] Since antiquity the land of the pygmies was thought to be in eastern Asia. See l. 575n.

783–4] See *Æneid* vi 451–4.

795 close recess] secret meeting-place.

conclave] here used to refer to an assembly of cardinals met to elect a pope.

797 Frequent] crowded.

Book II

2 *Ormus*] a trading city on an island at the mouth of the Persian Gulf.

9 success] result.

11–15 Powers, Dominions, Vertues] three of the orders of angels.

28 Thunderer] classical epithet for Jove.

51 sentence] judgement, opinion.

69] Tartarus was the place of the damned in the classical underworld.

73–4] See I 266n.

79 Insulting] means both 'contemptuously abusing' and 'assaulting'.

81] Milton asserts the falseness of the boast by the allusion to *Æneid* vi 126–9.

87 utter] acts as both verb and adjective.

89 exercise] afflict.

97 essential] essence.

104 fatal] means both 'destined' and 'ruinous'.

106 denounc'd] portended.

124 fact] feat of valour or skill.

156 Belike] in all likelihood.

165 What] what about the occasion.

amain] in haste.

170] Isa. xxx. 33.

174] Horace, *Odes* I. ii. 2–3.

180–82] Cf. the punishment of Ajax (*Æneid* i 44–5).

190–91] Cf. Milton's translation of Psalm ii. 4 (ll. 8–9).

218 temper] temperament (the balance of humours).

220 light] means both 'brighter' and 'easier to bear'.

224 For happy] in terms of happiness.

238 publish] announce.

243 Halleluiahs] refers to the heavenly songs of Rev. xix. 1–7, but the origin of the word as transliteration of the Hebrew injunction 'praise Jah' (Jehovah) is relevant here.

245] Ambrosia is the food of the gods.

249–51] The object of 'persue' is 'state'.

256 easie yoke] Matt. xi. 30.

263–7] Exod. xix. 16–20, II Chron. v. 13–vi. 1.

278 sensible] perception through the senses.

297 pollicy] statesmanship. The word was often used pejoratively to refer to political cunning.

302 Front] forehead or face.

306 *Atlantean*] Atlas, one of the Titans, was condemned to carry the heavens on his shoulders as a punishment for his part in the invasion of the heavens.

312 style] ceremonial designation.

324 first and last] Rev. i. 11.

327 Iron Scepter] See Milton's translation of Psalm ii. 9 (1. 20).

336 to] to the limit of.

352] Isa. xiii. 12–13; Heb. vi. 17; *Iliad* i 530; *Æneid* ix 106.

367 punie] means 'born later' (*puis né*), 'inferior in rank' (cf. ll. 349–50, Psalm viii. 5) and 'weak'.

375 Original] progenitor, i.e. Adam.

376 Advise] ponder.

377 sit in darkness] Psalm cvii. 10–11.

387 States] the 'estates' of Parliament.

391 Synod] means 'assembly of clergy' and secondarily, 'conjunction of stars'.

402–4] Isa. vi. 8.

404 tempt] risk of perils of.

406 palpable obscure] See XII 184–8n.

407 uncouth] unknown.

409 abrupt] abyss.

432–3] Cf. *Æneid* vi 126–9, and Dante, *Inferno* xxxiv. 95.

434 convex] the vault of hell.

439 unessential] without being, uncreated (cf. l. 150).

441 abortive] rendering fruitless.

452 Refusing] if I refuse.

457 intend] consider.

461 deceive] beguile.

468 rais'd] inspired with courage.

478 awful] full of awe.

504 anow] enough.

512 Globe] used in the Latin sense of 'a throng of people'.

513 imblazonrie] heraldic devices.

horrent] bristling.

517 Alchymie] brass (i.e. trumpets).

521–69] *Iliad* xxiii 287–897, *Æneid* v 104–603, vi 642–59.

522 Powers] here means 'armies'.

530 *Pythian*] The Pythian games were held at Delphi.

539 *Typhœan*] See I 197–200n. The word 'Typhon' also meant 'whirlwind' (see l. 541).

542–6] Hercules (*Alcides*) mortally wounded the Centaur Nessus, who took his revenge by telling Deianira (Hercules' wife) that she should soak a garment in Nessus' blood in order to revive Hercules' love for her. Hercules, returning from a victory in *Œchalia*, put on the poisoned robe, which corroded his flesh. Distracted with pain, Hercules blamed his attendant *Lichas* (who had brought the robe) and threw him from the top of *Œta*, a mountain in southern Thessaly, into the Eubœan (*Euboic*) sea. See *Metamorphoses* ix 134 ff., and cf. *Procan* 10–12.

552 partial] biased.

564 Apathie] refers to the Stoic ideal of calmness, dispassionateness (ἀπάθεια); cf. *PR* IV 300–309.

575–81] The epithet which Milton applies to each of the four rivers of Hades is a translation of its Greek name.

592–4] According to an ancient tradition which survived into the Renaissance, Lake Serbonis (near the Egyptian coast) had swallowed whole armies. *Damiata*, modern Damietta, is a city at the eastern mouth of the Nile.

595 frore] cold, frosty.

596 Furies] The Roman name for the Erinyes, the avenging goddesses. On harpies see *Comus* 605n.

611 *Medusa*] See *Comus* 446–51n.

614] *Tantalus* was condemned to stand in a pool in Tartarus; the water in the pool receded when he tried to drink. (*Odyssey* xi 582–92).

628] See *Comus* 446–51n., and 516n.; *Æneid* vi 287–9. The *Hydras* are sea-serpents, not the *Hydras* of *Comus* 604.

632 Explores] used in the Latin sense of 'tests'.

639 *Ternate, Tidore*] Two tiny islands of the Moluccas.

641 *Ethiopian*] Indian Ocean.

Cape] Cape of Good Hope.

642 Ply stemming] make headway against the wind.

Pole] South Pole.

647 impal'd] surrounded, fenced in.

648–889] The allegory of Sin and Death is based on James i. 15, and examples of expansions of the allegory exist in patristic, medieval, and Renaissance literature.

652 Voluminous] consisting of many coils.

654 cry] pack.

655] On Cerberus see *Allegro* 1–2n.

660 *Scylla*] See *Comus* 256–8n. According to an ancient Christian tradition Scylla was a symbol of sin.

661 *Trinacrian*] Sicilian.

662 Night-Hag] Hecate, goddess of witchcraft.

665 labouring] suffering eclipse. Cf. *faticosa Luna* (*Sonnet* IV 12).

673] Rev. vi. 2.

677 admir'd] wondered.

692] Rev. xii. 4. Cf. *PL* I 633.

693 Conjur'd] sworn together in a conspiracy. Cf. *conjurata* in *Novembris* 202.

701] I Kings xii. 11.

708–11] Comets were traditionally an ominous sign; see *Æneid* x 272–5. The 'hair' of l. 710 alludes to the Greek phrase for a comet, 'long-haired (κομήτης) star'.

718 mid air] see *Fair Infant* 16n.

752–9] The primary allusion is to the myth of Athena's birth from the head of Zeus, but as that myth was seen in the Renaissance as a pagan counterpart to the generation of God the Son, the passage can also be seen as a parody of that event.

815 lore] lesson.

825 pretences] assertions of claims.

829 unfounded] bottomless.

842 buxom] unresisting.

883 *Erebus*] here refers to hell.

891 hoarie Deep] Job xli. 32.

904] *Barca* and *Cyrene* were cities in Cyrenaica, a Roman province in the northeast of modern Libya.

905] The atoms are enlisted ('levied') to provide weight for ('poise') and thus stabilize the wings.

919 frith] firth.

922 *Bellona*] Roman goddess of war.

927 Vanns] fans, i.e. wings.

933 pennons] used in the Latin sense of 'wings'.

934 fadom] fathom.

937 Instinct] impelled, animated, inflamed.

939] The *Syrtes* were two sandbanks near Tripoli. Acts xxvii. 17 refers to quicksands (from σύρτιν), and in the R.V., Syrtis (from Σύρτιν).

943–7] Griffins were monsters who guarded the gold of Scythia against the one-eyed *Arimaspians*.

959–67] Cf. *Æneid* vi 273–81.

964 *Orcus*, *Ades*] both are names for Pluto (or Hades), the god of the underworld.

988 Anarch] Chaos.

989 incompos'd] wanting in composure.

990] Mark i. 24.

1004 heaven] the earth's sky (in 1006, God's heaven).

1005] Homer's golden chain (*Iliad* viii 18–27), a traditional symbol of the order and harmony of the universe.

1017–18] The *Argo*, with Jason and his Argonauts on board, passed through the Bosporus, narrowly missing the Symplegades ('justling Rocks').

1019–20] See *Comus* 256–58n., and *Odyssey* xii 234–59.

1026] Matt. vii. 13.

1043 holds] remains in.

1048–50] Rev. xxi. 16, 19–21. Cf. *PL* X 381.

Book III

1 first-born] Col. i. 15.

3 God is Light] I John i. 5.

4] I Tim. vi. 16.

6 effluence] emanation.

increate] uncreated.

7 hears't thou rather] a Latinism meaning 'would you prefer to be called'. Cf. *Libenter audis* (*Salsillum* 26) and *æquior audis* (*Damonis* 209).

10 invest] cover, surround.

12–16] The 'void and formless infinite' is Chaos, as is 'middle darkness'; the 'Stygian Pool' is hell, as is 'utter' (i.e. outer) darkness.

17 Orphean] See Allegro 145–50n.

19 heav'nly Muse] Urania. See VII 1–39.

25–6 drop serene, dim suffusion] translations of gutta serena and suffusio nigra, medical terms for diseases of the eye.

26–9] Virgil, Georgics ii 475–89.

30 Sion] here represents the Hebrew poetry of the Old Testament. Cf. PR IV 347.

35 Thamyris] mythical Thracian bard blinded by the Muses (Iliad ii 594–600). Mæonides] Homer.

36 Tiresias] The blind prophet of Thebes, 'whose blindness gave him profound light' (Idea 25). Cf. Elegia VI 68, and Marvell's 'On PL', ll. 43–44 (p. 155). Phineus] See Rousium 33–6n.

38 numbers] 'metrical feet', hence 'lines, verses'.
Bird] nightingale.

39 darkling] in the dark.

60 Sanctities] a metonymy for 'angels'.

61 his sight] the sight of him.

72 sublime] means 'aloft', and refers to Satan's flight.

73 stoop] 'swoop down', a term from falconry.

74 bare outside] see 416–19n.

129 first sort] the rebellious angels.

136 Spirits elect] the good angels. I Tim. v. 21.

139–40] Heb. i. 3.

153–4] Gen. xviii. 25.

156 Adversarie] See I 82n.

168–9] Æneid i 664, Matt. iii. 17, John i. 18.

180–81] Psalm xxxix. 4.

183–5] Matt. xxii. 14.

189] Ezek. xxxvi. 26.

206 Affecting] seeking.

208 sacred] primarily 'dedicated', but also 'accursed'.
devote] doomed.

215] I Pet. iii. 18.

216 charitie] the 'love' of Rom. v. 8 (ἀγάπη, translated into Latin as caritas).

218] Rev. viii. 1.

225] Col. ii. 9.

231 unprevented] unanticipated (i.e. not achieved by prayer). On grace preceding prayer see XI 3n. Contrast Milton's translation of Psalm lxxxviii. 13 (ll. 55–6).

241 wreck] wreak.

247–9] Psalm xvi. 10.

252–3] I Cor. xv. 55–6.

255] Psalm lxviii. 18, Eph. iv. 8. 'Maugre' means 'notwithstanding the power of'.

259] I Cor. xv. 26.

276 complacence] source of pleasure and satisfaction.

287–9] I Cor. xv. 22.

290–91 merit/Imputed] refers to the theological doctrine whereby the sins of mankind are imputed to Christ, and his righteousness or merits are imputed to mankind. See Romans iv. 3–8, and cf. PL XII 294–5, 408–9.

293 transplanted] refers to the theological doctrine whereby God the Father is said to 'plant' or 'engraft' believers in Christ, thus rendering them fit for their eventual union with the body of Christ. Cf. XII 7n.

299 Giving] submitting.

317–18] Matt. xxviii. 18.

320] See Col. i. 16 (where Milton's 'Princedoms' are called 'principalities').

321–2] Phil. ii. 10.

323–4] Matt. xxiv. 30–31.

327–9] 1 Cor. xv. 51–2.

334–5] II Pet. iii. 12–13.

343] John v. 23.

352–61] Amarant ('*Amarantus*' in *Lycidas* 149) is a flower that was an ancient symbol of immortality. In 1 Pet. i. 4 and v. 4 the crown of glory 'that fadeth not away' is said in the Greek to be ἀμαράντινον, i.e. unfading, imperishable (cf. l. 360).

370 exempt] excluded from participation.

375–9] I Tim. vi. 16.

381–2] Isa. vi. 2.

383] Col. i. 15–17; Rev. iii. 14.

416–19] The 'starry Sphear' is the sphere of the fixed stars; the opaque ('opacous') Globe is the created universe; the 'round World' is Earth; the 'first convex' (i.e. first sphere) is the *primum mobile*, the 'bare outside of this World' of l. 74. Cf. ll. 481–3n.

431 *Imaus*] mountain range extending from the Himalayas to the Arctic Ocean.

436 *Hydaspes*] modern Jhelum, in Pakistan.

438 *Sericana*] Cathay, here apparently not distinguished from China (but cf. XI 388, 90).

452 painful] painstaking, laborious.

456 unkindly] contrary to the usual course of nature.

459 some] Ariosto. Milton's Paradise of Fools (ll. 444–97) is loosely modelled on a lunar limbo described in *Orlando Furioso* xxxiv.

461 Translated Saints] 'Translated' is the term used in Heb. xi. 5 for the conveyance of Enoch to heaven without death (Gen. v. 24); Elijah was similarly honoured (II Kings ii. 1–18).

463–5] Gen. vi. 2–4; cf. *PL* V 447–8, XI 621–2.

466–7] Gen. xi. 1–9. *Sennaär* is the LXX and Vulgate form of 'Shinar' (verse 2). Cf. XII 38–62.

469–71] There are conflicting accounts of the death of the philosopher and statesman *Empedocles*; according to one tradition he committed suicide to hide his own mortality.

471–3] *Cleombrotus* was so eager to enjoy the immortality described by Plato in *Phædo* that he drowned himself.

474] In Catholic theology a limbo is provided for those who die in original sin, but are guiltless of personal sin. 'Embryoes and Idiots' were consigned to this *limbus infantum*.

474–5] The satire is directed against four orders of mendicant friars: Augustinian Hermits ('Eremits'), Carmelites (White Friars), Dominicans (Black Friars), and Franciscans (Grey Friars).

477 *Golgotha*] The Hebrew name for Calvary, where Jesus was crucified.

481–3] Medieval Ptolemaic astronomy assumed the existence of ten spheres; seven were planetary spheres, the eighth was the sphere of the fixed stars (the 'starry sphere' of l. 416), the ninth was the 'Crystallin Sphear', and the tenth was the *primum mobile* (see *Fair Infant* 39n.). The 'trepidation' (i.e. libration, oscillation) of the eighth and ninth spheres was held to be responsible for the precession of the equinoxes.

484–5] Matt. xvi. 19. Cf. *Lycidas* 108–31.

492 Dispenses] dispensations.

501 traveld] means both 'experienced in travel' and 'wearied'.

502 degrees] steps.

510–15] Gen. xxviii, John i. 51.

518 Viewless] invisible.

Sea] described in 'The Argument' (p. 200) as 'the waters above the Firmament'.

521 Wafted by Angels] refers to Lazarus (Luke xvi. 22).

522] describes Elijah (2 Kings ii. 11). Cf. *Bombardicam* I, 7–8, *Eliensis* 49–50, *PR* II 16–17. 'Rapt' means 'carried away'.

535–6] The fountain Leddan, the largest source of the Jordan, is on the western side of the city of Dan, which in late Greek is called *Paneas* (modern Baniyas, in Syria). The formula 'from Dan even to Beer-sheba' is common in the O.T., and refers to the extreme northern and southern points of Israel.

558 fleecie Starr] Aries, the Ram.

564 marble] smooth as marble.

568] See *Comus* 392–4n.

575 center] centric (orbit). A centric orbit has the earth or sun at its centre; an eccentric orbit does not. In the Ptolemaic system eccentric orbits were used to account for irregularities in planetary motion. Ll. 574–6 accommodate the possibility of either a Ptolemaic or a Copernican universe.

577 Aloof] apart from.

588–90] Sun-spots had been observed by Galileo in 1610, and by Fabricius in 1611.

596–8] Exod. xxviii. 17–20. 'Chrysolite' appears as the first stone in the fourth row in the LXX and Vulgate.

600–601] The 'philosophers' stone' was supposed by alchemists to possess the property of changing other metals into gold or silver.

602–3 binde . . . *Hermes*] solidify mercury.

604 *Proteus*] Greek sea god who had the power to assume any form he wished, hence an appropriate metaphor for the alchemical transmutation of matter.

605 Limbec] alembic.

606 here] in the sun.

607 *Elixir*] a substance such as the philosophers' stone which would change metals into gold.

608 Potable] drinkable.

609 Arch-chimic] chief of alchemists, so called because its rays were said to penetrate the surface of the earth and produce precious stones. Cf. *PL* V 300–302, VI 477–81.

610 Humor] moisture.

618 still direct] Before the Fall occasioned the 'changes in the Heav'ns' described in *PL* X 668–91, the sun's ecliptic coincided with the earth's equator, and 'direct' beams were therefore a daily occurrence.

623] Rev. xix. 17.

627 Illustrious] lustrous, shining.

634 casts] decides.

643 succinct] modifies 'habit', and means 'not ample or full, close-fitting, scant'.

648 *Uriel*] The name means in Hebrew 'flame (or light) of God', but in the O.T. it is never used of an angel. Milton probably had access to the tradition embodied in the pseudepigraphical Ethiopic Book of Enoch (xx. 2), where Uriel is described as 'the angel who is over the world and Tartarus'.

648–9] Rev. i. 4.

671–2] Echoes Herod's words in Matt. ii. 8.

706–7] Prov. iii. 19.

709 mould] substance.

716 quintessence] the 'fifth essence', the substance of which heavenly bodies were composed, was 'ether'. Cf. *PL* VII 243–4.

730 triform] Diana was thought to be triform for several reasons, among which was conformity to the three phases of the moon. Cf. *Eliensis* 56–7.

742 *Niphates*] mountain on the border of Armenia and Assyria.

Book IV

1–12] On the 'warning voice' which John heard see Rev. xii. 3–12.

11 wreck] wreak, avenge.

17 Engin] The primary meaning is 'cannon', and the secondary 'plot'.

27–8] 'Eden' means 'pleasure, delight' in Hebrew.

31 revolving] deliberating, meditating.

37] John iii. 20.

38–9] Rev. ii. 5.

50 sdeind] disdained.

53 still] continually.

66, 67, 71 thou] Satan addresses himself.

79–80] Heb. xii. 17.

110] Isa. v. 20.

115 pale] pallor.

123 couch't] hidden.

126 *Assyrian* mount] Niphates (III 742).

134 champain] free from woods and enclosures.

149 enameld] beautified with various colours.

153 of] expresses transformation from one condition to another.

162 *Sabean*] of Sabæa, i.e. Sheba, modern Yemen.

166–71] In the apocryphal Tobit, *Asmodeus* (*Asmadai* in *PL* VI 365, and *Asmodai* in *PR* II 151) is the evil spirit who kills Sara's seven husbands, and is exorcised by Tobias ('*Tobits* Son'), who on the advice of the angel Raphael burns the heart and liver of a fish, the smell of which drives the spirit 'into the utmost parts of Egypt, and the angel bound him' (Tobit viii. 3). In the Greek version of Tobit Asmodeus is merely an evil spirit (τὸ πονηρὸν δαιμόνιον), but Milton probably knew that in the Aramaic and Hebrew versions he is 'King of the Shedhim (i.e. demons)'.

176 had perplext] would have entangled.

193 lewd] evil, unprincipled.

211 *Auran*] the Vulgate form for Hauran (Ezek. xlvii. 16, 18), a tract of land east of the Jordan.

212] Seleucus Nicator, Alexander's general, built nine cities called *Seleucia*, one of which, on the Tigris, was called 'the Great' to distinguish it from others of the same name. Cf. *PR* III 291.

214 *Telassar*] II Kings xix. 12; Isa. xxxvii. 12.

219 blooming] causing to flourish.

223 River] Identified as the Tigris in *PL* IX 71–3.

229 Fountain] The Vulgate version of Gen. ii. 6 has a fountain instead of mist; *Sed fons ascendebat e terra*.

239 error] used in the Latin sense of 'wandering'.

242 Knots] alludes to the dying fashion for formal geometrical garden designs.

boon] bountiful.

246 Imbrownd] darkened.

250–51] See *Comus* 392–4n.

255 irriguous] well-watered.

256 without Thorn the Rose] a common patristic inference from Gen. iii. 18.

266 Universal *Pan*] here means universal nature, but cf. *Nativity* 89n.

267 *Graces, Hours*] See *Allegro* 12–16n. and *Comus* 985n.

268–72] Proserpina, daughter of *Ceres*, was carried off by *Dis* (Pluto) while gathering flowers (near *Enna*, according to *Metamorphoses* v 385–95). Proserpina was never allowed to leave the underworld permanently, because she had eaten the pomegranate of Jove, which in the Renaissance was identified with the apple which Eve ate.

272–4] *Daphne* is here a grove near Antioch, beside the river *Orontes*; in antiquity it had an oracle of Apollo (hence 'inspir'd') and a stream named Castalia after the spring on Parnassus. Here the nymph *Daphne*, daughter of the river-god Peneus, was turned into a laurel (see *Comus* 660–1) to protect herself from the ravages of Apollo. Cf. *Elegia* V 13, *Elegia* VII 33, and *PR* II 187.

275–9] *Cham* is the Vulgate name for Ham, the son of Noah, who was commonly identified with *Ammon*, *Libyan Jove* (called *Libyc Hammon* in *Nativity* 203), the Egyptian god. According to Diodorus Siculus (*Library* iii. 67–70) the Lybian King *Ammon* (who was identified with the god Ammon) became the lover of the nymph *Amalthea*, who gave birth to *Bacchus*. Ammon hid his lover and their child on Nysa, an island in the 'River *Triton*' near modern Tunis, in order to protect them from the wrath of his wife *Rhea*.

280–85] The sons ('issue') of Abyssinian ('*Abassin*') kings were raised in seclusion in palaces on 'Mount *Amara*', on the equator ('*Ethiop* Line').

300 Front] forehead.

sublime] means both 'exalted, lofty' and 'raised up'.

301–5] See I Cor. xi. 7–15 (and A.V. marginal note to v. 10). *Hyacinthin* may allude to the hair of Odysseus (*Odyssey* vi 230–31) or to Hyacinth, the boy whom Apollo loved (see *Fair Infant* 23–6n.).

310 coy] modest, shy, quiet.

313 dishonest] unchaste, lewd.

321] The clasping of hands is a traditional symbol of the pledging of faith. Cf. IV 488–9, 689, 739, IX 385–6, 1037, XII 648.

329 *Zephyr*] the west wind.

332 Nectarine] as sweet as nectar, the drink of the gods.

337 purpose] conversation.

341 chase] habitat of wild animals.

344 Ounces] See *Comus* 71n.

Pards] The name was used of both panthers and leopards.

348 Insinuating] penetrating by sinuous windings.

349 breaded] braided.

354 Ocean Iles] The Azores.

361–2] Psalm viii. 5; Heb. ii. 7.

380–81] Matt. x. 8.

404 Purlieu] tract of land on the edge of a forest.

410 him all eare] ambiguous: 'him' may be Adam or Satan, and 'all eare' can apply to Adam or Eve or Satan.

411] The first 'sole' means 'only', the second 'unique, unrivalled'.

443 Head] I Cor. xi. 3.

447 odds] construed as singular in the seventeenth century, and means 'the amount by which one thing exceeds or excels another'.

460–66] Alludes to Ovid's story of Narcissus. See *Comus* 229n.

470 stays] waits for.

478 Platan] plane tree.

486 individual] inseparable. Cf. *Time* 12.

499–501] *Iliad* xiv 346–51; Virgil, *Georgics* ii 325–7.

539 utmost Longitude] the extreme west.

541 with right aspect] directly.

549 *Gabriel*] means 'man of God' or 'strength of God' in Hebrew. *Gabriel* is an archangel, and his traditional function in Christian (and Moslem) thought is to reveal God. In Moslem and Cabbalistic traditions (though not in the Bible) he is a warrior (cf. l. 576). Milton seems to have had access to the tradition embodied in the Book of Enoch (xx. 7) that Gabriel was responsible for Paradise and the Cherubim.

557 thwarts] traverses.

561 by Lot] like the porters of the temple. I Chron. xxvi. 13.

567 Gods latest Image] His first image was the Son (III 63).

describ'd] descried.

568 Gait] journey.

580 vigilance] guard.

592–7] Ptolemaic and Copernican cosmologies are presented as alternatives; hence the 'prime Orb' may be the sun or the first sphere. 'Volubil' means 'capable of rotation on its axis'.

608 Apparent] manifest.

628 manuring] cultivating.

640 seasons] times of day.

642 charm] song.

688 Divide] means both 'divide into watches' and 'execute florid variations' (cf. *Passion* 4n.).

691 Planter] 'God planted a garden' (Gen. ii. 8); God is also a Planter in the sense of the founder of a colony.

699 flourisht] adorned with flowers.

703 Emblem] inlay.

707–8] *Pan*, *Silvanus*, and *Faunus* are often not clearly distinguished from one another, but are commonly mentioned together. Cf. *Comus* 267, *PR* II 190–91.

711 Hymenæan] wedding hymn; Hymen was the god of marriage. Cf. *Elegia* V 105–8 and *PL* XI 590–91.

712 genial] presiding over marriage and generation.

714–19] Prometheus ('fore-thought') and Epimetheus ('after-thought') were the two sons of the Titan *Japhet*. Prometheus 'stole *Joves* authentic [i.e. original] fire', and the gods took their revenge by having *Hermes* (see *Comus* 636n.) present *Pandora* ('all . . . gifts') to Epimetheus ('th'unwiser Son'), who opened Pandora's box of gifts and thus released all life's ills upon the world.

724–5] Psalm lxxiv. 16. 'Pole' means 'sky'.

735 gift of sleep] Psalm cxxvii. 2; *Iliad* ix 712–13, *Æneid* ii 268–9.

744–9] I Tim. iv. 1–3.

751 proprietie] ownership, proprietorship.

756 Charities] love, natural affections.

761] Heb. xiii. 4.

763] Cupid's sharp 'golden shafts' kindled love; his blunt leaden shafts put love to flight (*Metamorphoses* i 468–71).

769–70] Alludes to the ancient *paraklausithuron*, a serenade sung by a lover standing in the cold at his mistress' locked door. 'Starv'd' means both 'benumbed with cold' and 'starved for love'.

773 repaird] replaced.

776–7] Because the earth is smaller than the sun, the earth's shadow is cone-shaped. When the axis of the cone is halfway between the horizon and the zenith ('Half way up Hill'), the time in Paradise is nine o'clock.

778 Ivorie Port] In classical literature false dreams pass through an ivory gate, so it is appropriate that cherubim about to interrupt a false dream do likewise (*Odyssey* xix 592 ff., *Æneid* vi 893 ff).

782 *Uzziel*] means in Hebrew 'my strength is God'. The word is never used as an angel's name in the Bible, but according to a Rabbinical tradition *Uzziel* was one of the seven angels in front of the throne of God.

785] 'Shield' is left, 'Spear' is right in classical military parlance.

788 *Ithuriel*] means in Hebrew 'discovery of God'. The name does not occur in the Bible.

Zephon] means in Hebrew 'searcher'. The name is not used as an angel's name in the Bible.

793 Who] one who.

805] In Renaissance physiology 'spirits' were fluids permeating the blood and chief organs of the body; they were distinguished as animal, natural, and vital. Animal spirits (from *anima*, soul) were seated in the brain, and controlled sensation and voluntary motion.

840 obscure] dark.

869 port] bearing.

879 transgressions] means both 'sins' and (etymologically) 'the action of passing over or beyond (a boundary)'.

896 object] adduce as an objection.

899 durance] imprisonment, constraint.

911 However] howsoever.

926 stood] withstood.

940 mid Air] See *Fair Infant* 16n.

942 gay] brilliantly good (here used ironically).

962 arreed] advise.

965–7] Rev. xx. 1–3.

971] A 'limitarie' is a guard at a boundary. On Gabriel's responsibility for the cherubim see 549n.

976 road of Heav'n] the Milky Way. Cf. VII 577–81.

977–1015] Cf. *Æneid* xii 661–952.

978 mooned horns] crescent formation.

980–85] *Iliad* ii 147–50; Virgil, *Georgics* i 226.

980 ported] held diagonally across and close to the body, so that the blade is opposite the middle of the left shoulder.

981 *Ceres*] corn (*Ceres* is the goddess of agriculture).

983 careful] anxious, full of care.

987 *Teneriff*] mountain on Canary Island of same name.

Atlas] alludes to the Titan (see II. 306n.) and to 'Mount Atlas' (see XI. 402n.).

992 Cope] vault.

997–8] The constellation Libra (the Scales) is between Scorpio and Virgo (here called *Astrea* because in the Golden Age she lived on earth; see *Nativity* 141n.). The 'golden Scales' of Zeus often appear in classical epic (e.g. *Iliad* viii 69–72).

999–1001] a common Old Testament metaphor (e.g. Isa. xl. 12); 'ponders' means both 'weighs' and 'considers' (see I Sam. ii. 3).

1010] Isa. x. 6.

1012] Dan. v. 27.

Book V

1 rosie steps] Imitates the description in Homer and Hesiod of the dawn (Eos, Aurora) as 'rosy-fingered' (ῥοδοδάκτυλος).

2] *Metamorphoses* xiii 621–2.

16] *Zephyrus*, the west wind, 'breathes the Spring' (*L'Allegro* 18) and thus produces flowers, of which *Flora* was the goddess.

17–25] Cf. the aubade in Song of Solomon ii. 10–13. Satan's serenade (38–41) parodies the same passage.

56–7 dewie . . . Ambrosia] *Æneid* i 403–4.

84 savourie] means both 'gratifying to the sense of smell' and 'spiritually delightful or edifying'.

94 sad] gravely, seriously.

117 God] means 'angel', but may also mean 'God'.

124 Then] probably means 'than'.

130–31] Luke vii. 38.

145 Orisons] prayers.

150 numerous] measured, rhythmic.

153–208] This hymn is based on Psalm cxlviii, and on The Song of the Three Holy Children (35–66), a LXX addition to the Book of Daniel. This apocryphal passage later became the Canticle *Benedicite*, which appears in the Book of Common Prayer.

165] Rev. xxii. 13.

166 Fairest of Starrs] Hesperus (IV 605) here re-appears as Phosphorous, or Lucifer.

177 five other wandring Fires] Four of the planets are Mercury, Mars, Jupiter, and Saturn; the fifth may be Venus, or, if 'other' excludes Venus (which appeared in 1. 166) the earth may be intended (cf. VIII 128–9). 'Wandring Fires' approximates the Greek phrase for planets, αστέρες πλανῆται (wandering stars).

181–2] On the cycle of the group of four ('quaternion') elements see ll. 414–26.

215–19] A traditional idea, both in antiquity (e.g. Virgil, *Georgics* i 2, Horace, *Odes* II. xv. 4, IV. v. 30) and the Renaissance. Cf. *Damonis* 65 and *PL* IX 217.

224 *Raphael*] The name means 'God heals' in Hebrew; it does not occur in the canonical scriptures, but the angel Raphael appears in both the apocryphal Book of Tobit and the pseudepigraphical Book of Enoch. On his functions see Tobit xii. 15; on the service rendered to Tobias (ll. 222–3) see IV 166–71n.

249 Ardors] flames; the word may indicate seraphim (cf. fierie Seraphim, II 512; the word 'seraph' derives from the Hebrew verbal root meaning 'to burn') or angels in general (Psalm civ. 4).

261–3] Cf. I 288–91n.

264–5] *Delos* is a tiny island regarded in antiquity as the centre of the *Cyclades*, the islands of the south Ægean. *Samos* is an island off the coast of western Asia Minor.

266–70] Cf. the descent of Mercury in *Æneid* iv 238–58.

270 buxom] unresisting.

272–4] The Phoenix is a mythical bird which every 500 years was consumed by fire in its own nest, whereupon a new phoenix would rise from the ashes and fly to Heliopolis, the city of the sun, to deposit 'his reliques' in the temple. The names Thebes and Heliopolis were used interchangeably in the Renaissance. *Egyptian* distinguishes this city from Boeotian Thebes. Cf. *Damonis* 185–9, *SA* 1699–1707.

277–85] Isa. vi. 2.

285 *Maia*'s son] Mercury. Cf. 266-70n.

293 Cassia, Nard] Exod. xxx. 24; Mark xiv. 3. Cf. *Comus* 990.

297 enormous] deviating from ordinary rule, unusual.

299ff.] The scene in which Adam and Eve entertain Raphæl is modelled on the
scene in Gen. xviii in which Abraham and Sarah receive a theophanic visitation.

300-302] Cf. III 609n.

338 Earth all-bearing Mother] translates the classical Greek title παμμήτωρ γῆ
the classical Latin *Magna Mater* (cf. VII 281n.) and the post-classical *Omni-
parens* (cf. *Naturum* 9-10).

339-41] 'middle shore' includes the Black Sea (indicated by *Pontus*, a district on
the south coast) and the Mediterranean (indicated by the *Punic*, or Carthaginian coast). *Alcinous* was the king of the Phæacians in the mythical island of
Scheria. On the Garden of Alcinous cf. *Elegia* III 43-4, *PL* IX 441, and
Odyssey vii 112-32.

345 moust] unfermented wine.

meathes] mead, here non-alcoholic.

349 unfum'd] not burned for incense.

371] Raphael is an archangel, not a virtue, so the phrase may imitate Homeric
diction and mean 'the virtuous angel'. Cf. VI 355.

378 *Pomona*] Roman goddess of fruit trees, in Renaissance art often portrayed
with a pruning-knife in her hand. Cf. IX 393.

381-2] Alludes to the judgement of Paris (on Mount *Ida*, now Kaz Dag, near
Troy), who chose Venus over Juno and Minerva as the most beautiful goddess.
On Eve as Venus see VIII 46-7n., 60-63n.

385-7] Luke i 28. Cf. X 183n., XI 158-60, XII 379, *PR* II 67-8.

394-5] In a late tradition the Horæ came to represent the four seasons, two of
which are here represented as dancing hand in hand. On the simultaneity of
spring and autumn in Paradise see IV 148.

407-13] Milton's affirmation of the corporeity of angels is clarified by his description of 'first matter' in ll. 473-6. Broadly speaking, Milton's position aligns him
with Platonic, Patristic, and Protestant views, and against the Aristotelian,
Scholastic, and Counter-Reformation position.

433 nice] fastidious, difficult to please.

434-8] 'Seemingly' is almost a technical term, for it refers to the Docetist view
(from δοκεῖν, to seem) that the earthly bodies of spiritual beings (especially
Christ, but also the angels) were apparent rather than real. Milton's view that
Raphael physically ate is resolutely Protestant, for in Tobit, which Catholics
accepted as canonical and Protestants usually rejected from the canon,
Raphael claims that his eating was illusory ('ye did see a vision' Tobit xii. 19).
Milton's use of 'transubstantiate' as a digestive term is consonant with the
anti-Catholic emphasis of the passage.

484] On 'Spirits' and 'animal' spirits see IV 805n. The 'vital Spirits' were seated in
the heart, and sustained life.

501] Isa. i. 19-20.

503 Whose progenie you are] Alludes to Paul's use of the phrase in Acts xvii. 28;
Paul was quoting the phrase from Aratus' astronomical poem *Phænomena*.

557 Worthy of Sacred silence] Horace, *Odes* II. xiii. 29.

566 remorse] sorrow, pity, compassion.

571 dispenst] permitted.

580-82] Aristotle's description of time as the measure of motion (first used by
Milton in *Hobson* II 7) is here used to discredit the Platonic and Aristotelian

notion that time and motion cannot exist in eternity, i.e. without reference to the created world.

583] The 'great Year' or Platonic year was the period (variously reckoned) after which all the heavenly bodies were supposed to return to their original positions.

589 Gonfalons] banners.

601] Col. i. 16.

603–6] See Heb. i. 5, and Milton's translation of Psalm ii. 6–9 (ll. 11–21).

607–8] Isa. xlv. 23; Phil. ii. 9–11.

610 individual] cf. *Time* 12n.

613 blessed vision] cf. I 684n.

614 utter] outer.

618 solemn days] days marked by the celebration of special observances or rites.

645–6] Rev. xxi. 25.

647] Psalm cxxi. 4.

658 former name] According to a medieval tradition Satan's former name was Lucifer. Cf. VII 131–3.

664 *Messiah* King anointed] *Messiah* means 'anointed' in Hebrew.

669 dislodge] a military term meaning 'to leave a place of encampment'.

671 subordinate] presumably Beëlzebub, who is not named in Book V.

673] Alludes to *Iliad* ii. 23; cf. *Novembris* 92, *Æneid* iv 267, 560.

689 North] the traditional home of Satan; cf. Isa. xiv. 13.

697 several] separately.

708–9] Satan imitates ('with lies') Christ as 'Morning Starr'; both identifications are Biblical (Isa. xiv. 12; Rev. xxii. 16). Cf. *PR* I 294.

713] Rev. iv. 5.

734 Light'ning] Cf. Matt. xxviii. 3.

736 in derision] Cf. Milton's translation of Psalm ii. 4 (ll. 8–9).

739 Illustrates] renders illustrious.

750 triple Degrees] In a tradition originating in the scheme of Dionysius the Pseudo-Areopagite, the nine orders of angels were divided into three groups of three.

754 into Longitude] flat.

805 *Abdiel*] The name means in Hebrew 'servant of God'; in the Bible it is used only as a human name.

821 unsucceeded] having no successor, everlasting.

822–5] See Rom. ix. 20 and A.V. marginal note, where 'disputest with God' is listed as an alternative reading.

835–40] Col. i. 16–17.

864–5] Psalm xlv. 4.

872] Ezek. i. 24; Rev. xix. 6.

886–7] Cf. II 327–8 and 327n.

890 wicked Tents] See Num. xvi. 26 and Milton's translation of Psalm lxxxiv. 10 (ll. 37–40).

devoted] consigned to destruction, doomed.

906 retorted] thrown back. In the phrase 'he turned' Milton recapitulates the root-meaning of retort, which is 'to turn or twist'.

907] II Pet. ii. 1.

Book VI

1 Angel] Abdiel.

2–4] *Metamorphoses* ii 112–14. On 'rosie hand' cf. V 1n.

4–7] Hesiod, *Theogony* 736–57.

19 in procinct] prepared, in readiness.

29–30] Matt. xxv. 21, II Tim. iv. 7. On 'Servant of God' cf. V 805n.

33–4] Psalm lxix. 7.

42 Right reason] a theological term, inherited from the Scholastic (and ultimately Stoic) idea of *recta ratio*, which describes the faculty implanted in man which manifests itself both as conscience and as an ability to distinguish truth from falsehood.

44 *Michael*] The archangel *Michael* (Hebrew 'who is like God?') was traditionally regarded as 'Prince of Angels' (l.281), though Protestants often dissented from this tradition. On Michael's role in the war in heaven see Rev. xii. (cf. Dan. xii. 1).

56–60] Cf. *Nativity* 158–9n.

58 reluctant] means both 'struggling, writhing' (cf. X 515) and 'unwilling, averse'.

60 gan] began to.

62 Quadrate] square or rectangle.

69 obvious] lying in the way.

73–76] Gen. ii. 20, *Iliad* ii 459–63, *Æneid* vii 699–701.

78 terrene] earth.

93 hosting] hostile encounter.

108 edge] cf. I 276n.

115 realtie] sincerity, honesty.

120 tri'd] proved by trial.

129 prevention] stopping another person in the execution of his designs.

137–9] Matt. iii. 9.

148 my Sect] the primary meaning is 'those of my party', but the phrase probably glances at the Royalists' derisive use of the word to describe various dissenting groups.

182 lewdly] means both 'foolishly' and 'wickedly'.

209 brayd] made the harsh jarring sound of thunder (not of an animal).

210 madding] frenzied.

216 Battels main] the main bodies of the armies, as distinct from the van (1. 107) or the wings.

225 combustion] commotion, tumult (an exceedingly common meaning in the seventeenth century).

229 numberd such] so numerous.

236 ridges of . . . Warr] probably imitates an Homeric phrase (πολέμοιο γέφυραι), the precise meaning of which is uncertain. Milton *may* have understood the phrase to mean 'the ground which divided two lines of battle'.

259 Intestin War] civil war.

282 Adversarie] See I 82n.

296 parle] discussion between enemies under a truce.

313 aspect] the relative positions of the heavenly bodies. Renaissance astrologers distinguisned five positions, two of which (including 'opposition', l. 314) were deemed 'malign'. Cf. X 658–9.

320 prevention] anticipation.

321] Jer. 1. 25.

326 shar'd] 'cut into parts', as 'cut off'.

329 griding] piercing, wounding; cutting keenly and painfully through.

discontinuous] producing a separation of the tissues of the body; gaping.

332–3] 'Sanguin' means 'blood-red', but also modifies 'humor', and thus refers (in the physiological theory of the 'cardinal humours') to Satan's loss of confidence of success. Sanguine humour is 'Nectarous' because it is produced by the digestion of food and drink, and the angelic drink is nectar (V 633).

346 Reins] kidneys.

355 might of] imitates Homeric diction, and means 'mighty'.

357 King] See I 392n.

359-60] II Kings xix. 22.

365] *Adramelec* was a god of Assyrian origin brought to Samaria from Sepharvaim (II Kings xvii. 31). On *Asmadai* see IV 166-71n.

370 Atheist] impious.

371] *Ariel* means 'lion of God' in Hebrew, and in the O.T. is used as a human name and a name for Jerusalem; in a later tradition he was thought to be an angel or an evil demon. *Arioc* means 'like a Lion' and in the O.T. is used of various kings; in a later tradition he was identified with the spirit of revenge.

372] *Ramiel* means 'thunder of God' in Hebrew, and in the Book of Enoch refers to a fallen angel.

393 Defensive scarce] scarcely capable of defence.

404 unobnoxious] not liable.

410 foughten field] battle-field.

411 prevalent] prevailing, victorious.

429 Of] in.

447 *Nisroc*] The Hebrew name for an Assyrian god (II Kings xix. 37).

471 main] highly important.

485 th' other bore] the touch-hole.

514 Concocted] maturated (i.e. purified) by heating (an alchemical term). adusted] dried up with heat (cf. XII 635).

518 found] cast, mould.

519 incentive] kindling.

520 pernicious] means both 'rapid' (from *pernix*) and 'destructive' (from *perniciosus*).

521 conscious] possessing a guilty knowledge. Cf. Milton's use of *conscia* in *Novembris* 150 and (especially) *Naturam* 65.

535 *Zophiel*] The name means 'spy of God'; it does not occur in the Bible.

541 Sad] grave, serious.

549 took Alarm] took up arms.

553 Training] hauling.

555 At interview] within mutual view.

560 composure] a settled condition of affairs; public tranquillity.

560-67] As Raphael observes (l. 568), the lines contain 'ambiguous words': 'brest' means 'heart' (as the seat of affections) and, as a military term, 'the broad even front of a moving company'; 'overture' means 'opening of negotiations with a view to a settlement', and 'orifice', i.e. the mouths of the cannons (l. 577); 'touch' plays on the technical meaning of 'touch-powder', i.e. the priming powder for the cannons (the same pun occurs in ll. 479, 485, 520, 584); the puns on 'discharge' and 'loud' are obvious.

581 amus'd] put in a muse, absorbed.

587 Emboweld] 'disembowelled', or possibly 'filled the bowels of'.

598 dissipation] scattering, dispersal.

605] means 'in position to fire their second volley'.

611-12] 'Brest' repeats the pun of l. 560, and 'front' introduces a parallel play on the meanings 'the face as expressive of emotion' (here candour) and 'the foremost line of an army'.

613 composition] truce.

625 understand] means both 'comprehend' and 'be supported'.

635] *Æneid* i 150.

646 Amaze] panic.

654 Main] entire, solid.

665 jaculation] hurling.

674 advis'd] advisedly.

679 Assessor] 'one who sits beside', hence sharing his rank and dignity.

681–2] Col. i. 15.

692 Insensibly] imperceptibly.

698 main] entirety, universe.

701 sufferd] allowed.

709 Unction] anointing (cf. III 317, V 605).

734] Psalm cxxxix. 21.

749–59] The imagery is based on Ezek. i. and x. Cf. *Penseroso* 53 and *Passion* 36–40n.

752 instinct] impelled, moved.

761 *Urim*] Exod. xxviii. 30.

763–4] The eagle is the imperial bird of Jove, and the thunderbolt his weapon and the weapon of God in the O.T.

766 bickering] flashing, gleaming.

767] Rev. v. 11.

769–70] Psalm lxviii. 17.

771] Psalm xviii. 10; II Sam. xxii. 11.

773 Illustrious] lustrous, shining.

776] Matt. xxiv. 30.

777 reduc'd] led back.

785 obdur'd] hardened in wickedness.

788] imitates *Æneid* i 11.

789–91, 801] Exod. xiv. 4, 8, 13.

808] a Biblical commonplace (e.g. Deut. xxxii. 35).

815] The concluding doxology of the Lord's Prayer (Matt. vi. 13) was not part of the English liturgy until it was incorporated in the 1662 Book of Common Prayer.

827–32] See 749–59n.

833] II Sam. xxii. 8.

838 Plagues] used in the Greek and Latin sense of 'blows, strokes, wounds'.

845–6] Ezek. x. 9–14. 'Distinct' means 'adorned'.

868 ruining] falling headlong.

874–5] Isa. v. 14.

909 weaker] i.e. weaker vessel (I Pet. iii. 7).

Book VII

1 *Urania*] In early antiquity *Urania* ('heavenly one') was the name of one of the nine muses, and in late Roman times she was identified specifically as the muse of astronomy. In the Renaissance she was transformed by Du Bartas into the muse of Christian poetry.

3 *Olympian* Hill] Mount Olympus, the home of the gods on the border of Macedonia and Thessaly.

4] Pegasus, the winged horse, created with his hoof Hippocrene (literally 'horse-spring'), the Muses' spring on Mount Helicon.

8–12] See Prov. viii. 22–31. Milton's 'play' reflects the Vulgate (*ludens*) rather than the A.V. ('rejoicing') or the LXX (εὐφραινόμην, rejoicing). Cf. the apocryphal Wisdom of Solomon vii–viii.

17–20] *Bellerophon* tried to ride Pegasus to heaven, and was toppled from his mount by Jove, whereupon he fell onto the '*Aleian* field', Homer's 'plain of wandering'. 'Clime' means both 'region' and 'climb'; 'erroneous' refers to both physical and moral wandering.

22 Diurnal Sphear] the firmament, which appears to revolve daily around the earth.

23 rapt above the Pole] carried away in spirit above the celestial pole.

24–8] The lines refer to the 'dangers' of Milton's situation after the Restoration, when those who had served in Cromwell's government became liable to persecution.

32–8] Cf. *Lycidas* 58–63n. *Rhodope* is a mountain range on the border of Thrace and Macedonia.

52 admiration] wonder, astonishment.

59 repeal'd] abandoned.

63 conspicuous] visible.

67 current] flowing.

72 Divine Interpreter] a comparison of Raphael to Mercury, messenger of the gods ('*interpres divum*', *Æneid* iv 378).

83 seemd] seemed fitting, appropriate.

94 Absolv'd] completed.

97] Job xxxvi. 24.

103 unapparent Deep] invisible chaos.

106 watch] stay awake (cf. I 332).

116 inferr] cause to be, render.

131 *Lucifer*] See V 658n.

143 fraud] Milton's occasional use of the word in a passive sense (meaning 'in the state of being defrauded or deceived') may imitate the Latin *fraus*; the usage is unique to Milton. Cf. *PL* IX 643, *PR* I 372.

144] Job vii. 10.

162 inhabit lax] 'Lax' means 'so as to have ample room'. The phrase is a Latinism, and imitates *Habitare laxe et magnifice voluit* (Cicero, *De domo sua* xliv. 115).

182–3] Luke ii. 14.

201] Zech. vi. 1.

204] Ezek. i. 20.

205–9] Psalm xxiv. 7.

217 Omnific] all-creating.

224 fervid] burning. Cf. VI 832.

225] Prov. viii. 27; Dante, *Paradiso* xix. 40–42.

236] 'Vertue' is divine power and influence; 'vital warmth' alludes to the *primus calor* which figures in Renaissance Neoplatonist accounts of the creation.

239] 'Founded' means 'moulded, cast'; 'conglob'd' means 'formed into a ball'.

243–4] See III 716n.

247–9] Milton recapitulates the traditional solution to the problem that light was created on the first day, but the sun, moon and stars on the fourth. On the 'Tabernacle' see Psalm xix. 4.

264 expanse] Cf. A.V. and R.V. marginal notes to Gen. i. 6, and *PL* VII 340.

267, 269 Round, World] the universe.

279–82] Renaissance Neoplatonists assumed the existence of a *primus humor* (cf. 236n.), which was a generative ('genial') moisture.

281 great Mother] in antiquity Cybele was honoured as Magna Mater. Cf. V 338n. and *Arcades* 21n.

283–306] Psalm civ. 6–10.

302 error] the primary (Latinate) sense is 'winding course', but the juxtaposition of the word with 'Serpent' brings out the secondary sense, and thus connects the phrase with the fall.

308 congregated Waters] cf. *congregationesque aquarum*, the Vulgate rendering of Gen. i. 10.

317–19] Cf. the apocryphal II Esdras vi. 44.

322 humble] low-growing.

323 implicit] entangled.

325 gemmd] budded (a Latinism).

366] Venus has 'horns' when near to the conjunction, like the moon (cf. Milton's translation of Psalm cxxxvi. 9, l. 34).

367 tincture] an infusion of a quality.

368 Thir small peculiar] i.e. the small amount of light inherent in them.

373 Longitude] course.

376] Job xxxviii. 31.

382 dividual] divided.

402 Sculls] schools.

406 dropt] speckled.

409 smooth] smooth sea.

412–15] Cf. I 200–208n.

419 kindly] pertaining to nature or birth.

421 summd thir Penns] brought their feathers to full growth. Cf. *PR* I 14.

422 despis'd] looked down upon.

429–30 mutual . . . flight] Birds flying in a 'wedge' were thought to rest their beaks on those in front.

432 floats] undulates.

439 mantling] forming a mantle.

444 other] the peacock.

457 wonns] lives.

466 Ounce] See *Comus* 71n.

467 Libbard] leopard.

471 *Behemoth*] tentatively identified as the elephant in the A.V. marginal note to Job xl. 15.

474 River Horse] translates the Greek 'hippopotamus',

482 Minims of Nature] the smallest forms of animal life.

483 corpulence] bulk.

involv'd] coiled.

484] Isa. xxx. 6.

485 Emmet] ant.

490] Worker bees were thought to be female, and drones male.

504 Frequent] abundantly.

509 Front] face.

511 Magnanimous] An Aristotelian term meaning 'greatsouledness' or 'high-mindedness'; when blended with Christian ideas by scholastic philosophers it came to mean 'fortitude' or 'lofty courage'.

519–20] See the Vulgate rendering of Gen. i. 26. Expositors of this verse usually distinguished between the *Imago Dei*, which was obscured, but not lost at the fall, and the *Similitudo Dei*, which was destroyed by original sin but could be restored by God (traditionally through baptism). For Milton's view, see XI 511–25.

557 Idea] The term is used in the Platonic sense of 'ideal form'.

563 station] an astronomical term which refers to the apparent standing still of a
   planet at its apogee and perigee, here applied to the position of the planets at
   creation.

564 Pomp] triumphal procession.

565–7] Psalm xxiv. 7–9.

577–9] On the Milky Way as a road to the house of Jove see *Metamorphoses* i
   168–71. Cf. *Eliensis* 60–64.

596 Dulcimer] not the stringed instrument, but the *symphonia* of Dan. iii. 5, 15,
   translated in the A.V. as 'dulcimer'.

599–600] Rev. viii. 3–5.

605 Giant Angels] a comparison of Satan and his followers to the giants who in
   classical mythology rebelled against Jove.

619 *Hyaline*] the 'sea of glass like unto crystal' ($\theta\acute{\alpha}\lambda\alpha\sigma\sigma\alpha\ \acute{\upsilon}\alpha\lambda\acute{\iota}\nu\eta$) of Rev. iv. 6,
   xv. 2, and the waters above the firmament of *PL* III 518–19, VII 268–71.

620 immense] immeasurable.

624 nether Ocean] i.e. the ocean of the Earth, as opposed to the waters above the
   firmament.

631–2] Virgil, *Georgics* ii 458–60.

632 persevere] a technical theological term referring to steady continuance in the
   faith and life proper to the attainment of eternal life.

634 *Halleluiahs*] See II 243n.

Book VIII

2 Charming] In Milton's time the word was still strongly felt as a metaphor, and
   meant 'acting upon as with a charm'.

14 solution] explanation, answer.

19 numberd] numerous.

22 officiate] supply.

23 punctual] like a point, minute.

36 sumless] incalculable.

45 visit] examine.

46–7] The response of the fruit and flowers constitutes a comparison of Eve to
   Venus, who was in early antiquity an Italic goddess of vegetation, the guardian
   of gardens.

60–63] Another comparison of Eve to Venus, here as the goddess of love on
   whom the Graces (see *L'Allegro* 12–16n.) attended. Cf. V 381–2. 'Pomp'
   means 'train'.

65 facil] mild, courteous, fluent.

78 wide] wide of the mark, mistaken.

82 To save appearances] a scholastic term (originally Greek) referring to the
   construction of hypotheses which satisfactorily explain the observed facts.

83] See III 575n.

84 Epicycle] In the Ptolemaic system each of the seven planets was supposed to
   revolve in a circle, the centre of which moved along a greater circle concentric
   with the earth; this hypothesis helped to account for irregularities in planetary
   motion.

99 Officious] attentive.

102] Job xxxviii. 5.

126 wandring] See V 177n.

127] Copernicus showed that the stations (see VII 563n.) and retrogressions
   (apparent movements from east to west) of the planets were necessary consequences of the revolution of the planets (including the earth) around the sun.

128–9] The six planets are the moon, Mercury, Venus, Mars, Jupiter, and Saturn. In Ptolemaic astronomy the seventh planet is the sun; in Copernican astronomy, the earth.

130] Two of the motions are the daily rotation of the earth, and its annual revolution around the sun. If Raphael is speaking proleptically of the post-lapsarian universe, the third motion would be the alteration in the plane of the earth's equator which causes its axis to describe a cone in space, a phenomenon to which Copernicus attributed the precession of the seasons (cf. III 481–3n.). If, as seems more likely, he is speaking of the prelapsarian universe, then the third motion would probably be Copernicus' notion of the progressive (but fluctuating) motion of the earth's apse-line.

132] i.e. moving in contrary directions on inclined ecliptic planes.

134 rhomb] the *primum mobile* (see *Fair Infant* 39n.).

141 transpicuous] pervious to vision.

150 Male and Femal] original and reflected.

157 this habitable] imitates ἡ οἰκουμένη (sc. γῆ), the inhabited (world), a term used by the Greeks to designate the Greek world, as opposed to barbarian lands.

158 obvious] open.

164 inoffensive] means both 'unoffending' and (etymologically) 'free from hindrance'.

166] Copernican cosmology assumed an atmosphere which moved with the earth to account for the absence of high winds caused by the rotation of the earth.

167 Solicit] disturb, disquiet.

168] Eccles. xii. 13.

195 fond impertinence] foolish irrelevance.

197 to seek] deficient.

225] Rev. xxii. 8–9.

230 uncouth] strange, unfamiliar.

239 state] dignified observance of ceremony.

242–2] *Æneid* vi 557–9.

256 reeking] steaming.

263 Lapse] flow.

268 went] walked.

281] Acts xvii. 28.

292] Imitates *Iliad* ii 20, where Oneiros, god of dreams, stands at the bedside of Agamemnon.

320 Till and keep] The A.V. makes 'dressing' the garden a pre-lapsarian obligation (Gen. ii. 15) and 'tilling' a postlapsarian obligation (Gen. iii. 23). In the Hebrew, Greek (LXX) and Latin (Vulgate) versions, however, the same word is used in both verses.

330–31 inevitably . . . mortal] a traditional interpretation of Gen. ii. 17, overcoming the difficulty that Adam did not die on the day that he ate the fruit by interpreting death as inevitable mortality. Cf. X 49–52, 210–11.

332 lose] means both 'dissolve, violate' and 'lose'.

337 purpose] discourse.

371 Replenish] fully and abundantly stocked.

379–80] Gen. xviii. 30.

384–9] an extended musical metaphor. 'Intense' means 'taut' (etymologically), and 'remiss' means 'diminished in tension'; the human string is thus higher in pitch than the animal string.

396 converse] associate familiarly, consort.

402 in pleasure] plays on 'pleasure' as the literal meaning of 'Eden' in Hebrew.

406–7] Cf. Horace, *Odes* I. xii. 17–18.

415–20] Aristotle, *Eudemian Ethics* 1244b, 1245b.

421] 'Numbers' carries the Latin sense of 'parts' as well as its modern sense; 'absolute' means 'complete, perfect'.

427–8] Imitates Cicero's famous phrase, *Nunquam minus solus, quam cum solis* ('never less alone than when alone'), *De Republica* I. xvii. 27, *De Officiis* III. i. 1. Cf. *PL* IX 249, *PR* I 301–2.

433 complacence] See III 276n.

435 permissive] acting under permission.

450 other self] translates the Greek ἕτερος αὐτός and the Latin *alter ego*, both of which are used of very intimate friends. Cf. l. 495, and X 128.

453 earthly, Heav'nly] i.e. nature.

462 Abstract] withdrawn.

as in a trance] Milton follows the LXX version of Gen. ii. 21 (ἔκστασιν, the word translated in *Acts* x. 10, xxii. 17 as 'trance'); in the A.V. and Vulgate Adam falls into a 'deep sleep'.

466 cordial spirits] the 'vital Spirits' of V 484; 'cordial' means 'of the heart'.

476 her Air inspir'd] means both 'her manner and appearance inspired' and 'her breath breathed'.

490 aloud] i.e. saying aloud.

502 conscience] inward knowledge, consciousness.

504 obvious] open to influence.

508 Honour] Heb. xiii. 4.

509 obsequious] obedient, dutiful, prompt to serve.

518 Bird] the nightingale.

519 Ev'ning Starr] Hesperus. Cf. XI 588–9.

536 subducting] taking away.

547 absolute] See 421n.

556 Occasionally] incidentally, i.e. on the occasion of Adam's request for a companion.

557 Greatness of mind] magnanimity. See VII 511n.

574 Head] I Cor. xi. 3.

598 genial] see IV 712n.

610–11] *Metamorphoses* vii 20–21.

631 green Cape] Cape Verde.

verdant Iles] the Cape Verde Islands.

632 *Hesperean* sets] i.e. sets in the west.

634–5] I John v. 3.

639 persevering] See VII 632n.

647 whose] him whose.

Book IX

2 familiar] The primary meaning is 'as in a family', but the word also evokes the phrase 'familiar (i.e. guardian) angel'.

5 Venial] permissible, blameless.

14–16] 'The wrauth/Of stern *Achilles*' is the subject announced at the beginning of the *Iliad*; 'his Foe' is Hector.

17] In the *Æneid* Turnus is the suitor of *Lavinia*; he is killed by *Æneas*, who marries *Lavinia* himself.

18–19] In the *Odyssey* '*Neptune*'s ire' is directed against Odysseus ('the *Greek*') who had blinded Neptune's son, the Cyclops Polyphemus; in the *Æneid* Juno's ire is directed against Æneas, '*Cytherea*'s (i.e. Venus') Son', who is so described because Juno's ire was prompted by Paris' judgement in favour of Venus (see V 381–2n.). 'Perplexd' means 'tormented'.

21 Celestial Patroness] Urania. See VII 1n.

34–8] Alludes to the characteristic preoccupations of romance epic. 'Tilting Furniture' is armour; 'Impreses' are emblems or devices, usually with a motto; 'Caparisons' are the armour of horses; 'Bases' are the cloth housings of horses; 'Sewers' are waiters, and 'Seneshals' are stewards.

54 improv'd] increased or augmented (in evil).

56 maugre] in spite of.

63–6] For the first three nights Satan circles the earth at the equator, which before the fall was on the same plane as the ecliptic. For the next four nights he follows the lines of the colures, i.e. the two great circles intersecting rectangularly at the poles, one passing through the equinoctial points of the ecliptic, and the other the solstitial points. It is difficult to understand how Satan could have stayed in continual darkness, for before the fall both poles were in perpetual light (cf. X, 680–87), and even after the fall one is always light.

73 Fountain] See IV 229n.

75 involv'd] enveloped.

76–78] Satan travels northwards past *Pontus* (Pontus Euxinus, the Black Sea), 'the Pool/*Mæotis*' (Palus *Mæotis*, the Sea of Asov), and 'the River *Ob*', which flows into Obskaya Guba and thence into the Arctic Ocean.

81–2] Satan travels westwards past the *Orontes* River, in Turkey and Syria (see IV 272–4n.) to the Pacific Ocean, which is 'barrd' (see Job xxxviii. 8–11) by *Darien* (a district in Panama), and thence to India.

89 Imp] child.

95 Doubt] suspicion.

112 gradual] arranged in grades (cf. V 483).

155–7] Psalms civ. 4, xci. 11, Heb. i. 14.

170 obnoxious] exposed, liable (to an influence).

185 horrid] means both 'shaggy, rough' and 'causing horror'.

186 nocent] means both 'guilty' and 'harmful'.

188 brutal] pertaining to animals.

195–7] Gen. viii. 21.

200 season] i.e. early morning.

217 where to climb] i.e. on the elm. See V 215–19n.

218 Spring] a plantation of young trees.

219 redress] set upright again, direct to the right course.

229 motion'd] offered a plan.

233] Prov. xxxi. 27.

249] Cf. VIII 427–8n.

265 Or] whether.

270 Virgin] innocent, chaste.

292 entire] free from reproach, blameless.

293 diffident] distrustful (cf. VIII 562).

296 asperses] injuriously and falsely bespatters.

310 Access] increase.

320 Less] too little (by analogy to the Latin comparative *minor*).

sincere] pure. The Protestant catch-phrase *fides sincera* derives from the use of the word in I Pet. ii. 2.

328 affronts] means both 'insults' and, as Eve's use of 'front' in l. 330 indicates, 'sets face to face'.

341 no *Eden*] i.e. no pleasure. See IV 27–8n.

352 Reason . . . right] See VI 42n.

353 still erect] unceasingly alert (with a suggestion of 'directed upwards').

367 approve] prove.

371 securer] more overconfident.

385–6] Cf. IV 321n.; 'light' means both 'swift, agile' and 'unsteady, susceptible to slight pressure'.

387] *Oreads* are mountain nymphs, the favourite companions of Diana (*Æneid* i 500), and *Dryads* are nymphs of forests and groves; both are mortal (*Metamorphoses* viii 771). *Delia* is Diana, who is so called after her birthplace, Delos.

393] *Pales* was the Roman goddess of flocks and shepherds; on *Pomona* see V 378n.

395 *Vertumnus*] a Roman deity associated with the changing seasons and the effect of the seasons or vegetation; he assumed a series of disguises, and was thus able to seduce *Pomona* (*Metamorphoses* xiv 623–771).

395–6] See IV 268–72n.

421 hap] fortune, chance.

436 voluble] moving rapidly with an undulating movement.

437 Arborets] little trees, shrubs.

438 hand] handiwork.

440] See *Comus* 995–1110n.

441] See V 339–41n. '*Laertes* Son' is Odysseus.

442–3] Solomon married a daughter of the Pharaoh (I Kings iii. 1); on the garden see Song of Solomon, passim. Solomon is 'Sapient' in Kings and Chronicles, but Milton also exploits the Latin sense of wisdom (*sapientia*) as a kind of taste. (cf. ll. 1017–20).

446 annoy] affect injuriously.

450 tedded] spread out for drying.

453 for] because of.

456 Plat] patch of ground.

472 gratulating] manifesting joy (in meeting Eve).

481 opportune] conveniently exposed.

491 not] if not.

496 indented] having a zigzag course.

503 redundant] in swelling waves.

505–6] *Cadmus*, son of the King of Tyre, went in his old age to *Illyria* (an ancient kingdom which corresponds to modern Albania), where he and his wife Harmonia (*Hermione*) were turned into serpents (*Metamorphoses* iv 563–603).

506–7] *Epidaurus* was the sanctuary of Aesculapius (the god of healing), who turned himself into a serpent to travel to Rome to deal with a plague (*Metamorphoses* xv 622–744). Cf. *Elegia* VII 46.

507–9] *Ammonian Jove* (see IV 275–9n.) assumed the form of a serpent and became the father of Alexander the Great, whose mother was *Olympias*. Cf. *Elegia* IV 25–6n., *PR* III 84.

508–10] The Capitol is the hill in Rome on which stood the Temple of Jupiter (hence *Capitoline*). In antiquity many parallels were drawn between the lives of *Scipio* Africanus and Alexander, and *Scipio* was accordingly said to have been the son of Jupiter Capitolinus, who took the form of a serpent.

510 tract] track, course.

510–14] The initial letters of these lines may be a deliberate acrostic: S-A-T-A-N.

522] The 'Herd disguis'd' are those who had been turned into wolves and lions by Circe. Homer compares them to dogs fawning on their master (*Odyssey* x 212–19).

525 enameld] Cf. IV 149n.

530 Organic] like an organ or instrument.

impulse] the primary meaning is 'application of sudden force', but the word also carries the secondary meaning of 'a suggestion coming from an evil spirit'.

558 demurr] to hesitate about.

579 savourie] Cf. V 84n.

581–3] Serpents were believed to sharpen their sight with fennel, and to suck milk from animals. Fennel was also a common emblem of pride.

605 Middle] i.e. between heaven and earth.

609] Horace, *Odes* I. xii. 18.

612 universal Dame] mistress of the universe.

613 spirited] means both 'lively' and 'possessed by a spirit'.

614 amaz'd] means 'bewildered', but also refers to the agent of bewilderment, the serpent's 'Maze' (l. 499).

624 Bearth] birth.

629 blowing] blooming.

635 Compact] composed.

643 fraud] Cf. VII 143n.

654] Rom. ii. 14.

680 Science] knowledge.

687 To] as well as.

713–14] parodies a common N.T. metaphor (e.g. Eph. iv. 22–4, Col. iii. 1–10).

717 participating] partaking of.

722 they all] i.e. they produce all.

731 import] involve as a consequence.

732 humane] means both 'human' and 'gracious'.

758 In plain] plainly.

771 Author unsuspect] authority not subject to suspicion.

792 eating] i.e. that she was eating. The phrase imitates a Greek construction in which the verb 'to know' is followed by a participle (in the nominative) without repetition of subject.

795 vertuous, precious] most virtuous, most precious; in Greek and Latin the positive can stand for the superlative.

811–13] Job xxii. 13–14, Psalms x. 11, xciv. 7.

815 safe] unlikely to intervene, not at present dangerous.

832–3] Horace, *Odes* III. ix. 24.

837 sciential] infused with knowledge.

838–41] Cf. *Iliad* xxii 437 ff.

845 divine] diviner.

846 measure] i.e. his heartbeat.

854 Apologie] defence (not an expression of regret).

864 tasted] if tasted.

887 distemper] an imbalance of the humours, or (possibly) intoxication (cf. l. 793).

890 Astonied] dazed, dismayed.

Blank] means both 'speechless' and 'pale' (cf. l. 894).

892–3] Cf. Statius, *Thebaid* vii. 148–50.

901 devote] doomed.

928 Fact] evil deed.

947–8] Deut. xxxii. 27; on 'Adversary' see I 82n.

953 Certain] resolved.

976 eminently] According to a scholastic tradition which survived in Reformation theology God was said to possess the excellencies of human character – in this case love – not 'formally', as animals possess them, but 'eminently', i.e. in a higher sense. Eve's use of the word is thus blasphemous.

980 oblige] make subject to a penalty.

984 event] outcome, consequence.

998–9] I Tim. ii. 14.

1003–4] Original Sin is the theological doctrine according to which the sin of Adam was transmitted to all his descendants.

1017–20] Cf. 442–3n. for the play on 'Sapience'. 'Savour' refers to both taste and perception (cf. V 84n.).

1029–33] Cf. *Iliad* iii 442 ff., xiv 292 ff.

1034 toy] caressing.

1037] Cf. IV 321n.

1042–4] Prov. vii., esp. v. 18.

1050 unkindly fumes] unnatural vapours. Cf. V 5.

conscious] Cf. VI 521n.

1059–62] Judges xvi. Samson is a *Danite* because his father Manoah was 'of the family of the Danites' (Judges xiii. 2); on *Dalilah* as a Philistine see *SA* 216n.

1090 them] the 'shapes' of l. 1082.

1094 obnoxious] liable (Cf. *SA* 106).

1103 *Malabar* (modern Kurala) is on the south-west coast of India; *Decan* is the Indian peninsula.

1111 *Amazonian* Targe] i.e. the crescent-shaped shield of the Amazons, a mythical race of warrior women.

1121] Psalm cxxxvii. 1.

1140 approve] prove.

1141 ow] means both 'owe' and own'.

1144] *Iliad* xiv 83.

1155 Head] I Cor. xi. 3.

1175 confidence, secure] both words mean 'overconfident'.

1177 Matter] pretext, occasion.

Book X

10 Complete] fully equipped or endowed (modifies 'mind').

12 still] invariably, always.

19 this] this time.

31 approv'd] confirmed. Cf. Argument, 'approve thir vigilance'.

33] Rev. iv. 5.

40 speed] attain his purpose.

48 rests] remains.

49–52] See VIII 330–31n.

56–7] John v. 22.

70–71] Matt. iii. 17, xii. 18.

77 deriv'd] diverted.

79 Them] justice and mercy.

92 cadence] used in the Latin sense of 'falling, sinking down'.

98 soft windes] The A.V. marginal note to Gen. iii. 8 proposes 'wind' instead of 'cool' and *Vulgate* has *auram* (gentle breeze).

106 obvious] coming in the way (i.e. to meet).

112 apparent] evident.

128 other self] see VIII 450n.

149–50] I Cor. xi. 8–9.

151 real] royal.

156 person] rôle.

157 few] few words.

165 unable] modifies 'Serpent'.

183 *Mary* second *Eve*] a common Patristic idea, often illustrated in the middle ages by the conceit that the Latin form of her name (*Eva*) spelt backwards was the first word (*Ave*) of the angel's address to Mary.

184] Luke x. 18.

185] Eph. ii. 2.

186–7] Col. ii. 14–15.

188] Psalm lxviii. 18, Eph. iv.8.

189–90] Rom. xvi. 20. See the A.V. marginal note, which proposes 'tread' instead of 'bruise', presumably reflecting an uneasiness which Milton may have shared, about the precise meaning of the word translated as 'bruise' in Gen. iii. 15.

210–11] See VIII 330–31n.; 'denounc't' means 'proclaimed in the manner of a warning'.

214] Phil. ii. 7.

215] John xiii. 5.

216] Heb. ii. 13.

217–18 or . . . or] either . . . or.

222] Isa. lxi. 10.

235] II Kings vii. 3.

236 Author] begetter.

260–61 intercourse/Or transmigration] travel between two places, either both ways ('intercourse') or one way ('transmigration').

266 err] mistake.

281 Sagacious] acute in olfactory perception.

288 shoaling] assembling in shoals.

290 *Cronian* Sea] The Arctic Ocean.

291 th' imagind way] the north-east passage.

292 *Petsora*] Pechora, a river in northern Russia.

294 petrific] having the power to petrify.

296 *Delos*] See V 264–5n. *Delos* was created as a floating island by Neptune, and later anchored by Jove to provide a place for Latona to give birth to her twins (see *Sonnet* XII 5–7n.).

297] On *Gorgonian* see *Comus* 446–51n.; 'rigor' means 'stiffness, hardness'.

298 *Asphaltic* slime] *Asphaltic* renders the LXX of Gen. xi. 3 (ἀσφαλτος); 'slime' is the A.V. reading. The Vulgate says *bitumen*, which Milton uses in XII 41.

302 Wall] the 'Orb' of II 1029, and the 'firm . . . Globe' of III 418.

303 fenceless] defenceless.

305 inoffensive] used in the Latin sense of 'free from hindrance, uninterrupted'.

306–11] *Xerxes*, King of Persia, was the son of Darius, who had built his palace in *Susa* (now Shush, in Iran), a city associated by Æschylus and Herodotus with Memnon (on whom see *Penseroso* 18n., *Novembris* 133–5n.). In 480 BC *Xerxes* began his preparations for a punitive invasion of Greece by building a bridge across the *Hellespont* (the modern Dardanelles); when this bridge was swept away by a storm, *Xerxes* ordered the sea to be scourged.

313 Pontifical] Milton plays on the apparent etymology of the word – *pontem* (from *pons*, bridge), *-ficus* (making, from *facere*) – and also utilizes the ordinary

meaning of 'episcopal' or 'popish'.

328–9] The *Centaure* (Sagittarius), *Scorpion*, and *Aries* (the Ram) are respectively the ninth, eighth, and first signs of the zodiac.

347 foot] the end of the slope of the bridge.

348 Pontifice] means both 'bridge' and 'priest, bishop, pope'.

364 consequence] the relation of a result to its cause.

375 foil] defeat, disgrace. The etymological sense of 'that which is trampled under foot' may be relevant in view of Milton's repeated allusions to Gen. iii. 15.

378 doom] judgement, condemnation.

381 Quadrature] square. See II 1048–50n.

382 trie] demonstrate.

386–7] See I 82n.

399–402] Rom. v. 12–21.

409 No detriment] alludes to the charge given when the *decretum ultimum* was passed by the Roman Senate in times of national crisis giving the two consuls dictatorial power: *ne quid respublica detrimenti capiat* ('that the state suffer no harm').

be strong] Deut. xxxi. 7.

412–13] 'Blasted' means 'perniciously breathed upon'; malign planets normally 'blasted', and were not themselves the objects of a blast. Similarly planets 'struck' ('strook'), and were not themselves stricken by malign influence, and eclipses were normally apparent rather than real.

425–6] Cf. V 658n.

432 *Astracan*] Astrakhan, a Tartan khanate on the lower Volga.

433 *Bactrian Sophi*] Bactria (modern Afghanistan) was subject to Persia, and the Bactrian Sophi was the Shah of Persia.

434 Crescent] the emblem of the Turkish sultans.

435 Realm of *Aladule*] Armenia, of which *Aladule* was the last king before the Turkish conquest.

436 *Tauris, Casbeen*] now Tabriz and Kasvin, in Iran; both are former Persian capitals.

444 *Plutonian*] refers to Pluto, god of the underworld.

445 state] canopy.

457 *Divan*] an oriental council of state, especially the Turkish council.

471 unreal] unformed.

475 uncouth] strange, unfamiliar.

477 unoriginal] uncreated.

480 Protesting] appealing to.

506–14] Cf. the transformation of Cadmus (IX 505–6n.), and similar transformations described in Lucan *Pharsalia* ix. 700–733, Dante, *Inferno* xxiv, xxv. 'Supplanted', means 'tripped up'.

515 Reluctant] struggling, writhing.

523 complicated] means both 'complex' and 'turned together'.

524 *Amphisbæna*] The name means 'going both ways' in Greek, and refers to a serpent with a head at each end.

525 *Cerastes*] a horned serpent.

Hydrus] a water-snake (not the *Hydras* of *Comus* 604, nor the *Hydras* of *PL* II 628 and *Sonnet* XVI.7).

Ellops] here refers to a kind of serpent.

526 *Dipsas*] a serpent whose bite caused raging thirst.

526–7] When Perseus was crossing Libya, drops of blood from the head of the *Gorgon* (Medusa) fell on the soil and were changed into snakes, which is why

Libya is full of deadly serpents (*Metamorphoses* iv 617–20).

528 *Ophiusa*] in Greek means 'full of serpents'. In antiquity the name was applied to at least three different islands.

529–31] The *Pythian* Vale is Delphi, where the serpent whom Apollo slew had lived. Cf. *Elegia* VII 31–32. In the Greek of the LXX and the N.T. a *Python* is a possessing spirit (e.g. Acts xvi. 16).

536 Sublime] exalted in feeling, elated.

546 exploding] used in the Latin sense of 'hissing (an actor) off the stage'.

560 *Megæra*] a fury; see II 596n.

562] The Dead Sea ('bituminous Lake') is associated with *Sodom* in the apocryphal II Esdras v. 7. In a popular tradition originating in Josephus the fruit growing on the site of Sodom was said to contain ashes from the fire which destroyed the city. (Gen. xix. 24, Deut. xxxii. 32).

565 gust] gusto.

568 drugd] nauseated.

579 purchase] booty.

581] The name *Ophion* derives from the Greek word for 'serpent', and refers to a Titan, the husband of *Eurynome* (which means 'wide-ruling' in Greek); they ruled *Olympus* (see VII 2n.) until they were overthrown by *Saturn* and Rhea (*Ops*), whose son *Jove* was associated with Mount Dicte, in Crete. *Dictæan* was one of Jove's epithets. Cf. I 509–21n. *Ophion* was traditionally associated with Satan.

587 actual] Actual sin is a technical theological term for a sin which is the outcome of a free personal act of the individual will, and is therefore to be contrasted with original sin (see IX 1003–4n.). On sin 'in body' see 816n.

590 pale Horse] Rev. vi. 8.

601 unhide-bound] having loose skin.

624 conniving] remaining inactive.

633] I Sam. xxv. 29.

638–9] II Pet. iii. 7–13.

641–3] Rev. xix. 6.

643–4] Rev. xv. 3, xvi. 7.

645 extenuate] disparage.

648] Rev. xxi. 2.

656 blanc] white, pale.

657] See V 177n.

659 *Sextile*, *Square*, *Trine*, and *Opposite* are 'aspects' (see VI 313n.) of 60, 90, 120, and 180 degrees respectively.

661 Synod] conjunction, the fifth 'position' (often not called an aspect) of the heavenly bodies. Cf. *PR* IV 385n.

668 Some] Those who advocate the Copernican model, according to which the axis of the earth ('Centric Globe') is tilted.

671 Some] Those who advocate the Ptolemaic model, according to which the plane of the sun's orbit is tilted.

673–8] The sun travels through the signs of the zodiac. Before the fall it is in *Aries*, the first sign (l. 329); it now travels to the second sign, *Taurus* (in which are the Pleiades, 'the Sev'n *Atlantic* Sisters'), the third sign, Gemini ('the *Spartan* Twins'), and the fourth sign, Cancer ('the *Tropic* Crab'). Cancer represents the furthest retreat of the sun (i.e. the summer solstice), after which the sun descends quickly ('thence down amain') to the fifth sign, *Leo* (the Lion), the sixth, Virgo ('the *Virgin*'), the seventh, Libra ('the *Scales*'), and continues on this route through Scorpio and Sagittarius 'as deep as *Capricorn*' (the Goat), the tenth sign (i.e. the winter solstice). This journey brings the seasons to each region ('Clime').

686 *Estotiland*] the name referred vaguely to the coast of modern Labrador, or an island off its coast.

687 *Magellan*] either Argentina or the Straits of Magellan.

688 *Thyestean* Banquet] Thyestes, the son of Pelops, suffered from the curse which weighed on '*Pelops* line' (see *Penseroso* 99n.). His brother Atreus (whose wife Thyestes had seduced) killed one of Thyestes' sons and served him to Thyestes as food. According to Seneca, the sun changed course to avoid seeing the banquet (*Thyestes* 776–8).

693 sideral] from the stars.

696 *Norumbega*] New England and the maritime provinces of Canada.

Samoed] north-eastern Siberia.

697 brazen Dungeon] See *Elegia* IV 5–6n.

699–706] Milton is naming the winds. *Boreas* is north; *Cæcias*, northeast; *Argestes*, northwest; *Thrascias*, north-northwest; *Notus*, south; *Afer*, southwest; *Levant*, the vernacular name for the eastern wind; *Ponent*, a mediæval term for the west wind; *Eurus*, the southeast wind; *Zephir*, the west wind; *Sirocco*, *Libecchio*, Italian names for the southeast and southwest winds.

718] Isa. lvii. 20 may be the ultimate source of this commonplace.

738 own] own curses.

740 light] plays on the meanings 'alight' and 'not heavy'.

743–4] Isa. xlv. 9.

748 equal] used in the Latin sense of 'fair, equitable, just'.

762] Isa. xlv. 10.

792] Adam temporarily advocates the mortalist heresy, according to which both the spiritual and corporeal elements in man die at the same time (and are later resurrected together).

803–4] *Satisfaction* is a technical theological term for the payment of a penalty due to God on account of sin. Protestant theologians inherited Anselm's doctrine that Christ's death was a sufficient vicarious satisfaction for the sins of the world (cf. XII 419).

804–8] Adam appeals to a Scholastic axiom, according to which *omne efficiens agit secundum vires recipientis, non suas* (every cause acts according to the powers of its recipient, not its own powers).

816 incorporate] refers to Paul's doctrine of the 'body of sin' (*corpus peccati*; Rom. vi. 6).

867] According to a patristic tradition which drew on Philo, the Hebrew word for Eve means 'serpent'.

872 pretended] held in front as a covering.

884–8] Eve was traditionally thought to have been formed from a bent (hence morally defective) supernumerary rib. Sinister means 'left' (the original Latin sense) as well as 'corrupt, evil'.

888–95] Cf. Euripides, *Hippolytus* 616–19.

930–31] Psalm li. 4.

959 elsewhere] probably heaven, but possibly 'the place of judgement' (l. 932).

969 event] outcome, consequence.

979 our descent perplex] our descendants torment.

995] Cf. Dante, *Inferno* iv. 42.

996 object] Eve.

1045 Reluctance] resistance, opposition.

1052] John xvi. 21.

1053] Luke i. 42.
1068 shroud] shelter. Cf. *Comus* 147.
1069 diurnal Starr] the sun.
1071 foment] means 'cherish with heat, warm' (cf. IV 669) and also draws on the Latin *fomentum*, which could mean 'kindling-wood'.
1073 attrite] means 'worn or ground down by friction', but inasmuch as the word may be thought to reflect Adam's state of mind, it may carry some of its usual theological sense (originally Scholastic, and later Protestant) of 'having a sorrow for sin which proceeds from a sense of fear rather than (as does contrition, l. 1103) from the love of God'.
1075 Tine] kindle.
1078 supplie] serve as a substitute for.
1090–91] Dante, *Inferno* iv. 25–7 (cf. l. 995n.). 'Frequenting' means 'filling'.

Book XI

2 Mercie-seat] Exod. xxv. 17–22.
3 Prevenient Grace] An ancient technical theological term (*gratia præveniens*) for the kind of grace that precedes the free determination of the will. Cf. III 231n.
3–5] Ezek. xi. 19.
5–7] Rom. viii. 26.
8 port] bearing (cf. IV 869).
10–14] *Deucalion* (the son of Prometheus) and *Pyrrha* built a small boat and so became the sole survivors when Zeus destroyed mankind with a universal flood. When the waters receded the ship landed on Mount Parnassus, and *Deucalion* and *Pyrrha* consulted the Delphic oracle (which was dedicated to *Themis*, i.e. Justitia, before it became Apollo's) about repopulating the earth. (*Metamorphoses* i. 313–437).
15–16 nor . . . frustrate] Alludes to Milton's 'Paradise of Fools' (III 444–97, esp. 487–9).
18, 24] Rev. viii. 3.
33–4] I John ii. 1–2.
35 ingraft] Rom. xi. 16–24. See III 293n.
44] John xvii. 11, 21–3.
59 fondly] foolishly.
65 renovation] renewal of the body at the resurrection.
66] II Pet. iii. 13.
74 *Oreb*] See I 7–8n.
78 *Amarantin*] See III 352–61n.
86 defended] forbidden.
91 motions] stirrings of the soul, inward promptings. Cf. *PR* I 290, *SA* 1382.
93 Self-left] left to itself.
99 *Michael*] See VI 44n.
102 in behalf of] with regard to.
106 denounce] See X 210–11n.
111 excess] Cf. *Circumcision* 24n.
128] See VI 753 ('four Faces each') and VI 749–59n.
129 double *Janus*] Janus, the god of gates and of the course of the year, was described and depicted in late antiquity as *quadrifrons* (four-faced).
131–3] *Argus*, the son of Arestor, was a giant with one hundred eyes, of which only one pair slept at a time. Juno ordered him to guard Io, whom Jove had turned into a heifer. *Hermes* (Mercury) charmed Argus to sleep with his pipe of reeds ('Pastoral Reed') and his sleep-producing wand ('opiate Rod'), and then

slew him. (*Metamorphoses* i 568–779). Cf. *Novembris* 185–6.

135] *Leucothea* (see *Comus* 874n.) was identified by the Romans with *Mater Matuta*, a goddess of dawn.

142] James i. 17.

144 prevalent] powerful.

157–8] I Sam. xv. 32.

158] Cf. V 385–7n.

180] Phil. iv. 11.

185 Bird of *Jove*, stoopt] the eagle, having swooped.

187 Beast] lion.

204] Isa. xvi. 3.

209] Rev. xxi. 11.

213–15] Gen. xxxii. 1–2. *Mahanaim* means 'two camps' in Hebrew (cf. LXX, παρεμβολαί, and Vulgate, *id est*, *Castra*), Milton's 'field Paviliond'.

216–20] II Kings vi. 13–18, 'One man' is Elisha, for the capture of whom 'the *Syrian King*' beseiged *Dothan*.

227 determin] cause to end.

242 *Melibæan*] Melibœa, in Thessaly, was famous in antiquity for its purple dye.

243 *Sarra*] Tyre, which was also famous for its dye.

244] See *Comus* 83n.

247] Cf. VI 250, 320–23.

249 State] stateliness of bearing.

267 Discoverd] revealed.

283 to] compared with.

293 damp] dazed or stupefied condition (i.e. the bound senses of l. 265).

298] Dan. x. 13, and A.V. marginal note.

309 can] knows.

316] Gen. iv. 14.

338 virtual] effective, potent, powerful.

374 obvious] exposed.

377] Ezek. xl. 2.

381–4] Cf. *PR* III 251 ff.

388 *Cambalu*] capital of Cathay, and seat of the Khan.

389 *Samarchand*] Samarkand, in modern Uzbekistan, about 150 miles from the *Oxus* River (now Amu-Darya), was the seat of *Temir* Lang, Marlowe's Tamburlaine.

390] Peking (*Paquin*) was the seat of the Chinese (*Sinæan*) Kings; here China is clearly distinguished from Cathay (l. 388). Contrast III 438n.

391] *Agra*, in Uttar Pradesh (northern India), and *Lahor* (Lahore), in the Punjab (Pakistan), are both former *Mogul* capitals. 'Great *Mogul*' was the usual European designation for the emperor of Delhi, which after 1526 was the capital of a huge Mogul empire.

392 golden *Chersonese*] *Aurea Chersonesus*, so called because of its fabled wealth, was rather vaguely identified with the area east of India, possibly the Malay Peninsula. Cf. *PR* IV 74.

393] *Ecbatan*, now Hamadan, a Median city which was the summer capital of Persian kings.

394] *Hispahan*, now Isfahan, replaced Kazvin (X 436n.) as the Persian capital in the sixteenth century.

395–6] *Bizance* (Byzantium, later Constantinople and now Istanbul) was after 1453 the seat of the Turkish Sultans, who belonged to a tribe that had originally come from Turkestan (*Turchestan*), in central Asia.

397 *Negus*] the Amharic term for the title of the supreme ruler of Abyssinia (now Ethiopia).

398] *Ercoco* (modern Arkiko) is a port on the Red Sea near Massawa.

399] *Mombaza* (Mombasa, in Kenya), *Quiloa* (Kilwa Kisiwani, in Tanzania), and *Melind* (Malindi, in Kenya) were all Moslem colonies on the coast of East Africa.

400] *Sofala*, a port south of the Zambezi (in modern Mozambique), was sometimes identified with *Ophir*, which is mentioned many times in the O.T. as the source of Solomon's gold.

402] The *Niger* River is in modern Guinea and Mali, and the *Atlas* mountains in Morocco.

403 *Almansor*] The mediæval Spanish and Latin name for Mansur, who was Caliph of Cordova from 978–1002.

Fez] part of the Sultanate of Fez and Morocco.

Sus] a province of southern Morocco, once an independent kingdom.

404] *Tremisen*, now Tlemcen, in Algeria, was once an independent sultanate.

407 *Motezume*] Montezuma II, last ruler of the Aztec empire, in Mexico, was defeated by Cortés.

408–9] Cuzco (*Cusco*), the Inca capital (in modern Peru) was the seat of Atahuallpa (*Atabalipa*), who was defeated by Pizarro.

10–11] Manoa, or *El Dorado*, the mythical golden city supposed to be in *Guiana*, had not been plundered by the Spanish, who are here called '*Geryons* Sons'. Geryon was a three-headed monster who ruled Erythea, a mythical island which the Greeks situated somewhere in the west. Geryon, who was eventually slain by Hercules, is associated with Spain by Spenser, *Faerie Queene* V. x. 8–10.

412] Cf. *Iliad* v 127, *Æneid* ii 604–5.

414 *Euphrasie*] the name of a medicinal plant (eyebright), and (etymologically, from εὐφρασία), 'good cheer'.

Rue] the name of a medicinal plant, and (in a common play on the word), 'pity, compassion'. Shakespeare twice calls it 'herb of grace.'

416] Psalm xxxvi. 9.

427–60] For the story of Cain and Abel see Gen. iv.

433 grassie sord] sward, turf.

436 Uncull'd] not chosen or selected.

457 Fact] evil deed.

458–60] Heb. xi. 4.

468–70] The details are those of the classical underworld (see *Metamorphoses* iv 432–45, and the famous description in *Æneid* vi).

486 Moon-struck madness] lunacy, i.e. intermittent insanity caused by the changes of the moon (*luna*).

487 Marasmus] wasting away of the body.

504–6] Adam's response is Stoical (cf. Seneca, *Ad Marciam: De Consolatione* xxii. 3).

511–25] See VII 519–20n.

519 Inductive] inducing, leading on.

531 not too much] Alludes to the ancient aphorism μηδὲν ἄγαν (or *ne quid nimis*), nothing in excess.

535–7] The ultimate source of the comparison is Cicero's essay *De Senectute* 19.

553–4] A classical commonplace (e.g. Horace, *Odes*, I. ix. 9, Martial, *Epigrams* X. xlvii. 13, Seneca, *Epistles* lxv. 18).

560 who] Jubal. Gen. iv. 21.

561 volant] moving rapidly and lightly.

562 Instinct] impelled, animated.

proportions] melodies, harmony.

564 one] Tubal-cain. Gen. iv. 22.

566 casual] accidental (used of unfortunate events).

573 Fusil] formed by melting or casting.

574–627] Gen. vi. 2–4, the substance of which is recapitulated in ll. 621–2; cf. III 463–5, V 447–8.

578–9] According to an ancient tradition (e.g. Josephus, *Antiquities* I. ii. 3) the descendants of Seth discovered astronomy, the study of God's 'works/Not hid'.

588 Ev'ning Star] Hesperus, which is also 'Loves Harbinger' in VIII 519–20.

590–91 invoke/*Hymen*] See IV 711n.

607–8] Psalm lxxxiv. 10. Cain's descendant Jabal 'was the father of such as dwell in tents' (Gen. iv. 20).

609–12] The children of Cain were believed to have invented the arts (Gen. iv. 16–22).

619 appetence] desire, appetite.

620 troule] wag.

621–2] See 574–627n. Milton dissents from the common patristic idea that the 'Sons of God' were fallen angels, and aligns himself with those (such as Augustine) who identified them with the descendants of Seth.

624 traines] deceits, snares.

632–3] In sixteenth- and seventeenth-century popular etymology 'woman' was said to mean 'woe of man'.

638–73] Imitates the scenes depicted on the shields of Achilles (*Iliad* xviii 478–540) and Æneas (*Æneid* viii 626–728).

641 Concourse] hostile encounter.

642 emprise] chivalric prowess.

656 Scale] ladder.

665 one] Enoch (Gen. v. 21–4, Heb. xi. 5, Jude 14–15).

669 Exploded] See X 546n.

670–71] Milton probably had access to the tradition embodied in the pseudepigraphical Ethiopic Book of Enoch (xiv. 8–9) that the translation of Enoch (see III 461n.) was initiated by an invitation extended by the clouds.

688–9] Gen. vi. 4.

700 sev'nth from thee] Jude 14; Gen. v. 3–18.

706] A conflation of the tradition described in 670–71n. with the description of the translation of Elijah (II Kings ii. 11).

707 walk with God] Gen. v. 24.

714–18] Luke xvii. 26–7; 'luxurie' means 'lust'.

717 passing faire] 'Faire' means 'beautiful woman', and 'passing' plays on the senses 'passing by' and 'exceedingly'.

719–53] Gen. vi. 5 – vii. 24; Heb. xi. 7.

719 Reverend Sire] Noah.

723–5] I Pet. iii. 18–21.

734] Insects were added to the Biblical passenger-list by those Renaissance commentators on Genesis who had rejected the traditional belief that insects arose spontaneously from putrefaction and instead believed with Milton that insects were generated in the same way as other animals (cf. IV 704, VII 476).

738–53] Many of the details are drawn from Ovid's account of the universal flood in *Metamorphoses* i 253–347. Cf. *PL* XI 10–14n.

753 bottom] boat.

765–6] Matt. vi. 34.

773–4 neither . . . And] Imitates the Latin construction *'neque . . . et'*.

787–807] Milton's description is designed to embrace the seventeenth century as well as the time of the flood.

821 devote] doomed.

824–7] Gen. vii. 11. 'Cataracts' transliterates the LXX (καταρράκται) or the Vulgate (*cataractæ*); the Greek term probably and the Latin term certainly mean 'flood-gates', which is the A.V. marginal reading. The A.V. 'windows' translates the Hebrew word for 'lattices, windows' (cf. Isa. lx. 8, where the same Hebrew word is used).

833] The 'great River' is probably the Euphrates (Gen. xv. 18), and the 'Gulf' the Persian Gulf.

834 salt] i.e. barren (a common O.T. usage).

835 Orcs] whales, ferocious sea-monsters.

Sea-mews] gulls.

840 hull] drift.

842 North-wind] Gen. viii. 1; *Metamorphoses* i 328.

848–9] Gen. viii. 2.

850–54] Gen. viii. 4–5; *Metamorphoses* i 343–45.

865–701] Gen. ix. 8–17.

866] The three colours (red, yellow, blue) are arranged in bands ('listed').

886–90] Gen. vi. 6–12.

898–901] Gen. viii. 22; II Pet. iii. 6–13.

Book XII

1 baits] used of travellers who stop at an inn.

7 second stock] literally Noah, and typologically Christ, in whom believers were said to be 'engrafted'. Cf. III 293n.

18–21] Deut. xiv. 23–6.

24–37] On Nimrod see Gen. x. 8–10.

36] The popular derivation of Nimrod from *marad*, to rebel, rests on a false etymology.

38–62] On the Tower of Babel see Gen. xi. 1–9 and cf. *PL* III 466–8. Although Nimrod is associated with Babel in Gen. x. 10, the tradition that he built the tower seems to have been initiated by Josephus (*Antiquities* I. iv. 2, vi. 2).

41 bituminous] see X 298n.

gurge] whirlpool.

43 cast] resolve.

53 various] causing difference or dissimilarity.

62 Confusion] See Gen. xi. 9, A.V. marginal note. The Hebrew text contains a play on the words 'confound' (*balal*) and *Babel* (Babylon). Cf. l. 343.

84 right Reason] see VI 42n.

85 dividual] separate, distinct, particular.

101–4] On Ham and Canaan see Gen. ix. 22–27.

111–113] Among the several kinds of election distinguished by Protestant theologians were the general, or national election of the Jews (who are thus called 'peculiar', i.e. specially chosen) and the election of an individual (such as Abraham, or the apostles) to a particular office. Neither of these should be confused with the individual election to salvation (a doctrine related to predestination). Cf. 'Race elect', l. 214.

113–64] On Abraham see Gen. xi. 27 – xxv. 10.

114–15] Joshua xxiv. 2.

117] Gen. ix. 28.

120–30] Gen. xii. 1–3, Gal. iii. 6–18, Acts vii. 2–7, Heb. xi. 8.

130–1] *Haran* is a city of northwestern Mesopotamia (now Turkey). Line 114 suggests that Milton thought *Ur* was east of the Euphrates (cf. Acts vii. 2), so the 'Ford to *Haran*' cannot be across the Euphrates, but must rather be across one of the tributaries coming from the north-east (cf. *PR* III 257).

132 servitude] slaves and servants.

135–7] Gen. xii. 5–6.

139 *Hamath*] a city and ancient kingdom on the Orontes (now Hama, in Syria).

141] Mount *Hermon*, on the border of Lebanon and Syria, was the highest mountain of Palestine. In the Hebrew of the O.T. the Mediterranean is variously called the 'Hinder (i.e. western) Sea' (e.g. Zech. xiv. 8), the 'Great Sea' (e.g. Num. xxxiv. 6), or simply 'The Sea' (e.g. Num. xxxiv. 5).

144–5] Mount *Carmel* is a promontory near Haifa. The belief that the Jordan is 'double-founted' is at least as old as Jerome, who argued that the springs 'Jor' and 'Dan' ran together into a river appropriately called 'Jordan'. In fact the Hebrew word for Jordan is not related to 'Dan'.

146] *Senir* was the Amorite name for Mount Hermon (Deut. iii. 9), which was commonly represented on seventeenth-century maps as a range of hills.

147–8] Gen. xxii. 18.

152] In Gen. xvii. 5 Abram's name is changed to Abraham, and the termination *-raham* is connected with the Hebrew word for multitude to make the name mean 'father of a multitude' (see A.V. marginal note).

153] The son is Isaac, the grandchild Jacob.

155–64] Gen. xxxix-1. The 'younger Son' is Joseph.

164–8] Exod. i. The king is named as Busiris in I 307 (see I 306–11n.).

169–90] Exod. iii–xii.

173 denies] refuses.

179 Murren] murrain, cattle plague.

180 Botches, blaines] boils, blisters.

184–8] Cf. I 338–43. The darkness is palpable in Exod. x. 21, where the Vulgate reading is *palpari queant*.

191] Pharaoh is identified with the crocodile ('River-dragon') in Ezek. xxix. 3.

194–214] Exod. xiv. 5–31.

200–204] Exod. xiii. 21–2.

207 defends] repels.

210 craze] shatter (cf. I 311).

214 Warr] army.

214–20] Exod. xiii. 17–18. On 'Race elect' see 111–13n.

224–6] Exod. xxiv. 1–11; Num. xi. 16–25.

225 Senat] See Acts v. 21; the Greek word which is there translated 'senate' (γερουσία) is sometimes used in the LXX to mean 'Sanhedrin' (συνέδριον), which is the word translated as 'council' in the same passage. It therefore seems likely that Milton saw this 'Senat' as the beginning of the Sanhedrin.

227–30] Exod. xix. 16–20.

232–4] Heb. viii. 3–5.

235–8] Exod. xx. 18–20.

238–44] Deut. xviii. 15–19; Acts iii. 22, vii. 37.

245–56] Exod. xxv, xxvi, xxxvii; Heb. ix.

256–8] Exod. xl. 34–8.

263–7] Joshua x. 12–13. *Israel* is Jacob (Gen. xxxii. 28).

276–7 see/His day] John viii. 56.

285–306] A characteristically Protestant statement of the relation of the Mosaic law of the O.T. covenant to the 'better Cov'nant' of 'righteousness . . . by Faith imputed'. The doctrine is broadly based on the epistles to the Romans, Hebrews, and Galatians.

288 pravitie] depravity.

294–5] See III 290–91n.

307–9] Deut. xxxiv.

310] *Jesus* is the Greek form of the Hebrew *Joshua*, who is so called in the LXX and N.T. (e.g. Heb. iv. 8).

321–4] On the promise which David ('second') received see II Sam. vii. 16.

325–7] A common O.T. prophecy (e.g. Psalm lxxxix. 36–7), applied to Jesus in the N.T. (e.g. Luke i. 32).

330] a characteristic theme of Messianic prophecies (e.g. Dan. vii. 14, Luke i. 33).

332–4] On the Temple of Solomon ('next Son') see I Kings v.–ix. 9, II Chronicles ii.–v.

343] See XII 62n.

344–7] Refers to the Babylonian Captivity. Under Nebuchadnezzar Jews were deported to Babylon in 597 and 586 BC (II Kings xxiv. 14–16; xxv. 11); they were allowed to return after the Persian King Cyrus captured Babylon in 538 BC (Ezra ii). On the estimate of 'sev'ntie years' see Jer. xxv. 12.

348–50] Ezra, Neh. i–vi. The kings are Cyrus, Artaxerxes, and Darius.

353–8] See the apocryphal II Macc. iii–vi. 'They' (l. 356) are the Hasmonæan dynasty, one of whom, Aristobulus I, seized civil power and became the first person to assume the title 'King of the Jews'. The 'stranger' is Antipater, who in 47 BC was appointed by Julius Caesar procurator of Judæa, as a reward for services rendered against Pompey; he was the father of Herod the Great.

360–69] Matt. ii, Luke ii.

369–71] Psalm ii. 8; *Æneid* i 278–9, 287.

373 Surcharg'd] overwhelmed.

379–82] Luke i. 28–35.

383 capital] means both 'on the head' and 'fatal'.

393 recure] heal, make whole.

394–5] I John iii. 8.

396 want] lack.

401 appaid] satisfied.

403–4] Rom. xiii. 10.

408–9] See III 290–91n.

410 legal] in accordance with the Mosaic law.

415–17] Col. ii. 14.

419 satisfaction] See X 803–4n.

441–5] Milton concurred with many Protestants in asserting that baptism was for 'them who shall believe' rather than for infants, in asserting that one should be baptized in running ('profluent') water rather than in a font, and in emphasizing that baptism is a 'sign' in the face of counter-Reformation assertions (at the Council of Trent) that it is more than a sign. 'Washing' renders the original meaning (in Greek) of the word 'baptize'.

453–5] Rev. xx. 1–3, Eph. ii. 2.

460 judge . . . dead] this common N.T. phrase (e.g. II Tim. iv. 1) also occurs in the Apostles' Creed.

469–78] Adam recapitulates the traditional parodox of the 'fortunate fall' (*felix culpa*) and the traditional assertion that man's salvation is 'more wonderful' than God's act of creation.

478] Rom. v. 20.

486 Comforter] The Holy Spirit (John xv. 26).

488–9] Gal. v. 6, Hebrews viii. 10.

491–2] Eph. vi. 11–17.

493] Psalm lvi. 11.

497–502] Acts ii.

505 race well run] a N.T. metaphor (e.g. Hebrews xii. 1).

508] Cf. Acts xx. 29, *Sonnet* XVII 14, *Lycidas* 113–31.

511–14] a characteristically Protestant assertion of the right of the believer to interpret Scripture guided solely by the Holy Spirit without reference to any authority or tradition.

525–6] II Cor. iii. 17.

527] I Cor. iii. 17.

532–3] John iv. 23–4.

539] Rom. viii. 22.

540] See Acts iii. 19, where the phrase καιροὶ ἀναψύξεως, translated quite correctly as 'times of refreshing' in the A.V., could also be translated 'times of respiration' (i.e. respite).

545–6] Matt. xxiv. 30.

565] Psalm cxlv. 9.

566] Rom. xii. 21.

567–8] I Cor. i. 27.

581–7] II Pet. i. 5–7, I Cor. xiii, *PL* III 216n.

588–9 top/Of Speculation] The primary meaning is 'place which affords an extensive view', and the secondary sense is 'limit of theological speculation'.

591–2 expect/Thir motion] await their order to move.

593 remove] departure.

602] Gen. v. 5.

630 marish] marsh.

634–6] According to an ancient tradition the 'flaming sword' of Gen. iii. 24 was the heat of the tropics (hence '*Libyan*'). On 'adust' see VI 514n.

640 subjected] subjacent, situated at a lower level.

648] Cf. IV 321n.

PARADISE REGAIN'D

The poem was written between 1665 and 1670, but the precise period of composition is not known. In the notes which follow I do not attempt to list allusions to the two Biblical accounts of the temptation in Matthew iv. 1–11 and Luke iv. 1–13.

Book I

1–2] Cf. *Æneid* i 1–4.

2–4] Rom. v. 19.

7] Isa. li. 3.

8 Eremite] used in the Greek sense of 'desert-dweller' (ἐρημίτης).

14] See *PL* VII 421n.

18–32] See Matt. iii, Mark i. 2–11, Luke iii. 1–22, John i. 6–34.

19] Isa. lviii. 1.

33 Adversary] Satan. See *PL* I 82n.

33–4] Job i. 7.

39 mid-air] See *Fair Infant* 16n.

42 Consistory] means 'council', and is here used with ironic reference to the

ecclesiastical sense of an assembly of cardinals convoked by the Pope and, in the Anglican church, a bishop's court.

44–5] Eph. ii. 2.

48 as] i.e. as reckoned according to.

51 facil] easily led.

53 attending when] awaiting (me) until.

53–5] Gen. iii. 15.

62 infring'd] shattered, broken.

73 Pretends] professes.

74] I John iii. 3.

87 obtains] used in the Latin sense of 'holds'.

97 coucht] means both 'hidden' and 'expressed in words'.

112 main] highly important.

113 Dictator] In the seventeenth century the word was used with reference to the institution of the dictatorship in early Republican Rome, when a 'dictator' was a magistrate invested with absolute but temporary power in times of military (and later domestic) crisis.

117 gods] According to a patristic tradition (embodied in *PL* I 356–522) the fallen angels became pagan gods.

128 frequence] assembly.

129–40] *Gabriel* (on whom see *PL* IV 549n.) here appears as the angel of the annunciation. See Luke i. 26–55.

147–9] Job i–ii. Cf. I 368–70, 424–6, III 64–8, 95. The comparison of Jesus to Job may be traced to Gregory's *Moralia in Job*.

157–8] Cf. *Æneid* xi 156–7.

161] I Cor. i. 27.

171 hand] i.e. the hand which plays a musical instrument.

176] John x. 15.

182 Vigils] prayers sung at a nocturnal service.

184 *Bethabara*] John i. 28.

204–5] John xviii. 37.

206–7] Cf. *Æneid* ix 311.

207–8] Cf. Milton's translation of Psalm i. 2 (l. 5).

209–14] Luke ii. 46–50. The 'Feast' is Passover. 'Admir'd' means 'marvelled at'.

238–54] Matt. i–ii, Luke i–ii.

255–8] Luke ii. 25–38.

259 revolv'd] searched through, studied.

266–7] Isa. liii. 6.

270–89] See 18–32n.

279 hardly won] with difficulty persuaded.

281 eternal doors] Psalm xxiv. 7 (*portæ æternales* Vulgate).

286–7] Gal. iv. 4.

290 motion] See *PL* XI 91n.

294 Morning Star] Rev. xxii. 16.

296 horrid] bristling.

301–2] See *PL* VIII 427–8n.

310–13] Mark i. 13. The docility of the animals derives from various O.T. prophecies (e.g. Isa. xi. 6–9). One of the eight Hebrew words used for 'serpent' in the Old Testament is *saraph*, 'fiery serpent' (e.g. Num. xxi. 6–8). 'Worm' is used in a general sense: in Micah vii. 17, on which l. 312 is based, the A.V. marginal note to 'worms' is 'creeping things'.

334 Fame . . . out] i.e. news (Latin *fama*, report) also reaches us.

339 stubs] stumps.

349–50] Christ's answer (Matt. iv. 4, Luke iv. 4) is a quotation from Deut. viii. 3.

351–2] Exod. xxiv. 18, xxxiv. 28, Deut. ix. 9.

353–4] I Kings xix. 8.

363 unconniving] refers to God's eye, which never closes (cf. Latin *inconivus*).

371–6] I Kings xxii. 20–38; II Chron. xviii. 19–34. The identification of this 'lying spirit' with Satan is suggested in the cross-reference to Job i. 6 in the A.V. marginal note to II Chronicles xviii. 20. On 'fraud' see *PL* VII 143n.

393–6] According to a patristic tradition fallen angels were responsible for the oracular pronouncements of classical antiquity.

414 emptied] See *Circumcision* 20n.

428] I Kings xxii. 6.

447 President] presiding.

454 retrench] cut short.

456] Cf. *Nativity* 173; Micah v. 12.

462] John xvi. 13.

477 quit] discharged.

486–90] Satan assumes with scholastic and counter-Reformation theologians that the sacraments confer grace *ex opere operato*, through the act performed, regardless of the subjective attitude of the minister (or the recipient).

500 sullen] of a dark and dull colour.

Book II

1–7] John i. 35–41. *Messiah* is the Hebrew term which was translated into the Greek of the LXX and the New Testament as χριστός, Christ. Both words mean 'the anointed one'.

15] Exod. xxxii. 1.

16–17] Elijah is called 'the Tishbite' in I Kings xvii. 1; the precise meaning of the term is not known, but see 312–14n. On his second coming see Mal. iv. 5. See *PL* III 522n.

18–19] II Kings ii. 15–17.

20–24] On *Bethabara* see John i. 28; on Jericho as 'City of Palms' see Deut. xxxiv. 3. On *Ænon* and *Salem* see John iii. 23; *Salem* is 'Old' in deference to a patristic tradition which identified the 'Salim' of John the Baptist with the *Salem* of Melchizedek (Gen. xiv. 18, Heb. vii. 1–2). *Machærus* was a fortress overlooking the Dead Sea from the east; John the Baptist was imprisoned and executed there. *Genezaret* is the name of the Sea of Galilee in I Macc. xi. 67, Luke v. 1., and in Josephus. *Perea* is the name given by Josephus to the district described in Rabbinical literature and the N.T. as 'beyond Jordan' (e.g. Matt. xix. 1).

34] John i. 14.

36] Acts i. 6.

40 rapt] carried away.

44] Psalm ii. 2.

50 Anointed] See 1–7n.

67–8] Cf. *PL* V 385–7n.

87–91] Luke ii. 34–5; cf. I 255–8.

92 Exaltation] Miriam, the Hebrew form of Mary, is of uncertain etymology, but was sometimes believed to mean 'exaltation'.

96–9] Luke ii. 42–51.

103–4] Luke ii. 19.

115 preface] used in the etymological sense of 'something said before', with reference to I 483–5.

116 vacant] unoccupied.

117] See *Fair Infant* 16n.

120 blank] disconcerted, resourceless.

130 frequence] assembly.

131 tasted] experienced, examined.

139 amplitude of mind] magnanimity; see *PL* VII 511n.

147 old Serpent] Rev. xii. 9, xx. 2.

150 *Belial*] Cf. *PL* I 490–505, II 109–17, and I 490n.

151 *Asmodai*] See *PL* IV 166–71n.

152 Incubus] an evil spirit that had sexual intercourse with women while they slept.

169–71] I Kings xi. 1–8.

178–81] Gen. vi. 1–4. Cf. *PL* III 463–5, V 447–8, XI 574–627.

186–8] *Calisto*, one of the 'Nymphs of *Diana*'s train' (l. 355), was the mother by Zeus of Arcas (see *Comus* 340n.); *Clymene*, an oceanid, was the mother by Helius of Phæthon; on *Daphne* see *PL* IV 272–4n.; on *Semele* see *Elegia* V 91n.; *Antiopa* was the mother by Zeus of Amphion and Zethus; *Amymone* was the mother by Poseidon of Nauphius; *Syrinx* was pursued by Pan and changed into a reed.

191 haunts] habits.

196–8] The '*Pellean* Conqueror' is Alexander the Great (born at Pella, in Macedonia), who in 333 BC (at the age of twenty-three) captured and treated honourably the wife and daughters of Darius.

199–200] In 210 BC Scipio Africanus, aged twenty-four, restored a beautiful Spanish captive to her lover after the fall of New Carthage.

205–6] Matt. xii. 42.

214–15] *Iliad* xiv 214 ff.

222–3] Alludes to Ovid's remark about the peacock (*Ars Amatoria* i. 627–8).

236–7] Matt. xii. 45.

259] John iv. 34.

266–9] I Kings xvii. 3–7; 'ravenous' is a pun.

270–76] I Kings xix. 3–8.

278] Dan. i. 8–19.

302 officious] Satan uses the word in the sense 'eager to serve or please' (cf. Latin *officiosus*), but by the seventeenth century the word had also come to mean 'unduly forward in proferring services'.

308–10] Gen. xxi. 9–21. Ismael is here called by the name of his eldest son *Nebaioth* (Gen. xxv. 13).

310–12] Exod. xvi. 35.

312–14] I Kings xix. 3–8. *Thebez* is Milton's conjectural identification of the place signified by the word 'Tishbite' (l. 16).

327–8 nor . . . unclean] a falsehood. See 345n.

328–9 or . . . Idols] Acts xv. 29, I Cor. viii. 4–13, x. 25–31.

329 those . . . refuse] Dan. i. 8.

344 Gris-amber] ambergris, a morbid secretion in the intestines of the sperm-whale, used in cookery to impart a sweet odour to food.

345 shell] The Mosaic dietary laws forbid as 'an abomination' all fish without fins or scales (Lev. xi. 9–12).

347] *Pontus*, i.e. Pontus Euxinus, the Black Sea, was famous in antiquity for its fish; *Lucrine* Bay, a salt-water lagoon in Campania, was famous in antiquity for its shellfish.

353] On *Ganymed* and *Hylas* see *Elegia* VII 21–4n.

355 *Naiades*] river and fountain nymphs.

356] '*Amalthea*'s horn' is the Greek phrase (κέρας Ἀμαλθείας) equivalent to the Latin *cornu copiæ*, the horn of plenty. Milton seems to allude specifically to the horn of Achelous, which the naiades filled with fruit and flowers (*Metamorphoses* ix 87–8).

357] See *Comus* 392–4n.

360] *Logres* is the area of England east of the Severn and south of the Humber. *Lyones* is a mythical country (associated with Arthur), once located between Land's End and the Scilly Isles, and now covered by the sea.

361] In Malory both *Lancelot* and *Pelleas* have amorous adventures. *Pellenore* may be an allusion to Pellenore's son Percivale, whose experience of a banquet and sexual temptation bears some resemblance to that of Milton's Christ (*Morte d'Arthur* xiv. 9).

365 *Flora*] Roman goddess of flowers.

368 What doubts] Why hesitates.

370 Defends] forbids.

384] Psalm lxxviii. 19.

401 fet] fetched.

403 Harpies] See *Comus* 604n.

414] Matt. xiii. 55.

423–5] See *PL* XII 353–8n.

429] Hag. ii. 8.

439] On *Gideon* see Judges vi–viii; on *Jephtha* see Judges xi–xii; on David, 'the Shepherd lad', see Psalm lxxviii. 70–71, Ezek. xxxiv. 23–4.

441–2] Luke i. 32–3.

446] Lucius Quinctius Cincinnatus was a farmer who in 458 BC was appointed dictator and defeated the Aequi. Gaius Fabricius Luscinus, consul in 282 and 278 BC, was famous for his poverty, austerity, and incorruptibility. Manius Curius Dentatus was a Roman plebeian hero, famous for his humble birth, incorruptibility, and frugality. Marcus Atilius Regulus, a hero of the first Punic War (255 BC), was according to legend tortured to death in Carthage (see Horace, *Odes* III. v).

453 toil] trap, snare.

458 for that] because.

466–7] Prov. xvi. 32.

481–3] Seneca, *Thyestes* 529. Milton may have in mind the abdications of Diocletian (in AD 305), the Emperor Charles V (1555), and Christina of Sweden (1654). On 'magnanimous' see *PL* VII 511n.

Book III

13–15] The precise meaning of *Urim* and *Thummim* is not known. The vocalization of the words indicates that Massoretic scholars connected *Urim* with light, and *Thummim* with perfection, or innocence. The plural form is probably not intended to indicate plurality (as the R.V. marginal note to Exod. xxviii. 30 would have it) but is rather an intensive plural. *Urim* and *Thummim* are associated with the breastplate of Aaron in Exod. xxviii. 30 and Lev. viii. 8. They are most clearly oracular in the LXX text of I Sam. xiv. 41–42, part of which may be translated 'And Saul said, If the guilt be in me or in Jonathan my son, give Urim, O Lord God of Israel; but if you say it is in my people Israel, give Thummim'.

22 Affecting] seeking.

27 erected] exalted.

31–4] Jesus was 'about thirty' at his baptism (Luke iii. 23). Philip of Macedon's son was Alexander the Great, who in 334 BC (aged twenty-two) crossed the Hellespont and 'won *Asia*', and in 330 assumed the throne of the empire which *Cyrus* had founded.

34–5] *Scipio* was sent to Spain as proconsul in 210 BC, aged twenty-four, and eight years later defeated the Carthaginians in the battle of Zama, thus ending the Second Punic War.

35–6] Pompey defeated Mithridates VI, King of Pontus, in 66 BC, (when he was forty) and in 61 BC returned to Italy to celebrate the most magnificent triumph which Rome had ever witnessed. Pompey had been granted a triumph in 81 BC (though he was merely an *eques*, and not legally qualified for one) and another in 71 BC. Even if Satan is referring to this earliest triumph, he certainly misrepresents Pompey's age during the Mithridatic War.

39–42] According to Plutarch, in 68 BC Caesar (aged thirty) read the history of Alexander's campaigns, and wept because Alexander, at his age, was the king of so many people, whereas Caesar had yet to achieve a brilliant success (*Life of Caesar* xi. 3).

62 divulges] publicly proclaims.

64–8] Cf. I 147–9n.

81 titl'd Gods] The title *divus* was accorded to deceased Roman emperors, and from the time of Domitian emperors were regarded as gods during their lifetime. Antiochus II of Syria had assumed the title ὁ θεός (a god). Cf. Acts ii. 22, where the voice of Herod Agrippa I is said to be that of a god.

82 Benefactors] The title εὐεργέτης (benefactor) was conferred on various persons by the Greeks, and was enjoyed by two of the Macedonian kings of Egypt, Ptolemy III and Ptolemy VIII. Cf. Luke xxii. 25, which refers to the title.

Deliverers] The title Σωτήρ (deliverer, saviour) was anciently used of deities, and in Hellenistic times it was used of kings to imply deification. The most famous holder of the title was probably Ptolemy I. In the LXX the word is used of various warriors, and of God; in the N.T. it is often applied to Christ.

84] The 'Son of *Jove*' is Alexander (see *PL* IX 507–9n.); the son of *Mars* is Romulus, first king of Rome and (after his translation to heaven) the god Quirinus.

91–2] II Pet. i. 6.

96–9] According to an ancient tradition the teaching and death of Socrates foreshadowed that of Christ.

101–2] See 34–5n.

106–7] John v. 31–32, vii. 18, viii. 50.

119 Barbarous] non-Hellenic.

138 recreant] false, apostate.

146 not] nothing.

153] Luke i. 32.

154] The gospels are silent about the ancestry of Mary, but according to a patristic tradition she was descended from David.

157–60] In AD 6 *Judæa* was annexed to the province of Syria, and was thereafter ruled by procurators. *Tiberius* was Roman emperor from AD 14–37. From AD 26–36 the procurator of *Judæa* was Pontius Pilate; Josephus and Philo both testify to the intemperance of his rule (*Antiquities* xviii. 3, *Jewish War* ii. 8 ff.; *Legatio ad Gaium* xxxviii).

160–63] In 169 BC Antiochus IV had pillaged the temple, and had forced the Jews to offer swine on the altar; he later rededicated the temple to Olympian Zeus, thus precipitating the Maccabean revolt. In 63 BC Pompey had entered the

Holy of Holies with several of his officers. When Pontius Pilate had arrived in Judæa in AD 26 he had offended the Jews by bringing images of the emperor into Jerusalem.

165–70] The revolt led by Mattathias and his son Judas Maccabeus began in *Modin*, the location of which has not been established with certainty. See I Macc. ii–ix.

173 Occasion] opportunity, the forelock of which was proverbial.

175] Psalm lxix. 9, John ii. 17.

182–3] Eccles. iii. 1.

187] Acts i.7.

194–6] A classical commonplace, a version of which occurs in Matt. xx. 26–7.

221–2] Isa. xxv. 4–5.

234] Luke ii. 41.

242 he] Saul; I Sam. ix–x. 1.

247 inform] train.

249 Mysteries] In Milton's time the word 'mystery' retained the senses of two different Latin roots, and meant both 'skill, occupation' (from *ministerium*) and 'secret' (from *mysterium*).

255–6] The 'two rivers' are the Euphrates and the Tigris. The Greek word Tigris was known in antiquity to derive from the Persian word *tigra*, 'an arrow', hence Milton's 'straight'.

257 Champain] Mesopotamia.

271 Araxes] now Aras, a river which rises in eastern Turkey, and forms the Soviet-Iranian border as it flows to the Caspian.

274 drouth] desert.

275–9] *Ninus* was the legendary eponymous founder of Nineveh, the Assyrian capital on the Tigris. On the 'several days journey' requisite to walk around it see Jonah iii. 3. Shalmaneser (or Salmanasar in II Esdras xiii. 40), King of Assyria from 727–2 BC, made Hoshea of Samaria 'his servant' (II Kings xvii. 3), and later beseiged Samaria, and 'carried Israel away into Assyria' (II Kings xvii. 4–6).

280–84] See *PL* XII 344–7n.; 'wonder of all tongues' refers to such wonders as the temple of Bel and the hanging gardens, but also glances at the confusion of tongues (*PL* XII 38–62).

284–9] *Persepolis* was the summer capital of Persia, and *Susa* (see *PL* X 306–11n.) the winter residence of the kings on the banks of the *Choaspes*, which according to an ancient tradition was 'the drink of none but Kings'. *Bactra* (now Balkh, in Afganistan) was the capital of the Persian province of Bactria (cf. *PL* X 433n.). On *Ecbatana* see *PL* XI 393n. *Hecatompylos* ('Hundred-gated') was a royal residence of Parthian kings; its location is not known.

290–92] *Emathian* refers to the Macedonian successors of Alexander, the Seleucids. On *Selucia* see *PL* IV 212n. *Nisibis* is modern Nusaybin, in Turkey. *Artaxata* was the ancient capital of Armenia. *Teredon* was an ancient Babylonian city near the confluence of the Tigris and Euphrates. *Tesiphon*, or *Ctesiphon* (l. 300), on the Tigris near Selucia, was the winter capital of Parthia.

294–7] The *Parthian* Empire was founded by *Arsaces* in 247 BC in the Selucid satrapy of Parthia, south of the Caspian Sea. The Seleucid capital was *Antioch*.

298–336] Milton's account of a war between the Scythians (an ancient tribe of south Russia) and the Parthians does not refer to any specific historical event.

302 Sogdiana] an ancient province of the Achæmenian Empire, and the north-

eastern limit of Alexander's empire. At the time of Christ it was not a Parthian province, but was occupied by the Scythians.

306] Many classical authors testify to the fact that Parthian horsemen often shot their arrows backwards while in real or pretended flight. Cf. *Elegia* VII 36.

316–21] *Arachosia*, called White India by the Parthians, was their easternmost province; it occupied an area that straddles modern Afganistan and Pakistan. *Candaor* (now Kendahar, in Afganistan) was the frontier city of the Parthian empire. *Margiana* was a province centred on the ancient town of Merv (now Mary, Turkman SSR). *Hyrcania* was a province south-east of the Caspian Sea. *Iberia* (modern Georgia) was a vassal state rather than a province, as were *Atropatia* (now Azerbaijan SSR) and *Adiabene* (the ancient Assyria). Ancient *Media* was divided into four provinces by the Parthians. *Susiana* (modern Ilam, in south-west Iran) was a rebellious vassal state. *Balsara* (modern Basra) was not founded until AD 636; it was built on the joint stream that unites the Tigris and the Euphrates, and at the time of Christ the site was probably part of the Persian Gulf. Christ has viewed the Parthian Empire in a huge semi-circle from east to north to west.

328 Cuirassiers] horse soldiers wearing cuirasses, i.e. body armour consisting of a breastplate and a backplate.

329 endors] used in the etymological sense of 'carrying on the back'.

337–43] In Boiardo's *Orlando Innamorato* I. x–xiv, *Agrican*, the Tartar king, besieges with 2,200,000 men *Albracca*, the city of *Gallaphrone*, king of Cathay, in order to win the latter's daughter, the fair *Angelica*. At the beginning of the poem Angelica had won the heart of the *douzepers* (the twelve 'Peers of Charlemane'), including Orlando, and of the pagan (*Paynim*) knights. 'Prowest' means 'most gallant'.

353] David's struggle ('endevor') for the throne is described in I Sam. xvi–II Sam. v.

358 opposite] opposed.

359] The hostility of the Jews to the Samaritans was proverbial (John iv. 9, viii. 48).

361–2] Although the peace between Rome and Parthia established by Augustus lasted until AD 58, the Romans had periodically prepared for war during the time of Christ, and enmity between Rome and Parthia had previously been well established by the invasions of Sulla, Pompey, Crassus, and Antony.

364–8] 'Of late' is an exaggeration, and the captivity of *Antigonus* is a fabrication. *Antigonus*, the last member of the cadet branch of the Hasmonæan dynasty (see *PL* XII 353–8n.), supported the Parthian invasion of Judæa in 40 BC and was made king. He then mutilated his uncle *Hyrcanus* II (whom Caesar had appointed ethnarch) to render him ineligible for priestly office, and gave him to the Parthians as a prisoner. Herod fled to Rome, where he was appointed King of Judæa, and three years later re-captured Jerusalem, and deposed and crucified Antigonus. 'Maugre' means 'in spite of'.

373–8] David ruled all twelve tribes. After the death of Solomon in 933 BC the tribes of Judah and Benjamin attached themselves to Rehoboam, and the other ten tribes, including the 'two of Joseph' (Manasseh and Ephraim), followed Jeroboam, and in 721 BC were carried away to Assyria, and placed 'in Halah and in Habor . . . and in the cities of the Medes' (II Kings xviii. 11).

384] See I Kings iv. 21, where 'the river' is the Euphrates.

396–7] John vii. 6.

409–12] I Chron. xxi. 1–14.

414–19] The 'captive Tribes' are the ten tribes in Assyria. Jereboam erected calves of gold at Bethel and Dan in imitation of the gods of Egypt (I Kings xii.

28; cf. *PL* I 482–5 and notes). On *Baäl* and *Ashtaroth* see *Nativity* 197–200 and notes, and cf. *PL* I 421–3.

425] Rom. ii. 25.

431–2] Jer. v. 19.

436 *Assyrian* flood] Euphrates; see Isa. xi. 15–16.

438] Exod. xiv. 21–2, Joshua iii. 14–17.

Book IV

1 Perplext] distressed.

success] result.

15–17] *Iliad* ii 469–71, xvi 641–3, xvii 570–72. Cf. *Novembris* 178–9.

18–20] *Iliad* xv 618–21, *Æneid* vii 586–90.

27–33] The long and narrow plain of Lazio (Latium) lies south-west of the Apennines ('a ridge of hills'), which protect it from the north wind (*Septentrion*). The river is the Tiber, and the 'Imperial City' Rome.

40 Parallax] difference of the apparent position of an object caused by an actual change of position of the point of observation.

47 Capitol] one of the 'sev'n small Hills'.

49] The '*Tarpeian* rock' is the steep cliff that surrounds much of the Capitoline hill. The citadel (*arx*) was on the northern summit of the hill, and the Temple of Jupiter on the southern summit.

50–54] The *Palatine* is another of Rome's seven hills. Milton's description of the 'Imperial Palace' (presumably the Domus Tiberiana, on the west corner of the hill) is speculative: its location makes terraces possible, but Roman buildings did not have turrets and spires.

59 hand] handiwork.

63] Under Tiberius the election of the 'Pretors' (who then numbered about 14) was transferred to the Senate, who appointed them as civil magistrates. They sometimes acted as provincial governors. Under the emperors a proconsul was the governor of a senatorial province.

65] Lictors were officers attending upon magistrates; they carried bundles of rods (*fasces*) before the magistrates as an emblem of their power.

66] There were ten cohorts in a legion, and a legion under the Empire numbered about six thousand men. 'Turmes' were troops of about thirty horsemen.

68–9] The chief Roman road to south Italy was the Via Appia, which ended at Brindisi. The Via Æmelia ran from Rimini to Piacenza.

69–79] *Syene* (modern Aswan, in Egypt) was the southernmost limit of the Roman Empire. The Island of *Meroe* is the region bounded on three sides by the Nile, the Atbara, and the Blue Nile; as it lies between the Tropic of Cancer and the Equator, shadows fall to the south in summer and the north in winter. *Bocchus* was the king of ancient Mauretania (modern Morocco and coastal Algeria, not modern Mauritania) at the time of the Jugurthine War (111–106 BC); the 'Black-moor Sea' is the portion of the Mediterranean off the coast of Mauretania. On 'golden *Chersoness*' see *PL* XI 392n. The *Taprobane* described by ancient writers was identified in Milton's time with either Ceylon or Sumatra. *Gallia* (Gaul) encompassed modern France and Belgium, and parts of Holland, Germany, and Switzerland. *Gades* was the Latin name for Cadiz. As Britain had not yet been conquered in the reign of Tiberius, 'the *Brittish* West' is probably Brittany, which was part of the imperial province of Lugudunensis. The *Scythians* were a south Russian tribe who by the time of Tiberius had been displaced by the *Sarmatians*, a related tribe. Until Dacia was invaded in AD 101, the Danube (*Danubius*) was the north-east frontier of the empire. The *Tauric* Pool is the Sea of Azov, on the shores of which was the Bosporan Kingdom, the ruler of which had been given his royal title by Tiberius.

90–97] The emperor is Tiberius (42 BC–AD 37), whose sons – Drusus, Germanius (an adopted son), and an infant – were all dead by AD 23. He returned to Capri (*Capreæ*) in AD 26. His 'wicked Favourite' was Sejanus, who after being denounced by Tiberius was executed in AD 31. Stories of Tiberius' vice on Capri (recounted by Seutonius and Tacitus) lack serious evidence. He was indeed hated by the Romans, who welcomed the news of his death.

103–4] Luke iv. 6.

115] *Citron* is the wood of the highly-prized citrus tree; *Atlantic* means 'from the Atlas mountains'.

117–18] Wines from these three Italian districts (all south of Rome) and two Greek islands were all mentioned by Roman writers.

119] Ancient writers describe 'Myrrhine cups' and bowls (*murrina vasa*), but the identity and provenance of myrrha were (and are) disputed.

136 Peeling] plundering.

142 Scene] stage performance, play.

147–8] Dan. iv. 10–12.

149–50] Dan. ii. 31–5.

151] Luke i. 33.

157 nice] fastidious, difficult to please.

201 Tetrarchs] Rulers of fourth parts (like Herod Antipas and his brother Philip, Luke iii. 1).

203] II Cor. iv. 4.

215–20] Luke ii. 41–50. On '*Moses* Chair', from which the law was expounded, see Exod. xviii. 13–16 and Matt. xxiii. 2.

226 *Pentateuch*] the first five books of the O.T.

228 To admiration] admirably.

235 evinc't] overcome.

236 specular] cf. *PL* XII 588–9n.

240] Athens and Sparta had been described in antiquity as the eyes of Greece; here 'eye' means 'the seat of intelligence or light'.

244–6] Plato established his school in the Academy, a wooded park in a suburb of Athens. Nearby was Colonus, which according to its most famous demesman, Sophocles, was the home of many nightingales (*Oedipus at Colonus* 671).

247–50] *Hymettus* is a range of hills south-east of Athens; Hymettus honey was famed for its pale colour and sweet flavour. Bees were said to have fed the infant Plato with honey. Plato's *Phædrus* is set beside the *Ilissus*, a small river which rises in Hymettus.

250–53] Alexander's tutor was Aristotle, who founded his school, the *Lyceum*, in a park north-east of Athens (not 'within the walls'). The *Stoa Poikile* ('painted *Stoa*'), was a covered colonnade on the north side of the Athenian market-place; Zeno and his followers taught in this stoa, and so were called Stoics.

257] The lyric poems of Sappho and Alcæus are written in the Æolian dialect (Lesbos, where both were born, belonged to the Æolians), and are here called 'charms' in imitation of Latin *carmen* (song). Pindar wrote in the *Dorian* dialect.

259] *Melesigenes* is an Homeric epithet commonly used in the ancient lives of Homer; it affirms that he was born near the river Meles (near Smyrna, modern Izmir); 'thence' refers to 'Blind', for according to an ancient popular etymology Homer (ὅμηρος) was the Cumean word for 'blind'.

260] *Greek Anthology* ix. 455.

262] *Iambic* refers to the metre of the dialogue in Greek tragedy (iambic trimeter acatalectic); the *Chorus* is written in various metres. Cf. Milton's preface to *SA*.

264] probably refers specifically to the style of Euripides, which was said by Quintilian (X. i. 68) to be *sententiis densus* (dense with philosophical aphorisms).

270] The naval dockyard at Pireus was called the Arsenal, which Demosthenes could be said to have shaken when on his advice public funds were directed from its construction to the war against Philip of Macedon; 'fulmind' means 'sent forth lightning and thunder' (cf. Aristophanes' comment on Pericles in *Acharnians* 530–31).

273–4] According to Cicero, Socrates was the first to call philosophy down from heaven (*Tusculan Disputations* V. iv. 10). He is said to have a small house (οἰκίδιον) in Aristophanes, *Clouds* 92.

275–6] Plato, *Apology* 21.

276–7] On Socrates as the fountain of philosophy see Quintilian I. x. 13, and cf. Milton's *Hæc ego mente* 5.

278] According to an ancient distinction Academic philosophy had three phases: Plato founded the Old Academy, Arcesilias the Middle Academy, and Carneades the New Academy.

279–80] *Peripatetics* were Aristotelians, so called from the covered walk (περίπατος) in the buildings which Theophrastus provided for the school. The 'Sect *Epicurean*' descended from Socrates through his friend Aristippus, whose grandson (also Aristippus) founded the Cyrenaics, the intellectual pioneers of Epicureanism. Similarly, the *Stoics* descended from Socrates through his friend Aristhenes, whose Cynic sect influenced Stoic doctrine. See *Comus* 706–7n.

293–4 first] Socrates. See Plato, *Apology* 21–3.

295 next] Plato. Cf. *Idea* 38.

296 third sort] the Sceptics, founded by Pyrrhon. A form of scepticism was also espoused by Arcesilias and Carneades (l. 278n.).

297–8 Others] Aristotle and the Peripatetics.

299 he] Epicurus. Precedents for Milton's libellous misrepresentation of Epicureanism can be found in the attacks of other ancient schools and of Patristic and Renaissance authors.

300–309] Cf. *PL* II 564n.

319–21] Cf. *Passion* 56n.

321–2] Eccles. xii. 12.

328 Crude] unable to digest.

329 worth a spunge] means both 'worth very little' and 'worthy to be obliterated'.

335 artful terms] probably refers to the rubrics in the Massoretic and LXX texts of the Psalms.

336–7] Psalm cxxxvii. 1–3.

338] The idea that the arts were original to the Jews, who while in bondage had passed them on to the Egyptians, who in turn bequeathed them to the Greeks, was a Patristic and Renaissance commonplace.

347] Cf. *PL* III 30n.

351 Unless] refers back to 'unworthy' (l. 346).

354 Statists] statesmen.

384] an analogy to a large book ('Voluminous') and to single letters ('characters') in the book.

385] Conjunction, the apparent proximity of two heavenly bodies, is an unfavourable sign in astrology. Cf. *PL* X 661n. 'Spell' means 'interpret' (cf. *Penseroso* 170–71).

393 Rubric] a title or caption written in red letters.

402 jaunt] fatiguing journey.

409–10] 'Either Tropic' means north (Cancer) and south (Capricorn); the 'ends of Heav'n' are presumably east and west.

411 abortive] probably means 'unnaturally premature'.

412–13] Cf. Aeschylus, *Agamemnon* 650–51; 'ruin' means both 'falling' and 'destruction'.

413–14] Cf. *Elegia* IV 5–6n.

415 hinges] cardinal points (Latin *cardo*, hinge).

419 shrouded] sheltered.

427 amice] an article of costume (variously a cap, hood, or cape) made of, or lined with, grey fur.

453] *Æneid* i 133–4.

454 flaws] squalls.

455] Cf. *Comus* 597n.

457 main] universe.

518–20] See Job i. 6, and Milton's translation of Psalm lxxxii. 6.

524 collect] infer.

529 composition] truce.

542 *Hippogrif*] a fabulous creature, half horse ('hippo' means 'horse'), half griffin. Ariosto's *ippogrifo* carries his heroes on their journeys.

546–8] Milton draws on Josephus (*Jewish War* V. v. 6) for his description of the temple which Herod the Great built.

549] The meaning of 'pinnacle' ($\pi\tau\epsilon\rho\acute{\upsilon}\gamma\iota o\nu$, Vulgate *pinnaculum* and *pinna*) in Matt. iv. 5 and Luke iv. 9 was (and is) disputed; in Milton's time it was variously identified as a parapet, the ridge of the roof, the flat roof, a spire, etc.

563–8] *Antæus* was a giant who when wrestling renewed his strength by touching his mother Gæa (the earth). Hercules was the son of Zeus and Alceme (hence *Joves*), whose husband Amphitryon was the son of Alcæus (hence *Alcides*). At *Irassa*, in Libya, Hercules lifted *Antæus* off the ground and strangled him.

572–5] The *Theban* monster is the Sphinx, who leapt to her death from the acropolis at Thebes ('*Ismenian* steep', so called from the river Ismenus) after Oedipus answered her riddle.

578 triumphals] tokens of success.

581 Globe] used in the Latin sense of a throng.

583 Vans] fans, i.e. wings.

589] Gen. ii. 9, Rev. xxii. 2, 14. 'Ambrosial' here means 'heavenly' and 'fragrant'.

605 debell] vanquish, expel by force of arms.

611] Psalm cxxiv. 7.

619 Autumnal Star] a meteor or comet. Cf. *PL* II 708–11.

620–21] Gen. iii. 15, Mal. iv. 3, Luke x. 18, and Rom. xvi. 20 (on which see *PL* X 189–90n.).

624 *Abaddon*] In his translation of Psalm lxxxviii. 11 Milton translates this Hebrew word as 'perdition'. Elsewhere it refers to the destruction associated with *Sheol* (Job xxvi. 6, Prov. xv. 11, xxvii. 20) and with death (Job xxviii. 22). Cf. Rev. ix. 11.

628] Rev. xviii. 2.

630–32] Matt. viii. 28–33.

636] Matt. xi. 29.

SAMSON AGONISTES

The date of composition is not known. The traditional assumption has been that it was composed between 1666 and 1670, but arguments have been advanced for dates in the 1640s and 1650s. The notes that follow do not attempt to list allusions to the story of Samson as recounted in Judges xiii–xvi.

Title-page] In Milton's time the word *Samson* was popularly (and incorrectly) believed to mean 'there the second time'. *Agonistes*, a transliteration of a Greek word, could refer to a combatant at the national games, a pleader, or an actor; it could also refer to one who struggles for something, or to a champion (of virtue or truth). In the Greek text of Luke xxii. 44 Christ's 'agony' is an 'agonia' (ἀγωνία), a mental and spiritual struggle. The idea of the Christian life as a spiritual struggle may originate in Paul's injunction to 'fight the good fight of faith' (I Tim. vi. 12).

   The words in Greek are the opening words of Aristotle's definition of tragedy with a Latin translation of those words ('Tragedy is the imitation of a serious action') and of the passage at the end of the definition which deals with catharsis. Milton translates and amplifies this passage in the opening sentence of his preface.

'Of that sort of Dramatic Poem'.

16–18] David *Paræus* (1548–62), an eminent German theologian whom Milton often cites in his prose works, is here mentioned as the author of a commentary translated as *On the Divine Apocalypse* in 1644.

20–21] *Dionysius* I (*c.* 430–367 BC), tyrant of Syracuse, often contended for the prize of tragedy at Athens, and in the year of his death won first prize at the Athenian Lenaea with his *Ransoming of Hector*.

24–6] The mistaken notion that the Stoic philosopher and the tragedian were separate people originated in late antiquity and still prevailed in Milton's time.

26–9] *Gregory Nazianzen* (329–89) was long thought to have written *Christus Patiens*, but his authorship is now doubted.

37 Prologue] a prefatory speech outside the play, not to be confused with Aristotle's notion of a prologue (πρόλογος), the portion of the play that precedes the first chorus (in *SA* ll. 1–114).

38] Martial prefaces five of the twelve books of his *Epigrams* with prose epistles. In the preface to Book ii he makes his friend Decianus object to the use of an epistle.

47–52] The *Strophe* ('turning') was the stanza sung by the chorus as they moved from right to left across the orchestra; the *Antistrophe* ('counter-turn') was the metrically identical stanza sung in reply as they moved from left to right. The 'Epode' was the conclusion of the song, distinct in metre, sung as they stood still. *Monostrophic* refers to the repetition of a single strophe. *Apolelymenon* means 'freed', i.e. from stanzaic patterns. *Allæostropha* means 'of irregular strophes'. Cf. the postscript to *Ad Joannem Rousium*.

55 produc't . . . Act] echoes Horace's injunction that plays should not extend beyond the fifth act (*neu sit quinto productior actu*).

56] 'Style' in Aristotle's *Poetics* (xxii) means diction; 'uniformitie' probably refers to Aristotle's insistence on consistency of characterization (xv).

57] According to Aristotle's *Poetics* (x) plot is either simple ('explicit') or complex ('intricate').

58 *œconomy*] management, arrangement, called by Aristotle the 'putting together of the incidents' (*Poetics* vi).

63–5] 'Unity of time' in Aristotle's *Poetics* (v) is not a rule, but an observation to the effect that tragedy 'tries' to confine itself to one day. Unity of time became a precept at the hands of Castelvetro and other Renaissance theorists. 'Best example' must exclude plays by Aeschylus (*Persians*, *Agamemnon*, and *Eumenides*), Sophocles (*Trachiniæ*), and Euripides (*Suppliants*), for these five plays (and others no longer extant) do not observe the unity of time.

'The Argument' 20] *Catastrophe* ('overturning') is used in the dramatic sense of 'the change which produces the conclusion or final event; the dénouement'.

The Play

1–2] Cf. the opening of Sophocles' *Oedipus at Colonus*, where the blind Oedipus is led by his daughter Antigone; and see also Euripides, *Phoenician Women* 834–5.

11 day-spring] dawn.

13 *Dagon*] See *Nativity* 199n. and cf. *PL* I 457–66.

16 popular] of the populace.

31 person separate to God] renders the literal meaning of *Nazarite* (l. 318). See Num. vi. 1–21, Judges xiii. 5, 7.

53–6] a classical commonplace (e.g. Horace, *Odes* III. iv. 65).

77 still] invariably.

87 silent] not shining (cf. Latin *luna silens*).

89 vacant] at leisure (cf. Latin *vacare*).

92–3] The idea that the soul is 'all in every part' of the body is a patristic and Renaissance commonplace.

95 obvious] exposed.

106 obnoxious] exposed to harm.

131 forgery] the act of forging metal.

132 Cuirass] See *PR* III 328n.

133 *Chalybean*] The Chalybes were a Black Sea tribe famed in Greek legend as the first workers in iron.

136 insupportably] irresistibly.

138] See *PL* I 464–6n.

144 foreskins] uncircumcised Philistines.

145 *Ramath-lechi*] For the popular etymology see Judges xv. 17; the phrase probably means 'the height of the jawbone' (see A.V. and R.V. marginal notes).

147] See *PL* I 464–6n.

148] *Hebron* was anciently called Kirjath-arba (Joshua xiv. 15) i.e. the city of Arba. Arba was the father of Anak, whose descendants (the Anakim) were giants (Joshua xv. 13–14, Num. xiii. 32–3, Deut. i. 28, ii. 10–21, ix. 1–2).

149] In the Jerusalem Targum the prohibition in Exod. xvi. 29 forbids walking more than 2,000 ells (c. 1200 yards) on the sabbath. See Acts i. 12.

150 whom] Atlas, on whom see *PL* II 306n.

181 *Eshtaol, Zora*] towns variously allotted to Judah (Joshua xv. 33, where they are 'in the valley') and Dan (e.g. Joshua xix. 41); Milton chooses the latter. Between the two cities Samson began to be moved by the Spirit of the Lord (Judges xiii. 25) and was later buried (Judges xvi. 31).

203] Job xxx. 9 (Vulgate has *proverbium*).

216] The Bible does not state that Dalila was a Philistine, nor that she was married to Samson. There is strong patristic support for Milton's assumptions, but some exegetical traditions made her an Israelite and Samson's mistress (l. 537). Cf. *PL* IX 1061.

247 ambition] used in the Latin sense of 'canvassing'.

266] 'by this' means 'by this time'; on *Gath* (here used synecdochically for Philistia) see *PL* I 464–6n.

277–81] Judges viii. 1–17. *Madian* is the Vulgate form, and also occurs in A.V. Judith ii. 26 and Acts vii. 29.

282–89] Judges xi and xii. 1–6.

291   mine] my people.

295   think not God] i.e. think that there is no God.

296–8] Psalm xiv. 1, Eccles. ii. 14; 'obscure' means 'in darkness'.

312 obstriction] obligation (coined by Milton from mediæval Latin *obstrictionem*). In Samson's time Jews were not specifically forbidden to marry Philistines, though social contact with Gentiles was certainly forbidden by N.T. times (John xviii. 28, Acts x. 28). Milton may have had in mind Paul's injunction against marriage with unbelievers (II Cor. vi. 14). See also 380n. and 857–61n.

318–19] See 31n. There was no Nazaritic vow of celibacy; such a vow is an inference from the strong ascetic element in the abstinence from wine and strong drink (see ll. 541–52).

327   careful] full of grief.

328   advise] ponder.

333   uncouth] strange, unknown.

373   Appoint] arraign.

380] The Philistines were immigrants into Canaan from Caphtor (see l. 1713, Jer. xlvii. 4, Amos ix. 7), but Milton's use of the term *Canaanite* to describe them may imply an extension of the injunction against marrying members of the seven autochthonous nations (Deut. vii. 3) to the current inhabitants, the Philistines.

394   capital] plays on the meanings 'relating to the head', 'important', and 'fatal'.

405   over-watcht] wearied with too much watching.

424   state not] have no opinion on.

439] The second 'them' imitates the Latin dative of disadvantage, and means 'to their loss'.

466   connive] remain inactive.

469   discomfit] defeat.

471   blank] disconcert.

493   fact] evil deed.

500–501] Alludes to the myth of Tantalus, who was punished for betraying the gods' secrets; on his punishment see *PL* II 614n.

509   his debt] i.e. the debt due to him.

524   magnanimous] See *PL* VII 511n.

528] See 148n.

531   my affront] an encounter with me.

533   venereal trains] snares of sexual desire.

541–52] Cf. 31n., 318–19n. On l. 545 cf. Judges ix. 13.

557   liquid] clear.

560   boots] avails, profits.

568   redundant] abounding to excess or fullness.

571   craze] render infirm.

582] The word which Milton transcribes as *lechi* (l. 145) may in Judges xv. 19 refer to either the jawbone or the place named after the jawbone. In A.V. and Vulgate the water comes from the jaw. Milton's 'dry ground' places him in the other tradition, that of the Chaldee Paraphrase, the LXX, Josephus, and the A.V. margin.

594 genial] pertaining to genius or natural disposition.

600 humours black] melancholy.

609 reins] kidneys.

612 accidents] used in the medical sense of 'symptoms'.

624 apprehensive] pertaining to sensuous or mental impressions.

625 exulcerate] cause ulcers in.

639 nerve] muscle.

657 Consolatories] *Consolationes* are very common in the literature of antiquity; they range from simple letters to philosophical treatises (see e.g. Plutarch, *Consolatio ad Uxorem*). Later Christian consolers (Ambrose, Jerome, Paulinus of Nova) shifted the emphasis of the consolation from reasoned argument (l. 658) to feeling (l. 663).

667–70] Cf. Psalm viii. 4, Job vii. 17–20, and the speech of the chorus in Seneca, *Hippolytus* 1123 ff.

678–704] If *SA* was written after the Restoration, these lines may allude to the indignities suffered by the Commonwealth leaders at the hands of the Restoration government. Ll. 693–4 may be a specific allusion (phrased in Homeric language: *Iliad* i 4–5) to the disinterment of the bodies of Bradshaw, Cromwell, and Ireton from Westminster Abbey; their bodies (and possibly Pride's) were hanged publicly for a day and reburied at Tyburn. Lambert and Martin (Parliamentary generals) were imprisoned ('captiv'd'), and Vane (on whom see Milton's *Sonnet* XVIII) was condemned to death by a tribunal which Milton would doubtless have regarded as 'unjust'.

715 *Tarsus*] 'Ship of Tarshish' is a common O.T. expression for a large and strong ship, and Tarshish is a maritime country somewhere far to the west of Palestine. Milton's spelling *may* suggest that he identified Tarshish with Tarsus, the chief city of ancient Cicilia.

716] *Javan* is Ionia (see *PL* I 508n.), and *Gadier* was the Greek name for Cadiz.

736 fact] evil deed.

748 *Hyæna*] The note on Ecclus. xiii. 18 in the Geneva Bible explains that the hyena 'counterfaiteth the voyce of men, and so enticeth them out of their houses and devoureth them'; cf. Pliny, *Naturalis Historia* viii. 44.

800–802] In the A.V. of Judges xvi. 5 the stated motive is affliction, which follows Vulgate *affligere*; according to the A.V. marginal note the stated motive is only humiliation, which follows LXX ταπείνωσαι.

857–61] The priest is Milton's invention, and is probably meant to emphasize the analogy to seventeenth-century views about marriage with unbelievers (cf. 312n.).

885–6] Gen. ii. 24.

913 sensibly] acutely, intensely.

926 grateful] agreeable, pleasing to the mind and senses.

934–5] Alludes to the myth of Circe, on which see *Comus* 50n.

936–7] Psalm lviii. 4.

981] See *PL* I 464–6n.

987 odours] Jer. xxxiv. 5.

988–90] The killing of *Sisera* by *Jaël* is described in Judges iv. 4–22, and celebrated (in verse) in Judges v. 2–31. 'Mount *Ephraim*' is here mentioned as the home of Deborah, the prophetess who 'judged Israel at that time' (Judges iv. 4).

993 piety] used in the sense of Latin *pietas*, the Roman attitude of dutiful respect for gods, relatives, and (in this case) homeland.

1000 aggravate] make more grievous and burdensome.

1006 passion] the primary sense is 'suffering', but the word could also refer to a sexual impulse (as in *PL* I 454).

1008] Cf. Terence, *Andria* III. iii. 23.

1012 inherit] keep.

1020] In Greek antiquity 'Paranymph' meant 'friend of the bridegroom' (the modern 'best man'). Milton follows the Vulgate rendering of Judges xiv. 20 in interpreting the word 'friend' in this technical sense (Vulgate uses *pronubus*).

1038 Intestin] internal, domestic.

1046–9] Prov. xxxi. 10–28.

1062 contracted] drawn together.

1068] In the A.V. of II Sam. xxi the Hebrew word *Harapha* is treated as a common noun and translated as 'the giant'; the A.V. marginal notes to verses 16, 18, and 20 record the minority view (in which Milton seems to concur) that *Harapha* is a proper name (cf. LXX Ῥαφά) and that the Philistine champions should be called 'the sons of Rapha' (see ll. 1248–9). *Harapha* means 'to become limp or slack', and is often used in a spiritual or moral sense (e.g. Joshua xviii. 3, Prov. xxiv. 10, Jer. vi. 24).

1075 fraught] freight, the cargo of a ship.

1080–1] On *Og* see Milton's Psalm 136, 69n. On *Anak* see *SA* 148n. The *Emims* were a race of giants (Deut. ii. 10–11) living on the plain of *Kiriathaim* (Gen. xiv. 5, A.V. marginal note).

1087 camp or listed field] 'Camp' is used in the Latin sense of 'plain, field'; a 'listed field' is one converted into lists for tilting.

1093 Gives] shackles.

1109 assassinated] treacherously wounded.

1113 Close-] secretly.

1120–21] 'Brigandine' is body armour composed of iron rings or small thin iron plates sewed onto canvas, linen, or leather; an 'Habergeon' is a sleeveless coat of mail or scale armour; 'Vant-brass' is armour for the forearm, and 'Greves' are armour for the leg below the knee.

1122–3] On the comparison of the spear to the weaver's beam see I Sam. xvii. 7, II Sam. xxi. 19, I Chron. xx. 5; 'sev'n-times-folded' alludes to the shield of Ajax, which was made with the hides of seven bulls (*Iliad* vii 220). David confronted Goliath with a staff (I Sam. xvii. 40, 43).

1139–40] Alludes to the oath taken before the judges by medieval combatants; each combatant had to swear that he was not aided by magic, and trusted only in God.

1169 thine] thy people.

1197] Cf. Josephus, *Antiquities* V. viii. 6.

1204 underminers] secret assailants.

1220 appellant] the challenger in single combat.

1223 enforce] exertion.

1231 *Baäl-zebub*] See *Nativity* 197n. and *PL* I 81n.

1234 van] vanguard.

1237 baffl'd] disgraced, dishonoured.

1242 *Astaroth*] See *Nativity* 200n.

1245 unconsci'nable] unreasonably excessive.

1248–9] In II Sam. xxi. 15–22 four sons of Rapha (see 1068n.) are described, one of whom is named as Goliath. A comparison with I Chron. xx. 5 led the A.V. translators to refer to this giant as 'the brother of Goliath', who thus became a fifth son. Milton may have identified this Goliath with the giant whom David killed (I Sam. xvii).

1279 magnitude of mind] See *PL* VII 511n.

1303 quaint] skilfully made.

1307 voluble] rapid and ready of speech.

1309 remark] mark, distinguish.

1320] Exod. xx. 4–5.

1325 Antics] clowns.

1342 Joind] enjoined.

1369 sentence] aphorism (i.e. line 1368).

1377 dispense with] grant a relaxation of the strict letter of the law in a special case.

1382 motions] See *PL* XI 91n.

1461–71] If *SA* was written after the Restoration, these lines could be a topical allusion to the attitudes of various groups aligned with the new government towards Commonwealth figures (such as Milton himself). On 'magnanimity' see *PL* VII 511n.

1529 dole] plays on the meanings 'grief', sorrow' and 'that which is charitably doled out'.

1538 baits] used of travellers who stop at an inn.

1570] Cf. Sophocles, *Electra* 673.

1596 Occasions] affairs, business.

1605 theatre] In the Hebrew, LXX, Vulgate and A.V. of Judges xvi. 27 the building is called a house and has 3,000 people on the roof. In Milton's account the common people stand outside the building (l. 1659) rather than on top of it.

1608 sort] rank.

1610 banks] benches.

1619 Cataphracts] soldiers in full armour; Milton took this sense of the word directly from Latin *cataphractus*, Greek κατάφρακτος, 'clad in full armour'.

1647–8] Cf. *PL* I 230–7n.

1659 vulgar] the common people (Latin *vulgus*).

1671 fat] The Mosaic law forbade the eating of animal fat (Lev. iii. 17).

1674] Shiloh (*Silo*) was the site of the principal Jewish sanctuary at the time of the Judges (Judges xviii. 31); 'bright' probably alludes to the presence of the *Shekinah*, the glory of God dwelling among men (see John i. 14 for a probable N.T. expression of the idea).

1685 sense reprobate] Rom. i. 28.

1692 Dragon] a huge serpent or snake (cf. *PL* X 529 and Rev. xii. 9).

1695 villatic] used in the sense of Latin *villaticus*, belonging to a *villa*, i.e. a country house or farm.

1699–707] Cf. *PL* V 272–4n. and *Damonis* 185–9. 'Embost' is used of a hunted animal which has taken shelter in a wood; 'secular' means 'living for an age'.

1713 *Caphtor*] See 380n.

1727 lavers] water-jugs or basins.

1745–8] Cf. the final chorus used by Euripides in *Alcestis*, *Andromache*, *Bacchæ*, and *Helena*.

1749] Psalm xxvii. 9, xxx. 7, civ. 29.

1751 in place] in presence, at hand.

1755 acquist] acquisition.